D1488424

THE STACKPOLE SOCIAL SCIENCE SERIES

Laurence Foster, General Editor

THE DEVELOPMENT

OF

HISTORIOGRAPHY

Edited by

MATTHEW A. FITZSIMONS
University of Notre Dame

ALFRED G. PUNDT
Pennsylvania State University

and

CHARLES E. NOWELL
University of Illinois

THE STACKPOLE COMPANY
Harrisburg, Pennsylvania

Preface

A reasonably comprehensive and up-to-date volume on the history of historical writing has been a necessity for a long time. Earlier works are either too bulky or insufficiently comprehensive and inevitably somewhat out-of-date. This last point has special force, for recent years have seen a growing interest in historiography and a corresponding increase of monographs and articles in that field. The present volume is designed to meet this need, so frequently expressed by students and teachers.

This book, then, attempts to present an account of the development of historical writing from its beginnings to the present. The usefulness of such a project may be manifold. First of all, the volume describes the many meanings and functions which the inquiry into the past has had for man in various centuries and stages of civilizations. For several thousand years history has been prized as a teacher or supporter of morality and as a branch of literature. At the same time historians have sought to explain events by using concepts and ideas borrowed from practically all natural sciences and philosophical and theological systems. Thus, the history of history may claim a place in intellectual and literary history and may serve as a liberalizing and broadening influence for those who all too readily accept modern historical production as the climax of human achievement. The critical methods of modern history represent a great intellectual advance but it does not follow that contemporary historians have generally risen to their opportunity, to what has been called "the dignity of history."

It is hoped that this book will induce readers to turn to the great masters, the charming and discursive Herodotus, the masterful Thucydides, the mordant Tacitus, the sonorous and ironic Gibbon and the father of modern critical history, Ranke. These and a host of others represent various forms of history dealing with the persistent problems of human existence. Even such lesser figures as Orosius, Giraldus Cambrensis and Gilbert Burnet provide exciting reading which gives more intimate and direct glimpses into the past than we may easily get in any other way.

Or again, it can be profitable to inquire into the role of historical views in the developments of civilization; to speculate about the minor position of history in the thirteenth century, to assess its role in the Renaissance, the Reformation and the Enlightenment, to note its powerful stimulus in the Romantic movement and the extraordinary influence of myth and history in the story of nationalism. Indeed, in *History and Human Relations* the English historian, Professor Butterfield, confessed that he had been so appalled by the evils which bad history had brought to the world, and had wondered whether it would not be well for the world to forget its past. His conclusion, however, is that we must study and teach history precisely because there is so much bad history in the world already. Man would not be man without memory, and, as Cicero put it, history is the life of memory.

This book may serve another use: to persuade the reader to formulate his own definition of history. Having witnessed the evils of the confusion of history with philosophy, science and religion, he may wish to establish the sphere of history with clarity and firmness. He may, then, be alert against efforts to merge the past into the role of prophetic books for the present. The past by itself is no sufficient guide, and only the self-deceived will say so.

Ironically our own age which has seen the wide acceptance of critical history has also witnessed the emergence of totalitarian movements, Fascist and Communist, which pretend to have the laws of history and the key to the future. This belief withers the life of critical history. Is this, perhaps, a truth which the history of history suggests: that an anxious age in its confusion and emptiness worships history and in the act of worship destroys the dignity of history.

Authors of Chapters

HENRY ADAMS: 13
University of California
Santa Barbara, California

E. GEORGIADES ARNAKIS: 6
University of Kansas City
Kansas City, Missouri

SHERMAN B. BARNES: 11
Kent State University
Kent, Ohio

STEPHEN BORSODY: 24
Pennsylvania College for Women
Pittsburgh, Pennsylvania

ANTHONY F. CZAJKOWSKI: 21
Formerly, St. Louis University,
St. Louis, Missouri

KARL H. DANNENFELDT: 1, 7
Elmira College
Elmira, New York

HAROLD E. DAVIS: 32
American University
Washington, D. C.

GLENN S. DUMKE: co-author: 31
Occidental College
Los Angeles, California

JAMES C. FINDLEY: co-author: 31
Deep Springs College
Deep Springs, California

MATTHEW A. FITZSIMONS: 8, 9,
10, 16
University of Notre Dame
Notre Dame, Indiana

CHARLES W. HALLBERG: 14, 17
Queens College
Flushing, New York

LOUIS KESTENBERG: 18
University of Houston
Houston, Texas

SAMSON B. KNOLL: 23
Menlo School and College
Menlo Park, California

BENOIT LACROIX: 2, 3
L'Université de Montreal
Montreal, Canada

JAMES M. MORLEY: 28
Union College
Schenectady, New York

CHARLES E. NOWELL: 27
University of Illinois
Urbana, Illinois

ALFRED G. PUNDT: 12
Pennsylvania State University
State College, Pennsylvania

JOSEPH S. ROUCEK: 22
University of Bridgeport
Bridgeport, Connecticut

J. C. RUSSELL: 4, 5
University of New Mexico
Albuquerque, New Mexico

PHILLIP R. SHRIVER: 30
Kent State University
Kent, Ohio

ALFRED A. SKERPAN: 26
Kent State University
Kent, Ohio

LESLIE F. SMITH: 19, 20
University of Oklahoma
Norman, Oklahoma

GEORGE WASKOVICH: 25
Hunter College
New York, New York

HERBERT WENDER: 15
Long Island University
Brooklyn, New York

PHILIP YAMPOLSKY: 29
Columbia University
New York, New York

Table of Contents

CHAPTER 3—CAROLINGIAN HUMANISM AND ITS HISTORIOGRAPHY

CHAPTER 4—RENAISSANCE OF THE TWELFTH CENTURY

CHAPTER 10—POLITICAL HISTORIES AND MEMOIRS IN THE SEVENTH CENTURY

CHAPTER 11—THE AGE OF ENLIGHTENMENT

CHAPTER 14—THE INTRODUCTION OF CRITICAL HISTORICAL SCHOLARSHIP IN FRANCE, ENGLAND, AND ITALY

CHAPTER 15—GERMAN HISTORIOGRAPHY IN THE SECOND HALF OF THE NINETEENTH CENTURY

Part II. TWENTIETH CENTURY TENDENCIES
CHAPTER 16—BRITISH HISTORIOGRAPHY OF THE TWENTIETH CENTURY

CHAPTER 17—TWENTIETH CENTURY PROGRESS IN FRANCE

CHAPTER 18—GERMAN HISTORIOGRAPHY IN THE TWENTIETH CENTURY

CHAPTER 19—THE LOW COUNTRIES

CHAPTER 20—THE SCANDINAVIAN COUNTRIES

CHAPTER 21—TWENTIETH CENTURY TENDENCIES—POLAND AND BALTIC COUNTRIES

CHAPTER 31—TWENTIETH CENTURY TENDENCIES IN AMERICAN HISTORIOGRAPHY

CHAPTER 32—TWENTIETH CENTURY TENDENCIES—LATIN AMERICA

INTRODUCTION

By Philip S. Miller
Lincoln University

"Alas, there is no history," was the lament of a modern writer, weary, if not of this world, weary, at least, of our world's picture of the past. Whether there is history or not, there can be no denying the existence of historians. Their mere presence in the world and their assiduous activity is a hard if troublesome fact. If there were no historians we should have to invent them and set them to doing just what they are now trying to do—give an account of past events as they actually occurred. And such activity when continued for centuries will itself become the object of historical study. It is this study which in this volume is called the history of historiography.

Ranke's aim to give an account of "how things actually occurred" is in its simplest meaning not at all revolutionary. It has been the implied intention of every historian, chronicler and annalist whatever subsidiary motives gave form to his work. The reciter of the tales of his childhood (unless he is deliberately fictitious), the war veteran who describes a campaign and the general who writes his memoirs are all aiming at the reconstruction of a part of the past as they believe it to have taken place. But the history of historiography reveals that this aim becomes complicated whenever two or more persons are writing about the same period or when the subject matter has more than ordinary interest. The history of the development of the shotgun, I understand, has been "definitively" written, which means that no one has challenged the narrative. Up until now it meets the requirement of J. B. Bury, the Cambridge historian, that when history is once a science there will "no longer be divers schools of history" but only one history accepted by all just as there is only one elementary algebra. But let the subject begin to have more than ordinary meaning, then the history of it will be this man's history and that man's history. Such works may agree in general matters of fact and yet the final pictures of the past may be contradictory. The reasons for the disagreement are not easily discoverable. The simplest difference and the one most easily detected is in the handling of sources. But modern historians of every description agree in general upon the principles of historical method so that when, in both cases, the sources are used according to the accepted canons of criticism, the reasons for disagreement lie far deeper. It is these reasons which are present in all historical writing. To lay them bare is the function of the study of historiography.

THE HISTORIAN AS A NARRATOR

Several reasons lie in the nature of the historian's task. The historian must be more than a collector of data and his published work must be more than a summary of a statistical report. He is properly a narrator. The one great lesson taught by Herodotus is that history is a literary form, that it can be interesting and must be readable. This high requirement taxes the talent of the best historian. He is more than an examiner of old documents. The connection of events described in his documents, the tracing of influences and the motives behind human action—all these distinguish the historian from the antiquarian. The line between historian and antiquarian is not easily drawn, yet somewhere there is a line which divides them. A specialized monograph written by a specialist for the delectation of other specialists rarely rises to the dignity of history, no matter how necessary it may be as ground work for the larger super-structure.

In abridgements of history (history is used in this chapter in the sense of a written account of the past) and in surveys of world history the writer's world view becomes highly important. The honest belief that human events are controlled by economic factors, that history teaches morality, that patriotic and national biases are commendable, gives to many a historical work its form and flavor. The presupposition that there are "iron laws" of history, which the Enlightenment historian identified with the laws of physics and mathematics, may render a work unacceptable to the critics of today, for the extension of the laws of nature to include organic evolution wrought havoc with the "iron laws." For when evolution is included in natural law, a small factor ignored in the rubbish of a former age may be what develops and not the germ which the individual historian sees under his historical microscope. The very idea of natural law in our modern sense militates against the writing of any history. Everything hangs together in nature, the known and the unknown, the apparently trivial as well as the supposedly consequential. To reconstruct the past is impossible because everything in the past should be reproduced. Nothing is so delusive as the notion that the selection of the important elements of a period can be unerringly made by the wisest historian. The important elements are important because of a particular point of view. The only way to reproduce the past would be to turn back the clock and cut out a section of the past, very much like a slice of sausage—an utterly fantastic idea. It is this discouraging situation which requires all historical writers to superimpose upon a period some conceptions that are not a part of it with no other purpose than the minimum aim of making it intelligible to us, so that the historian becomes a theorist even before he has written a word of history.

Unconscious Assumptions

But there are assumptions made unconsciously. The historian does not stand apart from his time and age. An historian of the Enlightenment will never be confused with a nineteenth century historian no matter what his theme. It is rather alarming that in the following pages historians can be classified under the rubrics of "Enlightenment," "Romantic," "Economic," terms which are applicable to the worlds of literature and philosophy. What can these designations have to do with history when these categories refer not to the subject matter but to the historian himself? This coincidence of the historian with the intellectual climate of his time is so general and undeniable that the suspicion does not lie far away that history is no more than one form of literary expression of the period in which the author lives.

Nor will the reply be satisfactory that all this was true of past historians but now that we stand on the ground of scientific method, things are different. This is a naive judgment that our age is an absolute than which there is none higher, a *ne plus ultra*. This position is illustrated in the nineteenth century historian when writing about the Middle Ages. When medieval institutions and beliefs are portrayed, frequently a now-we-know-better attitude peeps through the narrative, an attitude seldom challenged because it is seldom noticed. Another assumption lying very close to this is the uncritical acceptance of our age as one to which all other ages are preparatory. We stand rather presumptuously with the biblical writer "upon whom the ends of the world are come." The struggles of the past are evaluated as important or unimportant only in so far as they contribute to what our age approves. An incident, small in a former age and actually insignificant if the age is studied for its own sake, becomes for us very important because we see it in an inkling of a turn to, *e.g.,* freedom or popular government. It must follow that the resultant picture must have some perversions and must be out of focus. The careful study of historians as men with the passions of men will bring these tendencies to light even when the work is a truly great achievement.

The uncertainty, however, which arises when the pictures of the past are out of focus is no argument against historical study. Historical study is a healthy activity in every civilized society. Cicero commends history by saying (*Orator* 120): "not to know what took place before you were born is to remain forever a child." All societies urgently strive to grow out of childhood into maturity. Preoccupation with the present will occasionally exclude interest in the past, yet again and again there will be an urge to see how the present came to be what it is and what roots the present has in the past. The past has gone forever and the difficulties encountered in trying to recreate it are compounded by the fact that in addition to the problems of sources and bare incidents, the historian is a problem in himself. He is human and the greater he is, the greater will his interest be in all things human. Many of the greatest historians were also great personalities and many of them have been men of affairs. Thucydides and Polybius, Grote and Bancroft, Ranke and Mommsen were not political innocents but had experience in the political world. They did not observe human affairs, timidly and uneasily and uncertainly as from a cloister. Their convictions and their prejudices were strong so that they became problems in themselves, *e.g.,* events in history which the student of historiography ought to examine. But this can be said in their defense: to expect from them what they never intended to give is to misread their works.

CAN WE LIMIT THE MEANING OF HISTORY?

But can we call literary productions "history" when the works in question do not meet our ideas of what history ought to be? May we not refuse the word "history" to what does not meet our requirements? Frequently, we speak of "history" as if the word had been copyrighted by some historical association and as if we had the right to read into the past a standard which was not then known and which might not have been adopted, had it been known. "Livy," we say complacently, "does not meet the severe standards of modern scientific history." Do we meet Livy's standards? Livy thought very highly of the speeches which he put into the mouths of his leading characters. He devoted much time to those rhetorical creations. Were he with us today, he might have reasons for this device which have never occurred to us. Another example of our judgments may be pointed out in our estimates of Herodotus and Thucydides. Both have received the praise of later generations but our estimate is somewhat as follows: "Thucydides comes nearer to our standards than Herodotus because Herodotus explains human events under the influence of divine intervention especially to punish *Hybris,* while Thucydides seeks only human motives to explain events." It is quite fashionable to praise Thucydides strongly and Herodotus faintly. Yet from whom have we learned more, from Herodotus or from Thucydides? Thucydides does not leave us in the dark as to what he considered the advantages of his method. He steps out from behind the curtain of anonymity and tells us (1) that his speeches express the ideas which he believes the actors would most naturally have in their minds, and that he is proud of his method; (2) that he intends his work to be not a prize essay but a handbook for statesmen because similar events in the future will follow from similar causes. No modern historian would follow Thucydides in the first, and few would agree with him on the second. On the other hand, from Herodotus, whose slight concession to divine intervention (Herodotus is far from the later theological interpretation of history) is out of fashion, historians have learned actually more than they have from Thucydides. The other qualities of Thucydides in style and compactness of thought, can be praised but hardly imitated. Orthodoxy in history claims for itself in every generation an authority which it cannot historically defend and finds its nemesis in the "history" of the next generation.

How does a historian conceive of his own work? In the case of a great historian, who is serious in his devotion to Clio (who incidentally is one of the Muses and not one of the Cyclops) is a question of great moment. He does not conceal his purpose and accordingly it is not a great feat for the modern student to discover it. We shall select several types of historical writers to show what history means to them, types which the student of historiography must examine with as much detachment as possible.

I. *The Historian as Patriot.* The historian as patriot is often what Wilhelm Schlegel called him: "a prophet who looks backward." He sees in the past the small beginnings of what are now great and glorious institutions. He finds there glorious institutions which have degenerated in his day. If he lives in a period of national humiliation or social corruption his patriotism leads him to study the past to improve the present. Tacitus, in a period of imperial tyranny and oppression, used the past to castigate the present. His essay on the ancient

Germans is a patriotic tract. The ancient Germans had all the good qualities which his age lacked. In his life of Agricola he portrays an old Roman of the primary virtues. The patriot historian is known also in modern times and in all lands. In the time of German humiliation after the Napoleonic wars, Luden in his *History of the German People* set a light shining in the past as a point from which the German people could go forward. He tried to raise his countrymen from the despair which had overtaken them. In his classroom at the University of Jena he lectured to crowds: "I wish that we Germans would study like children the life of our beloved parents, dominated by the holy thought of the Fatherland." In France, the poor boy who had become a Professor of History, Jules Michelet (1798-1874) wrote the history of France with a passionate love for the French people in their long struggle for liberty and justice. He never forgot the grinding poverty of the French peasant and when praised for his work he said: "If I am superior to other historians it is because I have loved more." In England, Freeman makes devotion to the early ages of England his guiding star. Liberty too was his theme.

These historians whom I have mentioned as patriots were also great and good men. Noble in their lives, they made history a school of virtue. The patriot cannot be objective. He must take sides and one-sidedness may distort his work. The great danger is that lesser men and less scrupulous men turn patriotic history into a weapon of fiery nationalism. The excessive nationalism of many Europeans is partly due to the patriot as historian. But there is a difference between true love of country and hatred of foreigners. History loses one of its motives when all patriotism is shunned in its pages. To avoid a real danger it is not necessary to avoid one of the noblest emotions—the love of country.

II. *The Historian as Judge and Censor of Morals.* The belief is very old that history provides a demonstration of the eternal power of justice and that the historian must severely condemn wrong. The historian Tacitus (*Annals* 3.65) states his view of the function of history: "This I hold to be the chief office of history, to rescue virtuous actions from oblivion, and to make men fear the infamy which posterity will surely attach to vile words and deeds." Two-fold is its function: to immortalize the right and to pillory the wrong. If "posterity" happened to be a Tacitus, a wrong-doer had good reason to fear. In small, compact and biting phrases Tacitus was able to sentence to lasting ignominy those whose sycophancy and corruptions supported a Roman tyrant.

Lord Acton, one of the most learned men of modern Europe and during his later years Professor of Modern History at Cambridge, believed strongly that an historian had to be a judge, even a "hanging judge." Hesitation on the part of the historian to brand injustice was a betrayal of the historian's trust. To his students in an inaugural lecture he said: "The inflexible integrity of the moral code is to me the secret of the authority, the dignity and the utility of history."

In Germany, Schlosser of Heidelberg was a famous representative of the same austere view. He declared that it was his object in teaching history to wean away his contemporaries from evil. A man of noble character and fine ideals, he conceived it as his function as a university professor to make history a guide to life. He lamented that his disciple Gervinus neglected to stress the moral law just as Lord Acton was saddened by his teacher Döllinger's caution in denouncing evil and injustice in public characters of the past. Lord Acton's aim for history was: "to develop and perfect and arm conscience," Schlosser's was: to be a guide to life; and Ranke's to describe the past "wie es eigentlich gewesen." The difference is important. History becomes on the first view a subject providing moral discipline as the Herbartian educators claimed it was; in the second case, history may enlighten and inform but it is not a discipline in virtue.

The assumption of the historian as judge is that the events of the past, when surveyed over a long period, reveal a moral pattern, an historical justice. Butterfield *(The Whig Interpretation of History)* denies that it is the function of the historian to act as judge and censor. He becomes "a judge when by qualifications he is fitted to be a detective." Yet it is a likely conclusion from the study of history that the decline of public virtues like honesty and fidelity, and the increase of luxury and irresponsible power will destroy the institutions of society. It is uncertain, however, whether we can go beyond this humble statement on the lessons of history.

III. *The Historian as a Detached Observer.* It is not lack of character nor of strong personal conviction that leads some historians to stand outside of the stream of events. It is rather the ambition to make history a science parallel to the exact natural sciences. Whether anyone can stand outside of the stream of events, especially the stream of modern history, is denied by many. Theodor Mommsen in his early days, after he had been a liberal journalist, had this to say: "Those who have lived through historical events, as I have, begin to see that history is neither written nor made without love and hate." His *History of Rome* shows Mommsen right in the fight and taking sides, yet it is one of the few histories of Rome which will always deserve reading. Perhaps too much has been made of objectivity and, as Paul Schrecker suggests, "if the paradigm had not been political history" no one would have thought of making objectivity the centerpiece of historical method. In non-political subjects such as art, folklore and language the subjectivity of the author has done little harm. The unpleasant situation which the detached observer must always face is this: that if, in the presence of injustice and wrong, he resolves to say nothing, the reading public will likely conclude that he has nothing to say.

These and other roles have been played by historians. How far their productions have been adversely affected by assuming the position of patriot, judge or detached observer is a question which depends upon the answer to another: whether their use of the sources was honest and whether their narrative has the ring of authenticity and truth. But their purpose in writing history is a sacred choice of their own. No authority exists to keep them from assuming such functions and the study of historiography places in high relief their own intentions for praise or blame.

RELATION TO THE HISTORY OF PHILOSOPHY AND OF LITERATURE

Our discussion has already suggested that history is not a study isolated from other disciplines. The influence of the ideas of ethics and the presence of the historian's point of view really belong to philosophy. The literary excellence of a few histories gives them a place in literature. It follows that the history of historiography stands as a parallel to the history of literature and the history of philosophy and impinges upon both. Not only in such massive works as Spengler's *Decline of the West*, a book saturated with philosophy, are history and philosophy bed-fellows, but the very urge to study the past and to understand it is akin to the urge of the philosopher to understand reality. The interplay between history and philosophy cannot be avoided without impoverishing both.

History is also related to literature and the best histories are occasionally works of literature. Schiller's *Thirty Year's War* may be bad history in places but the magnificent thought-structure and the largeness of view make it literature. But the relation between history and literature is nicely balanced only when a serious study of sources is united with the power of historical imagination so that the portrayal of the past has both form and truth.

Historical method has developed largely by observing the faults and failures of predecessors. It is much easier to learn how not to write history than how to write it. The pitfalls of the historian are like the bear-trap in the forest, seen only after someone has been so unfortunate as to step into it. Method has developed but slowly and then largely by learning what not to do.

But the study of historiography does not end with skepticism regarding the value and the validity of history. Its method of tracing the development of history as a written form places the work of the historian in its proper setting. Finality is not the standard of good historical work. Nor is "definitive" an adjective which has any special meaning outside of book-reviews. Since history is a part of the activity of men standing in a certain culture, its constant revision is a necessity. Just as travelers in the Alps, rising from one peak to another, find the vista changing, so every observer from a new position of human culture will find that the bird's eye view has changed from what it had been at a previous vantage point. The one standard which the study of historiography will support will be something like this: that history is the estimate of the past from the standpoint of the present and that a study of the past for its own sake, not for any advantage of propaganda or party, is proper history; and that the historian who lives his period and steeps himself in its life and thought from all possible sources is the proper historian. With the Wise Man of Ecclesiastes we can say: "Much study [of the sources] is a weariness of the flesh and of the making of [history] books there is no end." There can be no end because our own constantly changing culture requires an adjustment between its changes and its elements of permanence. Any period of

INTRODUCTION

civilization reveals itself not more clearly in any other matter than in its attention to history: its effort to understand its own past and to come to grips with its meaning, not meaning only in a narrow sense of the present, but meaning as a past expression of the human spirit.

Chapter 1

THE HERITAGE OF ANTIQUITY

By Karl H. Dannenfeldt

ORIENTAL

Egyptian Records. True history as we know it, the critical research and narrative of a historian, did not appear until long after man had acquired the ability to record his myths and legends, his traditions and deeds. The nations of the ancient Near East left numerous inscriptions and records, but no scribe wrote the history of his land and its people. Of all the Egyptian inscriptions which chance and the favorable climate of the Nile Valley have preserved on metal, clay, wood and papyrus, only a few may be called historical in nature. There are a few annalistic lists of royal names, with accompanying chronicles concerning the celebration of religious festivals, several descriptions of military campaigns, and biographical details on tomb walls—all very important to the modern Egyptologist in his reconstruction of the history of Egypt, but not really historical literature. In the Egyptian view of the world as a static order championed and maintained by the divine Pharaoh, historical incidents and facts were considered relatively unimportant. They were either not recorded or considered subsidiary to the greater theological truths.[1] It was only in the third century B.C. that the priest Manetho, more Greek than Egyptian, wrote "a history of his own country in the Greek tongue, translating it, as he says, out of their sacred records."[2] Manetho gave the modern historian the division of Egyptian history according to thirty dynasties, but his apparently excellent work has been lost; only excerpts are to be found in the writings of Josephus, Sextus Julius Africanus and Eusebius.

Assyrian, Persian, Babylonian Sources. The cuneiform texts of the early cultures of the Mesopotamian area are of a nature similar to the hieroglyphic records of Egypt. Archaeologists have uncovered and translated royal inscriptions, lists of kings, myths, date lists and chronicles—all saturated with religious ideas and customs. The historical facts, all too often, are meager, king-centered, and untrustworthy. The royal annals of the Assyrians are probably quite trustworthy, though they lack the exactness which characterized their business accounts.[3] Early in the fourth century B.C., Ctesias of Cnidus wrote in Greek a number of historical works, among them a *Persian History* and an *Assyrian History*. The fragments of these works that remain show that Ctesias did not make proper use of the excellent sources at his command. A century later a

---

[1] Henri Frankfort, *Kingship and the Gods*, pp. 9, 26, 56, 57, 149, and 347.
[2] Flavius Josephus, *Against Apion*, I, 14.
[3] Albert T. E. Olmstead, "Assyrian Historiography" in *The University of Missouri Studies*, III, No. 1 and David Luckenbill, *Ancient Records of Assyria and Babylonia*, I, pp. 25-26.

Babylonian priest of Bel named Berossus wrote a history of Babylonia which, however, contains much that is legendary.[4]

Jewish Writings. Compared with those of other ancient peoples, the historical books of the relatively small nation of the Hebrews are noteworthy and unique.[5] The monuments of Hebrew historiography are to be found in the Old Testament, covering the period from the Creation to the time of the Maccabees. Though less detailed than Babylonian writing, it has unity, beauty and many more personalities. A philosophy of history was its novel and unique contribution. Hebrew history is based on written sources such as the authoritative chronicles of the kings of Judah and Israel, on oral traditions, knowledge of contemporary affairs, codes, songs, poetry and hymns; all used without critical examination and judgment. The authorship of many books is disputed or unknown, but the writer of the objective history of David, often thought to be the high priest, Abiathar, achieved an outstandingly genuine contemporary historical work.[6]

In the Old Testament, the historical narrative, despite the predominant religious theme and viewpoint, exhibits a high degree of literary skill, a feeling for the dramatic and exaltation of the role of the individual. To the Hebrew author, it was most important to explain the happenings of history, to show that the history of the past as shaped by God contained principles which could be used for guidance in the shaping of contemporary and future events.

The greatest of the Hebrew historians was Flavius Josephus,[7] born about 37 A.D. of a priestly family. He became active in the rebellion against Rome; but when captured, supported the Romans and gained the favor of Vespasian. After being with Titus at the destruction of Jerusalem in 70, Josephus went to Rome to devote himself to writing. His *Jewish War*, beginning with the capture of Jerusalem by Antiochus IV, Epiphanes recounts in great detail the events of the Great Rebellion (67-70). The seven books, written first in Aramaic, were translated by Josephus into Greek. His *Antiquities of the Jews*, a much larger work, traces the glories of Jewish history from Creation to the twelfth year of Nero's reign. Besides an extraordinary *Autobiography*, Josephus also wrote an apologetic tract entitled *Against Apion*, in which, after a long introductory attack on the prestige of the Greek historians, he skillfully argues the Jewish claim to a great antiquity and cultural superiority. To support his contention he introduced, often *verbatim*, important excerpts from Manetho, Berossus, Chairemon, Megasthenes and other oriental writers whose works are now lost.

EARLY GREEK

Rise of Greek Historical Literature. In the period from Homer to Herodotus

---

[4] Berossus' work is lost except for portions which have been preserved by Josephus, Eusebius and others; cf. Paul Schnabel, *Berossos und die Babylonisch-Hellenistische Literatur*.
[5] William A. Irwin, "The Hebrews," in *The Intellectual Adventure of Ancient Man*, pp. 318-325; Curt Wachsmuth, *Einleitung in das Studium der Alten Geschichte*, pp. 415-435; A. T. E. Olmstead, "Hebrew History and Historical Method," in *Persecution and Liberty: Essays in Honor of George Lincoln Burr*, pp. 21-54; and Julius A. Bewer, *The Literature of the Old Testament in Its Historical Development*.
[6] Olmstead, "Hebrew History," p. 33, calls him "our first great historian." The *First Book of Maccabees*, which the Catholic Church includes in the Scriptural Canon but Protestants list among the *Apocrypha*, is also an example of excellent Hebrew historical writing.
[7] Alfred von Gutschmid, *Kleine Schriften*, IV, pp. 336-385; and H. St. John Thackeray, *Josephus, the Man and the Historian*.

(*ca.* 484-*ca.* 425 B.C.) the Homeric epics were everywhere accepted, praised and imitated. These epics satisfied the historical interest of many generations. Developments were already under way, however, which were to bring about the writing of true history. Mythological tradition was elaborated, chronologically arranged and systematized. Historical inquiry was stimulated by the interest in colonization, and local city histories and geographical guidebooks appeared. Greeks began to travel extensively, and the Persian conquest of the Ionian Greek cities in the sixth century produced a stimulating contact of cultures. Also of great importance for the rise of historical literature was the development of a spirit of skepticism and criticism among the scientific and philosophical schools of Ionia.

The first prose writers appeared about the middle of the sixth century. They were called *logographoi* and wrote mostly myths, genealogies, legends and the chronicles of cities. It was among the Ionian prose writers who recorded "sayings" *(logoi)* that we find the first historians.[8] Of these Hecataeus of Miletus, who wrote late in the sixth century,[9] and Hellanicus of Lesbos[10] were the most important.

Herodotus. A contemporary of the latter, Herodotus, has often been called the "Father of History," for his history of the wars between the Greeks and the Persians was the first comprehensive work in which the advances of his predecessors were combined with criticisms and an excellent style. He was born of a noble family in Halicarnassus in Asia Minor about the year 484 B.C., but was banished from his native city at an early age. He settled first at Samos, then at Athens, and in 443 B.C. became one of the first colonists who founded Thurii in southern Italy. He died in the early years of the Peloponnesian War *(ca.* 425). He traveled extensively in the Persian Empire, in Greece, Italy, Asia Minor, the Black Sea area and Egypt.[11]

As he states in the opening sentence to his history, his researches were recorded in the hope of preserving the "great and wonderful actions of the Greeks and Barbarians," and the causes for the conflict between them.[12] He sought, in a heroic prose epic almost Homeric in spirit, to narrate the enmity and struggles between Europe and Asia from mythical times, dwelling especially on the period from the reign of Croesus, the last Lydian King (560-546 B.C.), to the capture of Sestos in the Hellespont by the victorious Athenians in 478 B.C. In contrasting the freedom-loving Greek and the autocratically-ruled Asiatic and their different civilizations, Herodotus found it necessary to introduce lengthy digressions. "My story is looking for additions" he writes (IV. 30) as one tale leads to another, as one land involves descriptions of its neighbors.

Herodotus' history was later divided into nine books, each named after a

[8] J. B. Bury, *The Ancient Greek Historians*, pp. 1-35; Lionel Pearson, *Early Ionian Historians*, pp. 1-24.

[9] F. Jacoby, *Die Fragmente der griechischen Historiker*, I, pp. 1-47; 317-375; Pearson, *op. cit.*, pp. 25-108.

[10] F. Jacoby, *gr. Hist.*, pp. 104-52; 430-475; Pearson, *op. cit.*, pp. 152-235.

[11] Cf., T. R. Glover, *Herodotus*, Chapter 1.

[12] To Herodotus the word "researches" meant inquiry, investigation. A "historian" was one who sought the truth and it is only since the time of Polybius that the word "history" has been applied to the written narrative that resulted from such inquiry after truth.
Cf. Shotwell, *The History of History*, pp. 8-9, 168-170.

muse, by an Alexandrian editor. The first five books narrate the rise of Persia under Cyrus, the history of Egypt, the events which marked the accession of Darius and the history of Scythia and the Ionian rebellion. The remaining four books tell the stories of Marathon, Thermopylae, Salamis, Plataea and Mycale. His travels and early life under Persian rule had so broadened his sympathies that his *History* is remarkably free of bias and prejudice, although his sentiments are pro-Athenian.

Herodotus collected his data from a variety of sources: from his own observations, eye-witnesses, old family legends and traditions, oracles, lists of satraps, Egyptian priests and the earlier logographers. Yet he did not credulously record, without criticism or evaluation, the vast amount of material told him by his informants. Herodotus was a religious man and believed in a divine providence, yet he was cautious in relating tales of the intervention of the gods in the affairs of men (VII. 129). Although Herodotus is poor on motivation and interpretation, weak as a linguist (I. 139), given to exaggeration of numbers, and lacking in an understanding of military strategy, his "researches," his criticism, his naivete and charming style have made his *History* a valuable historical work and literary classic.

Thucydides. Herodotus may be called the Father of History, but it was his younger contemporary, Thucydides (*ca.* 455-*ca.* 400), who became the first critical and scientific historian. He was active in Athenian politics and affairs, and in 424 was elected one of the generals of Athens and placed in command of the Athenian naval forces off Amphipolis in Thrace. When this stronghold was lost, Thucydides was exiled and thereby given the opportunity and leisure to observe and record the course of the war. After living in exile for twenty years, Thucydides returned to Athens in 403 and died several years later, leaving his great work finished only to the year 411.

He began to write, he tells us, at the very beginning the war, clearly realizing its significance for the history of Greece and of his native city Athens. His writing reflects the intellectual and spiritual movements of his day, and he was also the first to apply to the writing of history the scientific methods of the Hippocratic school of medicine.[13] Thus, unlike his predecessors, Thucydides sought the causes of events in a critical study of men, their actions and emotions. Seeking to impart an exact knowledge of what happened, he studied or copied documents, talked with numerous eye witnesses, visited the scenes of action and then subjected all his findings to severe tests for accuracy (I. 22). His objectivity is extraordinary.

Thucydides chose a rather limited subject, the "history of the war between the Peloponnesians and the Athenians." To this program he adhered closely—perhaps too closely—throughout. He assumed a knowledge of the contemporary political and cultural institutions and sternly eliminated from his history all references to miracles and legends. Long digressions, too, are rare.[14] Thucydides neglected many of the social and economic phases of Periclean Athens and

---

[13] Charles N. Cochrane, *Thucydides and the Science of History*. For an opposing view see F. M. Cornford, *Thucydides Mythistoricus*.
[14] John H. Finley, "The Unity of Thucydides' History," *Athenian Studies Presented to W. S. Ferguson*, pp. 294-297.

the Peloponnesian War. This is particularly evident in his treatment of causation which, although advanced and showing a keen insight into affairs and events, emphasizes the military and diplomatic aspects of the intricate political situation of his day.[15]

Thucydides introduced speeches into his narrative to present his analysis and interpretation of a situation. These speeches, taking up almost a fourth of the work, summarize the forces and issues that shaped events and movements. Rhetorical in style, they also heighten the dramatic elements in his story. Thucydides was careful to explain that the speeches are not verbatim reports but that he, after careful inquiry, made the speakers say what the occasion, in his opinion, would have demanded (I. 22). Herodotus had inserted a few speeches into his history, but with Thucydides this literary device became an essential part of classical writing.

Thucydides also introduced a pragmatic element into Greek historiography. He felt that human nature was consistent, though often modified by *Tyche* (chance), and that the accurate picture of contemporary conditions and events which he was describing would help politicians and generals to shape the future (I. 23).

Xenophon. The works of Xenophon (434-354 B.C.), highly respected by the ancients for their admirable style, are, in the modern estimate, representative of the decline in historical writing in the fourth century B.C.[16] Yet Xenophon is an important historian because his *Hellenica*, beginning about 411 B.C., is the only continuous account which we possess of the period from the Peloponnesian War to 362 B.C. A journalist and biographer more than a historian, his personalities are sharply delineated. His narrative is vivid and fairly accurate, but because of his devotion to Sparta and Agesilaus he is often subjective and biased. His *Anabasis* is an accurate personal memoir of his career as a soldier of fortune during the revolt of Cyrus the Younger.

Lesser Early Greek Writers. Isocrates (436-338 B.C.), the proponent of Pan-Hellenic unity under Macedonian rule, greatly influenced the historical writing of the fourth and subsequent centuries. His artistic but too formal and artificial prose and his rhetorical and elaborate oratory contributed to the later prominence of rhetoric and moralization in literature and history.[17] The *Histories* of Ephorus of Cyme (*d.ca.* 330)[18] and the *Hellenica* and the *Philippica* of Theopompus of Chios[19] were the most important historical writings of the fourth century rhetoricians. A fragment of what was apparently a more detailed and valuable history than Xenophon's *Hellenica* was found at Oxyrhynchus in Egypt and published in 1909 as the *Hellenica Oxyrhynchus.* Of unknown authorship, the fragment gives a thorough account

---

[15] On Thucydides' treatment of causation see Cornford, *op. cit.,* pp. 1-14, 52-76, 244-250; G. B. Grundy, *Thucydides and the History of His Age,* pp. 315-332; Bury, *op cit.,* pp. 92-101; and S. B. Smith, "The Economic Motive in Thucydides," in *Harvard Studies in Classical Philology,* LI (1940), pp. 267-301.

[16] Alfred von Gutschmid, *Kleine Schriften,* IV, pp. 328-335.

[17] Hermann Peter, *Wahrheit und Kunst,* pp. 144-183.

[18] F. Jacoby, *gr. Hist.,* IIA, No. 70, 37-109 and IIC, 22-103; G. L. Barber, *The Historian Ephorus.*

[19] F. Jacoby, *gr. Hist.,* IIB, No. 115, 526-617 and IID, 351-403; Kurt von Fritz, "The Historian Theopompos," *American Historical Review,* XLVI (1941), pp. 765-787.

of the years 397-396, including an analysis of the Boeotian federal constitution.[20]

A characteristic type of historical writing of the fourth and third centuries B.C. was the *Atthis*. These were dry, objective and factual histories of Athens of which only fragments remain. The Atthidographers, differing from the rhetorical school of Isocrates, were concerned with religious history, ritual and mythology and with the development and chronology of Athenian demoeratic institutions.[21] The *Atthis (ca.* 326 B.C.) of Androtian,[22] a work later used by Aristotle in his *Constitution of Athens,* and that of Philochorus (*ca.* 320-260)[23] are the outstanding examples.

LATER GREEK

Timaeus. The spectacular conquests of Alexander stimulated the writing of histories and biographies, but unfortunately most of the historical writings of the Hellenistic age have disappeared. Among the greater losses are the *History* of Hieronymus of Cardia, an accurate and objective study of the period 323-266 B.C., and the historical memoirs of Aristobulus and Ptolemy I. Timaeus of Tauromenium in Sicily (*ca.* 345-250 B.C.) wrote a history of the West Greeks in Sicily and Italy from the earliest times to 264 B.C.,[24] introducing into historical chronology the system of dating events by Olympiads. If one is to believe Polybius, he was uncritical, an untrustworthy observer, given to vulgar abuse and to the reporting of wonders.[25]

Polybius. Deserving to rank with Herodotus and Thucydides is Polybius of Megalopolis (*ca.* 198-117 B.C.), the first Greek historian since the days of Xenophon whose works have survived in sufficient amount to warrant critical analysis.[26] He was the son of Lycortes, a general of the Achaean League, and was active in the political and military affairs of his native city. Brought as a hostage to Rome in 168 B.C., he gained there the friendship of Scipio Africanus and an admiration for the political institutions of the new rapidly rising power in the Mediterranean.

After his return to Greece, Polybius travelled extensively and completed his important *Histories.* In forty books, of which only five complete books and numerous lengthy fragments have survived, he described the First Punic War and the rise of the Achaean League, and then related the story of the fifty-three years between 220 and 167 B.C., in which period "almost the whole inhabited world" was conquered by Rome. His original plan had embraced only this period in which Rome's power reached its culmination, but the importance of the Third Punic War (149-146) and the wars in Greece led Polybius to include these contemporary events.

[20] F. Jacoby, *gr. Hist.,* IIA, No. 66, pp. 17-35 and IIC, pp. 6-20; Herbert Bloch, "Studies in Historical Literature of the Fourth Century B. C.," in *Athenian Studies Presented to W. S. Ferguson,* pp. 303-341; Peter, *op. cit.,* pp. 136-143.
[21] L. Pearson, *The Local Historians of Athens.*
[22] Karl and Theodore Müller, *Fragmenta Historicorum graecorum,* I, pp. 371-377.
[23] Photius has preserved Philochorus' explanation of the procedure of ostracism, the most complete account available; *Ibid.,* Fg. 79b.
[24] *Ibid.,* I, pp. 193-233.
[25] Polybius, *Histories,* XII. Eratosthenes of Alexandria (*ca.* 276-194 B.C.), Apollodorus of Athens (*ca.* 140 B.C.) and Castor of Rhodes (*ca.* 150 B.C.) continued the chronological studies of Timaeus on a more scientific basis.
[26] Richard Lacqueur, *Polybius;* Bury, *op. cit.,* pp. 191-220; Otto Cuntz, *Polybius und Sein Werk.*

Polybius, comparing history to the science of medicine, states (XII. 25-28) that the three divisions of the science of true history are the study and arrangement of written documents, the knowledge gained by travel and by study of the topography and physiography of land and sea, and finally experience in political affairs. A historian, he writes, must make statements and judgments which concur with the actions themselves, for truth is all-important; without it history is but an unprofitable story (I. 14). Polybius included no legends or miracles in his writing, and he scorned the rhetorical and episodic histories of the past. His descriptions and narratives are generally carefully done and his concept of history is comprehensive. Many times Polybius states that history should have a practical, didactic and pragmatic character.[27] He felt that the precedents which he recorded would be of great value in training for public office and that the heroic deeds which he described would inspire soldiers and statesmen of the future. Polybius sought to distinguish between cause and occasion, but his view of historical causation is rather superficial and external, and in the early parts of his work (I. 4; VIII. 4.3) he makes allowance for the mutability of *Tyche* (chance) along with the ordinary and natural causes. His style is dry; the artistry which is evident in the work of Thucydides is lacking. Polybius' work was continued by the versatile stoic, Poseidonius (*ca.* 135-50 B.C.) and by Strabo (*ca.* 64 B.C.-19 A.D.), the geographer.

Nicholas, Diodorus and Dionysius. Military conquest by Rome did not end the production of Greek literature. Nicholas of Damascus (b. *ca.* 64 B.C) compiled a world history now almost entirely lost. Diodorus Siculus (*ca.* 80-29 B.C) wrote his uncritical and rhetorical *Library,* or universal history, in an unsuccessful attempt to synthesize all history from the earliest mythological ages to Caesar's Gallic Wars. Also under Augustus, Dionysius of Halicarnassus published in Rome his *Archaeologia* which described the rise of Rome to the First Punic War (264 B.C.) and explained history as "philosophy teaching by example."

Plutarch. The writing of Greek historical biographies reached its culmination in the *Parallel Lives* of Plutarch (*ca.* 50-*ca.* 120 A.D). These interesting and often invaluable accounts of the lives of forty-six Greeks and Romans, arranged in pairs, are the work of a moralist who sought to present the personalities of the world's great and thus inculcate a desire for virtue and excellence.

Arrian, Appion and Dion. During the renaissance of Greek learning under Hadrian and his successors, Arrian (*ca.* 95-175 A.D.) composed his excellent *Anabasis of Alexander,* while Appion completed his history of Rome about 160 A.D. The latter work is inferior, marred by excessive rhetoric and affected by the imperial court. In the third century, Dion or Cassius Dio Coccijanus (155-*ca.* 235), the most important Greek historian of the Empire, composed a detailed and exact *History of Rome* in eighty books which covered the entire history of Rome to the year 229 A.D. Unfortunately, only books 36 to 60, giving the history of the important period 68 B.C.-

---

[27] Polybius, *Histories,* III. 31; IX. 9.

54 A.D., have survived in entirety. With the exception of an inferior history of the Empire by Herodian and some other historical writings by Dexippus, Dion is the last of the long list of eminent Greek historians.

ROMAN

Pictor and Cato. The early and great influence of Greek historiography on the Romans is evident from the fact that several of the early Roman annalists wrote in Greek. Thus the earliest Roman historian of whom we know was Quintus Fabius Pictor (b. *ca.* 254 B.C.) who wrote a valuable history of early Rome in Greek, not because Latin had not yet been sufficiently developed, but because he wished to present to the Greeks the Roman point of view on the Punic Wars. The *Origines* of M. Porcius Cato (d. 149 B.C.) was the earliest Latin prose history. It was an accurate and original account of the history of Rome and Italy from the origin of the city to the Lusitanian War of his day.[28]

Caesar. The Gracchan period, the civil wars with their stirring events, and the increasing emphasis on the role of the individual in politics led to the writing of a number of pamphlets and monographs on personalities and their deeds. Julius Caesar (100-44 B.C.) undertook to present his own case in his *Commentarii de bello Gallico,* in seven books which describes his activities in Gaul from 58-52 B.C. In a simple, lucid style, and writing in the third person, he cleverly sought to justify his actions and positions to the Romans. The work is marked by the objectivity of the author as well as by its accuracy.[29] After the Civil Wars, Caesar wrote his *Commentarii de bello civili* in the same interesting and clear manner, exercising the same simplicity and restraint as in his earlier work.

Sallust. More important than Caesar as a historian was his officer and partisan, Gaius Sallustius Crispus (87-35 B.C.). His *Conspiracy of Catiline* describes the Catilinian plot during the consulship of Cicero in 63 B.C. while his *Jugurtha* traces the rise of Jugurtha to power in Numidia and the subsequent war with Rome (111-104 B.C.). The fragments that survive of a third work entitled *Historiarum libri quinque* show that in this mature work Sallust related the history of the wars in the seventies and sixties.

In these brilliant monographs, which were very popular during the Middle Ages, there is a moralistic tone which decries the venality, the selfishness and the evil habits which wealth, luxury and power had brought to the governing aristocracy of his day. The character and personality of many famous people are carefully and sharply delineated in his works. His language is so trenchant, concise and replete with archaisms as to be ambiguous at times. Sallust is weak in chronology and his geographical descriptions are frequently inaccurate. His attempts to achieve high artistry and a dramatic effect often forced him to sacrifice the accuracy of his narrative, although in

---

[28] The fragments of these early Roman historians can be found in Hermann Peter, *Historicorum romanorum reliquiae,* I. See also M. L. W. Laistner, *The Greater Roman Historians,* Chap. II; Wilhelm Soltau, *Die Anfänge der roemischen Geschichtschreibung;* Tenney Frank, "Roman Historiography Before Caesar," in *American Historical Review,* XXXII (1927), pp. 232-240, and Chap. VI of his *Life and Literature in the Roman Republic.*
[29] T. Rice Holmes, *Caesar's Conquest of Gaul,* pp. 211-256.

historical reliability he does not approach Thucydides, whom he may have taken for his model.[30]

Livy. The historiographical writings of the Republic culminated in the signal work of Titus Livius (59 B.C-17 A.D.). The one hundred and forty-two books of his chief work, *From the Founding of the City,* traced the history of his nation from the founding of Rome to the death of Drusus, the younger brother of Tiberius, in 9 B.C. Unfortunately, only thirty-five books have survived. These books are I to X, which carry the story to the Third Sammite War (293 B.C.), and books XXI-XLV, the last five in truncated fragments, relating the events from the Second Punic War (218 B.C.) to the end of the Macedonian Wars in 167 B.C. Of the other books much has been preserved in fragmentary excerpts and in epitomes.[31]

Livy's impressive history of Rome was intended to extol the civic virtues of the founders and upholders of the Republic and to recall the qualities of the national character which had made Rome the mistress of the world. He recognized the paucity of early records and, without intending to establish their accuracy, recorded the legends of early Rome, after warning his readers of their unreliability. Their uncritical insertion has contributed much to our understanding of the *ethos* of the Fathers of the Republic, and archaeological evidence has in numerous cases substantiated their credibility. Livy, more than other ancient historians, mentions the names of many of his sources. Fabius Pictor, Claudius Quadrigarius, Coelius Antipater, Valerius Antias and Polybius are frequently cited.[32]

Livy exhibited the deficiencies common to most ancient historians. His patriotism did not compensate for his unfamiliarity with political economy and jurisprudence. His geography is weak, his knowledge of military affairs inadequate, and he may be criticized for anachronisms and faulty chronology. Livy was deeply religious and frequently included prodigies and many omens in his narrative—all contributing, however, to the portrayal of the early Roman spirit. In keeping with the rhetorical writing of his time, Livy inserted many fictitious speeches into his narrative, which give us a much better appreciation of the character of the speaker and of the artistry and genius of the author. For his lucid and honest narrative, Livy rightly deserves to be considered one of the greatest figures in Roman literature.

Tacitus. Primarily because of the loss of personal liberties, the Latin literature of the first century A. D. declined in quality from the heights reached in the brilliant age of Augustus. Numerous historical works of questionable value were written but, except for fragments, little besides the names of the historians is known. The senatorial view of Tiberius and imperial Rome was expressed by Cornelius Tacitus, four of whose extant works are historical in

---

[30] On Sallust see especially Laistner, *op. cit.,* Chap. III and H. Peter, *Wahrheit und Kunst,* pp. 339-348. Other historians of this period were C. Asinius Pollio and Pompeius Trogus. T. Pomponius Atticus, Cornelius Nepos and M. Terentius Varro undertook chronological works to fix the early dates in Roman history.

[31] Hermann Peter, *Die geschichtliche Literatur über die romische Kaiserzeit bis Theodosius I und ihre Quellen,* II, pp. 341-348. On Livy see Laistner, *op. cit.,* Chaps. IV and V.

[33] On the sources of Livy see especially Heinrich Nissen, *Kritische Untersuchen über die Quellen der vierten und funften Dekade des Livius* and Wilhelm Soltau, *Livius' Geschichtswerk, seine Komposition, und seine Quellen.*

nature. His *Life and Death of Agricola* is a biography of his father-in-law, Julius Agricola, composed in 98 A. D. when the mild reigns of Nerva and Trajan once again encouraged free expression after the silence enforced by the tyrannical Domitian.[33] Historical and topographical materials are secondary in the work, but the *Agricola* does contain geographic and ethnographic data on the early Britons. The ethnographic element is enlarged in the monograph *Germania*, which Tacitus also wrote in 98 A. D., and which contains a general description of the land of the Germans and the customs and morals of single tribes. In his *Histories*, Tacitus narrated in twelve or fourteen books the events of Roman history from 69 A. D. to the death of Domitian in 96, but only the first four and part of the fifth book have survived. His other major work, the *Annals*, was concerned with the period from the death of Augustus in 14 A. D. to January 1, 69 A. D. Of the original sixteen books, only books I to IV, parts V and VI, and almost all of XI-XVI are extant.[34]

In these two major works of Tacitus, the *Histories* and the *Annals*, his narrative is rich in detail and moral dignity, varied in structure and expression so as to maintain interest and written in a concise and vigorous style. Personalities are clearly portrayed and their characters distinctly depicted, for the keen insight of Tacitus saw beneath the external and superficial. Tacitus claimed to write without passion and partiality,[35] but his preconceived opinions and views are developed by means of innuendo and insinuation. The prejudices of Tacitus, however, in favor of the senatorial faction are more evident in the *Histories* than in the *Annals* where the gradual decline of the senate in power and dignity is contemptuously presented. Tacitus also believed that the glories of Rome had departed and that the paucity of great wars and the abundance of misery made the writing of his histories a pleasureless and mournful task.[36] To Tacitus, the function of history was to give praise where praise was due, to show the evil consequences of malicious and immoral acts, and to instruct the statesmen of the future by relating the experiences of others.[37]

Suetonius. A younger contemporary of Tacitus, Suetonius Tranquillus *(ca. 75-160 A.D.)*, wrote *The Lives of the Caesars*, portraying concisely and clearly the personalities and characters of the twelve rulers from Caesar to Domitian. Suetonius consulted the documents of the imperial archives, but his biographies contain many anecdotes, trivialities, physical descriptions, omens, and obscure details, all in marked contrast to the serious work of Tacitus. Suetonius did not arrange his data chronologically nor did he write rhetorically. His interesting biographies were to become the models for much later writing.[38]

Ammianus. Under the Antonines, Greek historical writing experienced a temporary revival, while Latin literature declined. Some epitomes of earlier works were composed and attempts were made to continue the biographical work

---

[33] On the literary character and antecedents of the *Agricola* see D. R. Stuart, *Epochs of Greek and Roman Biography*, pp. 235-253.
[34] Gaston Boissier, *Tacitus and Other Roman Studies*, trans. by W. G. Hutchison; Laistner, *op. cit.*, Chaps. VI and VII; H. Peter, *Geschichtliche Literatur*, II, pp. 42-67.
[35] *Annals*, I. i. i.
[36] *Annals*, IV, 32-33.
[37] *Ibid.*, III. 65; IV, 32-33.
[38] Friedrich Leo, *Die griechisch-romische Biographie nach ihrer litterarischen Form;* pp. 268-314.

of Suetonius. Ancient Latin literature almost seemed to have reached its lowest ebb when it was briefly revived by the excellent historical work of Ammianus Marcellinus. Ammianus was born of Greek parentage in Antioch about 330 A.D. In his *History*, the first thirteen books of which are now lost, he narrated the events of Roman history from the reign of Nerva (96 A.D.) to the death of Valens at Adrianople in 378, Book XIV beginning with the year 353. The impartiality, truthfulness and accuracy of this soldier, his wide reading and his vivid portrayal of the Roman world of the fourth century, make the reader overlook the harshness and clumsiness of his style. His work is a fitting finale to Roman historical writing.[39]

EARLY CHRISTIANS

Sextus Julius Africanus. While Roman historians were recording the vicissitudes of the Empire, the early historians of the Christian Church were seeking to show that the Hebrew-Christian culture was more ancient than that of the pagan civilizations and furnish secular proof of the unique and historic character of their religion. The literary device best suited to this purpose was the chronicle. Justus of Tiberias, Julius Cassianus and Clement of Alexandria had early attempted chronology studies, but Sextus Julius Africanus *(ca. 180-ca. 250)* was the first to write a comprehensive and scholarly chronicle of world history from the Christian position. His *Five Books of Chronicles,* written in Greek but no longer extant, was an exhaustive compilation of historical data, sacred and profane, from Creation to the year of 221 A.D.[40]

Eusebius of Caesarea. The most complete chronological study of this period and certainly the most influential, was the unified system established by Eusebius Pamphilus. Eusebius was born about the year 260, probably in Palestine, and was educated in the school of the learned Pamphilus, whose name he assumed. About 313 Eusebius was elected Bishop of Caesarea and soon became involved in the Arian controversy. He died about 340, after a lifetime of untiring research and literary activity. One of his many works is a *Chronicle* written in Greek early in the fourth century.[41] The *Chronographia*, the first of its two parts, outlines the history of the nations of antiquity and is based on the writings of the Old Testament authors, Diodorus, Manetho, Porphyry, Castor, Dionysius of Halicarnassus, Josephus and many others. The second part of the *Chronicle*, the more important part, consists of synchronistic tables which are known as the *Chronological Canons*. Beginning with the birth of Abraham (2016 B.C.), the chronological data of various nations is compiled in parallel columns. Brief notices of the outstanding events in Jewish and profane history are placed beside the appropriate column. Unfortunately, no copy of the original Greek text of the *Chronicle* has survived. The *Canons* were, however, translated into Latin by the learned Jerome in 379 A.D. This translation,

---

[39] See Laistner, *op. cit.*, Chap. XIII; Terrot R. Glover, *Life and Letters in the Fourth Century*, Chap. II; H. Peter, *Geschichtliche Literatur*, II, pp. 117-130.
[40] Martin J. Routh, *Reliquiae sacrae*, II, pp. 221ff.; Heinrich Gelzer, *Sextus Julius Africanus und die byzantinische Chronographie*.
[41] J. P. Migne, ed., *Patrologiae graecae*, XIX, cols. 101-598; Alfred Schoene, *Die Weltchronik des Eusebius*; Gelzer, *op. cit.*, II, pp. 23-107; F. J. Foakes-Jackson, *Eusebius Pamphili*, pp. 143-149.

hastily dictated and augmented, was to become the basis and model for most medieval annals and chronicles in western Europe.

Despite the appearance of other chronicles, notably those of Q. Julius Hilarianus[42] and Sulpicius Severus,[43] that of Eusebius and Jerome was the most widely used and quite naturally invited extension. Prosper of Aquitaine (b. *ca.* 390) continued the chronicle to the year 455.[44] Later Hydatius *(ca.* 427-*ca.* 270), a Spanish bishop, brought the work up to the year 467.[45] Marcellinus Comes further extended the work to 534, Victor Tunnunensis, to 563, and John Biclarensis to the year 590.

Lactantius. While these Christian writers compiled chronicles, others were engaged in more comprehensive and detailed histories. Such a work is the *De mortibus persecutorum* of L. Caecilius Firmianus Lactantius of Nicomedia *(ca.* 260-*ca.* 340) which contains frightful descriptions of the horrible fate of the persecutors of Christians from the time of Nero to Diocletian.[46] The work is important for our understanding of the Diocletian system of government.

Eusebius of Caesarea. But the pioneer in ecclesiastical history, whom we mentioned above, was Eusebius of Caesarea, being as he himself said, "the first to enter upon the subject."[47] Apologetic in character, his Greek *Ecclesiastical History* is an erudite amplification and extension of the events he had earlier listed in his *Chronological Canons.*[48] His purpose in writing, explained in the first book and maintained throughout, was to trace carefully the antiquity of the Christian religion and to make clear the continuity and spread of the Church since the days of Christ. To this end he recorded the succession of bishops in the important sees, listed the great Christian teachers and writers, narrated the stories of persecution and miracles, and quoted long citations as documentary evidence that the Christian Church was a divine institution with historical antiquity and continuity.

The *Ecclesiastical History* of Eusebius was revised by the author four times, until the ten books brought the history of the Church to the year 323 A.D. The *History* was rather poorly translated in the troubled days of the early fifth century by Tyrannius Rufinus, who added two chapters of his own describing the period 324 to the death of Theodosius (395 A.D.). Later in the century three Church historians, Socrates and Sozomen of Constantinople and Bishop Theodoret of Eastern Syria, each extended the *History* of Eusebius in Greek. Socrates, the best historian of the three, continued the history to the year 439.

Jerome. To acquaint the pagans with the ever increasing number of Christian literary works and to defend the Church against the accusations as to the lowly and uneducated character of its members, it was important that a list of the significant Christian authors and their works be compiled. Jerome *(ca.* 348-420)

---

[42] J. P. Migne, ed., *Patrologiae latinae,* XIII, cols. 1097-1114.
[43] Migne, *Pat. lat.,* XX, cols. 95-248; Gelzer, *op. cit.,* ii, pp. 107-121, Glover, *Life and Letters,* Chap. XII.
[44] Migne, *Pat. lat.,* LI, col. 535-606, 859-866; Theodor Mommsen in *Monumenta Germaniae Historica, Auctorum Antiquissimorum,* IX, "Chronica Minora I," pp. 341ff.
[45] Migne, *Pat. lat.,* LI, cols. 873-890.
[46] *Ibid.,* VII, cols. 157-276; *Ante-Nicene Fathers* ed. by Roberts and J. Donaldson, VII, pp. 301-322.
[47] Eusebius, *Ecclesiastical History,* I, i.
[48] F. J. Foakes-Jackson, *op. cit.,* pp. 61ff; Migne, *Pat. graecae,* XX, cols. 9-906.

undertook this task when in 392 he wrote his *De viris illustribus,* a catalogue of one hundred thirty-five authors beginning with Peter. Following the example and style of Suetonius, Jerome devoted a chapter to each author, giving biographical and literary-historical data.[49]

Augustine. The famous edict issued in Milan in 313 had assured the dominance of Christianity within the Roman Empire, but the collapse of the once well-organized Roman rule in the fourth and fifth centuries caused men to question the new religion. Especially after the six-day sack of Rome by Alaric the Goth in 410, it was felt that this was the punishment for the desertion of the old gods and for the widespread adoption of Christianity. It was from Africa that the formal refutation came to this claim that the civilization of the ancient world had been ruined by the Christian religion. Its author was the greatest of the Church Fathers, Aurelius Augustinus (354-430), the bishop of Hippo. Born a pagan, later, an adherent of the Manichaean heresy and a follower of Neo-Platonism, he was won to the Church in 387 by Ambrose of Milan. Ordained a priest in 391 and consecrated a bishop five years later, Augustine spent the remainder of his life opposing the Donatists, Manichaeans and Pelagians. His writings are varied and his influence, both in the Church of his day and for all time since, has been enormous.

In 426, after thirteen years of labor, Augustine completed his *De Civitate Dei,* the Christian reply to the pagan charge. The twenty-two books of the *City of God* form a Christian apology and while not in reality a historical work, yet in historiography this mighty treatise marks the beginning of the teleological interpretation of history.[50] To Augustine, the history of the world is the long unfolding of God's will, and the earth merely the scene of perpetual conflict between two cities or states; an earthly one, composed of all those who seek reward and happiness on this earth, and a heavenly one *(Civitas Dei),* composed of all faithful Christians who are but pilgrims in this world. The end of the conflict between these two polities will be the Last Judgment, where the citizens of the *Civitas Dei* will obtain immortality while those of the city of the unrighteous will be condemned. All human history leads but to this great occasion and has no other meaning.

The construction of the picture of the two Cities, curiously fused and intertwined, begins with the eleventh book. The history of the earthly, unrighteous community Augustine traced from the secular records as found in Cicero, Varro, Jerome's version of Eusebius' *Chronicle,* Plato, Sallust, Pliny the Elder, Vergil and others, while the history of the citizens of the City of God is drawn from the Scriptures, the only history of importance.

Orosius. In the year 414 a young Spanish presbyter named Orosius came to Augustine for advice and instruction. Sent on to Jerome at Bethlehem, Orosius in 415 entered the lists as an opponent of Pelagius. Returning to the West in the next year, Orosius was instructed by Augustine to prepare a summary of world history.

---

[49] Migne, *Pat lat.,* XXIII, cols. 631-720.
[50] *Ibid.,* XL; Ernst Troeltsch, *Augustin, die christliche Antike und das Mittelalter* and Heinrich Scholz, *Glaube und Unglaube in der Weltgeschichte* stress the apologetic character of the work and deny that it can be termed a philosophy of history.

Completed about 418, this compendium, entitled *Historiarum adversus paganos libri septem,*[51] was to supplement with historical data Augustine's *City of God.* The history of Orosius recounted the numerous evils, disasters, catastrophes, wars and crimes which marked the pre-Christian period in world history. His *historia calamitatum,* after a geographical sketch, begins with the evils which were introduced into the world by the Babylonian ruler Ninus and which have since beset mankind. The tribulations of those who lived in the Babylonian, Macedonian, Carthaginian and Roman kingdoms are recounted in dreary detail, with occasional remarks as to the comparative minuteness of the "present troubles." These the historian apologist narrates extensively, giving descriptions of Stilicho, Alaric, Athaulf and Wallia, and the sack of Rome (to Orosius, mild).

Writing in clear and forcible Latin, Orosius extracted his stories of disaster from a variety of sources. The chronological structure is based on Jerome's extension of the *Chronicle* of Eusebius. Suetonius, Tacitus and other Latin historians were searched for calamitous details, and the influence of the first five books of Augustine's *City of God* is evident throughout. With this endorsement by Augustine, the *Histories* of Orosius, inaccurate as they were, became the standard manual for non-Scriptural history in the Middle Ages.

Victor. The persecution of the orthodox Christians of Africa by the Arian Vandals is described in a work entitled *Historia persecutionis Africanae provinciae,* which Victor, Bishop of Vita in Africa, wrote about 486 A. D. Victor's account is highly colored and biased, but important as a regional study of the late fifth century.[52]

Jerome's biographical work on ecclesiastical writers was continued about 495 A. D. by Gennadius, Presbyter of Massilia. His important *De viris illustribus* contains descriptions of the lives and writings of one hundred Christian writers of the fifth century.[53]

Severinus. This account of the historical writing of the classical period may be concluded with the biography of Saint Severinus of Noricum written by his pupil Eugippius (*ca.* 455-*ca.* 543). His *Vita S. Severeini,* written in the plebeian Latin of the early sixth century, is anecdotal in character, relating in chronological order the wonders, prophecies and deeds of the saint. The work is important for an exact description of the conditions in Noricum during the collapse of Roman rule there.[54]

[51] Migne, *Pat. lat.,* XXXI, cols. 663-1174; *Seven Books of History Against the Pagans,* trans., by I. W. Raymond; W. M. T. Gable, "Orosius," in *Church Historians* ed. by P. Guilday, pp. 30-70.
[52] Migne, *Pat. lat.,* LVIII, cols. 179-260.
[53] *Ibid.,* LVIII, cols. 1059-1120.
[54] Wilhelm Wattenbach, *Deutschlands Geschichtsquellen im Mittelalter* (seventh ed.) I, 50-56; *Mon. Ger. Auct. Ant.,* I, ii, 1-36.

Chapter 2

EARLY MEDIEVAL HISTORIOGRAPHY*

By Benoit Lacroix, O. P.

THE sack of Rome by Alaric in 410 threw the Romans into consternation. A barbarian had just seized the city; a new civilization was on the way. To the Romans, accustomed to glory and success, this new turn of events caused shock and drove them to soul-searching. The pagans queried the historians. The Christians sought an answer from God. In the face of pagan arguments and Christian doubts, Augustine, Bishop of Hippo, felt obliged to turn to a rereading of history and to write on the subject. After acquainting himself with the historical writing of his compatriots, he began, in 413, to compose, and, until 426, to publish month by month his lengthy *City of God*.

Augustine's Influence on Orosius. In 417 or 418 he sought the help of his disciple Orosius, a Spanish refugee and encouraged him to write a work which completed Augustine's views. In composing the seven books of the *History against the Pagans,* Orosius accepted Augustine's views, but, dealing more concretely with the tragic event of 410, he placed it in its human and historical context. To the historian of these texts, the other writings of the period after 410, for example, *On the Governance of God* by Salvian of Marseilles (fifth century), seem to be only the epilogue of an inevitable development. Jerome, Augustine, and Orosius had vainly hoped and believed that Rome would once again recover. But the accounts in shorter form of those who continued the history of Jerome (after 378), for example, that of Prosper of Aquitaine (378-455), demonstrate that the Romans were no longer by themselves. The barbarians occupy an increasingly prominent place in the texts. Salvian praised their natural virtues. Idatius (died after 468 when his chronicle ended) spoke severely of the *Suevi*. By the sixth century, the chroniclers introduced new tribes into written history and devoted increasing attention to them. These chroniclers were: Chancellor Marcellinus (source for the period from 378-534), Victor of Tunnuna (source for the period from 444-566), Marius of Avenches (to 581), John of Biclaro or John the Goth, bishop of Girona, who continued the work of Victor of Tunnuna to 590, as Victor did that of Prosper.

The first barbarian to write history, Jordanes, is of the sixth century. He wrote a parallel history of the Romans and Goths. There we are in the age of pioneers, of founders. In the West Latin medieval historiography witnessed the progressive fusion of three traditions, represented by three different groups of historians: 1. The Jewish tradition extending from Moses and those who summarized and followed him to Flavius Josephus whom St. Jerome

---

* Translated by James A. Corbett.

(d. 420) and Cassiodorus (d. 575) accepted as the last of the Jewish historians. 2. The Graeco-Roman tradition, which was pagan and represented especially by Herodotus and Thucydides among the Greeks, and Livy and Sallust among the Romans. 3. The distinct Christian tradition, of more recent origin, for Eusebius of Caesarea (d. 338), Jerome and Orosius are its first great names.

In this period, also, St. Augustine (d. 430) had, so to speak, saved historiography, its texts and the reputation of its authors, when he recognized in his *De Doctrina Christiana (On Christian Doctrine,* II, 27), written in 397, that history, even history written by pagans, is a "useful discipline for the cultivated Christian, for it can confirm his faith by verifying the content and authenticity of the facts which support it." The texts of secular history bear witness to the reality of sin, of the Incarnation, the Passion, the Resurrection, etc. . . . Without knowing it Augustine had given the rule, the text which became the *authority* on which generations of monks and clerics would rely when reading, copying and transcribing the texts of pagan historiography and when writing in their own turn the history of their own times. But one history alone dominates all others: the history of salvation contained in the Bible. In these Latin Middle Ages, everything is said, done and written in the name of the Bible. Little by little the three traditions, the three groups of historians become fused into one, to the advantage of the Christian element. This group, new but profoundly dependent on the past, comprise the major historians known to the Middle Ages. These historians first of all retained the names of all the biblical authors, that of Flavius Josephus, the names of a few pagan historians, who soon took the place of such mere retailers of information as Florus, Justin and Trogus Pompeius, and Eutropius. Sallust owes a part of his medieval reputation to the admiration that St. Augustine professed for him. The same is true of Livy, and, to a lesser extent, of Tacitus.

MID-SIXTH CENTURY HISTORIANS

The first formal list of Christian historians that we have dates from the mid-sixth century. It was compiled by Cassiodorus around 550-560. In this matter his inspiration and model was St. Jerome's *De viris illustribus (On Distinguished Men)*. Cassiodorus *(Institutiones,* I, 17) particularly mentioned apart from those authors already named (Flavius Josephus, Eusebius, Jerome, and Orosius), Rufinus (d. 410), translator and continuer of the *Ecclesiastical History* of Eusebius, Epiphanus (sixth century) who prepared a Latin version (the *Tripartite History*) of the Greek continuation (to 349) of the same work by Socrates, Sozomenus and Theodoretus and Prosper of Aquitaine sought to deal with the whole period of time since Adam. Cassiodorus, himself, must be considered as one of the greatest promoters of historical learning at this time. The Vivarium, where he retired at the end of his life, is the first historical center of Christian Europe. Cassiodorus, also, prepared an abridgement of history. Jordanes, the only "barbarian" by birth who contributed to the historiography of the invasion, used and, thus in a measure preserved, the lost *History of the Goths (De rebus geticis)* of Cassiodorus, in the writing of his *Romana et Getica (Roman and Gothic Affairs)*. This is a clumsy but precious history, for Jordanes introduces us to a "new world." He preceded that new group of non-Roman historians, who may be called the founders of medieval historiography: Gregory of Tours (d. 593), Isidore of Seville (d. 636); Bede (d. 735), and Paul the Deacon (d. 787).

GREGORY OF TOURS IN FRANKISH GAUL

Two dates are all-important for the history of Latin literature between the "official" fall of the Roman Empire in the west (476) and the accession of Pepin (741). The first is the date (597) of the sending of the Roman Latin missionaries to England by Pope Gregory the Great. The second is the date (718) of the departure of Winfred of Wessex (Boniface) and his companions for Germany. It is in this period that there occurs what Christopher Dawson has happily called *The Making of Europe*. Gaul passed to the Franks. Italy became Lombard. Africa, and, in 711, Spain are lost to the Arabs. England and Ireland, more isolated, share in the general misfortune. In the history of literature, it is a time of impoverishment and adaptation, of dissipation of energy and of decline to the point of disappearance of the old centers of culture. Without schools, learning became a matter of private initiative. "Woe to our times," cried Gregory of Tours at the end of the sixth century, "for the study of letters has perished amongst us."[1] The schools of grammar, where formerly the ancient learned to read and love Sallust and Livy, have disappeared. Frankish Gaul, one of the first European nations to develop a certain degree of national unity, thanks to the Merovingian monarchy, had on the testimony of Gregory, himself, very few competent rhetoricians. A rustic and primitive Latin takes the place of the ancient Roman Latin. "Many lament it" but it was Gregory, himself Bishop of Tours since 573, who, although busy with his own pastoral duties, had to take the initiative in writing history. He had to do the job because, he explained, to the regret of everyone there could not be found "a single grammarian sufficiently competent in the art of writing to narrate, either in prose or verse, what had happened in the land of the Franks."[2]

His Work. It goes without saying that the writing of history is not the primary duty of a bishop. But because Gregory was the only one who knew a little Latin—and that, on his own recognition, was pretty rustic and barely grammatical—he had to do the writing. Matter is more important than form; and truth takes precedence over beauty. Gregory decided that when one man alone can suitably do the job, that everyone agrees is necessary, it is better to write even clumsily than to prolong indefinitely a silence that everyone regrets.[3]

Gregory's work is a kind of chronicle, in ten books that have been called *Historia francorum,* but could well have been called a chronicle. The history begins with Adam and ends in 591.

As a bishop, Gregory had to preach and instruct men in matters of faith.

---

[1] Gregory of Tours, *The History of the Franks,* translated with an introduction by O. M. Dalton (Oxford: Clarendon Press, 1927), V, Preface.
[2] *Ibid.*
[3] *Ibid.,* **X,** 31.

By the time he had finished Book II on the Merovingian period, he had already written a number of hagiographical works. Among these works are: *De virtutibus sancti Martini (On the Virtues of St. Martin)*, *De gloria sanctorum (On the Glory of the Saints)*, a commentary on the psalms, and an ecclesiastical calendar. The work of the historian is thus only a part of the teaching of the bishop.

Judgment of the Historian. The first point, which is basic for the understanding of all medieval Latin historiography, is the primacy of the narrative and of truth over any aesthetic consideration. The true takes precedence over the beautiful; the demands of the narrative come before style and even grammar. Gregory knew that it was necessary to write well; he could not do so. But he wrote to preserve the truth from oblivion.

The fact that to relate the history of the Franks, Gregory felt obliged to go back to Adam, is a second point to stress for it illustrates the essentially universalist viewpoint of medieval historiography. Even in the case of a small local history the historian is obliged to graft it upon the whole history of the past. In his own way, Gregory of Tours carried on the precedent inaugurated by Eusebius in his chronological tables, and followed by Prosper of Aquitaine in his *Chronicon,* and Sulpicius Severus (fifth century) in his *Two Books of Chronicles.* The Frankish story, which only begins at the end of Book I of the *History of the Franks,* going back to a single man, appears as the unfolding in a particular country, the land of the Gauls, of the brief history of the human race. As the Franks are human and Gregory wishes to tell their history, he thought it proper briefly to recall their remote origins; that is to say, to go back to the first man, Adam, ancestor of all the others.

Gregory mixes up his methods and literary genres. The *writer of history,* such as he was, often influenced, to the point of effacement during entire pages, the *historian* that he tried to be. This confusion is paid for by the loss of precision and a concise style. The *History of the Franks* illustrates a third noteworthy point about medieval historiography: literary genres were not so rigorously distinguished in the Middle Ages as they are today. From the standpoint of proper historical information, hagiography enables us to understand the psychology of its authors, the tastes of their epoch and the color and tone of their surroundings. Most of the Latin historians of the Middle Ages, bishops, priests, and monks wrote hagiographical works. They did so just as modern historians, at one time or another, write essays on subjects peripherally related to their professional interests.

Of course, in Gregory's time, there was no such thing as a professional historian. As history, however, liberal and literally written, was not recognized as an autonomous discipline, it usually happened, as in the case of Gregory of Tours, that the historian was also a hagiographer. He was intrusted with the care of souls, responsible for a diocese or abbey, or was busily committed to the royal and political life of his surroundings. To understand Gregory and his successors, it is important to stress the fact that a medieval historian cannot be explained without an account of his milieu, which he seeks to serve and for which he writes.

From a literary and methodological point of view, Gregory, as an historian, is characterized by his concern about chronology and narration, basic in all true historical writing. The historian of Tours first located events in time and then narrated them. He did not attempt to prove them, nor to defend them. Essentially he was a narrator. And one may find almost any kind of story in the *History of the Franks*. The author brusquely leads us from one fact to another, from one person to another. He mentions a king then passes on to a bishop, he stops in the midst of details about a war, relates some small personal adventure, leads us back to the Merovingian court, notices a "miraculous" event, and, soon after, tells us about the temperature and the yield of the harvests. All is mixed together without transition and without warning. Without any selection based on preconception, he relates all that he knows or has heard. He does not paint his environment; he photographs it. But in spite of this mixture, he maintains—and never voluntarily betrays—an order, the order of history as it happens: the chronological order. It is the only order that Gregory recognized.

Gregory's Literary Methods. Gregory's Latin is clumsy and his literary methods are sometimes very dubious. But he remains the historian *par excellence* of the Merovingian age, because in spite of everything, he rigorously preserved, in their natural order, the sequence of events. It did not matter to him that in recalling events in their sequence he mingled pleasant and tragic events, and the history of a faithful king or of "an impious wretch." "Indeed, I do not believe that lack of sense will be imputed to me for having mixed together the goodness of happy people and the wretchedness of the unhappy, because in this respect it is not the writer who gives the command, but the order of time." [4] Perfect objectivity! It is not the historian who arranges the facts to suit his logic or his classicism; the facts themselves guide the historian. The facts are set down "confusedly" in the order in which they take place and they remain the masters. The history of God itself (the Bible), Gregory queries as if to justify himself, Is it not composed of the same, mysterious interplay of good and evil, of temporal and spiritual developments?

This concern for observing the order of events, even if it is confused, is a feature peculiar to the Middle Ages and to antiquity. The annalistic form of history no longer is to our taste, but it is well to remember that it did please the ancients.

We should also note in Gregory an instinctive need, a compulsion to tell us stories. This feeling is characteristic of young and nomadic civilizations, where oral tradition plays a very important role. Older and more restrained civilizations are more profoundly impressed by the conventions of writing. Gregory always draws his inspiration from oral tradition, which he prefers, both as a matter of taste and because of his circumstances. As "letters have decayed" in his time, he does not have to deal with contemporary written sources. This insistence upon the fact *recounted,* this instinctive preference for oral tradition and the search for eyewitness testimony are additional

---

[4] *Ibid.*

traits of early medieval historiography. They are well revealed in Gregory, its first Frankish representative.

There remains the question of his interpretation of facts. This is the weak and, for us, disconcerting part of medieval historiography. The interplay of facts, advanced by Gregory, may be summed up in this phrase: God punishes the wicked and rewards the good. Instead of surrendering discreetly to the sometimes inscrutable judgments of God as do the authors of the Bible which he invokes, Gregory oversimplifies things by identifying the good man or the bad man according to the good or bad fortune which happens to him. Clovis is blessed for all the hatchet blows which cut off the necks of the "bad heretics"; but Gontran is handled roughly by the things which happen to him and by the historian who recalls them with satisfaction: "It was, I believe, an effect of Providence for he proposed to send into exile a great number of bishops."[5]

Thus, war, pestilence, and a military defeat appear like God's chastisements of particular persons. Salvian of Marseilles had already written in *On the Governance of God* that God judges men as He leads them. Gregory, like the majority of the historians in the Middle Ages, even the laymen, believed this. The fundamental thesis which supports all these judgments is clearly of scriptural inspiration, but a misunderstood one. The historians, beginning with Gregory of Tours, do not hesitate to recall the texts needed to support it. They too readily applied precise Biblical texts to facts which were not those of the Old Testament. Gregory of Tours read the history of France in the light of Jewish history but without any nuances. In brief, Gregory of Tours represented the historiography of his time both in taste for narrative and his desire to promote the religious education of his readers by offering a moral interpretation of the facts. The *History of the Franks* illustrates well the first type, simple and naive, natural and without artificial imitation, of medieval historiography. Most of the subsequent historians would resemble him: they too would be narrators, just as dependent on their immediate sources, oral tradition and eyewitnesses, and just as overloaded with digressions and hasty judgments. The *History of the Franks* remains for the knowledge of medieval historiography what the histories of Herodotus are for the knowledge of Greek historiography: the first work which makes possible a judgment of the progress of the others. The modern historians who have studied the "ten books of history" of Gregory of Tours know how these "texts" synthetize the preoccupations and the thoughts of a cleric, bishop and Frank at the end of the sixth century. Almost in spite of himself, he had to improvise in order to save his people from the misfortune of being ignored any longer.

Isidore of Seville

Spain has always been the land of surprises for the historian of western Latin culture. In mid-seventh century, while everywhere else major religious and social changes were taking place, there were first rate men of letters at Toledo. One of them, Isidore, Bishop of Seville, drawn to history more

---

[5] *Ibid.*, V, 36.

by events than by taste and personal aptitudes, is worthy of study because he was for Spain, the Goths, and the Vandals and *Suevi,* what Gregory of Tours was for the Franks. In temperament and performance, Isidore was more of an encyclopedist. This was what the times called for. Isidore taught that historiography was above all a kind of *Narratio rei gestae per quam ea quae in preterito facta sunt dinoscuntur,* that is to say, the account of an event which had occurred thanks to which posterity is instructed about the past.[6] This was the only definition of history with which the Latin Middle Ages were familiar. He would likewise remind it that history lends itself to several literary forms depending upon whether it is presented as a chronological recapitulation verified by events (Chronicle), or it is restricted to a more limited period: it may for example be written from day to day (cf. diary), monthly (calendar), annually (annals), or extend over a longer period (history).

All these notions and divisions are derived from the ancient world. Isidore repeats them without discussing them. Through him they reached the Middle Ages and were accepted in those times. On this matter, the Middle Ages did not invent any more than Isidore did; the two accepted the authority of the ancients.

Six Ages of World History. What the Latin Middle Ages and Isidore added was their historical writings. Isidore wrote about 615 a sort of universal chronicle, a short survey of times from creation to his own day. Eusebius and Jerome were the primary sources for this writing which has nothing very original about it unless it be that he published an essentially biblical division of history often pointed out by St. Augustine. The history of the world was divided into six ages which Isidore enumerated as follows: (1) From Adam to Noah, (2) From Noah to Abraham, (3) From Abraham to David, (4) From David to the Babylonian Captivity, (5) From the Babylonian Captivity to the Coming of Christ, and (6) From the Coming of Christ to the Final Resurrection.

This division of history passed from Isidore to Bede and through them to the whole Latin Middle Ages. One still finds it in the national chronicles of the sixteenth century. Thus, what we call the Middle Ages was not in the eyes of Isidore and his successors, the Middle Ages. We are all, they would say, in the sixth and last age, this unique and Christian age of the Redemption. Any other division of history would be in their eyes handy but provisional and accidental.

Isidore also reminded the Middle Ages that its first historian was not Herodotus but Moses.[7] He learned this from Jerome with whose work he was very familiar.

The *Historia de regibus Gothorum, Vandalorum et Suevorum. (History of the Kings of the Goths, the Vandals and the Suevi),* another work of Isidore of Seville, along with a few notes of Idatius (fifth century), remains our principal source for our knowledge of Visigothic Spain up to 621, of

---

[6] *Etymologies,* I, 41.
[7] *Etymologies,* I & II; VI, 2.

the Vandals from 408 to 522 and of the Suevi up to 585. Isidore did not have time to write more. Even if he had so desired, in this period of crisis and surprises he probably would not have obtained the materials necessary to write history successfully.

Of Isidore we can truthfully say that the encyclopedist won out over the historian, that his contribution to written history is small enough, but important because it is unique. He was a man of his times: attentive to the past, anxious to save the essentials of a tradition and capable of foreseeing the historical importance of contemporary events whether they be the deeds of the Visigoths, or Vandals or Suevi.

BEDE IN ENGLAND

Until the end of the sixth century, Anglo-Saxon England was pagan. Ireland, isolated, but already the land of saints and holy adventures, multiplied Christian undertakings. Occupied with a multiplicity of undertakings in Ireland and on the continent, she only had time to live her history, not to write it. As a result we shall never know the true celtic Christian history of Ireland and its neighbors, for example, Cornwall and Wales, at the beginning of the Middle Ages. Even the apostolate of St. Patrick (461) is hardly known to us, except from imperfect sources which give us rather the spirit than the facts. The invectives of Gildas, who wrote about 540 on the *De exicidio et conquestu Britanniae (The Fall and Conquest of Britain)*, tell us more about the personal reaction of the author than of the facts themselves. Such texts do not succeed in reviving the past. We must therefore give up trying to know from these contemporary narrative sources the true history of this past which was not however without its beauty, for legend alone has been able to draw so much beauty from them.

Romanized, Christianized and Latinized England holds a surprise for the historian of historical texts for it offers us, in the eighth century, the Venerable Bede (d. 735) one of the greatest historians of all time, one we are tempted to call the Thucydides of the Latin Middle Ages, in comparison with Gregory of Tours who is their Herodotus. A modern reader will learn more about these four centuries from reading the *Ecclesiastical History of the English People* (ed. Plummer, 2 vols.) than from reading any more recent work, however modern and careful its method may be. Bede's merit is not only that he puts together, reestablished or related from other sources (Pliny, Solinus, Prosper of Aquitaine, Gildas, Orosius, etc.) the facts from the very early Roman origins of England up to 731, but at the same time he captures the spirit and the habits of the period. The whole is written in a precise Latin which, unlike that of Gildas, and especially Gregory of Tours, attains a certain elegance while carefully adhering to the truth. Bede, like Gregory of Tours, did not disdain anecdotes or stories, but he was more rigorous in his method. He wrote the history of the English Church and he does not even think of going back to the Deluge as the chroniclers did. He began with a "profane" fact: Caesar's expeditions. But he is not writing "profane" history but rather the history of the Church in Britain, the people of the British Isles and everything that interested them at the time. He presented facts about episcopal, royal and monastic life as well; brief lives of saints; transcriptions of epitaphs, of letters and hymns, without overlooking astronomical details. Everything became Church history because the Church encompassed the whole of life. The Christian life was not divided into civil life, military life and ecclesiastical life. History is one; it is made of a little of everything. For Bede the important thing was not to classify and to distinguish the facts, but to make a general choice of them. The true law of history is not to create a plan and to organize everything according to this plan but rather to note in order and relation to a given place as many and as diverse facts as possible. Bede wrote that "the true law of history is quite simply to say posterity is what is said here and there." [8] The historian found the source of what he related in the eyewitness who records his own experience; *ex mea ipsa cognition escire potui* (I know from my own experience), or he has heard the ancients relate the fact *(ex traditione majorum)* or has read what he is going to write *(ex litteris antiquorum).*

Bede enumerated his written sources. He tested oral traditions; he asked old people preferably, trustworthy persons or several witnesses at once.[9] Like all his fellow historians of the Middle Ages, he tried to justify his judgments or his remarks with a biblical text. He did it carefully with soberness and appropriateness.

Bede and His Contemporaries. Bede is distinguished from the contemporaries by the fact that he devoted special attention to chronology and a concern which with him was almost a cult. Here he can be compared with Eusebius of Caesarea of whom he is, in many ways, the perfect disciple. This carefulness stems from the fact that Bede, like Eusebius, was a chronographer of highest value before he became a historian. He was largely responsible for introducing into the west our present practice of dating events from the Incarnation. He wrote in 703 a *De temporibus libris,* which in 725 became the *De ratione temporum (On the Reckoning of Time).* This was very competently edited in 1934 by C. W. Jones. The same editor also presented the text of an *Epistola de sex hujus seculi aetatibus (Letter on the Six Ages of the World)* in which Bede taught his readers the essentials of the tradition on the division of history and reminded them that it is not only man who has his ages, but all humanity, comparable to a little world and to a microcosm constantly growing.

The *Ecclesiastical History,* all the narrative work of Bede, his lives of saints like his chronographic works, represented in the Anglo-Saxon and Germanic world of the Latin Middle Ages the first attempt to write a sustained history of large scope. This first effort is a masterpiece. This Benedictine monk who, as he tells us, passed his life singing in Church, writing and teaching *(Eccl. Hist.)* and was a born historian. His piety, love of God and fidelity to the monastic rule made him conscientious and methodical. His is one of the greatest names of the Middle Ages. William of Malmesbury (twelfth century)

⁸ *Hist. Ecc.,* p. 8.
⁹ *Ibid.,* I, 2: III, 15 and 16.

who comes close to him can only imitate him. It is understandable that Abelard
at the Abbey of St. Denis, where he sought refuge, consoled himself for his
calamities by rereading the finest pages of Bede's History. All the pioneers
and promoters of medieval Latin culture, Alcuin (eighth century), Rhabannus
Maurus (ninth century), Hugh of St. Victor (twelfth century), looked on
Bede as an authority. In the *Paradise* of Dante (X, 130-131) Bede is at the
side of Isidore.

ITALY: PAUL THE DEACON AND THE "LIBER PONTIFICALIS"

After the Heruli and the Visigothic period, and the Vandal pillaging, there
was a short Byzantine restoration, and then the appearance of the Lombard
threat which the alliance of the Pope with the Franks of the eighth century
caused to fail. Between 476 and the union of the papacy with an extraterritorial
temporal power, we find very few historians in Italy, the land of Livy and
Tacitus. We have to wait until the eighth century to find the first great name
of medieval Italian historiography; and then it is a Lombard.

Paul the Deacon or Paul Warnefried, born between 720-730 of a Lombard
family, was a professional historian, the first one of the Middle Ages. He
won the favor of Charlemagne who had him come to the royal court between
782-786.

This Lombard first wrote the "national" history of his people. *The History
of the Lombards* in six books is a much more "secular" history than that of
Bede even though both authors were Benedictines. The nature of the facts
obliged the historian to accept things as they were. Now the Lombards were
not the most devout of people at the time. However that may be, anyone who
wishes to know the history of the Lombards from the origins up to 774 can
read no better text than that written by Paul the Deacon in the middle of the
eighth century. The most reluctantly done work of Paul the Deacon, but also
the most picturesque, is his Christian revision of the *Breviarium* of the pagan
Eutropius. Eutropius had drawn up in the second half of the fourth century a
sort of summary in ten books of all Roman history from its origins to the death
of Julian the Apostate (d. 363). Originally, Queen Adelperga had asked him
for a book for her son. By this time the Lombards had become Christians and
the *Breviarium* of Eutropius was a pagan work. The Queen, therefore, wanted
a revision of the work. Paul the Deacon then prepared a revised, corrected
and considerably expanded edition of the *Breviarium* which later became the
Historia Romana in sixteen books and, soon after subsequent revisions by other
authors, the *Historia Miscella* in twenty-four books (tenth century).

How does a pagan work become a Christian one? Paul the Deacon explained: he first gave biblical dimensions to Roman history. It no longer
began with Romulus but with Adam. Paul adapted the Roman accounts to
biblical accounts; he introduced on this occasion, biblical texts. This was what
the Queen wanted most (cf. prologue). Then he carried the history up to 565
by giving it more and more a Christian atmosphere. The *Breviarium* of
Eutropius thus became a Christian *Historia Romana*. This is a surprising and

very concrete example of the tastes of the times and of the passage of the Greco-Roman tradition to the new medieval tradition.

The most important source for the history of the popes is still the *Liber Pontificalis*. Far from being complete this collection of biographies is often overly brief, yet it gives us the names, dates, places and facts. They are of great value, for they are found nowhere else. One of the characteristic facts of medieval Italian and German historiography is that one learns most about the political history of the period from the history of the popes. The *Liber Pontificalis in quo continentur acta beatorum pontificum urbis Romae* (in which are contained the acts of the blessed Popes of Rome), begun in the sixth century, became by the eighth century the major archivistic source for Roman life and for the relations between the religious and the lay power. The narrations are less diffuse there than in the histories but the facts are better dated and placed in better perspective. The modern historian will read the *History of the Lombards* with pleasure but he will learn more by consulting the *Liber Pontificalis* in the great and learned two volume edition by Msgr. Duchesne (Paris, 1886-1892).

Chapter 3

CAROLINGIAN HUMANISM AND ITS HISTORIOGRAPHY*
By Benoit Lacroix, O. P.

FOR the purpose of this paper, it may be well to define humanism. In its most objective and literal meaning humanism for a historian consists in being a historian and in putting in the service of man in his own age all that he is and all that he knows.

HISTORICAL WRITING AND ITS PLACES OF ORIGIN

In the time of Charlemagne and his successors, there developed in England as well as in Italy and Germany three categories of historiography. These three categories derived from three different places of origin: bishoprics, monasteries, and princely courts. Each type sought to relate what had been learned about an age or a person.

Bishoprics. From the bishoprics came the numerous *Gesta* of the bishops. Conspicuous examples of this type are the *Gesta episcoporum* (of Metz) by Paul the Deacon and the *Liber Pontificalis* of Ravenna (ninth century). There are also the histories of particular churches, such as the history of the Church of Rheims by Flodoard (d. 966). Moreover, two bishops revived the genre of the universal chronicle: Freculf of Lisieux (853) and Ado of Vienne (874). In the tenth century the monk Richer wrote his famous *History of France* under the watchful eye of Archbishop Gerbert of Rheims. The principal part of the work known as *The Annals of Saint-Bertin* (the best source for the reign of Charles the Bald) was composed by bishops Prudentius of Troyes and Hincmar.

In Germany, even more than in France, historiography revolved around the life of the bishops and thus is rich in factual detail. The spirited Liutprand of Cremon (ca. 972) wrote a *Liber de rebus gestis Ottonis Magni (Book of the Deeds of Otto the Great)* comparable in some respects to the *Rerum gestarum Saxonicarum Libri (the Deeds of the Saxons)* of Widukind, written at Corvey around 967. The *Vita Brunonis (Life of Bruno)* by Ruotger gives a good account of the vigorous physique of the famous brother of Otto, the Archbishop of Cologne.

Moreover, the larger part of the narrative literature on the investiture controversy should be viewed in its religious and episcopal context. The *Annales* of Lambert of Hersfeld, a principal source for that controversy, in effect simply report the facts as they were seen in the bishoprics and the courts. There is no theory in all this literature, which consists mainly of facts and anecdotes.

Objectivity. The histories inform the reader of what has happened without

---

* Translated by James A. Corbett.

trying to preach what should have happened. The objectivity is brutal but real. The reader recognizes the side on which the sympathies of the historian lie. But he learns this from the things that have happened and not from theories adjusted to history. True objectivity and true humanism require no more. The historian of this German period is not evasive about his narrative nor does he play at pseudo-objectivity. Herein lies his merit.

Biography won out over annals, which were declining as an historical form because personalities (popes and emperors) were the centers around whom controversies of the period raged. Sometimes biographies and official acts (letters, diplomas, controversial writings) tell us more about the true history of Germany and Italy—their history is inseparable—from the time of Charles the Fat to Henry IV than do such annals as the *Annales Altahenses;* the *Annals of Quedlinburg; Annals of Rome;* the *Annals of Bari;* the *Beneventan Annals* and the work of the *Annalista Saxo;* and such chronicles as those of Sigebert of Gembloux, Hermann of Reichenau and Ekkehard of Aura.

Monastic Historical Writing. Alongside of and in close relationship with episcopal historiography there is the historical writing of the monasteries. The monastic historians and hagiographers increase in number. Their duty, as well as their value, was generally to serve immediately their abbot and their brother monks. Paul the Deacon composed the *History of the Lombards* for the monks of Monte Cassino, and the history was read aloud in the refectory. Bede named the abbot of his monastery in the dedication of his *Ecclesiastical History.* Some abbots themselves wrote in the intervals between divine office: Regino, Abbot of Prüm, wrote a chronicle which is essential for the understanding of the Carolingian Empire until 906. In the ninth century, the Abbot Lupus of Ferrieres corrected a text of Suetonius with his own hand. In fact, the monks were the best historians during the period from the beginning of the ninth century to the middle of the twelfth century. The monastic life itself, its veneration of traditions and the selfish interest in history taken by kings and dukes, encouraged the more talented monks to devote their leisure to the composition of annals and chronicles. These works are sometimes overloaded with facts, stories, and anecdotes too local and prolix to be useful for general history.

The monasteries produced *Miracula, Translationes, Virtutes, Necrologies,* and *Obituaries,* not to mention numerous *Lives.* The monastery was such a favorite and obvious place for historical work that even in the time of Louis VI the great Abbey of Saint-Denys became the official center of Capetian historiography. There, the monks were occupied in composing the royal annals. They preserved the documents and, without break or interruption, constructed that great monument of French historiography, known as *les Grandes Chroniques.*

THE ROYAL COURT AND LAY HISTORIANS

Nonetheless, it was in the courts, especially those of Charlemagne and Charles the Bald, that there appeared the two greatest lay historians of the early Middle Ages: Einhard (d. 840) and Nithard (d. 844).

Einhard. In his *Vita Caroli,* written between 817 and 822, Einhard recounted the life of Charlemagne. In its technique and biographical form it is directly inspired by the *Life of Augustus* by Suetonius. As Einhard himself has told us, he had been a pupil of the Benedictines of Fulda and became the friend and confidant of the great Charlemagne. His position, therefore, was uniquely favorable for the writing of history.

Of his reasons for writing he said: "Gratitude toward the man who has supported me . . ., the friendship and debt which I owe to him and his memory, a debt so great that I would appear as an ingrate and would justly be judged as such if forgetfully . . ., I was silent about the glories and illustrious deeds of the man to whom I owe so much and permitted his life to remain unknown."

His Model: Suetonius. He was "conscious of being able to provide more of the truth than anyone else." But in order to make his own style at least somewhat worthy of his subject, as Cicero would have it, Einhard, for lack of competence and "with the boldness of a barbarian hardly accustomed to Latin composition," decided to follow a model. The framework of the facts would be the same as that of the *Life of Augustus* by Suetonius; the facts would vary and, therefore, so would the story. This is another example of humanism; in this instance the historian has not hesitated to imitate Suetonius in order to make himself better understood by his contemporaries and to honor the figure of his beloved emperor.

Nithard and Carolingian Disintegration. While Einhard gloried in having such great deeds to relate, Nithard grieved over the painful necessity of instructing posterity in the events of the fratricidal war that broke out among the sons of Louis the Pious. His *Four Books of Histories*, which contain the text of the famous Strasburg Oath, provide only a sequence of doleful episodes which the historian would have curtailed (he began to write in 841), had not Charles the Bald constantly urged him to continue. "You know," Nithard wrote, "how I have been buffeted by storms in discharging this obligation." When he completed Book II on June 25, 841, Nithard felt unable to continue. He could no longer bear to hear evil spoken of his family and, of course, "it was even more painful for him to speak of it himself."[1] But here again, he yielded to the argument that he must serve his contemporaries. The prologue to the last book reveals an historian so open minded in the face of facts that he concluded by accepting contradictory facts. Nithard indicated that he had only one desire: "to get away from politics," to leave them and to rest. But once more he was sustained by the thought of his obligation to his fellow men, who at some future time would wish to know what had happened in 844 "in both camps." He resumed his writing. "I have absolutely no idea where I shall end. While waiting . . . I shall be occupied in setting down in writing the deeds of our princes and great men so that, as I have been ordered, their memory will be retained."[2]

Nithard was a layman. He died on the battlefield in June, 844, or May, 845.

[1] *Four Books of Histories*, III, preface.
[2] *Ibid.*, IV.

His history stops with his death and constitutes one of the finest examples of all time of fidelity to historiography.

We cannot list here the contemporary sources of Nithard's histories. They have all been given in Potthast, Gross, Molinier or Wattenbach (Holtzmann). All these historians, however, wrote with the same idea Einhard and Nithard had: to save the past from oblivion and for the instruction of posterity. They wrote much more for others than for themselves. Their humanism as historians is profoundly objective, sometime naive, but rarely egotistical.

THE CAROLINGIAN TRADITION CONTINUED

Alfred the Great. The impetus given to letters in France in the eighth century by Charlemagne was reproduced a century later in England, thanks to Alfred the Great (901) who had a special predilection for history. He translated Bede's *Ecclesiastical History* into Anglo-Saxon and also made a rather free translation of *The History against the Pagans* by Orosius to which he added his own moral commentaries.

Norman historiography of the eleventh and twelfth centuries which is so "royalist," so "ducal," even epic, appears as an even more definitive continuation of this courtly historiography begun in the courts of France and England in the ninth and tenth centuries. Dudo of St. Quentin, William of Jumieges, Ordericus Vitalis and William of Poitiers (eleventh century) were all monks; yet we must keep in mind that what they relate took place more often at the court than in the monastery.

In Germany and Italy the historical writing of this period is entirely different; it is primarily papal or episcopal. The narrative source for those lands derives not from the initiative of the kings who, moreover, are emperors there, but from the initiative of popes and bishops. The religious, political and social events express this literary fact. There historiography was, as medieval men would say, the mirror of the times.

In short, we find among historiographers just about everywhere in Europe the visible but often imperfect expressions of a desire to make history serve the collectivity. With great candor (Nithard) or with grim bravery (Liutprand), the historian believed it his duty to forget himself in order to tell his readers what he believed to be the truth of things.

The historian wrote at a time when literary glory was not a possible end, when the state was not yet stable reality. His motives for writing appear to be pure, rarely vain. If he writes, it is only for his readers. Of this objective form of humanism Nithard especially makes us aware. It is as though we were back in the times of the modest Herodotus.

HISTORY AND THE TRIVIUM

Thanks to the expansion of monasticism, to the aggressive authority of Charlemagne, his example and the counsel of his select entourage, many schools and centers of culture developed in the eighth and succeeding centuries. These schools, run by ecclesiastics, were attended by future historians, even the lay historians. Einhard learned to write at Fulda. With the return to the study of the *trivium* history was saved, for the *trivium* involved the study of grammar, rhetoric and dialect. Grammar, the beginning of everything, encouraged a return to the classics and therefore to the Roman historians. These were copied read and studied as in the time of Cicero and Quintilian. In the ninth century as in the time of St. Augustine, grammar was defined as the science of the interpretation of the poets and historians (Rhabbanus Maurus, *De clericorum institutione (On the Education of Clerics)*, III, 18; *Etymologies of Isidore of Seville*, I 81). History was not useful simply because it made for a better reading of the Scriptures. It can even be said that history was a necessary subject from the moment the study of grammar was revived.

INFLUENCE OF THE CLASSICAL HISTORIANS

Once ancient historiography was revived the historians who wanted to continue it and imitate it multiplied. Hence a new form of humanism; for humanism can be understood in its historical and more modern meaning of a return to antiquity. This return, expressing itself first on the literary, textual and pedagogical level, soon manifested itself on a level even more essential for historiography, namely, that of the motives for writing history.

Why did the ancients write history? Flavius Josephus summed it up rather sharply: "Some anxious to acquire fame wish to show off their literary talent; others wish to flatter the persons of whom they write . . .; others feel themselves constrained by the urgency of the events in which they have taken part to describe them as they really happened by writing a general history of them; finally, many were led to write history for the general public because of the ignorance of certain fundamental facts people should know."[3] The best Greek historians—Herodotus, Thucydides, and Polybius—wished to serve truth first and through it, their contemporaries. "Who does not know," Cicero wrote,[4] "that the first law of historical writing is the truth?" To the desire to speak and serve the truth the Romans added, with emphasis, the objective of instructing the man in his duties. Thus, with Suetonius,[5] Livy[6] and even Cicero,[7] history entered into the service of moral and political man. *Historia magistra vitae!*

What were the reasons for writing history in the time of Charlemagne? Almost the same, apart from literary glory. The annalists sought to inform their contemporaries. Einhard wished to praise the man whose merits he had witnessed. Nithard hoped to save posterity from error and prejudice. Each one wished to tell the truth as he knew it. From this point of view there can be no doubt about the humanism of the Carolingian historians even if in practice many an imperfection slipped in.

HISTORICAL FORM: ANNALS

The outstanding fact about patristic historiography is the renewal of the chronicle. The original fact about Carolingian historiography is the return to

---

[3] *Jewish Antiquities*, Prologue, 1 and 2.
[4] *On the Orator*, II, 15, 62.
[5] *The Jugurthine War*, IV-V.
[6] *Ab urbe condita*, Preface.
[7] *On the Orator*, II, 9.

annals. At first a simple catalogue of liturgical or royal dates and names (bishops, abbots, kings, dukes), the annals soon became, from the seventh century on, more and more accounts of facts selected to illustrate and locate a given year in the irrevocable march of time. In a given year, a certain king died, a pope was elected, and a certain duke was killed; this is followed by accounts of the events. The next year provides another series of events. The Carolingian annals, the *Annales Laurissenses majores* from 741-788 (the *Annals of Lorch,* also called the *Royal Annals*); the *Annales Einhardi* (741-820-829); the *Annales Metenses* were all written by different authors—clerics, monks and a few laymen. In spite of the importance of the facts related, each author wrote little or nothing of what he himself thought about them. He devoted himself entirely to saying what happened. His duty was to relate and that is all he did.

Their Character and Value. It would be appropriate to recall here the names, if we knew them, of the numerous authors who wrote from 741 to the beginning of the tenth century in order to tell us what happened at court, in the abbeys and bishoprics. We have only a small part of these annals; the rest have been lost or destroyed. These annals of all sorts, of kingdoms, monasteries or duchies, contain the best texts for the study of feudalism. It is a difficult and sometimes a disconcerting task to find them. Soon the annals developed and expanded so that a reading of them, folio by folio, suggests that they have become histories. This is particularly true of Capetian France. Contrary to the method of the historian or the chronicler, the annalist did not refer to the distant past; he did not cite his sources; he wrote from year to year. He did not foresee nor plan beyond what the calendar required. There is no division of his work into books and chapters.

Furthermore, the writing of annals was essentially a collective work; several authors participated in it. Each one in his own way and turn followed the course of the years. When the annals break off, it is because there was no one to continue them. War or disinterest on the part of the superior, king, bishop or abbot, caused these terminations.

Annals Not an Original Medieval Creation. The writing of annals is the big fact of Carolingian historiography. This is its chief characteristic and one worthy of attention because the annals represent an objective, immediate historiography written as events occurred, without literary or technical pretentions, apart from recording events as long as they are not of such a kind as to prevent the historian from describing them. It is my conviction, moreover—and even without the support of explicit texts which have disappeared—that annals are not an original, independent medieval creation. The Middle Ages simply renewed the ancient historical form of which Isidore of Seville spoke in his *Etymologies* and of which Tacitus, well known at this period, also made use.

By this simple fact, taken in connection with so many others, we see that in matters of methodology, the medieval period was hardly original. Rather it wished to walk in the footsteps of the ancients. We shall not forget that it learned to write and to read history as the ancients did by studying the same "classical" texts. From this point of view its humanism is school-bookish and not very active.

A TIME OF TROUBLE: HISTORICAL GAPS

Those familiar with the history of the tumult and destruction which went on in France, Germany, and Italy at the end of the ninth and the early tenth century are not surprised to find annals ending suddenly. The great *Annals of Lorsch* stop in 829. The *Annals of Fulda,* so well maintained from 838 to 863, and from 863 to 887, and then continued at Regensburg, stop suddenly in 901. The *Annals of Xanten* in a similar way stop in 882; those of St. Waast of Arras in 900. From 906 to 950 there is practically everywhere the great silence of an iron age. Even in the British Isles from which the first Christian annals probably came (the *Annals of Lindisfarne,* 532-993) the late ninth and early tenth centuries are a dead period. The *Historia Britonnum* of the pseudo-Nennius, more annals than history, becomes thinner and thinner from 796 to 994. The *Chronicle of Northumbria* stops in 802; the *Annals of Alfred* do not go beyond 887 and the *Chronicle of Ethelwold* stops in 974. The *Encomium Emmae,* the first source of value since the reign of Alfred, is useful only after 1012.

After Paul the Deacon there is silence at Monte Cassino. Leo Marsicanus (fl. 1075) resumed the tradition but in another age which is characterized by another kind of historiography, less stereotyped in its forms and, in a general way, closer to oral tradition.

NATURE OF CAROLINGIAN HUMANISM

The orientation of the humanism of the historians of the eight and ninth centuries is not so very different from that of the first Greek and Roman historians, if we overlook the style, were it not that it is first of all primarily religious and in a very special way.

Herodotus did not like to bring the gods into history; Thucydides was just as discreet. Polybius referred to fortune and chance. The Christian Cassidorus protested against these vague and contradictory appeals (*Institutiones* I, 17). According to him every event ought to be explained first by the will of God, the creator of all things. The *fortuna jubente* (dictate of Fortune) of the ancients became, in the Christian historians, *Deo permettente* (with God's permission), *Deo jubente* (by divine command), *judicio Dei* (the judgment of God), *divina gratia disponente* (by the disposition of divine grace). Gregory of Tours wrote the long *Credo* of his faith before the first chapter of Book I of his *History of the Franks* in order to identify his work in the eyes of posterity, to distinguish it from all others, heretical or pagan works.

RELIGIOUS EXPLANATION OF EVENTS

The Christian *Credo* became the first principle of explanation of all the accounts which came afterwards. We have seen how scriptural texts, increasingly numerous after the eighth century, within the narrative and between the facts which elicit them from the historians, express the Christian meaning of

history. Everything happens: good and evil. The good occurs through and
for the good; the evil through and for the wicked. What is bad for a bad
man can become a good for good men. Each fact had a meaning. The historian sometimes tried to find this meaning, but he did so crudely. The
particular and immediate meaning of events escaped him and he did not
always wish to resign himself to it. But for himself he wished to find and
understand an explanation. This involved him in errors of perspective. It often
makes him seem ridiculous in the eyes of scholars today who are more skep-
tical, or less firm in the Christian faith. The scholar is more interested in
precision than interpretation. In the Middle Ages the historian often enough
simply recorded the superstitions of his milieu. As an historian he had every
right to do this, for his first function is to relate what was said and done
around him. In brief, the historian in the Middle Ages ought more often
to be blamed than praised for the way in which he interpreted and judged
particular facts.

View of Unity of History and of Progress. Medieval historiography, especially Carolingian historiography, proved to be more exact and sober when
it dealt with another more fundamental aspect of history: its unity. Here
the Bible, even where it was not explicitly cited, guided thought. In fact, all
historians of the period recognized that there is only one history, the history
of salvation begun with Adam. Its first pages were written by Moses and
its last by the author of the Apocalypse. Between these two terms, the creation of man and his final resurrection foreseen by the Scriptures, the historian
in the Middle Ages, coming after the fathers, the prophets, the evangelists
and the first Christian historians (Eusebius and Jerome), added his few words
and in his own way related a part of the *Gesta Dei* which took place through
men's actions as the irreversible course of time proceeded.

The unity of human history and the constant progress of this history along
a given path which continues with the ages are two notable aspects of the
religious humanism of this new historiography, aspects which are easy to
verify in the texts. The texts presuppose these views and perpetuate them.
This linear and progressive concept of time on which the division of history
into six ages is inscribed (recalled by Freculf of Lisieux and so many others)
and the major fact of the Incarnation (which in the tenth century was used
to date the new era) will be definitively expressed in the *Two Cities* of the
Cistercian Bishop Otto of Freising (twelfth century).

Interpretation and Moralizing. Another aspect of the same humanism is that
the individual is seen as part of a whole which is the true universe, the cosmos.
Events never happen in isolation. They, too, form part of the whole. This
whole, this universe, comes from God as does man. Human actions have,
because of this unity and because of God who permits it, even cosmic consequences. Nithard felt this profoundly when he compared the Carolingian
period with that of the grandchildren of Louis the Pious.

How did it happen that in the time of Charlemagne everything went so
well? "There was abundance and joy . . . The very elements themselves
were favorable to each king." But now: "Everywhere there is misery and

sadness." It is cold; it snows. The Scripture had foreseen this in the statement: "the universe will struggle against the fools." Let everyone learn, Nithard concluded, that he who commits the folly of neglecting public interest and gives himself over like a fool to his personal and egotistical desires, thereby offends the Creator so much that he even makes all the elements oppose his extravagance. Today the kings are divided; it used to be that "as the people walked in the same straight path, the public way of the Lord, peace and concord reigned everywhere." This association of the cosmos and man is frequent in the Middle Ages. Ordinarily, a text of Scripture was to confirm it. Even where there was a mixture of superstition the historian, who was not always aware of it, knew how to justify his account by scriptural texts which supported what he said.

This form of interpretation of the historians of the period, strongly dominated by the reading of Scripture, is, however, also tied up with a Roman and Latin desire to moralize about everything. Tacitus himself did not write a single section of his *Histories* or his *Annals* without raising the moral problem of the individual and the collective responsibility of those who make history.

In the Middle Ages, the biblical element pervades and dominates all interpretation. That is why we may speak of a religious humanism in Carolingian and medieval historiography. The public always wanted the historian to express himself with scriptural texts. Bede, for example, was anxious about the fate of his *Ecclesiastical History,* not because he feared, like Gregory of Tours, that his book would be destroyed by the wicked or the ignorant, but because he was afraid that the king would be less interested in what he said than in the biblical texts which accompanied it. "I cannot recommend strongly enough to your zeal not only the scriptural texts but that you know also the *gesta* and the sayings of our ancestors." Adelperga also wanted scriptural texts in the *Breviarium* of Eutropius.

Christian Humanism

The Bible provided the bearings for all the interpretations, both the very general ones and the hasty and rash ones, of Carolingian historiography. The Bible directed and dictated its spirit. Thus, it may be said that this humanism is Christian, although this does not mean that it is always a perfect representation of Christian humanism or that this classification is exclusively adequate.

With Norman historiography (beginning in the tenth century) and that of the Crusades as well as the birth of European nationalism, historiography was to experience a new flowering at the end of the eleventh century. The literary and epic element which had been missing since the time of Livy became fashionable again. Historiography still remained in the hands of monks and clerics. Under the pressure of the times they secularized it. Gradually, though vaguely, there appeared the very "modern" division of religious or ecclesiastical history and profane or secular history: a division which has remained one of the chief characteristics of contemporary historiography and distinguishes it from the unifying and at times oversimplified perspectives of medieval historical thought.

Chapter 4

RENAISSANCE OF THE TWELFTH CENTURY
By J. G. Russell

General Character of the Intellectual Revival

DURING THE COURSE of the tenth century, both the tempo and character of European civilization underwent significant changes. The population grew more rapidly than during the several preceding centuries. There was a notable quickening of trade and there were many evidences of growing intellectual and political interests and ambitions. The restless vikings left their mark on Iceland, Greenland, England, France, Southern Italy and Russia. Meanwhile, the cities of Italy and elsewhere grew rapidly in commercial and industrial strength as their merchants traversed the water and land routes of the known world. The thrust of these movements caused Christian Europe to shift from a defensive toward an aggressive position in its relations with the pagan and Mohammedan states of the Slavic northeast, in Spain, in Italy and especially in the Near East.

This expansive elan pervaded the European intellectual world as well. Since it was chiefly a Latin world, the revival of learning, usually called the Renaissance of the twelfth century, was actually a re-examination of earlier Latin literature accompanied by a modest literary development of its own. The Latin Classics aroused more interest than during the preceding millenium. Roman Law was studied ardently at Bologna and influenced political thinking in many lands. The study of theology, particularly at the University of Paris, occupied many of the better minds of the day. Much rhymed poetry, expressive of deep emotions, was written. An interest in science led to extensive translations from the Arabic as well as from Greek in Spain and Italy. As one would expect, this intellectual enthusiasm institutionalized itself in an increasing number of schools of higher learning and eventually the university.

Inferior Status of Historical Studies

These developments were reflected in quantitative, if not qualitative, changes in the historiographical activities of the period. But in this period, no office of historian existed, nor did anyone devote full time to the teaching of history. This subject remained as it had been, a part of grammar, and was treated as such—hence, there was no historian to define the functions of his office or consider rigorously the implications of history as a field of knowledge.[1]

[1] On the place of history in the schools see E. M. Sanford, "The Study of Ancient History in the Middle Ages," *Journal of the History of Ideas*, V (1944), especially pp. 28-32; 21-43. The finest study of this period is C. H. Haskins, *"The Renaissance of the Twelfth Century;* see also Robert S. Lopez, "Still Another Renaissance," *The American Historical Review*, LVIII, No. 1 (October, 1951), pp. 1-22.

The writing of history was largely determined in the later medieval period by the patrons of the historians, the function and purpose of their writing, and by the personalities of the writers themselves. The chief patrons were monastic houses and reigning families. However, feudal lords and cathedral chapters often also fostered this work. Some of the rising communes patronized history but they did not wield an outstanding influence upon historical writing until the thirteenth century. The literary tradition also tended to remain unchanged although the growing influence of the classics appears in greater dependence upon them, resulting in an increase in the size of accounts. The subject matter tended to be general or miscellaneous, although such spectacular movements as the Crusades, the rise of the communes, and the development of national monarchy were bound to excite historical interest.

PATRONS AND LITERARY CENTERS[2]

Monasteries. The monasteries continued to be the great literary centers. More learned men lived together there than elsewhere, thus providing each other with an intellectual stimulus. They had access to history books and often also to extensive collections of documents, together with the leisure to read and study them. Furthermore, the officials of the monastery often travelled widely and all travellers usually availed themselves of monastic hospitality. The chronicler, Gervase of Canterbury, tells us that he wrote at the instance of fellow monks: he, like many other chroniclers, was a sacristan in charge of the books of the house.[3]

Monastic libraries were usually collections of books housed in conveniently placed closet or press, often in the passage between the choir and the chapter house. Many medieval volumes still bear the press marks, usually of three characters (for instance, A·II c), where the first, indicates the tier of the press, the second, the shelf, and the third, the place in the division of the shelf. Occasionally an attempt at alphabetical arrangement was made, and the results recorded in a list or catalogue. As a rule, the monastic library had a collection of the Fathers, but rarely had the classical historians or books defining chronology and lengths of reigns or other books of ready reference.[4] "The work of the historians never attained the same degree of popularity in the medieval libraries as did other types of literature." Nevertheless, the number of medieval histories in some libraries must have been considerable, to judge from the number of authors cited by some writers.

After 1050, there was a tremendous increase in the number of religious houses established. The great Cluniac Reform was followed by numerous foundations of Cistercian monks and Austin canons, and, to a lesser extent, of Benedictine and Premonstratensian houses. However, the number of chronicles did not increase in the same proportion. The newer houses were often smaller, poorer and, at least after the first generation, less attractive to intellectually gifted young men. The newer orders like that of Cluny, for example,

---

² On intellectual centers see especially C. H. Haskins, *op. cit.,* pp. 32-69.
³ *Gesta Regum,* II, p. 3.
⁴ J. S. Beddie, "Libraries in the Twelfth Century: Their Catalogues and Contents," *Haskins Anniversary Essays,* pp. 1-24, especially p. 18.

either burdened their members with more religious services, or like the Cistercians, located them in country districts unfavorable to intellectual stimulus. So, while houses of all groups wrote chronicles, for the most part, they are the work of the great Benedictine houses, usually located in the urban centers.

Royal Courts. The royal courts often included men of learning as well as men of action. The court of Henry II of England, as well as the Norman court of Sicily, was famous for such groups. These courts were centers of the kinds of activity which would normally find their way into the chronicles. However, the medieval king and his court were usually migratory. At that time books were heavy and could not be readily transported with the court. The royal clerks were also usually too busy to write history on the move even if they were so inclined. Except for a few countries, records were seldom enrolled and properly recorded. Even the thought of attaining perpetual fame in this world was essentially a secular idea—the careers of few rulers were exemplary enough to justify their biographies as works of edification. Thus, clerks usually postponed their writing until they were away from the court.

The close association of the monastery of St. Denis with the French kings is paralleled by a series of chronicles emanating from that house, probably initiated by the great abbot Suger (*ca.* 1081-1151) and covering the history of France. This series continued into the fifteenth century.[5]

The only case in which a medieval European historian seems to have been expressly employed to write a history was that of William (1130-84), who became archbishop of Tyre and the greatest historian of the Crusades.[6] He was apparently chosen by King Amaury of Jerusalem about 1167 to write the record of the king's deeds, which were already noteworthy and promised to achieve even greater fame in the future. This effort was a spectacular success and suggests what might have been produced by similar encouragements. For the most part, such cases of association of prominent historians with great courts were more or less accidental. The court of Henry II of England was remarkable for its writing, but the two historians of his reign, Roger of Hoveden and whoever wrote the chronicle dedicated to Abbot Benedict of Peterborough, were only casually associated with it and received no known patronage.[7] A member of that court, the witty Welshman, Walter Map, wrote *Courtiers Trifles* giving a candid account of its activities[8] and explaining tacitly why so little writing was done there.

Cathedral Chapters. A third center of history writing was the cathedral. Learned men belonged to the Cathedral Chapters and, although frequently busy or even away from the cathedral, they often had much time at their disposal and could enjoy greater stability than the royal court. Moreover, the

[5] A. Molinier, *Les Sources de l'histoire de France,* II, pp. 181-184; III, pp. 97-104.
[6] A. C. Krey, "William of Tyre, the Making of an Historian in the Middle Ages," *Speculum* XVI (1941), pp. 149-166. William's chronicle is edited in the *Recueil des Historiens des Croisades, Historiens Occidentau* I (1844); it is translated by A. C. Krey and E. A. Babcock, *A History of Deeds Done Beyond the Sea,* 2 vols.
[7] C. H. Haskins, "Henry II as a Patron of Literature," *Essays in Mediaeval History Presented to Thomas Frederick Tout,* (1925), pp. 71-77.
[8] Edited by M. R. James; translated by M. B. Ogle, and F. Tupper, *Master Walter Map's Book, de Nugis Curialium.* Map lived through the reign of Henry II (1154-1189) and died about 1209; he was a clerk, precentor of Lincoln.

eleventh and twelfth centuries saw the chapters better equipped to serve as intellectual centers than a later date. The chapter, then, was closely knit, often eating together and drawing its expenses from common endowments. Subsequently, it became the practice for the common funds to be divided into prebends and for the chapter members to go their separate ways. Furthermore, their schools were at their height, during the eleventh and twelfth centuries, often drawing excellent teachers and students. Later, they were to be overshadowed by the rising universities. In this period, too, many canons and even bishops wrote history. Proportionately, they probably furnished as many historians as did the monasteries. Like the monasteries, they often had libraries and were located in situations favorable for the accumulation of news.[9]

The members of cathedral chapters occasionally made use of official journeys to seek information. Thus, Henry, Archdeacon of Huntingdon (d. *ca.* 1158), tells how he stopped at Bec in 1139[10] and was shown a copy of Geoffrey of Monmouth's book by another famous chronicler, Robert of Torigni. Henry apparently grew up in the episcopal family of Lincoln and was encouraged to write a history of the English from the time of Caesar. He commences Book III as follows:[11]

> Now (1088) I have to deal with events which have passed under my own observation, or which have been told me by eye-witnesses of them. I have to relate how the Almighty alienated both favour and rank from the English nation as it deserved, and caused it to . cease to be a people. It will appear also how he began to afflict the Normans themselves, the instruments of his will with various calamities.

Henry's views are a characteristic rationalization of the ruling class, but Henry was also too honest to pass over certain obvious failings of the Normans.

Cities. Parallel to and part of the general growth in population was the rapid increase in the size of communes and cities of Europe in this period. This development was more rapid in northern Italy than elsewhere, producing, with the aid of widespread lay education, the earliest civic chronicles. Most of them were anonymous, even those of the great cities of Venice and Florence in this period.[12] There were few civic chronicles in the rest of Europe. The most remarkable achievement in the encouragement of history writing occurred in Genoa.

On the basis of existing evidence the first official recognition of civic history was by Genoa, whose consuls and council in 1152 honored the historian Caffaro of Caschifellone by decreeing that his history should be copied with care and preserved in the city archives. Caffaro was about 72 then, but continued to write history until within three years of his death at the age of 86. In addition to the annals, he wrote accounts of two Genoese expeditions in which he participated. He was apparently an able citizen who served his city

[9] The French chapters seem to have produced little.
[10] *Chronicles of the Reigns of Stephen, Henry II and Richard I,* IV, pp. 65-75.
[11] Henry's chronicle is translated by Thomas Forester. The quotation is from p. 222. Another cathedral writer of England was Ralph de Diceto, who was dean of London, and thus in an excellent position to write his histories, edited by W. Stubbs, *Opera Historica.*
[12] U. Balzani, *Early Chronicles of Europe: Italy,* pp. 293-315. For Caffaro in Genoa, pp. 303-304.

well in many ways. The city commissioned the chancellor Obertus (1164-73), and later, the notary Ottobonus (1189-96), to continue *The Chronicle*.[13] These writers were laymen who shared in civic life and thus brought to their writing an exact and detailed knowledge of city life.

Papacy. Although the Church was the greatest European institution of the period, no general church history was then written. The chief focus of ecclesiastical interest was theological rather than historical. Instead of producing a great church history, the ecclesiastical writers have left us a series of great theological works. The most widely used of these was the Sentences of Peter Lombard. There is little history in it, since it is mainly devoted to theological relationships in which the earth and its inhabitants occupy only a minor part.

HISTORICAL TRADITION AND CRITICISM

Medieval histories fall into three main types: past history based upon earlier writings, general chronicles of miscellaneous subject matter, and specialized accounts. The first usually took the form of a world chronicle, of which there were very many. The second and third were often discussions or records of current events. The value of the first has been overlooked by modern historians who have emphasized the other types. However, in a study of historiography the former are also important, especially when studied for a critique of historical sources for a particular period.

Popular Histories. The study of past history naturally involved the composition of a pattern of universal history. This had been standardized for the Middle Ages by Eusebius and Jerome and placed into chronological periods for the six days of eternity of which the sixth began with the birth of Christ and continued to the present. The seventh began with the end of the Earth. As a pattern, it was an idea which was only occasionally followed. Within this framework there was room for individual differences. "It was not until the twelfth century that chroniclers began to copy standard epitomes of earlier history without reworking the material."[14] In England, however, the influence of Bede was very powerful upon the leading twelfth century historians,[15] while Orosius' *History Against the Pagans* set the pattern for ancient History.

The greatest twelfth century follower of Bede was William of Malmesbury (?-1142) whose chief works were: *Lives of the Kings of England* and *Lives of the Bishops and Abbots of England.* His easy running account may be illustrated by a paragraph about the well-known historian, Marianus Scotus:[16]

> During this emperor's reign (Henry IV, 1056-1106), flourished Marianus Scotus, first a monk of Fulda, afterwards a recluse at Mainz, who, by renouncing the present life, secured the happiness of that which is to come. During his long continued leisure, he examined

[13] These Genoese chronicles are edited by Pertz, *Cafari et Continuatorum Annales Januenses*, M. G. H. SS XVIII.

[14] E. M. Sanford, "The Study of Ancient History in the Middle Ages," *Journal of the History of Ideas.* V (1944). p. 32; H. Buttenwieser, "Popular Authors of the Middle Ages: The Testimony of the Manuscripts." *Speculum.* XVII (1942), pp. 50-55.

[15] H. Richter, *Englische Geschichtsschreiber des 12 Jahrhunderts*, especially emphasizes this influence.

[16] Quotation from J. A. Giles, *William of Malmesbury's Chronicle of the Kings of England*, pp. 317-89. William's works are edited in the Rolls Series. The work of Marianus, The *Chronographia*, is edited by D. G. Waitz, M.G.H. SS V, pp. 481-564 (without the first two parts). It is also edited in Migne, *Patrologia latina*, CXLV.

the writers on chronology, and discovered the disagreement of the cyclès of Dionysius the Little with the evangelical computation. Wherefore reckoning every year from the beginning of the world he added twenty-two, which were wanting, to the above mentioned cycles; but he had few or no followers of his opinion. Wherefore, I am often led to wonder, why such unhappiness should attach to the learned of our time, that in so great a number of scholars and students, pale with watching, scarcely one can obtain unqualified commendation for knowledge. So much does ancient custom please, and so little encouragement, though deserved, is given to new discoveries, however consistent with truth. All are anxious to grovel in the old track, and everything modern is contemned: and therefore as patronage alone can foster genius, when that is withheld, every exertion languishes.

Marianus' attempt to revise chronology was not very successful, yet his work was immensely popular. He was used and commented upon by a second great twelfth century historian, Ordericus Vitalis, whose work had very limited circulation. Ordericus was a monk of St. Evroul in Normandy (1075-ca. 1141). In his first book, he includes material chronologically up to his own day. The second book is concerned largely with the apostles and the popes. The third book deals with St. Evroul and Norman affairs. The other ten books, telling of more recent centuries, are heterogeneous in character, but present a tremendous amount of valuable information.[17]

Sigebert of Gembloux (d. 1112), has been called "the best of the universal chroniclers of the Middle Ages," although this claim is much disputed.[18] His *Chronographia* used more than fifty other works as sources and in turn was copied by more than that number of later writers.

Study of Classical History. The tradition, as presented by the standard epitomes, could only be improved by a study of classical and early medieval sources themselves and by the development of historical criticism. There was much ancient history reproduced in the writings of the chroniclers, some directly; even more was probably taken from those collections of excerpts called florilegia such as the *Liber Floridus* (1120), canon of Lambert of St. Omer in Flemish Belgium.[19] It included maps, genealogies, and discussions of chronology which might be useful to the historian. It is heavily local in its choice of subject matter but draws from a very wide circle of histories and other literature.

The study of the classics was hindered by the inaccessibility of some of the greatest historians, particularly of the Greeks, and by the lack of interest in their study.[20] To this, Lambert of Hersfeld [21] (d. *ca.* 1088), however, is an

---

[17] Ordericus Vitalis, *The Ecclesiastical History of England and Normandy*, translated by Forester.
[18] Statement of A. Molinier, *Les Sources de l'historie de France*, I, iii, No. 2193. Thompson and Holm. *A History of Historical Writing*, p. 191, suggests Ekkehard of Urach, whose works are edited by D. G. Waitz, M.G.H. SS VI, pp. 1-127. Sigebert's work is edited by D. L. C. Bethman, M.G.H. SS. VI, 300-374. He wrote much else, including a *De Scriptoribus Ecclesiasticis*. Sigebert's sources and users are given in the edition of his work, pp. 271-275.
[19] E. M. Sanford, "The Liber Floridus," *Catholic Historical Review*, XXVI (1941), pp. 469-478.
[20] J. S. Beddie, "The Ancient Classics in the Medieval Libraries," *Speculum*, V (1930), pp. 3-20, especially pp. 12-13.
[21] Edited by V. C. L. Hesse, M.G.H. SS. V, pp. 134-263. Good short accounts of Lambert in Barnes, p. 83, and Thompson, p. 187.

exception. His works provide "An excellent illustration of the effective use of Livy, Sallust, and Suetonius by a medieval scholar who could profit both by their historical content and by their rhetorical values." Even Lambert's very marked bias with respect to the history of his own time had classical precedents.[22] Lambert illustrates what might have been done if the historical effort of his time had been organized professionally. The general tendency was to copy what one had rather than to seek for better authorities or for original sources.

In contrast to Lambert's historical achievement, may be placed the inaccuracy of Geoffrey of Monmouth's *Historia Regum Brittaniae,* if indeed that work is to be considered as history rather than propaganda or fable.[23] His account of the genealogy and succession of kings contradicted Bede's evidence. If Geoffrey's picture of Arthur was true, Arthur must have been a greater ruler than Alexander and a greater prophet than Isaiah. These are the criticisms which a canon of Newburgh in England, William (1136-*ca.* 1198), voiced in the last half of the twelfth century against the authenticity of Geoffrey's books. The brilliance of this insight into ancient history immediately arouses one's curiosity about what William might have done to vulnerable sources, but in settling the starting point of his excellent history within a century, of his own time, William did not seek the opportunity.[24] Of the two, however, Geoffrey's work was immensely more popular and was used by even reputable historians during the rest of the Middle Ages.

Historical Criticism. A penetrating historical critic of the twelfth century is Otto of Freising (*ca.* 1110-58). He records the story of the destruction of Mohammedan idols by Bishop Tiemo in the east, but doubts the story because Mohammedans do not have idols.[25] Indeed, his description of Mohammedanism is very fair considering the scope of knowledge in his day. Even more important is his denial of the validity of the Donation of Constantine. Imperial advocates, he states, point out that Constantine actually gave the western half of the Empire to his son, which would not have been done by so devout a ruler if he had given it previously to the Church, nor would the great Theodosius have appropriated it later if it had belonged to the pope.[26] Here, of course, the sharpening impetus of controversy to criticism is clear. Otto, a Cistercian monk and later bishop, was a member of the German imperial house, and had studied at the University of Paris. There he may have been a student of Hugh of St. Victor (d. 1143), whose *Book of the Three Most Important Factors in Events* represented a real, though not very influential, attempt to inculcate accuracy in describing historical incidents.[27]

[22] E. M. Sanford, "The Study of Ancient History in the Middle Ages," *Journal of the History of Ideas, V* (1944), p. 23.
[23] G. H. Gerould, "King Arthur and Politics," *Speculum,* II (1927), pp. 33-51. Geoffrey lived about 1100-1152 and was an archdeacon of Llandaff and bishop of St. Asaph. As the fountainhead of Arthurian romance his history has a very large literature.
[24] *The Chronicles of the Reigns of Stephen, Henry II, and Richard I,* ed. Richard Howlett, I, 11-19.
[25] Translated by C. C. Mierow, *The Two Cities by Otto Bishop of Freising,* especially p. 412. Edited by A. Hofmeister, in *Scriptores Rerum Germanicarum.*
[26] Otto, iv, 3.
[27] The manuscript has not been published. For an edition of the prologue and a brief discussion of the work, see William M. Green, "Hugo of St. Victor, De Tribus Maximis Circumstantiis Gestorum," *Speculum,* XVIII (1943), pp. 484-493.

The principles which had interested Hugh had already been tried in a series of notable works by Gregory of Catino, a monk of Farfa in Italy, just before the end of the eleventh century. He drew up first of all a great register of the many documents of Farfa, charters from popes, emperors and other feudal lords, the famous Farfa Register, or, as he liked to call it, the *Liber Gemniagraphus sive Cleronomialis Farfensis.* He was very careful to copy correctly, even including all of the witnesses in the charters, and tried not to guess in regard to words difficult to read in the text.[28] He followed this with another register of temporary contracts and less important documents, the *Largitorum,* and a topographical index of the Register called the *Floriger Cartarum.* On the basis of these great collections, he wrote a *Chronicle of Farfa,* mostly about the monastery. The idea of proceeding from a careful edition of documents to a narrative history was excellent, even though in execution the narrative tended to resemble a string of documents. This promising development was followed only in a few places, mostly in the south of Italy.[29]

Outside of strictly historical literature, historical criticism of a high order was presented by Guibert de Nogent (1053-1124), in his book on relics and their authentication. Again a very practical matter had forced decisions and thus had necessitated some method of criticism.[30] Guibert also wrote a story of the First Crusade, *Gesta Dei per Francos,* and an autobiography.[31] All of these works were well done.

A serious deficiency of much of medieval historical writing was the absence of historical sense.[32] Like the painters and sculptors in dealing with Biblical characters, they imagined that people of ancient times dressed as in their own time. Presumably they thought and acted much the same, and used the same languages. The result was that anachronisms abounded.

The writing of contemporary history involved other types of historical study. The sources were usually common information which was in circulation and which was known to the historian in the monastery. The difference in the historians of that age lay chiefly in their instinct for accuracy; few of them apparently took the trouble to check their information. Some believed more easily than others; most of them accepted even Geoffrey of Monmouth uncritically. Then, too, some had better channels of news than others. One of the best contemporary statements of a sound historical approach appears in the chronicle of Helmold, Priest of Bosau (*ca.* 1120-72), entitled *The Chronicle of the Slavs.*[33]

In portraying deeds of men, as in chiseling out the most subtle

---

[28] Cf. U. Balzani, *Early Chroniclers of Europe: Italy,* pp. 149-160; *Il Regesto de Farfa,* ed. I. Georgi and U. Balzani (1879-1888) ; *Liber Largitorius,* ed. G. Zuchetti; *Il Chronicon Farfense,* ed. Balzani.
[29] At St. Vincent on the Volturno about 1119 (Balzani, pp. 159-160), Monte Cassino by Peter the Deacon (ca. 1107-1140).
[30] C. H. Haskins, *The Renaissance of the Twelfth Century,* p. 235. Edited in Migne, *Patrologia Latina,* CLVI.
[31] *Gesta,* edited in *Recueil des historiens des croisades, historiens occidentaux,* IV (1879) ; the *Vita,* ed. G. Bourgin, *Guibert de Nogent: Sa Vie,* 1053-1124.
[32] T. F. Tout, *Collected Papers,* III, 7.
[33] *The Chronicle of the Slavs* by Helmold, Priest of Bosau, translated with an introduction by F. J. Tschan, pp. 251-252; edited by B. Schmeidler.

carving, there ought to be a sincere concern that one be not led from the way of truth by favor, by hatred, or by fear. (I dedicate this book to the venerable lords and brethren of Lubeck) in the hope of rendering honor to men of the present day and of contributing profit through the knowledge of facts to men of the future. And I hope that I shall not be without some little gain from the prayers of the great men who may read this little book.

Hagiography. The pattern of hagiography was well established so that a capable writer could produce a creditable biography with no great difficulty. The early life, miracles at conception or birth, schooling, and early temptations of saints seldom occupied much space. The adult life was usually given in detail, since normally much more was known about it in the twelfth century than had been the case earlier. The miracles performed or witnessed by saints are described in detail. The biography was nearly always a straightforward account, which runs to many modern printed pages with a minimum of embellishment. As history they are often quite useful—much can be learned from even the shortest of them, because they frequently present information which chroniclers seldom recorded. The miracles with their illustrations of psychoneurotic behavior, have not been sufficiently studied by modern historians. Of autobiography, there was little; what there was is interesting for the presentation had to be original as there was no tradition for the autobiographer to follow.[34]

Functions and Purposes of Historical Writing

Medieval historical writing was neither a full time occupation, nor professional. Some of it is definitely designed for edification, and probably all of it was considered so. Other writers were impressed by the greatness of such movements as the Crusades, particularly of those in which they participated. Occasionally the writing was used to defend a position or a course of action in the past. Finally, much medieval historical literature had no other object than to record current events of general interest. Naturally, the function and purpose of the writing influenced the author's form and the organization of his composition.

Recording of Current Events. The mind of the twelfth century was a good bit like that of the modern newspaper reader. It was interested in the lives and deaths of outstanding world leaders (popes, kings, lords), of important local characters, and in great and unusual events. These accounts were often arranged in approximately chronological order, particularly local events, since they were usually recorded in the more extensive chronicles not long after they happened. News items of distant events came in more slowly and might find their way into chronicles only after local events of earlier months. Within each year almost no attempt was normally made to arrange items by subject matter. Monks wrote surprisingly little about their own religious houses; their attention was largely centered upon the outside world.

An exception to this rule is the great historian of the mother house of the

[34] See the excellent pages of Haskins on this topic, *The Renaissance of the Twelfth Century,* pp. 253-260; *The Confessions of St. Augustine* offered one model.

Benedictines, Monte Cassino, Leo Marsicanus of Ostia (*ca.* 1046-1117), keeper of the archives and librarian of his house. Abbot Oderisius first invited him to write a biography of the abbot who became Pope Stephen IX. This work was subsequently enlarged into a full length story of the monastery. Leo explained his method of collection:[35]

> Then I sought out such little writing as seemed to treat of the matter, composed in a ragged style and briefly, and chief of these the chronicle of the Abbot John—also I collected the books necessary for this task, namely the history of the Longobards, and the chronicles of the Roman emperors, and pontiffs; likewise searched diligently for privileges and charters as well as concessions and documents with various titles (such as those of Roman pontiffs, of various emperors, kings, princes, dukes, counts, and other illustrious and faithful men) that were left to us after the two destructions by fire of this convent although I could not find even all of them; lastly I questioned scrupulously all who had either heard of or seen any deeds of modern times or of abbots.

Such careful methods were characteristic of Leo, who produced an admirable and unusual work. He later became a cardinal and a very distinguished churchman.

Unfortunately, this fine work did not necessarily establish a tradition at Monte Cassino. A successor of Leo as keeper of the archives and librarian was Peter the Deacon (*ca.* 1107-1140), who continued the chronicle of the house and copied out great cartularies of the documents of the house. He was always interesting but frequently inaccurate, especially where the interests of his family or the monastery were concerned, and very gullible. Peter also wrote saints' lives and a series of biographies of the great monks of Monte Cassino. He was thus remarkable for his versatility. With him, outstanding historical writing ceased at Monte Cassino.[36] Thus, the historical accounts of even one of the greatest of the medieval monastic houses were incidental rather than a primary interest of its librarians and keepers of archives.

Close to documentary history and its emphasis upon administration are treatises upon its practices, like the account of English law, possibly by Ranulf of Glanvill, and of the Exchequer by Richard FitzNeal,[37] treasurer of England, 1158-98, and bishop of London, 1189-98. Both of them give an intimate view of the working of a remarkably efficient medieval government. They give, of course, a much better view than that derived from occasional items and even running accounts of important events in the chronicle of Roger of Hoveden,

---

[35] Balzani, *Chroniclers of Early Europe: Italy,* pp. 169-170. His work is edited by W. Wattenbach, M.G.H. SS. VII, p. 574. Another exception was Jocelin of Brakelond of the Abbey of Bury St. Edmunds, England, whose chronicle covers the years 1173-1203 and is largely devoted to his house. It is edited by T. Arnold, *Memorials of St. Edmunds,* and J. G. Rokewode (Camden Soc., London, 1840), and translated by T. E. Tomlins, *Monastic and Social Life in the Twelfth Century.* It is the basis for Carlyle's *Past and Present.*

[36] Balzani, pp. 174-180 for Peter the Deacon. Peter has been edited by W. Wattenbach, M.G.H. SS. VII, p. 727.

[37] Glanvill is edited by G. E. Woodbine, *Glanvill: De Legibus et Consuutudinibus Angliae.* FitzNeal is edited by A. Hughes, C. G. Crump, and C. Johnson; translaed in E. F. Henderson, *Select Historical Documents of the Middle Ages,* pp. 20-134. *Chronica Rogeri de Hovedene,* ed. W. Stubbs, translated by H. T. Riley; Haskins, *The Renaissance of the Twelfth Century,* pp. 261-262.

who shared to some extent in the governmental machine of England. These two types of materials enable the historian to gain a well-rounded picture of contemporary practical politics.

Those writings which were polemical and written to prove a case often made important contributions to historical criticism. The long series of pamphlets which grew out of the controversy between the emperor and the pope in the latter half of the eleventh century stimulated political theory in a remarkable fashion.[38] The pity is that except in the case of Thomas Becket the English were not aroused in the same way in the twelfth century. Even polemical pamphlets illustrating the trends of thought in the time of the formation of the English constitution would have been invaluable.

Pride in Achievement. Pride in achievement was one of the causes for the writing of history. Sometimes this pride is not easily distinguishable from special pleading, as is the case of Archbishop Romuald of Salerno (1153-1181), who, by virtue of his high office, was a constant attendant at the court of the Norman kings of Sicily. He was an outstanding diplomat and participated in many of the great events of the period, such as the diplomatic negotiations at Venice in 1177 involving the emperor, the pope, the communes of northern Italy and his own master, William II. Romuald of Salerno obviously had a fine education and wrote in an eloquent style and for the most part accurately, if from the royal point of view. His contemporary, Hugo Falcandus, wrote from the standpoint of the barons of the kingdom, who, like most feudal barons, were frequently in rebellion against the king and saw historical events in a quite different light. He apparently came from outside of the Norman kingdom but had been well received there; he wrote excellent Latin, was reasonably impartial and very discerning in regard to events in that kingdom.[39]

Edification. The types of historical material suitable for edification were several; prominent among them were the saints' lives, the stories of missionary effort and of the crusades and even the general chronicles. Indeed, one phase of scriptural interpretation practised constantly in sermons, as well as in the theological classroom, was called the historical and involved an historical explanation of the text. The methods of interpretation naturally spread beyond Scriptural texts, and thus the use of history was very practical.[40] Hagiography was also used constantly in the monasteries, where private and public reading of the lives of the saints was a constant form of edification. The chronicles of Helmold, mentioned above, and of Adam of Bremen tell of the advance of Christendom in northern Europe.[41]

The Crusades naturally inspired authors to write; they were important as wars and even more as holy ventures upon a vast scale in an ecclesiastical age.

[38] Edited in the M.G.H., *Libelli de Lite.* Discussed thoroughly by A. J. Carlyle, *A History of Mediaeval Political Theory in the West*, IV; C. H. McIlwain, *The Growth of Political Thought in the West.*

[39] Balzani, pp. 230-235; the works of Romuald and Hugo are edited in Muratori, VII; Romuald also by Ardnt, M.G.H. SS. XIX, p. 398 and Hugo by Siracusa.

[40] Harry Caplan, "The Four Senses of Scriptural Interpretation and the Mediaeval Theory of Preaching," *Speculum*, IV (1929), pp. 282-290; F. Fellner, "The 'Two Cities' of Otto of Freising and Its Influence on the Catholic Philosophy of History," *Catholic Historical Review*, XX (1934), pp. 154-174.

[41] Adam of Bremen, remarkable for geographic information as well as historical, is edited by B. Schmeidler, *Gesta Hammaburgensis Ecclesiae Pontificum.*

Each Crusade had its chroniclers as did usually each contingent within the Crusade. Most of the accounts were written by clerks accompanying the troops, who wrote them upon their return to Europe.[42] The most important and comprehensive was by William, Archbishop of Tyre (1130-84). Led for the most part by distinguished rulers or nobles, the Crusades, in many respects, resemble ordinary feudal wars and operations, but they were also a manifestation of expansion on the part of the dominant class, an expansion that failed.

While the greater crusading efforts were led by great feudal lords, at least two expeditions led by lesser people succeeded spectacularly: the Crusade of 1147 which captured Lisbon and that of 1189 which took Silves. Both cities remained permanently a part of Portugal.[43] In contrast to the heroics, the bitter hostility among Christians and the feudal instability of the Near East Crusades, these ventures were more sober and probably better organized; the chronicles about them are businesslike and detailed.

One purpose of historical study is to analyze the present in terms of the past, to try to see what has been the course of human events in order to understand the world today, and, perhaps, to gauge the possibilities of the future. This was not a medieval aim, because the Middle Ages had its own philosophy of history; it thought that it knew, as far as was necessary, what had happened in the past and that it could prophesy with reasonable accuracy about the future. Thus, it was only natural that Bishop Otto of Freising should include a book on the future in his great work on universal history. *The Book of Revelation* was of tremendous value because of its vivid picture of the future. In a sense, then, since the answers to the main questions about the past and future of the human race were known, the answers to the lesser questions of history were unimportant; therefore historical criticism was not particularly necessary.

PERSONALITY

The Twelfth Century Renaissance was not an individualistic age like the better known and later Renaissance. Rather conventional by tradition, its historians could not appeal to great audiences, and, thus, had no incentive for popular writing. The scholars, such as Abelard, who craved intellectual leadership or the admiration of even the academic audience, might better teach theology or the arts at the schools. History had few attractions for dynamic and vibrant personalities. The chroniclers wrote in terms of men or of incidents rather than of institutions or culture as a whole, while leaving relatively little information about themselves. A very large portion of the monastic chronicles and even of other historical literature is anonymous, and thus gives little idea of the writers or of the circumstances of writing. The tradition is one in which the subject matter is personal but authorship is quite impersonal. The few but rather well-known autobiographies include those by Peter Abelard, Guibert of Nogent, Gerald of Wales, and Jocelin of Brakelond.[44]

An Official as Historian. These, however, are not really typical twelfth centry

---

[42] See Thompson and Holm, *A History of Historical Writing*, Chapter XVIII.
[43] C. W. Davis, ed. *De expugnatione lyxbonensi; narratio de itinere navali peregrinorum hierosolymam tendentium et sylviam capientium*, Proceedings of the American Philosophical Society, LXXXI (1939), pp. 590-676.
[44] On Autobiography see C. H. Haskins, *Renaissance of the Twelfth Century*, pp. 253-260.

historians. The career of William, Archbishop of Tyre, can be cited as an example of the more professional historians. He was not trained especially as a historian, but had such a career offered him as part of an official and clerical career by King Amaury in 1167. His education as an historian was partly by experience in the diplomatic and clerical world of the day and partly by the reading of chronicles, both Latin and Arabic. His shift from theoretical to acutal knowledge of politics seems to have been accompanied by a growing faith in the importance of mankind in his own history. His work then became characterized by six qualities which indicated an essential greatness of mind: objectivity, freedom from prejudice, critical attitude toward his sources, wide range of interests, analysis of cause and effect, and concern about style. His faults were carelessness about chronology and professional bias in favor of the Church.[45]

A Scholarly Historian. Interest in scholars and intellectual history appears in the chronicle of Robert of Torigni, who became Abbot of Mont Saint-Michel (1154-86). He is conventional in relying heavily upon Sigebert of Gembloux for history before his own time, but Robert's work records, as few others do, events of consequence for intellectual history: the translations of James of Venice in 1128; Gratian's *Decretals* in 1130; the death of Hugh of St. Victor in 1143, who left many books as a monument to his knowledge; the death of Abbot Rogert, "erudite in both Scriptures"; the law book of Master Vacarius in England; the elevation of Geoffrey Arthur (of Monmouth) to a bishopric in 1152, "who translated the history of the Kings of Britain from Celtic to Latin"; the translation of a Greek book at the request of Pope Eugenius in 1152; the death of Bishop Gilbert of Poitiers, "who commented brilliantly upon the Psalms and Pauline Epistles" in 1154; the long series of translations from the Greek by Burgundio the Pisan in 1181. The chronicle, also, records the usual data, but was wide in its reach. The Mount was a very revered shrine, visited by many important people who became Robert's informants.[46]

The Typical Historian. What then was the twelfth century historian? He was obviously not a professional; none was paid for writing history and none taught history as a discipline. He did not have even the idea of history as the changing, developing culture of the past. He had no function in society as a historian; his history writing might interest or flatter or edify but it conveyed little understanding of the past. In short, history was essentially a pleasant hobby for a variety of men. Some of these were men of importance in the world, some were obscure monks in lesser monasteries. But even the historian's historian, Sigebert of Gembloux, was the author of a rather meager chronicle in comparison with the fuller histories of his own day. The brilliant and detailed accounts were written by men whose individual genius was not overcome by the jejune tradition of the time or whose interest in a great endeavor led irresistibly to a full and interesting exposition.

Nevertheless, historical writing did advance in this period. The chronicles

[45] Krey (note 6), especially, pp. 162-3.
[46] *Chronicles of the Reigns of Stephen, Henry II, and Richard I,* ed. R. Howlett, IV, pp. 114-299.

increased both in yearly material recorded and in breadth of interest. The conception of a philosophy of history was carried further by such writers as Otto of Freising. Well organized biographies of saints and some good character sketches of secular leaders appear. A beginning is made in the keeping of archives and in the production of records. Even criticism advanced occasionally in such writers as William of Newburgh and Guibert of Nogent. And if Geoffrey of Monmouth did appear then—well, he did help with a long and entertaining series of stories about King Arthur. With the growth of literacy and the appearance of advanced schools, history might expect a brilliant future, particularly if the processes of definition applied to theology would be applied to history.

Chapter 5

THE THIRTEENTH CENTURY
By J. G. Russell

FROM 1200 UNTIL the Black Death of 1348 most of the movements of the preceding age acquired momentum. The kingdoms of England, France and Spain increased in strength. The larger Italian and other commercial centers strengthened their economic and usually their political positions. Exceptions to this were the states of eastern Europe and the Near East where a Mohammedan revival reduced the Christian influence. Nearly everywhere, population increased markedly until the catastrophe of the plague decimated the peoples. Although the Church tightened its discipline following the Fourth Lateran Council of 1215 the trend was distinctly secular.[1] Furthermore, the secular elements, which had intellectual aspirations, regarded French as the language of polite society.

Nevertheless, the Latin ecclesiastical world was still very strong. Literacy spread, encouraged by an increasing number of schools and universities. Scholarly vision improved with the invention of the eyeglass, offset somewhat by a degeneration of handwriting and student note-taking. The introduction of materials translated from Arabic and Greek broadened and strengthened the academic curriculum. The thirteenth century saw a magnificent series of encyclopaedic treatises upon various phases of knowledge, integrating great areas of information, illustrated by such names as Albertus Magnus, Thomas Aquinas, Roger Bacon, Duns Scotus, and hundreds of others. History writing might be expected to reveal the influence of these developments. But there was no marked change. The tradition of the chronicle in narrative writing and of the saint's life in biography remained standard. Such alterations as occurred seem largely to have resulted from the increase of secular patrons, kings, nobles and cities who pressed for the use of the vernacular as the means of expression.

PATRONS AND LITERARY CENTERS

The patrons and literary centers remained for the most part as they had been in the preceding period. Many of the monasteries which had been outstanding in the twelfth century receded in importance compared with other centers. Only in England did the monasteries retain their earlier preeminence. Royal courts held somewhat the same position, while the lesser feudal courts slightly improved their place. On the other hand, the cities, particularly in Italy and the Mediterranean areas, became much more important in the historical field. The rise of universities, however, was not an important influence on the writing of history.

---

[1] On this secularization see especially J. R. Strayer, "Laicization of French and English Society in the Thirteenth Century," *Speculum*, XV (1940), pp. 76-86.

Monasteries. During the thirteenth century the chief patrons of historical writing in England, France and Germany were the monasteries. In the contest for outstanding men of learning they tended to lose to the new mendicant orders. This was probably the main reason for the decline of the monastery as an intellectual center, and it affected monastic historical writing as well as all forms of monastic literary writing. Nevertheless, the great Benedictine houses with their prestige, their libraries, their large numbers of intelligent monks, and their literary traditions were always attractive to considerable numbers of able men.[2] Their work was not so spectacular but it was substantial.

The thirteenth century was a difficult time for the monasteries. They found the new economic conditions based upon a wider use of a money economy, a serious problem.[3] They frequently faced heavy and costly litigation for their lands and other holdings. The great intellectual controversies centered in the universities, hence the monasteries were now out of the main arena of intellectual struggle. At the same time the sources of monastic history improved as many houses copied their documents in great volumes called cartularies, which rendered their early history more accessible. In Italy, in the preceding century, this process had been the inspiration for some chronicles; few appear in the thirteenth century.[4]

The members of the new mendicant orders, especially the Franciscans and Dominicans, were in a favorable position to write history. The more able of them were often dispatched upon important secular journeys and most had some traveling experience. The Franciscans, John of Plano Carpini and William of Rouysbrock, got as far as China.[5] A most interesting account is that of the well known Italian, Salimbene, a Franciscan from Parma, who saw a great deal of southern France and northern Italy and heard much about the world in which he lived. But, these were new orders and they had no background beyond the thirteenth century to draw upon, except that of the Church,—and Church history was not a flourishing study.

Kings. The importance of royal households as patrons of history and as literary centers varied with the strength of the king and the interests of the court. The destruction of the invulnerability of the Byzantine capital reduced that court's importance as a historical center; the same is true of the German empire, which no longer seemed to have encouraged historians. On the other hand, the Iberian peninsula enjoyed a historical golden age. Frederick II had a very intellectual court but its interests were primarily scientific.[6] The courts of France and England provided some, though not very much patronage of history. The conditions at the court should have been better. More books came into circulation and the number of literate clerks at court increased. This grew, in part, out of the need for keeping records which now became an in-

---

[2] The output of English Benedictine houses is catalogued in J. C. Russell, *Dictionary of Writers of Thirteenth Century England.*
[3] See the very good discussion of phases of thirteenth century monasticism in D. Knowles, *The Religious Orders in England.*
[4] One in England: *Chronicon Monasterii de Abingdon,* ed. by J. Stevenson.
[5] *Texts and Versions of John de Plano Carpini and William de Rubruquis,* ed. by C. R. Beazley.
[6] C. H. Haskins, "Science at the Court of the Emperor Frederick II," *Studies in the History of Mediaeval Science,* pp. 242-271.

creasingly important part of royal administration. The volume became so large in some countries that some provision for depositing them became advisable; the mishaps to which the records of King John of England and of the Emperor Frederick II fell prey pointed up the danger of carrying valuables with the court. The ambulatory character of the court handicapped the writing of history at the court still more. Many chroniclers alleged that they were urged to write by royalty; in most cases patronage probably did not go much further.

The relationship of the kings of France to the royal abbey of St. Denis is worth noting. The tradition, started probably by Suger in the previous century, was continued by a series of monks of that house who worked upon the rather second-rate compilation known as the *Grandes Chroniques de St. Denis* or *de France*. The most famous of these writers was William of Nangis (d. 1300). He is reported to have been the historiographer of the royal house,[7] but his position was probably not very official. He was custodian of the charters of his own abbey. He based his history upon such standard works as Sigebert of Gembloux, Martin of Troppau and Vincent of Beauvais, supplemented by many other sources; he wrote in both Latin and French. Vincent of Beauvais (ca. 1190-1264), a Dominican, wrote under the patronage of Louis IX, who got him appointed lector in a monastic house. If Louis IX did not appoint the first Regius Professor of History, he at least made an early grant-in-aid of research for assistance in copying manuscripts.[8]

In England, Henry III (1216-72) was acquainted with the reputation of Matthew Paris[9] (?—ca. 1259), the great chronicler of St. Albans, and showed his favor in ways of which Matthew was proud. In October, 1247, the king invited the chronicler to sit near him at the celebration of the Feast of St. Edward the Confessor so that he might write a better account of the occasion. Twelve years later when the king stopped at St. Albans he had a long and well remembered conversation with Matthew. Apparently his interest went no further; and he reserved his patronage more for poets.[10] Edward I (1272-1307) made remrakable use of history writing on one occasion; in 1291 he asked the monasteries of England to send information from their chronicles about the relationship of the Scottish and English crowns.[11]

More direct patronage appears in the Spanish peninsula. There Fernando III (1199-1252) is alleged to have requested Archbishop Rodrigo of Toledo to write his great history. The next king, Alfonso X, had history as one of the fields of knowledge in which he and eminent scholars worked laboriously.[12] Two kings of Aragon, Jayme I (1213-76) and Pedro III (1286-85), as well

---

[7] A. Molinier, *Les Sources de l'histoire de France*, III, No. 2532; Thompson and Holm, *A History of Historical Writing*, p. 271. Thompson says that he was custodian of the charters of France. He is edited in *Recueil des Historiens des Gaules et de France*, XX, 466. Cf. also L. Delisle, *Mémoire sur les Ouvrages de Guillavme de Nangis*.

[8] Others associated with Saint Louis IX wrote upon his life: Godeffroi de Beaulieu, his confessor (Molinier, III, No. 2542); Guillaume de Chartres, a chaplain (Molinier, III, No. 2543); Guillaume de S. Pathus, the queen's confessor (Molinier, III, No. 2544).

[9] *Chronica Majora*, IV, 644, V, 617-618. For Matthew see below note 47.

[10] J. C. Russell and J. P. Heironimus, *The Shorter Latin Poems of Master Henry of Avranches* etc., pp. 137-142.

[11] V. H. Galbraith, *Roger Wendover and Matthew Paris*, pp. 43-44.

[12] On these writers see the works of B. Sánchez Alonso, *Historia de la Historiographia Española*, ch. III.

as two writers close to other kings, Desclot and Muntaner, wrote outstanding history. Many of the data in these accounts are very accurate and are no doubt derived in part from documents as well as from memory. The prevalence of royal interest and even participation in history writing is unusual and striking. It may have been the result of the Arabic tradition of learned secular rulers.[13]

Feudal Lords. In the thirteenth and fourteenth centuries, the feudal lords increasingly employed clerks to keep their legal and financial records. With increasing literacy and records the feudal court should have been a more promising center for historical writing than it was. There are instances— Robert of Clari is one—of writing by ordinary knights, presumably for similar courts. However, for the most part, little history was written there, although if one includes the history written in monasteries for their lay patrons, the amount was considerable. There is an interesting, unpublished chronicle which deals largely with the Mortimer family, while another chronicle, also unpublished, of the monastery of Hagneby in England has the Neville family as its chief interest.[14]

Cities. After 1200 the cities in Europe grew rapidly in population and even more in energy and enthusiasm. Literacy became more necessary to keep the ever increasing records of commerce and of government, and as a basis for that legal education into which great numbers entered. This emphasis upon literacy, schools and records formed a congenial atmosphere, for the production of history. The writers were clerks who had entered minor orders or laymen whose interests were literary. German and, more especially, Italian cities led in the development of civic history. Even in England it was a member of a German migrant family, Arnald FitzThedmar (1201-75) who wrote the first important city chronicle, that of London. He was a merchant, an alderman of the city and apparently keeper of the city records for a time. Although the chronicle is entitled *Chronicle of the Mayors and Sheriffs* it includes much about the kingdom as a whole.[15]

The official encouragement by the Genoese government of an outstanding group of historians continued into the thirteenth century with the writing by Marchisius (1220-4), Bartholomeus (1224-48), and d'Oria (1269-94).[16] Then this city, which had made such a brilliant start, lapsed into the taciturnity which distinguished it in the later Middle Ages and produced little history.[17] Much progress in this direction was in Padua and Verona rather than in Venice and Florence where anonymous productions were still current. The second half of the thirteenth century and the early fourteenth century saw great historical writing in these cities, but this was the result of general literary interest rather than of official encouragement, of which there is very little evidence.

This study of patronage reveals that it is not the size of the city nor the

---

[13] See J. C. Russell, "Chroniclers of Medieval Spain," *Hispanic Review*, VI (1938), pp. 218-235.
[14] Cambridge, C. C. C., MS 339, fos. 34v-47v for the Mortimer chronicle: London, British Museum, *MS Cotton, Vesp.* B i, fos. 1-61v for Hagneby.
[15] Edited by T. Stapleton, translated by H. Riley, *Chronicles of the Mayors and Sheriffs of London* (London, 1863).
[16] Ed. Pertz in M.G.H. SS. XVIII, pp. 115-356.
[17] On the taciturnity of the Genoese see R. Lopez, "European Merchants in the Medieval Indies: The Evidence of Commercial Documents," *Journal of Economic History*, III (1943), pp. 168-174.

power of the feudal lords which promoted the patronage of chronicles. Instead, it appears to have been the independent spirit of the city or lord. Not every free city or independent lord fostered a chronicle, but more chronicles come from these centers than from those under the control of feudal superiors.

THE TRADITION AND HISTORICAL CRITICISM

The rise of universities somehow failed to influence the study of history very much. History was not a special field in the curriculum of the day. It fell in with grammar and thus was, so far as it was studied at all, identified with literature. The rules of logic were seldom applied to it. Furthermore, medieval people were not historically minded; they did not realize that earlier people thought and acted differently from themselves. They did not create a hypothetical memory necessary to reconstruct the past. The past to the medieval mind was apparently a better present, a Golden Age, an idealized era only qualitatively different from the contemporary scene, sharing the same ideas and institutions but using them more efficiently.

It is unfortunate that the medieval university did not take history more seriously, since it was very good at taking a limited subject matter and by scholastic processes extracting all that could be drawn from the evidence. This is precisely what historians have to do.

Popular Compendia. The compendia of history of Marianus Scotus and Sigebert of Gembloux which had been so popular in the previous century as bases for chronicles remained so for the thirteenth century. The latter had its own favorites as well. One was the quite dry chronological list prepared by the Dominican Martin of Troppau (Martinus Polonus, d. 1278) ; it was a convenient list for those houses which desired a good directory of dates and persons. Martin wrote under papal patronage and carried his work to 1277.[18] Other popular works were longer and fuller. A much fuller work which had a wide vogue was the *Speculum Historiale.*

The first effects of the university upon historical writings, so small for the most part, appears in the form of composition by Vincent, rather than in any noticeable change in historical criticism. His *Speculum Historiale* was a typical scholastic encyclopedia of knowledge. However, large as it was, it was only one part of his *Speculum Maius,* which included a *Speculum Naturale* and a *Speculum Doctrinale.*[19] The pattern allowed for breadth of historical exposition so that it contained not merely political and anecdotal history, but even much discussion of pagan religion and of other topics connected with the New History of this century. Vincent was a kind of educational expert in his day, but his work was not well arranged and followed the tradition of the *florilegia* rather than the universal chronicles.

The work of Vincent of Beauvais was more in line, in some respects, with the historical tradition of the Arabic historians than of the western European scholars. The Arabs were not limited by the tradition of western history and

---

18 His *Chronicon Pontificum et Imperatorum* is edited by Weiland, M.G.H. SS XXII, pp. 377-475.
19 B. L. Ullman, "A Project for a New Edition of Vincent of Beauvais," *Speculum,* VIII (1933), pp. 312-326; edited (Douai, 1624).

often cast their net widely, but seldom ordered their histories logically. An exception who made the most of his tradition was Ibn-Khaldun (1352-1406) whose history is probably the supreme historical achievement of the medieval world. In his *Prologomena* he discusses causes of historical change and the influence of geography in an extraordinarily mature fashion.[20]

In Spain, a notable tradition of historiography was evolving in the thirteenth century. "It appears first in the west (Asturias, Leon, Castile) with the works of Alfonso III (866-910), Bishop Sisnand, Bishop Sampiro *(ca.* 1041) and Bishop Pelayo *(ca.* 1143), which added to an Isidorian group of writings, formed a *Corpus Pelagianum.*"[21] The culmination of this Spanish tradition was by Alfonso X (the Wise) and his collaborators (1252-84), who followed the Pelayan tradition in a great *Primera Cronica General de España.* Then, like Vincent of Beauvais, they compiled a vast *General Estoria,* a world history,[22] one part of an encyclopedic effort which included a *lapidario* and a code of law. It was the last of the series and probably represents Alfonso's most mature achievement. Its success was largely the result of the wisdom and direct supervision of the king and the great collection of source materials which Alfonso and his predecessors had amassed. Alfonso's mind was that of a collector and antiquary rather than that of a trained historian. His belief in Goeffrey of Monmouth and other myths is rather characteristic.

Several explanations of Alfonso's work have been advanced: to bring the political achievement of the Reconquest to a peak with the accession of the king to the position of Holy Roman Emperor, to reestablish the Isidorian scientific tradition of integrated knowledge, to equate Christian culture with the Mohammedan by joining Romance and Semitic knowledge, and to popularize knowledge by publishing it in the vernacular.[23] Alfonso's interest in astronomy, mineralogy and law would suggest, however, that the primary emphasis was upon knowledge rather than political ambitions. Alfonso's effort, it should be noted, was outside of the universities which, unfortunately, did not feel the stimulating influence of such an undertaking.

Progress of Criticism. Historical criticism, if anything, tended to decline in this period. The possibility of improvement depended largely upon acceptance of history as a definite subject in the medieval curricula of the universities and that never occurred. The development of ecclesiastical history made little progress and with it went the chance of improving that type of history. On the other hand, the great contemporary secular urge inevitably increased the scope of vernacular history. This, however, did not entail any refinement of criticism. This history emphasized brilliance of exposition and vividness of style rather than accuracy of information and sharpening of method. It could hardly be expected that the secular or the city audience of the new history would be fastidious or critical in evaluating the data presented to it. The very novelty of

[20] Prologomena edited in *Notes et Extraits des Manuscrits XVI;* excerpts translated by D. B. MacDonald; see also M. A. Enan, *Ibn Khaldun, His Life and Work.*
[21] B. Sánchez Alonso, *Historia de la Historiografía Española,* I, 110-140.
[22] See introductions to these: A. G. Solalinde, *Alfonso el Sabio General Historia* I and J. Filgueira Valverde, *Primera Cronica General de España,* and D. Donald, "Suetonius in the Primera Cronica General" through the "Speculum Historiale," *Hispanic Review,* XI (1943), pp. 95-115.
[23] Valverde, *loc. cit.*

the effort worked against the prospect of good historical method; its brilliance caused the listeners or readers to forget the problems of accuracy involved in the story. The *chansons des gestes* had been popular in the preceding period, particularly among the courts. A clientele habituated to the long and detailed epics and *chansons* would expect the same characteristics in its history.

French was the language of European feudal society of the thirteenth century, so that even the chronicle of Venice and the *Travels of Marco Polo* were written in that language. It perhaps explains the vernacular writing of the crusading accounts of Villehardouin, Robert of Clari, and Joinville. French also was used by the Englishman, Peter Langtoft.[24] The use of the vernacular became a part of the historical tradition of other countries besides France. It was, if anything, even stronger in Spain. The great chronicles written under the direction of Alfonso X were written in Spanish. In Aragon great historical works were composed in the vernacular by Jayme I, Pedro III, Muntaner and Desclot.[25] These were largely histories of the royal family of Aragon in Aragon, Navarre, Catalonia, Mallorca, and Sicily. The writing was in an easy narrative style which often portrayed vivid color and action.

Chronicles were, as usual, copied from earlier histories; the evidence about the actual process is not always clear. However, William of Bougeville, a monk of Bec, compiled a chronicle which he named *One from All*. He says that he saw many histories and chronicles at the excellent church of Bury St. Edmunds, at St. Albans and at Westminster, as well as at St. Denis in Paris.[26] He evidently knew where the greatest collections were to be found. Since he seems to have served as prior at the cell of St. Neot in England, he may have taken side journeys on his way from the mother house to the cell to improve his knowledge of history.

There was much criticism of documents and seals in the thirteenth century; this was naturally a function of the courts. Thus, Innocent III wrote a letter to the chapter of Milan, explaining how one should approach the question of such forgeries; he was doubtless explaining the techniques used by the Curia.[27] English courts occasionally faced the same situation in regard to private charters. Richard Morius, chronicler of Dunstable and former professor of law, tells how a judge showed that a charter had been washed and rewritten in bad grammar and thus was false.[28] However, the only treatise dealing with the subject was by a versatile historian, Bernard Cui,[29] but this essay hardly touched upon the field of history.

FUNCTIONS AND PURPOSES OF WRITING

Certain changes in patronage from the twelfth to the thirteenth centuries seemed to foreshadow alterations in the functions and purposes of historical

[24] Ed. T. Wright.
[25] B. Sánchez Alonso, *Historia de la Historiografía Española*, I, 235-245.
[26] J. S. Russell, *Dictionary of Writers of Thirteenth Century England*, pp. 184-185. He left the cell without permission but the mistake was condoned. Perhaps it was because of the merit of his historical activities. The *Unus Omnium* has survived only in fragments.
[27] Tout, "Medieval Forgers and Forgeries," *Collected Papers*, III (1934), pp. 126-127. The letter was published by Baluze in *Epistolae Innocentii III*, I, 101.
[28] *Annales Monastici*, ed. H. R. Luard, 111, 66.
[29] Tout, *op. cit.*, p. 127.

writing. The growth of archival and record collections might suggest that more chronicles would be written for the purpose of record. The increase in the power of the Papacy would seem to suggest a great history of the Church as an institution. Yet, just as the universities grew without including much history in their curricula, so also did the other expectations foreseen for that discipline fail to materialize. Functions and purposes remained surprisingly the same, with some change of emphasis.

Little Official Writing. One reason alleged for this namely, official activity, must be written off at once. The statement that royal or monastic historiographers were appointed by the kings of France and Spain[30] and by the monastery of St. Albans,[31] runs against the whole trend of attitudes towards history in the thirteenth or even the fourteenth century. History was not a professional subject. One would expect that payments would be made to a royal historiographer and that, following the death of one, others would continue the office. It is really unbelievable that such a position, once established, should be left vacant in an age which saw many historians eager for preferment.

If there is little evidence that scholars were employed to examine the past, there is also no evidence of an official effort to explain current law. The great work of Bracton upon English law and of Beaumanoir upon the customary law of France were private efforts. Both are of tremendous importance to the modern historian and were doubtless so to the contemporary lawyer. Henry of Bratton (d. 1268), to use the correct form of the name, was a very distinguished lawyer and justice at a time when the legal profession was developing ideas and principles for the common law of England. His work, *Treatise on the Laws and Customs of the Kingdom of England,* reflects a fine insight into the operation and principles of law at that time.[32] Philip of Remi, Sire de Beaumanoir (d. 1296), does the same for France in the second half of the thirteenth century.[33] Both volumes were designed for information, rather than for the encouragement of legal change, for the very practical purpose of aiding lawyers to know and understand the law.

General Chronicles. The general chronicle remained annalistic in form; it continued to present news in medieval fashion, chiefly events of interest to the local people. Usually the monastery itself provided some news: deaths and promotions of abbots and priors and occasionally of others, events in the lives of the patrons of the monastery, catastrophes and unusual incidents in the community. Despite some variety inspired by the location or personality of the writer the idea of news remained about the same.

Among chroniclers of the thirteenth century, Roger of Wendover (d. 1236), occupies a respectable position in spite of his evident credulity with respect to accounts of the past. His monastery of St. Albans was on the main road north of London, about a day's journey from the city. Many travelers stopped there

---

[30] Thompson and Holm, *A History of Historical Writing,* p. 271, calls William of Nangis an official historian but gives no evidence.
[31] Thompson and Holm, pp. 276-278, quotes C. Jenkins but omits part of the quotation which gives the statement precisely the opposite meaning. The *Monastic Chronicler,* p. 67. Jenkins says that there is no evidence that Paris was an official historian.
[32] In process of being edited by G. E. Woodbine, I; II (1922); III (1940), and IV (1942).
[33] *Coutumes de Beauvaisis,* ed. Salmon. He was also a poet.

and left information for both Roger and his contemporary and successor, Matthew Paris. Illustrative of the types of information and length devoted to each year, are the items for the year, 1227:[34]

> extorsion of Money by Henry III, cancellation of charters by Henry at the Council of Oxford, return of English messengers from a vain mission to France, return of king's brother Richard, consecration of the bishop of Rochester, knighting of the justiciar by the king, disturbance of barons against the king, Alpine hermit's sayings, crusade preached in England, letter of Pope Gregory IX on the crusade, hindrance to the crusade by the emperor, death of St. Francis, confirmation of the Franciscan order by the pope, preaching and death of Francis, concourse of people at his funeral.

Some of the items doubtless came from Master Honorius and his roll of information about the crusade which he was preaching. While monastic chronicles existed throughout most of Europe during this period they were more meager on the continent.

The general chronicle gives some idea of what the medieval mind considered newsworthy. The more specialized accounts, for the most part, present the same types of news, but naturally have more unity and coherence than the ordinary chronicles. Pride in achievement is one obvious purpose for the writing of many of these accounts, either from the standpoint of association or participation in the movements.

Mendicant History. The rapid rise of the new mendicant orders and their remarkable achievements inaugurated some historical accounts of them. Perhaps the best of these is the treatise of Thomas of Eccleston on the coming of the friars minor to England, an interesting story of the first generation of Franciscans in that country. The story which has few chronological guides includes many phases of Franciscan life: the early hardships, the building program, the admission of both humble and well placed people, studies, and simple anecdotes with respect to the early austerity. Thomas tells of Walter of Maddeley who found some shoes and wore them. Falling asleep, he dreamed that he was attacked by thieves in a perilous valley between Oxford and Gloucester. In terror he said that he was a Franciscan, thrust out his feet to show them and was disconcerted to find shoes on them. He woke up so shaken by the dream that he threw the shoes away.[35]

The great intellectual achievements of the Franciscans and Dominicans at the universities must be traced largely through the theological and other treatises written there, for none thought to write formal intellectual history. Similarly, the intellectual efforts of the court of Frederick II found no historian. The two chroniclers of this period, Richard of San Germano and Nicholas of Iamsilla, were both apparently royal notaries and thus officials associated to some extent with the emperor. They were more concerned with his political activities than with his intellectual interest. Richard (d. 1243) was born near

---

[34] *Rogeri de Wendover Liber qui dicitur Flores Historiarum*, ed. H. G. Hewlett, II, pp. 317-333.
[35] Collatio vi. Best edition by A. G. Little, *Tractatus fr Thome Vulgo Dicti de Eccleston de Adventu Fratrum Minorum in Angliam;* older edition by Brewer, trans. by E. G. Salter in the *Coming of the Friars Minor to England and Germany.*

the abbey of Monte Cassino, a notable center of history writing, as we have seen. He wrote the *Chronica Regni Siciliae* marked by temperate and accurate reporting. Nicholas (d. *ca.* 1258), was as ardent a partisan of Frederick II as his contemporary, Saba Malaspina, was of the popes of that time.[36]

City Chronicles. In the thirteenth century, the great achievements of the communes of Italy stimulated the writing of history, principally by laymen who were connected with the archives of the city and had participated in the activities of the city. Genoa led in the movement by giving official encouragement to historiography. The last of the Genoese chroniclers of great importance was James D'Oria (1234-94), grandson of the famous admiral. James also took part in naval action and later was a kind of archivist, making use of the documents in his chronicle. He had had the good education which sons of the wealthier families often enjoyed. From his education and his experience he had gained a broad view of what constituted history for a commercial republic, such as Genoa.[37]

The amount of chronicle writing to some extent varies with the power of the cities. Thus, Padua and Verona, which were relatively less powerful in the second than in the first half of the thirteenth century, had their best chroniclers in the first part. In Padua a scholar who had studied at Bologna, Rolandinus, wrote the history of his city for the years 1200-60. He was contemporary with much of this period, for he became a doctor in grammar and rhetoric as early as 1221. His work was read publicly at the University of Padua in 1262 and honored by academic approval. Yet apparently, Rolandinus taught grammar and rhetoric of which, of course, history was a part. His history was of a narrative type and in the professor's mind involved few problems of historical criticism.[38]

The period from 1260 to the Black Death saw the flowering of civic history writing in Italy; smaller cities such as Padua, Vicenza and Siena had [39] outstanding historians as did the great cities of Florence, Genoa, and Venice. Two great historians of Vicenza and Padua were friends: Ferreto de Ferreti and Albertino Mussato (1261-1330).[40] Ferreto wrote a history of Italy from 1250 to 1318, making good use of his classical studies, depicting persons and scenes brilliantly and recording rumors of scandal in the best classical manner. Albertino, by his great intellectual ability, rose from comparative poverty to a high position in the state. He thus was enabled to write history as he participated in it and to do it well, since he had made his living with his pen.

The literature of Florence blossomed forth in the last quarter of the thirteenth century and continued well past our period. In the historical field the great names are Dino Compagni and the Villani. The first (1260-1323) was by trade a silk merchant who in his early manhood served the city in important capacities. He was an honest, pleasant person who was forced out of politics by

[36] Balzani, *Early Chroniclers of Europe: Italy*, pp. 236-238; Richard is edited by Pertz, M.G.H., SS XIX, pp. 321-384; Nicholas is edited in Del Re, *Cronisti e Scrittori Sincroni Napoletani, II*; so is Saba Malaspina.
[37] Balzani, pp. 306-308. Edited Pertz, *Cafari et Continuatorum Annales Inuenses*, M.G.H., SS. XVIII, pp. 288-356; he shared in pp. 267-288.
[38] Balzani, pp. 274-275. Rolandinus is edited by Jaffe in M.G.H., SS. XIX, pp. 32-147.
[39] Balzani, pp. 271-272.
[40] Balzani, pp. 272-291; he is somewhat overwhelmed by Mussato. The works of the two are edited in Muratori, IX and X; see also C. Cibilla, *Le Obere de Ferreto de' Ferreti*.

its increasing roughness and brutality. He then devoted himself to the writing of history and to his trade. Dino intended to portray the greatness and refinement of early Florence hoping to persuade people to return to its former simple and gracious life. He had the medieval inability to understand change and thought that, if decadence could be eliminated, the city would return to its early simplicity and happiness.[41]

Giovanni Villani (d. 1348), also of the merchant class of Florence, was so impressed by the Jubilee at Rome in 1300, with its hundreds of thousands of pilgrims, and by the City itself that he began a great world chronicle from the beginning of time, centering largely in Italy and carrying it on to the time of his death in the Great Plague. Villani was an important citizen of Florence, engaged from time to time in commissions for the city, such as supervising the mint and rebuilding the city walls. He also participated in intercity affairs and thus acquired by experience a variety of information. His writing was rather in the conventional type of the chronicle than a well integrated history. After his death his chronicle was continued first by his brother Matteo and then by his nephew Filippo.[42]

The Venetian story was told anonymously until the end of the thirteenth century, when it was written in French by Martin da Canale, who has been mentioned earlier. He was followed by Andreas Dandolo (ca. 1300-54), of the great family of that name. He participated in civic affairs and drew his information largely from earlier chronicles of the city. Not very critical nor even a very good writer he managed to incorporate most of the earlier data satisfactorily and to give a reasonably good account of the history of the city.[43]

Edification. Edification was the professed purpose of most of the medieval historical writing. This was natural since education was still largely confined to churchmen or, at any rate, dominated by the Church ideals and inspiration. The motive of edification, of course, is especially revealed in the saints' lives written in the century. The number of canonizations declined markedly in the thirteenth and fourteenth centuries, but there were very revered saints, such as Francis in Italy, Dominic in Spain, Louis IX in France, and Edmund in England; their biographies were very full and quite interesting.

Even history as a whole served edification in the views of some of the writers of the period. Thus, St. Bonaventure believed in a trinity of historical ages: the age of the law of nature, the age of the law of Holy Scripture, and the age of the law of Grace, all foreknown to God.

> If everything is created by God and if there is a providence of God which disposes of the flow of events as well as their status, then it follows immediately that all events of this world are foreknown and predisposed by God. Consequently, what we call history was first a conception or an artistic composition of God which now

[41] Balzani, pp. 317-329; *The Chronicle of Dino Compagni*, translated by Benecke and Howell; new edition in *Muratori*, IX.
[42] Balzani, pp. 329-335. Partially translated by P. H. Wickstead and R. E. Selfe; ed. *Muratori*, XIII.
[43] Balzani, pp. 293-302. Martin is edited by G. Galvani, *La Chronique des Veniciens de Maistre Martin da Canal, Archivio Storico Italiano*, 1st series, VIII (1845), pp. 268-766. Dandolo in Muratori, XII.

through the ages takes place like the play of a drama. Though it is played by various creatures, nevertheless its author is the triune God, and consequently history, too, bears the mark of the Blessed Trinity.[44]

Dante's philosophy of history must be worked out from scattered items but seems to have followed the ecclesiastical pattern of emphasis upon human progress, Divine Providence, freedom and the Fall.[45]

> "History is the movement of humanity towards peace, not merely towards the temporal peace of an ordered Church and State with Grace and Law; but onwards and upwards to an Eternal Peace in the ordered Will of God."

PERSONALITY

The increased secularization evident in the thirteenth century suggests that the personality of its authors might stand out more than in the more impersonal twelfth century. This seems to be true, although there is almost as little autobiographical writing as before. The interests of the chroniclers do seem to appear more clearly. Many historians left enough clues which make identification possible and sometimes sufficient data to write a fairly satisfactory biography. The educational system in which most chroniclers were trained had become somewhat stabilized by the thirteenth century. Cathedral schools were mostly on the secondary level. Schools within the monasteries ceased to function; even monks attended either outside schools or the universities, if they had not finished their education (as most must have done) before they entered religion. Thus, elementary and secondary education was general and tended to become standardized over Europe.

Standardization, however, was very limited because no very strong idea of the exact character of history had been formed. As discussed above, history did not become an autonomous division of the university curriculum. Furthermore, no one historian stood out as "The Historian" in the same way that Aristotle is "The Philosopher." There was no manual of historiography comparable to the *Sentences* of Peter Lombard which could mold historical writing into one pattern. There was, of course, historical tradition, but its limitations were not great, since it was a tradition of a historical backbone to which the individual writers might add flesh and blood. There was ample opportunity for historians to follow their own bent. Sometimes they were influenced by their training in law, art, or other interest. Sometimes they revealed the bias of their own group within a country or the force of unusual personality.

A Lawyer Historian. Richard de Morius (Morins) of England was a good contemporary example of a chronicler interested in law. He had been a professor of law at Bologna and author of famous legal treatises before he

[44] Philotheus Boehner, *The History of the Franciscan School* (St. Bonaventure, New York, mimeographed, 1944; re-mimeographed, Duns Scotus College, 1947), II, p. 81. This passage was pointed out to me by Fr. Robert Wilken, O.F.M.
[45] G. G. Walsh, "Dante's Philosophy of History," *Catholic Historical Review*, XX (1934), pp. 117-134. The quotation is on the last page.

became prior of Dunstable in 1202. From this year until his death in 1242 he wrote the conventional type of chronicle to which he added a heavy emphasis upon law. He records many instances in which he served as papal legate in legal cases and many disputes in which his own house was involved. This included a long and fierce legal battle between it and the town of Dunstable, a struggle so serious that the townsmen declared they preferred to go to hell rather than give in. Yet Richard tells also of the religious side of his house's history and even had visions himself.[46]

An Artist Historian. The achievement of Matthew Paris, monk of St. Albans (?-1259?), included, in part, the writing of a wide variety of historical types of literature. They included the typical general chronicle, more direct historical accounts, and saints' lives in both Latin and the vernacular. His main effort was the *Chronica Majora* from the beginning of time to 1259, a tremendous work of five stout volumes in its published form. It is arranged by year, with a summary of events and of the characteristics of the year at the end of each annual account. It covers a very wide range of human interests and even items from the distant East as well as from his own neighborhood. The chronicle had an appendix of documents, another stout volume, to which references from the *Chronica Majora* are made by footnote-like signs. Paris was also an artist, illustrating his text with coats of arms, pictures, and maps. These are quite modern developments which seldom appeared in historical works until recently. His *Historia Anglorum* is shorter and concentrates more upon English affairs. He seems to have reserved much of the material about his abbey of St. Albans for his section of the *Deeds of the Abbots of St. Albans.*[47]

Feudal Historians. The influence of social status upon historical attitudes is well illustrated by two French accounts by participants in the Fourth Crusade (1202-04), Robert of Clari and Geoffrey of Villehardouin. For the most part they tell the same story, supplementing each other in detail. The magnificence of the great Venetian fleet, the skill of the crusaders in taking Constantinople, the internal difficulties of the victors and the untimely deaths of most of the leaders stand out in both. These stories presuppose a feudal public accustomed to long and elaborate narration, probably of the exploits of Roland, Arthur and Charlemagne. The literary background thus would have provided a suitable pattern of heroic exploits.

One was a leader, Geoffrey (ca. 1160-1213), Marshal of Champaign and later of Romania,[48] and the other, Robert, just a knight.[49] A difference is in the disposal of their time. Robert, who obviously had a lot of spare time, saw the marvels of the city and wrote of them at considerable length; Geoffrey said little about them. Robert complained of the greediness of the great and

[46] *Annales Monastici*, ed. H. R. Luard, III, introduction, pp. 1-158. For his life and identification as a law writer see Russell, *Dictionary of Writers of Thirteenth Century England*, pp. 111-113.
[47] Miriam H. Marshall, "Thirteenth Century Culture as Illustrated by Matthew Paris," *Speculum*, XIV (1939), pp. 465-477. His knowledge of the classics was extensive. F. M. Powicke, "Notes on the Compilation of the *Chronica Majora* of Matthew Paris," *Modern Philology*, XXXVIII (1941), pp. 305-317. V. H. Galbraith, *Roger Wendover and Matthew Paris*.
[48] Conveniently translated in Everyman's edition by F. Marzials.
[49] *The Conquest of Constantinople*, trans. by E. H. McNeal, ed. P. Lauer. Marvels on pp. 101-113: lack of generosity, p. 121.

of their lack of generosity toward the ordinary soldiers, a condition never mentioned by Geoffrey. A more serious discrepancy appears in their accounts of why they went to Constantinople instead of to the Holy Land. Geoffrey says that the claimant to the Byzantine throne, in whose name the crusaders turned aside, was already in Verona and pressed his claims on the crusaders; Robert says that the crusaders first sought an excuse for attacking the Empire and then thought of the young claimant.[50]

Another interesting memoir writer was Jean of Joinville (1224-1317), a feudal lord of modest pretension. He accompanied Louis IX upon his crusade to Egypt and Palestine. He first wrote his memoirs some twenty years later, a few years after he rejected Louis' request to join him in his second and fatal crusade to Tunis in 1270. However, he did not publish them at the time and held them as he lived on decade after decade. Finally, in 1309, when he was about 85, he rewrote or completed them for Jeanne of Navarre, Queen of France, calling them, *Le Livre des saintes paroles et des bonnes actions de Saint Louis.* He was at this time a patriarch of the French feudality. This chatty recital is full of interest, wit, pathos, and heroism in turn. One incident, as the survivors of the debacle in Egypt sailed toward Palestine, illustrates difference of attitude toward tragedy:[51]

> One day Louis asked what the Count of Anjou (his brother) was doing: and they told him that he was playing at tables with my Lord of Nemours. And he went thither tottering, for he was weak by reason of sickness; and he took the dice and the tables, and threw them into the sea; and he was very wroth with his brother because he had so soon taken to playing at dice. But my Lord Walter came off best, for he threw all the moneys on the table into his lap—and they were many—and carried them away.

Influence of Accident. An interesting case of accidental influence appears in the chronicle of a monk of Westminster, probably Robert of Reading. Theoretically, since Westminster was a royal foundation, closely associated with the English kings, the chronicle should have been very royalist. However, this monk spent some time in the royal prison for being implicated, with all the monks of Westminster, in the theft of the royal treasury from the crypt of their chapter house in 1303.[52] Robert's account of what happened placed the blame on one culprit who confessed that he had bored through thirteen feet of stone wall from a busy courtyard. He covered his work by sowing hemp at Christmas time which, before the end of April, was able to "afford sufficient green cover to hide the hole in the wall and to secrete gleaming articles of silver within its thick recesses." [53] It is no wonder that Robert accepted the culprit's confession gladly, even with its amazing account of what could not have taken place.

Humane Historian. There is little accidental about the chronicle of the

[50] Geoffrey, p. 18; Robert, pp. 45-46.
[51] *Memoirs of the Crusades,* translated by F. Marzials, p. 236; also by E. Wedgewood, *The Memoirs of the Lord of Joinville;* ed., N. de Wailly.
[52] Tout, *Collected Papers,* "A Mediaeval Burglary," III, pp. 93-115.
[53] *Ibid.,* pp. 106, 110, Robert's chronicle is edited by H. R. Luard in the *Flores Historiarum.* For the years 1302-26 see Tout, pp. 113-114.

Italian Franciscan, Salimbene (1221-*ca.* 1290) given the unusual character of his mind.[54] Like most chronicles, his work is largely about people and events of the area with which he was acquainted. He had a wide range of interests, both religious and secular, and tells tales of edification as well as of scandal or of mere interest. He enables one to identify the little known Franciscan, Maurice, who wrote a very popular compendium of sermon topics; Maurice had, indeed, asked Salimbene to assist him. He records the life of his generation of Franciscans: the great failure, Elias of Cortona, as well as the great followers of Francis. The chronicle is distinguished by a mass of details about the more personal aspects of life which few chroniclers mention. Almost every phase of life seems to be touched upon without any real effort at chronology.

---

[54] Edited by O. Holder-Egger, M.G.H., S.S. XXXII; translation by G. G. Coulton.

Chapter 6

THE EASTERN IMPERIAL TRADITION
By G. Georgiades Arnakis

THE BYZANTINE IMPACT

THE Roman imperial tradition, which in Western Europe was little more than a memory after the flood of the warlike peoples, continued uninterrupted in the East, whither, in 330 A.D., Constantine the Great transferred the capital of the Empire. Though the barbarians managed to spread into the eastern provinces, too, Constantine's City (Constantinople), built on the site of old Byzantium and frequently referred to as New Rome, was spared the humiliating ordeal that the Eternal City experienced in 410. The new capital grew to be the home of about one million people, the queen amidst a score of thriving cities. Western Europe, with its large towns destroyed, thereby deprived of urban culture, fell back upon a provincial, rural economy. The West sank into the Dark Ages. Feudalism appeared there as a protection of the individual from the effects of disorder and political chaos. The Eastern Empire, on the other hand, remained a well-organized, compact political unit—the heir of the Graeco-oriental culture, the champion of Christianity, and the embodiment of the Roman imperial ideal.

Constantinople overcame the crisis produced by the Gothic infiltration in the fourth century and assimilated in the interests of the Empire and Christianity large masses of heterogeneous people. It drove back successive currents of invading Goths, Avars, Persians, Arabs, Bulgarians, Russians, Pechenegs, and Turks, each of which might have conquered Europe. Throughout long centuries, the Byzantine Empire, as later historians called it, stood as an advanced outpost whose task it was to preserve and protect the valuable cultural tradition of Europe from the alien invader. Thus, it gave a chance to the new nations of Europe to grow into maturity. At the same time, it spread the Christian religion to the Serbs, the Bulgarians, the Rumanians, the Czechs, the Hungarians, and the Russians, and thus it brought new peoples, possessing youthful dynamism, into the orbit of civilization. Unlike the Western Church, it allowed these peoples to use their vernacular as a medium of religious expression and it also helped them to develop their cultural potentialities.

At last it fell a victim to its own magnificent achievement. When the Western peoples became of age, they organized commerce and trade on an ambitious scale, they built towns and cathedrals and they moved over into the East during the period of the Crusades. The Byzantine Empire, worn out by constant warfare in the service of Christianity and of the Roman imperial ideal and still enjoying the economic security of a workable measure of state capitalism and planned economy, failed to keep pace with the changing times; it became inflexible and stagnant; it was no longer able to protect itself from the new, aggressive commercialism of the West, and internal disintegration set in apace. The neighboring Slavs took up arms against it and the Fourth Crusade brought about its downfall by capturing Constantinople and dismembering the provinces in 1204. The Byzantine era came to an end.

The Ottoman Turks. The successor states—Greek and Slav—and the restored empire at Constantinople (1261-1453) were but shadows of the former Byzantine Empire and spent their energies in fratricidal wars. The commercial towns of the West took control of the East's resources while a new enemy developed to deal a mortal blow to Eastern Christendom. From northwestern Asia Minor the Ottoman Turks, inspired by the religion of Mohammed and assisted by the manpower and the political experience of the Byzantines, invaded Europe (1354), conquered Thrace (1361), Albania (1386), Serbia (1389), Bulgaria (1393), Greece (1444), and, at last, entered the Imperial City itself on May 29, 1453.

Now firmly established in the Balkans, the Turks absorbed the most virile elements of the local populations, completed the conquest of the Near East, and thrust their new weight against the heart of Europe. Vienna, the seat of the Holy Roman Empire, was besieged in 1529 and again in 1683. There, the Turks were repulsed by European armies and natural adversities, but even the enlightened eighteenth century regarded them as a menace to Christendom. Then internal decay, largely due to a prolonged era of material prosperity among a race of warriors, made them soft and harmless. By the end of the eighteenth century, the Ottoman Empire was steadily losing ground and prestige before the rising power of Russia. By the middle of the nineteenth century the sultan was widely known as "the sick man of the Bosporus," and only the rivalries and intrigues of the Western powers postponed the dismemberment of his empire. One by one the peoples of the Balkans—Greeks, Serbs, Rumanians, Bulgarians, and Albanians,—who had so prematurely succumbed to the Turk, arose from national torpor, threw off the alien yoke, and took their places in the family of Christian nations. This began with the opening of the nineteenth century and was completed by the eve of the First World War. The ideals of the French Revolution had found eager followers among the oppressed peoples of the Balkan peninsula, notably among the Greeks and Serbs.

Until the era of the French Revolution and the advent of nationalism and liberal ideas in the Near East, the peoples that had been associated with the Byzantine Empire lived under the imperial tradition.

THE EASTERN ROMAN EMPIRE

As far back as the seventh century, when Latin was no longer the language of the Empire, all racial groups that were identified with Christianity called themselves *Romaioi* (Romans). They were proud of their "Roman" law— recodified and Christianized, but essentially Roman—and they thought of their Empire as the *Oecumene* (the inhabited world), which included everything that was not wilderness and barbarism. No matter what reverses they suffered, they believed that the Empire was one and indivisible. The new peoples in East and West were mere "barbarian intruders" who might be subjugated sooner or later but never recognized as equals. Their rulers were styled as *rex, hegemon, despot, satrap,* never as *basileus,* a term reserved for the emperor exclusively.

On the other hand, the neighboring peoples in their apogee made a claim to the Roman imperial heritage. For example, the Bulgarian king Symeon (893-927) proclaimed himself "Emperor of the Romans" and fought hard for the possession of Constantinople. The attempt was repeated, with disastrous effects on Bulgaria, by Samuel (977-1014), who yielded before the might of Basil the Slayer-of-the-Bulgarians. The revived Bulgarian kingdom likewise had imperial ambitions, which were realized when Pope Innocent III proclaimed Joanitsis emperor (1204). The Serbs, for a long time after their emancipation, were content with lesser imperial titles, but in 1346 the conquering Stephen Dushan assumed the title of "Emperor and Autocrator of the Serbs and the Romans." All the newly Christianized peoples, without exception, coveted Byzantine court titles for their rulers and considered themselves fortunate if they got them. The emperor would grant them judiciously, for it was known that they had an appeasing effect on aggressive neighbors.

Even those Asiatics who considered the Christians as infidels came under the spell of imperial traditionalism. The Arabs, whether Omayyads reigning at Damascus (661-750) or Abbasids at Baghdad (750-*ca.* 1100), adopted many Byzantine traditions and institutions. Byzantine influence was inevitable in all expressions of life, since the manpower that developed Arabic culture was largely drawn from the former subjects of the Eastern Roman Empire who had turned Moslem. The same is true of the Seljuks (1071-1243). From ancient Iconium, henceforth called Konya, they governed the eastern half of Asia Minor as Turks and Moslems, but they had come so effectively under Byzantine influence that they called themselves *Rūm* (Roman) Seljuks. The Ottoman Turks, who succeeded in placing the crescent of Islam on the domes of Constantinople, came more directly under the Eastern Roman traditionalism.

After the fall of Constantinople, the Russians, unwilling to recognize the Turks as heirs to the Empire, regarded themselves as the unique successor state. Moscow was spoken of as the Third Rome, and the double-headed eagle of Byzantium found its place on the banners of the Romanovs. The idea of a restored Byzantine Empire, under Russian influence, was never forgotten by the czars. The "Greek project" of Catherine II is perhaps the most spectacular but by no means the only expression of this idea. Nor was it for the first time during World War I that Russia planned to take possession of Constantinople, which was called Tsargrad. The Greeks, too, cherished a similar dream. For ages it was kindled by legends touching the chords of religious mysticism and in the nineteenth century it developed into the "Great Idea." The rest of the Balkan nations would not remain strangers to such a dream.

BYZANTINE AND POST-BYZANTINE HISTORIANS

The fact that the imperial tradition remained uninterrupted in the East from the fall of the old Roman Empire to the beginning of modern times was undoubtedly the most significant influence in Byzantine and post-Byzantine historiography. One of its main results was the continuity of historical writing. Another was the tendency to draw upon tradition and to imitate prototypes to an extent which was unknown in the West.

The Greek language possesses great flexibility and, because of long usage by great masters, lends itself peculiarly as a medium of historiography. For most of the Eastern historians, writing in Greek was an aesthetic accomplishment. Fascinated by the beauty of the language and cognizant of their responsibility as contributors of a venerable tradition, these writers offer nothing new by way of technique or philosophy. Instead, they seek to preserve true records of important areas of human experience that would otherwise have been lost to posterity. Herein lie their value and importance.

THE BEGINNINGS OF THE EASTERN ROMAN EMPIRE

Eastern Roman historiography—like Eastern Roman history—begins, perhaps a little arbitrarily, with the year 395 A.D., when the Empire was divided between the two sons of Theodosius I. The century that began a few years after the division is the era of great church historians who continued the tradition of Eusebius (ca. 265-ca. 340). Socrates, a lawyer of Byzantium (d. after 450), wrote a documented account of the years 305-439;[1] his contemporary Sozomenus, a lawyer from Palestine (d. 447), described the events from 324 to 439[2] and wrote a chronicle from the birth of Christ to the death of Licinius (325), which is lost; and Theodoretus, Bishop of Cyrrhus in Syria (ca. 395-457), covered the period 323-428, substantiating his account with documents and reports of eye-witnesses.[3] The three histories, which are parallel most of the way, were condensed into the Latin Historia Tripartita of Cassiodorus, who relied upon his friend Epiphanius for the translations. The Historia Tripartita, extended to 518, became a basic handbook of history in the West during the medieval period. It is no longer extant.

Comparatively few historical works written in the fifth century have come down to our time. From later sources and from a number of fragments that have survived we learn that Eunapius of Sardis (d. ca. 414) continued the Chronicle of Dexippus from 270 to 404; Zosimus, a pagan historian, building on these two, carried the narrative to 410; Olympiodorus, another pagan, drawing information from Zosimus and others, wrote an account of the period

---

[1] Edited by R. Hussey; Migne, PG, LXVII, cols. 33-841. Translated into English with an excellent introduction by A. C. Zenos, A Select Library of the Nicene and Post-Nicene Fathers of the Christian Church—2nd series, II, 1-178. For Socrates, see the article in Catholic Encyclopedia, XIV, 118-119.
[2] Edited by R. Hussey; Migne, PG, LXVII, cols. 844-1630. Translated by C. D. Hartranft, Nicene and Post-Nicene Fathers, 2nd series, II, 179-427. The article in Catholic Encyclopedia, XIV, 165-166, is very good.
[3] Edited by T. Gaisford. PG, LXXXII, cols. 879-1280. Translated by Blomfield Jackson, Nicene and Post-Nicene Fathers, 2nd series, III, 1-348. See article in Catholic Encyclopedia, XIV, 574-575.

407-425; Priscus, the ambassador to Attila, dealt with the years 433-474; Malchus of Philadelphia-in-Syria continued the history of Prisus to 480, paying attention to Italy as well as to the East; Eustathius of Epiphania published a world chronicle to 502; and, finally, Hesychius of Miletus wrote another world chronicle which closes with the year 518.

THE ERA OF JUSTINIAN

Hesychius takes us to the first year of the reign of Justin I (518-527), uncle and predecessor of Justinian (527-565), with whom he was associated from the very beginning. The era of Justinian—and, in general, the sixth century—is rich in historical works of importance. Besides the well known Procopius, we have Agathias, Menander, Evagrius, together with others whose works have been lost, save a few fragmentary excerpts.[4]

The greatest representative of the period is undoubtedly Procopius. He was born in Caesarea of Palestine toward the close of the fifth century, and by the year 527 had become legal counselor and secretary to General Belisarius, whose star was beginning to rise. In that capacity Procopius took part in the expeditions in North Africa, Italy, and Persia. Thus he could easily follow the struggles of Justinian to reclaim the lost provinces and to rebuild the Empire on a Christian basis. Procopius relied upon personal memories and notes, in the same way as Thucydides in the fifth century B.C.

A comparison of the *History* of Thucydides with the *Histories* of Procopius shows that the Byzantine historian had something of the penetrating insight and philosophical approach as well as the descriptive power of his Athenian predecessor. However, he lacked the cold impartiality of the latter, particularly with regard to political personalities—a fact which we can easily understand if we remember that his career was closely related to Belisarius and Justinian. As far as the Christian religion is concerned, he could afford to be much more detached. He does not give the impression that he shares the militant Christianity of his time, though there can be no doubt that he was a Christian.

The works of Procopius consist of the *Histories,* the book *On the Buildings (De Aedificiis),* and the *Anecdota.*[5]

The *Histories,* divided into eight books, deal with the wars fought in the reign of Justinian. The first two books describe the war against the Persians, the next two are on the Vandals in Africa, the following three are about the

---

[4] John Lydus wrote the history of Justinian's Persian wars; Peter the Patrician, who served as ambassador to Queen Amalasuntha and to the King of Persia, was the author of a book of *Histories;* the period after Justinian was described by Theophanes of Byzantium, who dealt with the years 566-581 and whose excerpts on the introduction of silk and on the Turks were preserved by Photius; John of Epiphania wrote about the Persian wars of 572-593; and John of Ephesus wrote in Syriac a chronicle from Julius Caesar to Maurice (584). Most of the fragmentary historical works are accessible in L. Dindorf, *Historici graeci minores,* 2 vols., and C. Müller, *Fragmenta historicorum graecorum,* 5 vols.

[5] The first complete edition of the works of Procopius was by Maltretus, in 2 vols.; reprinted (Venice, 1729); revised by K. W. Dindorf, 3 vols.; new edition by J. Haury, *Procopii Caesariensis opera omnia,* 3 vols. Haury's text was reproduced with a few changes and with an English translation by H. B. Dewing, in 7 vols. For literature on Procopius see K. Krumbacher, *Geschichte der byzantinischen Litteratur* (2nd ed., Munich, 1897), II, pp. 938-940. Some recent studies on Procopius: J. Haury, *Prokop und Kaiser Justinian,*" *Byzantinische Zeitschrift,* XXXVII (1937), pp. 1-9; G. Downey, "The Composition of Procopius' De Aedificiis," *Transactions of the American Philological Association,* LXXVIII (1947), pp. 171-183; A. Freixas, "Temas de Procopio de Cesarea," *Anales de Historia Antigua e Medieval,* pp. 36-66.

Goths of Italy, and the last is a general résumé of events to the year 554. While following the course of military operations, the historian takes us on excursions to the background of the various peoples, so that the *Histories* are by no means a dull narrative of war. Nor does he ignore the internal affairs of the Empire. We read interesting pages on such events as the Nika riot (532) and the great plague (540), which is described in perfect Thucydidean style. The greatest part of the work was probably written before 545 and the first seven books were published together in 550 or 551. The last book was published later.

The work *On the Buildings,* divided into six books, is characterized by unreserved admiration for Justinian's personality and achievement. Abandoning the calm tone of the previous narrative, Procopius, in a style that befits a panegyric, describes the ambitious building projects of the emperor: in Constantinople (Book I) ; in Mesopotamia and Syria (Book II) ; in Armenia and the Pontus (Book III) ; in the European provinces (Book IV) ; in Asia Minor and Palestine (Book V) ; and in Egypt and the rest of Byzantine Africa (Book VI).

After reading these laudatory descriptions, one wonders what made Procopius write his *Anecdota*—i.e. his unpublished ("unpublishable" might be a better word) history of Justinian, Theodora, and their friends. Written shortly after the publication of the *Histories* and circulated after the emperor's death, this *Secret History* (as it is usually called in English) comprises seven books of scandal and crime that must have been a shock to Byzantine society. The doubtful past of Theodora, the empress, is exposed with all the lascivious relish of a scandal-seeker; Belisarius, the great leader of men on the battlefield, is held to ridicule as a mere plaything in the hands of an unfaithful, licentious wife; Justinian is described as a ruthless, unscrupulous tyrant; and, in general, every dark recess is explored in order to belittle the heroes of the *Histories.* "It was not possible," says Procopius, "as long as the agents of these deeds were still alive, to record the facts in the proper way; for no one could avoid the multitudes of spies, nor could anyone escape the worst kind of death, if detected. I could not trust even my closest relatives. Then, too, with regard to many facts described in previous books, I was obliged to conceal the real motives that prompted them. Therefore, it will be necessary for me to disclose the facts that have been kept secret and also to reveal the causes of events that have already been mentioned." In the light of the above statement, Procopius felt a need to present the other side of the picture, and at the same time he wanted a plausible excuse to ease his conscience; for his master Thucydides would hardly have written libel or obscenity.

Agathias, a younger contemporary of Procopius, born at Myrrhina in western Asia Minor, was a poet, an orator, and a lawyer. His work, entitled *On the Reign of Justinian,* was written after the death of the emperor.[6] It covers the years 532-558. For unknown reasons, it was not completed. The historian, an unusually broadminded man for his time, wanted to become thoroughly

---

[6] Edited by B. G. Niebuhr; reprinted in *PG,* LXXX, cols. 1248-1608. For literature see Krumbacher, *op. cit.,* pp. 242-243.

familiar with the Persian wars and he worked hard with Persian sources. But he did not have the wide range of military and political information that made the work of Procopius so valuable.

The history of Agathias was continued by Menander, usually surnamed Protector because he belonged to the imperial bodyguard. Like Agathias, Menander was a man with legal training. In a style which is imitative of his colleague's poetic prose, he described the events of the years 558-582. Unfortunately, only fragments of his book have survived.[7]

Menander's work was used by Evagrius of Epiphania (ca. 536-ca. 594), who compiled an *Ecclesiastical History* in six books.[8] It covers the period between 431 and 593. It includes large areas of political history, too, and in connection with the era of Justinian the author relies upon the *Histories* of Procopius.

THE STRUGGLE WITH THE PERSIANS AND THE ARABS

For the last quarter of the sixth century and for the beginning of the seventh century we have the work of Theophylactus Simocattes, a widely read gentleman from Egypt who became imperial secretary and prefect under Emperor Heraclius (610-641). Theophylactus wrote a *History* in eight books which deals with the reigns of Tiberius (578-582) and Maurice (582-602).[9] The writer's erudite work is a mixture of historical facts, naive legends, and amusing superstitions, which, coupled with the peculiarities of his language, make his account interesting as a piece of medieval popular historiography. Medieval readers were very fond of his daring similes, subtleties, and euphuistic verbosity.

Even more interesting as a literary curiosity is the *Chronicle* of John Malalas.[10] It is written in a language which could easily be understood by the masses of the seventh century. It is a naive compilation of facts, trivialities, and monstrosities, derived from the Bible, ancient and contemporary historians, and from his own memory—all put together in a careless, uncritical manner, so that the author's childish imagination is allowed full play. The *Chronicle* of Malalas was translated in the tenth century into Old Slavic and Georgian and it attracted much attention in later times.

The writings of Theophylactus Simocattes and John Malalas are exceptional cases among Byzantine chronicles, for the quality of Byzantine chronicles is usually much higher.[11] The *Paschal Chronicle*,[12] for example, is a reliable source for the wars with the Persians in the seventh century and for the siege

---

[7] Included in vols. I and II of *Porphyrogeniti excerpta historica*, ed. F. Boissevain, C. de Boor, Th. Büttner-Wobst. For literature see Krumbacher, *op. cit.*, pp. 243-244.
[8] Edited by J. Bidez and C. Parmentier: *PG*, CXXXVI, 2, cols. 2405-2906.
[9] Edited by I. Bekker (Bonn, 1834). Best edition by C. de Boor. On Theophylactus see N. H. Baynes, "The Literary Composition of the History of Theophylactus Simocatta," *Xenia* (75th Anniversary of the University of Athens, 1912), pp. 32-41.
[10] Edited by W. Dindorf; reprinted in *PG*, XCVII, cols. 9-790. On Malalas there is extensive bibliography; see Krumbacher, *op. cit.*, pp. 332-334; and Potthast, *op. cit.*, I, p. 670.
[11] The period before Heraclius is covered by the chronicle of John of Antioch (from Adam to 610 A.D.). Edited by C. Müller, *Fragmenta historicorum graecorum*, IV, pp. 535-622; V, pp. 27-28. For the period before Heraclius we also have the church chronicle of Nicephorus Callistus Xanthopulus, who wrote it in the beginning of the fourteenth century. *PG*, CXLV, cols. 549-1331; CXLVI, cols. 1-632.
[12] Edited by Du Cange; revised by L. Dindorf, in 2 vols.; vol. II contains the preface and commentary of Du Cange.

of Constantinople by the Avars (626). For the siege of Constantinople and for the Persian wars of Heraclius we also have the poems of George Pisides,[13] who was in the City when the Avars threatened it. The last years of Heraclius, which coincide with the rise of Islam, are depicted in a universal chronicle written by John of Nikiou, a Coptic bishop in Egypt, who lived in the second half of the seventh century. The original Greek text of Bishop John has been lost, but we have a translation in Ethiopian,[14] which, in turn, is a translation from Arabic.

The period from the death of Heraclius (641) to the death of Constantine V (775) is poor in contemporary sources, partly because the iconophile monks destroyed all unfriendly writings that fell into their hands. At the turn of the century, however, we have the *Chronicle* of Theophanes the Confessor *(ca.* 758-*ca.* 817), which covers the long, barren period in the best possible way and comes down to the year 813. It was begun at the request of George Synkellus (d. 810), who wrote a chronicle from the Creation to the accession of Diocletian (284), and wanted somebody to continue the work which his death would leave unfinished. Quite loyally, Theophanes continued from the point at which his friend left off.[15]

Theophanes, an officer and a member of the aristocracy, though married, lived the life of a monk. As a staunch opponent of iconoclasm, he suffered persecutions and exile. After a two-year imprisonment in Constantinople he was sent to the island of Samothrace, where he died. For the events of his own time he carried on independent investigation and consulted sources which have not survived his *Chronicle.*

A contemporary of Theophanes was Nicephorus, Patriarch of Constantinople from 806 to 815. Like Theophanes, he was an iconophile. Emperor Leo the Armenian, the enemy of icon-worshippers, deposed the recalcitrant ecclesiastic, who turned to historiography and wrote a *Concise History (Historia Syntomos)* of the years 602-769.[16] In accuracy and judgment Nicephorus is much inferior to Theophanes. The close similarity between their works, which at times becomes verbatim repetition, suggests that the patriarch and the monk used a common source, which has remained unknown.[17]

The *Chronicle* of Theophanes was carried on to the year 961 by a group of anonymous authors, usually referred to as the "Continuators of Theophanes."[18]

---

[13] The poems of Pisides were published by Bekker in the same volume with the history of Patriarch Nicephorus.

[14] Edited with a French translation by H. Zotenberg, in *Notices et extraits des manuscrits de la Bibliothèque Nationale,* XXIV, part I (1883), pp. 125-608. For literature see Krumbacher, *op. cit.,* p. 404.

[15] The *Chronicle* of George Synkellus was edited in 2 vols., by W. Dindorf on the basis of the Paris edition of 1652 (Bonn, 1829). There is a new edition by H. Gelzer and W. Reichardt. The *Chronicle* of Theophanes was edited by J. Classen; and by C. de Boor, in 2 vols. The latter edition is an excellent piece of work. For important bibliography, see Krumbacher, *op. cit.,* pp. 346-347. In addition, E. W. Brooks, "The Chronology of Theophanes," *Byzantinische Zeitschrift,* VIII (1899), pp. 82-97. V. Grumel, "L'année du monde dans la chronographie de Theophane," *Echos d'Orient,* XXXVII (1934), pp. 396-408.

[16] Edited by Bekker. The same volume contains the works of Paul Silentiarius and George Pisides. Bekker's revision is reprinted in *PG,* C, cols. 876-994. A reliable edition is that of C. de Boor. For bibliography see Krumbacher, *op. cit.,* pp. 351-352.

[17] The chronicles of George Synkellus, Theophanes, and Nicephorus were translated into Latin and were united in a *Chronographia tripartita* by Anastasius the Librarian, in the days of Pope Hadrian (867-872). It has been included in the Bonn edition of Theophanes (vol. II, ed. Bekker, 1841) and in the edition by C. de Boor (vol. II, pp. 33-346).

[18] Under the title *Theophanes Continuatus* it was edited by Bekker (Bonn, 1838). For bibliography see Krumbacher, *op. cit.,* p. 349.

The new work is divided into six books. The sixth book has been attributed to Theodore Daphnopates. Since there is a tendency to present the Phrygian emperors (Michael II, Theophilus, and Michael III) in shady colors and to extol the Macedonian dynasty, it is safe to assume that the continuation of Theophanes belongs to the Macedonian era.

The story of the Phrygian dynasty and of the rise of the Macedonian is also recorded in the *Four Books of History* by Joseph Genesius.[19] They deal with the period from Leo the Armenian (813) to the death of Basil I (886). Genesius, who wrote between 945 and 959, included in his narrative a number of legends and miracles, but he also consulted written sources, some of which do not exist today.

The monastic historical tradition is best represented by George Monachus or Hamartolus (the Monk or the Sinner) who wrote a *Chronicle* in four books,[20] from the Creation to the death of Theophilus (842). Later hands continued this chronicle to 948, to 1071, to 1081, and to 1143—the year of conclusion depending upon the manuscript we may have in mind. Because of numerous interpolations by later hands this chronicle tires and confuses the reader.

The Macedonian Dynasty

The Macedonian era (867-1056) is identified with a revival of art and literature and with epic struggles in East and in West conducted under Basil I, Nicephorus Phocas, John Tsimiskes, and Basil II the Slayer-of-the-Bulgarians. It was a long and glorious era for the Empire. Even after the male Macedonian line had died out, the memory of their heroism made the people feel respect for the worthless old women, Zoë and Theodora, the lawful heirs to the throne.

The dominant intellectual figure at the opening of this great epoch is Photius, patriarch of Constantinople (858-867 and 877-886) at a time when the rivalry between the Eastern and the Western Churches grew into open conflict. The main importance of Photius in historiography, as well as in the history of literature, lies in the fact that he and his assistants prepared critical comments and summaries of about 280 books, as a part of a projected work of general reference called *Myriobiblos (Ten Thousand Books)*.[21] It is our only source of information about many important works that can no longer be found.

The revival of learning, of which Photius is the best representative, extended to the imperial palace, which had never ceased to be a center of culture. Even the emperors of this period devoted themselves to literary pursuits. Leo VI wrote the *Book of the Prefect (Eparchiacon Biblion)*,[22] which, though not historical in scope, is a source of information for the historian. His son, Constantine VII Porphyrogennetus, published four works, one of which may be styled as pure history and the other three as works of historical interest.

The purely historical work of Constantine Porphyrogennetus is a biography of

[19] Published in the Bonn series (1834). For editions and bibliography see Krumbacher, *op. cit.*, p. 265.
[20] Published together with *Theophanes Continuatus*. The Migne, *PG*, CX, is a reprint of E. Muralt's unsatisfactory edition. The best edition is that of C. de Boor, in 2 vols. The Greek text and an Old Slavic version have been published by V. M. Istrin, *The Chronicle of George Hamartolus in Its Old Slavo-Russian Version*, in 3 vols. (introd. in Russian).
[21] In connection with the *Myriobiblos*, see Krumbacher, *op. cit.*, pp. 518-519.
[22] Edited by J. Nicole; translated into French by same.

Basil I, the founder of the Macedonian dynasty.[23] The crowned historian had a natural bias for his grandfather and tended to present in a favorable light even the dark deeds which placed him on the throne in 867.

Constantine VII's other works are:[24] *To His Son Romanus* or *On the Administration of the Empire (De administrando imperio)*, a political geography of the peoples surrounding the Empire and instructions as to how to deal with them; *About Themes (De thematibus)*, another book of geography, which is our main source for the domestic affairs of the Empire and for its administrative machinery; and *About Imperial Etiquette (De ceremoniis)*, a detailed and somewhat tedious description of court life.

Besides Porphyrogennetus, in the tenth century we have John Cameniates, a priest of Thessalonica, who wrote a vivid description of the siege of that city by the Arabs (904) ; [25] Symeon Magister or Logothetes,[26] the writer of a *Chronicle* from the Creation to the death of Romanus Lecapenus (948), which exists in an Old Slavic version; Leo the Grammarian, another chronicler who covered the same period; [27] and Leo Diaconus (the Deacon), whose *Ten Books of History* [28] deal with the years 959-975. Leo Diaconus is the most important historian of the period. His work is a sober, documented, contemporary account of the eventful reigns of Nicephorus Phocas and John Tsimiskes. Leo Diaconus is an eyewitness of many of the events he describes and is fairly impartial.

The same thing cannot be said of Constantine-Michael Psellus, the continuator of Leo Diaconus. Psellus *(ca.* 1018-*ca.* 1090) is one of the most interesting characters in Byzantine society. A man of encyclopedic education and versatility, he lived at a time when learning was again respected, and he served as imperial secretary, minister, and chancellor of the university. At a time of trouble and corruption he held high posts under four emperors. So he must have been an unusually adaptable man, a man well-versed in the ways of the world. For a while he retired to a monastery on Mt. Olympus in Bithynia, where he continued writing, but he was too worldly to ignore the alluring life of the capital for long and soon returned to society.

A man of such character was suited to the role of a court poet or chronicler, but not to the unselfish mission of a historian. His *Chronicle*,[29] extending from

[23] Edited by Bekker in the volume of *Theophanes Continuatus*, pp. 211-353.
[24] Edited by Bekker, in 3 vols. For bibliography and for older editions, see Krumbacher, *op. cit.*, pp. 255-257. New editions of *De administrando imperio* by Gy. Moravcsik, with an English translation by R. J. Jenkins; *De thematibus* by A. Pertusi, in *Studi e Testi*, 160 (1952) ; and *De ceremoniis*, with a French translation in 2 vols. by A. Vogt. Cf. for translation of difficult terms and corrections in *De ceremoniis*, R. Guilland, "Sur quelques terms du Livre des Cérémonies de Constantin Porphyrogénète," *Revue des Etudes Grecques*, LVIII (1945), pp. 196-211; and Ph. Koukoulès, "Corrections and Translations . . ." *Epeteris Hetairias Byzantinon Spoudon*, XIX (1949), pp. 75-115.
[25] Edited by Bekker in *Theophanes Continuatus*, pp. 487-600.
[26] He has been identified with Symeon Metaphrastes, the biographer of saints and writer of hymns. See Krumbacher, *op. cit.*, pp. 358-361. S. Eustratiades, in his article on Symeon, written in Greek, in *Epeteris Hetairias Byzantinon Spoudon*, VIII (1931), pp. 47-65, is inclined to place him in the eleventh century. The Greek chronicle wrongly attributed to Symeon was edited by Bekker, in *Theophanes Continuatus*, pp. 603-760.
[27] Edited by Bekker.
[28] Edited by B. Hase; reprinted in *PG*, CXVII, cols. 635-926.
[29] Edited by K. N. Sathas, in *Bibliotheca graeca medii aevi*, IV (1874). New edition and French translation by E. Renault, Michel Psellos: *Chronographie, ou Histoire d'un siècle de Byzance*, 2 vols. For bibliography see Krumbacher, *op cit.*, p. 443; Potthast, *op. cit.*, II, pp. 943-4. Recent studies of Psellus are the following: G. Redl, "La chronologie appliquée de Michel Psellos," *Byzantion*, IV (1929), pp. 197-236. J. B. Bury, *Selected Essays* (ed. H. Temperley), pp. 126-214. J. Sykoutris, "Zum Geschichtswerk des Psellos," *Byzantinische Zeitschrift*, XXX (1930), pp. 61-71; J. Hussey, "Michael Psellos—The Byzantine Historian," *Speculum*, X (1935), pp. 81-90.

976 to 1077, includes the struggle between the Greeks and the Bulgarians for the control of the Balkan peninsula and, in its last chapters, the appearance of the Turks in Asia Minor. Psellus did not seek to penetrate very deeply into the past, nor did he feel any anxiety for the future. He gave vivid, witty characterizations of men and women, adding a word of flattery in the right direction and was always inclined to exaggerate trifles of private interest. An event with far-reaching consequences, such as the battle of Mandjikert (1071), did not engage his attention more than the rheumatism of Constantine Monomachus.

TURKISH INVASIONS AND THE CRUSADES

The appearance and the expansion of the Turks are more fully presented in the works of Michael Attaliates, Nicephorus Bryennius, Anna Comnena, and John Cinnamus. Furthermore, Anna Comnena is our main Greek source about the First Crusade and John Cinnamus about the Second. In the meantime, the once glorious Macedonian dynasty had been succeeded by a series of six emperors (Michael VI, Isaac Comnenus, Constantine X, Romanus IV, Michael VII, and Nicephorus Botaniates), whose brief reigns form an era of transition between the Macedonians and the Comneni. The latter rose to the throne with Alexius I in 1081, and begin another period of Byzantine achievement.

Attaliates. Michael Attaliates, as his surname indicates, hailed from Attalia; and his family background explains his interest in Asia Minor. In the capacity of military judge, he accompanied Romanus IV (1067-1071) on his expedition against the Turks. His observations, therefore, are valuable as those of a competent eye-witness, particularly as to the decisive battle of Mandjikert. At the same time, he was acquainted with the complicated back-stage politics, the intrigues in the palace, the doubtful role of women and eunuchs and the rivalries of army officers.

In the *History,*[30] completed shortly before 1080, while Botaniates was still on the throne, he deals with the years 1034-1079. Though he expressed his intention to continue, he did not do so, either because of death or because of the fall of his patron, Botaniates, to whom the work was dedicated.[31]

Bryennius. Attaliates' work was completed and carried on by Nicephorus Bryennius, the son-in-law of Alexius I. Bryennius, a distinguished general, was born in 1062 at Adrianople of a noble military family and died in or shortly after 1137. As he had a prominent part in political and military affairs and close relations with the imperial family, he was able to write a well-informed

---

[30] Edited by W. Brunet de Presle and published by Bekker in the Bonn Corpus (1853). For bibliography see Krumbacher, *op. cit.,* p. 271.
[31] Attaliates' work was incorporated in the *Chronicle* of John Skylitzes (d. ca. 1081), which surveys the years 811-1079. This chronicle was edited by Bekker in vol. II of Cedrenus, pp. 641-744; reprinted in *PG,* CXXII, cols 368-476. The *Chronicle* of Skylitzes in a somewhat modified form, became a part of the *Synopsis of History* compiled by George Cedrenus, at the end of the eleventh or at the beginning of the twelfth century. It starts from the Creation and it reaches the year 1057. The work of Cedrenus was edited by A. Fabrotus, in 2 vols.; Bekker in the Bonn series, in 2 vols., revised the Paris edition and reprinted Fabrotus' commentary. For bibliography on Skylitzes and Cedrenus, see Krumbacher, *op. cit.,* pp. 365-369. In addition, note K. Schweinburg, "Die ursprüngliche Form der Kedrenchronik," *Byzantinische Zeitschrift,* XXX (1930), pp. 68-77. For a discussion of the date of the Russian campaign of Tsimiskes see D. Anastassevic, in *Byzantion,* VI (1931), pp. 337-342, and in *Byzantinische Zeitschrift,* XXXI (1931), pp. 328-333. The period up to 1081 is covered by the chronicle of Constantine Manasses, a twelfth century writer. His work is in verse. Edited by Bekker, in the same volume with Joel and Acropolites. *PG,* CXXVII, cols. 216-472.

account of the rise of the Comnenian dynasty. He began with a brief sketch of the career of the father of Alexius I and he went on to describe the reign of Michael VII, the revolt of Nicephorus Botaniates, and the first year of his reign (1078). The central thread is the rise of Alexius Comnenus during those critical years. Since it was for the most part contemporary history, he had to rely upon his memory and upon information from older men. For the generation that preceded him, he used Psellus, Attaliates, and Skylitzes. His style—terse, clear, and military—reminds us of Xenophon. But a certain carelessness in the arrangement of the material and the title *Material for History* lead one to think that it was meant as the basis for another work, or at least that it was not in its final form.[32]

Anna Comnena. The work of Bryennius was taken up by his wife, Anna Comnena *(ca.* 1083-1148), perhaps the best educated woman of the Middle Ages. Under the epic title *Alexiad,* she wrote the story of her father and his times, in the language of Thucydides and Polybius.[33] Her life was one of devotion to two men—her husband and her father—and her book begins with the death of the former (1137) and closes with the death of the latter (1118?). In the introduction she says that her husband stopped writing history when he reached the year 1078 because he did not have time to spare from his military duties; then he died leaving his book unfinished. "So," says Anna, "I decided to write what my father did, in order that such deeds may not pass unnoticed by posterity."

She took up the narrative from the time when Alexius was fourteen years old, on the eve of the battle of Mandjikert. As an historian, she was fully aware of the importance of the three main political realities of her time—i.e. the establishment of the Normans in Southern Italy, the Turkish advance, and the First Crusade—and she tried to describe and interpret them as best she could. She consulted her notes and her friends, she wrote from personal memory, and she used a Latin chronicle on Robert Guiscard, which is now lost. Undoubtedly she was impressed by the magnitude of the Crusade and sensed its far-reaching effects, but shared the attitude of her countrymen, which was one of skepticism and mistrust of the movement. To her the Crusaders were little more than barbarian intruders, much like the Asiatic Turks. The year 1204 came to justify her attitude.

Zonaras. The work of Anna Comnena is not our only source about the reign of Alexius I. We have the *Abridged History (Epitomè Historion)* of John

---

[32] The Paris edition by P. Possinus (1661) was reprinted by A. Meineke. For a general study of Bryennius, see J. Seger, *Nikephoros Bryenniis.* Further bibliography in Krumbacher, *op. cit.,* pp. 273-274.

[33] In the Bonn Corpus the *Alexiad* is edited by L. Schopen (vol. I, 1839) and by A. Reifferscheid (vol. II, 1878). Reifferscheid edited the entire work in 2 vols. (Teubner: Leipzig, 1884). There is an excellent edition, with a French translation, by B. Leib, in 3 vols. English translation by E. A. S. Dawes, *The Alexiad.* The best detailed work is by Georgina Buckler, *Anna Comnena.* There is an extensive bibliography in Krumbacher, *op. cit.,* pp. 277-279, to which the following must be added: Sophia Antoniades, "Description in the Alexiad," *Hellenica,* V (1932), pp. 255-276 (in Greek); Ch. Diehl, "Anne Comnène," in *Figures byzantines,* II, pp. 26-52; W. Miller, "A Byzantine Bluestocking—Anna Comnena," in *Essays on the Latin Orient,* pp. 533-550: J. McCabe, *The Empresses of Constantinople,* pp. 197-217; Naomi Mitchison, *Anna Comnena;* E. Oster, *Anna Komnena,* in 2 vols.; L. du Sommerard, *Deux princesses d'Orient au XIIe siècle—Anna Comnène témoin des Croisades: Agnes de France,* pp. 1-199.

Zonaras [34]—a chronicle in 18 books, from the Creation to the death of Alexius (1118). Writing in the reign of Manuel Comnenus (1143-1180), Zonaras was able to gather reliable information from older contemporaries and from state documents, while for the earlier times he depended upon the Bible, Herodotus, Xenophon, Josephus, Arrian, Plutarch, Dio Casius, Eusebius, and most of the Byzantine authors, especially Psellus. Zonaras was a man of the world—he had served as commander of the imperial guard and director of the imperial chancery—but his chronicle belongs to the last years of his life, which were spent in a monastery on one of the Princes Islands.

Cinnamus. The work of Zonaras and the Anna Comnena found a continuator in John Cinnamus *(ca.* 1143-*ca.* 1190), who wrote a *History* in seven books dealing with the years 1118-1176. A man of devotion and loyalty, Cinnamus served as secretary to Emperor Manuel Comnenus and accompanied him on his expeditions. The *History,* preserved in a single manuscript, remained practically unknown among the Byzantines.[35] In the clear, readable style of Xenophon, it tells of the reign of John Comnenus in the first book, and it goes on to give, in the other six books, a detailed account of the eventful era of Manuel.

Acominatus. The story of the Fourth Crusade and of the fall of Constantinople in 1204 is vividly narrated by Nicetas Acominatus. Nicetas and his brother Michael, bishop of Athens, were born at Chonae in Phrygia in the middle of the twelfth century. At an early age, Nicetas came to the capital, where he distinguished himself in a number of high offices. When the Fourth Crusade was starting out, he happened to be governor of Philippopolis. He was also an eye-witness of the conquest of Constantinople by the Crusaders.

His *History* [36] is divided into twenty-one books and covers the period from 1180 to 1206. After an introduction in which he sums up the reigns of John and Manuel Comnenus, he proceeds to depict the domestic struggles, the adventurous career of Andronicus Comnenus, the accession of Isaac Angelus, the reign of Alexius III, the events of 1203-1204, with the capture of Constantinople forming the climax, and the establishment of the Latin Empire under Baldwin I and his brother Henry. The narrative ends with the second year of Henry (1206). It was written at Nicaea, where the historian had found refuge under the Lascarids. He died shortly after writing his book.

THE LASCARIDS AND THE PALEOLOGI

Acropolites. The Empire of Nicaea, the most important of Byzantium's successor states, was fortunate to find a historian in the person of George Acropolites (1217-1282). Born of noble parents in Constantinople, at the age of 16 he fled Latin oppression and sought a future in the new Greek capital. There he

[34] Ed. Pinder, in 2 vols.; *PG,* CXXXIV, CXXXV, cols. 1-438. Revised edition by L. Dindorf, in 6 vols.; Book XII-XIII edited by Th. Büttner-Wobst. For bibliography see Krumbacher, *op. cit.,* pp. 374-376.
   A parallel chronicle was written by Michael Glycas, a contemporary of Zonaras. Edited by Bekker; *PG,* CLVIII, cols. 1-624. It is one of Bekker's worst editions. The Paris edition by Phil. Labbaeus (1660) is better; reprinted.
[35] Edited by Du Cange, with valuable commentary, in the Paris Corpus; reprinted 1729. Revised edition after a collation with the Codex Vaticanus, by A. Meineke; reprinted in *PG,* CXXXIII, cols. 299-678. For bibliography see Krumbacher, *op. cit.,* p. 281.
[36] Edited by Bekker; *PG,* CXXXIX, cols. 287-1088. About Nicetas Acominatos see C. Neumann, *Griechische Geschichtsschreiber und Geschichtsquellen im 12. Jahrhundert* (Leipzig, 1888), pp. 103ff; Th. Uspenski, *The Byzantine Author Nicetas Acominatos Choniates* (in Russian).

was educated under Theodore Hexapterigus and Nicephorus Blemmydes, and he came to play a leading part at the palace as teacher to Theodore II Lascaris and as a great logothete. Neither high office, however, nor academic dignity saved him from a public spanking in the presence of the emperor when the latter got angry over an argument concerning a proposed treaty with the Bulgarians. Not long after this amusing incident, for which Acropolites is our only source, the emperor made the humiliated scholar commander-in-chief in the war against Michael Angelus of Epirus; Acropolites was defeated and captured; he remained a prisoner for two years, until he was liberated after the victories of Michael Paleologus, who in the meantime had proclaimed himself emperor after a bloody *coup d'état.*

Thus began the era of the Paleologi, who reigned until 1453. Acropolites continued his leading part under the new regime. In 1261 he composed the prayers that were recited from the Golden Gate during the celebrations of the liberation of the city. Later, in 1274, he was a delegate at the Council of Lyons, where he signed the act of union of the churches.

The *Chronicle* [37] of Acropolites has survived in two forms—a first draft and a revised version. In three of the manuscripts we have a revision and interpolations by Theodore Scutariotes, a scholarly friend of the author. The *Chronicle* covers the years 1203-1261, continuing Nicetas Acominatus.[38] It is a realistic, truthful account written in a clear, if occasionally pompous, style. Acropolites believes that the historian must write "with no motives of hatred or favor, but only for the sake of history, so that the good or bad deeds of certain men may not be committed to the bottom of Oblivion, which is the child of Time."

Pachymeres. The connecting link between the Empire of Nicaea and the restored Empire at Constantinople is the history of George Pachymeres (1242-1310). Like Acropolites, he was a student of the philosopher and theologian Nicephorus Blemmydes. At Constantinople he established his reputation as an author on law, rhetoric, and astronomy; he occupied various high offices, and he took part in the religious squabbles about the union of the churches, which was the thorny problem of his time.

His historical work consists of two books, taking their respective names from the two emperors under whom he lived—*Michael Paleologus* and *Andronicus Paleologus.*[39] They are detailed narratives of those two eventful reigns, with

[37] Edited by Bekker, with the commentary and notes of the Paris edition by Leo Allatius (1651) ; *PG,* CXL, cols. 969-1220 ; best edition by A. Heisenberg; vol. II contains the *scripta minora* of Acropolites. For bibliography see Krumbacher, *op. cit.,* pp. 287-288.

[38] Parallel accounts of the period before and after the Fourth Crusade are given by the following writers: (1) Joel, who wrote a chronicle which begins with the Creation and reaches 1204. Edited by Bekker; *PG,* CXXXIX, cols. 223-288. (2) John of Sicily, whose chronicle, half lost, reached the same year. Edited by A. Heinrich. (3) Ephraim, whose chronicle in verse was composed in the beginning of the fourteenth century and surveys the era from Julius Caesar to the Latin conquest of Constantinople. Edited by Bekker; *PG,* CXLIII, cols. 1-380. (4) The *Synopsis Sathas,* so called after the Greek scholar who discovered it, is a chronicle from the Creation to 1261. Edited by K. N. Sathas, *Bibliotheca graeca medii aevi,* VII (1894), pp. 1-556. (5) The period of the Latin conquest in the Peloponnesus is depicted in the *Chronicle of Morea,* composed in verse by an unknown poet around 1300. It deals mainly with the years 1204-1292, with a brief introduction which takes us to the First Crusade. Edited by J. Schmitt.

[39] Edited by P. Possinus, in 2 vols.; revised by Bekker, in 2 vols, who included the notes of Possinus. For bibliography see Krumbacher, *op. cit.,* pp. 390-391. Newer studies are: V. Laurent, "Les manuscripts de l'Histoire Byzantine de Georges Pachymère," *Byzantion,* V (1929-30), pp. 129-205 ; "L'Histoire Byzantine de Georges Pachymère," *Byzantion,* VI (1931), pp. 355-364; B. Mystakides, "Pachymeres, protecdicus and dicaeophylax, and M. Crusius," *Enaisima* dedicated to Archbishop Chr. Papadopoulos, pp. 214-232 (in Greek).

emphasis upon ecclesiastical affairs, which were known to the author from close observation. At the same time, Pachymeres does not lose sight of the effects of the expanding commercialism of Genoa and Venice and he also follows the rapid growth of the Ottoman Turks. Long before the Turks captured Brusa (1326), Pachymeres was the first historian to mention Atman (Othman, Osman), in connection with the battle of Bapheus—the first important victory of the Osmanlis against the Empire (1301).

Pachymeres writes in an archaic Greek style, which does not lack individuality. It is characterized by long, involved sentences and congested verbosity. He is also lengthily digressive. Furthermore, he shows his unusual erudition by frequent references to classical literature and mythology. He discovers and brings into use old, obsolete names of places, and he has his own way of referring to the months of the year with old Athenian names.[40]

As the reader struggles through the two volumes of Pachymeres, he gets the feeling that the author is trying to escape from the reality of his time into the worlds of religion and antiquity. This other-worldiness, which is perhaps the most peculiar aspect of Byzantine decadence, becomes more apparent in subsequent years, as the Turks approach the Imperial City and the forces of disintegration, which led to the fall of the Empire in 1204, appear to be at work again under strikingly analogous circumstances. Pachymeres and his contemporaries do not seem to be aware of the ominous signs of the times. They allow their interests to be absorbed by ecclesiastical squabbles, metaphysical speculation, and dogmatic hairsplitting. Their spiritual attitude makes the death of the Empire seem natural and inevitable.

Gregoras. The unrealism of the dying Byzantine world is the most noticeable trait in the writings of Nicephorus Gregoras (1295-ca. 1359), whose *Roman History* covers the years 1204-1359, and affords a sequel to the work of Pachymeres.[41] Both Gregoras and Pachymeres belonged to the circle of scholars that surrounded Emperor Andronicus II (1282-1328). When the emperor fell as a result of the war with his grandson Andronicus III, Gregoras lost his fortune, became a teacher, and got involved in the *hesychast* (quietist) controversy as an exponent of Western scholasticism against the Athonite mysticism which finally prevailed. Gregoras was excommunicated and imprisoned.

Gregoras was too active in the quarrels of his time to be impartial, too absorbed in theology to be aware of what was happening in the world. His religious philippics cover hundreds of pages, but an event like the fall of Nicaea, where the Christian creed was formulated in 325 A.D., receives no more than a sentence: [42] "At this time the barbarians took Nicaea, the great and populous city, having besieged it with famine and with troops."

Cantacuzenus. Perhaps the most biased writer in this time of religious and political fanaticism was the emperor John VI Cantacuzenus, who usurped the crown a few years after the death of Andronicus III and fought another civil

---

[40] G. Georgiades Arnakis, "The Names of the Months in the History of Georgius Pachymeres," *Byzantinisch-neugriechische Jahrbücher.* XVIII (1949).
[41] Edited by Schopen, vols. I and II, and by Bekker, vol. III; reprinted in *PG,* CXLVIII-CXLIX, cols. 1-502. For bibliography see Krumbacher, *op. cit.,* pp. 296-298. There is a valuable monograph by R. Guilland, *Essai sur Nicêphore Grégoras,* which discusses Gregoras from every aspect.
[42] Bonn edition, I, p. 458.

war in order to maintain his position. Overthrown in 1355, he became a monk and spent nearly thirty years trying to justify his political career. His story is told in the third person by a fictitious character called Christodulus, who, at the start, promises to tell it truthfully.[43] Rarely, however, has a more misleading narrative been produced in the name of truth.

With writers like Cantacuzenus and Gregoras, the fourteenth century is a barren period in Byzantine historiography. In the second half of the century we miss even these one-sided and historically poor records. They would have described the decline and the humiliation of the Empire at the time when John V, Manuel II, and John VIII went out to the West to implore assistance against the threatening Turk. Their story remained to be told by the historians who lived at the time of the fall of Constantinople.[44]

THE HISTORIANS OF THE FALL

The first of the so-called "historians of the fall" is George Phrantzes (also called Sphrantzes), secretary to Manuel II and trusted friend of Constantine XI. His life reflects all the vicissitudes of his times. Taken prisoner during the sack of the City, he was subsequently liberated and he fled to the court of Thomas, despot of Mistra. When the Peloponnesus was conquered, he went to Italy. He ended his days as a monk on the island of Corfu, where he completed his chronicle.[45]

The Phrantzes chronicle came down to our times in two forms—the shorter (Chronicon minus) and the longer (Chronicon majus). The former, now recognized as the genuine work of Phrantzes, covers the years 1413-1478, while the latter, which is believed to be a revision and an expansion of the original, goes back to 1258—that is, to the beginning of the Palaeologian era. It is divided into four books, as follows: Book I takes us to the death of Manuel II (1425); Books II and III are on the reigns of John VIII and Constantine XI respectively, culminating in the fall of Constantinople; and Book IV deals with the struggle in the Peloponnesus and the consolidation of Turkish authority in the Balkans until 1478.

For the period prior to 1350 the compiler of the longer chronicle made ample use of the Roman History of Gregoras; for the second half of the fourteenth

[43] Edited by Schopen, in 3 vols. with the notes of the Paris edition of 1645; PG, CLIII-CLIV, cols. 1-710. The main work on Cantacuzenus is still V. Parisot, Cantacuzène—Homme d'état et historien. For further bibliography see Krumbacher, op. cit., p. 300.

[44] There are two exceptions to this long period of silence in the first half of the fifteenth century: the brief narrative of John Cananus concerning the siege of Constantinople by Murad II (1422), and the work of John Anagnostes on the conquest of Thessalonica by the same ruler (1430). In the Bonn Corpus, Bekker published the work of Cananus and Anagnostes in the same volume with Phrantzes; in PG, they are in vol. CLVI, cols. 61-81, and 583-632 respectively.
In Cyprus, in the same period, we have the Chronicle of Machairas, which is mainly of local interest. It begins with Constantine the Great and it reaches the year 1432. The Cypriote writer is loyal to the memory of the Byzantine Empire and considers the house of Lusignan as foreign in ruders. The best edition is by R. M. Dawkins, in 2 vols., Leontios Makhairasā—Recietal concerning the Sweet Land of Cyprus, Entitled "Chronicle."

[45] In the Bonn Corpus, edited by Bekker (1838); reprinted in PG, CLVI, cols. 551-1080. New edition of the first two books by J. B. Papadopoulos. Krumbacher, op. cit., pp. 308-309, mentions useful bibliography, to which we must add: J. B. Papadopoulos, "John VII Palaeologus and the Chronicle of Phrantzes" (in Greek), Byzantinische Zeitschrift, XXXII (1932), pp. 257-262; id. "Phrantzès est-il réelement l'auteur de la grande chronique qui porte son nom?" Bulletin de l'Institut Archéologique Bulgare, IX (1935), pp. 177-189; id. "Corrections in the Great Chronicle of Phrantzes" (in Greek), Hellenica, VII (1934), pp. 271-273; R. J. Loenertz, "Autour du Chronicon Majus attribué à Georges Phrantzès," Miscellanea G. Mercati, III Studi e Testi, 123, 1948), pp. 273-311. Loenertz rejected the authorship of Phrantzes as regards the longer chronicle.

and the early part of the fifteenth century he borrowed from sources that do not exist today, some of them on the Ottoman Turks; and for the events of his time he relied largely upon his own memory.

Both chronicles, previously regarded as equally authentic, are written in a simple language, which is very near to the Greek spoken in the fifteenth century. Phrantzes and the compiler evince the same personality, the same general attitudes: a strong opposition to Catholicism and, at the same time, unmitigated enmity toward the Turks and loyalty to the memory of the Palaeologi. This thought pattern is somewhat unusual, since the Greeks of the fifteenth century were inclined to show preference either for the Moslem East as against the Catholic West, or for the West as a possible ally against the East, and they resented the advances that their rulers made in the direction of the pope or of the sultan.

Ducas, the second "historian of the fall," does not share the isolationism of Phrantzes. He is decidedly pro-Western. At the same time, he is familiar with the rising power of the Osmanlis. As secretary to the Genoese podesta of Phocaea he visited the court of Mehmed II and saw the preparations for the siege of Constantinople. Later, he revisited the sultan as ambassador of Gattilusio, Prince of Lesbos, in order to pay the tribute for the island. His book which bears no title, begins with the year 1341 and closes with 1462, when Lesbos was annexed by the Turks.[46]

Ducas is the supplement of Phrantzes. He mentions the events of his time with less bias than Phrantzes, but for earlier events must be used with caution. Unlike Phrantzes, Ducas is friendly to the West and he shares the opinion that the hatred of the Greeks for the Catholics was not unconnected with the sad fate of the City.

Laonicus Chalcocondyles of Athens is unique not only because he is the sole Athenian writer of the Byzantine era, but also because he is the first Greek historian to write from the standpoint of the rising Ottoman Empire, not condemning it but accepting it as the central reality of his time.[47] The history of the Turks is a new subject in Greek historiography. Chalcocondyles writes in the style of Thucydides and Herodotus to record the story of the descendants of Osman. He begins with 1298 and ends with 1463, thus tracing the growth of the Turkish nation from Osman to Mehmed the Conqueror. He is familiar with Turkish and Greek material, but he is not always able to discriminate between fact and fiction. He is misinformed about the geography of Western Europe and his chronology is not always reliable. He must, therefore, be read with extreme caution. Nevertheless, he is an important source on early Turkish history, at least as important as Ashikpashazade, the chief Turkish historian of the middle of the fifteenth century.

---

[46] Edited by Bekker; PG, CLVII, cols. 739-1166. To the important bibliography in Krumbacher, op. cit., p. 307, we must add W. Miller, "The Historians Dukas and Frandzes," Journal of Hellenic Studies, XLVI (1926), pp. 63-71.
[47] The work of Chalcocondyles was edited by Bekker; PG, CLIX. New edition by E. Darkó, in 2 vols. Bibliography in Krumbacher, op. cit., pp. 304-305, to which must be added: K. Güterbock, "Laonikos Chalkondyles," Zeitschrift für Völkerrecht und Bundesstaatsrecht, IV (1910), pp. 72-102. W. Miller, "The Last Athenian Historian—Laonikos Chalcocondyles," Journal of Hellenic Studies, XLII (1922), pp. 37-49.

The last "historian of the fall" is Critobulus of Imbros. He was a feudal lord on his native island, who saw that the safest course of action lay in accepting the Turk as his master. He was a learned man, and he set out to write the biography of Mehmed the Conqueror, in the style of Thucydides.[48] He spares himself no pains extolling the Conqueror in the most servile manner. For the last enthusiasts of Greek culture in the East it was grievous to use the language of Thucydides for such a purpose. Quite appropriately he has been called the first Phanariote, in the sense that he was the first prominent Greek to occupy a trusted position under the Turk. He was Mehmed's private secretary.

After 1453

After the fall of Constantinople the stream of Greek historiography became thin and irregular. In the last quarter of the sixteenth century we meet Manuel Malaxus of Nauplia, who composed a chronicle from the Creation to 1573. At about the same time we have the *Patriarchal History,* covering the years 1454-1578. Two generations later, Dorotheus, bishop of Monemvasi, completed his *Chronicle* (from the Creation to 1629) ; and Caesarius Dapontes, in the third quarter of the eighteenth century, wrote a *Book of Kings* in verse.[49]

The post-Byzantine era, which is a transition from medieval to modern civilization among the peoples of the Balkans—a transition that was unusually long because of the stagnant character of the Turkish domination—comes to a close at the time of the French Revolution, when the concepts of freedom and nationalism spread to the Near East. The most prominent representative of the new era is Regas of Velestino (1757-1798), the poet-martyr, who strove to promote a liberation movement among the Greeks and the other peoples of the Balkan peninsula. Regas was a romantic idealist who envisaged a federation organized as a sequel to the Byzantine Empire on the principles of liberty, equality, and fraternity. At the same time, advocates of an orthodox and more practicable type of nationalism were getting ahead in their work of enlightenment. The well-known classical scholars Eugenius Voulgaris and Adamantius Korais (Coray) among the Greeks and Father Paissy, a monk from Mt. Athos who wrote a popular nationalist history in simplified Slavic and became a pioneer among the Bulgarians, are typical leaders of the new movement.

The Moslems

The development of Arabic historiography from tribal genealogies to detailed narratives of significant events and great periods is one of the most remarkable achievements of Islamic culture—an achievement which wins admiration if we remember that Arabic as a medium of expression lacked the cultivated background of Greek and Latin. A careful comparison, however, will show that the chroniclers and historians of the Arabic-speaking peoples at the time of their grandeur, in the ninth and tenth centuries, did not lag behind those of Western Europe or of the Byzantine Empire. Compared with the writings of either group

---

[48] Edited by C. Müller, *Fragmenta historicorum graecorum,* V, pp. 40-161. Bibliography in Krumbacher, *op. cit.,* pp. 310-312, to which we must add N. P. Andriotes, "Critobulus of Imbros and His Historical Work" (in Greek), *Hellenica,* II (1928), pp. 167-200.
[49] In connection with these works, see K. N. Sathas, *Modern Greek Literature* (1453-1821) (in Greek).

as to extent and scope, Arabic historiography is by no means less impressive. As a general characteristic it evinces a poetic approach to the subject and a keen interest in the human element, which is hard to find in Europe before the Renaissance. It was probably due to the worldly appeal of Mohammedanism, which sought to unite earthly and heavenly bliss into a perfect physical-spiritual reality.[50]

FROM MOHAMMED TO THE FALL OF THE OMAYYAD DYNASTY

At a very early stage, Arabic historiography came under the influence of the Persian literary tradition, because many authors were Persian-born or Persian-trained and relied upon Old Persian sources and prototypes. The most important of these works was the *Khudai-namè (Book of Kings)*, which covers a period of three hundred years, from the accession of the Sassanid dynasty (226 A.D.) to the defeat of the Byzantines near Nisibis (526). In the middle of the eighth century it was translated from Old Persian into Arabic by Ibn al-Muqaffa and in the ninth into New Persian by Abul Mansur.[51] In the latter form it became the basis of Firdusi's poetic romance, the *Shah-namé*. Firdusi (932-1025) revised and popularized the almost forgotten history of the Old Persian Empire.

The first Arab writer whose work has been preserved is Ibn Ishaq (d. 767), the biographer of the Prophet. The *Life of the Prophet* [52] exists in a later version, after a recension by Ibn Hisham, who lived and wrote in Fustat (Old Cairo) in the first quarter of the ninth century.

At about the same time we have the *Book of Conquests (Kitab al-Maghazi)* by al-Waqidi (d. *ca.* 822), which tells of the expansion of Islam in a popular, romantic style.[53] The same story is told by al-Mada'ini, in another *Book of Conquests*. Al-Mada'ini (d. *ca.* 830) is also the author of a *History of the Khalifs Ta'rikh al-Khulafa)*.[54]

THE ABBASIDS

In the next generation we have al-Yaqubi, a great traveller, who wrote two historical works, one on the non-Moslem peoples (his account of India is particularly good)[55] and another on Islamic developments to the year 872.[56] The interesting story of the movement of Islam to the West is told by al-Baladhuri (d. 892), in his book *Futuh al-Buldan*,[57] in which he gives detailed information about each area conquered. Ibn Qutaybah (d. 889), a scholar of Persian origin, who was born and died at Baghdad, wrote several books in Arabic. His *Kitab ul-Ma'arif (Book of Knowledge)*,[58] a manual of history, deserves special mention because of its value as a contemporary record and because it has preserved

---

[50] The student may consult to his advantage the works of C. Brockelmann, H. A. R. Gibb, R. A. Nicholson, and others.
[51] See F. Gabrieli, "L'opera di Ibn al-Muqaffa," *Rivista degli Studi Orientali*, XIII (1932), pp. 197-247.
[52] Edited by F. Wüstenfeld, in 2 vols. German translation by Weil—inaccurate.
[53] About one third of his work was edited by A. von Kremer. Translation of sections into German by J. Wellhausen.
[54] See D. S. Margoliouth, *Lectures on Arabic Historians*, pp. 85-92.
[55] Edited by M. T. Houtsma, in 2 vols. Sections on Asia Minor translated by E. W. Brooks, *Journal of Hellenic Studies*, XVIII (1898).
[56] Edited by M. J. de Goeje.
[57] Under the title *Liber expugnationis regionum*, it was edited by M. J. de Goeje, in 2 vols. Translated by P. K. Hitti and F. C. Murgotten, *The Origins of the Islamic State*, 2 vols.
[58] Edited by F. Wüstenfeld.

important material from older sources, among them fragments of lost Persian histories. Equally broad in its scope, reminding us of the best universal chronicles of Christendom, is ad-Dinawari's *Book of Long Narratives*.[59] Perhaps the greatest Moslem historian of the Abbasid period is Tabari (838-923), whose full name is Abu Jafar Mohammed Ibn Jarir ut-Tabari. As his name indicates, he was born in Tabaristan, a region south of the Caspian Sea. A diligent scholar and a tireless traveller, he became familiar with Persian and Arabic history and preserved information from books that have been lost, for example, an account of the reign of Chosroes, the enemy of Justinian. Tabari's monumental work bears the title *History of the Prophets and Kings (Ta'rikh ur-Rusul wa'-Muluk)* but it is usually mentioned by Western historians as the *Annals of Tabari*.[60] It covers the story of mankind from the Creation to the year 915.

Another great historian of the first part of the tenth century is Mas'udi (d. *ca.* 956). Like Tabari, he was a traveller and his main work, entitled *Meadows of Gold (Muruj ed-Dhahab)*, is important from the point of view of geography and ethnology as well as of history.[61] It is also valuable for its fairly objective information concerning the Omayyad dynasty, which writers of the Abbasid period tended to underestimate. The policy of the Abbasids was to obliterate even the memory of their vanquished predecessors and most historians were more or less influenced by that attitude. Mas'udi was one of the few exceptions. Toward the end of his life, he produced the *Kitab ut-Tanbih wa'-Ishraf*,[62] which is a summary and a completion of his former writings.

Tabari's and Mas'udi's work was continued and completed by Miskawayh (d. 1032). His narrative is important for the expeditions of Nicephorus Phocas, whose victories over the Arabs were a prelude to the last phase of the Abbasid Khalifate. Miskawayh's history was, in turn, continued by Rudhrawai (d *ca.* 1090).[63] But the leading Moslem historian of the eleventh century was al-Biruni (d. 1048).

Mas'udi, Maskawayh, Rudhrawari, and al-Biruni lived at the time when the Abbasids were declining. Already in 945 the khalif had proclaimed Muizz al-Dawla, one of his rebel vassals, Prince of Princes. In the east, Subaktagin, the Turkish emir of Ghazna, carved off large slices of territory and sought to expand into India. His successor, Mahmud the Idol-breaker, conquered Khorasan and overran the Indian sub-continent. He was very fond of scholars and took them to his court, sometimes against their will. The well-known poet Firdusi was one of his protegées and al-Biruni, the historian mentioned above, was another. The latter wrote the *Vestiges of the Past (Athar al-*

---

[59] Edited by V. Guirgass.
[60] Edited by J. Barth, Th. Nöldeke, P. de Jong, E. Prym, H. Thorbecke, M. J. de Goeje and others, in 3 series, 13 vols. of text and 2 vols. of commentary. French translation by H. Zotenberg, 4 vols.
[61] Under the title *Prata aurea* it was edited and translated into French by C. Barbier de Meynard and Pavet de Courteille, in 9 vols.
[62] *Liber commotionis et recognitionis*, published by J. M. de Goeje. Translated into French by B. Carra de Vaux (*Le livre de l'avertissement et de la revision*). In connection with Mas'udi's see R. A. Nicholson, *A Literary History of the Arabs*, pp. 352ff.
[63] Miskawaihi, Abu Shuja Rudhrawari and Hilal ibn Muhassin—*The Eclipse of the Abbasid Caliphate*, edited and translated by H. F. Amedroz and D. S. Margoliouth, in 7 vols.

Baqiyah),[64] a universal chronicle, and a history of India, which is still indispensable to the Indologist.[65]

THE RISE OF THE SELJUK TURKS

The Crusades. Al-Biruni was the last great Oriental historian to survey a united Eastern Mohammedan world. Shortly after his death, the house of Ghazna was overthrown by the Seljuks. Half a dozen other dynasties came to control large areas and were hungry for more. In the general disorder that ensued the khalif still held his throne but practically all authority had slipped from his hands. The leading role now belonged to the Seljuk Turks, who won the battle of Mandjikert in 1071.[66] In spite of the civil war that divided them at the turn of the century, their western branch, firmly established at Konya, retained its predominant position.

The First Crusade passed through Seljuk territories and liberated Jerusalem in 1099. Three generations later, Saladin made himself master of Egypt, united the Fertile Crescent under his authority, and drove out the Crusaders (1187). It was then that Emperor Frederick Barbarossa, Richard the Lionhearted, and Philip II of France led the Third Crusade against the Moslems (1189-1192). At about this time, Temujin, better known as Genghis Khan, was getting ready to lead his Mongolian hordes to the West. His lieutenants beat the forces of the Seljuk Empire at Kösedagh, in 1243, and prepared Asia Minor for the rise of the Ottoman Turks.[67]

Moslem historiography throughout this eventful period was rich and varied. Historians devoted books to wars, heresies, peoples, countries, provinces, cities, buildings, dynasties, and personalities. Local histories became very popular. Each city could boast of its chronicle, each country had records of its past.

AFRICA AND SPAIN

Egypt, whose history in previous centuries was written by men like al-Qurashi (d. 871), al-Kindi (d 961), and Ibn Zulaq (d. 997), now found able historians in the persons of el-Musebbihi (d. 1030), el-Kudai (d. 1062), al-Maqrizi (d. 1442), al-Ayni (d. after 1471), and Ibn TaghriCirdi (d. 1468). The last-mentioned is perhaps the most important of all, as he presents a wide variety of information—political, military, economic, social, scientific—in an objective, trustworthy manner.[68]

Spain, which had known Arab rule since Tariq's memorable crossing in 711, had its own development and its own historiography. It was not, however, of a strictly local character, for it very often surveyed the entire Mediterranean world. Al-Razi (d. 937), Ibn Abd Rabbini (d. 940), Ibn al-Qutiya (d. 961), Arib ben Said (d. 998), Abu el-Bekri (d. 1094), el-Idrisi (d. 1154), Ibn Jubair (d. 1217), Ibn ul-Idari (d. 1292), al Maqqari (d. 1632) and many

---

[64] Edited by C. E. Sachau. English translation by same, *The Chronology of Ancient Nations.*
[65] Edited by Sachau; English translation.
[66] The importance of the battle was recognized by Arabic historians. See C. Cahen, "La campagne de Mantzıkert d'après les sources musulmanes." *Byzantion,* IX (1934), pp. 613-642.
[67] On the rise of the Ottoman Turks, see G. Georgiades Arnakis, *The Early Osmanlis,* in Greek, with a detailed summary in English.
[68] The first two volumes of his *Annals* were edited by T. G. J. Juynbol and B. F. Matthes, and the rest of the work was edited by W. Popper.

others wrote about the Arab conquest of Spain and the kingdom of the Moors or described their journeys from Spain to North Africa and the Middle East. In the fourteenth century North Africa produced perhaps the greatest Moslem historian of all time. Ibn Khaldun was born at Tunis in 1332 and died at Cairo in 1406. He was undoubtedly a walking encyclopedia, commanding vast areas of knowledge, but at the same time he was an independent thinker and an indefatigable research worker. He is generally recognized as a leading philosopher of history.[69] For him political history is simply one of the several branches of history, which he defines as "the science that deals with the social phenomena of man's life." His voluminous production falls into two groups: the *Prolegomena (Muqaddimah)*;[70] a general introduction to history, with discussions of the problems of interpretation and causation, and the *Book of Instructive Examples (Kitab el-Ibar)*, [71] which is a detailed universal history covering the growth of civilization, the Arabs and the other peoples from antiquity to his time, with ample treatment of the tribes of North Africa.

THE HISTORIANS OF THE SELJUKS AND OF THE EARLY OSMANLIS

The rising power of the Turks found its worthy historians, too. The westward march of the sultan of Kharezm Jelal ed Din Mankobirti was recorded by Mohammed en-Nesawi.[72] The story of the Seljuks was told by Anushirwan ben Khalid,[73] Ibn Bibi,[74] and Kerim ed-Din Mahmud.[75] For the conflict between the East and West we have the Damascus *Chronicle*,[76] which surveys the period from 1056 to 1160. It is the work of al-Qualanisi, who lived at Damascus in the first half of the twelfth century. As to the struggles of Saladin, our sources include the writings of two contemporaries—Ibn al-Athir and Baha ad-Din,—the former an opponent and the latter an admirer of the sultan.[77] The period of the Mongol invasion is recorded by Abul Fida of Damascus in his universal chronicle,[78] which extends to 1328, and by the Jacobite bishop of Aleppo, Gregory Abul-Faraj (also known as Bar Hebraeus), who wrote a chronicle in Syriac reaching the year 1286.[79] The Turkish principalities, which sprang up in Asia Minor after the fall of the Seljuks, are described by the great traveller Ibn Batutta,[80] who visited them about the year 1333, and

---

[69] N. Schmidt, *Ibn Khaldun;* G. Bouthal, *Ibn Khaldun: sa philosophie sociale;* E. Rosenthal, *Ibn Khalduns Gedanken über den Staat;* A. von Kremer, *Ibn Khaldun als Kulturhistoriker der islamischen Völker.*

[70] Edited by E. Quatremère, *Notices et extraits des manuscrits de la Bibliothèque Imperiale,* XVI, 1, XVII, 1, XVIII, 1 (1859). French translation by MacGuckin de Slane, *ibid.* XIX, 1 (1862), XX, 1 (1862), XXI, 1 (1865) ; published separately, in 3 vols.

[71] Published in 7 vols. from Cairo mss. French translation, *Histoire des Berbères,* 4 vols. ; new edition by P. Casanova, 2 vols. The sections dealing with the Latin kingdoms of Syria were translated into German by C. J. Tornberg, in R. Röhricht, *Quellenbeiträge zur Geschichte der Kreuzzüge,* pp. 214ff. For a complete list of translations see N. Schmidt, *op. cit.,* pp. 57-60.

[72] Translated into French by O. Houdas (Paris, 1895).

[73] Edited by M. Th. Houtsma, *Histoire des Seldjoucides de l'Iraq par al-Bondari.*

[74] Edited by Houtsma, in *Recueil de textes relatifs à l'histoire des Seldjoucides,* IV. Translated into French by Ch. Schéfer, in *Bibliothèque de l'Ecole des langues vivantes orientales,* series 3, vol. V.

[75] Sections of his Seljuk history translated into German by Fikret Issiltan.

[76] Edited and translated by H. A. R. Gibb.

[77] See H. A. R. Gibb, "The Arabic Sources for the Life of Saladin," *Speculum,* XXV (1950), pp. 58-72.

[78] Edited with a Latin translation by J. J. Reiske and published by J. G. C. Adler, in 5 vols.

[79] Facsimile of the Syriac text and English translation by E. A. Wallis Budge, in 2 vols.

[80] Edited and translated by C. Defrémery and B. Sanguinetti, in 4 vols. English translation by H. A. R. Gibb, *Travels in Asia and Africa.*

by Shihab ed-Din al-Umari (d. 1355), who collected information about them, while he was a prisoner in Egypt.[81]

The Ottoman Turks have no historiography of their own prior to the fifteenth century. Their first historian worthy of the name is Ashikpashazade, a contemporary of Mehmed the Conqueror, for whose reign he is our chief Turkish authority.[82] He wrote in simple Turkish, unaffected by the Arabic and Persian literary tradition. The era of Selim I and Suleyman the Magnificent abounds in court poets and historians who praise the deeds of the descendants of Osman in poetic, lavishly ornamented language. The most outstanding are Idris, who wrote the *Eight Heavens (Hesht Bihisht)* in Persian, and Neshri, whose *View of the World (Jihan-numa)* was compiled in Osmanli Turkish. None of them, however, have the objective approach which was so common among the Arabs or the Byzantines. Some semblance of impartiality can be noticed in the *Travels of Evliya Tchelebi* (1611-1680), who was fond of historical digression but was often misinformed. Much better informed though no broader in his views is Haji Kalfa (1609-1658), the author of a *Jihan-numa* and of a bibliographical encyclopedia.

Ottoman historiography is voluminous during the four centuries after Mehmed the Conqueror, but, as far as intrinsic merit is concerned, it never rises above the average production of the Arabs.

---

[81] *Al-Umari's Bericht über Anatolien*, ed. Franz Taeschner. Translated into French by E. Quatremère, in *Notices et extraits*, XIII (1838).

[82] Franz Babinger in his invaluable book *Die Geschichtsschreiber der Osmanen und ihre Werke*, studies 376 historians up to the middle of the nineteenth century. Of these only about ten belong to the period before the fall of Constantinople.

Chapter 7

THE ITALIAN RENAISSANCE

By Karl H. Dannenfeldt

CHANGING economic conditions and the growth of the Italian communes in the twelfth and thirteenth centuries brought about corresponding changes in the social, religious, cultural and intellectual life of the Italians. An increasing secularism, a new spirit and new attitudes gradually turned men from the old order of the Middle Ages. Man's life here on earth assumed a dignity and value which it had not known for centuries. These changes were long in developing and were accompanied by stress and strain, but all fields of knowledge and endeavor, including the writing of history, were slowly transformed or modified by them.

The gradual transition from medieval historiography to the humanistic histories of the Italian Renaissance is already evident in certain of the Latin historical writings of the late twelfth and thirteenth centuries. Attempts to entertain the reader through diverting and amusing incidents replace the medieval predilection to moralize and edify, and complete characterizations and anecdotes emphasized the role of personalities in history. Pride and self-praise, so seldom found in medieval history, mark the transitional writings to an increasing degree. The influence of classical antiquity, however, which was to become so marked in Italian historiography of the fourteenth and fifteenth centuries, was not yet apparent.[1]

THIRTEENTH CENTURY HISTORIOGRAPHY

In the troubled thirteenth century, Italian historiography continued to rid itself of medievel forms, concepts and purposes. Near the middle of the century, Sanzanome, a Florentine notary, wrote his *Gesta Florentinorum* to popularize the city's history from its legendary origins to the year 1231. His work is the first history of Florence of known authorship and, although somewhat rhetorical in style and written without historical perspective, it foreshadows the many chronicles and histories to be written later about the cultured city on the Arno.[2] Rolandius of Padua, also a notary, composed twelve books on the history of Padua from 1200 to 1260, which, although rhetorical in nature, are much advanced in style and content.[3]

At the end of the thirteenth century, Riccobaldo da Ferrara wrote a universal

---

[1] For the medieval and early Renaissance historians of Italy see Ugo Balzani, *Early Chroniclers of Europe: Italy*, and Bernhard Schmeidler, *Italienische Geschichtschreiber des 12. and 13. Jahrhunderts.*
[2] Otto Hartwig, *Quellen und Forschungen zur Ältesten Geschichte der Städt Florenz*, Part I, pp. iii-xv, 1-34; Paul Scheffer-Boichorst, *Florentiner Studien* pp. 250-259. On an early thirteenth century anonymous work used by Sanzanome, The *Chronica de Origine Civitatis*, see Hartwig, *op. cit.*, pp. xv-xliii, 37-69.
[3] *Rolandini Patavini Chronica* in *Monumenta Germaniae Historica Scriptorum*, ed. by G. H. Pertz, *et al.* (32 vols.), XIX, pp. 32-147.

history entitled *Pomarium* and a *Historia Imperatorum Romano Germanicorum* in which are already evident the new forces and interests that were to be characteristic of the historical writing in the next two centuries in Italy. Calling his contemporaries the "modern ones,"[4] he considered the previous periods of history as completed and closed. Another unusual feature of his work is that he disparages the coarseness of the customs and culture of the Italians in the period before the death of Frederick II, after whose reign great changes had occurred in Italian life. His history, largely based on the *Chronicle* of Jerome, contains much of a religious nature, and the many wonders of the earlier centuries are not questioned. Unlike the earlier chroniclers, in his *Compilatio chronologica* Riccobaldo systematically includes in each reign a list of the famous men of the period, both clerical and lay. Livy, Suetonius, Florus, Justinus and the *Scriptores historiae augustae* are among his sources for Roman history, and his writing is replete with classical words and place-names.

This interest in the Latin classics is still external and medieval in character. There are missing the spirit of antiquity, the conscious desire to model one's life and morals after the ancients, the surrender to the ancient world, the classical attitude toward life and the yearning to know the language and literature of ancient Greece—all the things which are so pronounced among the humanists who followed the path opened by Petrarch.

Mussatus. The changing view toward classical antiquity is found in the historical works of Albertius Mussatus (1261-1330), a distinguished author and political leader of Padua.[5] Mussatus wrote in excellent Latin an impartial history of the deeds of Henry VII of Luxembourg, who had accepted the invitation of the Ghibelline faction to come to Italy for the imperial crown. This *De Getis Henrici VII. Caesaris* shows that Mussatus was a friend and admirer of the emperor, but praiseworthy deeds and faults are told with impartiality.[6] After the death of Henry in 1313, Mussatus wrote a second history, *De Gestis Italicorum post Henricum VII. Caesarem,* narrating in twelve books the events in Italy, and in particular those in Padua, between 1313 and 1329.[7] The histories of Mussatus are sources of primary importance, for his knowledge of contemporary Italian affairs gained as a councilor, soldier, ambassador and statesman, makes his works authoritative and comprehensive. He patterned his work after that of Livy, making much use, like the Roman, of indirect discourse and applying Roman names to the officials and institutions of fourteenth century Italy. Like the classical writers whom he admired so much, he wrote in the third person when describing events in which he himself took part.

Villani. Also representative of the departure from the traditional medieval chronicle and yet revealing the strength of that tradition is the *Florentine Chronicle* of Giovanni Villani (*ca.* 1272-1348).[8] This chronicle, originally

4 Riccobaldo, "Praefatio," *Historia Imperatorum,* in *Rerum Italicarum Scriptores ab Anno Aerae Christianae 500 ad 1500,* ed. by Locovico A. Muratori, IX, 105; cf. also Schmeidler, *op. cit.,* pp. 55-64.
5 On Mussatus as a poet and historian see Gustav Koerting, *Die Anfänge der Renaissance-Litteratur in Italien,* pp. 302-355.
6 Muratori, X, pp. 5-568.
7 *Ibid.,* pp. 573-768.
8 G. Villani, *Cronaca di Firenze* in Muratori, XIII, pp. 5-1002 and an edition by F. Gherardi-Dragomanni (4 vols.).

ending in 1348 when the author died of the Black Death, was extended by his brother Matteo and his grandson Filippo to the year 1364. Although the chronicle begins with early biblical times and is quite general in scope, the central theme is the rise of Florence to its position of power and glory. It remained a popular work for centuries and in 1539 even comforted Benvenuto Cellini in his noisome prison in S. Angelo.[9]

Giovanni Villani, the best of the three chroniclers, was a busy merchant, well-traveled and active in the public affairs of Florence. His experience in business and in political life is reflected in the merchant viewpoint of his work, in the details of economic life which he includes and in his exact knowledge of the political vicissitudes of Florence. Villani belonged to the successful Black party of the Guelphs, but factional considerations do not play a great part in his patriotism for the city-state which to him is greater than the party.

He began his great chronicle, he tells us (VIII, 36), after a visit to Rome in the Jubilee year 1300. There the sight of the great ruins and the reading of the works of Vergil, Sallust, Lucan, Livy and others prompted Villani to record the history of Florence, "the daughter and offspring of Rome." For the foundation of Florence and its early history he used the legendary material of Sanzanome's *Gesta Florentinorum*.[10] He is uncritical also in his use of later materials, but when in the greater part of his chronicle, he describes the events in his own lifetime, he shows the care with which he gathered facts to supplement his own shrewd and accurate observations. Florentine life is depicted in genuine detail—politics, art, customs, trade and society. His recording of statistical data, unusual in early historians, adds immensely to the value of the chronicle. However, he seldom portrays the inner life which produced the wonderful culture and institutions of Florence.

The medieval element is still strong in Villani, for to him the history of the world is the story of man's sin and God's will and judgment.[11] There is also a moral purpose in his chronicles, for he wished to present the past so that the citizens would in the future "practice virtue and flee vice, and stoutly bear their misfortunes for the welfare of the Republic" (I. i). Villani believed in an association of astrology and history; the favorable and unfavorable conjunction of the planets were signs of God's will. Astrological observations also enter into his attempt (XII, 40) to found a new chronological scheme for Florentine history. Villani accepted the medieval belief in the *translatio imperii* through the Pope from the Greeks to the French, thence to the Italians and finally to the Germans (VIII, 101).

Villani the Historian. As a historian writing in a transitional period, Villani also shows certain characteristics generally associated with the later humanists. He praises the style and form of the classical authors and declares his intention of imitating them "as a pupil," but, although he does evince some enthusiasm for the rhetorical form, his style remains simple and slovenly. He admired the

---

[9] *The Autobiography of Benvenuto Cellini*, Book I, Chap. CXVII.
[10] Otto Hartwig, *op. cit.*, Part II, pp. 247-271.
[11] Ernst Mehl, *Die Weltanschauung des Giovanni Villani*, pp. 126-139.

beginnings of the new art in the genius of Giotto (XI, 12), was aware of the world about him and felt deeply the reality of facts. Villani had some knowledge of the Latin classics, but the spirit of antiquity which inspired the humanists was lacking.[12]

The secularizing tendencies of the twelfth and thirteenth centuries gradually turned the minds and hearts of the Italians away from the essentially religious viewpoint of the Middle Ages and led them to discover values in this world, in man and in nature. A part of this movement, called humanism, was a new interest in classical literature. The humanists turned to the descriptions of the advanced, highly secularized civilizations of antiquity, which aproximated their own, for guidance in all aspects of society and culture, and for approbation of their feeling of individuality and their desire for fame. The Latin of Cicero and others was the object of veneration and emulation.

Petrarch. Of this new spirit of antiquity, this conscious submergence of oneself in the life and feeling of the ancients, Francesco Petrarch (1304-1374) was the herald. The son of a lawyer who had been exiled with Dante and other *Bianchi* in 1302, Petrarch received his education in Carpentras and Montpellier in France and Bologna. Although trained in law, his chief interest was in classical literature, especially the writings of Cicero and Vergil. As a humanist he turned against the scholasticism and the crabbed Latin of his day and set the example for others in the use of pure Latin and style of the classical authors. Petrarch's passion for antiquity caused him to denounce his own age, and letters written to Cicero, Seneca, Varro, Livy, Vergil, Homer and others show the intensity of the spirit which led him to treat them as contemporaries.

Petrarch was also interested in the history of antiquity.[13] He writes, "That I might forget (my own age) I have constantly tried to place myself in spirit in other ages; and therefore I took pleasure in history."[14] His interest in the glorious past, when Rome had ruled the civilized world, was prompted also by a patriotism that was cosmopolitan and Italian rather than centered on any particular city-state; a patriotism which was spurred on by the hope of once again establishing a strong and united Italy. It was this latter utopian wish that led Petrarch to become the first humanist historian. In his biographical history of Rome, now called the *Liber de viris illustribus,* Petrarch joyously described the lives of thirty-one heroes from Romulus to Caesar. Alexander the Great, Pyrrhus, and Hannibal were the only non-Romans included

Petrarch was psychologically unsuited to write biographies and was uncritical in his use of sources, but he did discard the medieval legends about the ancient Roman leaders. The authenticity, the motives and the time of writing of his sources were not investigated. If the work was ancient, it was assumed to be an excellent source. However, his reading was wide and with few exceptions he employed all the historians that were available. In another work intended

[12] *Ibid.,* pp. 18-19. Robert Davidsohn, *Geschichte von Florenz,* IV, i, p. 32, points out that Villani (I, 38) was one of the first to call attention to the traces of ancient construction exposed by excavation.
[13] See especially Gustav Koerting, *Petrarca's Leben und Werke,* pp. 592-617.
[14] F. Petrarch, "Epistola ad posteros" in *Epistolae de Rebus Familiaribus et Variae,* ed. by I. Fracassetti, I, p. 4.

for moral instruction and called *Rerum memorandarum libri IV*, Petrarch collected historical anecdotes. Most of the accounts are concerned with ancient Greeks and Romans but a few dealing with men of his own age, like King Robert of Sicily, Dante and others, are included.

Besides thus laying a foundation, humble and weak as it was, for the future historians who were influenced greatly by his admiration and esteem for the ancient Romans, Petrarch also contributed to the establishment of certain historical concepts.[15] He distinguished between an "ancient" period which lasted until "the name of Christ was celebrated at Rome and venerated by the Roman emperors" and the "modern" period which extended from that time to his own day.[16] This latter period Petrarch viewed as an era of decline and retrogression, thereby originating the conception of a dark and barbaric Middle Ages, an idea which lasted much too long in historiography.[17] To Petrarch, the only history worth knowing was that of the Romans. Consequently, he controverted the medieval theory of the continuity of a Roman Empire enervated and almost destroyed by the barbarians. He was not aware of the new age which he inaugurated and thus did not use the threefold division of ancient, medieval and modern which the later humanists expressed.

Boccaccio. The influence of Petrarch was first seen in the writings of his friend, Giovanni Boccaccio (1313-1375), the author of the *Decameron*. Two of his historical works, *On Famous Women* and *On the Fortunes of Great Men* were supplementary to Petrarch's biographical works. They, too, were written in Latin and gave evidence of wide reading in classical literature. Boccaccio's most important historical work was his eulogistic Italian *Life of Dante*, the first lengthy biography of a poet and a work which served as a model for later humanistic writings of that type.[18]

The historians of the fifteenth and sixteenth centuries were in a much more favorable position than Petrarch and Boccaccio to write histories. Most of them were laymen with political experience and a knowledge of contemporary events. Their knowledge of the past had been increased through the large number of newly discovered classical works, both in Latin and Greek. These texts had been made more accurate and meaningful by the growing art of criticism and by classical philology. The secular spirit of the Renaissance led them to seek only human motives and deeds in history and omit the wonders and supernatural elements of the medieval chronicles. The writing of history gave to the humanist an excellent means for the employment of the ornate and refined Latinity gained from the study of ancient literature. Local patriotism also prompted humanists to record the history of their city or state, and whereas Petrarch had confined his research to the Romans, the later humanists, beginning with ancient Rome, continued the story through to their own day, the latter period receiving the greater emphasis.

---

[15] Theodor Mommsen, "Petrarch's Conception of the 'Dark Ages'," *Speculum*, XVII (1942), pp. 228ff.
[16] Petrarch, *Epistolae de Rebus Familiaribus*, VI, p. 2; ed. I. Fracassetti, I, p. 314.
[17] Mommsen, *op. cit.*, pp. 226-242.
[18] The biography, a work of love, is uncritical and leaves much to be desired; cf. Gustav Koerting, *Boccaccio's Leben und Werke*, pp. 707-710.

FLORENTINES

Bruni. Humanism and the revival of antiquity was quite universal in Italy but is was the scholarship and literary activity of the Florentines which established their city as the intellectual center of Italy. Here Coluccio Salutati (1330-1406) and Luigi Marsigli (d. 1394) had early instilled an admiration for classical literature and a cultivated style of writing. Florence had led the way in Greek scholarship when its university had engaged Chrysoloras in 1396 to teach Greek. Thus Leonardo Bruni (1369-1444) inspired by Salutati and instructed in Greek by Chrysoloras, became an enthusiastic classical scholar and the author of the first humanistic history. Born at Arezzo and therefore often called Leonardo Aretino, he studied law in Florence but turned to classical literature. An excellent Latinist, he served as a papal secretary from 1405 to 1415, with the exception of the years 1410 and 1411, which were spent in the Chancery at Florence. He returned to Florence at the end of his service in Rome and in 1427 was reappointed Chancellor of the city, which office he held until his death in 1444. In 1415 he began his annalistic *History of the Florentine People,* a political history in twelve books.[19] The first book summarized Florentine history from the founding of the city to the death of Frederick II (1250). The remaining books were a detailed exposition of events to 1402.

With the exception of some long rhetorical speeches and frequent use of Roman terms, the style of Bruni is clear and simple. Critical in the use of his sources, the old legends of the founding of the city are not included and events in history are no longer attributed to Divine Providence.[20] His practical experience as an official of a free republic is apparent in his interpretation of history and in the emphasis he places on the importance of the communes in Italian history.[21] To him the end of the Roman Republic and the rise of the emperors in Rome was the the begining of a period of decadence. Crimes and revolts followed the decline in morals under the Empire and the barbarians invaded the void created when the capital was moved to Constantinople and the West left unprotected. Bruni rejects the medieval theory of the *translatio imperii,* for to him the Roman Empire ceased to exist when it fell before the barbarian invasions. For Italy the period of decline which began with the Caesars in Rome came to an end when the emperors residing in Germany left Italy to her own devices.[22]

Bruni also wrote a work entitled *Commentary on Contemporary Events in Italy* which pretended to be a history of the culture of his age, but which was more of a memoir than a history. His *Greek History,* his *Punic Wars*

---

[19] L. Bruni, *Historiarum Florentini Populi Libri XII,* in Muratori, Vol. XIX, part 3 (New edition by E. Samtini).

[20] Bruni considered the study of history of practical value in that it brought about an understanding of the origins and development of events and the achievements of peoples and kings, enlarged one's foresight in contemporary affairs, furnished lessons of inspiration and warning, and contained many examples of moral precepts; cf. his *De Studiis et Litteris ad Illustrem Dominan Baptistam de Malatesta Tractatulus,* p. 10 and W. H. Woodward, *Vittorino de Feltre and Other Humanist Educators,* p. 128.

[21] Cf. B. L. Ullman, "Leonardo Bruni and Humanistic Historiography" in *Medievalia et Humanistica,* IV (1946), pp. 59-60 on his "central theme of democratic liberty."

[22] For a discussion of his new periodization and his views of the medieval Empire see W. K. Ferguson, *The Renaissance in Historical Thought,* pp. 9-11.

and his *War of the Italians against the Goths* are merely free translations of Xenophon, Polybius, and Procopius, made without the proper acknowledgement as to his sources.

Bruni's style and periodization were much copied by later humanists. In Florence his influence lasted to the end of the century and can be seen, for example, in the humanistic treatment of the First Crusade by Benedetto de' Accolti (1415-1466), whose work contained much excellent material and rejected many of the wonders and legends. Bartolomeo della Scala (ca. 1430-1497) in his *History of Florence* and Giannozzo Manetti (1396-1459) in his *History of Pistoia*, also show the influence of Bruni.[23]

Poggio. Poggio Bracciolini (1380-1458), also a Chancellor of Florence, wrote a *History of the Florentine People* which covered with much rhetoric the period from 1352 to 1455.[24] Though stylistically purer and more impersonal than the work of Bruni, the historical content falls far short of the standard established by his predecessor in office. Concerned only with the political history and wars of Florence he slighted much in his narrative so that Machiavelli later complained of his negligence.[25] Like Bruni, Poggio felt that the continuity of the Roman Empire was spurious and that the selection of German emperors was based on an invention of the German Pope Gregory V.[26]

Florence was not alone in producing humanist historians. In Naples, Lorenzo Valla (*ca.* 1407-1457), the philologist and moral-philosopher, wrote in 1445 a *History of King Ferdinand of Aragon* for King Alphonso I. This short work, though ably composed with great clarity and really an introduction to an intended history of King Alphonso's reign, was more concerned with the private life of Frederick than with history. It was as an historical critic that Valla achieved his greatest success. He was the first to examine critically the ancient histories and documents which the humanists considered inviolable. The first of two critical works was directed against the papacy and attacked the authenticity of the document confirming the extensive temporal power which Constantine was said to have given the bishop of Rome. The treatise was written in 1440 and is entitled *The Discourse of Lorenzo Valla on the Forgery of the Alleged Donation of Constantine.*[27] Nicholas of Cusa, the German prelate, had earlier doubted the authenticity of the document in his *De concordantia catholica*, yet Valla, by his study of words and his exhaustive use of internal criticism, showed the philological and historical absurdities of the document and furnished the final proof of the forgery. In his second critical study, *Duo Tarquinii*, Valla dared to question parts of Livy's history of the early Romans, an act which gained for him the hatred of many humanists who were passionate champions of the ancient Roman historian.

Despite their preoccupation with classical literature, the humanists did not neglect the period between the Roman Empire and their own day. The patriotic

[23] Eduard Fueter, *Geschichte der Neueren Historiographie*, pp. 24-25.
[24] *Poggio Bracciolini Historiarum Florentini Populi Libri VIII*, in Muratori, XX, pp. 193-434.
[25] N. Machiavelli, "Proemio," in *Delle Istorie Fiorentine di Niccolo Machiavelli*, p. ix.
[26] Poggio, *Historiarum*, VII (Muratori, XX, p. 381).
[27] It was first published by Ulrich von Hutten in 1517. An English translation has been made by C. B. Coleman, *The Treatise of Lorenzo Valla On the Donation of Constantine.*

histories of the various city-states, which the humanists often began with the founding of the city, necessarily described the rise of the city during the medieval period. Matteo Palmieri (1406-1475) of Florence wrote a chronicle covering the period 449-1449 which was a continuation of that of Prosper of Aquitaine. The most scholarly of humanist historians, Flavio Biondo of Forli (1388-1463), also wrote on the medieval period in his *History since the Decline of the Power of the Romans.*[28] The entire work covers the history of Italy and of the Eastern Empire from the sack of Rome by the Goths in 410 (his date, 412) to the year 1442. The history is divided into decades (ten books) of which there are three complete and two books of a fourth.

Biondo, or, as he was called in Latin, Blondus, wrote this careful and erudite work with little attention to humanistic form and style. He felt that while much had been written on the period when Rome was at its height, the age between Orosius and his own lacked proper historical analysis. This defect he intended to remedy.[29] Biondo's work shows the results of humanistic historical criticism, for he has made careful studies of the best sources for each century, discarding legends and wonders. His neglect of the classical style caused his history to be little appreciated by his fellow humanists, but later historians frequently drew material, often without acknowledgement, from the plentiful data it contained. Biondo's views of the Middle Ages are quite original.[30] Bruni had dated the decline of Rome from the rise of the Caesars, but Biondo argued that the actual decline began in 412 and continued only until the time of Charlemagne, with whose reign he began his second decade. The other works of Biondo are more archeological than historical in character. They include his *Rome Established, Illustrated Italy* and *Rome Triumphant.*

Piccolomini. Many of the Renaissance popes patronized humanist historians but only one, Aeneas Sylvius Piccolomini (1405-1465), became a historian in his own right. His first work was entitled *Commentaries on the Council of Basle,* although only the events pertaining to the description of Eugenius IV and the election of Felix V are narrated. The description of the Council gave him opportunity to record his keen observations and reproduce with great rhetoric the speeches made by the members of the Conclave.[31] His unfinished *History of Frederick III* deals only with the coronation and marriage of the Emperor in 1452 and the unrest in Austria at that time. Aeneas Sylvius' interest in northern countries is also evident in his *Germania,* in a *History of Bohemia* and in his epitomization of Jordanes' *History of the Goths.* He also recast in a humanistic style the first two decades of the *History* of Biondo. His *History of Europe* and the *Cosmography,* both unfinished, combine history and geography and contain notices of customs and ways of life which he had observed himself or extracted from classical authors. He closed his literary activity with the *Commentaries,* a bid for fame. Autobiographical in

[28] This *Historiarum ab Inclinatione Romanorum Imperii Decades* was completed in 1453 but was first published in Venice in 1483.
[29] F. Biondo, *Historiarum ab Inclinatione Romananorum Imperii Decades,* Vol. II, pp. 3-4.
[30] See the detailed study in Ferguson, *op. cit.,* pp. 11-14.
[31] Of the three books, the second has been lost; of Aeneas Sylvius Piccolomini, *Opera,* pp. 1ff. The best biography of Aeneas Sylvius is that of Georg Voigt, *Enea Silvio de' Piccolomini als Papst Pius der Zweite, und sein Zeitalter,* 3 vols. in 2.

nature and written in the third person, these are full of digressions and rhetorical speeches but in general reveal an observant scholar, rich in experience and political wisdom.

Aeneas Sylvius' historical works, all written in classical Latin, are generally superficial and were not a major contribution to humanistic historiography, but they influenced later German historians to introduce into their works geographical and legal material and caused them to be semi-critical of legends on the origin of their race. His writings on Germany, which reveal an accurate knowledge and a keen interest, may also have contributed to the tendency of the German humanists to exhibit such an exaggerated patriotism.[32]

Local patriotism and the secular viewpoint of the humanists delayed for a long time the writing of a humanistic universal history. This popular type of medieval writing with its theological basis and theological emphasis is still to be found in the *Chronica universale* of Archbishop Antonio Pierozzi of Florence. Using the medieval chroniclers instead of the classical authors, Antonio followed both the chronological scheme of six ages, of which Augustine had written in the last chapter of his *De civitate Dei*, and the division into four world monarchies, thus recognizing no break in the continuity of the Roman Empire.[33] The humanistic element is stronger in the *Supplementum chronicarum* (1483) of Jacobus Phillippus Foresta of Bergamo. Here the classical authors are frequently cited and the scheme of the four monarchies disappears, though that of the six ages was retained.[34]

Sabellicus. The only world history to be written by a humanist was that of the Venetian Marcantonio Coccio (1435-1506), better known as Sabellicus. In his *History of the World to the Year of Human Salavation 1504*, first published in Venice in 1498-1504, Sabellicus presented an annalistic arrangement of world political history in the humanistic style and method of Bruni, writing from the Roman-Italian point of view and emphasizing the history of Rome and Venice. For ancient history, Sabellicus used the classical works. The chronicle of Eusebius in Jerome's version formed the basis for his chronology while Biondo's work was especially used for later history. Sabellicus' work reveals no deep philosophical grasp, but he did improve on the medieval chroniclers in removing fables and tales of the supernatural from his history and, by diminishing the usual preponderance of Hebrew history, he established a better historical perspective. He ignored the system of the four monarchies and in the eighth ennead began what today would be called medieval history with the founding of Venice.[35]

Earlier, in 1487, Sabellicus had published a *History of Venice from the Founding of the City*, a humanistic state-history, written at the instigation of the Venetian government. Bruni again was his guide in style, while the history of Biondo was used extensively. Sabellicus lacked the scholarly ability and the practical experience in political affairs to make this a successful work.

[32] Paul Joachimsen, *Geschichtsauffassung und Geschichtschreibung in Deutschland unter dem Einfluss des Humanismus.* Part I, pp. 32-36 and Fue·er, *op. cit.*, p. 118.
[33] Antonio died in 1459 and his work was printed in 1484; cf. Joachimsen, *op cit.*, pp. 80-81.
[34] *Ibid.*, pp. 82-86.
[35] Ferguson, *op. cit.*, pp. 16-17. The seventh ended with the sack of Rome in 412 (Biondo's date).

He neglected the important religious and economic factors in Venetian history and his facts are confused in humanistic rhetorical elaborations.[36]

Machiavelli. The preoccupation of the humanist historians with political history is nowhere better seen than in the late *Quattrocento* and the early sixteenth century when the republican government which Bruni portrayed was dying. The greatest of these historians was Niccolo Machiavelli (1469-1527), politician, statesman, diplomat, poet and political philosopher. Living in an age of intrigue and realistic power politics, Machiavelli was stimulated by his experiences and travels, and by the vicissitudes of Florence to analyze the men and conditions which made Italy the battleground of Europe. Forced to retire from public life in 1512, he found leisure to record his political philosophy in *The Prince* and in the more comprehensive *The Discourses on the First Decade of Titus Livius.* His plans for the organization of militia instead of mercenary troops were propounded in his *Art of War.*

Late in the year 1520, Machiavelli was commissioned by Cardinal Giulio de' Medici, later Pope Clement VII, to compose a history of Florence. Five years later the eight books of the *History of Florence,* written in Italian, were presented to Clement VII in Rome. Believing the histories of Bruni and Poggio to be sufficient for the earlier history of Florence, Machiavelli limited his first book to a rapid survey of the history of Italy from the "decline of the Roman Empire" to 1434, in which year the Medici were recalled to Florence. Much of this condensation, in many places inaccurate and incomplete, was taken from Biondo.[37] Machiavelli was little interested in medieval history, but his keen insight saw historical causation in human motives and found in the deeds of the Middle Ages principles of political action for his own day.

The remaining books trace the rise of Florence from its founding to the death of Lorenzo de' Medici in 1492.[38] For his data he borrowed heavily from the chronicle of Giovanni Villani, the history of Francesco Sforza by Giovanni Simonetta of Milan and the earlier history of Florence by Cavalcanti. The inner political development of Florence, despite the complexities of the party strife and unrest which led to the despotism of the Medici, is clearly portrayed with many personal observations and comments. In the latter half of his history. Machiavelli dealt with external affairs and wars rather than with an account of the loss of liberty under the Medici for whom he was writing. He did not hesitate, however, to cite the papacy as the cause of the disunity and weakness of Italy, a weakness increased by the employment of perfidious *condottieri* and unreliable mercenary troops. His last two books relate with much eloquence the conspiracies by which the democratic elements in the various cities of Italy sought to regain freedom from the despots, and the history ends with praise for the character and deeds of Lorenzo the Magnificent.

---

[36] M. Coccio Sabellico, *Historiae Rerum Venetarum ab Urbe Condita Libri XXXIII,* in *Degli 'Istorici delle cose Veneziane,* Vol. I; Fueter, *op. cit.,* pp. 30-33. That part of Sabellicus' work which dealt with the origin of Venice was much inferior to the critical *History of the Origins and Growth of the City of the Venetians to 809* by Bernardo Giustiniani (1408-1489) of Venice; cf. Fueter, *op. cit.,* pp. 113-115. Other Venetian historians were Cardinal Pietro Bembo (1470-1547), Francesco Contarini (1421-1460), and Paolo Paruta (1540-1598).
[37] P. Villari, *Niccolo Machiavelli,* II (fourth ed.), 422-423, 434-440.
[38] Fragments and materials for a continuation were found after his death.

Machiavelli's invaluable history, despite its inaccuracies, marks the beginning of modern historiography. Written in the late Renaissance, its form and style are more advanced than those of the earlier humanistic writings. Machiavelli wrote a rationalistic and natural political history in clear, precise and vigorous language. Only in the speeches in his work does he abandon his realistic idiom for the rhetorical embellishments of his predecessors. Generally, too, he arranged his materials topically instead of in the usual annalistic form. Ethics, sentiment and religion play no part in his history.

Guicciardini. Also contemporary with Machiavelli was the realistic and able historian, Francesco Guicciardini (1483-1540). Born of an influential family, he studied law in Florence, Ferrara, Padua and Pisa. In 1512, he was sent by the city of Florence to the court of Ferdinand of Aragon, the first step in a long and busy career as diplomat and statesman. Leo X appointed him Governor of Reggio, Modena and Parma, and in 1526, he became a high officer in the army of the pope. Five years later he was elevated by the pope to the important post of Governor of Bologna, which position he held for three years. A firm adherent of the Medici party in Florence, he supported both Duke Alessandro and Duke Cosimo, but retired from active life in 1537 and died three years later.

Early in life Guicciardini composed a *History of Florence* which revealed an extraordinary keenness of perception and understanding.[39] This work, which unfortunately was not published until 1859, narrated with great clarity the events from the Ciompi Revolt in 1378 to the year 1509. Guicciardini, intending the history for his own use, emphasized the events of his story more than the form and style. His use of indirect discourse instead of rhetorical speeches also showed an advance over the earlier humanistic writing. Less philosophical than Machiavelli, he nevertheless analyzed with care the complex political situations in Florence. Although a member of a family that had long been active in the rule of Florence, his impartiality is unique. His resignation, impassivity, and even contempt, are in sharp contrast to the patriotism and illusions of Machiavelli. In general, Guicciardini sought no principles or rules in his exposition of the origins, causes and developments of events, but he did see intrigue and design as the source of political events.[40]

Late in life, Guicciardini wrote in Italian his realistic *History of Italy*.[41] The twenty books of this unique general Italian history relate the tragic events between 1492 and 1534. As in his earlier work, here too we find the same disillusionment and self-interest, the same clear insight based on wide experience, and the same lucid and dispassionate writing. His knowledge of the intricate politics and diplomacy of Italy enabled Guicciardini to write a signal work of great breadth and compass, while careful analysis of men and events disclosed the motivation, whether good or evil, which incited men to action. Much archival material was reworded by the historian and introduced

---

[39] F. Guicciardini, *Storie Florentine*, in *Opere*, ed. by G. Canestrini, III. An unfinished, preliminary study for a second Florentine history has been discovered recently and edited by Roberto Ridolfi, *Le Cose Fiorentine dall' Anno 1375.*
[40] Fueter, *op. cit.*, p. 75 and "Guicciardini als Historiker," in *Historische Zeitschrift*, C (1908), pp. 486-540.
[41] F. Guicciardini, *Storia D'Italia*, ed. by C. Panigade, (4 vols.).

into his history. As Guicciardini intended his *History of Italy* for the public, his style and form differ from the natural simplicity and spontaniety of his earlier work. The involved and intricate subject matter of his history of Italian politics led him to write complicated and wearisome periods, an artifice which in no way, however, obscures the clarity of presentation. Detailed description of battles, an annalistic arrangement, the use of direct discourse and rhetorical speeches show concessions to the humanistic conventions.[42]

Giovio. Quite different from the usual humanistic histories and yet well within the pattern as set by Bruni were the works of Paolo Giovio or Paulus Jovius (1483-1552). A humanist doctor, professor of rhetoric, and bishop, Jovius combined historical writing and journalism.[43] He became "the first great reporter and interviewer," who could write on anything even if he did not understand it.[44] He had no knowledge of politics and no deep philosophical insight into history, yet his uncritical reporting was accepted by a credulous public. His most famous historical work is the Latin *History of His Own Time,* originally intended to be an extended work of forty-five books covering the period 1494 to 1547; however, books five to ten and nineteen to twenty-four were either never written or soon suppressed. Jovius was among the first to see that the history of Italy and its city-states could only be understood in relation to the general European political scene. His *History* and other works include cultural and ethnographic materials on many and various peoples. Among his other writings are an Italian *Commentary on the Affairs of the Turks* (1531) and a large number of biographical works. Of these latter writings his two *Elogies* were biographical works on military heroes and illustrious authors from many lands and times. They are important as the first biographies composed to accompany portraits of the persons described.

HUMANISTIC BIOGRAPHY

These studies by Jovius were a part of the biographical literature which the humanists had developed, for the Renaissance idea of fame and individuality naturally led to the description for posterity of the characteristics and *virtu* of outstanding men. The literary portraits presented cultural and social aspects of the age, thus supplementing the histories of the humanists which were almost purely political and diplomatic. Suetonius, Nepos and Plutarch served as models and all too often limited or even completely stifled the native Italian aptitude and disposition to describe accurately the characteristics of the great. Petrarch and Boccaccio had led the way, but Filippo Villani (*ca.* 1325-1405), the nephew of the chronicler, Giovanni Villani, really established the writing of historical biographies as an important form of humanistic activity. Late in the fourteenth century he wrote his *Book Concerning the Famous Citizens of the City of Florence* in which he briefly characterized the leading Florentines of the past and present. His style is poor, but the essential internal and external characteristics are sketched in such a manner as to mark his work as an advance in biographical writing. Another Florentine, Pietro Riccio

---

[42] Ranke, *Sämmtliche Werke,* XXXIV, pp. 6-9, 19-24 severely criticizes the annalistic arrangement and the speeches of the *History of Italy.*
[43] *Ibid.,* pp. 70-78.
[44] Fueter, *op. cit.,* pp. 53-54.

(*d. ca.* 1505), better known as Crinitius, wrote the first critical history of literature in the form of biographical descriptions of Roman poets.[45]

Humanistic biographical writing culminated in the interesting Italian work of Giorgio Vasari of Arezzo (1511-1574),[46] whose *Lives of the Most Eminent Painters, Sculptors and Architects* is an all-important source for the history of the artists of the Italian Renaissance.[47] Vasari was a painter and architect who had travelled widely and was personally acquainted with many artists. He collected a vast amount of data from such historians as Giovanni and Matteo Villani, Paulus Diaconus and Machiavelli, and from the study of letters, chronicles, inscriptions, traditions, portraits, and from personal observation. His work is marked by his impartiality, his understanding of artistic technique, and by his charming style. The anecdotes and gossip he included may be considered a weakness but they assist in making the artists he describes more human and alive.[48] Despite his claim of "accuracy and good faith" his chronology is often in error. In this history of art, the first of its kind, Vasari depreciates Greek (Byzantine) and Gothic art. He dates the renaissance (rinascita) in art from the naturalism of Cimabue and Giotto.

The height of the Italian Renaissance had been passed when the eminent and prolific historian Carlo Sigonius (*ca.* 1525-1584), a professor of Greek and humanistic learning at Modena and other northern Italian cities, wrote his histories.[49] Among his numerous Latin historical works are a *History of the Western Empire,* a work of twenty books covering the history of Italy from Diocletian to Justinian, and a *History of Rulers of Italy* which continued Italian history to the year 1268. He also wrote an unfinished *History of the Church* in fourteen books and a *History of Bologna* which narrated the growth of that city to the year 1267. Among his critical rationalistic writings on ancient history were his *De republica Atheniensium* and *Fasti consulares ac triumphi acti a Romulo rege usque ad Tiberium Caesarem.* In these historical works, Sigonius sought to remain scholarly and yet to employ the humanistic forms of Bruni. Despite his excellent use of source materials, a true historical perspective is often lacking, and documents and invented speeches occur side by side.[50]

Italian Renaissance historiography may be said to close with the writings of Sigonius. The restraining hand of the Roman Inquisition and the political disturbances in Italy hindered the continuation of humanistic learning and historiography. Italian scholarship continued in the courts of those countries which were now being influenced by the Italian Renaissance. Thus, Peter Martyr of Anghera, Lucio Marineo, Polydore Vergil and others devoted their talents to the writing of humanistic histories of Spain and the countries north of the Alps.

---

[45] Crinitius, *De Poetis Latinis Libri V;* cf. Fueter, *op. cit.,* pp. 95-96. Other outstanding biographies were the *Vita Phillippi Mariae Vicecomitis* and the *Vita Francisci Sfortiae* of Pier Candido Decembri (1399-1477) and the *Vite di Uomini Illustri del Secolo XV* of Vespasiani da Bisicci (d. 1498).

[46] Wolfgang Kallab "Vasaristudien," in *Quellenschriften Fur Kunstgeschichte,* XV (1908).

[47] G. Vasari, *Le vite de 'piu eccelenti architetti, pittori, ed scultori ataliani da comibue insino a tempi nostri.*

[48] In the revised edition of 1568 the number of biographies was increased from 133 to 161.

[49] Giovanni Franciosi, "Della Vita e delle Opere di Carlo Signoio," in *Pensieri e Discorsi in Materia di Letters,* pp. 33-72.

[50] Fueter, *op. cit.,* p. 131.

Chapter 8

HUMANISM BEYOND THE ALPS

By Matthew A. Fitzsimons

INTRODUCTION

THE EUROPEAN countries north of the Alps had their own Renaissance, which began at different times in each country. This movement, as a rule, had a threefold character: 1) a reaction against medieval scholasticism which favored the study of moral philosophy, supported by the study of the Bible, the Church Fathers and the ancient classics; 2) a patriotic inspiration; and 3) the influence of the Italian Renaissance. In France, England, Spain, and Scotland, the patriotic inspiration supported the respective monarchs. In Germany, the patriotic inspiration was doomed to frustration. The Low Countries, which became a part of the Habsburg Empire, did not reveal the same patriotic excitement, and their greatest scholar, Erasmus, was preeminently a citizen of the Christian Commonwealth of Europe.

CHARACTERISTICS OF HUMANIST HISTORICAL SCHOLARSHIP

The historical writing of the late fifteenth and sixteenth centuries reflects the varied interests of the humanists beyond the Alps. The prestige of Italian achievements caused Louis XII of France and Henry VII of England to entrust the histories of their countries to critical scholars and masters of elegant Latin. The reaction against scholasticism which favored the Erasmian *eloquens et insipiens pietas* stimulated a searching study of the text of Scriptures and of the writings of the Fathers. This studious emphasis upon the sources of Christian belief and Church history and this identification of learning and piety were, however, soon directed to the apologetic ends of Protestant and Catholic controversialists. In Italy the humanists were often proudly conscious of their own Roman heritage. This patriotic and literary self-consciousness was paralleled in the north by the previously mentioned return to the supposedly simpler and surer fonts of Christian life and by self-conscious patriotism, which involved either an elaboration or affirmation of national legends and historical traditions or, as in Germany, involved the discovery of and search for a national character. As in Italy, where the humanists eagerly collected the remains of the ancient world, so beyond the Alps a host of antiquaries collected material about their own countries. Classical scholarship and, to a lesser extent, the demands of learned controversy spurred considerable advances in the critical handling of texts and sources; however, the progress made in classical studies was not regularly carried over to other phases of historical writing. Finally, by the end of the century, there was the clear recognition and reluctant acceptance of the religious disunity of Europe. The northern humanists had, as a rule, been patriotic, and the cosmopolitanism of Erasmus was unique. Europe was divided politically and religiously. But there was a secular and cultural unity in the international acceptance of humanism and classical education.

NORTHERN HUMANIST VIEWS ABOUT THE NATURE OF HISTORY

Moral Examples. The function of history was generally agreed upon. This conception was an amalgam of traditional elements with some new emphases arising from the literary culture of the Renaissance. As a rule, history was thought to belong to the field of moral philosophy. History was "philosophy teaching by examples." From this point of view, history reinforced the precepts of morality and made vivid and concrete to the unimaginative, what the able moral philosopher already knew. But as men reflected on the scope of history, they also realized that history was an inadequate moral teacher. Thus, in true Aristotelian fashion, men like Sir Philip Sidney argued that since history dealt with individual events, it was inferior to poetry, which could present truths of universal importance. The fact that it rained today does not mean that it will rain tomorrow.[1]

Revelation of Providence. Closely allied to this point of view is the conception of history as the revelation of God's providence. The historian presents the theatre of God's judgments. Admittedly, this conception is not a very fruitful one for historical science, but it pervades the writing of this period. The historians did not believe that they could explain everything. Philippe de Commines (1447-1511) frequently saw events develop so differently from human plans and abilities, that he regularly attributed the inexplicable and the unexpected to divine intervention. The humanist historians did not see God's hand so readily as some of the chroniclers of the Middle Ages and the popular historians of the sixteenth century. They were discriminating in their acceptance of miracles but they did believe in Providence. Where historians did not accept Providence, they turned, as Machiavelli did, to the pagan concept of Fortune—or, as equally characteristic of the age, they mingled references to Fortune and to Providence. This was true of Sir Walter Raleigh, who, however, with eloquent melancholy, registered God's judgments on all human vanity—and what finally was not vanity—in his *History of the World* (1614).

Prudence. History could make a claim to an independent position in its role as a teacher of prudence. Man might know all the rules of morality and, nonetheless, fail in the conduct of his affairs. Prudence could not be formally taught but was the fruit of experience. But history, especially the narratives of men who had practical contact with weighty affairs, could supply men with this experience. Where men did not successfully practice the prudence, which they had learned, they could at least learn to resign themselves to the ways

---

1 Philip Sidney, *The Defense of Poesy,* ed. by A. S. Cook, pp. 13-23. Sidney further wrote: "The historian, being captivated to the trueth of a foolish world, is many times a terror from well doing, and an encouragement to unbrideled wickedness." Quoted in *The Anglica Historia of Polydore Vergil* A.D. 1485-1537, edited with a translation by Denys Hay, Camden Series, LXXIV, p. xxxviii.

of Providence or Fortune, and thereby avoid the undignified futility of prolonged complaints and repining.

Monument against Oblivion. History was also the life of memory.[2] The historian preserved the fame of men and events. This function goes back to the days of Herodotus and Homer. But it had a special poignancy in the sixteenth century. Scholars were very conscious of the vast world of antiquity which they had rediscovered, and all of this knowledge recovered from oblivion was made possible by literary remains. The historian proudly claimed the function of preserving the records of memorable events. As a moralist, his censure of evil and praise of the good shaped the future fame of men and acted as a deterrent for later ages, which would fear the stigma of wrongdoing and seek the praise due to noble deeds. In addition, the historian was called upon to celebrate the preeminence of his own country.

Periodization of History. The divisions of universal history were at first conventional. There was the Christian tradition with its emphasis upon the creation, man's fall, the history of the Jews under the Law, and the Redemption. This was more fully elaborated by a deeper knowledge of pagan history. The breadth of universal history was further extended by the discovery of the Americas and by closer and more direct contact with the people of Asia. The French, English, and Spaniards all had legends about their national ancestry, and with a learned ingenuity that sometimes amounted to perverseness, their historians traced their origins to the Trojans and the descendants of Noah. They had been once a part of the Roman Empire and proudly related their own people to this empire; simultaneously they recounted their entrance into the Christian community. The French were conscious of their own powerful monarchy and lovingly recounted its recent triumphs over England and Burgundy. The Spaniards saw their own kingdoms united and a new era of history opening for themselves with the conquest of the last Moorish stronghold of Granada. English historians warmly hailed the peace and security which the Tudors had given their subjects. The Germans discovered themselves in Tacitus' *Germania* and proudly recounted their part in the Holy Roman Empire of the German nation, sometimes relating it to the *Book of Daniel's* vision of the Four Monarchies.

Method: Conflict of Art and Criticism. As for historical method, older practices often survived except in the editing of classical texts and the Scriptures. The humanist historians usually aimed to write their narratives in a polished and uniform style. They borrowed extensively from older material, although as a rule they preferred to rephrase their source material. Some humanists contented themselves with the arrangement and polished presentation of readily available material. Others ranged farther afield and collected inscriptions, coins, and all texts which they could locate. But, as a rule, those who labored so earnestly were rarely able to master their material, and presented the fruits of their labors not in faultless organization and

---

[2] Much of this sixteenth century conception of history was frequently expressed in the words of Cicero's *De Oratore*, II, ix, p. 36; II, xi-xv. This view is well presented in the poem (probably Ben Jonson's) prefaced to Raleigh's *History of the World:* "From Death and dark Oblivion (near the same) The Mistress of Man's life, grave History, Raising the World to good or evil Fame, Doth vindicate it to Eternity."

style but in the fumbling manner of Flavio Biondo's *Italia illustrata*. In general, their critical principle may be summarized in the statement that an old source was a good one. Where there were contradictory sources, the historian often chose one account rather arbitrarily or presented both sides with the proposal that the reader could make his own choice. This learned but unfinished presentation was in great vogue by the middle of the century, when the practice of the frequent citation of authorities became not unusual. The classical models and stylistic requirements sanctioned the use of contrived speeches, which, however, rarely had the sharpness of Thucydides. During the century, Livy lost some of his prestige, and the more pragmatic historians modeled themselves on Polybius and Tacitus. So closely did they follow their models that freqently they took individual sentences verbatim from the classical authors. A story which illustrates this also reveals one of the contemporary dangers which faced the historian. John Hayward wrote a *History of the Life and Reign of Henry IV* (1599), which was remarkable for its psychological keenness. The work dealt at length with the deposition of Richard II and was published at the very time when the Earl of Essex was preparing his ill-fated rising against Queen Elizabeth. The Queen, perceiving in the timeliness of this history's account of a deposition an invitation to take similar action against herself, consulted Francis Bacon about the possibility of charging the imprisoned Hayward with treason. Bacon suggested that, while a charge of treason could not be maintained, a charge of felony would be in order, for Hayward had literally plundered Tacitus.[3]

ERASMUS

Search for a Patron. The controversial figure of Erasmus (1466-1536) towers over the early part of this period. Erasmus, a priest's son, was reared by guardians who urged him to enter the religious life. His own studious interests pointed to the same course, although he later protested that the choice had been forced upon him. His distaste for monastic life, despite his composition of an eloquent though conventional *De contemptu mundi,* shaped much of his life. The opportunity to leave his monastery of Steyn came when he was offered the post of Latin Secretary to the Bishop of Cambrai. Subsequently, he went to Paris to study for his doctorate in theology and his mission also provided an excuse for absenting himself from his religious community. Not until he had won European fame was he given papal permission to be secularized and, thus, was freed from the fear of returning to Steyn. All of his life this sensitive man suffered the embarrassments and humiliations of a search for patronage.

Opposition to Scholasticism. Erasmus received his early training in the schools of the Brothers of the Common Life. From them he received a classical education which opened to him a world of incomparable elegance and wit. Erasmus thought in literary images derived from the classics, perhaps to the point of obscuring his vision of reality. His teachers, also, probably contributed to his later religious views. The Brothers of the Common Life were

---

[3] Sidney Lee, "Sir John Hayward," *Dictionary of National Biography,* Vol. IX, p. 311.

hostile to the pretentions and quarrels of the scholastic philosophers. Their attitude was most notably expressed in Thomas à Kempis' *Imitation of Christ,* which emphasizes the pride and vanity of philosophical and even theological pursuits and asserts the primacy of a humble and earnest moral life. Erasmus also reacted against the intellectual formulation of religious beliefs, partly because of the "barbarous" Latin of the philosophers and theologians, partly because of an understandable impatience with their overelaborate allegorical interpretation of the Scripture, which, thereby, lost its meaning in the ingenuity of human explanation.

Biblical and Patriotic Humanism. Erasmus, then, would have swept aside the whole intellectual formulation of religious teaching, a formulation which he neither knew deeply nor appreciated. He believed that the philosophy of Christ was simple and could readily be found in the *New Testament,* which, he hoped, would be made available to all men. With bitterness and piercing wit he attacked the multitude of abuses in the religious life of his time. His cherished means of stimulating the rebirth of culture was a union of the grace, eloquence and learning of the ancients with the philosophy of Christ as expounded in the *New Testament* and in the earliest sources of the Christian tradition, the Church Fathers. His optimism about the nature of man and his religious naivete, from the standpoint of the orthodox Christian, are revealed in the fact that Erasmus did not think of Christ as the Redeemer of sinful men but as the divine philosopher whose life should be the model of all Christians. This optimism and naivete is the cause of his ambiguous relation to the Reformation, for he drew back in horror from Luther's teaching of the utter corruption of man's nature.

The fame of Erasmus was already established when he entered upon the preparation of his Greek edition of the *New Testament* (1516). He had been attracted to this study by an early reading of Lorenzo Valla's *Annotationes in Novum Testamentum,* by the encouragement of John Colet, the English scholar, and by his veneration for St. Jerome, who compiled the Latin Vulgate text.

Erasmus believed that his edition was based on ancient manuscripts but he was mistaken in this, for none of the versions which he used were earlier than the eleventh century. He could have learned this only by a careful study of handwriting, which was beyond his interests. His edition was accompanied by an elegant Latin translation, notes and paraphrases. Characteristically, he professed considerable humility and in his preface, disclaimed all pretense of displaying his erudition, of "putting perfume in soup."[4] But his notes carried on his own struggle for the restoration of the *philosophia Christi,* and the later editions multiplied his caustic and sometimes petulant criticisms against his adversaries.

His edition was soon caught in the tumult of the Reformation. With the strong assertion of the Church's teaching authority at the Council of Trent, Erasmus' edition was cast aside by Catholic circles, and with them, the Vulgate remained the authorized version of the Scripture.

---

[4] John J. Mangan, *Life, Character and Influence of Desiderius Erasmus of Rotterdam,* vol. II, p. 7. For a brief estimate of Erasmus' work on St. Jerome see *Erasmi Opuscula,* ed. W. K. Ferguson, pp. 125-130.

The popularity and circulation of Erasmus' edition indicates that it answered a deeply felt need of the time. The same point emerges from a consideration of the vast edition (published 1522) of the Bible (the Complutensian Polyglot) in Hebrew, Greek, and Latin, undertaken at the University of Alcala under the patronage of Cardinal Ximenes. Erasmus' more venturesome criticism has won for him the position of founder of modern biblical studies.

HUMANIST PATRIOTISM

The German Empire. Erasmus himself was a cosmopolitan and his influence was international, but the humanists of the various countries were very patriotic, and, while venerating the ancient classics and imitating Italian Renaissance historians, they proudly proclaimed the glories of their own people and history. This is particularly and pathetically true of Germany. German scholars had become conscious of their national identity and could boast of the heroic courage of the Germans who had not been subjugated by Imperial Rome. This boast was all the more heatedly made because Germany was not politically unified and, thus, could not offer effective resistance to the increasing financial demands of the Renaissance papacy. The German humanists could, with some pride, deal with the history of Bavaria or Saxony. But the only focus of their patriotism as Germans was the Holy Roman Empire.

Conflict of Local and Imperial Interests. Maximilian I (1459-1529), the ruler of this Empire, had as the core of his strength the family possessions of the Habsburgs. The Emperor in spite of his financial straits was a knightly figure, given to grandiose dreams, and capable of rallying patriotic Germans to himself. This personal influence was of the greatest importance, for Germany was the restless center of a multitude of conflicting interests and discontents. The rulers of the territorial states followed exclusively self-centered policies and responded not at all to the literary patriotism of the humanists. The towns, seats of an advancing capitalism, which involved tense social and economic struggles within the towns and a darkly understood threat to the countryside, were prepared to abide by their own leagues, and, at heavy cost, to maintain their privileges. The rich merchants were often generous benefactors of the Church, proud of their cities, and ambiguously responsive to the patriotism of the humanists. The knights, a class doomed to political and economic extinction, had their position proudly expressed by Ulrich von Hutten and by following Franz von Sickingen (1523), were soon to accomplish their own destruction. Even Maximilian can not be regarded as a simple force for unity. He worked for the German Empire only so far as its interests coincided with his dynastic interests. Thus, the Empire's very diversity nullified its common action. This may be seen most clearly in the failure of the reform of the Reich (1495) attempted by Berthold of Henneberg. His proposed reform, as enacted, protected the separate interests of the princes, and Maximilian felt compelled to sabotage the reforms which served such an end.

Imperial Patriotism: Cuspinianus. Maximilian was the patron of such patriotic German humanists as Conrad Celtes and, at the same time, the patron of Austrian and Habsburg historical writing. Johannes Spiessheimer (Latin name,

Cuspinianus, 1473-1529), a versatile humanist, physician, teacher of rhetoric, diplomat, and collector, was Maximilian's court historian. In 1512 he finished a history of the Emperors, *Caesares* or *Kaiserbuch*. This work is the compilation of a talented and courtly dilletante. It is highly derivative and as an imperial work betrays a sharp anti-papal bias. His *Austria* (finished in 1528) is a description of Austria, an amalgam of geography, genealogy and history in the manner of Flavio Biondo and Aeneas Sylvius. In his travels, Cuspinianus became interested in the Eastern Roman Empire and his works are notable for a fuller treatment of the Eastern Emperors than was usual in the compilations of his contemporaries.

Trithemius. Johannes Trithemius (1462-1516), the Benedictine Abbot of Sponheim, was closely associated with Maximilian. The learned abbot, who shared with the Emperor an indulgence in fantastic speculations, left behind a mass of works, read and respected until the rise of the modern historical school. He was a tireless collector, and compiled catalogues of famous Germans and of ecclesiastical writers. Especially on early German history he used very untrustworthy sources. His *Compendium de origine gentis Francorum* (first printed in 1515) served, among other purposes, to prove the Frankish, non-Roman origins of the Holy Roman Empire, thus glorifying his Emperor Maximilian. In historical writing Trithemius is notable for his collections, his wide but indiscriminate erudition, and for his rather Carolingian interpretation of German history. In religion, unlike most of his humanist friends, he cherished the monastic life and, like them, identified Church reform with improvements in education.

Mingling of Patriotic and Religious Interests. The German humanists, following the leadership of Erasmus, criticized abuses within the church. They criticized the scholastic philosophers, and added their influence to the support of Reuchlin's Hebrew studies, which had been bitterly opposed by the Dominicans. Ulrich von Hutten's contribution to the *Letters of Obscure Men,* the coarse and witty humanist reply to the Dominicans, expressed the range of humanist hostility to the *status quo*—humanist learning against scholastic philosophy, German hostility to the privileges of Rome. In attacking abuses in the Church, the humanists not only gave vent to their own feelings of superiority against the Italians, but to a widespread German feeling that the reform of the Church had been hindered by the clergy.

Wimpfeling. German historical writing in this period still concerned itself with world history.[5] The first German humanist to attempt a presentation of German history, is the theology professor, Jakob Wimpfeling (1450-1528), who taught at both Heidelberg and Strasbourg. In his *Epitome Rerum Germanicarum usque ad nostra tempora* (to 1504), published in 1504, he praised the glories of Germany and, in his praise of Alsace, revealed his local patriotism. The *Epitome* is a general German history, which deals with the early German tribes as well as the glories of the Holy Roman Empire. Wimpfeling had a

---

[5] Hartmann Schedel (d. 1514), a physician of Nurnberg, published in 1493 his *Liber Chronicorum,* which ranged from Adam to Maximilian I and even to the Last Judgment. Though Schedel was familiar with many Italian writers, he used Vincent of Beauvais as a source for his account of the Trojan War. Fueter, *Geschichte der Neueren Historiographie,* pp. 184-185.

considerable knowledge of the Roman and medieval sources of German history. He was, however, not a researcher in compiling his history, and though he patriotically attacked modern Italian writers, he borrowed extensively from them. But his ardor for the fame of Germany and his credulity were proof against the critical example of his models. He is silent or ingenuous about events not favorable to Germany, and typically revealed his patriotism in contemptuous and bitter remarks about Frenchmen. When the French humanist, Gaguin, went to Germany to explain Charles VIII's marriage to Maximilian's fiancee, Anne of Brittany, Wimpfeling favored Gaguin with letters that bitterly attacked France.

Krantz. Contemporary with Wimpfeling was Albert Krantz (*ca.* 1450-1517), also a professor of theology, who devoted himself to the history of Saxony and of the Scandinavian world, which he came to know during his residence in the towns of the Hanseatic League. His *Saxonia* (published 1520) and *Metropolis,* a history of the churches established in Saxony by Charlemagne, attempt to follow the model of Biondo's *Italia illustrata. Vandalia* (pub. 1519), a history of the Wends on the eastern German seacoast, revealed the fanciful side of Krantz's philology. He identified the Wends with the Vandals, and thus extended the scope of his history from the Wendish lands to the African Vandal kingdom. This ingenious philology was not peculiar to Krantz, who was among the most learned and critical of the German historians. In his works, some of which he carried on to his own historical period and all of which he left incomplete, he used only older sources for his earlier history. He shared the patriotism of the humanists and was particularly bitter against the Italians, whom he accused of suppressing parts of Tacitus favorable to the Germans.

Aventinus. A similar but more controversial work was done for Bavaria by Johannes Thurmaier (called Aventinus after the Latinized name of his birthplace Abensberg). Aventinus (1477-1534) received the education of a humanist and planned to write in elegant Latin a *Germania Illustrata.* He never carried this project beyond an account of the earliest Germans. Between 1519 and 1521, as official Bavarian historiographer, he wrote *Annales ducum Boiariae* (to 1460), of which the complete text was not published until 1580. He became a Protestant and revealed an unrestrained hatred for the clergy. Between 1526 and 1533, he prepared a German version, *Bayerische Chronik* (to 1508), which was even more bitter against the clergy, and displayed a rare purism about the use of German. Aventinus was widely read and, in following the Italians, attempted, albeit rather carelessly, to give references for his narrative. In spite of his stylistic accomplishments and his erudition, his works do not bear comparison with his Italian models, Biondo and Bruni. The narrative of Bavarian history is often lost in his account of general German history, and the facts of Bavarian history are often transformed into fanciful heroic tales. Nor, apart from this, was his critical talent of a high order. He identified the Illyrians with the Bavarians and was, thus, able to pride himself on descent from Alexander the Great.

Celtes and the Pagan Extreme. In contemporary influence the greatest of the

German humanists was Conrad Celtes (1459-1508), who enjoyed the favor of Maximilian and was professor of rhetoric at Vienna. Celtes was keenly aware of living in an age of great possibilities. He is an interesting combination of humanist and patriot. Indeed, he aimed at a specifically German education to produce a German self-consciousness. In 1500 he published an edition of Tacitus' *Germania*. He travelled widely in Germany and formed circles of humanists, who devoted themselves to the patriotic, learned and anti-Roman tasks which Celtes favored. Celtes planned a *Germania illustrata*, but his own historical works are slight, apart from an edition of some medieval German plays. In his poetry, his *De situ et moribus Germaniae*,[6] for example, he celebrates the unconquered German people, their masculine pursuits—even the German voice has no womanish sound!—and advances one of his favorite ideas, that the barbarian Germans had their own culture and philosophy, akin to the philosophy of the Greeks. In his glorification of the primitive German past, Celtes reveals the anti-Christian tendency which appeared in some of the humanist patriots. The various written works of Celtes are much less important than his influence in forming humanist circles in Germany and in inspiring the humanists to patriotic historical labors.[7]

Beatus Rhenanus: Friend of Erasmus. The most impressive achievement of patriotic German humanist scholarship is the work of Beatus Rhenanus (1486-1547). Rhenanus, of Alsatian origin, was a friend and correspondent of Erasmus, and his own deep religious feeling kept him free from the extravagance of Celtes. He lived in Basel and Strasbourg during the years when those cities were the most active centers of Protestantism. His hope of writing a *Germania illustrata* produced only a book on early German history, *Rerum Germanicarum libri tres* (Basel, 1531). He recognized that the great work on all of Germany could be done only after scholars had worked on all the provinces of Germany. But as he pursued his studies he became convinced that in the field of early German history the whole job remained to be done. He travelled extensively to see remains and inscriptions and to check his identification of contemporary sites with towns mentioned on Roman itineraries. He rejected most of the mythical material on the German tribes. Nor was he hostile, as Wimpfeling and Celtes had been, to the classical writers. He described the early Germans as a barbarian and cultureless people, who had to be studied through the literary remains of the Romans. These barbarians had been free, although the period of Frankish dominance was a time of servitude, because the Franks had taken over Roman ways. Christianity removed German barbarism; and, with the free German empire of the Ottos came letters and civility. This account extends to the middle of book two. The remainder deals with problems of criticism and topography. In the course of the work he presented brief histories of Schlettstadt, his birthplace, and Basel.

---

[6] Celtes' poem is reprinted in the Strasbourg edition (1610) of the *Rerum Germanicarum* of Beatus Rhenanus, pp. 729-738.

[7] A valuable account of Celtes may be found in Willy Andreas, *Deutschland vor der Reformation*, pp. 67, 71, 143-144, 217. Dubravius, 1489-1553, Bishop of Olmutz, had been a student under Celtes at Vienna. The Bishop, who fought in the defense of Vienna against the Turks in 1529, was an antiquary and author of a *History of Bohemia*.

In general, his merits are his wide and careful learning and his critical habits of mind. Unfortunately, in the field of philology, though he was far less fanciful than most of his contemporaries, he was often wrong in his derivations. Like the other German humanists he never grappled with relatively modern German history; and this failure of the Germans resulted in their historical writing remaining more the sagas of a glorious past and the general treasury of moral examples than the teacher of political prudence.

FRENCH HUMANISM

Patriotic. French historical writing does not reveal the richness of Germany and produced no work comparable to the *Memoirs* of Commines, who was not a humanist. Jacques Lefevre d'Etaples, under strong Italian influence, sought to restore the text of Aristotle which, he believed, had been corrupted by the scholastic commentators. Like Colet and Erasmus, he devoted his biblical studies, especially on the Psalms and the Epistles of St. Paul, to establishing the texts and to a simple rendition of their meaning. Robert Gaguin (1433-1501) dreamed of securing royal support for his project of writing a humanist Latin history of France. He failed to receive royal support but did publish a *Compendium de Origine et gestis Francorum* (1495), a history which was humanist in style, but which hardly disturbed the legends and traditions of the *Grandes Chroniques*.

Paulus Aemilius: An Italian Master. The most finished piece of historical writing in France was the work of Paulus Aemilius of Verona.[8] In 1499, Louis XII commissioned him to write a history of the French monarchy. In his *Ten Books on the Deeds of the French,* Paulus surveyed the history of the French from their "Trojan beginnings" to the early years of the reign of Charles VIII. Not only the style, but the approach is humanist. He divided his material by reigns, and within this framework he frequently indicated a deeper comprehension of the course of events than the conventional division would promise. Making a courtly reservation he passed rapidly from the Trojan legend to the time of Clovis. In serving his royal masters he was rather anti-papal and Gallican. He quoted his sources rarely. As for the purpose of history, his views are conventional. A man should not be a stranger in his own country and history can make him familiar. From history, and particularly from the history of the ancient and most warlike Franks, a man learns to seek virtue, to be prudent, and to steel himself against the ravages of Fortune.

Pithou. The dissolution of the monasteries in Germany and England provided antiquaries with vast quantities of documents for the study of the past. One of the greatest French collectors was Pierre Pithou (1539-1596), whose interests and learning foreshadow the seventeenth century age of erudition in France. Trained in the law, Pithou was a *politique* and a vigorous defender of the Gallican Church's liberties. While pursuing his aim of publishing the sources of medieval history, he edited, among other works, the capitularies of Charlemagne, and the histories of Paul the Deacon and Otto of Freising.

---

[8] Pauli Aemylii Veronensis, *historici clarissimi de Rebus Gestis Francorum . . . libri Decem.*

ENGLISH HUMANISM

More and Hall. In England the humanist influences manifest many of the same tendencies found in France and Germany. St. Thomas More wrote a remarkably serene and well rounded *History of King Richard the Third.*[9] This lively vernacular biography assumes, in characteristic Tudor fashion, the monstrous evils of rebellion, but unlike the strident but equally lively Edward Hall's *The Union of the two Noble and Illustre Families of Lancastre and York* (1542), it recounts with artistic restraint the ills attendant upon the seeking of a throne by violence.

Polydore Vergil: An Italian Master. An admirably simple Latin style, a sense of form which caused the author to abandon the form of annals, and the broader perspective of a foreigner, characterize the *Historia Anglica* (1534) of Polydore Vergil of Urbino, an Italian cleric. Polydore Vergil, a famous humanist and author of a work on the inventors of the arts, was asked by Henry VII to write the history of England. After making diligent search for sources which in his day were still scattered in the monasteries and not generally known or accessible, Polydore wrote a history of England reign by reign. These labors engaged much of his time for nearly thirty years. Lacking written materials about the reigns of Henry VII and Henry VIII, "I betook myself to every man of age who was pointed out to me as having been formerly occupied in important and public affairs, and from all such I obtained information about the events up to the year 1500." For the later years he depended upon the notes of memorable events which he himself made for the years he was in England.[10]

Polydore was critical of the old monastic chronicles, and among them allowed the title of true history only to the works of William of Malmesbury and Matthew Paris. "I call those which were composed of old by monks who were wont to engage in such writing in English monasteries mere annals, and in such records bald statements of events are sometimes made inconsistent with other statements and not infrequently mingled with obvious errors. Reports of things that have taken place, as they were talked about on the highways, were noted down by the monks in their studies from the descriptions of travellers and from popular rumor which reached them."[11] Nonetheless, from these works, "so lacking in form and style that they really are like food without seasoning," and from the annals of England's neighbors, Polydore believed that he could get the material for a new history of England.[12]

The avowed purpose of Polydore's work was to write the history of England, so that oblivion would not crush the memory of "The great deeds of English kings and those of this noble people." Polydore is the proud artist, preserving man's knowledge of his past and contributing to man's moral education by recalling the glory of good men and the infamy of evil deeds. Unlike the more

---

[9] In *The English Works of Sir Thomas More,* ed. W. E. Campbell.
[10] F. A. Gasquet, "Some Materials for a new edition of Polydore Vergil's History," *Transactions of the Royal Historical Society,* New Series, XVI (London, 1902), p. 11; "Preface" to Book XXVII, *Polydori Vergilii Urbinatis Anglicae Historiae Libri Vigintiseptem,* p. 619.
[11] Gasquet, *op. cit.,* p. 3. Cardinal Gasquet's quotations are from a manuscript first draft of Polydore's history now in the Vatican.
[12] Polydore Vergil, *op. cit.,* "Letter of Dedication to Henry VIII."

provincial Edward Hall, who celebrated the security of the Tudor monarchy, Polydore saw in the centuries of his history a succession of strong governments disintegrating into anarchy and rebellion.[13]

Polydore's rejection of the fables of Goeffrey of Monmouth aroused the wrath of such patriotic antiquaries[14] as John Leland, and Tudor nationalism led even the classical scholar, Sir Henry Savile, to criticize the history as the work of a foreigner. But the work was enormously and justly popular. Parts of it in translation were incorporated into other English histories and provided English writers with a model of their own history, critically written and free of the constraining form of annals.

Patriotic Antiquarianism: Camden's Britannia. Antiquarianism became a veritable passion in England during the late sixteenth and early seventeenth centuries. Its greatest production in the form of *Italia illustrata* was William Camden's *Britannia* or a *Chorographical Description of Britain, Scotland, Ireland and the adjacent islands from the most remote antiquity.* The first edition, a small octavo volume (1586), gave place to five new editions during Camden's lifetime (1551-1623), so that the sixth edition (1607) was a monumental folio volume of 850 pages, several times translated, and edited as a useful survey of Britain as late as 1806.

Camden was of humble origin and earned his living as a teacher in Westminster School. His talents and amiability won for him the support of powerful men, including Lord Burghley, and the friendship of many of the great scholars of his time. By chorography, Camden meant a description of the location and physical features of a region, an account of the memorable events anciently and more recently associated with a region, and some indication of its peculiarities along with a record of its noble families. The scope of chorography, as Camden understood it, could be extended to anything that concerned Britain or that had happened in it, and strained philological derivations could support very far-ranging identifications, for Camden identified the Britons with the Cimbri and the latter, in turn, descended from Gomer, the grandson of Noah. Such a work was endless, and could have been finished at all only by a man of unusual ambition, endurance and will. Only the comparative formlessness of chorography could provide a form for his all-embracing patriotism.

HUMANIST CLASSICAL SCHOLARSHIP

Estienne and Lipsius. It is impossible to catalogue the various advances made by classical scholars in the sixteenth century. Some of the most important work was done by lexicographers. Robert Estienne (1503-1559) published a Greek edition of the *New Testament,* largely based on Erasmus. In 1532, he published a dictionary, *Thesaurus linguae latinae,* and Henri Estienne (1531-98), another member of this printing family, published in 1572 a Greek dictionary in five volumes. Justus Lipsius (1547-1606) was famous in his own time for

---

[13] *Idem:* also Gasquet, *op. cit.,* pp. 10-11, the translation and the editor's introduction, mentioned in note 1, are worth consulting.
[14] The phenomenon of patriotic antiquarianism connected with humanism was general. In Spain, for example, Elio Antonio de Lebrixa worked on the Antiquities of Spain. See M. Bataillon, *Erasme et L'Espagne,* p. 29.

his religious vacillations and for his great edition of Tacitus (first edition, 1575). This Belgian scholar systematically collated versions and ranged far into the history of antiquity to explain his text. His greatest historical work dealt with the Roman Army, although he had an antiquarian interest in the history of Brabant.

Scaliger. The effusive and self-admiring humanists justly exhausted their epithets on the French Huguenot scholar, Joseph Scaliger (1540-1606). He had a wide knowledge of languages, science and the classics. His editions of classical authors were remarkably dependable. But his greatest achievement was *De Emendatione Temporum* (1583), a work based on a deep knowledge of astronomy and astronomical systems, a work which charted the way for a sure framework of chronology. In it he explained the calendars of various peoples and after solving the problems of the various systems he assembled a collection of dates. In an important sequel, *Thesaurus Temporum* (1606), he reconstructed the chronological tables of Eusebius, thereby providing an invaluable basis for a correct chronology in ancient history.

Chapter 9

CHURCH HISTORY DURING THE PROTESTANT REFORMATION AND THE CATHOLIC REFORM

By Matthew A. Fitzsimons

THE REFORMATION AND HISTORICAL APOLOGETICS

THE Protestant Reformation involved a rejection of some of the doctrines and of the teaching authority of the Catholic Church. Against the authority of the pope and of the Council of Trent, the Protestants appealed to Scripture or to the history of the early Church. This appeal involved historical issues, and the great mass of Protestant historical writing aimed to demonstrate Protestant conformity with Scripture and the Fathers or to prove the perversion of Christ's teachings by papal usurpation. The Catholics replied by affirming the continuity of Church teaching from the times of Christ, and by insisting that the Scriptures and Church traditions were both valid sources of Christian belief. At the Council of Trent, Catholic doctrine was defined and the reform movement within the Church secured a vigorous renewal of discipline and morals. This Council stimulated the Catholic apologists to further historical writings against the Protestants, and itself proved to be a famous and controversial subject of history.

The Catholic renewal was paralleled by the development of an aggressive Protestantism, Calvinism, which also provided Protestants with a more systematic formulation of their beliefs. The religious change, in general, was tangled in politics, for it involved a serious change in the relationship of Church and temporal rules. Thus, a number of the histories of Church affairs in the sixteenth century may be as readily classed as political histories.

All of this historical apologetics is heatedly partisan and, often enough, quite uncritically partisan, for religious and political interest combined to command man's deepest loyalties. Later Protestant writers have been appalled by the bitterness of Catholic apologists much as Catholic writers have found the Protestant apologists equally offensive. Instead of such selective indignation it would be well if the contemporary conditions were kept in mind. In defending their religious beliefs Catholics and Protestants were defending doctrines believed to be divinely ordained. Where appeals were made to Scripture or to early Church traditions or to the traditions of the Universal Church, the authors had already taken a stand. Nor had they elaborate means of testing and criticizing documents. Often enough texts were tortured to prove a point, but the torturing was more the unconscious work of *parti pris* than deliberate distortion. In the minds of the contending parties truth was already established.

Where the literal rather than the historical meaning of a source was favorable, the literal was accepted. This was not sheer expediency, for controversialists were strongly influenced by habits of thought drawn from Scriptural exegesis or from the study of canon law. At any rate, where men defended absolute and eternal values, and readily saw the features of Anti-Christ beneath the mask of an opponent, where charity had fled from the Christian, it was hardly to be expected that scholarly dispassionateness would be prized. Fundamentally the Protestant was a heretic and enemy to the Catholic, and to the Protestant the Catholic was a supporter of a perverted Christianity.

THE INFLUENCE OF MELANCHTHON

In the course of his struggle Luther made use of some of the historical achievements of the humanists, notably Valla's work on the *Donation of Constantine* and the materials of the German humanists, and borrowed heavily from the invective imagery of such medieval opponents of the papacy as the Spiritual Franciscans. Luther himself composed a chronicle, *Supputatio* (1541), but his importance in the realm of historical studies is limited to the inspiration which he gave them. He was aware of the historical implications of his position and characteristically regretted in 1520 his failure to read in history and poetry and the time he had wasted on the inanities of the philosophers and the sophists.[1]

The Greek scholar, Philip Melanchthon (1497-1560), who became Luther's disciple, exercised the widest influence on German historical studies. Melanchthon was a teacher all his life and put his impress upon the curricula of German universities, where the first academic study of history took place. A nephew of Reuchlin, Melanchthon was acquainted with Hebrew, but his earliest interest and ambition was to prepare a new edition of Aristotle. His Greek and Hebrew studies reveal the influence of Erasmus and in his first lecture at Wittenberg (1518) Melanchthon developed an Erasmian view of European history. He described the decline of letters as beginning in the fifth century and, after a few sporadic revivals, the rebirth of the arts and letters in recent years. Indeed, in Melanchthon's mind the revival of letters and of evangelical truth became inextricably intermingled.

Apart from incidental references to historical matters, Melanchthon's main historical work was his rewriting of the *Chronicle* (1532) of Johannes Carion, a German work which he elaborately revised and translated into Latin (1558 & 1560). This universal chronicle, an historical textbook in Germany for some two hundred years, divided the history of the world into three ages of two thousand years each.[2] The first period extended from the creation and man's fall to the time of Abraham, and Melanchthon's exclusive source for this section is the Bible. For the next division man lived under the Law, and here Melanchthon used his extensive knowledge of classical authors to fill out his story. The last age, not yet finished, is the age of man under the Gospel.

---

[1] For Luther's historical knowledge see Ernst Schafer, *Luther as a Student of Church History* (in German).
[2] "Chronicon Carionis" (Latin), Vol. XII, columns 711-1094 in Bretschneider, Ed., *Corpus Reformatorum*.

Intermixed in this pattern is the historical succession of the Four Monarchies of Daniel's vision. Not that Melanchthon limited himself to the Four Monarchies, but he believed that there were only four whose extent merited the name—the Turks were only a pagan tyranny!

This *Chronicle* marks a turning away from secular humanist historical writing, for Melanchthon emphasized the role of God in history. There was, he said, a special need of history in the Church, for God wanted man to know His ways.[3] God preserves the kingdoms of this world, which in their turn should be the shepherds of the Church. In harmony with Lutheran views on Church and state, Melanchthon stressed the position of the temporal ruler and attacked papal usurpation. His political history is rather an account of the deeds of kings than a history of kingdoms. All kingdoms fall and God transfers power from one ruler to another. Melanchthon was also interested in the history of learning,[4] but here again his work is devoted to the achievements of individual great men. This emphasis on the individual was essential to a history conceived as a part of moral philosophy, as a treasury of examples and God's judgments. The *Chronicle* reveals the enormous learning of the author but there is no important critical advance in his work, for, though he used an astonishingly wide range of sources, his selection was often dictated by *parti pris* and sometimes by apparent caprice.

THE MAGDEBURG CENTURIES

The most sustained historical attack of the Lutheran Reformers was the work of Matthias Vlacich, Latinized as Flacius Illyricus (1520-1575) and his associates, the Magdeburg Centuriators. Flacius Illyricus, the vehement defender of Lutheran orthodoxy against Catholics and compromising Lutherans, was born in Venetian Istria, and early manifested a desire to enter the Franciscan Order. An uncle, sympathetic to Lutheranism, was responsible for sending him to Germany, where he studied at such German universities as Tübingen and Wittenberg. He was a precocious and prodigious scholar. In 1544 he became Professor of Hebrew at Wittenberg, but his bitter disagreements with Melanchthon caused his resignation in 1549. One of the occasions of their dispute was the Interim, a political, Erasmian attempt to end the religious divisions in Germany on a basis unacceptable to Catholics and Lutherans alike. Thereafter, Flacius went to the more orthodox Magdeburg, and from 1557 to 1561 he was a professor at Jena. His defense of Lutheran teachings there also caused him to attack the temporal authorities and forced him into a wandering life.

Flacius. Flacius was as indefatigable a collector of manuscripts as the humanists. His numerous works, as a rule only incidentally historical, reveal an extensive familiarity with the works not only of the past but of his own time. He was the friend and correspondent of Matthew Parker, Archbishop of Canterbury, to whom he wrote that the desire to defend the truth of the Protestant position and to overthrow the papal tyranny was the inspiration of his labors in Church history.[5] Indeed, only his boundless hatred for the papacy could have

---

[3] *Ibid.,* cols. 714, 721-722.
[4] *Ibid.,* cols. 787-788.

sustained him in his enormous labors,[6] and the demands of controversy caused the broadening of his erudition. Thus in 1550 and again in 1556 and 1557 he engaged in controversy with Catholics over the history of the Mass, and in the course of the controversy he drew upon a number of medieval chronicles and doctrinal works in addition to making a collection of liturgical texts. As early as 1552 he wrote to a friend about his efforts to get support for a Church history from the German princes. His preface to the *Catalogus testium veritatis* (1556) called for a history of the Church from the birth of Christ to his own times, a history which would reveal the persistence of pure doctrine and the extent of its corruption, a history which would be a treasury ready for all possible necessities. In his project he directed his associates, particularly Gallus, Judex and Wigand, to search for manuscripts and material for his work.[7]

The first volume of the work appeared in 1559 and the last volume, covering the thirteenth century, appeared in 1574. This was the only edition of the work in its original form, for though the work was important in the history of Protestant apologetics, it was not long used as a major work. As a history its very construction is dictated by its apologetic purpose. The division into centuries is some improvement over the annalistic form but no more than that. Each century in turn is divided into sixteen chapters and these divisions, especially chapter four (doctrine), chapter six (liturgy and ceremonies), chapter seven (government of the church) and chapter nine (synods), largely serve controversial purposes. Nonetheless, they take a very wide view of the history of the Church. Each century also attempted to deal with libraries and schools.[8] There are chapters on religions outside the Church, and this also affords an opportunity to compare the Pope with Mohammed.[9] Like Melanchthon, the authors argue that the more men are delighted by accounts of the great deeds of the pagans, the more should they be delighted by Church history with its account of the ways of God.[10]

The great merit of the work is its revelation of vast masses of source material. As a rule a source is accepted if favorable to the book's thesis. If source material is favorable to the papacy, it may be subjected to highly critical and sometimes fruitful scrutiny. The thesis of the work is the warfare between good and evil, between evangelical truth and the intrigues of Anti-Christ. Decay in the purity of religious belief is seen as early as the second century.[11] and by the seventh century the truly faithful are not so numerous. In the dedication of the *Tenth Century* to Adolph Riedesel, they noted, "It is not to

[5] *Correspondence of Matthew Parker*, edited for the Parker Society by Bruce and Perowne, pp. 139-140.
[6] Emil Menke Gluckert, *The Historical Writing of the Reformation and the Counter Reformation* (in German).
[7] These were "the several laborious and pious men in the city of Magdeburg" referred to on the title page, which gives the title as *Ecclesiastica Historia . . . secundum singulas centurias*.
[8] *Ecclesiastical History, First Century*, (in Latin), ch VII.
[9] *Seventh Century*, ch. XV, columns 595-596, and in the *Thirteenth Century*, "Dedication" a2.
[10] *First Century*, ch. XVI.
[11] *Second Century*, "Dedication to John Frederick II of Saxony," pp. aa2v and aa3. They also noted that no doctrine was obscured so quickly as that on free will. They gave four main reasons for departure from true doctrine: (1) an excessive love of human writings and commentaries, (2) the pope's authority, (3) the multiplication of indifferent, but also unscriptural practices, (4) the oppression of those who thought and felt righteously. *Ninth Century*, (Basel, no date), "Dedication." a3.

be doubted that the Church of God existed in the tenth century but it is exceedingly difficult to say which it is and where it is."[12]

THE COMMENTARIES OF SLEIDANUS

The works of Melanchthon and Flacius are strongly influenced by their theological interests and apologetic purposes. The most famous account of events in Germany during the careers of Luther and Charles V is the work of Johann Philippi (1507-1556) of Schleiden (his name was latinized as Sleidanus), a humanist-trained diplomat. Sleidanus was associated with some of the most important events in the political development of the German Reformation. A friend of Johannes Sturm, the Strasbourg educator, in 1536 he succeeded to Sturm's position as secretary to Cardinal Jean du Bellay in correspondence with the German Protestant forces. While in this key position Sleidanus translated Froissart into Latin and, later, at Strasbourg did the same for Commines' *Memoirs*. In his dedications he expressed the belief that his was a century of wonderful and significant events and uttered the hope that the memory of such wonders should not be lost for lack of a historian. The hope was a formulation of his own ambition.[13] He left the French service in which he had had the chance of becoming acquainted with the currents of French and German politics, and settled in Strasbourg, where in 1545 he joyously and confidently began his laborious work. The busy, strategically located city was a valuable place for securing news and documents. By the fall of 1547 he had brought his story in four books up to 1525. With the outbreak of the last desperate war for the Protestant cause he had to leave his work and did not resume it until 1552 when the German religious wars had all but ended. He finished his history in 1555, covering the events in Germany to that very year in twenty-five books. His death occurred the next year.

Sleidanus, following the example of Caesar, called his history, *Commentaries-Commentariorum de statu religionis et reipublicae, Carolo V. caesare, libri XXV*—and in their bald narrative they are reminiscent of Caesar. But Sleidanus' work is more important than readable. He aimed to present a true account of his age of religious change, and his history abounds in documents and summaries of documents.[14] His presentation of sources as a guarantee of impartiality is a notable advance. But the annalistic form of the history destroys almost all narrative interest. Sleidanus was industrious in collecting sources but he had no vision of continuity to enable him to organize his material.

He began with the year 1517 and proceeded through the years when Luther broke with the Catholic Church, but he offered no intelligible picture of the sweep and revolutionary changes of those years. In every age God

---

[12] *Tenth Century*, "Dedication," a2v.
[13] "The recital of those things, which approach nearest our own times, have more force and efficacy both to informe our Judgments and delight our Fancies." This is from Sleidanus' Dedicatory Letter to an English translation of *The History of Philip de Commines*, 3rd edition.
[14] For true history and profitable "The councils and designs of those who manage affairs" must "be clearly demonstrated in their true colours." "There is hardly one that takes upon him to write a History, who doth declare the designs and councils of those concerning whom he treateth in such terms and clearness as he ought to do." *Ibid.*

raises up great princes, when religion or the commonwealth is to be changed. The alteration in his own time is all the more remarkable, "for the beginning was ful small, and in manner to be contemned, and one man alone susteined the malice and violence of all the world." [15] Rarely, however, did the author achieve such heights, for he declared his intention as follows: "All these things I recite plainly, simply, and truely as everye thing was done: neither use I also any collour of Rhetorick, nor write anything in the hatred or favor of any man . . . . . I frame my stile only, and use mine own words, that the speache may be alwaies like and equal, and I bestowe eche thing in his place, as they followed in order."

He was familiar with Luther's writings but did not appreciate the importance of the Reformation writings of 1520 and 1521. These criticisms are made in conscious reaction against the prevalent tendency to overpraise the *Commentaries*. Sleidanus attempted to present the story as he knew it, but the result of his labors is a rather highly selected brief for the Protestant cause. This comparison is not capricious, for he was a trained jurist and his work served as a source for later German lawyers.

Sleidanus' history, then, is important for its advance in method, and, as with many advances in method, it has been uncritically praised. A noteworthy point is that it was the Reformation rather than humanist patriotism which produced the first major contemporary history of sixteenth century German affairs.

Controversy Extends the Fields of Study

The necessity of defending the Protestant settlement of religion in England inspired a considerable widening of historical studies. Matthew Parker, Elizabeth's Archbishop of Canterbury, sponsored Anglo-Saxon studies in his apologetic work. "We be careful to reedify a decayed temple." In harmony with Flacius Illyricus, he believed that the tyranny of the popes and the obscuring of truth could be shown in the actual history of the Church. With the help of his secretary and fellow student, John Joscelyn, he published in 1567 the first book printed in Anglo-Saxon, *A Testimony of Antiquitie,* which argued that true doctrine may be found in the sermons of former ages, and presented some of the homilies of Alefric.[16]

Another Protestant apologist was the vitriolic John Bale (1495-1563), who compiled catalogues of English writers and a vigorous *Lives of the Popes,* mainly variations on the theme that the Papacy represented Anti-Christ.

John Foxe. Possibly the most important English Church history, in terms of popular influence, is John Foxe's *Book of Martyrs.* John Foxe (1516-1587) began this work as a Latin treatise, *A Narrative of Events within the Church* (Basel, 1559). His purpose was to demonstrate that not the Protestants but the Catholics were "new nothings." Upon the accession of Elizabeth he returned to

---

[15] From the Dedication to Prince Augustus of Saxony in John Day's translation, *A Famous Chronicle of oure time, called Sleidanes Commentaries.*
[16] The earlier quotation occurs in a letter of Parker to Cecil, in *Correspondence of Matthew Parker,* edited for the Parker Society by Bruce and Perowne, p. 147; cf. Eleanor N. Adams, *Old English Scholarship in England from 1566-1800,* p. 23. The influence of the Reformation on the study of vernacular and national languages is well known through the translations of Luther and Calvin.

England and, indignant at Mary Tudor's persecutions, added enormously to his original work, which was issued in 1563 as *Acts and Monuments*. It is a bitter and highly partisan volume, inaccurate in details but impressive for its research in such sources as bishops' registers and narrative accounts by friends of Mary's victims. Like Flacius Illyricus, he wished to show the continuity of true believers through the ages. In typical Tudor fashion he criticized the popes as promoters of political sedition. Among his martyrs and heroes are King John and Henry IV of Canossa fame, for martyrdom is a matter of the cause and not the punishment. "One Cranmer is worth six hundred Beckets." [17] The book gained poignancy from its author's closeness to many of the events he described, and from his grim urging to his readers to be worthy of these sacrifices and to be ready to imitate them.[18]

English historical apologetics in general was concerned with a wider field of history than earlier Calvinist writing usually was, for the Elizabethan religious settlement did not and could not appeal to Scripture alone as the Calvinists had done. The intimate and indissoluble commonwealth of Church and state, which Richard Hooker defended in *The Laws of Ecclesiastical Polity*, was concretely embodied in the Elizabethan Society of Antiquaries. The members later included Archbishop Whitgift, Lord Burghley and William Camden. Though the antiquaries largely limited themselves to political subjects, these subjects themselves were full of implications about the sphere of Church and state.[19] The mistrust of James I caused the Society to suspend its meetings in 1604. Religious and political controversy, however, compelled James to look for a similar instrument.[20] In 1609, Matthew Sutcliffe, Dean of Exeter, with royal approval planned to establish a College at Chelsea on the Thames. There, seventeen theologians and two historians were to prepare arguments against the Catholic controversialists, especially Jesuits.

When the assassination of Henry IV in 1610 made the future status and support of Isaac Casaubon (1559-1614) uncertain, that great scholar was invited to England, where he was provided with a pension of £300 and was "to be used as we shall see cause for the service of the Church." [21] Casaubon had taught at Geneva and had found many friends in France. His learned reputation was almost legendary, and his editions of Athenaeus and Polybius were universally admired. His interest in Church history separated him from the Calvinists and made the Anglican Church more congenial to him. In England he was used more for controversial purposes, and, instead of writing a Church history, he projected a series of criticisms of the *Ecclesiastical Annals* of Cardinal Baronius. He proposed to follow Baronius volume by volume but covered only one-half of the first volume of Baronius in 800 pages with his *Exercitationes*

---

[17] Quoted by J. F. Mozley, *John Foxe and His Book*, p. 134.

[18] A work which was a model for Foxe, was *The Book of Martyrs . . . From the Time of John Huss to the Present* (1554) by the Frenchman, Jean Crespin. It is based on a very wide range of sources and is written with deep feeling.

[19] Fitzsimons, "Politics and Men of Learning in England, 1540-1640," *Review of Politics*, VI (1944), 460-464; Butterfield, *The Englishman and His History*, pp. 31-33.

[20] For some of these arguments, see C. H. McIlwain's "Introduction" to *The Political Works of James I*, pp. XV-CXI; also E. A. Ryan, S. J., *The Historical Scholarship of Bellarmine*.

[21] Mark Pattison, *Isaac Casaubon*, p. 318.

in Baronium, which, on its completion in 1614, was rushed to the Frankfurt Book Fair.

THE ANNALS OF CARDINAL BARONIUS

From the beginning of the Reformation, Catholic controversialists had been busy replying to their adversaries. Implicit in all their arguments was the belief that the Church had always been the same and that its doctrine had not changed. In the first half of the sixteenth century the Church had gained notably in vigor through the founding of new religious orders and the reform of older orders. Apart from the Jesuits, one of the most notable of these orders was the Oratorians, an association of secular priests living according to a religious rule. In their preaching these followers of St. Philip Neri (1515-1595) stressed practical subjects,—the lives of the saints and Church history. This preoccupation and the prominence of the Oratorians at Rome and in Italy made it fitting that one of their number, Caesar Baronius, should have undertaken the task of replying to the Magdeburg Centuriators with a history of the Catholic Church from the birth of Christ.

Baronius (1538-1607) was born at Sora near Naples, and after studies in philosophy, theology and law, he joined the Oratorians at the age of 19. St. Philip Neri, his religious superior, directed him to the study of Church history. Baronius pursued his studies as a matter of religious obedience, and was compelled to lecture and work through the course of Church history seven different times for over thirty years before he published his first volume.[22] He had advantages over the Centuriators in that he had access to the vast resources of the Vatican collections and that he had the support of the wealth and numbers of the Catholic Church. But his labors were colossal. He worked by himself, doing his own note-taking, and even his humility and selfless devotion did not deter him from speaking of his labors as a painful and difficult journey in which he was sustained by God's help.[23] Casaubon's biographer, Mark Pattison, wrote: "Perhaps no modern historian, not Gibbon or Grote, ever devoted the whole of a life so entirely to one historical work, or made such a noviciate." [24]

Baronius' volumes were read long after modern critical methods had developed, and his work, therefore, has been more searchingly examined than the *Magdeburg Centuries.* Under the spell of this criticism the originality of Baronius' investigation and his pioneering in sources have not received their proper credit. As librarian at the Vatican, Baronius was the first to use a staggering range of material. The purpose of his *Annals* was to enable the reader to perceive that "the Catholic faith had always been one and the same, the one Church had always continued the same, though it had been troubled by the changes of events and times." [25] Impelled by this motive, Baronius, as a rule, supported the claims of the Church against the temporal powers, for example, in Germany and in Henry II's quarrel with St. Thomas à Becket. Indeed, Philip III of Spain was offended by Baronius' rejection of Spanish claims to Sicily as a papal fief. Each

---

[22] Baronius described this labor in the Dedication of the first volume to Pope Sixtus V and under the year 57. *Annales Ecclesiastici,* vol. I, p. 555.
[23] *Ibid.,* p. 3.
[24] Pattison, *op. cit.,* p. 364.
[25] *Annales Ecclesiastici,* vol. III, "Preface to the Pious Reader, Eager for Truth."

volume was not uniformly devoted to a century. The first covered the first century, the second concluded at 305, but it took the author three more volumes to reach the year 440. Each was dedicated to a pope or an emperor or king. The ninth volume (1600) was presented to Henry IV of France.

In writing "against the innovators of our time and in behalf of the antiquity of sacred traditions and of the power of the Catholic Church" [26] he chose the form of annals. He explained his choice by noting that in ancient times history was a term used to describe events which the author experienced and about which he offered reflections. The form of annals called for a less ornate style, such as Baronius preferred, and imposed on him the necessity of placing every event in its temporal order.[27] But there was in this choice an act of faith that the whole range of human events would support the validity of the Catholic Church. Nonetheless, the choice of form was unfortunate, for the bulk of Baronius' mistakes were wrong dates. Where he himself was doubtful, his form still compelled him to assign a specific date to everything. Other mistakes arose from his inadequate knowledge of Greek. Besides, Baronius' critical powers were not of the highest order, even though he remarked in his Dedication of the first volume that nothing is more dangerous in historical writing than to trust another author on any matter.

OPPOSITION TO TRIDENTINE REFORM: SARPI

Baronius is a typical figure of the Catholic Reform period. Paolo Sarpi (1552-1623), a Venetian historian of the Council of Trent, is a more puzzling figure, who, however, has been more appreciated by modern writers. The reasons for this are numerous, though the most important are the liveliness of his style, his wit, intelligence and his exceedingly critical attitude toward the Council of Trent. At an early age Sarpi entered the order of Servite friars and while quite young revealed remarkable talents. He was trained in theology and canon law, and was interested in such subjects as chemistry and anatomy. For a short period he was associated with Charles Borromeo of Milan. By the time he was 27 years old, he had become Provincial of his order and a later promotion compelled him to reside at Rome for three years. Quarrels in his own order embittered him against Roman intervention, but he was also suspect in the eyes of Church authorities because of his intimacy with Protestants.

In 1606 a long dispute between the Pope and the Republic of Venice came to a head when Pope Paul V imposed an interdict on the Republic. Sarpi, who lived the ascetic life of a friar, advised the Venetian authorities to disregard the ban. This was a characteristic action, for Sarpi was certainly hostile to the authority claimed by the popes and equally hostile to the spirit of the Catholic Reform with its carefully defined doctrine and rigorous discipline. During the course of the quarrel an attempt to assassinate Sarpi was made. Sarpi was eager to continue the fight and resented the conciliatory efforts of Henry IV. During these years Sarpi wrote his *History of the Council of Trent,* which was first printed in London in 1619. Naturally, the English Protestants welcomed the

[26] *Ibid.,* vol. I, "Dedication to Sixtus V."
[27] *Ibid.,* vol. I, "Preface," pp. 1-7.

book, and understandably enough the suspicion of Fra Paolo's Catholic orthodoxy increased.

Sarpi indicated that from his youth he had been interested in the Council of Trent and had for many years collected material from the writings, registers and oral testimony of its principal actors. To him, the Council represented the final and entirely unwanted consolidation of papal power. In place of reformation there had been deformation, and the schism of Christendom had not been healed but overwhelmingly confirmed. This great Council, the Iliad of his age as he called it,[28] had been long desired by some and frequently hindered by others, and "hath gotten a forme and conclusion contrary altogether to the designe of them that procured it, and to the feare of those, that with all diligence disturbed it, a cleere instruction for us to referre our selves to God, and not to trust in the wisedome of man." [29]

In his almost Erasmian dislike of the precise definition of doctrine and of doctrinal quarrels he could be very satirical. "Those that were read in the Ecclesiastical Story sayd that in all the Councels, held in the Church, from the Apostles time untill now, there were never so many Articles decided, as in this Session onely (to 1547); in which Aristotle had a great part, by having exactly distinguished all the kindes of causes, which if hee had not done, wee had wanted many Articles of Faith." [30] He further suggested that the papacy and the Council spent so much time on doctrinal matters in order to avoid disciplinary reform. "The Court of Rome, who stood all amazed at the very name of reformation, was well pleased to heare that the Councell entertained it selfe in preambles, hoping that time would bring foorth some remedie." [31] The death of Luther in 1546, he noted, caused rejoicings at Rome and Trent, for there Luther was considered as almost the total cause of all "the divisions and innovations introduced." "But those things that happened afterwards, even untill our age, have declared that Martin was onely one of the meanes, and that the causes were more potent and secret." [32] He sharply criticized the Council's reforming efforts as inadequate. "For to trust in God and the Pope that provision should be made of persons worthy to governe the Churches, belongeth rather to him that prayeth, then to him that reformeth. To renew the ancient Canons with one word onely, and one so generally was more to confirme the disuse of them." [33]

Sarpi's fame has remained considerable to our own day, and his talents certainly justify this fame. But secular historians have uncritically admired Sarpi's interpretation of Trent as a power struggle. Sarpi's history is witty and makes many telling points, but it missed the main achievement of the Council, that it reformed and reinvigorated the Church.[34]

---

[28] *The Historie of the Council of Trent,* translated by N. Brent, p. 2. The work originally was attributed to Pietro Soave Polano, an anagram of Sarpi's name.
[29] *Ibid.,* p. 1.
[30] *Ibid.,* p. 228.
[31] *Ibid.,* p. 148.
[32] *Ibid.,* p. 149.
[33] *Ibid.,* p. 229.
[34] The popularity of Sarpi's work, which was quickly published in Latin at London and Geneva, caused the Catholic authorities to prepare a reply. The task was entrusted to the Jesuis and carried out by Sforza Pallavicino (1607-1667), who completed Alciati's unfinished labors. Pallavicino's *History of the Council of Trent* (2 vols.) in Italian is less a formal history than an attempted refutation of Sarpi. The work is not as readable as Sarpi's but it has value for presenting more fully the concrete difficulties of the Council which ultimately make the critical position of Sarpi appear to be that of an idealist, indifferent to doctrine, and eager for a reformation beyond the powers of earthbound man.

THE BOLLANDISTS

This reform took its special shape in the Habsburg German lands, in the Spanish Netherlands and in France. Characteristically, Church historical scholarship achieved its most spectacular triumphs in the cooperative labors of the religious orders, notably the Jesuits and the Benedictines. The former, who played a great role in historical apologetics, sponsored the vast and as yet unfinished labors of studying the lives of the saints. The beginning of this project goes back to Father Herbert Rosweyde (1569-1629), who had been struck by the number of apocryphal stories in the accounts of the saints. He proposed in 1603 that he was willing to undertake a search through the hagiographical manuscripts of Belgium in order to present an historical *Acta sanctorum*. In the course of his work he edited a *Lives of the Fathers* (1615). Upon his death his material was made available to Father John Bollandus, from whom the group has been called the Bollandists. Bollandus (1596-1665) made Antwerp the seat of his labors and was fortunate to coopt for his labors Father Godfrey Henschenius, and Father Daniel Papebroche, who was the keenest and most industrious of the Bollandists. At first, the authors were rather sanguine and drastically underestimated the burden of their task. Originally, they had planned to edit the old manuscript lives of the saints with notes and general introductions. In the hands of Henschenius the plan was changed and Bollandus and Henschenius actually reworked their volume on the saints whose feasts occur in January, for their new plan called for a complete and fresh presentation of the lives of the saints. It should be noted that the division of the work was dictated by the Church's calendar and, thus, the authors could not specialize in a particular century but had to range over the ages. The first two volumes, dealing with January, were published in 1643 and fifteen years later the three volumes of February appeared. By 1688 the work had been completed to the end of May. These labors opened up tremendous vistas in medieval history, for the lives of the saints provided valuable source material, and promoted great advances in the critical handling of medieval documents, for the ambitious plans of the Bollandists compelled the authors to examine Merovingian charters, to be mistrustful of Spanish chronicles and the lives of Irish saints, etc.[35]

THE MAURISTS

In France, as in England, the seventeenth century witnessed a searching study of medieval history. For Church history French historical scholarship was particularly indebted to the efforts of the congregation of St. Maur to restore Benedictine scholarship to its former glories. These efforts are a characteristic part of the culture of the time, for just as Baroque Art frequently served the purpose of expressing specifically Catholic practices and piety, so the scholarship of the Maurists was dedicated to revealing the riches of medieval monasticism and the sanctity of the Benedictine Order. Among the Maurists the greatest names were Luc d'Achery (1609-1685) and his disciple, Jean Mabillon (1632-

---

[35] The work of the Bollandists was interrupted by the dissolution of the Jesuit Order in 1773, and even more seriously by the French Revolutionary Wars, and was resumed in 1837. See Hippolyte Delehaye, S. J., *The Work of the Bollandists*, pp. 7-56.

1707). When the former became librarian of Saint-Germain-des-Pres, he compiled an inventory of it, and subsequently edited the works of Lanfranc (1648) and Guibert (1651). Between 1655 and 1677, d'Achery edited in thirteen volumes his *Spicilegium Veterum aliquot scriptorum,* a critically treated collection of medieval documents. In his later years d'Achery was aided in his labors by Mabillon, an ascetic and zealous monk, who is as justly noted for his critical powers as for his industry. Among Mabillon's contributions to this age of erudition were *The Acts of the Benedictine Saints* (9 vols., 1669-1701), which goes from the sixth to the end of the eleventh centuries, and the *Annals of the Benedictine Order* (6 vols., 1703-1739). These works, written in an exquisite Latin style, are contributions of a highly critical talent to the study of the Middle Ages. But Mabillon is most famous for his *Six Books on Diplomatics* (in Latin, Paris, 1681), a scientific formulation of the principles of diplomatics, the study of ancient documents and charters. This work was the unusual and effective Benedictine reply to the Bollandist's questioning of the Merovingian charters of the Abbey of Saint Denis. Mabillon's reply sketched the operations of his science, the study of seals, forms, language, handwriting, paper and ink. The Bollandist, Father Papebroche, gave in completely. "The only satisfaction to be derived from having written on the subject is that it has been the occasion for the production of such an admirable work as yours." Mabillon replied: "Far from being proud of my success, I would prefer to be the writer of your letter, so full of humility, than to entertain any vain glory for my own work." [36]

Mabillon also wrote an impressive defense of monastic studies against Trappist criticism, and at St. Germain he participated in regular meetings with the greatest French medieval scholars.[37] In this group was Sebastian Le Nain de Tillemont (1637-1698), an indefatigable, accurate and modest student of Roman Imperial and early Church history. Tillemont was associated with the Jansenists at Port Royal and after its dissolution he retired to uninterrupted labors at his own home. He is a particularly good example of the erudite scholar of this age, whose research provided materials for the more brilliant and, sometimes, less industrious scholars of the eighteenth century. Tillemont's *History of the Emperors* (6 vols., 1690-1738) and *Memoirs on Church History of the First Six Centuries* (16 vols., 1693-1712) provided a guide to Edward Gibbon. In his *Memoirs* he wrote that he would use the talents God gave him and would, therefore, write not a history but a presentation of "the complete and simple truth of what has passed in the Church's first centuries." "He is content to seek for the truth of events; and provided that the truth is found, he does not fear the abuse of it: being certain that the truth can not be contrary to the truth, nor, as a result, to piety, which should be based on truth."[38]

THE CHURCH HISTORY OF ENGLAND: BURNET

In England a similar, though less fruitful, advance took place in the study

---

[36] *Ibid.,* p. 35.
[37] This group included the Maurist, Bernard de Montfaucon (1655-1741), a great student of antiquity, author of a basic work on Greek palaeography (1708), and editor of Athanasius, Origin and Chrysostom, and Du Cange.
[38] Tillemont, *Mémoires pour servir a l'histoire ecclesiastique,* Vol. I, viii-ix, and xiii.

of medieval Church history. Sir Henry Spelman (1564-1641) began an edition of the decrees of the Councils of the British Church, a work which was continued by David Wilkins. In general, the English medievalists were strong Anglicans and sought to establish the continuity of the Anglican with the medieval and early Church. James Ussher (1581-1656), Archbishop of Armagh, and compiler of a long-used system of Scriptural chronology which dated the year of the creation as 4004 B. C., was an able controversialist and prodigious worker. His work in history was strongly motivated by his recognition that the Catholics believed in the continuity of their Church.[39] Against this view Ussher wrote a *Discourse of the Religion Anciently Practiced by the Irish* (1623) and *Antiquities of the British Churches* (1639). Typical of his labors is the fact that he collated eleven manuscripts of Nennius' *Historia Britonum,* and that he worked in fields as far apart as Anglo-Saxon, Hebrew and Arabic. His thesis is rather in the grand line of Flacius and John Foxe. All these achievements of medieval scholarship were for a time abandoned in the eighteenth century.

This abandonment is portended in the attitude of Gilbert Burnet (1643-1715) toward medieval studies. Burnet, of Scottish origin, wrote a number of biographies and a *History of His Own Time.* In the field of Church history he essayed a *History of the Reformation* (3 vols., 1679, 1681 and 1714). This work is notable for its presentation of documentary source material in appendices. Burnet was fortunate in the time of publication of his first volume, for it appeared in the midst of the religious frenzy attending the Popish Plot. The author had industriously collected material, though he had difficulty in securing the use of Robert Cotton's library. On the strength of his success with the first volume, he advertised in the *London Gazette* for copies of English Reformation documents.[40] As an ardent Low Church Protestant, Burnet was a warm defender of the Reformation and this warmth as well as his hasty and careless copying of documents made him very inaccurate in details. Moreover, Burnet was not interested in the general subject of Church history, and in reply to a critic, Henry Wharton, he wrote: "The barbarous stile, the mixture of so much Fable, the great want of Judgement that runs thro' the Writings of the Monks has so disgusted me at their Works that I confess I could never bring myself to read them with Pleasure. If any one that has more Patience than I, can think it worth the while to search into that Rubbish, let him . . . have the Glory of it for his Pains."[41]

To Burnet the Reformation was a great movement of restoration of truth, of elimination of superstition and of the return of a proper order in Church and state. This history was a meditation on the Providence of God, in which it was revealed that God made use of even apparently unworthy agents for his ends. Such an approach permitted Burnet to present the weaknesses of the Reformers, although he has a rather simplified account of what happened.

---

[39] *The Works of Ussher,* edited by C. R. Elrington, Vol. I, 57.

[40] In his Preface he said that he published the first volume in the hope that people would communicate material to him. *The History of the Reformation of the Church of England,* ed. Rev. E. Nares, I, xxxv.

[41] Quoted in David C. Douglas, *English Scholars,* p. 192.

Central to his view is the importance of the invention of printing and the simultaneous revival of learning, which involved considerable anti-clericalism because the monks held all the benefices and discouraged the new learning as a nursery of heresy. "And the corruptions of their worship and doctrine were such, that a very small proportion of common sense, with but an overly looking on the New Testament, discovered them."[42]

BOSSUET

The work of Burnet, who became Bishop of Salisbury after the Glorious Revolution, served the controversial purposes of Jacques Benigne Bossuet (1627-1704), the French Bishop of Meaux. Bossuet wrote his *History of the Variations of the Protestant Churches* (1688) to convince the Protestants of the falsity of their beliefs. The author began with the statement that variations in faith are signs of falsehood and proceeded to narrate the variations and inconsistencies of their various confessions of faith and to note the "many subtleties, evasions, and equivocations" by which they labored to repair the divisions of "their disjointed reformation."[43] The instability of Protestantism, according to Bossuet, arising from the human love of novelty and the lack of authority, will drive the Protestants to ever more numerous divisions. His work is a polemic, but a polemic based on a considerable and careful use of the writings of Protestants and their confessions of faith.

In Burnet and Bossuet the respective positions of the Protestants and Catholics are expressed after more than a century and a half of Protestantism. Both men agreed in their belief in providence, and Bossuet gave wonderfully eloquent form to this belief in his *Discourse on Universal History* (1681) written for the education of the Dauphin. This *Discourse* goes from the Creation to the empire of Charlemagne, which, he believed, marked the end of the ancient World. He contrasted his universal history to national histories and compared his own to a general map on which the various countries could be located. "He it is who prepares effects in the remotest causes, and he it is who strikes those great strokes, the counter-stroke whereof is of such extensive consequence. When he means to let loose the latter, and to overturn empires, their counsels are weak and irregular . . . God sets right, when he pleases, the bewildered judgement, and he who insulted over the blindness of others, falls oftentimes into thicker darkness himself, without there needing any thing else to turn his head, than his long course of prosperity. Thus it is that God rules over all nations."[44] In his famous sermon on Providence, Bossuet argued that the freethinker denied providence because he does not see things from their proper point. This point was faith, and, unfortunately, while Bossuet defended Catholic orthodoxy, there was arising a generation many of whose leaders differed not about doctrine but actually denied the truth of Revelation and the whole content of Christian religious belief.

[42] Burnet, *op. cit.*, I, pp. 35, 49.
[43] *The History of the Variations of the Protestant Churches*, Vol. I, 1.
[44] *A Universal History*, p. 516.

Chapter 10

POLITICAL HISTORIES AND MEMOIRS IN THE SEVENTEENTH CENTURY

By Matthew A. Fitzsimons

CHARACTERISTICS OF HISTORIOGRAPHY AND CURRENTS OF THE AGE.

THE secular historical writing of the seventeenth century cannot be described in the comparatively simple terms used to characterize humanist historiography. The patriotic and religious concerns of the humanists persist but in new forms related to the national monarchies, the Protestant Churches and the post-Trent Catholic Church. The age was more notable for its collections than for its finished histories, although the work of amassing and editing documents was accompanied by an important advance in critical technique, which reveals itself in the writing of church and secular history. History, especially popular history, was still philosophy teaching by example, but its pragmatic value as a teacher of prudence was more and more emphasized beginning in the first half of the century. While the Bollandists and Maurists extended the range of medieval studies in France and the Spanish Netherlands, a host of antiquaries and scholars did the same work for England, Italy, Denmark, Sweden, and to a lesser extent, Germany. A greater awareness of human partisanship made the reading public, notably in England, welcome collections of documents on contemporary history. Interest in types and persons stimulated the writing of biographies, and the memoir is one of the most characteristic literary forms of the century. In biography, the age saw both the attempt to generalize a person into a type, for example, Izaak Walton's *Lives* of Hooker, Donne, Wotton, etc., and the prying curiosity about the individual of John Aubrey in his *Lives*. The memorialists drew their inspiration from a desire to justify themselves, a motive capable of the infinite variations of human vanity itself. Indeed, apart from the documented histories or collections, nearly all the major historical works of this century, are memorialist in form.

French Culture. The last point may properly suggest that the seventeenth century historians were peculiarly aware of the importance of contemporary events. In France the religious wars ended in the settlement of Henry IV, which upon his assassination was followed first by the weakness of the Regency and then by the absolutist architecture of Richelieu. The protests against the royal power in the Fronde, 1649-1652, failed but produced a spate of memoirs. Richelieu's intervention in the Thirty Years' War prepared for French predominance and the Reign of Louis XIV saw French culture enjoying a European eminence which exceeded the power of the Sun King. This culture, in harmony with its political setting, expressed itself in the veneration of regularity, clarity and order, ideals which were fostered by classical humanism, the Catholic Church and Cartesianism.

Italy remained divided, though the nationalist vision of Italian unity did not disappear. Germany suffered the anguish of the Thirty Years' War, whose end in practice ratified the sovereignty of the princely states. Twice in the century, Sweden produced meteors: Gustavus Adolphus, whose spectacular Protestant crusade was abruptly cut short by death, and Charles XII, an insensitive, single-minded warrior, whose blazing ambitions were first smothered in the Ukrainian plains and caused the impoverishment of his nation. This Swedish defeat was an incident in the rousing of Russia under Peter the Great.

While Spain declined to become the victim of a war over the succession to its throne, the Dutch founded an empire, gained their independence, fought grimly against the designs of Louis XIV, and against their English rivals in trade and empire, and, in providing a king to the English, joined their rivals in two coalitions against the French. This Glorious Revolution was the culmination of a century of strain in British institutions. King and parliament, wrangling over religious, economic, social and legal policies, finally resorted to Civil War. Parliament, able to draw on most of the resources of England, won, but lost its victory to the army it had created. Oliver Cromwell, commander of the army, struggled to make a revolutionary government acceptable to conservative Englishmen but his efforts were cut short by his death in 1658. The monarchy was restored, but some of the old difficulties continued, and when the lazy but pliable Charles II was succeeded by the Catholic James II (1685-88), who had the political qualities of a negative genius, James soon fled, to be aptly described in his exile by Mme de Sevigne: "When one listens to him one realizes why he is here." The Revolutionary settlements and subsequent developments established parliamentary supremacy at the very time when England was to achieve a preponderance of wealth and power comparable to France.

In the intellectual sphere, the seventeenth century saw the continuation of the work of Kepler and Galileo and its overpowering synthesis in the *Principia Mathematica* of Newton. The fame of Aristotle and the scholastics declined to be succeeded by the vogue of philosophers who sought in philosophy the unattainable certainty of mathematics, or by empirical philosophers, who swathed themselves in the prestige of the natural sciences. The political convulsions of the age produced a multitude of works to justify the security of absolutism or the rights of the governed. International conflict inspired numerous writings on international law and some projects for the organization of Europe. Economic policy won its share of writers and the beginnings of the study of economic statistics took place. In religion, though the eighteenth century was to dwarf its influence and content, England and France during the later seventeenth century revealed greater fervor and even fanaticism than during the first half of the century.

PROGRAMS FOR HISTORY

Bodin. From the middle of the sixteenth century onwards there appeared numerous works on the study and practice of history. The most fruitful one for the study of historiography is the *Method For the Easy Comprehension of History* (1566), by Jean Bodin (1530-1596), more famous for his writings on sovereignty and for his analysis of the price revolution. Bodin's work is important for historiography in spite of the fact that it is designed for readers of history rather than for writers of history. In part, its importance arises from the fact that Bodin definitely abandoned the theory of the four monarchies and in doing so recognized the divisions of Europe which the state system and the Reformation had produced. The historical conception of the four monarchies and of the one Christian Empire had in an imperfect way expressed the unity of Christendom. Bodin not only rejected these concepts but sought for a scheme of general history which was not seriously related to Christian beliefs. The earlier concepts were certainly narrow, and Bodin had the merit of attempting to bring into the scope of history all the people of the world. Although his aim is partly empirical and pragmatic (to teach prudence), Bodin sought to rise above the details of particular histories and to sketch the general laws of history, for "the arts and the disciplines . . . are not concerned with particulars, but with universals."[1] Universal history will reveal the relation of parts to the whole and, thereby, reveal human episodes recurring "as in a circle," so that man will be able to recognize these repetitions and to seek their causes. Bodin further stressed the necessity of observing time sequences, but his most influential point was his explanation of human diversity by differences of climate. Though this view was not original with him, his systematic formulation of the influence of climate is impressive. Not that he limited himself to a single determining influence, for Bodin, a complex and not always clear thinker, believed that history "mostly flows from the will of mankind, which ever vacillates and has no objective."[2] Moreover, Bodin believed in the significance of certain numbers and in the influence of the stars and planets. Interestingly enough, Bodin found the climate of France to be the proper human mean, and, thus, to him France presented a model of human achievement for the world. The *Method,* then, is important as a revelation of the complexities of sixteenth century thought, for its explanation of history, and for its critical account of ancient and modern historians.

Bacon. Francis Bacon (1561-1626), the famous essayist and literary promoter of experimental science, outlined a series of needed historical works as part of his design for *The Advancement of Learning* (1605). In the course of his exhortation that men abandon the subtle pursuit of words or the concepts of the intellect and bend their minds to the nature of things so that they could control the forces of nature, Bacon pointed to a number of subjects

---

[1] John Bodin, *Method for the Easy Comprehension of History,* translated by Beatrice Reynolds, p. 2.
[2] "Philosophy, which itself is called the 'guide of life,' would remain silent among dead things, even though the extreme limits of good and evil had been set, unless all sayings, deeds, and plans are considered in relation to the account of days long past. From these not only are present-day affairs readily interpreted but also future events are inferred, and we may acquire reliable maxims for what we should seek and avoid." *Ibid.,* p. 17.

which required historical investigation. He called for an elaborate history of learning, a history of the various sciences, a history of mechanical controls of nature, as well as a history of God's providences.[3] These recommendations bore fruit in the work of the Royal Society (1662). Bacon's empiricism is directly related to his interest in history, for he distrusted the abstractions of the mind. Indeed, in Bacon may be found the germs of the empirical and historical attitude which ultimately can arrive at no general values and conclusions. Because he was impatient with the wrangling that attended them, he argued that theology and moral philosophy had been pretty completely worked out. To the clergyman he urged the study of church history. "For it is not St. Augustine's nor St. Ambrose's works that will make so wise a divine, as ecclesiastical history, thoroughly read and observed."[4] Instead of studying moral philosophy, Bacon invited men to study the difficulties of applying its principles, and especially to study the passions and the differences in mankind that arise from such individual conditions as sex and profession. "Poets and writers of histories are the best doctors of this knowledge."[5]

ENGLISH HISTORICAL WRITING

Bacon's Henry VII. Bacon himself did not carry out his own program, and wrote only a political history, a *History of the Reign of Henry VII,* composed directly after his political disgrace in 1621. The *History* presents the pattern of a politic king. Not that Henry VII was always his model, for he used the faults of Henry as an occasion for moralizing. He noted that Henry had determined to depress all eminent persons of the line of York. "Wherein still the King, out of strength of will or weakness of judgment, did use to shew a little more of the party than of the king."[6] Perhaps he intended a lesson for King James in observing that Henry, while maintaining the laws, still suffered no impediment to his will. "And yet as he would sometimes strain up his laws to his prerogative, so would he also let down his prerogative to his Parliament."[7]

Bacon's artistic achievement in presenting the model of a political king was so great that the work was long assumed to have been based on a wide use of original sources. Wilhelm Busch has shown that the original authority for Bacon was Polydore Vergil as used by Hall.[8] The artistic achievement is all the more surprising because Bacon consulted his sources hastily and carelessly. His *History,* moreover, comes perilously close to what he called "ruminated history," books of policy, and he inevitably overstepped what he and most of his contemporaries professed to be the bounds of history, that is, the presentation of events, leaving the reader to draw his own counsels.[9] The "facts" and "events" which he wanted to present were not facts, for only

---

[3] Bacon, *The Advancement of Learning,* pp. 69-76.
[4] *Ibid.,* p. 70.
[5] *Ibid.,* p. 172.
[6] Bacon, *History of the Reign of Henry VII* in *The Works of Francis Bacon,* ed., Spedding, Ellis and Heath, XI, p. 51.
[7] *Ibid.,* p. 356.
[8] Wilhelm Busch, *England Under the Tudors,* trans., Alice M. Todd, I, p. 517.
[9] Bacon, *The Advancement of Learning,* p. 79.

too frequently the "events" were successful policies, already approved by *parti pris*.

Fulke Greville and Thomas Hobbes. There was, then, a more serious concern with the pragmatic value of history, accompanied by criticism of writers who catered to a demand for vulgar spectacles. The philosopher, Thomas Hobbes, compared the popular attitude toward history to the tastes of the people of Rome, who went to see the gladiators more "to behold their blood, than their skill in fencing." He regretted that people prefer to read about "bloody battles, and many thousands slain at once," than to "mind the art by which the affairs both of armies and cities be conducted to their ends."[10] John Donne, Anglican priest and poet, assailed many older historians, Holinshed, Hall and Stow as purveyors of "trivial household trash."[11] To regard history as a teacher not of general moral precepts but of prudence placed heavy demands on the writer. One historian expressed the hope that, in setting forth "what counsailles" famous men have undertaken and "lively patternes' both for private directions and for affairs of State," he would instruct the young and furnish old men with fuller "experience than the longest age of man can afford."[12] Such an ambition compelled men to search out papers of state, but when the poet Fulke Greville approached Secretary of State Robert Cecil with such a request, Cecil said "that upon second thought, he durst not presume to let the Councell-chest lie open to any man living, without his Majesties knowledge and approbation." Seeing that this would involve a complete censorship of his proposed Elizabethan history, Fulke Greville abandoned his project.[13]

Camden. The discreet William Camden, already famous as an antiquary, was more fortunate. In 1597, Robert Cecil's father, Lord Burghley, giving Camden access to his own and the Queen's papers, asked Camden to write a history of the beginnings of Elizabeth's reign. Camden was appalled by the mass of material, chronologically arranged, and upon Burghley's death (1598), abandoned his labors on this subject until 1608. He was urged on by many of his friends, including Jacques de Thou, a great French historian who admired the political wisdom of Elizabeth, and suggested to Camden that she would be a great subject for a history, if the necessary documents were available.[14] Camden resumed his labors, and in the perspective of James' reign, Elizabeth's rule appeared to be close to a golden age.

Drawing upon the resources of his own collection, the libraries of antiquarian friends and from many of the principal persons of the age, Camden wrote in Latin his *Annales,* translated as *The History of the Most Renowned and Victorious Princess Elizabeth* (London, 1688). He wrote in Latin, for he had no desire to permit himself to become the target of popular attacks. Not until after his death was the second part (1589-1603) of the history

---

[10] Thomas Hobbes "To the Readers," *The History of the Grecian War Written by Thucydides* in the *English Works of Thomas Hobbes,* ed., Sir William Molesworth, VIII, pp. vii-ix.
[11] Satire IV, 97-98. *The Complete Poems of John Donne,* ed. Roger Bennett, p. 102.
[12] A. P.'s preface "To the Reader," Hayward and Cotton, *The Histories of the Lives and Raignes of Henry the Third and Henry the Fourth,* no pagination.
[13] Fulke Greville, *The Life of the Renowned Sir Philip Sidney* (Chiswick: Caradoc Press, 1907), pp. 159-162.
[14] Thomas Smith, *The Correspondence of William Camden* (Largely in Latin), pp. 68-69.

published (1625) and no translation into English was permitted during his lifetime. In choosing the form of annals he was influenced by the fact that he was dealing with recent events, for which he could not always advance explanations that would dictate the organization of his material. The form made proper the simpler style of writing that he preferred, permitted a recording of the main events and some curiosities and did not force omissions for the sake of art. Camden thought of himself not as an artist but as a guide, teaching the wise and prudent man the nature of the state and the political world, and he expressed the hope that "in training up the minds of men to honesty and wisdom, I may thereby find a place amongst the petty writers of great matters."[15]

The work was of extraordinary value, because it was based on a truly vast range of source materials. Not until the late nineteenth century was Elizabeth's reign treated in fuller fashion. Camden was sensitive to the charge that he was a mere scholar and that, as Polybius had written, history could not be composed simply from a study of papers. For a reply Camden detailed his method and sources. "I have attained by them no less knowledge of those affairs than some others who have been long and deeply versed in state-matters."[16] Finally, though he had no avowed theme, he constantly celebrated Elizabeth's successful maintenance of government power which made for England's security.

Memoirs and Biography. After Camden, distinguished historical works in England are few. There was abundance of learned research, and the age produced the erudite legal and religious studies of the sharp-witted Erastian, John Selden (1584-1654), and an edition of the parliamentary journals of Elizabeth's reign by Simonds D'Ewes (1602-1650). The struggle between king and parliament and the social turbulence of the Commonwealth proliferated pamphlets and memoirs, which range from the universal types of Lord Clarendon and Thomas Fuller to the sententious and witty gossip of the Duchess of Newcastle (1623-73), who tells in a memoir of her husband that he changed his clothes frequently and "is neat and cleanly; which makes him to be somewhat long in dressing."[17] The philosopher Lord Herbert of Cherbury (1583-1648) wrote his autobiography to present the events which best revealed himself. The surprising result is "a portrait of a bully and a coxcomb . . . a catalogue of amatory triumphs" . . . revealing the author "as vain, foolish, blustering and ridiculous."[18] John Aubrey's *Lives* are the entertaining opposite of the character sketch, for they present notes and gossip on a multitude of individuals. Politically revealing are the memoirs of Edmund Ludlow (1617-1692), a republican soldier who wrote in exile after the Restoration, "having seen our cause betrayed, and the most solemn promises that could be made to the asserters of it, openly violated."[19]

For the factional and party conflicts of the century, two writers are par-

---

[15] Camden, *The History* . . . . . *Elizabeth,* "The Author to the Reader," no pagination.
[16] *Idem.*
[17] *Memoirs of the Duke of Newcastle,* ed. C. H. Firth, p. 112.
[18] Harold Nicolson, *The Development of English Biography,* p. 55.
[19] *The Memoirs of Edmund Ludlow,* ed. C. H. Firth, I, p. 9.

ticularly memorable, Lord Clarendon and Bishop Gilbert Burnet. Clarendon's historical work has all the grace and reticence of the early seventeenth century and his complex rhythmical sentences well express an attempt to explain the world by general character analysis. Burnet is closer to our own time, for he has few reticences and his paragraphs are the accumulation of individual details and qualities in fairly short sentences. Clarendon was, to antedate a term, a Tory, and Burnet a Whig.

Clarendon. Edward Hyde, Lord Clarendon (1609-1674), was a lawyer with literary and philosophical interests. As a traditional Tudor constitutionalist who believed that king and parliament should cooperate, he sided with the parliamentary opposition to Charles I, whose adviser he became in 1641 after the long parliament had drastically redressed the balance of the Constitution in favor of the Commons. During the war, Hyde served the king and also began the composition of a *History of the Rebellion,* a work not designed for the world but for King Charles and his counsellors, an explanation of the war's causes and of mistaken royal policies. At the end of two years, in 1648 he had brought the story to 1644. Later events delayed his labors and in 1652 he was called to the exiled court of the Royal Martyr's son, Charles II. Hyde was the chief royal adviser and the architect of the Restoration. But his very principles and conservatism made him an inadequate and unacceptable servant to the restored Charles. By 1667, he was impeached and fled to France. In the enforced leisure of exile and without documents, he began an *Autobiography,* a justification of his own career until the Restoration. He had completed this work, a more personal one enlivened with unforgetable character sketches, when his son visited him in 1671, bringing with him the manuscript of the unfinished *History.* Thereupon, Clarendon resolved to fuse the two works, thus producing a book of uneven merit and, sometimes, doubtful reliability, for the *Autobiography* was written in the self-deceiving world of an exile, who had to depend on his memory. Nonetheless, his combined *History* (published 1702-1704) has the advantages both of the more carefully and freshly recorded passages of the early *History* and of the masterly sketches of the *Autobiography.*

Clarendon's volumes express his constitutional views, the cause of his success at the Restoration and of his later downfall. His description of the Earl of Pembroke applied equally to himself. "He was a great lover of his country, and of the religion and justice, which he believed could only support it." He was as unsentimental about his own wives as about the Earl's unhappiness, for Clarendon also tells us that the Earl "paid much too dear for his wife's fortune, by taking her person into the bargain." [20] To Clarendon, the Duke of Buckingham's "kindness and affection to his friends was so vehement, that it was as so many marriages for better and worse, and so many leagues offensive and defensive." [21] Among the human agents contributing to a period of "prosperous wickedness" to the apostasy and confusion of the kingdom was the "unpolished integrity" of Archbishop Laud, whose greatest infirmity was

---

[20] Clarendon, *The History of the Rebellion and Civil Wars,* I, p. 95. The best edition is by W. D. Macray in six volumes.
[21] Clarendon, *The History of the Rebellion and Civil Wars,* I, pp. 51, 73.

"that he believed innocence of heart, . . . was a guard strong enough to secure any man in his voyage through this world, in what company soever he travelled." Clarendon is excellent for portraits and for constitutional issues. The motives of revolutionaries and Puritan zealots escaped him. He is not useful for the economic background of the rebellion, but in his own sphere of politics he is almost invariably illuminating and delightful. Thus, he wrote about the Londoners when King Charles was to be restored: "The city of London had had too great a hand in driving the father of the king from thence, not to appear equally zealous for his son's return thither." [22]

Burnet. Gilbert Burnet (1643-1715), who made an important contribution to Church history, wrote a remarkable *History of My Own Time,* which covered the early seventeenth century and became a practically continuous contemporary memoir for the last years of the Bishop's life. The author, who had a flair for uplifting biographies and deathbed scenes (see his studies of Justice Matthew Hale and of the death of the Earl of Rochester), composed *The Lives of the Dukes of Hamilton* (1673), which Professor Firth has called "the first political biography of the modern type."[23] In that work, Burnet presented a large collection of source material, for he argued that the partisanship and failings of historians had recently made people want to see the documents. They found the imaginary speeches distasteful, and "the World desires nothing so much as to see the Truth of things as they were really designed and acted, rather from some Original Papers, than from the Collections or Extracts of persons of whose Fidelity or Judgment they are not well assured." [24] In writing his memoirs, Burnet carried this process a step further, although in doing so he once again had to ask the reader to believe him. He recognized that documents alone do not give a full story. "For above thirty years, I have lived in such close intimacy with all who have had the chief conduct of affairs and have been so much trusted . . . that I have been able to penetrate far into the true secrets of counsels and designs." He proposed to give "a true view of men and counsels, leaving public transactions to gazettes and the public historians of the times." [25]

The *History* was begun in 1683 and continued over the years, with considerable revision of the whole work as he went along. In writing it and representing things in their natural colors, he intended to make himself and the reader wiser and better. With disarming candor, he warned the reader that he had a low view of men and tended to see things in their worst colors. As the friend of William and Mary, he took a dim view of Charles and James, but he adequately described the charm of Charles II, who once told him that "he was no atheist, but he could not think God would make a man miserable only for taking a little pleasure out of the way." [26] His volumes (published 1724-34) presented a Whig version of the Glorious Revolution and its subsequent fortunes. It is full of life, of the colors and prejudices of his time. Of

---

[22] *Ibid.,* I, p. 148; VII, p. 541.
[23] C. H. Firth, *Essays Historical and Literary,* p. 176.
[24] Burnet, *The Memoirs of the Lives and Actions of James and William, Dukes of Hamilton and Castelherald.* "The Preface," no pagination.
[25] Burnet, *History of My Own Time,* ed. O. Airy, Part I, Vol. I, p. xxxii.
[26] *Ibid.,* pp. 166-167.

course, some of the secret counsels are the wildest gossip, for Burnet did not discriminate critically in narrating the stratagems of his enemies.

FRENCH HISTORIANS AND MEMOIR WRITERS

De Thou, the Politique. Religious differences and political and constitutional claims produced the religious wars in France. Henry IV's efforts of reconstruction were largely influenced by political considerations. For the sake of domestic peace, the King became a Catholic and granted a regional toleration to French Protestants. In this work, the King[27] was a true *Politique,* a member of a party which in the interests of French strength was willing to recognize and accept the religious divisions of France. This party numbered among its members, the most important historians of early seventeenth century France, Jacques Auguste de Thou (1553-1617), whose *History of His Own Time* was a model for Burnet. After studying law, which was one of the most serious historical pursuits in France, de Thou became a state counsellor, and later, master of the Royal Library of Henry IV. He was a collector of books and manuscripts, and the friend of most of the contemporary great men of French letters, including Montaigne and Ronsard. His *History,* unfinished at his death, covered the history of Europe and of France in great detail, from 1546 to 1607, and for his work he called for help from a host of scholars and men of affairs. Thus, he appealed to Camden for guidance in English, Scottish and Irish matters.

In the prefatory letter of dedication,[28] de Thou argued at length the uselessness of religious persecution, and defended a policy of religious toleration with arguments drawn from the Church Fathers and because it contributed to political strength. The shadow of religious conflict, which had made him rather indifferent to religious confessions, pervades the history. "The scenes of my childhood recur to my mind, during the first religious commotions in France. At that time, men were not judged by their manners, or the innocency of their past life, but suspected for their countenance or cloaks; and from thence marked out by the eyes for slaughter. The flaming zeal, the malignity of factions, tore the kingdom to pieces, and endangered religion itself, while our rulers added not a little to these evils by partiality, fear, inconstancy, lethargy, silence and arrogance." [29]

This enormous annalistic history, (the London edition of 1733 consisting of seven large folios), was a stupendously erudite work. Its bulk and its Latin have rendered it unreadable, but it inflamed the passions of contemporaries. In 1609, it was placed on the Index, and de Thou had a heated controversy with Bellarmine. As a lawyer, de Thou was a Gallican. Moreover, he professed to follow Henry IV in speaking honorably of the Protestants and in not con-

---

[27] Henry IV was the admired subject of a biography (1626) by the patriotic Dutch historian, P. C. Hooft (1581-1647). The latter was profoundly influenced by Tacitus, and his terse Dutch style has something of the power of his model. He also wrote a moving *History of the Netherlands* (covering the years 1555-1587) to "put on record the piety of his countrymen, of his fellow citizens, and of his kinsfolk." Herbert Grierson, *Two Dutch Poets,* p. 11.

[28] Reprinted in Francois L'Honore, *Memoires de la Vie de Jacques de Thou,* and in J. Collinson, *Life of Thuanus.*

[29] Collinson, *op. cit.,* pp. 403-404.

cealing "the faults of our own party," for he believed that heresies "have gathered strength not more from the malice and intrigues of their supporters than from our own vices." [30] Like his royal master, he was full of distrust towards Spain.[31] In the *History*, he noticed even the most distant events. For the year 1596 he mentioned a Dutch voyage to Java and followed this with an account of betel nuts, Mohammedan marriage customs and the unsanitary water supply of the Javanese.[32]

Sully's Memoirs. The Wars of Religion and Henry IV are among the principal subjects of the memoirs of Maximilien de Bethune, Duc de Sully (1559-1641). This cautious and useful servant of Henry IV in the economic reconstruction of France was a Huguenot, who lost his power after Henry's assassination. In retirement, he compiled his *Oeconomies royales,* memoirs designed to do more than justice to his career. Sully had an intimate knowledge of the later phases of the religious wars and of his master's reign. With a corps of secretaries he prepared the material. Though Sully in public life was at least courtly enough, in his literary retirement his vanity reached insufferable heights. The memoirs, addressed to Sully, are in the second person, and his secretaries are properly admiring of him. "We have tried our best to speak of your greatness, to make known the fundamental causes of your advancement and of your employment in many great offices . . . with so much integrity, competence and diligence that your praises are still sounded in public and your return to office ardently desired." [33] To make these valuable memoirs more readable, they were elaborately reedited in the eighteenth century, and nearly all available copies are based on that plan. Sully's recollections give many important details about Henry's reign, ranging from financial policy to provisions for Henry's mistresses. Scattered through the pages are the outlines of a Grand Design, attributed to Henry IV and calling for an organization of Europe grounded upon the destruction of Habsburg power.

Richelieu. In the years after Henry's death French policy wavered and the nobility again proved to be a source of French political weakness. The dedicated servant of royal power, Armand du Plessis, Cardinal Richelieu (1585-1642), planned a history of the reign of Louis XIII, and with some co-workers compiled a large collection of notes, analyses and memoirs. Unlike Sully, Richelieu did not have the leisure of enforced retirement and, as a result, his design was never completed. In his *Memoirs* it is not easy to ascribe the form of particular passages to the Cardinal, although it is likely enough that the entire work expresses his thought. Of the retirement of Sully in 1611 the *Memoirs* acidly noted that the early years of Sully's service were profitable to France but that his later years saw him more self-regarding and less austere, though not overburdensome to the state.[34] A note of irony is

---

[30] *Ibid.,* pp. 423-424.

[31] "When the French decline, then the Spaniards begin to be masters." *Historiarum sui Temporis,* I, p. 14.

[32] *Ibid.,* V, p. 65. This *History* was a principal source for the extraordinarily popular *History of the Civil Wars in France,* 1559-1598 in Italian (Venice, 1630) by Davila, whose coursing style, narrative gifts and vision of the wars as simply selfish power struggles, appealed powerfully to his contemporaries.

[33] Quoted in Henri Carré, *Sully: Sa Vie et Son Oeuvre,* p. 372.

[34] *Mémoires du Cardinal de Richelieu,* Vol. I, ed. by Le Comte de Beaucaire, pp. 136-137.

sounded frequently in the *Memoirs*. There is a remarkable passage of reflections on the advantages of a proposed marriage and alliance treaty with England in 1624. These reflections reveal the Cardinal as a superb diplomat.[35] But Richelieu enjoyed the creation of historical situations more than he longed for literary creations. In the preface to his *Political Testament* he wrote: "I admit that it gives greater satisfaction to provide the matter of history instead of merely giving the latter its form; nevertheless, it has given me no little enjoyment to recreate here that which only with difficulty has become political reality." [36] The political reality which he created was the establishment of royal authority and, by intervention in the Thirty Years' War, the humiliation of Habsburg power.

De Retz. Memoir writing was so fashionable in France that even Louis XIV composed a history of the early years of his reign. The most famous memoirs, however, are those of Cardinal de Retz and of the Duc de Saint Simon. Jean de Gondi, Cardinal de Retz (1613-1679), who described himself as "the soul in the world perhaps the least ecclesiastical," wrote a lively, witty and unreliable history of his own turbulent and unedifying life. The author wards off criticism by his own candor. His first sentence begins with the avowal that he intended to write his life "even at the expense of my own reputation." [37]

Saint-Simon. Louis de Rouvroi, Duc de Saint-Simon (1675-1755), is perhaps the greatest of memoir writers. A man of high ambitions, resentful towards the crown which depressed the nobility, and compelled to live in the stately boredom of Versailles, he composed a vivid and detailed picture of the French Court, and was at the same time, the best witness against the political competence of the nobility. He began his journal in 1694 and continued his entries to 1723. In 1749, he secured a copy of Dangeau's *Journal,* a bare and useful chronicle of events at court, and used it in the revision of his *Memoirs* which he completed in 1751. Saint-Simon took a dim view of Louis XIV—to him Louis XIII, who had advanced the author's family, was the great king. Nonetheless, he recognized that Louis XIV labored hard at the business of kingship. Mme. de Maintenon is regularly described as the enchantress or the "Sultana." His sardonic account of the reception of the *History of France* by the Jesuit, Father Daniel,[38] is typical. "The sensation was, at first, so great that everyone, including the women, took it up. . . . On the affairs of the League and of Rome, it was a pleasure to watch him racing across the ice with his Jesuit skates. . . . The King spoke about it and asked some courtiers if they had read it. . . . Soon it appeared on all the tables of the courtiers at Versailles." [39]

HISTORICAL STUDIES IN ITALY

While the great abundance of memoirs, which added richness and problems

[35] *Ibid.,* Vol. IV, ed. by Lavallee (1920), pp. 37-67.

[36] Quoted in Otto von Simson, "Richelieu and Rubens," *The Review of Politics,* VI (1944), p. 423.

[37] *Memoirs of Cardinal de Retz,* pp. 1-3.

[38] Gabriel Daniel, S. J., published in 1713 a *History of France* (3 vols.). The work began with Clovis and reached the year 1610. Saint-Simon's harsh criticism does not do justice to the classic style, the critical talents and method of the author.

[39] Quoted in La Force "Le Centenaire de la Societe de l'Histoire de France" in *Revue des Deux Mondes,* series 8 (1934), p. 450.

to history, was peculiar to France, many other countries, including Bohemia,[40] delved into their past with antiquarian and patriotic fervor and erudite criticism. Italian writers labored both on general and local histories. "During the tranquil century before the Revolution, Italians studied the history of their country with diligence and success. Even such places as Parma, Verona, Brescia, became centers of obscure but faithful work. Osimo possessed annals as bulky as those of Rome. The story of the province of Trevisa was told in twenty volumes. . . . The best of all this national and municipal patriotism was given to the service of religion." [41] In this period the greatest figure in Italian learning was Ludovico Antonio Muratori (1672-1750), who in his own day was equally eminent as literary critic and historian. He was successively librarian at Milan and Modena, and before entering the priesthood, he had studied law. His edition of *Writers on Italian History from 500 to 1500* (27 volumes, 1723-1751) is still a basic work, for Muratori wrote excellent critical introductions. *The Annals of Italy From the Beginning of the Christian Era to 1500* (12 volumes, 1744-1749) was largely written in the course of one year. Among his other works are studies of inscriptions and many essays on medieval antiquities. He corresponded with Mabillon and Montfaucon, and these men along with Tillemont and Muratori provided the sure outlines for Gibbon's masterly history. Gibbon called Muratori "my guide and master in the history of Italy." [42]

German and Scandinavian Historical Writing

Pufendorf. The Thirty Years' War made Germany the battlefield of all western and northern Europe. This catastrophe produced no contemporary history of great significance. But it was the starting point for an imposing, collaborative work, *Theatrum Europeum* (in German, 21 folio volumes, Frankfort, 1662-1738). The scope of this work was all of Europe for the years 1618 to 1718. Its originator was Johannes Abelinus, but the volumes are more famous for the many vivid engravings by Matthew Merian and for the maps by Hollar.

Two German philosophers also made important contributions to German history. The political and legal philosopher, Samuel von Pufendorf (1632-1694), after teaching at the University of Lund, was in 1677 made Royal Historiographer of Sweden. In that capacity he wrote *Commentaries on Swedish Affairs* (from Gustavus Adolphus' intervention in the Thirty Years' War to the abdication of Christina) and a *History* of Charles X. Pufendorf then changed masters, for in 1686 he became historiographer of the Great Elector. The latter received good service, for he was the subject of a *Commentary* in 1695. Pufendorf used an abundance of archival material in his works, but he rarely went beyond the exposition and justification of the policies of his subjects. His works are primarily legal and diplomatic histories. While in Sweden he also composed a history textbook for Swedish gentlemen,

---

[40] The Jesuit, Father Balbin, collected and published a mass of material on Czech history.

[41] Lord Acton, *The History of Freedom and Other Essays*, p. 387.

[42] Gibbon, *The Decline and Fall of the Roman Empire*, Vol. II, p. 1437.

An Introduction to the History of the Principal Kingdoms and States of Europe.[43]

Leibniz. The versatile Gottfried Wilhelm Leibniz (1646-1716), who shared with Pufendorf the belief that the young should receive more training in facts than in philosophy, also wrote history. At a very young age he developed an ingenious project to persuade Louis XIV to turn his conquering zeal against Egypt rather than European states. The French Minister for Foreign Affairs wrote from the battlefield his reply that holy wars had gone out of fashion. In various works, written in behalf of the German princes against imperial claims, Leibniz revealed a wide knowledge of German history. His major historical work was done while he was employed by the princely house of Brunswick. *Origines Guelficae* (5 volumes) was not finished during his lifetime. With all the critical talent, though perhaps not the discrimination, of the French scholars of the Age of Erudition, he compiled and edited *Writers Illustrative of Brunswick Affairs* (3 volumes, Hanover, 1707-1711). This work amasses the fragments of earlier writers on the affairs of Brunswick. His comments and criticisms are often just, but the compilation itself is a rather curious thing, for so much of the material is out of context. In his introduction, Leibniz argued that historians, even in the revival of letters, had not supported their writings with documents. He conceded that such a practice was understandable in a contemporary history. For remote times, however, truth is more difficult to ascertain. He argued that the modern reading public is superior to the ancient reading public in that the modern reader demands proofs.[44]

Leibniz is an ambiguous figure, a man of the baroque age in his learning and infinite projects, but a man whose thought also looked forward to the Enlightenment. His fame in historical writing is, perhaps, more an indication of the comparative poverty of German historiography in an age that elsewhere witnessed extraordinary achievements in collecting, editing, criticism and memoir writing.

---

[43] This work was published at Frankfort (1682) and had a great vogue. It was translated into French and English, but the translators and edi ors adapted it as they saw fit. Pufendorf argued that the young should study modern history because it was useful. In treating the interests of the various states he considered their geography and the power of neighboring s:ates, but emphasized the variability of state in erests and power. He also expressed the opinion that there had been no civil government before the flood; if there had been, man would not have become so depraved that God drowned most of the human race.

[44] Leibniz, *Scriptores Rerum Brunsvicensium Illustrationi Inservientes,* I. al.

Chapter 11

THE AGE OF ENLIGHTENMENT

By Sherman B. Barnes

GENERAL ASSUMPTIONS AND OUTLOOK

IN THE history of western civilization the era from about 1715 to 1780 is known as the Enlightenment. This term, invented by Immanuel Kant (1724-1804), was used by Kant to designate the emancipation of reason from its previous state of minority. The expression mirrored the apocalyptic self-confidence of the *philosophes* that they could by reason's powers discover the natural laws of all human phenomena—ethics, jurisprudence, society, religion, art—just as Newton's *Principia* had proclaimed the laws of physics and astronomy. The historians of the Englightenment shared, in varying proportions, both the scientific and the humanitarian reforming zeal of the century.[1]

The great historians of the Age of Reason wrote history as a combination of synthesis, propaganda, and good style, for cultivated men of the world. To write history, as a *philosophe,* meant to write it in the service of a Creed— the Enlightenment Creed of Nature, Reason, Progress, and Humanity. This was what Voltaire meant by "philosophy of history," a phrase he coined. Insofar as history had a political goal, it was to instruct kings in the laws of reason and nature. Enlightenment historians wrote neither to flatter statesmen nor to impress antiquarian specialists.[2] With a few exceptions, such as Robertson and Vico, they were attached neither to state office nor to university teaching positions. They wrote for and from the standpoint of their own cultivated upper middle class and nobility, and not in behalf of their rulers. Their monumental histories of the eighteenth century were widely sold and read because of their judicious mixture of style, propaganda and synthetic power.

SUBJECTS OF ENLIGHTENMENT HISTORY

Enlightenment historians told more about trade, industry, social life, cultural developments, and the interrelations among these forces, than had been customary in the old political and theological histories. Montesquieu, Voltaire and Robertson, in dealing with Asia and America, brought the whole world into historiography. The narrow Europe-centric approach became antiquated. There was increased attention to primitive man and early civilizations, to the need for judging primitive man by standards other than those of civilized

---

[1] Eduard Fueter, *Geschichte der Neueren Historiographie,* p. 36.
[2] Erudite labors of collecting documents and laying foundations for future synthesis were continued in this era, but did not constitu e what was most characteristic. See Robert Flint, *Historical Philosophy in France and French Belgium and Switzerland,* pp. 245-261. An interesting example of the clash between exac , technical scholarship and the "philosophical" historiography of the eighteenth century appears in the fact that medieval studies, research in Saxon and in ecclesiastical history, actually withered in England after 1730, compared with the preceding seventy years. See David C. Douglas, *English Scholars.*

nations.[3] Man's very slow and gradual rise from savagery to civilization was better appreciated. Adam played a declining role, although still the starting point of many histories. Because the great historians of this era had wide interests and undertook large subjects, they usually relied on secondary books and hasty and incomplete exploration of original documents. But they subjected the works which they did consult to sharp criticism, picking to pieces legends, fables, miracles and all actions of men, deemed incomprehensible and contrary to their canons of common sense and daily experience. They rejected the authority of ancient historians, including the Bible and the Roman historians of early Rome, in many matters of fact. They improved the science of documentary analysis by asking whether witnesses were worthy of credence, enlightened, and contemporary with the deeds recorded. Pre-Renaissance documents were approached with a presumption of unreliability.

Concerning causation, the Enlightenment historians (Vico excepted) ignored the theological assumption that Divine Providence shapes the course of history. They were not agreed on what to substitute. However, they did not put serious stress on economic causes. Typical was Hume's view that men owed little of their "temper or genius to the air, food or climate." [4] A favorite theory was that the same human nature, operative in all times and places, was the underlying cause of "the vicissitudes of kingdoms and peoples." How the same laws of human nature could account for so many changes and diverse political and cultural forms was not well answered. Events were frequently attributed to conscious, rational motives. The founding of governments and churches was traced to deliberate acts of priests and lawgivers. Closely connected was the great man theory and the idea of historical change as catastrophic rather than evolutionary. Other causes mentioned were national character, chance, the spirit of the times, climate, religion and government. Causation theories were contradictory and groping, but the very real attempt to interpret and explain marked an advance over unthinking chronological annals of names, dates and events.[5]

THE AGE OF REASON

The Age of Reason looked with hostile eyes upon the ignorance and barbarism of the past, particularly the Christian medieval past, which was stigmatized as dark and replete with follies, superstitions, and crimes. Voltairean history was a long argument seeking to refute the past. Past ages were valued hardly at all for themselves and their own unique points of view but more for their present polemical value in the fight against obscurantism and tyranny. The Enlightenment poured the new wine of its philosophy into the ancient didactic practice of sermonizing from history, which now supplied object lessons or warnings of the errors of fanaticism, superstition and intolerance. What was vice, what was virtue, what was wisdom and what was a fault in the past, were all surprisingly obvious and clear. History, as Bolingbroke put it, was "philosophy teaching by examples how to conduct ourselves in all

---

[3] Fueter, *op. cit.*, p. 341.
[4] David Hume, *Essays, Moral, Literary and Political*, "Of Climate."
[5] Eduard Fueter, *op. cit.*, pp. 345-349.

the situations of private and public life . . ." [6] To know the absurd quarrels of the past, thought Voltaire, will help prevent their recurrence. It was not made very clear how the enlightened eighteenth century could have evolved from a past that was a record of "crimes, follies, and misfortunes." [7] The faith in Reason had its saints and miracles no less than the Church.

Although the Enlightenment historians subordinated sacred or church history to their avowedly profane or secular history, they unconsciously carried over into their writings three attitudes rooted in sacred history—dualism, eschatology, and cosmopolitanism. (1) *Dualism.* Voltaire and his school, inverting the Augustinian Two Cities, depicted the church as the earthly force of darkness obscuring the heavenly light of human reason and science. The Christian dualism of God and Satan was secularized into the struggle of Reason against Unreason.[8] (2) *Eschatology.* The Christian hope of a fulfillment in the historical process of God's promises of salvation was secularized into a belief in the goal of history as a fulfillment of man's growing power to achieve happiness on earth by his own science and wisdom.[9] (3) *Cosmopolitanism.* It was felt that history would best serve the cause of philosophy and reason if it were written on a scale broader than national history, just as universal Christian church histories had put religious belief above nationality or state loyalty.[10]

Vico's Providential-Cyclical Theory

Giambattista Vico (1668-1744) a poverty-stricken professor at the University of Naples, wrote a book so far ahead of his time that it did not achieve the recognition it deserved until the early nineteenth century. This work was *The Principles of a New Science of the Nature of Nations,* in Italian (1725).[11]

Vico put coherence and meaning in universal pre-history and classical antiquity.[12] His brilliant achievement was founded in a highly learned comparative and evolutionary analysis of early languages, fables, gods, poems, and laws.[13] He used these as sources from which to reconstruct the intellectual, political and economic outlooks and evolution of early man.[14] He repudiated the reading of reflective and universal moral ideas of later ages back into pre-history and classical antiquity.[15] With profound insight into the group mind, he saw Homer, Romulus, Lycurgus, Zoroaster and other ancient poets, sages and mythical heroes as collective or allegorical beings poetically imagined by early men to be the founders of civilization.

[6] Henry St. John, Vicount Bolingbroke, *Letters on the Study and Use of History* (1735), in *Works,* II, p. 191.
[7] Voltaire, *Essai sur les Moeurs et l'Esprit des Nations* (1754), ch. 197.
[8] See Morris Cohen, *The Meaning of Human History,* p. 12.
[9] See Karl Löwith, *Meaning in History,* p. 111.
[10] Eduard Fueter, *op. cit.,* p. 348.
[11] *The New Science of Giambattista Vico,* trans. into English by Thomas Goddard Bergin and Max Harold Fisch. *The Autobiography of Giambattista Vico,* trans. into English by Thomas Goddard Bergin and Max Harold Fisch, with a valuable analysis of *The New Science* and of Vico's reputation and influence.
[12] *The New Science* (Hereafter referred to as N.S.), Paragraph 357.
[13] N.S., p. 51; for another example of growing interest in the comparative method applied to primitive man see Lafitau, *Moeurs des Sauvages Ameriquains* (1724).
[14] N.S., p. 338.
[15] N.S., Ibid.

Each gentile civilization[16] went through successive stages of growth—the divine, the heroic, the human. The bestial and ferocious men of the two centuries after the universal flood were raised to social life, laws, family and agricultural life by the guidance of Providence. Religion arose from fear of natural phenomena such as thunderstorms. The family was the strongest institution. The rulers were both priests and fathers. Stern religions were needed to curb the proud and cruel. The weak became clients of the fathers. In the heroic age, the fathers submitted to the proud nobles most able to rule (Achilles is the symbol). The clients or serfs of the divine epoch became the plebeians of heroic aristocratic kingdoms. The ruling or hero class often regarded itself as of divine origin, the plebeians as of bestial origin. Reflection was in a rudimentary state, but was already "outlining in advance the principles of modern science."[17] In the human age, (Periclean Athens; Roman Empire) morality came under the rules of conscience and duty of universal scope. Government was either popular or monarchial. But a "barbarism or reflection"[18] and corruption crept in. "Men first feel necessity, then look for utility, next attend to comfort, still later amuse themselves with pleasure, thence grow dissolute in luxury, and finally go mad and waste their substance."[19] There is then a recurrence of a divine epoch (early Middle Ages) as the remedy Providence uses in the process of history for man's corruption. Kings, laws and warfare were again placed under the rule of the divine. The difference from the antique divine age was that Christianity replaced less humane religions. The feudal age from the 10th to the 14th century, Vico compared to the heroic age of early Rome and Greece. The modern "age of men" is marked by the transition from feudal aristocracy to popular and monarchical kingdoms in which the recovered Roman law with its teaching of natural equity is influential.

Vico regarded religion as the basic support for each regime; this was achieved by Providence dialectically using the passions and desires of individuals and groups to arrive at ends unknown to the actors in history. Seeking "to gratify their bestial lust"[20] men established families. Nobles abused their power over the plebeians and came under the laws establishing "popular liberty."[21] "The free peoples mean to shake off the yoke of their laws, and they become subject to monarchs."[22]

In two respects particularly, Vico profoundly deviated from what came to be the general trend in 18th century historiography. (1) He had no hope of a future fulfillment of ideals being developed in history, no illustrations of inevitable progress either secular or Christian; history was a scene of cycles and recurrences. (2) He regarded the return to barbaric conditions as a creative means by which mankind is saved from civilized self-destruction and

---

[16] He did not include the Hebrews in his *schema*. They were the most ancient people and were enlightened from the beginning by the true God. Thus, Vico adhered to the old distinction between profane and sacred history.
[17] Jules Michelet, *Oeuvres Choisies de Vico*, ii, p. 196.
[18] *N.S.*, p. 1106.
[19] *N.S.*, pp. 239, 241.
[20] N.S., p. 1108.
[21] N.S., *Ibid.*
[22] N.S., p. 1112.

brought back to that piety, faith and truth without which one "cannot really be wise." [23]

There was a basic philosophical presupposition which lay at the heart of Vico's historical speculations. It was a theory of the identity of knowing and doing which he reached after throwing off the Cartesian dualism and non-genetic mechanism. Rejecting the Cartesian clear and distinct idea as the criterion of truth, Vico held that man can best know what he himself has created. God can alone truly know the world of nature, for He has created it. History is well suited to be a field of human knowledge because it is made by the human mind. ". . . the world of human society has certainly been made by men, and its principles are therefore to be found within the modifications of our own human mind." [24] The past neglect of the "study of the world of nations" Vico explained by the fact that since the mind is "immersed and buried in the body" it was easier for it to study bodily things rather than itself.

THE LAWS AND HISTORY OF MONTESQUIEU

Charles-Louis de Secondat, Baron de La Brède et de Montesquieu (1689-1755), dislike petty details and chicanery, sold his Chief-Justiceship in the Parlement at Bordeaux and spent over twenty years preparing his main book, L'Esprit des Lois (1748). He had earlier written a satire on contemporary France, Les Lettres Persanes (1721), and a history of Rome, Considerations sur les causes de la grandeur des Romaines et de leur decadence (1734).

Basic Assumptions of Montesquieu. To understand Montesquieu, his four basic assumptions about the nature of law must first be stated. (1) Montesquieu regarded positive law as that which concretizes a primal sense of equity in relative, particular human environments. ". . . the political and civil laws of each nation ought to be only the particular cases in which human reason is applied." [25] (2) Each positive law is an expression or outgrowth of environmental forces both physical and moral, including climate, topography, manners, customs, religion, morals, commerce, money, population, the general spirit of a nation and the spirit of a time. The relations between each of these factors and to the laws must be studied. "Laws . . . are the necessary relations arising from the nature of things. In this sense all beings have their laws: the Deity his laws, the material world its laws, the intelligences superior to man their laws, the beasts their laws, man his laws." [26] (3) Each form of government is a body with a principle as its spirit which the lawgiver must heed if the state is to survive. He classified governments into monarchy, despotism, and republic. Honor is the principle of a monarchy, fear of a despotism, moderation of an aristocratic republic and virtue or public spirit of a democratic republic. (4) Positive laws can be altered to keep them in line with the principle on which the government rests.[27]

It is apparent that Montesquieu believed general laws, both of a physical

---

[23] N.S., 1112.
[24] N.S., p. 331. See R. G. Collingwood, The Idea of History, pp. 63-71, and Thomas Berry, The Historical Theory of Giambattista Vico.
[25] Esprit des Lois (hereinafter cited as EL), Book I, ch. III.
[26] EL. Book XIX, ch. IV.
[27] "The more the physical causes incline mankind to inaction, the more the moral causes should estrange them from it." EL, Book XIV, ch. V.

and moral nature, were at work in human institutions, in every state, "exalting, maintaining or overcoming it." His laws were a mixture of causal relations and moral maxims for the guidance of legislators.[28] He said that the laws illuminated history and history illustrated the laws.[29] Montesquieu's *leitmotiv* was not the evolution through time of particular growing institutions. On the contrary, he drew upon the laws and institutions of diverse times and places, primitive and civilized, to illustrate his timeless principles, with the result that the past lived in his static world of abstractions in spatial deployment instead of temporal succession.[30] The connections he pointed out were not portrayed merely as historical fact, but were elevated to doctrines of universal validity.[31] The most important exception was his truly evolutionary treatment of French and English freedoms as rooted in "our fathers, the Germans." In his treatment of how Germanic institutions changed in the course of time in early feudal France he made his closest approach to a true developmental historiography.[32]

One of Montesquieu's most important contributions to historical thought was his sense of the unique elements in different situations. In several places he expressed the important individualizing sentiment that "To apply the ideas of the present time to distant ages is the most fruitful source of error."[33] Moreover, he enjoyed the variety in human arrangements. In his *Voyages* he stated, "I would be angry if all men were the same. One travels in order to see different morals and ways, not in order to criticize." [34] Among the nations whose individuality he was most successful in penetrating were the Roman Republic, England, and the early Franco-German Middle Ages. Although, as is well known, he greatly admired the English constitution, nevertheless, he did not hold up England as a model to be imitated by other states. He saw that different national situations call for laws suitable to their peculiar circumstances. He admired Solon's statement that he had given the Athenians not the best laws but "the best they could bear." [35] There is no positive law or form of government that must be followed by all men. "If the people observe the laws, what signifies it whether these laws are the same?" [36]

Another merit in Montesquieu was his strong organic sense of the interdependence between the parts of a culture, between the physical and the human world and between human wisdom and eternal justice, the ultimate ground of all law. Unlike Voltaire, Montesquieu did not blur his perception by separating reason and unreason too sharply. Montesquieu calmly accepted irrational passions, loyalties, loves and atttachments as part of objective situations. He warned statesman to take account of the general spirit (folkspirit) of their nations and not overthrow customs of which the people were

---

[28] F. Meinecke, *Die Entstehung des Historismus*, pp. 150-153.

[29] EL., Book XXXI, ch. II.

[30] See Frank T. H. Fletcher, *Montesquieu and English Politics* (1750-1800), p. 73.

[31] F. Meinecke, *op. cit.*, p. 150.

[32] *Ibid.*, pp. 177-180.

[33] EL., Book XXX, ch. XI.

[34] F. Meinecke, *op. cit.*, p. 170.

[35] EL., Book XIX, ch. XXI.

[36] EL., Book XXIX, ch. XVI.

fond.[37] States could benefit from irrationalities: "No republic is so powerful as one where the laws are obeyed from fear and passion, not from reason, as in Rome and Sparta." [38]

Montesquieu's Treatment of Historical Sources. Perhaps because he regarded his sources as a lawyer regards statutes and precedents, Montesquieu undoubtedly was uncritical of them. He was behind his times in accepting unquestioningly the sources of Roman history before the Pyrrhic wars.[39] He was equally credulous of travellers' tales. At times he misread his sources[40] or juggled them to support his ideas.[41] His most thorough examination of primary sources was made in the documents of Merovingian Gaul, in spite of his feeling that they were "frigid, dry, insipid, and hard."

Montesquieu was received more warmly in England than by the French *philosophes.* Edmund Burke, liking his conservative trend and his sympathetic historical approach to institutions, called Montesquieu the greatest genius of the age. The list of translations, editions and imitations of Montesquieu, and scholarly researches into the English feudal past inspired in England by Montesquieu is a long one. The French *philosophes,* however, found elements of naturalism, pessimism, and relativism in Montesquieu that disturbed their reforming hopes. They resented Montesquieu's belief that in the nature of all things all human institutions and governments grow old and die, that nothing much can be done to remedy this fact.[42] In Germany, Arnold Heeren's (1760-1842) researches in economic history owed much to the stimulus he received from Montesquieu's grasp of relations between the commercial and political spheres.[43]

A Secular Historian of Civilization

Voltaire. François Marie Arouet, pen name Voltaire, (1694-1778), opened important new approaches in his two major histories, *Le Siècle de Louis XIV* (Berlin, 1751) and *Essai sur les moeurs et l'esprit des nations, et sur les principaux faits de l'histoire, depuis Charlemagne jusqu'à Louis XIII* (The Hague, 1754).[44] In place of history as a naive chronicle of unrelated events, of battles and court intrigues, Voltaire presented the history of civilization—the rise and fall of nations, governments, morals, economics, the arts and sciences, the history of opinion. The *Essai*—less objective, less accurate in details, less unified, but far bolder in scope than *Le Siècle de Louis XIV*—aimed to be a more truly universal history than Bossuet's *Discourse on Universal History.*

---

[37] F. Meinecke, *op. cit.,* p. 164.
[38] *Ibid.,* p. 146.
[39] See Robert Flint, *op. cit.,* pp. 254-261.
[40] For example, Jordanes had said that the Goths claimed Scandinavia as the populous *vagina gentium.* Montesquieu believed that Jordanes had said this himself. See Thor. J. Beck, *Northern Antiquities in French Learning and Literature,* 1775-1855, p. 33.
[41] How Montesquieu used his sources to support his ideas in the case of China is shown by Elie Carcassone, "La Chine dans L'Esprit des Lois," *Revue d'Histoire Litteraire de la France,* XXXI, pp. 193-205.
[42] See EL., Book IX, ch. I; Book XI, ch. VI; Book XXIX, ch. XVI; A. Sorel, *Montesquieu,* pp. 163ff; Gilbert Chinard, "Montesquieu's Historical Pessimism" in *Studies in the History of Culture,* pp. 161-173; Voltaire, *Commentaire sur l'Esprit des Lois* (1777), *Oeuvres Completes,* XXX; E. H. Price, "Montesquieu's Historical Conception to the Fundamental Law," *The Romanic Review,* XXXVIII (October, 1947), pp. 234-242.
[43] Eduard Fueter, *op. cit.,* p. 385.
[44] Minor works included *History of Charles XII* (1728); *Annals of the Empire since Charlemagne* (1753); *The History of the Parlement of Paris* (1769); *History of Russia under Peter the Great* (1759-1763). This last work was intended to please Catherine the Great.

This aim was polemical because Voltaire included America, Asia and the ancient civilizations to discredit biblical chronology and other biblical authority and to remove the Jews (Voltaire was anti-semitic) and the Christian Church from the pivotal place in world history accorded them by Bossuet. History on the world scale enabled Voltaire to praise Confucianism, Mohammedanism or the religion of the Incas to the detriment of the Christian Church.

To Voltaire the past was shrouded in crimes, follies, dogmatisms, credulity and ignorance. He regarded the fables and miracles which he exposed as intentional deceptions. Scheming priests and conquering tyrants were his devils. The people of republics abused their power as often as kings. He had a low view of human motives, classifying men as the rascally few and the imbecile multitude.

Light and happiness appeared in history only from man's own efforts—from thinkers, poets and benevolent princes. There were four happy ages—Periclean Athens, Augustan Rome, the Age of the Medici, and the Century of Louis XIV—when reason and refinement temporarily ruled over barbarism. He felt there was a "love of order which secretly animates the human race" and which has prevented its total ruin.[45] But he had only a tepid belief in progress, "men always being men" and half regarded it as an accident. "Nature has marked the limits of man's perfection.[46]

Though widely read and imitated by those of the same outlook, Voltaire was critized by Montesquieu as never able to write a good history because he wrote like a monk who writes only for the glory of his order,[47] and by Gibbon for his organization, his lack of research, his narration and his sectarian bigotry.[48] Edmund Burke said "Nobody has ever united blasphemy and obscenity so happily together." [49] In his research, he often said evil of the historians he pillaged[50] and mentioned sources he hardly used "in order to conceal his indebtedness to one he followed closely." [51]

AN OUTLINE FOR A UNIVERSAL HISTORY

Turgot. At the Sorbonne, in 1750, Anne Robert Jacques Turgot, (1727-1781), gave three discourses on universal history in which the ideas of continuity, progress and novelty were fundamental. Man, unlike other forms of life, acquires and transmits knowledge. In man, "reason, the passions, liberty unceasingly produce new events." Yet (unlike Voltaire) progress rests on conserving past achievements and not on eliminating vestiges of the ignorant past from the present. The course of history is a complex system of powerful intentions producing unforeseen results. Humanity, unknowingly and even in ages of retrogression, ever marches on to greater moral and intellectual perfection. Wars, conquests, migrations, the mingling of peoples,

---

45 *Essai,* ch. CXCVII.
46 *Essai, Ibid.*
47 Preserved Smith, *A History of Modern Culture,* II, p. 253.
48 D. M. Low, *Edward Gibbon 1737-1794,* pp. 120-121.
49 Anne M. Osborn, *op. cit.,* p. 8.
50 Letter of M. le Marquis d'Argens, Nov. 20, 1758, in M. de Lescure, ed., *Correspondence complete de la Marquise du Deffand avec ses amis le President Henault—Montesquieu—D'Alembert-Voltaire-Horace Walpole,* p. 236.
51 R. Lowenstein, *Voltaire as an Historian of Seventeenth Century French Drama,* p. 182. Lowenstein states that Voltaire did not read the majority of the plays available, p. 180.

the spread of commerce, the multiplication of inventions serve purposes of progress unknown to the participants. ". . . the blind passions have multiplied ideas, enlarged knowledge, and made minds more perfect, owing to the lack of a reason whose day had not yet arrived and which would have been less powerful if it had governed earlier." [52] This distinction between the visible events of history and the hidden meanings they contained for human progress probably was rooted in the Christian distinction between the will of God and the will of men. The new form of the idea was the conversion of Providence into Progress.[53]

The standards by which Turgot judged progress were human happiness, liberty, the rights of man, justice, respect for work and property, and enlightenment. He believed the greatest force at work in history for advancement of these values was Christianity, which had "given the passions the only check that could hold them in control." [54] He treated the Middle Ages as a time of progress, shown in the rise of towns, of the universities, of many inventions (clocks, windmills, paper, glass, compass, bills of exchange). He noted that "in the early Middle Ages the mechanical arts never suffered the same eclipse as did letters and speculative sciences." [55]

Two other aspects of Turgot's discussion of progress were outstanding. (1) He saw that progress was a process varying greatly in rate from one age and people to another. He offered various hypotheses on how to reconcile this with his belief in the uniformity of Nature.[56] (2) He advanced the idea that intellectual progress goes successively through three stages: the religious, the metaphysical (when men accounted for phenomena by "abstract essences and faculties"), and the scientific. Turgot intended no irreligious implication in the statement of this law, as was the case in Comte's later use of the law of three stages.[57]

A National Historian, David Hume

David Hume (1711-1776), was a Scotch philosopher who turned to history with the hope of winning literary fame. His major historical work was *The History of England from the Invasion of Julius Caesar to the Abdication of James II, 1688* (1754-1762), a book widely read for a hundred years.[58] Written in an easy, direct style, the content was largely political history arranged chronologically in order of reigns and dynasties. The slight amount of cultural, social and economic history was not well correlated. Hume relied for his information on existing secondary histories, rarely troubling to go to the sources for fresh facts or to find error of fact.[59]

[52] *Oeuvres*, II, p. 623.
[53] See K. Lowith, *op. cit.*, pp. 101-104.
[54] *Oeuvres*, II, p. 596.
[55] *Oeuvres*, II, p. 666.
[56] *Oeuvres*, II, p. 633.
[57] See Robert Flint, *op. cit.*, p. 287. For an introduction to the too little explored French historiography after Voltaire and Turgot through Condorcet (d. 1794), see F. Meinecke, *op. cit.*, ch. 4, and R. Flint, *op. cit.*, pp. 307-330.
[58] The first two volumes published were on the Stuart era (1754); the next two on the Tudors (1759); last he wrote the volumes on medieval England (1762). In 1757, he regretted that he had not begun with the accession of Henry VII. J. Y. T. Greig ed., *The Letters of David Hume*, I, pp. 251, 294.
[59] J. B. Black, *The Art of History*, pp. 90-91.

Hume's treatment of causation was weak because he relied on the theory of a uniform, normal human nature, the same for all times and places. "Ambition, avarice, self-love, vanity, friendship, generosity, public spirit: these passions have been, and still are, the causes of all the actions and enterprises of mankind.[60] Such a view, deductively applied, blocked appreciation of the unique and particular elements in various epochs and individuals. Hume, an empirical philosopher, was more speculative than empirical as a historian.[61] He set up his narrative according to what he thought was normal or natural, with the result that history was largely the same events repeated over and over. He advanced little beyond distinguishing between ages of cultivation and those of rude barbarism. He was biased against the latter for lacking trustworthy records and for having little instruction to offer enlightened ages. How development from the rude to the refined epochs, from primitive to advanced religions, took place was not a problem to Hume.[62] Hume felt that the physical factors of climate, tools, food, habitations had slight "discernible operation on the human mind." He set forth the general principle that "what depends upon few persons" is harder to account for by known causes than "what arises from a great number." [63]

Hume upheld the established Church of England as a rational middle way between the extremes of Catholic *superstition* and Protestant *enthusiasm*. He hated religion only when it bred frenzy and civil disorder.[64] Although despising their bigotry, he appreciated the contributions of the Puritans to freedom. He understood political and constitutional arguments much better than theological problems; these were two realms he did not interrelate well.[65] His bias was in favor of established governments. He disliked both despotism and revolutions. He felt that the rise of government by laws instead of by willful men was the key to English history; he recognized this development as an outgrowth of commerce and the rise of the middle classes.[66] Whigs called Hume a Tory and Tories believed him a Whig. There is much truth in Hume's claim that he was impartial in his excellent discussion of the constitutional issues of the seventeenth century. Hume explains why he was attacked by both parties. His views of things suited Whig principles; his representations of persons fitted Tory prejudices. "Nothing can so much prove that men commonly regard more persons than things as to find I am commonly numbered among the Tories." [67]

The classification of Hume as a member of the Voltairean school of historiography should not be emphasized too much. Hume disliked being called a pupil of Voltaire, insisting that his history was planned and largely

[60] *Ibid.*, p. 96.
[61] For relation of Hume's philosophy to his historiography see R. G. Collingwood, *The Idea of History*, pp. 73-76.
[62] J. B. Black, *op. cit.*, pp. 98, 104.
[63] As a consequence he judged that "the domestic and the gradual revolutions of a state must be a more proper subject of reasoning and observation, than the foreign and violent, which are commonly produced by single persons, and are more influenced by whim, folly, or caprice, than by general passions and interests." *Essays, Moral, Liberty and Political.*
[64] J. B. Black, *op. cit.*, p. 108.
[65] F. Meinecke, *op. cit.*, p. 243.
[66] F. Meinecke, *Ibid.*, p. 236.
[67] J. Y. T. Greig, *op. cit.*, I, p. 237. See E. C. Mossner, "Was Hume a Tory Historian?", *Journal of the History of Ideas*, II (April, 1941), pp. 225-236.

composed before the appearance of *Le Siecle de Louis XIV*.[68] In 1764, Voltaire wrote that he liked the philosophy of Hume more than his historical works.[69] Hume was nearer Montesquieu, with whom he corresponded, than Voltaire because of his understanding of the roles of authority, force and irrational factors in the origin of religion and government and because Hume's history was more national political history than history of civilization.[70]

A CLASSIC HISTORIAN, EDWARD GIBBON

Edward Gibbon (1737-1794) brought his youthful ambition for fame as a historian to a definite focus when on a visit to Rome.

> It was at Rome, on the 15th of October, 1764, as I sat musing amidst the ruins of the Capitol, while the bare-footed fryars were singing vespers in the temple of Jupiter, that the idea of writing the decline and fall of the city first started to my mind.[71]

The first edition of *The History of the Decline and Fall of the Roman Empire* appeared at London, 1776-1788.[72] Half of his stately narrative, the magnificent fulfillment of ambition, covered the Empire from the Principate to 476, the rise of Christianity and the founding of the Germanic kingdoms. The last half included the Byzantine Empire to 1453, the Bulgars, Russians, Magyars, the rise of Mohammedanism, the Holy Roman Empire, the Normans in Sicily and Italy, the Crusaders, the Tartars and Turks, and Rome in the Great Schism and Renaissance. For each subject, Gibbon claimed that he had examined "all of the original materials" in print.[73] He subordinated mastery of events to "system, connection, sequence,"[74] and, as a philosopher, to showing the constant and universal principles of morality and human nature. He judged his array of emperors, bishops, prophets, and monks in terms of whether they brought happiness to mankind; he felt they usually did not because they lacked the right principles of virtue. He assumed that heroes and great leaders were the most important causative force in history.

"Human nature" appeared in Gibbon now in the sense of the constant human passions[75] which shape history, and again in the sense of an absolute norm, according to which ethical judgments were made. He often referred to tyrannous misdeeds as "the disgrace and calamity of human nature;"[76] he left no doubt that human nature has its grandeur rights and dignity[77] which it is the function of civilization to protect.[78]

---

[68] J. Y. T. Greig, *op. cit.*, letter of 1755, i, p. 226. William Robertson (1721-1793), fellow country-man of Hume, acknowledge a debt to Voltaire much more than did Hume or Gibbon. This Presbyterian clergyman and professor learned from the free-thinker Voltaire to see significant institutional develop-men's in the Middle Ages! Hating despotism, he appreciated the greater freedom in the Middle Ages compared with the Roman Empire.

[69] M. de Lescure, *op. cit.*, p. 303; see Fueter, *op. cit.*, pp. 364-365.

[70] F. Meinecke, *op. cit.*, pp. 209-246.

[71] Edward Gibbon, *Autobiographic Memoirs*, in *The Life and Letters of Edward Gibbon*, pp. 66-79.

[72] Hereafter cited as *DF*. All references are to the critical edition by J. B. Bury.

[73] J. B. Black, *op. cit.*, p. 161.

[74] Edward Gibbon, *Miscellaneous Works*, IV, p. 63.

[75] "Man has much more to fear from the passions of his fellow creatures than from the convulsions of the elements." DF., III, p. 73.

[76] DF., I, p. 85, ch. III.

[77] DF., VII, p. 258, ch. LXIX.

[78] DF., VII, p. 205, ch. LXVIII.

It was not surprising to Gibbon that Rome fell when in the Empire the universally valid principles of freedom, virtue, honor and civic discipline that were the strength of the Republic became corrupted. The Republic was his "paradise lost." [79] The "long peace, and the uniform government of the Romans, introduced a slow and secret poison into the vitals of the Empire." [80] Too often Gibbon's words that "the condition of the human race was most happy and prosperous" from "the death of Domitian to the accession of Commodus" [81] have been cited, torn from their pessimistic context, to allege his satisfaction with the Empire during the Age of the Antonines. Gibbon subsequently stated, however, that Nerva, Trajan, Hadrian and the Antonines "delighted in the image of liberty" and *"deserved the honour of restoring the republic, had the Romans of their days been capable of enjoying a rational freedom."* (Italics mine) [82] He spoke of the shortness of the list of emperors "who added lustre to the imperial purple." [83] Gibbon preferred individual freedom and a system of independent, competing states (as Greece had and modern times have). He disliked despotic empires of any type.[84]

Gibbon's Treatment of Religion. Personally antagonistic to much in Christianity,[85] Gibbon was far from stating that that religion had had a wholly negative effect in history. He did not regard it as a major cause of the decline of the Empire.[86] He saw that it "broke the violence of the fall, and mollified the ferocious temper of the conquerors."[87] Throughout the Middle Ages he felt that the clergy "prevented the total extinction of letters" and exerted important humane influences for peace and protection of the defenseless.[88]

Gibbon is less convincing in his treatment of the inner history of Christianity itself. His thesis was that church history is a record of retrogression from the ethical teachings of Jesus. He spoke with respect of Christ's humanity,[89] of his "sublime simplicity" and "universal benevolence." [90] But he belittled the numbers and vain motives of the martyrs, regarded asceticism as absurd, and did not grasp the development of Christian philosophical theology. Toward miracles he was cold and agnostic. Christians have injured each other in their hates, intrigues and anathematizing more than the infidel ever hurt them. The Church of Rome, he stated, acquired her dominion by fraud.[91] On almost every development in the Church he offered the same judgment

---

[79] This is the thesis of the able article by Lewis P. Curtis, "Gibbon's Paradise Lost," in *The Age of Johnson: Essays Presented to Chauncey Brewster Tinker*, pp. 73-90; DF., IV, pp. 172-173.

[80] DF., I, pp. 61-62, ch. II.

[81] DF., I, pp. 85-86, ch. III.

[82] DF., I, pp. 85-86, ch. III; DF., IV, p. 174, ch. XXXVIII.

[83] DF., I, p. 312, ch. XI.

[84] F. Meinecke, *op. cit.,* p. 249; D. M. Low, *op. cit.,* p. 330.

[85] For his religious experiences see his Autobiographic Memoir, pp. 30, 39. Forced to leave Oxford at 16 because he became a Catholic, he was received back into Protestantism, Christmas Day, 1754.

[86] J. B. Black, *op. cit.,* pp. 170-172; DF., IV, p. 175.

[87] DF., IV, p. 175.

[88] DF., VI, p. 465.

[89] DF., V, p. 105.

[90] DF., II, p. 83.

[91] DF., II, p. 148; elsewhere he stated that the temporal power of the popes "insensibly arose from the calamities of the times." DF., V, p. 39.

he made on ritual: "the spirit of the Gospel evaporated in the pageantry of the Church.[92] The entire story was of the same human passions, tricks, frauds, impostures and ambitions constantly corrupting the Gospel.[93] His account of church history was learned, earnest and severe, yet no growth of truth or goodness took place within it; the church was statically the same in each century. "He never found the true causes of the good, but only for the evil in medieval civilization." [94] How a religion so static or retrogressive could accomplish the benefits he hinted that it did, Gibbon did not answer. Today eminent scholars reject his authority as a historian of Christianity.[95]

Gibbon did not perceive the individuality or uniqueness in persons or events. They were types. Persons were portrayed statically without inner struggle or development. Jargon adjectives were used—a person was "credulous," "crafty," "artful," "haughty," "intrepid," "profligate," "effeminate," etc. Constantine was a mixture of "rapaciousness and prodigality." His hero, Julian the Apostate, was characterized as "deserving the empire of the world." Gibbon lacked the sense of organic relatedness among the parts of a civilization. His account of Roman law, largely of Roman lawyers, was inorganically set apart in a separate chapter. Finally, his normative, censorious outlook rendered his narrative immobile, ungenetic, unappreciative of the uniqueness of persons and events.[96] Gibbons' power to portray the declining glory of classical culture was rooted in his sense of membership in and continuity with that culture. The portrait, based on extensive erudition and drawn with the literary strokes of a master stylist, is not only a historical masterpiece of eighteenth century scholarship but also an excellent expression of the enlightened century's culture and outlook.

An Historian of Culture, Johann Joachim Winckelmann

The most original German contributions to historiography in the Age of Reason were made by Johann Joachim Winckelmann (1717-1768)[97] and Justus Möser (1720-1794). Winckelmann's *Geschichte der Kunst des Alteriums* (Dresden, 1764), had great historiographical significance, although it was even more important as a theory of beauty. He did not try to write "a mere chronicle of epochs." Instead, he sought to show "the essential of art, of which the history of the individual artists has little bearing." [98] A vision of the grandeur, simplicity, nobility, serenity and good proportioning in Greek art, especially sculpture, possessed Winckelmann. Athenian art embodied the Only One Beauty, eternally perfect. He judged Persian, Etruscan, Phoenician and Egyptian art by the standards of Periclean Athens instead of seeing the art of each people from within their own circumstances and backgrounds.

[92] DF., V, p. 369.
[93] DF., II, p. 414; III, pp. 221-225; III, p. 215; F. Meinecke, *op. cit.*, p. 252.
[94] Statement of Bishop Grundvig, quoted in Kemp Malone, "Grundtvig's Philosophy of History," *Journal of the History of Ideas*, I (June, 1940), p. 282.
[95] See Shelby T. McCloy, *Gibbon's Antagonism to Christianity*, p. 367.
[96] See Carl L. Becker, *The Heavenly City of the Eighteenth Century Philosophers*, p. 117. See also Christopher Dawson, "Edward Gibbon," *British Academy Proceedings*, XX (1934), pp. 159-180.
[97] J. J. Winckelmann, *The History of Ancient Art*, tr. by G. Henry Lodge, M.D., I, p. 107. For the life of Winckelmann see Walter Pater, *The Renaissance*, pp. 147-193. The popular resentment over his murder by a thief at Trieste testifies to the esteem he had already won.
[98] Henry C. Hatfield, *Winckelmann and His German Critics 1755-1781*, pp. 90-93, for Herder's criticism of Winckelmann's absolutizing.

Nevertheless, although Winckelmann's thought was rooted in a normative classicism,[99] which deeply influenced the Hellenic revival of the coming century, his work also had historiographical importance. He set an example of writing on a theme in cultural history instead of on public affairs. Moreover, under Montesquieu's influence, he related Greek art to the total life of the Greeks, bringing in the influence of free government, the climate, economic conditions, the physique and the athletics of the Greeks, their national characteristics and trends in public opinion. He correlated the post-Alexandrine decline of freedom and the post-Alexandrine decline of art, which had become pedantic, imitative and emotional. Winckelmann probably had in mind the luxurious and grandiose decadence in Baroque art that was a sequel to the age of Michelangelo.[100] Winckelmann saw clearly, and in doing so went beyond his age, that works of art had their roots less in formal rules and willful creation than in social psychological factors of which the artist may not be conscious. Also in contrast to the progressive pattern of the age which saw perfection in the future, Winckelmann saw artistic perfection as having been already achieved in Greek art.[101]

Most important, perhaps, was the example Winckelmann gave for future historians of the possibilities latent in devoting one's whole soul enthusiastically to grasping the unique content of a total culture. Herder's organic view of history was fostered by Winckelmann's well-rounded view of Greek culture;[102] F. von Schlegel's *History of Greek Poetry* was modelled on Winckelmann.[103] Winckelmann's critical study from primary sources of one individual object —Greek art—pointed to the fruitful results of empathy or sympathy with the object studied. Mere factual antiquarianism was shown to be inadequate. So also were the usual patterns of Enlightened historiography.[104]

THE LEGACY OF THE ENLIGHTENMENT HISTORIANS

The patterns of Enlightenment historiography were attacked by the romanticist and nationalistic schools for their upper middle class prejudices: their attributing of laws, states, religions, and art to rational design; their failure to portray local color and uniqueness in the past; their judging of other times by the standards of their century; their weakness in grasping cultures as organic, evolving unities; and their interest in universal man with its corollary of relative indifference to national history, to the folk-spirit of nations as the subconscious moulder of history. Such criticisms, often rooted in new insights stirred by the French Revolution, did not kill the legacy from the Enlightenment historians. This legacy was absorbed in the world view of nineteenth century liberalism with its belief in progress as a law of history, in freedom, in religious toleration. Liberal historians, like Thierry and Guizot, appropriated romantic feeling and color for their histories, but

[99] F. Meinecke, *op. cit.*, p. 319 states "His was one of the last and perhaps the most beautiful victory of the old normative and absolute spirit."

[100] *Ibid.*, p. 316.

[101] E. Fueter, *op. cit.*, pp. 389-393.

[102] H. C. Hatfield, *op. cit.*, p. 93.

[103] Friedrich von Schlegel, *The Philosophy of History*, tr. by James Burton Robertson, p. 2.

[104] F. Meinecke, *op. cit.*, pp. 320-324.

even more they stood on the shoulders of Voltaire.[105] Furthermore, all historiographical art—which seeks to probe causes from a secular and human standpoint, which writes the history of civilization and ideas on a world scale, which assumes man's reason can shape events, which investigates the credibility of sources, which is bold enough to pose a thesis and affirm value judgments, which feels the dignity of the task of historiography—continues to enrich the heritage bequeathed us by the historians of the Age of Enlightenment.

---

[105] See the interesting comparison between the liberal historians of the first half of the nineteenth century and the historians of the Enlightenment in Fueter, *op. cit.* pp. 500-503. "The historiography of Liberalism was a direct continuation of that of the Enlightenment."

Chapter 12

THE RISE OF ROMANTICISM

By Alfred G. Pundt

The Romanticist Reaction

A LTHOUGH the rationalism of the eighteenth century dominated the outlook of central and western Europe for over a generation and inspired the achievements of great writers like Voltaire, Gibbon, Hume and Raynal, a reaction against it was inevitable. The seeds of this reaction had been sown centuries earlier. It had historical roots in the Protestant Reformation, with its stress on faith as against good works, in the early modern repudiation of geocentric astronomy and the Christian cosmology, and the consequent revolution in outlook and attitude. It was prepared by the English political revolutions of the seventeenth century which stressed the domain of the individual, by the pantheism of Spinoza and the pietism of the German and English Protestants and by the persistence of medieval esthetic ideals throughout most of central and western Europe. Some writers of the early eighteenth century such as Vico, Winckelmann, Shaftesbury and Muratori, had already protested the skepticism and intellectualism of the Enlightenment which, by impairing faith in the achievements and beliefs of the past while undermining the institutions of the present, was leaving a void in its wake. Finally, the French Revolution, which embodied a culmination of "enlightened" principles and embarked upon violence, terror and destruction in order to achieve them, turned conservatives, moderates and even most of the liberals away from the new dispensation.

It was the void left by this relaxation of social forms and the weakening of religious faith which romanticism sought to fill with a new faith and a new purpose. This new state of mind emerged in the 1770's and, by the turn of the century, had become general. It was heralded by a growing discontentment with the contemporary ideology, by an anxiety over the philosophical implications of human existence and a sadness without reason (the so-called *Weltschmerz* or *mal de siècle*). As Goethe observed, the classical outlook was healthy, the romanticist outlook was ill. This moral anxiety deeply influenced the literature, morals and politics of the late eighteenth and early nineteenth centuries and left an enduring impression upon contemporary historiography.

Chronological Scope and Character of Romanticism

While rationalism owed its original inspiration to a group of French *philosophes,* the romanticist movement first arose in Germany and England, some years before it made its debut in France. Romanticism made a peculiarly profound and enduring impression upon the life and outlook of Germany, where the literary aspect of the movement may be said to begin with Hamann,

Schelling and Herder in the 1770's and to reach its climax toward the turn of the century with the writings of Friedrich Schlegel, August Wilhelm Schlegel, Novalis (Friedrich von Hardenberg), Tieck and Wackenröder. The outstanding English literary romanticists include Southey, Coleridge, Scott, Wordsworth, Byron, Keats and Shelley. In France the impact of romanticism was felt later than in Germany and England but, if we may believe Brandes, the French romanticist writers constituted the greatest literary school of the nineteenth century.[1] The chief literary representatives of that school include Nodier, Hugo. Alexandre Dumas, Sainte-Beuve, Madame de Staël, Chateaubriand and de Vigny. In Italy, as in Germany, romanticism, as represented by the literary generation which included Foscolo, Leopardi, Manzoni, and Tommasseo, quickly identified itself with the contemporary political struggles for national unification.

The romanticist movement left its mark upon every phase of early nineteenth century European thought and culture. Its ideas and its inspiration were transmitted to the various media of artistic expression, to the realm of pedagogy and to the several social sciences. Its impact upon the realm of historiography was profound.

Feeling and Imagination. The romanticist reaction against late eighteenth century rationalism was particularly emphatic in the romanticist's stress upon the role of feeling and imagination. The protest against intellectualism was especially marked in Germany. Feeling was exalted above reason. As Faguet has pointed out, the romanticists abhorred reality and sought to escape it and imprison themselves in the sanctuaries of their personal feeling. Thus, Jean Paul Richter conceived romanticism as a yearning for indeterminate ideals of beauty and harmony. Not infrequently these nostalgic dreams of the romanticists fixed themselves upon concrete objectives. Most commonly their ideals embraced beauty in all its various forms, especially in its more colorful and striking manifestations.

Romanticists as Maladjusted Men. The desire to escape reality and the unappeasable yearning for unattainable objectives, made many of the romanticists profoundly and inconsolably unhappy. Thus, the romanticist poets often remained isolated, lonely and unadapted souls, spiritually living on the margin of contemporary society and not infrequently in conflict with it. Lacking a strong intellectual armor, many of these frustrated souls became profoundly depressed. In France and Germany, many of the romanticists experienced an attraction toward an unknown being and a happiness not of this world, a happiness which, like Novalis' blue flower, was unreal.

Love of Beauty. Their aversion to the ugliness of reality impelled the romanticists to seek solitude and beauty in nature. This love of solitude drove them to the country, the woods, the mountains, and the sea, not so much in order to describe natural beauty as to stimulate their reverie and cradle their melancholy. But the esthetic sensibilities of the romanticists also made them cherish the variety of nature's beauties, the picturesque, grandiose and exotic,

---

[1] Georg Brandes, *Main Currents in Nineteenth Century Literature*, V. p. 39.

storms and tempests, rains, winds, the pale moon, ancient ruins, etc. Often, as in the case of Byron, Shelley, and Hugo, the glorification of nature had a religious quality; nature became man's consoling and comforting confidante.

Religious Attitude. The romanticists' vague aspiration toward an ideal frequently resulted in a deepening and rejuvenation of religious sentiment. Nearly all of the romanticists had been reared as Christians. Most of them, however, soon abandoned the faith of their fathers. Their subsequent sentimental agony as well as their worship of tradition frequently led them back, if not to orthodoxy, at least to a faith and hope in God. Some representatives of this school, such as Manzoni and Pellico, never wavered from the old faith while others, notably Shelley, Leopardi, de Vigny and Michelet, drifted far from the established faiths. God was placed in the role of guardian of human liberties, of an inspiration to "pure" love and of a supreme authority called upon to sanction many activities condemned by law and the prejudices of man. This religion was dissociated from most elements of revealed Christianity and, at least among the early romanticists, occupied a position somewhere between pantheism and deism. Hence, among the romanticists, atheists were as rare as ardent Christians. In some parts of Europe, notably in Germany and Scandinavia, romanticism evinced a strong tendency toward a pietistic mysticism, a yearning for an ambiguous but nevertheless real in-dwelling consciousness of God and an interest in the occult. On the other hand, not a few German members of this school, notably Friedrich Schlegel, Friedrich von Stolberg and Zacharias Werner, abandoned Protestantism for the Catholic faith.[2]

Natural Rights. In their worship of God, of nature and of beauty, the romanticists were seeking to free themselves not only from reality but also from many everyday and irksome conventions and institutions, for the romanticists were at once idealists, individualists and revolutionaries. Many of the romanticists, for example, eschewed the bonds of legal wedlock on the assumption that love is a divine principle, that only God can unite two people in marriage and that the human heart must remain free to fix upon the objects of its yearning, all the conventions and laws of man notwithstanding, and that any loveless union is adulterous, regardless of any legal sanction. According to this doctrine the "natural rights" of men transcend the exigencies of society, tradition and orthodoxy. In a spirit reminiscent of the Enlightenment, the romanticists stressed the political and social freedom of the individual as against all forms of authoritarianism.

The Romanticists' Social and Political Conscience. Many of the romanticists found consolation for their frustration, disillusionment and martyrdom in a life of service and devotion to others. They became deeply solicitous of the humbler classes of society. In their desire to renovate society and elevate humanity they devoted themselves to various social causes. In many parts of Europe they were engaged in the early nineteenth century struggles for national independence. Some of them participated in the Greek war of independence. The Polish

---

[2] After a tumultuous life of adventure and licentiousness, the poet and dramatist Friedrich Ludwig Zacharias Werner finally abandoned Germany for Italy. While in Rome, where he passed the last years of his stormy career, Werner embraced the Catholic faith and was even ordained a priest.

romanticists took an active part in the abortive revolt of 1831. In France the first romanticists were champions of the monarchy but, toward 1830, they began to espouse liberal ideas. Thus, Hugo pleaded for the hapless victims of outmoded institutions and laws in the early 'thirties. George Sand and the historian Michelet eloquently espoused the rights of women and children. George Sand, who took a sympathetic interest in the first victims of modern industrial society in France, wrote in the early forties, *Le Compagnon du tour de France,* which recounted the customs and tribulations of the rapidly decaying French journeymen's associations. Foscolo, Manzoni and Leopardi strove to clear the alien rulers from Italian soil. Adam Mickiewicz, some years later, labored to keep the cause of Polish patriotism alive.

Interest in Particular, Strange and Bizarre Things. Apart from these essential features of romanticism, there were several other aspects of the movement that have a special bearing upon modern historiography. As a group, the romanticists were more interested in the particular, whereas the classicists in their search for universal values, emphasized the general and characteristic features of societies and institutions. The romanticists sought local color and were fascinated by the exotic and the remote, whether they were found in the distant past or in contemporary society. While the classicists conceived the world as a well-ordered and determinate community, the romanticists saw it as infinite, enormous, striking and disproportionate. They never ceased to be astonished and thrilled by the grandeur of nature or by the bizarre, fantastic and abnormal in human society. Not unlike children, the romanticists were charmed by curious legends, notably those peopled with strange and fantastic figures such as gnomes, dwarfs, nymphs, dragons, vampires and ghosts. They had a similar predilection for abnormal moral phenomena such as lovers consumed with passion, heroes capable of sublime devotion, criminals of satanic perversity, women of angelic virtue or diabolic perfidiousness, saints, martyrs, murderers, fiends, ascetics and angels. While many early romanticists were especially attracted by the world of the savage and of the peasant as such, the later romanticists were peculiarly susceptible to the charms of strange and exotic lands, customs and peoples. The picturesque descriptions of Hugo, Wordsworth, Scott, Heine, Gautier and Chateaubriand were charactertistic of this interest, as was the keen contemporary preoccupation of writers with many half-forgotten countries such as Egypt, Spain, Corsica, Sicily, the Crimea, Greece and the Near East.

Genetic Conception of History. But the romanticists widened the temporal as well as the spatial horizon of their generation. Their curiosity about little known or half-forgotten parts of the world, their preoccupation with the obscure and strange and their focus upon the particular and local necessarily awakened interest in long-neglected historical epochs as well. Their desire to see their own society, its mores, customs and institutions against the background of other and diverse civilizations found an analogue in their differentiation of eighteenth century European culture from that of other and chronologically more or less remote historical ages. Hence, while the classicists were peculiarly preoccupied with unchanging man's relentless struggle for a better world, the romanticists stressed the organic wholeness of a historical evolution in which man was inseparable from the various elements of his ever-changing environment.

Interest in the Middle Ages. Thus, reversing the classicists' disdain for medievalism, the romanticists eagerly recalled the past which they sought to reproduce as completely and faithfully as possible. The romanticists' attention was first called to medieval times by the extant artistic monuments and the poetry of that period. Many English writers of the mid-eighteenth century had already focussed attention upon the grandiose beauty of their old churches and abbeys, especially those that were more or less in ruins. In Germany, the pioneer work of Lessing, Herder and Winckelmann in re-awakening an enthusiasm for medieval art soon found an echo in literary, social, political and intellectual history. In France, Chateaubriand launched the crusade in favor of medieval art.

While the classical writers found nothing but coarseness, ignorance, barbarism and superstitution in Catholic-Feudal times, the romanticists saw in the Middle Ages, quaintness, charm, color and originality. As Friedrich Schlegel wrote, "if the middle ages are a night it is a night resplendent with stars." The initial preoccupation with the esthetic and literary aspects of medieval times with their architecture, sculpture, music, drama and ballads, was quickly followed by a curiosity about other features of medieval civilization, by a historical interest in the Papacy, the Empire, the chivalry of the Middle Ages, the Crusades, the baronial conflicts, the life in the castles, the character of the princely courts with their women, pages, retainers, etc.

It is both interesting and significant that the romanticist historians centered their attention chiefly upon the Middle Ages not only because it had been the most neglected period of literary history but also because they believed to have found in it the sources of national character, customs, and institutions. Indeed, in many cases the collection and subsequent study of old texts caused the developing scientific techniques of evaluation to be put into service of national prejudice. Thus in Prussia, Arnim and Kleist abandoned the romanticist ideas to launch a nationalist and conservative campaign against the cosmopolitanism and liberalism of the Enlightenment. The Polish writer Grabovsky saw the historical and nationalist as the predominant elements in romanticism. The Czech romanticists reproached the great Dubrovsky for lacking patriotic zeal. Only a few years after the Congress of Vienna, the Austrian government ordered the compilation of the songs of the various peoples of the polyglot monarchy. Hungarian literature of the early nineteenth century is replete with medieval national characters, tales, customs and ideas. Only in Russia and the Balkans, where the Middle Ages were associated with military occupation and oppression, was there comparatively little literary preoccupation with medieval national backgrounds.

THE GERMAN ROMANTICIST REACTION

Notwithstanding the fact that the first European reaction against the rationalism of the eighteenth century was founded by the widely read and influential works of the French-Swiss Rousseau, it was in Germany that the romanticist protest against the ideas of the Enlightenment made the deepest and widest impression. There the rationalist outlook had many devotees and had left innumerable enduring souvenirs. For, like England, Germany could regard the French revolutionary forces with some detachment, at least until she became embroiled with them in the course of the 1790's. Moreover, central Europe found itself in the throes of a vast literary renaissance during the latter part of the eighteenth century. Finally, the German predilection toward mysticism and obscurantism quickly responded to the anti-intellectual bias of romanticism.

Möser. Justus Möser (1720-94), a historian, statesman and publicist, became one of the earliest German critics of the Enlightenment. He was born and died in the old Westphalian city of Osnabruck, where he saw many years' service as administrator and councilor. Opposed t othe cosmopolitanism of the Enlightenment, to its stress upon the universal man and universal culture, Möser interested himself in the customs, dialects, mores, the economy and family life of localized regions and communities. His outstanding historical work (1768), the *History of Osnabrück (Onsabrückische Geschichte)*, dealing chiefly with the medieval social life of that city, was an example of this new type of local history. In his essay entitled *German History (Deutsche Geschichte)*, which was part of a symposium bearing the significant title *On German Character and Art (Von Deutscher Art und Kunst)*, he stressed the importance of writing German national history on the basis of many such localized studies. "There are many compelling motives for writing such a history," he pointed out. Above all, "it is necessary for everyone to illuminate his province in order to show it in a true light to this great (national) historian," he insisted. Such a history, he urged, must describe the dress of the times, the style of writing, law, etc. As such, it must embrace legal history, the history of religion, philosophy, the arts and sciences since even "every war is surrounded by a special set of circumstances and every diplomatic negotiation takes place in a peculiar and special atmosphere."[3]

Hamann. Much better known than Möser, in this connection, was his contemporary, Johann Georg Hamann (1730-88). The son of a surgeon, Hamann was born in Königsberg. His education, both at the hands of frequently changing private tutors and at the University of Königsberg, was fragmentary and unsystematic. After a few years' employment as private tutor, the restless Hamann embraced a business career which took him to England and France and left him poverty stricken, with a deep sense of frustration. Through his closest friend, Behrens, he was introduced to Kant, who exerted a profound influence upon him, brought him many benefactions and launched him upon a literary career. Hamann enjoyed a prolonged contact with Kant, whom he attacked for his abstract logic and his differentiation of matter and form. He also made the acquaintance of Moses Mendelssohn, whom he assailed for his anti-Christian bias.[4] Although most of his writings were in the form of short

---

[3] *Von Deutscher Art and Kunst,* p. 181.
[4] See Hamann's hostile review of Mendelssohn's prize-winning *Jerusalem* in J. G. Hamann, *Schriften,* p. 287.

essays and literary fragments, Hamann exerted a considerable influence upon many illustrious contemporaries, notably upon Johann Gottfried Herder and many of the *Sturm und Drang* poets who saw in the *Magus of the North* the prophetic oracle of a new dawn.[5]

As an admirer of Jean Jacques Rousseau and an early adversary of the Enlightenment, Hamann stressed the creative value of feeling and faith and condemned the intellectualism of rationalism. Much of this was probably due to his inability to reason abstractly. As he himself confessed, "as against Kant my poor head is like a broken vessel, clay against iron."[6] Hamann especially emphasized the importance of language and poetry as expressions of individual or group character. As he wrote in 1759, the visible character of our soul expresses itself through words. A man of deep religious faith, Hamann believed that the world was part of a divine design. He remarked, "a world without God is [like] a man without a head—without a heart, without a digestive tract and without sense organs." The unfolding of history revealed to him a philosophical pattern. "Without philosophy," Hamann insisted, "there is no history, and the one is revealed in the other."

√*Herder: Early Life.* Although, like his mentor Hamann, Herder did not bequeath to posterity any great historical writings, he nevertheless exerted a profound influence upon the historiography of romanticism. Johann Gottfried Herder (1744-1803), a philosopher, poet, preacher, anthropologist, and philologist, was an East Prussian. Taken to Königsberg in his late teens young Herder there abandoned his medical studies for theology, came under the intellectual sway of Hamann and soon found his way to the great philosopher Kant. After several years' teaching experience in Riga, Herder undertook a journey to France as a travel companion of the Prince of Holstein-Catin. He was deeply impressed by Paris, by its brilliant writers, its theatres, its art and its splendor.[7] Soon Herder made the acquaintance of Goethe, who had him brought to Weimar where he made a living as court preacher and where, together with Goethe, Wieland and Jean Paul (Jean Paul Friedrich Richter), he became a leading spirit of the *Sturm und Drang* and an implacable opponent of the ascendant rationalism of his time.

Herder's Ideas for the Philosophy of History of Humanity. Although Herder proved to be a poet of mediocre talents, he was a prodigious writer, and a lucid and brilliant stylist. His literary career began with anonymously published collections of German literary fragments which appeared in the 1760's. He wrote extensively on the origins of language, the spirit and character of German poetry and popular folklore and songs. Probably his most significant publication in these areas was his *Voices of the People in Song (Stimmen der Völker in Liedern)*, which appeared in 1778-1779. His *Ideas for the Philosophy of History of Humanity (Ideen zur Philosphie der Geschichte der Menschheit)*, appearing between 1784 and 1791 and describing his conceptions of history,

[5] Hamann was christened the *Magus of the North* by his friend the Swabian statesman and political theorist Friedrich Karl Freiherr von Moser.
[6] J. G. Hamann, *Schriften*, p. 336.
[7] See his travel diary of 1769, reprinted in *Herders Sämmtliche Werke*, edited by Bernhard Suphen, IV, p. 435.

was one of his most ambitious undertakings. Although it is not, properly speaking, a romanticist who appears in its pages, by directing attention toward the Middle Ages, his *Ideas* determined the historical orientation of a vast generation of German romanticists which included the Schlegel and Grimm brothers, Arnim, Brentano, Novalis and Tieck.

Herder's Concept of Evolution. The most significant contribution of Herder's *Ideas* is its emphasis upon the conscious process of evolution which underlies the development of organic life and of human civilization. As he says in the fifth book of the *Ideas,* "We have traced the rise in the form of organization from stones to crystals, from crystals to metals, from these to the creation of plants, from plants to animals and from these to man and, with it, the inherent forces and tendencies toward the diversification of creatures, forces, which, in so far as we can perceive them, unite in the form of man."[8] Anticipating the Darwinian theory of biological evolution, Herder, even assumed, for example, that man had, over a long period of development, evolved out of the primates. "He who has any doubts about this," he asserted, "should carefully compare the skulls of man with those of the primates and all such doubts must disappear."[9] This theme of evolution is implicit even in the organization of the *Ideas,* which begins with the earth as a planet, deals with the diverse species of animals and concludes with the story of man's interaction with his environment and his eventual emergence as an intelligent and self-conscious master of destiny. Thus, Herder assumed that all beings which have, at one time or another, inhabited the earth were conditioned by the requirements of their environment, by the conditions and circumstances of the various ages through which they have passed and by their inherited or acquired characteristics or traits. This genetic conception of history as an unending stream of interrelated phenomena in which man plays a significant active as well as passive role, underlies the entire philosophy of the *Ideas.*

Herder's Historical Objective. Behind this pattern of history, Herder saw a providential purpose. To him every successive civilization, while it built upon the ruins of its predecessors, simultaneously added something new. In this way man was gradually making his way to ever higher levels of civilization; not, as the rationalists imagined, as an accidental result of cumulative cultural progress, but toward objectives determined by God. Every new phase of civilization, according to Herder, thus brought man nearer to this divinely ordained purpose, a purpose which, however, was inherent in man himself. Herder loosely defined this purpose as humanity. To achieve this humanity, man had been endowed with senses, ambition, reason, freedom, health, language, art and religion.[10] Nature's greatest gift to man, Herder contended, was reason, and it was this reason which exalted man above the animal kingdom and made him free.

Diversity of Social and Biological Phenomena. In his ascent toward this humanity, said Herder, man was destined to spread throughout the world and,

---

[8] Johann Gottfried Herder, *Ideen zur Philosophie der Geschichte der Menschheit,* part 1, p. 164.
[9] *Herders Werke,* edited by Theodor Matthias, IV, p. 50.
[10] *Herders Werke,* IV, p. 249.

hence, to organize as many and as diverse civilizations as the circumstances of the varying and changing institutional and natural environments of the world might require. For in nature, Herder observed, no two leaves of the same tree are identical, much less two human faces or two civilizations.[11] Each such civilization, Herder went on, must necessarily develop all its potentialities within its given framework of time, space and circumstance. Man is, moreover, destined to pass through many stages and changes of culture and civilization, Herder argued, but in the course of all these vicissitudes reason and justice must increasingly prevail among men and must eventually lead them to an enduring humanity.[12] Hence, the story of mankind is, in essence, the story of man's moral education and progress.

National Culture. Herder defined national culture as the flower of a people's character. In the same way that a newborn child must learn, so must an unlettered people learn by experience and contact with others. But every national culture must complete the same life cycle that individual beings undergo, Herder asserted. As a plant withers it spreads its own seed and thus creative life is ever renewed.

The German Nation. Herder assumed that the German people possessed the characteristics of a nation held together by bonds of common solidarity, at least until the Germanic invasions of early medieval times. With the migrations, the nation lost its bonds of solidarity, for feudal warriors fought primarily for private gain, free men disappeared under the mounting pressure of baronial extortion and royal military preoccupations caused the delegation of legal authority to dukes, counts, barons, etc. The result of this was that national interests, still nebulously embodied in the monarch, were gradually transferred to his servants, warriors and lieutenants. Thus the selfish interests of warriors and clergy detroyed all ambition, enterprise and intellectual curiosity. The democratic German traditions barely survived the medieval extinction of liberty. Yet Herder reluctantly admits that the pressure of the clerical hierarchy was perhaps necessary to keep Europe from dissolving into anarchy and despotism. After the close of the Middle Ages, he goes on, the pressure of new exigencies, or crisis and danger, brought forth a third estate, in opposition to those of the nobility and clergy. This, he continues, is the estate of science, of useful labor, and of artistic creation, and it was this which gradually brought the age of knighthood and priesthood to an end.[13]

Herder's Genetic Concept of History. Constituting the philosophical connecting link between rationalism and romanticism and not a professional historian himself, Herder thus gave an entirely new direction to contemporary historiography. He emphasized the organic unity of the historical process, pointing out that man's life, outlook, aspirations, institutions and conventions are necessarily a product of the past and that nothing is impervious to the impact of this past. Herder also called special attention to the genetic character of historical change according to which every culture, building on the basis

[11] Herder, *Mensch und Geschichte, Sein Werk im Grundriss,* p. 241.
[12] *Ibid.,* p. 275.
[13] *Herders Ausgewählte Schriften,* edited by Bernhard Suphan, p. 493.

of preceding and ruined civilizations, strives for a higher humanity and justice and that the evolutionary process underlies all organic and institutional life. He stressed the interaction of civilizations, the influence of climate and the physical environment on man's development and the necessarily extensive variety of human cultures. Above all, Herder re-emphasized the Middle Ages as the gestation period of national character and the part which language, poetry, art and folklore played in the evolution and transmission of this national character. Herder's contributions in so many diverse areas of literary activity immediately and deeply influenced a generation of distinguished writers, which included Hegel, Görres, the Grimm brothers, Ranke, Eichhorn, Savigny, Michelet, Thierry and Guizot.

Müller. One of the first German writers to apply the romanticist conceptions to historical scholarship was the Swiss-born Johannes von Müller (1752-1809). Born in 1752, the son of a Calvinist preacher, the restless Müller began his professional career as private tutor in Geneva. After several years' teaching experience in Cassel he returned to Switzerland for a few years, following which he assumed a post as librarian and, subsequently, as diplomat for the Archbishop-Elector of Mainz. When the French occupied Mainz in 1792, Müller went to Vienna, and left there in 1804 to become official historiographer for the Hohenzollern dynasty. A political opportunist and an ambitious man of conservative temperament, the gifted Müller left Prussia in 1807 to become state secretary and superintendent of public instruction in the Kingdom of Westphalia, recently created by Napoleon.

Müller's Historical Works. Müller's various historical writings include the *Historical Essays (Essais historiques)*, published in 1781, and the *Twenty-four Books of General History (Vier-und-zwanzig Bücher Allgemeiner Geschichte)* which was a collection of his Geneva lectures published after his death in 1811; but his greatest work was a five-volume *History of the Swiss Confederation (Geschichten schweizerischer Eidgenossenschaft)*, published during the years 1786-1808. In fact, Müller had brought out volume one of a projected *Histories of the Swiss (Geschichten der Schweizer)* in 1780 but later re-wrote it, making altogether six revisions. In its completed and polished form, his *History of the Swiss Confederation* was a glowing eulogy of medieval Switzerland. The work was so well received that it went through many great enlarged editions.

Müller's History of the Swiss Confederation. Müller's original *History* began with the early twelfth century and concluded with the end of the fourteenth century. Although he thought of himself as a great modern historian and had consulted a wide variety of sources, his *History* leaned too heavily on the chronicles of the sixteenth-century Tschudi and suffered much from an uncritical acceptance of those sources. Müller's vanity and ambition caused him to inject a strongly patriotic note into his work which especially featured the life and work of cantonal and national political and religious leaders.[14] While his work was pervaded with sentimental tributes to his fellow Swiss and the

---

[14] Müller was disturbed by the lukewarm reception accorded his *History* in Zürich where he was rebuked for a lack of patriotic zeal in his treatment of local cantonal heroes.

Swiss struggle for independence, Müller's aristocratic bias caused him to over-look or ignore the growth of Swiss democratic institutions. Hence, although Müller's writings undoubtedly possessed literary brilliance, and were widely esteemed for their romantic approach to history, they have long since been overshadowed by the more thorough works of modern critical scholars.

Schiller. The famous dramatist and poet, Friedrich Schiller (1759-1805), took one of the characters made famous in Müller's *History* as the subject of his drama *Wilhelm Tell.* The brilliant literary style and warm sentimentalism of Schiller, the poet, was also reflected in his historical works. These include his *History of the Defection of the Netherlands from Spanish Rule (Geschichte des Abfalls der vereinigten Niederlande von der spanischen Regierung),* which appeared in 1788, and won for its author a professorship at the University of Jena, and *The History of the Thirty Years' War (Geschichte des dreissig-jährigen Krieges),* published during the years 1791-93. The Dutch conflict was seen as a saga of national liberation from foreign domination. As for *The History of the Thirty Years' War,* it was a dramatic conflict of irreconcilable religious and political forces replete with all the elements of suspense and pathos. Like Müller's historical writings, Schiller's histories and numerous historical plays endure as brilliant literary achievements but, because of their limited scope and their exclusion of valuable pertinent material, are no longer esteemed as satisfactory works of historical scholarship.

Luden. Another student of Müller who shared his enthusiasm for medieval Germany was Heinrich Luden (1780-1847). A native of Bremen and professor at the University of Jena during the larger part of his life, Luden sought the medieval roots of German national character. This was a prominent feature of his *History of the German People (Die Geschichte des deutschen Volkes)* published in twelve volumes during the years 1825-37, and covering the story of medieval Germany down to 1237. He also published a *General History of the Peoples and States of Medieval Times (Allgemeine Geschichte der Völker und Staaten des Mittelalters)* in the early 1820's and a short *History of the Germans (Geschichte der Deutschen)* twenty years later. Luden was an ardent German nationalist and liberal, who was dismayed by the Napoleonic con-quests of Germany and the subsequent political reaction in his country. Luden played a leading role in the founding of patriotic German student clubs *(Burschenschaften),* dedicated, among other things, to the achievement of national unification within the framework of liberal political institutions.

Voigt and Stenzel. Müller and his protégé Luden set a pattern of his-torical interest which conditioned the outlook of a whole generation of widely-read German romanticist historians. As a group, these writers combined an ardent and sympathetic interest in German medieval backgrounds with buoyant nationalism. Johannes Voigt (1786-1863) was the oldest of this group of romanticist historians and Luden's principal disciple. Voigt's first work (1815) described *Hildebrand as Pope Gregory VII and his Times (Hilde-brand als Papst Gregor VII und sein Zeitalter).* His greatest works were the *History of Marienburg (Geschichte Marienburgs),* published in 1824, and his

History of Prussia (Gechichte Preussens von den ältesten Zeiten bis zum Untergang der Herrschaft des deutschen Ordens) which, appearing during the years 1827-38, shed a welcome light upon a long obscure chapter in the rise of modern Prussia.[15] Another eminent member of this group was Gustav Adolf Harald Stenzel (1792-1854), who was also a disciple of Müller. Stenzel was so nationalistic as to interrupt his academic career in 1813 to volunteer for military service against Napoleon, in the course of which he was seriously wounded. His principal historical works include A History of Germany under the Franconian Emperors (Geschichte Deutschlands unter den fränkischen Kaisern), the result of eight years of diligent labor, which appeared in 1827 and 1828, incomplete histories of Prussia and Silesia and a voluminous collection of Silesian source material published under the title Scriptores rerum Silesciacarum. An official on the Silesian archival staff and a one-time friend and associate of Ranke, Stenzel won a solid reputation for his critical and methodical use of his sources, a reputation which, however, was marred by his attacks upon his famous rival, Ranke.

Raumer. A third and peculiarly interesting member of this group of German romanticist medievalists was Friedrich Ludwig Georg von Raumer (1781-1873). Raumer was a personal friend of Muller, who took a fatherly interest in the former and strongly urged upon him a careful study of the fifteenth century. A man of broad and highly varied interests, Raumer had traveled in Switzerland, Italy, France, England and America. In 1848, he became a member of the ill-fated Frankfurt Assembly and, subsequently, continued to strive for a liberal Germany. Raumer's fame as a historian rests chiefly upon his History of the Hohenstaufens and Their Times (Geschichte der Hohenstaufen und ihrer Zeit) published during the years 1823-25. This was at once a masterpiece of literary creation as well as a scholarly historical treatise. If it was tainted with a mildly nationalistic flavor,[16] it also showed a broad and profound human understanding.[17] His minor works include a treatise On Prussian Municipal Administration (Über die preussische Städteordnung), which appeared in 1828, and a History of Europe since the End of the Fifteenth Century (Geschichte Europas seit dem Ende des 15. Jahrhundert), published in 1832. Raumer's chief service as an historian derives from his reconstruction of a brilliant epoch of German imperial and medieval history, his integration of this "glorious" phase of medieval Germany into the framework of feudal Europe. Thus, notwithstanding his pro-Prussian and pro-German bias, the solid scholarship of his History of the Hohenstaufens established Raumer's reputation as one of the greatest German romanticist historians.

Schlosser. It is interesting that German romanticist historiography received its earliest impulse from Hamann and Herder, both of whom were East

---

[15] His Views of Nuremberg's Artistry and Craftmanship (Blicke in das kunst und gewerbliche Leben der Stadt Nürnberg), published in 1861 and reprinted as volume four of the Deutsche National-Bibliothek, edited by Ferdinand Schmidt, is a good example of Voigt's sympathetic interest in medieval German backgroupnds.
[16] See his comments on the Knights of the Teutonic Order in Friedrich von Raumer, Geschichte der Hohenstaufen und ihrer Zeit, second edition, VI, p. 777.
[17] See his sympathetic picture of Innocent III in the same set, II, p. 598.

Prussians, and that its last great exponents were professors of history at the University of Heidelberg, in southwestern Germany. Friedrich Christoph Schlosser (1776-1861) was the first of this latter group. Professor at the University of Frankfurt and, after 1817, at the University of Heidelberg, Schlosser's chief work was his *History of the Eighteenth Century (Geschichte des 18. Jahrhundert)*, which appeared in 1828, although his nineteen-volume *World History for the German People (Weltgeschichte für das deutsche Volk, 1843-57)*, made him more widely known among his contemporaries. With intellectual roots deep in the Enlightenment of the eighteenth century and moral roots in the idealistic philosophy of the early nineteenth century, Schlosser, like his English contemporary Macaulay, severely applied his own high ethical standards to the past. Hence, although supported by a solid foundation of prodigious research, Schlosser was full of reproach for the times and characters that came within the purview of his work. Like Herder and the early romanticist writers, Schlosser notably stressed the value of literary remains as testimonials of the past and was perhaps the last great German historian of the nineteenth century to write a universal history. Like Luden, Schlosser made his work a vehicle of liberal and nationalist propaganda addressed to a generation of Germans faced with unprecedented problems of political reconstruction.

Gervinus. Schlosser's student, one time colleague, and successor at Heidelberg was Georg Gottfried Gervinus (1805-71). Like Schlosser, Gervinus was especially interested in the literary movements of the past and, in the tradition of the early romanticists, saw in poetry the peculiar expression of national character. This interest was chiefly responsible for the *History of German National Poetic Literature (Geschichte der poetischen National-literatur der Deutschen, 1835-42)*, and his *History of German Poetry (Geschichte der deutschen Dichtung, 1853)*. Gervinus' reputation as a historian also owed much to his *History of the Nineteenth Century since the Treaties of Vienna (Geschichte des neunzehnten Jahrhunderts seit der Wiener Verträgen)*, published during the decade 1855-66. Like Luden and his teacher and colleague Schlosser, Gervinus was a man of extensive learning, of great resourcefulness as a research scholar, and a pronounced liberal and nationalist.

Häusser. Probably no other German historian so well embodies the transition between romanticism and nineteenth century nationalism as Ludwig Häusser (1818-67). A student of Schlosser and, for some years, a professor at the University of Heidelberg. Häusser was primarily a political historian.[18] He was deeply impressed by Prussia's role as the chief bulwark of German resistance to the Napoleonic tyranny and was painfully conscious and resentful of Germany's political insignificance. His chief historical works include the *History of the French Revolution (Geschichte der französischen Revolution 1789-1799)*, which appeared, after his death, in 1867, and the

---

[18] See his tribute to the Protestant reformers; his treatment of them was the occasion for a prolonged controversy among historians, in Ludwig Häusser, *The Period of the Reformation 1517-1648*, edited by Wilhelm Oncken and translated by Mrs. G. Sturge, p. 239.

History of Germany from the Death of Frederick the Great until the Founding of the German Confederation (Deutsche Geschichte vom Tode Friederichs des Grossen zur Gründung des deutschen Bundes, 1854-57). The latter of these works, tracing the impact of the French Revolution and Napoleon upon Germany, went through many editions and made its author well known to the general public. The year following his death saw the publication of *The Period of the Reformation 1517-1648 (Geschichte des Zeitalters der Reformation 1517-1648).* While Ranke and the contemporary school of critical historiography which he founded frowned upon Schlosser, Gervinus and Häusser as mediocre historians, the latter's stress on national backgrounds and character and ardent German chauvinism, enormously contributed to the rise and popularity of the so-called Prussian school of historiography. As such, Schlosser, Gervinus and Häusser constituted a logical political culmination of early nineteenth century German romanticism.

ENGLISH ROMANTICISM

The reaction to the Enlightenment was neither as intense nor as widespread in England as it was in Germany. In the first place, the Gallic influence had penetrated much less deeply in England, where the growth of indigenous arts had long been assiduously fostered. Secondly, England had a great and venerable tradition of modern national literature embodying, among others, the works of such great writers as Shakespeare, Milton, Swift, Pope and Fielding. Finally, England did not feel the impact of the French Revolution as quickly or as directly as did politically divided Germany. In its literary aspects, English romanticism began with imitations of Spenser and Milton and only gradually returned to Chaucer, to medieval poetry and translations of bardic and scaldic remains.[19] Moreover, romanticism was only one of the many contemporary currents in English literary life.

Burke. Although he is not, properly speaking, a representative of the romanticist school or of any school, Edmund Burke's political views made him one of the first English opponents of late eighteenth century rationalism. Edmund Burke (1729-97) was born in Dublin, Ireland, but spent most of his adult life in England, where he became a leading spirit of the Whig Party in parliament and made a reputation as a political theorist. Not a professional historian, Burke published many political works which had a profound bearing upon contemporary historiography. *A Vindication of Natural Society,* published in 1756, was a refutation of Bolingbroke's concept of natural religion. Three years later Burke launched the *Annual Register,* a chronology of contemporary events, which he edited until 1788. His *Observations on the Present State of the Nation* (1769), and his *Thoughts on the Cause of the Present Discontents* (1770) attacked George III for his efforts to undermine the English Cabinet system. Burke is perhaps best remembered for his brilliant defense of British liberties in Parliament, notably in connection with the American Revolution, and for his *Reflections on the Revolution in France,* which began as a letter to a French friend.

---

[19] Henry A. Beers, *A History of English Romanticism in the Eighteenth Century,* p. 381.

As he wrote to this friend in France ". . . the French Revolution is the most astounding that has hitherto happened in the World. The most wonderful things are brought about in many instances by means the most absurd and ridiculous, in the most ridiculous modes, and, apparently, by the most contemptible instruments." [20] Burke had a profound respect for tradition, which he believed was sanctioned by the usage of generations and, as such, had its basis in sound precedent. He bitterly condemned the French for their rash and ill-considered subversion of existing institutions and, especially, for their erroneous conceptions of English political usages. As he wrote in the *Reflections,*

> Our political system is placed in a just correspondence and symmetry with the order of the world, and with the mode of existence decreed to a permanent body composed of transitory parts; wherein, by the disposition of a stupendous wisdom, moulding together the great mysterious incorporation of the human race, the whole, at one time, is never old, or middle-aged, or young, but, in a condition of unchangeable constancy. . . . A spirit of innovation is generally the result of a selfish temper, and confined views. People will not look forward to posterity, who never look backward to their ancestors . . . the idea of inheritance furnishes a sure principle of conservation, and a sure principle of transmission; without at all excluding a principle of improvement.[21]

While Burke was thus pleading for a conservation of the accumulated achievements of the past and condemned the rationalists for their disdain of history, it was not until the 1790's, after the death of that great triumvirate, Hume, Robertson and Gibbon, that romanticism, properly speaking, made its debut in English historiography. The popular romanticist appeal to medieval lore, for example, found its first systematic historical expression in England in the writings of Whitaker, Pinkerton and Turner.

Whitaker. An Anglican clergyman, John Whitaker (1735-1808) owed his reputation as a historian chiefly to his painstaking *History of Manchester,* (1771). The second edition (1773) of this work brought the story through the Saxon period, although the unpublished manuscript had continued the account down to the fifteenth century. Whitaker also published *The Genuine History of the Britons* in 1772, *Mary Queen of Scots Vindicated* in 1787 and the scurrilous *Gibbon's History of the Decline and Fall of the Roman Empire.*[22] Whitaker's study of Manchester was the result of diligent and careful research, showed much originality and imagination and was especially noteworthy for its interest in social history and its sympathetic treatment of early medieval times.

Pinkerton. John Pinkerton (1758-1826) combined the study of medieval literature and folklore with a keen professional interest in the early medieval history of his native Scotland. Pinkerton's first literary excursion took the

---

[20] *The Works of Edmund Burke,* II, p. 284.
[21] *Ibid.,* p. 307.
[22] Gibbon had sent Whitaker the first draft of his *Decline and Fall,* excepting that chapter on Christianity. Whitaker resented this when the complete work was published, but he also was offended by the content of the missing chapter.

form of collections of Scottish ballads, not a few of which he forged. He was personally known to Gibbon, who esteemed him highly, both as a historian and for his prodigious learning. Pinkerton's *Dissertation on the Origin and Progress of the Scythians or Goths* (1789), attracted wide attention to this forgotten chapter of the past. Pinkerton's greatest historical writings, however, were the *Inquiry into the History of Scotland Preceding the Reign of Malcolm III* (1790), and *The History of Scotland from the Accession of the House of Stuart to that of Mary*, published seven years later. Written in a verbose style, both works were the product of painstaking research and a keen and sympathetic interest in the subject.

Turner. Probably the ablest of this group of English romanticist historians was a lawyer, Sharon Turner (1768-1847), and his principal work, the result of sixteen years of diligent labor, was *The History of the Anglo-Saxons,* published during the years 1799-1805. To quote Turner's own words:

> When the first volume appeared, the subject of Anglo-Saxon antiquities had been nearly forgotten by the British public; although a large part of what we most love and venerate in our customs, laws and institutions, originated among our Anglo-Saxon ancestors. . . . The Anglo-Saxon MSS. lay still unexamined, and neither their contents nor the important facts which the ancient writers and records of other nations had preserved of the transactions and fortunes of our ancestors had been ever made a part of our general history. . . . His (the author's) desire has been fulfilled—a taste for the history and remains of our Great Ancestors has revived and is visibly increasing.[23]

Thus Turner reconstructed the cultural and social background of the Anglo-Saxon conquerors of England, brought to light an array of hitherto unpublished material and created an active interest in early medieval English life.

The reviving interest in medieval life and customs was impressively exemplified in contemporary literature. The immense popularity of the Scottish poet Macpherson's *Fragments of Ancient Poetry* (1750), *Fingal* (1761) and *Temora* (1763), the latter two of which were represented to be the work of the Irish bard Ossian, were symptomatic of this awakening enthusiasm, as was the variable popular reception accorded to the no less spurious *Rowley Poems* published by the precocious young Chatterton.

Literary Exponents: Scott, Southey, Godwin, Chalmers. If English romanticism failed to produce a great historian it was, nevertheless, not without very distinguished literary exponents. Sir Walter Scott, whose medieval romances achieved a tremendous success,[24] was an outstanding literary member of that school in England. Scott wrote several historical works, including a *Life of Napoleon* (1827), *Tales of a Grandfather* (1828-30) and a *History of Scotland* (1830). Robert Southey's historical novels and poems also enjoyed a vast success. His greatest work, *The History of Portugal,*

---

[23] Sharon Turner, *The History of the Anglo-Saxon,* third edition, I, v and vi.
[24] Cf. Sir Herbert J. C. Grierson, *Sir Walter Scott,* p. 304.

inspired by a visit to that country, was left unfinished, but a part of it was published in the form of the brilliant *History of Brazil* (1810-19). Southey also gave posterity a sympathetic *Life of Wesley*. Southey's brother-in-law, Samuel Taylor Coleridge, also belongs to that school, as do Byron, Keats, Shelley and Wordsworth, not to mention William Godwin and George Chalmers in their respective fields of politics and history.

FRENCH ROMANTICISM

Chateaubriand. Aside from Rousseau, who fathered the romanticist movement, the first profound French reaction to the rationalist outlook found expression in the prolific and influential writings of François René, Vicomte de Chateaubriand (1768-1848). The son of a noble family in Brittany, Chateaubriand led an extremely strenuous and adventurous life, one that took him to America in 1791, to England as an *émigré* in 1794, back to France in 1800, into the French diplomatic and administrative service and, finally, to Greece, Turkey and Asia Minor. Meanwhile, Chateaubriand published a wide variety of works, including essays, memoirs, reviews, etc. The first of these works, his *Essai historique, politique et moral sur les Revolutions,* appeared in London in 1791, only to be subsequently repudiated by its author. His most important work was the famous *Génie du christianisme où beautés de la religion chrétienne,* which appeared in 1802. A man of deep insight, delicate feeling and melancholic temperament, Chateaubriand had early in life become a disciple of Rousseau. Filled with a spirit of adventure, an insatiable curiosity, a fine appreciation of abstract beauty and a warm attachment to nature, Chateaubriand also had a profound respect for human achievements and traditions. It is not surprising, therefore, that Chateaubriand had an extensive and almost professional acquaintance with the great historical literature of all times and an appreciation of sound historical method. As he says in his *Études historiques,* "History is not a work of philosophy, it is a painting; it is necessary to combine narration with the representation of the subject, that is, it is necessary simultaneously to design and to paint; it is necessary to give to men the language and the sentiments of their times, not to regard the past in the light of our own opinion." [25] As he says elsewhere in the same work, "four types of documents embrace the entire history of nations in a chronological order; poems, laws, chronicles of general facts and memoirs which picture social and private life. Men sing first; they write later."

Barante. One of the first romanticist historians in France was Amable Guillaume Prosper Brugière, Baron de Barante (1782-1866), a prefect under Napoleon, a deputy and director of internal revenue during the Restoration and an ambassador of Louis Philippe. His historical writings include *Histoire de la Convention Nationale* (1851-53) and *Histoire du Directoire de la République française* (1855), but his outstanding historical achievement was the *Histoire des ducs de Bourgogne de la maison de Valois,* which appeared during the years 1824-28 and which won for him admission to the French Academy. Recognized as chief of the French narrative historians,

---

[25] *Oeuvres Completes de Chateaubriand,* IX, p. 31.

Barante was primarily concerned not with the philosophical implications of history but with a faithful and vibrant reproduction of the past. Writing in a brilliant style and freely employing varied and colorful material, Barante won a very wide reading public. His lofty concept of historical writing is illustrated in the following passage:

> To deal with a question as it really was, and describe the political role of literature, was thus an act of candor; it was to call things by their proper names and exercise the right of being impartial. In showing that literature had to conform to the state of society, one may without injustice incur the reproach which does not fall upon one alone; in showing a feigned and superstitious awe for the regime which led France to the Revolution, in candidly pointing to the iniquitous and frivolous, one might also say that it (the old regime) was attacked and subverted in a manner similarly frivolous and a thousand times more iniquitous.[26]

Thierry. Much better known as an historian than Barante was Jacques Nicolas Augustin Thierry (1795-1856). Like so many of his contemporaries, Thierry early fell under the spell of Chateaubriand, whose *Les Martyrs* inspired him, although he imbibed much of his romantic enthusiasm for the past from Sir Walter Scott. A secretary to Saint-Simon for many years, Thierry soon acquired his employer's bourgeois and republican bias. This element was injected into his *Lettres sur l'histoire de France,* published in 1820, in which he takes the reader through the early medieval migrations, through the Norman conquest and describes the rise of the communes, in the course of which he pictures the various nations as achieving free and parliamentary institutions. As he wrote in 1827, "I always love liberty, but with an ever more impatient affection." At all times and in all countries, he argues, men with the most diverse opinions have sought liberty but "most of them died before having realized that which they abstractly anticipate." Like so many other romanticist historians, Thierry also felt that the study of history served an important moral function in instilling a patriotic sentiment. To quote from the *Lettres* in this connection:

> I believe that our patriotism will grow much in purity and firmness, if the knowledge of history and above all the history of France is more generally disseminated among us and becomes popular . . . . We should have more security and more confidence in the future if we knew that, even in the most difficult times, there was no want of champions, of justice or of liberty.[27]

Thierry's greatest work as an historian was his *Histoire de la Conquête de l'Angleterre par les Normands* (1825). This work so taxed his eyesight that by 1830 he was blind. This did not prevent him, however, from rejoicing over the 1830 Revolution, or from collaborating on the valuable *Recueil des monuments inedits de l'histoire de tiers état* (1850-70).

---

[26] Prosper Brugière de Barante, *Tableau de la Litterature française an dix-buitième siècle,* p. 6.
[27] Augustin Thierry, *Lettres sur l'histoire de France,* p. 12.

Michelet. By far the most distinguished figure among the French romanticist historians, however, was Jules Michelet (1798-1874). The son of a Paris printer whose business suffered severely from the rigors of the imperial censorship, Michelet embarked upon a different profession. Making a brilliant record as a student at the Lycée Charlemagne in Paris, Michelet subsequently enjoyed a distinguished career as a teacher. At the Collège de France he established close ties with his famous colleagues Quinet and Mickiewicz. The apostle of liberal ideas and a man of humanitarian impulses, Michelet vigorously opposed Guizot, Veuillot and Montalembert's ultramontane and conservative policy and, shortly after the *coup d'état* of December, 1851, his lectures at the Collège de France, in which he inveighed against the new regime, were suspended. Meanwhile, Michelet had been busy with his *Histoire de la Révolution,* which was published in 1851, and his momentous *Histoire de France* which by 1867 had brought the story down to the reign of Louis XVI. These works were preceded by many essays on modern and early modern European history.

Michelet's fame has gone far beyond his role as a romanticist historian. His writings reveal a fine spirit of impartiality and are the products of scrupulous research and authentic documentation. This is more especially true of the first part of his *History.* Michelet painted in broad picturesque and panoramic strokes and his work is replete with drama and suspense. His observation that history should constitute an integral resurrection of the past was exemplified in his work. To quote from his *Histoire de la Revolution:*

> Oh France, you have been redeemed! Oh world, you have been saved! . . . . I return to heaven, my young reader, whence I have so long awaited the rays of Joan of Arc . . . What is the old regime, the King, the priest, in the old monarchy? It is tyranny by God's grace. What is the Revolution? The reaction of equity, the belated return of eternal justice. Justice my Mother, law my Father, who are one in God.[28]

It is true that Michelet did not always reveal his sources and that he probably depended heavily upon secondary materials for the latter part of his *Histoire de France.* Moreover, Michelet was too eager to finish the work and hence proceeded much more rapidly than a careful collection and evaluation of all the pertinent data would have made possible. His work also suffered somewhat from his pretension to "divine" the character of a people or the outlook of an epoch, and to communicate with the "soul" of France. On the other hand, he wrote a lucid and brilliant style and quickly found a large and enduring audience.

---

[28] Michelet, *Histoire de la Revolution francaise,* I, cxxvii.

Chapter 13

FIRST HALF OF THE NINETEENTH CENTURY

By Henry M. Adams

THE catastrophic events which ushered in the nineteenth century left a legacy of problems and conflicts. Ten years of French revolutionary chaos, with its passionate battle cry of Liberty, Equality and Fraternity, and fifteen years of Napoleonic imperialism made order, stability, and peace the watchwords of the men who reorganized Europe in 1815 at Vienna.

Against the new liberal and national aims born of revolution and spread by war, they set conservative and aristocratic doctrines born of ancient tradition and maintained by privilege. This historic conflict marked by the revolutions of 1820, 1830, and 1848 in Europe, and by the reforms of the thirties and forties in England, politically dominated the first half of the nineteenth century.

This political conflict was paralleled by an economic one, which came with the spread of the Industrial Revolution from England to the continent, where it made itself felt by 1830 on the side of national independence in Belgium, by 1848 on the side of liberal Republicanism and Utopian Socialism in France, and on the side of national unity in Germany and Italy after mid-century.

The political and economic conflicts coexisted and often joined with social conflict which, after centuries of slow evolution, burst upon Europe with the French Revolution to set the middle class in search of political power, on the side of liberalism, nationalism, and industrialism. The socio-political, socio-economic conflict between the new institutionalized forces of liberalism, nationalism, industrialism, and their chief social exponent, the middle class, during the first half of the nineteenth century contended against the old institutionalized forces of monarchical conservatism in Church and State, a handicraft and agricultural economy, and their chief social exponents, the nobility and the peasantry.

The historiography of the first half of the nineteenth century reflects the very continuity of history of which the great thinkers of the age speak so eloquently. The great intellectual revolt against the rationalism and classicism of the Enlightenment which finds expression first in Rousseau and Herder, then in Schiller and Goethe, continues to dominate the currents of thought to which it gives its name, Romanticism, from the turn of the century to the revolution of 1848. Similarly, the cultural nationalism of Herder, the political liberalism and nationalism of the French Revolution, the transcendental idealism of Kant continue into the nineteenth century, to become, with some exceptions in the cases of liberalism, inextricably merged with romanticism. The writing and interpretation of history during this period, therefore, is deeply influenced by philosophical idealism, liberalism, nationalism, and above all, romanticism which "left its mark on every aspect of European culture, and nowhere more significantly than on the writing and interpretation of history." [1] Yet, out of this same intellectual climate there emerged, somewhat paradoxically, the German Historical School, which was destined to revolutionize the study and writing of history and which ever since has been symbolized by the name of its immortal exponent, Leopold von Ranke. Just as romanticism is both an outgrowth of, and a revolt against, classicism and rationalism, so the new historical criticism is both an outgrowth of, and a revolt against, romanticism.

GERMANY

The ideas of the German romanticists which found expression in literature and language, in philosophy and religion, in art and aesthetics, gave rise in history to a new romantic view and to a movement in historical learning known as the Historical School.

The Romantic View. The new romantic view of history was dynamic, developmental, and organic. It conceived of history as process, as eternally becoming, as a development governed by universal forces, unconscious, inexplicable, mysterious. It proclaimed the organic continuity of this development and the organic unity of any cultural complex. It emphasized one's own indigenous history as the creator of nationality and the source of lasting achievement. It endowed the individual state, nation, social group, and age, with the distinguishing quality of personality. It viewed past ages, especially the medieval, Christian, Gothic world, as valuable in themselves, and also as sources of the present to which by necessity they led. It developed the concepts of the spirit of the people *(Volksgeist)*, of the spirit of the times *(Zeitgeist)*, and of the spirit of the world *(Weltgeist)* into working principles fundamental to an understanding of historical development. It was based in the last analysis on philosophical idealism.

Historical School. The movement in historical learning known as the Historical School came into being with the University of Berlin in 1810. It embraced not only history *per se,* but all related subjects, philosophy and philology, literature and law, state and religion. It revived the entire past. It replaced the concept of the law of nature with those of nationality, of continuity, and of totality; principles first enunciated by Winckelmann, Wolf, and Herder. It brought to bear upon the study of history a critical method, and with it are associated in these early creative days the distinguished versatile scholars: Berthold Georg Niebuhr (1776-1831) in Roman history; Karl Friedrich Eichhorn (1781-1854) in German law; Friedrich Karl von Savigny (1779-1861) in Roman law; Philipp August Böckh (1785-1867) in classical philology; Jakob Grimm (1785-1863) in German philology; and Karl Otfried Müller (1797-1840) in Greek history.

Niebuhr, who introduced a new method in the study of early Roman history, opened a new era in the history of historical research. He united the romantic interest in origins, folksongs, and myth, and the philological method of Wolf,

---

[1] W. K. Ferguson, *The Renaissance in Historical Thought: Five Centuries of Interpretation,* p. 113.

with academic historical scholarship. Seeking to reconstruct a Roman national epic from Livy's *History,* he used the method which F. A. Wolf had applied to Homer. This method was, in essence, to examine and analyze the sources. It involved two processes: first, an analysis and division of the sources into older and newer, original and second-hand, trustworthy and untrustworthy; second, an analysis of the trustworthy sources to discover the conceptions and purposes of the author and their influence on his presentation of the facts.[2] The originality and fame of Niebuhr lie in his talented application of this method to Roman history, which resulted in his major work.[3]

Under the influence of the romantic view and of the national enthusiasm that came with the regeneration of Prussia, Eichhorn, by showing in his great work[4] that German law was a manifestation of the total national culture, founded a new discipline, the historical treatment of law, which received its fullest development in the writings of Savigny, of which the most significant was his monumental study of Roman law in the Middle Ages.[5]

The universality of these men, their capacity for mastering several fields of learning under the dynamic impetus of the romantic view, enabled them to glimpse the interrelationship of literature, philology, and history, and to draw into the historical field, Böckh, Bopp, and Grimm.

Böckh's editing of the series of Greek inscriptions, Bopp's founding of comparative philology, and Grimm's introduction of the comparative method to German philology prepared the ground for the brilliant and versatile Müller who, combining this knowledge and the method of Niebuhr, reconstructed the early history of Greece.[6] As a literary artist, he surpassed his predecessors. His "delicate balance of learning and art gave to the study of Greece, a truly Greek harmony of powers." [7]

Stein and the Monumenta. The same romantic national influence which gave rise to the Historical School and to the victory against Napoleon in 1813 inspired the historical contribution of the great political leader of Prussian regeneration, Baron Stein. Not a historian but a learned patron of history, he is responsible for initiating the collection and publishing of the sources of medieval German history. This publication, the *Monumenta Germaniae Historica,* was to become "the greatest historical collection in the world." [8]

Of all the many distinguished contributors to the writing and interpretation of history in Germany during this period, the two greatest in enduring influence upon historical thought are Hegel (1770-1831), in philosophical history, from whom stems "the greatest development of the *Geisteswissenschaften* the world has ever witnessed," [9] and Ranke (1795-1886), in scientific history, whose

---

[2] Eduard Fueter, *Geschichte der Neuren Historiographie,* pp. 462-464; who influences directly the statement of the method by R. G. Collingwood, *The Idea of History,* p. 130, who in turn refers to its origin in Vico.
[3] B. G. Niebuhr, *Römische Geschichte.*
[4] K. F. Eichhorn, *Deutscher Staats and Rechtsgeschichte.*
[5] F. K. von Savigny, *Geschichte des Römischen Rechts im Mittelalter.*
[6] K. Otfried Müller, *Geschichte der Hellenischen Stämme and Städte.*
[7] Emery Neff, *The Poetry of History,* p. 115.
[8] J. W. Thompson, *A History of Historical Writing,* II, p. 166; J. P. Elder and T. E. Mommsen, "The Monumenta Germaniae Historica; Present Status and Plans," *Speculum* (April, 1949), XXIV, pp. 307-308.
[9] Sidney Hook, " The Contemporary Significance of Hegel's Philosophy," *Philosophical Review,* XLI (May, 1932), pp. 237-238.

"supreme achievement was to raise the whole standard of scholarship and to make the German school of history the first in the world." [10]

Hegel. The importance of Hegel to history lies not in the writing of the history of a society or of an age, but rather in the profundity of his thinking about history. It is his concern with the meaning of history that places Hegel among the philosophers of history.[11]

In Hegel, learned in theology and philosophy, well-versed in the natural-sciences, and even a Greek enthusiast, the forces of the time moved most deeply. Closely associated with the romantic thinkers and the romantic ideas of the age, he brought to its systematic fulfillment the romantic view of the world and history. Intimately acquainted with the philosophical idealism of Fichte and Schelling, and with its Kantian origins, Hegel not only represented the culmination of, but the reaction to, this movement. Keenly alive to the practical political conditions and the problem of unity of his time, he absorbed the nationalist atmosphere after Jena and systematically developed the national solution in his political philosophy, a "phenomenon as significant in the creation of modern Germany as the careers of Stein and Hardenberg." [12]

Hegel's Views of History. At the same time, Hegel transcends the forces of his time, giving newer and deeper meaning to the strams of ideas from the past, which in his gigantic mind are fused into a great synthesis, a whole system of interrelated thought, art and religion, law and logic, philosophy and history. He sought to achieve a philosophy of culture, and in doing so gave to history many fruitful concepts.

Hegel's view of history is inescapably complex. As an idealist he conceived of ideas as existing outside as well as inside the mind, of the world as spiritual and containing its ultimate purpose in itself, and of material things as the expression of ideas. To Hegel all history was the history of thought. It was the task of the historian to understand what people thought, not what they did, since action was nothing but the expression of man's thought.

His view of history was rationalistic. The impelling force of the historical process was reason, but with a special meaning. Reason to Hegel was made up of rational and irrational elements in which the latter were essential to the former. In this way, Hegel unites human reason and human passion into an inseparable necessary whole, but in which the rational is dominant, possessing a special power, "the cunning of reason," which uses passion for its own ends. Thus, Hegel explains the fact that "the ultimate outcome of great historical action is always something which was not intended by men." [13]

Furthermore, Hegel viewed history not only as process but as logical process.

---

[10] G. P. Gooch, *Studies in German History*, p. 266.

[11] Karl Lowith, *Meaning in History: The Theological Implications of the Philosophy of History*, p. 57. Hegel is "the last philosopher of history because he is the last philosopher whose immense historical sense was still restrained and disciplined by the Christian tradition."

[12] G. H. Sabine, "Hegel's Political Philosophy," *Philosophical Review*, XLI (May, 1932), p. 282. "To suppose that Hegel desired to perpetuate the political state of affairs in Germany as it was in his lifetime is manifestly false." P. 280.

[13] Karl Löwith, *Meaning in History*, p. 55, claims "the cunning of reason" is merely Hegel's rational expression for divine providence. R. G. Collingwood, *The Idea of History*, p. 116, claims that this reason of Hegel is finite, not abstract or divine. Sidney Hook, "The Contemporary Significance of Hegel's Philosophy," *Philosophical Review*, XLI (May, 1932), p. 259, agrees with Löwith that this reason is absolute and a theodicy.

This conception was twofold. On the one hand, the events of history were the expression of thoughts, but there was no necessary connection between them. On the other hand, the thoughts which occasioned the events were logically connected, forming a process of logical concepts. The historian's task was not only to determine the events, but above all to discover the meaning of the logical concepts and thereby understand the course and events of history. Logic for Hegel meant a system of abstract entities, of "ideas," and in the case of history these "ideas" served as a logical framework. The historical activities of man take place by necessity in a natural environment. The content of these activities, that is, the particular thoughts behind them, are not determined by this natural environment, but by the "ideas." Thus, "logic is the key to history in the sense that man's thoughts and actions as studied by history follow a pattern which is the colored version of the pattern logic has already drawn in black and white." [14]

History became the organon of Hegel's thinking. In the course of history, he developed his system, a part of which was his philosophy of history, a universal history of mankind which traced the development of freedom from primitive times to Hegel's day. To Hegel, freedom and man's consciousness of freedom were the same thing and were identified with the moral reason of man. The history of the world, therefore, was the history of a process of thought, of dialectical concepts, of large, unconscious abstract forces, which summed up in themselves the multiplicity of events in which they were externally manifested. The mechanism of this development was the famous Hegelian dialectic of thesis, antithesis, synthesis, a way of looking at social phenomena, a principle of logical succession by which one concept or form of life, Greece, generates an opposite concept or form of life, Rome, and out of the interaction arises a new concept or form of life, the Christian world, which is not a fusion or mixture but a new, higher synthesis, and which will in turn generate a new thesis. At the same time, Hegel's history of the world, which is the history of the consciousness of freedom, is also the history of the world spirit, the *Weltgeist* which manifests itself in the spirit of the nation *(Volksgeist)*, which in turn creates the total culture of the nation through its individuals in whom its spirit is unconsciously manifested. Thus romanticism and rationalism, idealism and nationalism, philosophy and history unite in the great Hegel, whose lectures, published posthumously as *The Philosophy of History* (1837) [15] and *The History of Philosophy* (1833-1836) [16] were "to introduce a way of thinking about history that has exerted an incalculable influence on the historiography of the past century." [17]

Ranke. In Ranke the romantic and philosophical tendencies of the age, and the critical method of the Historical School unite to create the first German whose whole-hearted devotion to history for its own sake, whose understanding of history, whose mastery of historical criticism, whose artistic and instructive ability made him the first great historian of Germany.

His first work, *History of the Latin and Germanic Peoples, 1494-1514*

[14] R. G. Collingwood, *The Idea of History*, p. 124.
[15] G. F. Hegel, *Vorlesungen über die Philosophie der Geschichte*.
[16] G. F. Hegel, *Vorlesungen über die Geschichte der Philosophie*.
[17] W. K. Ferguson, *The Renaissance in Historical Thought: Five Centuries of Interpretation*, p. 169.

(1824)[18] brought him national recognition and a position at the University of Berlin. The work contained his famous declaration that he intended to show history "as it really happened," *wie es eigentlich gewesen ist,* and his equally famous appendix, *On the Criticism of Writers of Modern History,*[19] which inaugurated modern critical historiography.

In his critical appendix, Ranke applied the method of historical criticism to the historians who at that time were considered authoritative sources on the period, 1494-1514. He showed their general histories to be untrue. In doing so he established the principle that only original documents and archives were the proper sources for the reconstruction of history, and that that reconstruction should be the simple truth of what really happened.

The ideal which he set for himself was furthered by establishing at the University of Berlin a historical seminar where, under his talented guidance, students learned by experience with medieval documents, the method of source criticism and the writing of history.. In this way the school of Ranke was founded, out of which during the course of the century came many of Germany's foremost scholars to spread the ideal and method of Ranke throughout the realm of historical learning. Thus did Ranke become a tradition.

His second work[20] was superior to his first in clarity of style and breadth of content. His third work, *History of the Popes,*[21] brought him world admiration for the cool scholarly detachment and artistic skill with which it was written.

His writings on foreign countries, which included histories of England and of France, as well as the world, were surpassed by his writings on his own country, "not only because their bulk is greater and the research on which they rest of wider range, but also because historians, like other people, speak with special authority on the land of their birth."[22]

The nationalism which he avoided in the twenties made its influence felt in the forties, in his favorite work, *History of Germany in the Age of the Reformation,*[23] which became not only a historical classic of Protestant Germany, but the most controversial of his many books. In the same decade, he began his studies of Prussian history,[24] which twenty years later were completed along with the most important enterprise of his closing years, the editing of the Hardenberg papers.

The greatest master of historical criticism borrowed from romanticism the presuppositions of his historical writings. Yet he transcended their views, valuing only what harmonized with his realistic observation of life.

His conception of history, influenced by Wilhelm von Humboldt and Hegel, Niebuhr and Scott, was likewise influenced by the events of the times. The influence of the French Revolution upon general European history was the prototype for this theory of the significance of leading ideas, of dominating tenden-

[18] L. von Ranke, *Geschichte der Romanischen und Germanischen Völker 1494-1514.*
[19] L. von Ranke, *Zur Kritik Neurer Geschichtsschreiber.*
[20] L. von Ranke, *Fürsten und Wölker von Südeuropa im Sechzehnten und Siebzehnten Jahrhundert.*
[21] L. von Ranke, *Die Römischen Päpste, Ihre Kirche und Ihr Staat im Sechzehnten und Siebzehnten Jahrhundert.*
[22] G. P. Gooch, *Studies in German History,* p. 210.
[23] L. von Ranke, *Deutsche Geschichte im Zeitalter der Reformation.*
[24] L. von Ranke, *Zwölf Bücher Preussicher Geschichte.*

cies, in each century. Ranke became the greatest exponent of the theory, first formulated by von Humboldt, that purely intellectual forms could shape history, that observations of reality could be universalized into ideas, like the intellectual conflict between conservatives and liberals in the disunited Germany of this period. These ideas were not mystical, unconscious forces like *Volksgeist,* but concrete, conscious working forces in men. Hegel's conception of historical movements as the realization of an idea played a role in Ranke's systematic application of this theory. "Protestantism in Ranke is an 'idea' in the true Hegelian sense; a thought, a conception of man's life held by man himself . . . historically conditioned . . . a way in which people come to think at a certain time, and in accordance with which they organize their whole life, only to find that the idea changes by a dialectic of its own into a different idea and that the manner of life which expressed it will not hold together, but breaks up and transforms itself into the expression of a second idea which replaces the first." [25] Ranke applied this theory with more care than others. He was convinced that the historian has only to describe these dominant ideas, like other living forces, not to judge.

Ranke as an historian is at his best when analyzing historical problems or individuals, tracing the development of ideas or revealing the influence of international relationships upon the life of states. His character portraits reflect his extraordinary ability to penetrate to the inmost thoughts of an individual and bring him creatively to life. His mature style and composition combine a clarity and nuance of thoughtful expression with reflection and broad characterization. "He sought a compromise between the analytical method of the Enlightenment and the colorful living narrative of the romantics." [26]

The contributions of Ranke to historiography are many indeed. His collected works of some fifty-two volumes, containing historical writing of the highest order, serve as a model of quality and productivity. His perfection of historical criticism and his ideal of what historical reconstruction should be is not a "misleading of generations," [27] but a legacy of the dignity of historical truth as it has been understood by generations of historians ever since. His creation of the seminar as an instrument of historical instruction and his technique of education have served as the pedagogical ideal of historiography to this day. His furtherance of the critical study of medieval and modern history has been largely responsible for the position of those studies in historiography today. "The ideal of an imaginative reconstruction of the past which is scientific in its determinations and artistic in its formulation is the ideal to which the greatest historians have ever aspired." [28]

---

[25] R. G. Collingwood, *The Idea of History,* p. 122; Eduard Fueter, *Geschichte der Neueren Historiographie,* p. 425, claims that Ranke's theory of ideas should not be confused with Hegel's, which is theological.

[26] *Ibid.,* pp. 482-483.

[27] J. W. Thompson, *A History of Historical Writing,* II, p. 186. For the modern controversy on the limitations of Ranke see the articles of Charles Beard, Jan., 1934, XXXIX, pp. 219-231, and Oct., 1935, XLI, pp. 74-87; and of T. V. Smith, April, 1935, XL, pp. 439-449, in *American Historical Review.* For an unfavorable estimation of Ranke see Emery Neff, *The Poetry of History,* pp. 189-191. That contemporary (1934) thought may repudiate Ranke's ideal of objectivity is hardly sufficient grounds for minimizing his place in historiography. On Ranke's impartiality see G. P. Gooch, *Studies in German History,* p. 266.

[28] Morris R. Cohen, *The Meaning of Human History,* p. 34.

FRANCE

In France the currents of thought of this period find broad and deep manifestations in literature and art, in religion and politics, in historical writing and study. At the turn of the century, French romanticism, continuing the intellectual revolt of Rousseau, burst forth in the writings of René de Chateaubriand, whose new prose style and aesthetic-historical theories were to influence significantly the French romantic historians. "To those in revolt against the dryness and realism of the eighteenth century he opened up a new kingdom of feeling and imagination: to those who were disheartened by the iconoclasm of the Revolution he offered an idealized past." [29]

In his *Genius of Christianity*,[30] he combined the romantic view of the organic unity of art, religion, and nationality with aesthetic infatuation for medieval culture. In his *Martyrs* [31] he introduced into history the authenticity of natural background, of precise detail, of customs, manners, costumes, and speech, to produce the life of the past in all its living color. "Over old France, France of the great cathedrals, the talent of Chateaubriand, the enchanter, diffused a poetic charm." [32]

Into French romanticism at this time came German romantic thought through the writings of Mme. de Staël whose famous study, *Of Germany*,[33] influenced many generations of historians.[34] To the influence of Chateaubriand and Mme. de Staël there was added that of Walter Scott, whose historical novels with marvelous intensity revived the medieval world in the manner of Chateaubriand. They became the prototype of romantic historical writing, giving to it a color which it had not had before. The local historian, Baron Barante,[35] catered to this romantic taste. Barante wished to restore to history the charm of the historical novel. Thierry proposed the same objective, the same method, as Barante, but fulfilled it more effectively and more productively.[36] At the same time, Thierry is representative of another trend in French historiography, the liberal political, which unites the influence of men of politics with that of the men of letters, and which, as well as romanticism, shapes his writing of history.

Liberal Political Trend. Reflecting this double influence, political and literary, in their historical works are Adolphe Thiers (1787-1877), François Mignet (1796-1884), and François Guizot (1787-1874). To them history was a school of politics. The lessons which they took from history correspond marvelously with their personal programs. Society has evolved in one direction because it had to. All is inevitable, necessary, and unavoidable. "Open Guizot, open Thiers, open Mignet, you will see the same theory displayed by all and in all their works, at least in those which date from the Restoration." [37]

[29] C. Maxwell, "Chateaubriand and the French Romantics" in F. J. C. Hearnshaw, ed., *The Social and Political Ideas of Some Representative Thinkers of The Age of Reaction and Reconstruction,* p. 47.
[30] R. de Chateaubriand, *Le Génie du Christianisme.*
[31] R. de Chateaubriand, *Les Martyrs.*
[32] L. Halphen, *L'Histoire en France Depuis Cent Ans.*
[33] G. de Staël, *De L'Allemagne.*
[34] W. K. Ferguson, *The Renaissance in Historical Thought: Five Centuries of Interpretation,* pp. 124-125.
[35] B. de Barante, *Histoire des Ducs de Bourgogne.*
[36] A. Thierry, *Histoire de la Conquête de l'Angleterre Par les Normands* (Paris, 1825) and *Recits des Temps Merovingiens.*
[37] L. Halphen, *L'Histoire en France Depuis Cent Ans.*

In the twenties, Thiers and Mignet both published histories of the French Revolution which brought them national reputations. However, Thiers' fame as an historian lies in his narrative ability and his writing on the Napoleonic period,[38] while that of Mignet lies in his scholarly research and lucidity of style.

With Guizot this trend is perhaps best expressed for he made the history of the liberal bourgeoisie the history of France. His writings, based on his celebrated lectures,[39] brought him to the peak of his fame as an historian. Yet he "was essentially a thinker about history rather than an historical narrator." [40] Like Stein for Germany, he was responsible for the creation of source collections for France. His ideas in his writings and his furtherance of the study of history have given him a place in historiography which transcends the trend of which he was leader.

Michelet. In Jules Michelet, the greatest of French historians of the first half of the nineteenth century, are gathered all the currents of thought which shape the historical writing of this period—romanticism, nationalism, liberalism, and philosophical idealism. Every phase of the diverse influences of the time passed through his mind and left its mark. Out of his romantic temperament and the bitter experiences of his youth came his love for the people and for France which would create for him the goal of his teaching and writing, to restore the historical continuity of France, to arouse patriotic interest in the national past, "to teach France to Frenchmen." [41] Out of this same love came his passion for the liberalism of the early days of the Revolution and his volumes on its glorification. In the passage of his intellectual curiosity through language and literature to history and philosophy, seeking the synthesis and continuity of all knowledge, he discovered through his learned friends, Cousin and Quinet, the ideas of Herder and Vico, and the achievement, literary and linguistic, historical and philosophical of the German world poured thenceforth into his mind.

Michelet held that history was "a chain of ideas clothed for the imagination with concrete forms," [42] that history was a struggle between man and nature, spirit and matter, liberty and necessity, that it was marked by the twofold action of unity and dissolution through the centuries. Romantically seeking to synthesize the whole life of humanity, he based history on geography and to geography he added all the concrete aspects of life which would bring history before the eyes, in the manner of Barante and Thierry.

Out of his own crisis and the romantic, liberal national passion Michelet produced his *History of the Revolution,*[43] which represents "the summit and the center of all his creations" [44] and in which his "lyrical identification of himself with his themes reached its greatest intensity." [45] It was an attempt to evoke the spirit of a whole people. Everything is individualized, characters brilliantly painted, but the people are the hero. Every aspect of human toil, every

---

[38] A. Thiers, *Histoire du Consulat et de l'Empire.*
[39] F. Guizot, *Histoire de la Civilisation en Europe* and *Histoire de la Civilisation en France.*
[40] J. W. Thompson, *A History of Historical Writing,* II, p. 262.
[41] Anonymous, "Michelet as an Historian," *Quarterly Review,* Vol. 193, p. 135.
[42] G. Lanson, "Historic Method of Jules Michelet," *International Quarterly,* XI (1905), p. 90.
[43] J. Michelet, *Histoire de la Révolution.*
[44] Hans Kohn, *Prophets and Peoples, Studies in Nineteenth Century Nationalism,* p. 66.
[45] Emery Neff, *The Poetry of History,* p. 147.

manifestation of living concrete life passes in review. No trait of national thought or feeling escaped the piercing vision of Michelet. It was a national epic, partisan, based on historical documents arbitrarily used, but "the mood of the revolutionary period is restored with a power unequalled in historiography." [46]

In the same spirit of this tragic crisis, Michelet took up the continuity of his *History* where it had been broken off to write of the Revolution. In 1855, the seventh volume, entitled *The Renaissance*,[47] was published. Now a hater of the Church and the aristocracy, his view of the medieval world was no longer sympathetic. He saw in the sixteenth century a spirit more congenial to his tragic feelings, a spirit antithetical to the Middle Ages, and in the introduction to this volume appeared his epoch-making characterization, "the first attempt to isolate and characterize the Renaissance so-called as a period in general European history." [48]

In Michelet, the currents of thought of the period in France found their most significant expression, their weakness and their strength. Sensitive to the pathos of common life and to the meaning of a register of galley slaves, seeing with poetic vision and philosophical grasp the whole life of the past, feeling himself into the very stones and streams of his beloved France, he resurrected the past, as he intended, in a style which adapts itself by nature to every historical situation, which holds the reader by the force of its native melody, and through which history becomes art.

ITALY

During the first half of the nineteenth century, Italian literature, reflecting the currents of thought of the age, was devoted to the winning of national unity and independence. Its greatest literary achievements were a romantic historical novel of Manzoni[49] and the poetry of Leopardi. Historical writing, too, served similar purposes, inspired by romanticism, nationalism, and liberalism. From the cross currents, literary and historical, and marked by the traditional realities of papacy and regionalism, there emerged a school of historical writers called Catholic Liberal, or Neo-Guelf, which represented the best in the Italian historiography of this period.

Catholic Liberal School. Besides Manzoni it included among its members the Florentine, Count Gino Capponi (1793-1876), the Neapolitans, Carlo Troya (1785-1858) and Luigi Tosti (1811-1897), the Piedmontese, Cesare Balbo (1789-1853) and the Lombard, Cesare Cantù (1804-1895). All were Catholics in sentiment; all were fervid patriots and liberals. The fundamental motive of their historical writing was the defense and strengthening of the papacy and the support of the confederate solution of Italian unity under the Pope. The historical philosophy of Sismondi—that political liberty brings cultural greatness and the lack of it brings cultural decay—played a significant role in the works of Capponi, Troya, and Balbo. Count Capponi, although he wrote a history of

---

[46] Eduard Fueter, *Geschichte der Neueren Historiographie*, p. 454.

[47] J. Michelet, *La Renaissance*.

[48] W. K. Ferguson, *The Renaissance in Historical Thought: Five Centuries of Interpretation*, p. 174.

[49] A. Manzoni, *The Betrothed*, in Italian.

his native city, is famous in Italian culture as a patron "who by knowledge, zeal, and wealth, contributed more to Italian historical studies than any of his countrymen." [50]

Troya's and Tosti's works [51] are of historical importance because they are based on manuscript materials in the archives of Monte Cassino and other Italian monasteries. Balbo was one of the most popular Italian scholars. Independence from foreign control, the thesis of his two chief works,[52] was a fixed idea from which he never deviated. His writing is forceful, compact, and marked with strong national feeling.

Cantù, like Balbo, wrote in other literary forms before turning to history as a form of national education in the spirit of the men of the *Risorgimento*. Cantù's chief historical work [53] was a world history which dealt with the evolution of humanity. Its influence was very great and generations of Italians were to derive their historical knowledge from it. "No one of that school was more of a professional historian than he who covered the history of all the peoples and at all times, not only in their political aspects but also in their literary, religious, economic, and cultural aspects." [54] In similar fashion, he wrote the first complete history of the Italians.[55] On these beginnings, greater Italian historians would build.

ENGLAND

Between 1760 and 1830, English historical writing was in transition from the great eighteenth century masters to the beginning of a new creative period. During this time, English historical scholarship produced some minor studies of merit influenced by the currents of thought—romantic, national, and liberal— but the triumph of English romanticism was with the great poets and in prose with the historical novels of Walter Scott, who, as on the continent, was to inspire the revival of the past. Gradually, the influence of Niebuhr and Ranke crossed to the island after 1830 and English historical scholarship, near mid-century, laid the basis for its great advances during the last half of the century. Meanwhile, there arose two great men of letters whose historical writing and historical thinking have made them bywords, not only in historiography, but in the minds of generations of educated people ever since, Thomas Babington Macaulay (1800-1859) and Thomas Carlyle (1795-1881).

Macaulay. Macaulay was a partisan historian, a Whig patriot, who believed that English ascendancy in his day was the result of the victory of the Whigs in the Glorious Revolution of 1688. He set out to write a history which would manifest that progress through all aspects of English civilization. In the course of twenty years of extensive research, visiting the scenes he would describe, ransacking libraries, gathering materials and taking notes, he produced his famous and unfinished history [56] which, covering only twenty years of the

[50] G. P. Gooch, *History and Historians in the Nineteenth Century*, p. 439.
[51] C. Troya, *History of Italy in the Middle Ages*, in Italian; L. Tosti, *History of the Monastery of Mount Cassino*, in Italian, and *History of the Lombard League*, in Italian.
[52] C. Balbo, *History of Italy*, in Italian, and *Summary of the History of Italy*, in Italian.
[53] C. Cantú, *Universal History*, in Italian.
[54] B. Croce, *History of Italian Historiography in the Nineteenth Century*, in Italian, I, p. 198.
[55] C. Cantú, *History of the Italians*, in Italian.
[56] T. B. Macaulay, *The History of England from the Accession of James II.*

course of English history, from the accession of James II, is nevertheless a masterpiece of historical narrative. It read like a novel as he intended it should, and through its great popularity, he became the leading literary figure in the English-speaking world.

The greatness of Macaulay lay in his style, which was in part an innate talent, in part the influence of his reading, especially Scott, and in part the influence of his view of history.

His mastery of remarkable style in his twenties had been revealed in a brilliant essay on Milton, which appeared in 1825 in the *Edinburgh Review*. It inaugurated a series of historical essays which, appearing periodically during the following twenty years, brought him fame as an essayist. Each essay was an historical picture, painted, as it were, in a sparkling, polished prose, and full of information, illustrations, and analogies drawn from his vast reading, his extraordinary memory, and his practical experience in public affairs. They were not, however, of uniform worth. Some, like those on Chatham, Clive, and Hastings, were masterpieces. Others, like those on James I, and Frederick the Great, represent Macaulay at his worst. Through these thirty-six essays he contributed to the perfection of one of the highest and most difficult forms of historical writing.

Macaulay viewed history as a chaotic mass of disarranged phenomena. The historian's task was, through his selective skill and narrative ability, to bring order out of this chaos and create an artistic whole. History was a form of literature, an art, compounded of poetry and philosophy, which should reveal the character and spirit of the age, not an objective sequence or compilation of facts. The historian should make sweeping generalizations, should judge, and even prophesy. It is his own "positiveness, assertiveness, vituperative phraseology rather than his evidence" [57] for which he is condemned.

Carlyle. Even greater in his influence on the study and writing of history, because of his ideas, has been Carlyle, whose vividness of presentation equals that of Macauley and Michelet. Carlyle is perhaps the most controversial figure of all those who have contributed to historiography. The currents of thought of the age find deep and complex expression in this Scottish Calvinist romanticist whose melancholy was doubly brewed by that historic union. Steeped in his moral and religious inheritance he was philosophical in thought but not a systematic philosopher. Indebted for the saving of his soul to German philosophical idealism, to the currents of thought which flowed from Herder, Schiller, and Goethe, he made them the inspiration of his *Weltanschauung,* and his philosophy of history. A part of the continuity of English tradition, he admired the historical writing of the English masters but revolted with the romanticists, of whom he was the apotheosis, against rationalism. A moral patriot in the tradition of Burke and Scott, quite the opposite of the Whig, Macaulay, he wrote history to instruct the present not as an expression of progress but of catastrophe. "Every one of Carlyle's historical books serves a definite timely purpose."[58] Through his mind, as through that of Michelet,

[57] W. C. Abbott, "Macaulay and the New History," *Yale Review,* XLIII (March, 1929), p. 551.
[58] René Welleck, "Carlyle and the Philosophy of History," *Philological Quarterly,* XXIII (October, 1944), p. 72.

passed every phase of the diverse influences of the times, to leave its mark in some modified manner throughout his works. Out of Calvinistic morality, transcendental idealism, full-bodied romanticism, and prophetic nationalism, but not liberalism, flowed Carlyle's complex many-sided view of history, as art, as philosophy, as innumerable biographies, as resurrection, as dynamism, as instruction for the present.

Inseparable from his view of history is his view of the world and man. The nature and the origin of the universe is spiritual. Its spirituality is a divine creative force, the real, the true, which lies behind the world of appearance and which is felt or sensed intuitively, a mystery not to be learned scientifically. Every person partakes of this mysterious creative force in the depths of subconsciousness, and every social group, like the individual, acts out of this irrational force, thus producing history, which can only be human history. To grasp the spirit behind the facts of history is the task of the historian.

History becomes, therefore, a resurrection of the spirit of the past through the facts, and the more it reveals the character of the person, or the spirit of the scene depicted, the closer it will be to the truth. To so reconstruct the past, since the historian is a part of this mysterious creative force, it is necessary to relive through one's own spirit the spirit of the past to be written, and in this intuitive way pour out in prose such an account that the reader will relive it, as the writer did. To this end, the historian has to gather all the evidence meaningful to the spirit of that past as Carlyle did for the composition of his works. But he used the material subjectively, as he believed it should be used, not objectively in Ranke's sense.

The result of this view and method were the artistic "flame pictures," and character portraits for which he is justly famous. Of the three major works of Carlyle,[59] the greatest and most famous is the *French Revolution*. "No writer but Michelet has approached Carlyle in the power of rendering the atmosphere of horror and hope, of tense passion and animal fury"[60] which it reveals. His *Cromwell* has been praised for creating a sympathetic but objective portrait of the great Puritan leader. *The Life of Frederick the Great* provides a vivid account of military and diplomatic campaigns, but as history it "is disfigured by distortions, partisanship, biased judgment and significant omissions." [61] Of his many minor writings, through which he is equally well known, Book II of *Past and Present* is "the most perfect of Carlyle's historical writings in satisfying his own requirements."[62] And his portraits of Goethe, Schiller, and Jean Paul, his essays on Boswell and Burns, are as great achievements in literary history as his portraits in his major historical works.

The currents of thought of the first half of the nineteenth century shaped the historical writing of the age. Philosophical idealism stimulated the study of the philosophy of history and found its most famous exponent in Hegel.

[59] T. Carlyle, *The French Revolution, Letters and Speeches of Oliver Cromwell, Life of Frederick the Great.*

[60] G. P. Gooch, *History and Historians in the Nineteenth Century*, p. 325.

[61] J. S. Shapiro, *Liberalism and the Challenge of Fascism. Social Forces in England and France, 1815-1870*, p. 388.

[62] L. M. Young, *Thomas Carlyle and the Art of History*, pp. 124-125.

Romanticism and nationalism stimulated, on the one hand, the collecting, editing, and publishing of documents on the national past, and on the other, the study of language, of origins, of peoples, and the writing of romantic national history, which found its greatest masters in Michelet and Carlyle. Liberalism stimulated the study of the past for the lessons it taught the present and for the justification of the political power of the bourgeoisie and found its most famous spokesmen in Macaulay and Guizot. And historical criticism brought forth the ideal and method of objective history and found its greatest master in Ranke.

Chapter 14

THE INTRODUCTION OF CRITICAL HISTORICAL SCHOLARSHIP IN FRANCE, ENGLAND, AND ITALY

By Charles Hallberg

INFLUENCES ON NINETEENTH CENTURY HISTORICAL WRITING

H ISTORICAL writing in France, England and Italy during the second half of the nineteenth century was influenced by a great many factors. Among them were new developments in science, the spread of liberalism and nationalism, the revival of imperialism and the sharpening interest in the economic and social problems that grew out of modern industrialism. Such earlier movements as Romanticism and Positivism, the latter associated with Auguste Comte (1797-1858) and deriving its inspiration from the progress in science and technology, continued to exert an influence. But the most significant development in the historiography of the second half of the century was the introduction and diffusion of critical or scientific scholarship.

While the pace was set by the great German historians like Ranke, Waitz, Sybel, Jaffes and others, the new scientific history was furthered in France by Aulard, Fustel de Coulanges and Monod, in England by Gardiner, Maitland and Stubbs, and in Italy by Villari. With the introduction of the seminar method and more exacting standards of workmanship, there took place a gradual separation of history from *belles lettres* and a tendency for narrative to give way to monograph. More and more the writing of history became the work of the university-trained specialist rather than of the non-professional writer. Critical scholarship also meant specialization. While the emphasis was largely on political history, increasing attention was given to cultural, economic, religious and social developments.

There was considerable interest in the Middle Ages, an interest which had been encouraged by Romanticism. In France and England, many historians inquired into the origin and formation of feudalism. This interest was influenced by the prestige of science, for science provided not only a method of investigation but stimulated the historian to trace institutions to their origins. Although each country had its own peculiar historical developments and problems, the Great Revolution in France, the seventeenth century conflict between king and parliament in England, and the movement for independence and unity in Italy provided historians of these countries with dominant themes.

FRANCE: REVOLUTIONARY STUDIES

The scientific writing of history in France did not begin until the sixties—a generation after von Ranke inaugurated his famous seminar method in

Germany. The great French historians of the first half of the century were non-professionals like Guizot, Michelet, and Thiers. Now, no other subject exerted more influence over the historiography of nineteenth century France than that of the Great Revolution. During the first half of the century, Lamartine, Michelet, Mignet and Thiers had devoted themselves to it. Although Alexis de Tocqueville (1805-59) belongs to this earlier period, he approached the study of the Revolution in the spirit of modern critical scholarship. The son of a peer who had attained some recognition as an historian and philosopher and had served as prefect in the Restoration era, Alexis in 1827 became a magistrate at Versailles and four years later received permission to visit the United States in order to study its penal system. In 1835 appeared his famous classic of political science, *Democracy in America*.[1] Entering politics, he became Vice-President of the Assembly and in 1848, Foreign Minister, but retired after the *coup d'état* of 1851 and devoted the remainder of life to the study of the Old Regime. The first volume of *L'ancien regime* was published in 1856.[2] Based upon extensive research, especially in provincial archives, it maintained that the Revolution was the logical continuation of the Old Regime, that it changed less than had been supposed, and was less terrible than the lurid accounts of some writers suggested—conclusions generally accepted by later historians. *L'ancien régime* has remained a standard work in its field. Unfortunately, Tocqueville did not live to complete the second volume in which he intended to deal with the reform movements of the Revolution.

Taine. While Tocqueville wrote without passion and adhered to no particular theory of history, Hippolyte A. Taine (1828-92) approached the study of the Revolution in a far different spirit. One of the most versatile of nineteenth century writers, he was an advocate of Comte's Positivism and was especially influenced by the concept of the *milieu*. He maintained that the methods of science should be applied to the study of history. Few Frenchmen of his time had a more lively interest in German intellectual developments or a higher regard for German historical scholarship. While Taine wrote on various subjects, including art, literature, and philosophy, his most famous work is in the field of history: *The Origins of Contemporary France*.[3]

The first volume of this work, *The Ancient Regime,* is a fairly balanced account in which Taine attributes the Revolution to the *philosophes,* especially Rousseau. In the volumes on the Revolution, largely concerned with the Jacobins, he becomes more impassioned. Viewing the Revolution as a spontaneous eruption of anarchy, he depicts the Jacobins as monsters intoxicated by the heady wine of Rousseau's concept of popular sovereignty. With its abundance of insignificant details and serious omissions, the work does not satisfy modern standards of scholarship. The research was superficial and the method unscientific. Taine's principal contribution to historiography was in emphasizing the part played by the *milieu*—the geography, climate and resources of a country—which is clearly revealed in his *History of English Literature*.[4]

[1] Alexis de Tocqueville, *Democracy in America,* trans. by Henry Reeve, 3rd ed., 2 vols.
[2] Alexis de Tocqueville, *The Ancient Regime,* edited by G. W. Headlam.
[3] Hippolyte A. Taine, *The Origins of Contemporary France,* trans. by John Durand, I, *The Ancient Regime,* II, III and IV, *The French Revolution.*
[4] Hippolyte A. Taine, *History of English Literature,* trans. by H. Van Laun, 4 vols.

Aulard. The systematic study of the Revolution in France began with Alphonse Aulard (1849-1928). Entering the École Normale Supérieure at the age of eighteen, he interrupted his studies to serve in the Franco-Prussian War. His training was in literature rather than history, and from 1878 to 1884 he taught literature in the provinces. In 1884 he became professor of rhetoric at the Lycée Janson de Sally in Paris, and in the following year was appointed to the first chair of the history of the French Revolution which the municipality had endowed at the University of Paris, where he remained until his retirement. He had already acquired a reputation in the field of the French Revolution through his work, *L'eloquence parlementaire pendant la Révolution.*[5]

Aulard's principal work on the Revolution, though not his greatest contribution, *The French Revolution, a Political History, 1789-1804,* appeared in 1901.[6] The result of twenty years of patient research in the archives, largely in official sources, the study is almost exclusively political and frankly partisan in character, for Aulard did not conceal his hatred of the Old Regime and his admiration for the Revolution and Danton. In it, Aulard attempted to trace the development of democratic principles and was the first to point out that the republican idea was a fairly late occurrence in the history of France.

The minor writings of Aulard deal with various aspects of the Revolution: the religious cults, educational policies of Napoleon, the feudal regime, in which he turns to economic history, and a larger work based on articles contributed to periodicals, especially *La Révolution française,* of which he became editor in 1887. It is as an editor that Aulard made the most lasting contribution to the history of the Revolution. Of special significance is his collection of the documents of the Committee of Public Safety.[7]

Despite the limitations of his work—the emphasis on political history and his partisanship—Aulard was recognized as the historian of the Revolution. His influence upon French historiography and upon the political ideas of the Third Republic was considerable.

Sorel. Another historian whose main work falls within the period under discussion was Albert Sorel (1842-1906). After studying law, he entered the French Foreign Office in 1866, where he remained until the close of the Franco-Prussian War. In 1872 he became professor of history at the École in Paris and in 1898 at the military school of St. Cyr.

His chief work, *L'Europe et la Révolution française* (4 vols.), was based upon extensive research in the archives of France and Europe. It deals with the international aspects of the Revolution which Sorel represents as a continuation of the history of the Old Regime. The wars of the revolutionary period, he maintains, were inspired neither by the desire of the French to spread their principles nor by the desire of the European rulers to save the French monarchy. Austria, Prussia and Russia were more interested in Poland than in the fate of Louis XVI. Based on critical scholarship and written in

---

[5] Alphonse Aulard, *L'eloquence parlementaire pendant la Révolution* (3 vols.).
[6] Alphonse Aulard, *The French Revolution, a Political History, 1789-1804,* trans. by Bernard Miall (4 vols.).
[7] Alphonse Aulard (ed.), *Recueil des Actes du Comité de Salut Public, avec la Correspondance Officielle des Representants en Mission* (27 vols.). Aulard also edited documents on the Jacobin Club and on Paris in the periods of the Directory, the Consulate and the First Empire.

a lucid style, without noticeable bias, Sorel's work was the first adequate study of the diplomatic history of the French Revolution.[8]

THE MEDIEVAL FIELD

Some of the best historical writings in France in the second half of the nineteenth century were in the medieval field. France was fortunate in having a rather unique institution, the École des Chartes, where the systematic study of medieval history began as early as 1820 and where some of the most eminent scholars of the country, particularly archivists, received their training.

Fustel de Coulanges: the Origin of Feudalism. Outstanding among French medievalists and one of the great historians of the century was Numa Denys Fustel de Coulanges (1830-89). In the course of his studies, he worked at the École Française d'Athenes and spent two years in Greece collecting unpublished materials. After teaching in lycées in Amiens and Paris, he was appointed to the chair of medieval and modern history at the University of Strasbourg in 1860, remaining there for ten years.

The early interest of Fustel de Coulanges was in antiquity. *The Ancient City,*[9] which he published in 1864, became a classic of French historical literature. Preoccupation with the defeat of France in the Franco-Prussian War caused him to turn from the ancient world to questions affecting his own time and country. In the course of this, he also took up the study of the origins of feudalism, a subject which increased his anti-German sentiments. There existed at the time two schools of interpretation concerning the origins of feudalism, the German and the Roman. In an article which appeared in *Revue des Deux Mondes* (1872), Fustel de Coulanges declared that the German invasions of the fifth century left no permanent mark upon French institutions. This thesis was repeated in his *Histoire des institutions politiques de l'ancienne France* [10] (first volume published in 1874). Feudalism, he asserted, would have come even if there had been no Germanic invasions. Stung by the criticism which greeted this volume, largely on the ground that he had not proved his conclusions, Fustel de Coulanges set about to convince his critics. The next three volumes revealed his mastery of documentary evidence and of the analytical method.

Like Taine, Fustel de Coulanges was a Positivist. He regarded history as a science—the science of interpreting documents. The historian must know what texts exist, analyze them with an unbiased mind, and synthesize. Interested in institutions rather than individuals, Fustel de Coulanges tried to view the past through the eyes of contemporaries. As a master of the texts and of historical synthesis, he was undoubtedly one of the greatest of

---

[8] Among other French historians of the Revolution were Edgar Quinet, who defended the Revolution and attacked Catholicism; Mortimer Ternaux, whose history of the Terror is still important; and Wallon, an authority on the Revolutionary Tribunal. In the field of Napoleonic studies are Taine's volume on Napoleon which is biased against him and is based on questionable sources; the books of Frederic Masson giving intimate details of Napoleon's life; the more scholarly volumes of Vandal, especially his study of Napoleon and Alexander I; and the laudatory works of Henri Houssaye and Arthur Levy.

[9] Fustel de Coulanges, *The Ancient City*, trans. by Willard Small.

[10] Fustel de Coulanges, *Histoire des institutions politiques de l'ancienne France* (6 vols.); Volumes 1, 2, 5, and 6 were edited by Camille Julian.

his time. Yet neither his method nor his conclusions are entirely acceptable to modern scholars.

Monod: Scientific Scholarship. Less well-known than Fustel de Coulanges, though hardly less important in French historical scholarship, was Gabriel Monod (1844-1912). Upon the advice of Taine he studied in Germany, attending the lectures of Jaffe in Berlin and Waitz in Gottingen. He became a warm admirer of the German seminar method. Upon his return to France, he joined the École Pratique des Hautes Études, founded in 1868 by Victor Duruy, for the training of historical scholars. Here Monod offered a seminar in medieval history.[11]

His greatest contribution to historiography was the founding of the *Revue Historique,* the first issue of which appeared in January, 1876. As editor until his death in 1912, he was instrumental in publishing articles on all periods of history and in attracting contributions from outstanding historians of France and other countries. Monod's article in the first issue set the standard. There he directed attention to the shortcomings of French historical scholarship and the need for a scientific approach. French historiography is also indebted to him for his support of the seminar method and the introduction of the study of diplomatics which he brought back from Germany.[12]

CHURCH HISTORY

Renan. Apart from interest in the Revolution and the medieval period, French scholars were drawn into other fields of history.[13] Widely known for his history of the early church was Ernest Renan (1823-92), who was born in Brittany. As a young student he became interested in semitic philology and for a short time was professor of Hebrew and Chaldaic languages in the Collège de France. In 1863 appeared his *Life of Jesus* which was the first of several volumes in the series, *Histoire des origines du christianisme.*[14] Though less scholarly than some of the other volumes, the *Life of Jesus* is the best known of Renan's books. It depicts Jesus as a human being rather than as a god and was bitterly denounced by the clergy. In his old age, Renan brought forth the *History of the People of Israel,*[15] which explained the origins of the Old Testament in terms of the environment and racial characteristics of the Jews. Renan was one of the followers of Comte and an admirer of German scholarship. He combined a remarkable power of analysis with an exquisite literary style. His books, however, are more important as literature than as history.

---

[11] Monod was an authority on Merovingian and Carolingian sources.

[12] In the last half of the nineteeth century there appeared in France a number of historians of institutions and specialists in the medieval field. Among these were Leopold Delisle, a prolific writer and a "scientific" historian; Camille Jullian, the historian of ancient Gaul; Achille Luchaire, one of the greatest French medievalists and an outstanding authority on the eleventh, twelfth and thirteenth centuries; and Paul Marie Viollet, known for his works in the fields of French law and political institutions.

[13] In the history of the ancient east, including Egypt, Gaston Camille Charles Maspero was an outstanding figure. The works of Gaston Boissier in Roman history and of Alfred Rambaud in Byzantine history are noteworthy contributions. The economic life of antiquity was the subject of Paul Guiraud's studies. Few French historians of the period, however, were attracted to economic history. The best known before Henri See was Pierre Émile Levasseur who wrote a history of the working classes of France. Vicomte Georges d'Avenel's study of prices is also important although it is now regarded as unreliable.

[14] Ernest Renan, *Histoire des origines du christianisme* (7 vols.).

[15] Ernest Renan, *History of the People of Israel* (3 vols.)

The advance in French historiography during the second half of the nine-teenth century was indeed noteworthy. With the introduction of the German seminar, the training in critical methods of scholarship in such famous schools as the École des Chartes and the École Normale Supérieure, the founding of historical journals and the multiplication of historical societies, there took place an increasing specialization and a gradual separation of history from *belles lettres*. While the emphasis was chiefly on political de-velopments, one detects a growing interest in other aspects of history. In Aulard and Fustel de Coulanges, moreover, France had two of the great historians of the age.

ENGLAND

English historical scholarship in the second half of the nineteenth century was less advanced than in France or Germany. The systematic study of history at Cambridge and Oxford did not begin until the seventies, and there was much less emphasis upon scientific methods than in the great continental universities. English historians of the period were mainly interested in de-velopments of their own country—the rise of feudalism, the growth of the constitution, the Reformation, and the seventeenth century conflict between king and parliament. Although the volume of serious historical production was somewhat less than in France or Germany, English historians did turn out some remarkable works. Moreover, in no other country did the non-professional historian enjoy a higher standing.

NATIONALIST HISTORY

Froude. The first English historian to prepare a detailed history of England from unpublished manuscript sources was James Anthony Froude (1818-94). A disciple and biographer of Carlyle, an ardent nationalist and a bitter enemy of the Roman Church, Froude was a brilliant narrative writer. During the closing years of his life he was Regius Professor of History at Oxford. His *History of England from the Fall of Wolsey to the Defeat of the Spanish Armada*[16] is a monumental work based on manuscript sources, especially those at Simancas. In it he reveals not only his literary gifts and his Carlylean hero-worship but also his strong prejudices. Militantly Protestant, he regarded the Reformation as the greatest event in English history. His defense of Henry VIII, his dislike of Elizabeth, his hatred of Mary, Queen of Scots, and his vindication of Cranmer and exaltation of Lord Burghley, stand out in bold relief. Even more biased is his three-volume work, *The English in Ireland in the Eighteenth Century*,[17] in which he endeavored to show the futility of conciliating the Irish. On the other hand, Froude was fairly ob-jective in his biography of Carlyle.[18]

The bitter attacks made upon him by Freeman in the *Saturday Review* gave rise to the legend of Froude's constitutional inaccuracy and even charges of

---

[16] James A. Froude, *History of England from the Fall of Wolsey to the Defeat of the Spanish Armada* (12 vols.)
[17] James A. Froude, *The English in Ireland in the Eighteenth Century* (3 vols.)
[18] James A. Froude, *Thomas Carlyle, A History of the First Forty Years of His Life, 1795-1835* (2 vols.), and *Thomas Carlyle: A History of His Life in London, 1834-1881.*

dishonesty. There is no doubt that he was a very careless worker but more recent scholars have refuted the charges of dishonesty. It is, however, his partiality rather than his inaccuracies which has damaged his reputation. He was less a scientific historian than a great literary artist.

THE OXFORD SCHOOL

Freeman. Froude's critic, Edward Augustus Freeman (1823-92), was a political historian whose maxim, "history is past politics, and politics is present history," is widely known. With John R. Green and William Stubbs, he was a member of the so-called Oxford School of historians. In 1884, he succeeded Stubbs as Regius Professor at Oxford. For the first twenty years of his career as historian, he devoted himself to the classical world. His *History of Federal Government,*[19] of which only the first volume was published, established his reputation. Shifting his interest from ancient Greece to his native land, he wrote the *History of the Norman Conquest, Its Causes and Its Results,* his greatest work, where he represents the Conquest as far less cataclysmic than was generally supposed. Freeman was a prolific writer with a wide range of interests, including architecture and geography as well as history.

As a historian Freeman relied on his own library and disdained manuscript sources. Only printed materials were consulted in preparing his books. His chief interest was in political and military affairs; economic and social factors, religion and philosophy found little place in his works. He had a tendency towards repetition and the inclusion of many insignificant details. Like a number of his fellow English historians, he glorified the Anglo-Saxons. Freeman was a man of wide learning and had much influence in his day. His appreciation of the geographic factor in the study of the past and his emphasis on the continuity of history were important contributions to historiography.

Green. More original than Freeman although less productive as a writer was his close friend, John Richard Green (1837-83). One of the great amateur historians of England, he was educated at Oxford, entered the church, served as vicar for a number of years among the poor in the East End of London, and was influenced by the Christian Socialist movement. In 1869, he succeeded Stubbs as librarian of Lambeth.

Green's reputation as a historian is based upon a single book, *A Short History of the English People* (1874), which was an immediate success. Unlike Freeman's works, which were strictly political, Green deliberately minimized the role of dynasties and treated the life of the people as a whole. At the same time he shared Freeman's enthusiasm regarding the Teutonic influence on England's early history. An expanded version, *History of the English People,*[20] proved less successful.

To have compressed the life of a great nation into a single volume was in itself a significant contribution. Green combined a clear and vivid style with

---

[19] Edward A. Freeman, *History of Federal Government,* 1863.
[20] John R. Green, *History of the English People* (4 vols.)

a masterful organizing capacity. Omitting unessential details, he dealt with every aspect of the life of the English people. He studied the topography of the country and the boundaries of the towns. He was also keenly aware of the urban role in history.

Stubbs. It was the third member of the Oxford School, William Stubbs (1825-1901), who seriously applied more critical methods to the writing of history. Educated at Oxford, he entered the church, and for sixteen years was vicar at Navestock in Essex. He was librarian of Lambeth (1862-67), Regius Professor at Oxford (1867-84), and then became Bishop of Chester and Oxford.

While a student at Oxford, Stubbs spent many hours studying old manuscripts and acquired a first-hand knowledge of palaeography. His first writing, *Registrum Sacrum Anglicanum*[21] traced the succession of English bishops and was an important contribution to ecclesiastical history. His editions for the famous Rolls Series, beginning in 1863, advanced the critical study of English medieval manuscripts. In 1870 appeared his volume of *Select Charters,*[22] which included the important sources of early English constitutional history and was a brilliant work of editing. Stubbs' masterpiece, *Constitutional History of England,*[23] was a stupendous undertaking and was hailed by scholars throughout the world. It was the first critical study of English constitutional developments in the Middle Ages. Based on manuscript sources and written in a clear and vigorous style, it alternates analytical with narrative chapters and achieves a high degree of objectivity. The first volume, however, has been rendered obsolete by later research.

INSTITUTIONAL HISTORY

Seebohm. In the field of institutional history, England lagged behind France and Germany. Of greatest interest to the late nineteenth century European historian was the question of the origin and formation of feudalism and, as in France, this had produced two schools of interpretation, the German and the Roman. By 1880, the Germanic theory had gained acceptance in England through the writings of Freeman, Green and Stubbs. The outstanding Romanist after Palgrave was Sir Frederick Seebohm (1833-1912), local banker and magistrate, and an amateur historian. His chief work, *The English Village Community*[24] attacked the Mark theory which Kemble[25] had borrowed from German historians, and concluded that manorialism had existed in the Roman villa before the Anglo-Saxons. The book was based upon considerable research and was an important contribution to the institutional history of medieval England although its conclusion was later demolished by Vinogradoff.[26]

Maitland. The most brilliant of English institutional historians, Frederic

---

[21] William Stubbs, *Registrum Sacrum Anglicanum,* 1858.

[22] William Stubbs (ed.), *Select Charters* (2nd ed.)

[23] William Stubbs, *Constitutional History of England* (3 vols.)

[24] Sir Frederick Seebohm, *The English Village Community,* 1883.

[25] John M. Kemble, *The Saxons in England* (2 vols.) It first appeared in 1849.

[26] In his *Villainage in England,* first published in Russian in 1887, Vinogradoff rejected the Romanist theory advanced by Seebohm and maintained that the free village communities were agrarian rather than political and of German rather than Roman origin. His view has been accepted by later historians.

William Maitland (1850-1906), practiced law for a number of years before turning to teaching and the writing of history. From 1884 to his death he taught law at Cambridge and took a leading part in organizing the Selden Society in 1887, which published the sources for English legal history and for which he edited eight volumes.

Maitland's great contribution to English institutional history, *Domesday Book and Beyond*,[27] grappled with the problem of manorial origins in England and contended that the manor did not grow out of the Roman villa but was a unit of taxation and that it was not identical with the village. He asserted that free villages existed at early times and that no real manorial system was to be found until the twelfth century, thus indicating his leanings toward the Germanic School. In addition to this book and his work as editor for the Selden Society, he contributed to the *Cambridge Modern History* and published several volumes dealing with English legal history and the origin and privileges of towns. Maitland, with his mastery of critical analysis and synthesis and his flawless style of writing, is one of England's ablest and greatest historians.[28]

Other English Historians

Lord Acton: Moral Law in History. No survey of English historiography would be complete without the name of Lord Acton[29] (1834-1902), who, though he wrote little, achieved a great reputation for his erudition. Distantly related to the Gibbon family, he was born in Naples, the son of an English baronet and a German mother. He was educated in schools of France, England and Scotland, then for six years in Munich where he lived with the famous Catholic Church historian, Dollinger. Later he attended the lectures of Ranke and Bockh at Berlin. Then, he settled in England, served in the House of Commons (1859-65), later in the House of Lords, and in 1895 became Regius Professor at Cambridge. Lord Acton's liberal Catholicism is revealed in his writings, particularly in articles published in the *Rambler* and the *Home and Foreign Review*. He disliked ultramontanism and was very critical of the Vatican Council, which in 1870 promulgated the dogma of Papal Infallibility.

An article, "German Schools of History," which appeared in the first issue of the *English Historical Review* in 1886,[30] shows Lord Acton's wide learning. It is a study of the ideas influencing historical scholarship of the nineteenth century. His name is associated with the *Cambridge Modern History* which he was invited to edit and for which he prepared the outline. His brilliant and learned reviews in the *English Historical Review* are among his best writings. Though a man of world-wide reputation, he failed to produce a great work. His plan to write a history of liberty was abandoned because it was too enormous a task as he conceived it. Lord Acton was a moralist. To him history was not merely a record of the past but of the spiritual evolution

---

[27] Frederic W. Maitland, *Domesday Book and Beyond*, 1897.
[28] Other English institutional historians included Sir Henry Maine (1822-88), Mary Bateson (1865-1906), and John Horace Round, (1854-1928).
[29] Sir John Emerich Edward Dalberg, first Baron Acton of Aldenham and eighth baronet.
[30] Lord Acton, "German Schools of History," *English Historical Review* (Vol. I 1886), pp. 7-42.

of man. As he saw it, the historian was to pass formal judgment and to act as the guardian of morality.

Gardiner: the Puritan Revolution. With the possible exception of Stubbs, no historian of nineteenth century England set a higher standard for critical scholarship than Samuel Rawson Gardiner (1829-1902), a descendant of Cromwell. Educated at Oxford, he served from 1871 to 1885 as professor of history at King's College, London. Upon the death of Froude, he was offered the Regius professorship at Oxford but declined the honor in order to continue with his writings.

Gardiner was the great authority on seventeenth century England. In 1863 appeared the first two volumes of his monumental work, *A History of England from the Accession of James I to the Outbreak of the Great Civil War, 1603-1642.*[31] He also wrote on the history of the Civil War, the Commonwealth and the Protectorate, and on Cromwell. His works on the seventeenth century have successfully weathered all the subsequent storms of criticism.

An indefatigable worker and a master of several modern languages, Gardiner pursued his investigations in the British Public Record Office, the British Museum and in a number of European archives. He consulted not only manuscript materials but newspapers and a vast pamphlet literature. His work belongs to the field of political history and is characterized by its strict chronological arrangement and its spirit of impartiality. His chief limitation as a writer was a prosaic style. Gardiner was, however, a master of his craft and one of the most competent and trustworthy historians of nineteenth century England.

Creighton: the Papacy. While most of the major English historians of the period focused attention upon internal developments there were others, like Mandell Creighton (1843-1901), who looked beyond the Isles. Creighton received his education at Oxford, took Anglican orders, taught ecclesiastical history for six years at Cambridge, and in 1891 became Bishop of London. He was one of the founders of the *English Historical Review.* In 1882 appeared the first two volumes of his masterly work, *A History of the Papacy during the Period of the Reformation.*[32] He did not consult the archives as Ranke did, but his impartiality and sympathetic treatment of the papacy, his skillful use of the printed sources, and his clear and interesting style, make his work a significant contribution. Creighton's other writings on Simon de Montfort, the age of Elizabeth, and on Aneas Sylvius are of minor importance.

Seeley: the Cambridge School. Sir John Seeley (1824-95) is identified with the so-called Cambridge School of historians. Before his appointment as Regius Professor at Cambridge, he had established a reputation as author of *Ecce Homo,*[33] and as the editor of the first book of Livy. Seeley's most important historical writing, *The Expansion of England,*[34] dealt with the eighteenth century conflict between Britain and France and is recognized as a

[31] Samuel R. Gardiner, *A History of England from the Accession of James I to the Outbreak of the Great Civil War, 1604-1642* (10 vols.), 1883.
[32] Mandell Creighton, *A History of the Papacy during the Period of the Reformation* (5 vols.)
[33] Sir John R. Seeley, *Ecce Homo. A Survey of the Life and Work of Jesus Christ,* 5th ed.
[34] Sir John R. Seeley, *The Expansion of England,* 1883.

classic in the history of British imperialism. He had much the same detached manner of writing as Creighton. His main interest was in international problems which he dealt with in broad generalizations. He regarded history as a school of statesmanship and sought to derive practical lessons from it.

English Positivists: Buckle and Lecky. In England as in France, Comte's Positivism and mid-nineteenth century scientific discoveries exerted an influence on a number of writers. Among them were two brilliant amateur historians, Henry Thomas Buckle (1821-62) and William Edward Hartpole Lecky (1838-1903). Buckle's *History of Civilization in England*[35] set forth certain natural laws of historical development. It was his plan to apply these laws to a detailed study of English civilization, but he died before he could complete his task. Like Taine, he regarded history as an exact science but was severely criticized for this by other English historians.[36]

Lecky. Lecky, a disciple of Buckle, developed an early interest in the history of ideas and achieved a European reputation while still a young man. In 1865 appeared his famous work, *History of the Rise and Influence of the Spirit of Rationalism in Europe,*[37] in which he endeavored to show that the advance in European culture was the result of emancipation from theological ideas. This was followed four years later by *History of European Morals from Augustus to Charlemagne.*[38] After these histories of ideas, Lecky wrote *The History of England in the Eighteenth Century,*[39] his most important work. It is divided into two parts: England from 1714 to 1793 and Ireland from 1714 to 1801 and, in addition, gives an account of both the American and French Revolutions. The part dealing with Irish history is Lecky's chief contribution to nineteenth century historiography. The work, as a whole, treats of economic and social as well as political developments and is characterized by much the same spirit of impartiality as is found in Gardiner's writings. Lecky's last work, *Democracy and Liberty,* was a sharp criticism of democracy.[40]

Lesser Historians. English historians of the period showed a fairly wide range of interests. John Bagnell Bury is well known for his study of the Eastern Empire, his critical edition of Gibbon's monumental work, and his contributions to the *Cambridge Ancient History* and the *Cambridge Medieval History.* Bryce's *Holy Roman Empire* is a classic. In economic and social history, James Edwin Thorold Rogers attained a high level of scholarship, William Cunningham was less original though more productive, while William James Ashley introduced German economic thought. The study of the ancient east was aided by the work of Sir Henry Creswick Rawlinson in deciphering the old Persia cuneiform, while his younger brother, George, is known for a scholarly edition of Herodotus and for several volumes on ancient eastern kingdoms. One of the most critical of Old Testament scholars was W.

---

[35] Henry T. Buckle, *History of Civilization in England,* 2nd ed.
[36] Among the English writers who interpreted history in terms of science was Sir Leslie Stephen (1832-1904), famous as a biographer and for his books, *The Science of Ethics, History of English Thought in the Eighteenth Century* (2 vols.), and a sequel, *The English Utilitarians* (3 vols.)
[37] William E. H. Lecky, *History of the Rise and Influence of the Spirit of Rationalism in Europe* (2 vols.)
[38] William E. H. Lecky, *The History of European Morals from Augustus to Charlemagne* (2 vols.)
[39] William E. H. Lecky, *The History of England in the Eighteenth Century* (8 vols.)
[40] William E. H. Lecky, *Democracy and Liberty,* 1896.

Robertson Smith, whose most original contribution was on the religion of the Semites. Italian history attracted Thomas Hodgkin and John Addington Symonds (Renaissance).

Despite the eminence of some of her historians, England lagged behind France and Germany in the volume of serious historical studies. While scientific methods were employed by Gardiner, Maitland, Stubbs and others, there was not much effort to train students in the requirements of the craft. Oxford and Cambridge were not as yet comparable to Berlin or the École des Chartes and the École Normale Supérieure in promoting historical scholarship. Although the main emphasis of the period was on political history, there was, as in other countries, a broadening of interests and an increasing specialization.

ITALY

Italian historical writing of the nineteenth century owed much of its inspiration to the struggle for independence and unity. Important work was done in the publication of source materials and in the study of regional history, while German influence was apparent in the development of critical scholarship.

Villari. The outstanding Italian historian of the period was Pasquale Villari (1827-1917). His *Life and Times of Girolamo Savonarola*[41] won him a European reputation. Based upon ten years of archival research, it showed his warm admiration for the religious prophet, although more recent evidence does not sustain his highly laudatory account. In another study, *The Life and Times of Niccolo Machiavelli,*[42] Villari defended the famous Florentine diplomat against his critics. These two biographies were followed by a scholarly work on the history of Florence entitled, *The First Two Centuries of Florentine History.*[43] Villari's other writings dealt with medieval Italy and were of a popular nature.

Much of the historical writing of Italy in the second half of the century was nationalistic in character. There was a conscious effort on the part of some historians, such as Villari and Cesare Cantu (1804-95), to stimulate the interest of the people in the story of Italy's past. At the same time, Italian historians were beginning to adopt more scientific methods and to broaden the range of their interests.

---

[41] Pasquale Villari, *Life and Times of Girolamo Savonarola,* trans. by Linda Villari (2 vols.)
[42] Pasquale Villari, *The Life and Times of Niccolo Machiavelli,* trans. by Linda Villari (2 vols.)
[43] Pasquale Villari, *The First Two Centuries of Florentine History,* trans. by Linda Villari.

Chapter 15

GERMAN HISTORIOGRAPHY IN THE SECOND HALF OF THE NINETEENTH CENTURY

By Herbert Wender

THE SPIRITED controversy between supporters of factual history and exponents of colorful narration was not ended in the second half of the nineteenth century, for romanticism still flourished and the followers of Leopold von Ranke were legion. From time to time there appeared historians, such as Michelet or Mommsen, who were both artists and scholars and combined literary charm with scientific adequacy, but these were exceptional. Nationalism impelled many patriotic writers to select documents and manuscripts suitable to their bias and produce fascinating histories of their lands and heroes, their folk traits and customs. Other significant influences on late nineteenth century historiography were the growth of liberalism and democracy, theories of social evolution, concepts of environmentalism, imperialism, neo-mercantilism and the advances made in the fields of archaeology and anthropology.

Europe in the latter part of the century was characterized by the increasing ascendancy of the bourgeoisie, traditional champions of nationalism and democracy. Industrialization was spreading rapidly, accompanied by a growth in population, and the new factory proletariat, an increase in the wealth of nations and a rise in the standard of living. Capitalists manifested a lively interest in imperialism while labor unions strove to achieve greater class solidarity and demanded political and social reforms. Germany in this epic period of Bismarck experienced the striking triumph of nationalism, became firmly unified, conceded a measure of democracy to the masses and pioneered in the field of social reform. These economic, social and political forces naturally affected every phase of cultural evolution, historiography included.

THE PRUSSIAN SCHOOL

The gospel of nationalism formulated in Hegel's philosophy and dramatized by the iron chancellor's brilliant triumphs led many history professors in Germany to secede from the Ranke school of scientific detachment and become enthusiastic apostles of Prussian patriotism. They eulogized the Hohenzollerns, inflated their achievements and proclaimed the historic necessity of a German empire. It was the mission of Prussia, the most perfect state, to create a German fatherland which would become the highest expression of human reason, an infallible and ideal political system. These fervent purveyors of Prussian chauvinism and sycophantic champions of the Hohenzollern dynasty formed what is known as the Prussian school of historians.

Dahlmann. One of the first members of this school was Friedrich Dahlmann (1785-1860), who taught at the University of Kiel, then at Goettingen and finally at the University of Bonn. An ardent advocate of constitutional monarchy, he had participated in the ill-fated Frankfort Assembly. Dahlmann outwardly favored the then revolutionary type of constitutional government but his views were highly theoretical and he really preferred a strong centralized monarchy with little concern for individual freedom. In his books on government and on the English and French revolutions, he manifests a keen interest in constitutional problems and advises rulers as a matter of prudent politics to grant and preserve constitutions for their people.[1] The most judicious instrument of government is the constitution of England, which represents the development of the ancient Teutonic ideals and is a worthy paragon for modern Germans. Dahlmann was most famous as a political teacher and passionate propagandist who influenced many young college students through his patriotic lectures, pamphlets and books. In addition to the works mentioned above, he published three volumes on the history of Denmark and a survey of the principal sources and authorities of German history, which after a little elaboration and revision became a very thorough national bibliography.[2]

Haüsser. Another staunch member of the Prussian nationalist school was Ludwig Haüsser (1818-1867), who also furthered the cause of German unification under Prussian leadership. Although a southerner from the state of Baden, he was eager to see Prussia become the nucleus of a national union, for only Prussia could attain genuine unity of the Germans and create a strong and virile country with a powerful and commanding position in the world. Haüsser contributed much through his books and lectures to awakening political consciousness in the nation and disseminating good citizenship and patriotism, especially among the youth of the south German states. He advocated a constitutional monarchy with a liberal policy in education and religion, criticising both Protestant orthodoxy and Catholic ultramontanism.[3] His books include a vivid account of the Thirty Years War and the Palatinate and the history of Germany from 1786 to 1815. Writing for the general public with a conscious political purpose. Haüsser emphasized Prussia's services to the fatherland and glorified her role in freeing the Germans from Napoleon.[4]

Duncker. The historian Maximilian Duncker (1811-1886) also participated in current affairs, in the movement for German unity, the establishment of empire and in the extravagant praise of the Hohenzollern dynasty. In his opinion, the significant factor in German policy was force, not freedom, and when Bismarck quarreled with the Prussian Parliament he enthusiastically supported the great statesman. In addition to politics, which occupied much of his time and energy, Duncker served as director of the archives at Berlin

---

[1] F. Dahlmann, *Zwei Revolutionen.*

[2] G. Waitz, *Friedrich Christoph Dahlmann.*

[3] E. Marcks, *Ludwig Haeusser und die Politische Geschichtsschreibung;* W. Oncken in *Badische Biographien,* I, pp. 340-347.

[4] L. Haüsser, *Deutsche Geschichte vom Tode Friedrichs des Grossen Bis Zur Gruendung des Deutschen Bundes.*

and later as historiographer of Brandenburg.[5] All peoples of all times interested him—ancient, medieval, and modern—and his historic publications covered diverse fields. Not a profound scholar, his style and attitude were considered sober and moderate. The *History of Antiquity,* nine volumes based on recently discovered material, was Duncker's most important work.[6] It deals with the migration of various people—their political, social and religious struggles and organizations. Other noteworthy achievements of Duncker include a number of valuable essays, the editing of state papers of the Great Elector, and the correspondence of Frederick the Great.

Droysen. A more eminent figure of the Prussian school was Johann Gustav Droysen (1808-1884), professor of Kiel, Jena and Berlin and a prominent participant in the abortive Frankfort Assembly. As a young man he was very much interested in Greek life and literature and in the life of Alexander, but as he grew older he abandoned the ancients and plunged with great enthusiasm into modern history, current politics and the movement for German unification. Even in his early works, Droysen revealed a Prussian outlook and demonstrated that only by blood and iron could Philip and Alexander have united the centrifugal states into a strong empire and extend Greek *kultur* over the Orient. Dedicating all his efforts to love of fatherland, he now taught, lectured and wrote exclusively as a patriot. There is only one salvation for the German states—they must all be incorporated into Prussia, who would utilize her army, administration and financial system to establish the new empire under the aegis of the House of Hohenzollern. In his *Lectures on the Wars of Liberation,* Droysen expresses his faith in the association of people to form a fatherland; it is a divine plan, God's will, and therefore depriving Poland of its independence was a far greater crime than the execution of Louis XVI, and it was Prussian patriotism that defeated Napoleon.[7] The *Life of York* is an arresting biographical narrative of a great heroic figure of the triumphant wars of liberation. Droysen's most impressive work was his *History of Prussian Policy,* in which he depicts the origin, progress and character of the Prussian monarchy, and shows how it continually strove to develop into a German power, particularly during the reigns of the Great Elector, Frederick William the First, and Frederick the Great. This voluminous work is based entirely on documents, contains an enormous amount of new material and has been considered one of the greatest achievements of German scholarship.[8] In his *Principles of History,* he emphasizes free will and the responsibility of the individual, the power, majesty, and authority of the state. Droysen identified history with past politics and the glorious deeds of statesmen and soldiers, and asserted that the aim of the historian should be to understand and interpret events in the light of current needs and problems.[9]

Sybel. Heinrich von Sybel (1817-1895) began his career as a brilliant disciple of Ranke, but the stirring events in the middle of the century im-

[5] R. Haym, *Das Leben Max Dunckers.*
[6] M. Duncker, *Geschichte des Alterthums.*
[7] J. G. Droysen, *Vorlesungen ueber das Zeitalter der Freibeitskriege.*
[8] J. G. Droysen, *Geschichte der Preussischen Politik.*
[9] O. Hintze, in *Allgemeine Deutsche Biographie,* XLVIII (1904), pp. 82-114. F. Meinecke, "J. G. Droysen" in *Historische Zeitschrift,* CXLI (1929), pp. 249-287.

pelled him to abandon the methods of his master and become one of the
leading exponents of the Prussian school of history. Abandoning his role of
a neutral and scientific scholar, he became a fervent missionary of German
nationalism, a votary of the powerful Hohenzollern state. His first important
production was a *History of the First Crusade,* a simple story based on the
best authorities and devoid of many legendary prevarications about the saintly
seekers of the Holy Sepulcher. Sybel disparaged medieval historiography and
historians—pointing to their lack of judgment, and critical reflection, their
predilection for epics, myths and fiction, their propensity to forge documents
and fabricate history. A profound study of early Teutonic institutions led
Sybel to conclude that kingship was a Roman contribution to the Germans.[10]

Then, turning his attention to modern history, Sybel resolved to demonstrate the horrible dangers involved in radicalism and revolution by writing
a didactic brochure about the French Revolution denouncing especially its
socialistic tendencies. The pamphlet, however, developed into a massive
polemic, a five-volume work discrediting the entire movement and establishing
for the Prussian historian a prominent European reputation, particularly
among the many conservative politicians. Instead of the turbulent and inept
French variety of freedom and equality, Sybel offered Germans the wise
Prussian ideas of discipline, order and moderation. The principles of the
Revolution were repugnant, trivial, and disastrous, and in the far more
significant diplomatic conflict which ensued, he found that the French were
mad, the Austrians selfish, and the Russians avaricious. Only impeccable
Prussia stood out as the model state—a paragon of virtue.[11] In addition
to Austria, France and republicanism, Sybel had an aversion to Catholicism,
particularly ultramontanism, and consequently supported the *Kulturkampf.*
His last great work was the *Founding of the German Empire by William I.*[12]
Inspired by Bismarck, the seven-volume work is a highly partisan defense
of the chancellor's politics and diplomacy. William is treated with reverence
while Bismarck is portrayed in a pedantic, prosaic style as the faultless and
blameless hero of the great German drama. A man of fierce prejudice, Sybel
distorted history and held to the view that strong personalities aware of the
spirit of the times and propitious occasion lead the incompetent masses to
realize their ideals. One of Sybel's lasting contributions to historiography
was his establishment of the *Historische Zeitschrift*[13] (1859), which became
the world's foremost historical periodical.

Treitschke. The most popular German historian of the nineteenth century
and the last of the Prussian school was Heinrich von Treitschke (1834-1896),
eloquent, passionate, and chauvinistic. Objective history, he declared, is blood-
less history and the true historical sense must manifest the narrator's heart.
The Germans wanted an emperor, a state and a flag. Prussia, the only great
and chosen power, would provide those needs by annihilating the petty

[10] H. Sybel, *Entstehung des Deutschen Koenigthums.*
[11] H. Sybel, *Geschichte der Revolutionszeit von 1789-1800.*
[12] H. Sybel, *Die Begruendung des Deutschen Reiches unter Wilhelm I.*
[13] E. Marcks, *Maenner und Zeiten;* F. Meinecke, *Historische Zeitschrift,* LXXV (1895), pp.
390-395.

contemptible principalities and by creating a genuine Germany which would dominate Europe and become the cultural instructor among nations. When his dreams were realized he began to compose his scholarly, though unscientific masterpiece, five volumes of the *History of Germany in the 19th Century,* (1879-1894).[14] A literary artist of consummate skill, Treitschke gives an admirable and stimulating account of the men and policies, institutions and ideas that contributed to the development of the new Germany. Unlike other members of the Prussian school he devotes adequate attention to fundamental cultural forces, to poetry, art and science as well as politics, but his vehemence and vitality are blatant, brutal, and beastly, for he loved and he hated with elemental fury. Essentially, a poet and ardent patriot, Treitschke wrote history not to record facts but as an emotional propagandist to arouse and convert his readers.

As an official spokesman of German monarchy, Treitschke proclaimed the absolute superiority of the state, advocated an executive power independent of party majorities, and recommended stern discipline, virile training and blind obedience. Some rulers serve the state, he said, others serve themselves; for example, Napoleon was an egotistic monster, but Bismarck and Cavour were altruistic statesmen. Among the objects of his scorn and derision were Austria, France, Russia, England, the small German states, Jews, Catholics, socialists, democrats and pacifists. Armed conquest is necessary and desirable and the hope of abolishing war is not only preposterous, it is immoral. War is noble, glorious and sublime, it is the law of life and the will of God. Its banishment would convert the world into a sea of selfishness. When Treitschke passed away, the Prussian school disappeared, for there was no longer any reason for its existence. Its members had helped inculcate their countrymen with the spirit of patriotism and thus assisted in the regeneration of Germany.[15]

THE SCHOOL OF RANKE

Waitz. By the middle of the nineteenth century Ranke's influence on historiography was recognized throughout Europe, and in Germany many of his students achieved great distinction. One of the earliest and most prominent among these disciples was Georg Waitz (1813-1886), who devoted many years to the critical study of medieval source materials. He was one of the editors of the magnificent *Monumenta* containing an enormous compilation of documentary data on German history. At the University of Goettingen, Waitz created the foremost German historical school specializing in the Middle Ages which became a mecca for contemporary medievalists. But his most famous scientific production was *German Constitutional History,* dealing with the origins, customs and institutions of the early Teutonic tribes and dynasties. The work is erudite, thorough and meticulously documented, but is entirely devoid of literary skill or popular appeal and avoids any illuminating interpretation. It was written for scholars and is a valuable source for students of medieval German history.[16]

[14] H. Treitschke, *Deutsche Geschichte Im 19 Jahrhundert.*
[15] F. Meinecke, *Die Idee der Straatsraeson in der Neuerin Geschichte.*
[16] G. Waitz, *Deutsche Verfassurigssgeschicht.*

Giesebrecht. The second of Ranke's students to become famous was Wilhelm von Giesebrecht (1814-1889), who not only possessed vast factual knowledge but could also narrate the events in a charming literary style. His monumental work was the *History of the German Imperial Era* in five volumes, covering the story from the Carolingians to Barbarossa. It is a great historical drama, instructive, colorful and patriotic, written in a popular vein, yet scholastically sound. By his romantic glorification of the House of Hohenstaufen and his insufficient recognition of north Germans in relating the remarkable achievements of the medieval empire, Giesebrecht aroused the anger of the Prussian school of historians. In his opinion, the imperial crown had been beneficial to both Germany and Italy, while Sybel and his associates berated the Hohenstaufen rule and argued that the medieval emperors with their universal outlook greatly damaged the German nation. As a loyal follower of Ranke and naturally averse to strife, Giesebrecht held aloof from political disputation and remained unaffected by the keen controversy. Although he was a sincere patriot and was eager to see the revival of a glorious German empire it was evidently immaterial to him whether the new state would be dominated by a Hohenzollern or a Habsburg. Giesebrecht became widely known, trusted, and popular among many students of medieval history through his mastery of a single era, his moral animation, delightful diction, and discerning criticism of authorities.[17]

THE ECONOMIC SCHOOL

Roscher. The economic school of historical interpretation, founded by Ludwig Feuerbach and Karl Marx, was increasingly promoted in the late nineteenth century in most countries of Europe. One of the first German economic historians of this period was Wilhelm Roscher (1817-1894), who was trained under Ranke and was profoundly learned in economics and political theory as well as in history. He aimed to discover the fundamental forces that governed economic phenomena, to point out the interrelationship between social, economic and political institutions, and then to combine history and economics by means of basic laws. The progress of human culture is the stream of history which results from the confluence of many tributaries. According to Roscher, every nation develops like a living organism, passing through the definite stages of childhood, youth, maturity and old age. As an able linguist he became conversant with many fields and periods of history, and as an adept writer of lucid prose, his books enjoyed wide circulation.[18]

Schmoller. An eminent follower of Roscher was Gustav Schmoller (1838-1917), distinguished for his work in furthering the study of social science, collecting historical sources and editing historical investigations. He was the author of several excellent works, such as the history of German small industries in the nineteenth century, the guild and municipal organizations of Strasbourg, Prussian constitutional, administrative and financial history

---

[17] W. Giesebrecht, *Geschichte der Deutschen Kaiserzeit.*

[18] Max Weber, "Roschers historische methode" in *Gesammelte Aufsaetz Zur Wissenschaftslehre,* pp. 3-42. O. Hintze, "Roschers Politische Entwicklungsthreorie" in Schmoller's *Jahrbuch,* XXI (1897), pp. 767-811.

and contemporary social and industrial politics. Schmoller observed the intimate connection and interaction between state and society and pointed out that the prevailing economic institutions and processes determine the character of all other social and cultural expressions. He also believed that the growth of economic life and institutions is influenced more by the state than by individual action.[19]

Inama-Sternegg. German economic history, as an evolutionary development, was ably treated by the Austrian, Karl von Inama-Sternegg (1843-1908), who also emphasized the close connection between economic life and all other fields of endeavor. He discussed medieval industry, towns, markets, and guilds, but laid particular stress on the importance of the agrarian aspect of economic history.

Karl Wilhelm Nitzsch. Karl Wilhelm Nitzsch (1818-1880), devoted his attention to the economic problems in Rome during the period of the Gracchi and explained the causes for the decline and fall of the Republic. He also investigated medieval German life, including legal and constitutional institutions, and after a study of the relations between the bourgeoisie and functionaires he presented the theory that the free bourgeoisie stemmed essentially from the functionary ministerial class. Nitzsch's general thesis was that all elements in the life of a nation—cultural, political, social and economic—are inter-related, but the dominant force is economic. The bases of legal and constitutional history and of politics may be found in economic conditions, movements and class interest. Allowing for the influence of outstanding personalities and a limited amount of free will, Nitzsch held that historical phenomena cannot be explained either by nationality, race or political custom, but by an understanding of the social and economic factors which are fundamental.[20]

INTELLECTUAL AND CULTURAL HISTORY

Lamprecht. Most eminent among the advocates of intellectual and cultural history of this period was Karl Lamprecht (1856-1915), who became professor at Leipzig in 1891. His first important work was a substantial treatise on the economic history of medieval Germany in which he manifested interest in the growth of classes and economic mass movements and their effect on social, cultural, and intellectual life. In addition to this Marxian concept, Lamprecht also adapted to his interpretation of history Comte's idea of successive, collective psychic stages and the prevalent doctrine of evolution. Between the years, 1891 and 1909, there appeared the nineteen volumes of his very popular *German History* in which he introduced his favorite theories.[71] The academic conflict between proponents of political history and champions of cultural history, which had already begun, was greatly intensified by the publication of this revolutionary work. The conservatives contended that the aim of historiography should be the history of the state and the achievements

---

[19] G. Schmoller, *Die Soziale Frage.*
[20] H. Merzdorf, *Karl Wilhelm Nitzsek.* K. W. Nitzsch, *Geschichte des Deutschen Volkes bis zum Augsburger Religionsfrieden.*
[21] K. Lamprecht, *Deutsche, Geschichte.*

of eminent individuals. The new historians, however, would not only restrict their attention to politics and personalities, but would also deal with art, law, religion and economic movements—all to be correlated into an organic whole governed by comprehensive principles.

Lamprecht aimed to establish a science of history which conformed to general sociological laws. His views on periodization and the social psyche were demonstrated in the history of Germany; but he believed that they possessed universal validity and could be applied to all countries. There were six basic periods of mental growth, each accompanied by a corresponding material development. These stages were Symbolism, the primitive period of history; Typism, the early Middle Ages; Conventionalism, the later Middle Ages; Individualism, the sixteenth century to 1750; Subjectivism, romanticism and the industrial revolution; and the post-industrial revolution epoch without a ruling ideal but characterized by nervous tension, a spirit of speculation, speed and enterprise. History, according to Lamprecht, is not the mere collection of facts about states and personalities and the narration of how events happened, but must answer the question "How did it become?" This task called for a generic and genetic exposition involving a survey of society as a whole to ascertain the behavior patterns—material, cultural and intellectual. The basic element of society is not the individual but the national folk soul, and historians should devote more study to the collective work and condition of mankind and less to the lives of eminent men.[22]

Riehl. Cultural history, where the whole life of a people is portrayed, was founded by Voltaire, but its real significance was not recognized until the second half of the nineteenth century. Prominent among the pioneers of this school was Wilhelm Heinrich Riehl (1823-1897), a sociologist as well as historian. In his chief, work, *The Natural History of the German People,* Riehl endeavors to demonstrate his basic theory that the development of man is limited by the forces and conditions prescribed by nature. Geographical factors such as climate, soil and topography generally determine cultural diversity, differences in food, clothing, houses, and customs and beliefs. Peasants, because of their occupation and social condition, are inclined to be provincial and conservative, while townsmen tend to be cosmopolitan and progressive. There are then two adverse forces in operation, namely, inertia and movement, and it is the function of the state to maintain a balance between the two and thus promote the welfare and happiness of the people. The family also interested Riehl, who regarded it as an indispensable social nucleus and stabilizer. In connection with his cultural history he demonstrated the important part played by music, architecture and the plastic arts, and made a very thorough study of German local life, in the 17th and 18th centuries.[23]

Freytag. The events of 1848 drove Gustav Freytag (1816-1895), a poet and dramatist, to the study of history and politics. As a nationalist, he

[22] R. Koetschke and A. Tille, *Karl Lamprecht,* M. Ritter, *Die Entwicklung der Geschichtswissenschaft,* pp. 436-4461. E. J. Spiess, *Die Geschichtsphilosophie von Karl Lamprecht.*
[23] W. H. Riehl, *Kulturstudien ans Drei Jahrhunderten;* Henry Simonsfeld, *Wilhelm Heinrich Riehl Als Kulturhistoriker.*

favored the unification of Germany under the hegemony of Prussia and as a liberal he opposed both radicals and reactionaries and was even critical of the policies of Bismarck. The life of the common people attracted him most and he therefore made an immense collection of papers, pamphlets and wood-cuts relating and describing scenes, episodes and anecdotes of humble men and women. Freytag's most famous book is *Scenes from German History*, a five-volume survey of German popular life from barbarian times to the nineteenth century, a major contribution to the field of cultural history.[24] The work, published in five volumes, received a wide and popular appeal, the scholars praising the evidence of original research and scientific treatment while the general public applauded its patriotism and its colorful and artistic style. A champion of the German bourgeoisie, Freytag believed that national life and cultural productivity depend upon the virtues and conditions of the middle class, who constitute the core of the nation. He describes in graphic detail the character and achievements of salient national heroes, such as Charlemagne, Barbarossa, Luther and Frederick the Great, and his vivid portrayal strikingly suggests the magnitude of the moral and material misfortune of the Thirty Years War. Unlike many other authors, Freytag did not cherish the good old times but preferred the present and the future in which he saw the standard of living rising and man's soul becoming more free.[25]

Burckhardt. The greatest cultural historian of the nineteenth century was Jacob Christoph Burckhardt (1818-1897), a brilliant Swiss scholar. Having studied theology, history and art at Basel, Berlin and Bonn, he devoted his first works to Swiss and German church art, and his forte was in the field of art. Indeed, though he was interested in all aspects of civilization, Burckhardt in his *History of Greek Culture* presented a detailed, comprehensive and realistic survey, and, in rejecting the often romantic reverence for the Greeks, emphasized their flaws—slavery, intolerance and cruelties. Burckhardt also, points out the affinity between historic forces of contemporary and ancient civilization.[26] The *Age of Constantine the Great* depicted an important transition period in the life of the Roman Empire when people longed for novelty but suffered from insecurity, when disintegration and decay had set in, when the old world was dying—destroying itself and thereby making way for Christianity and the Middle Ages.[27]

But the most splendid contribution of Burckhardt was *The Civilization of the Renaissance in Italy*, an addition to the world's classics which greatly enhanced the prestige of cultural history and stimulated further research in the field.[28] In this magnificent and famous work, Burckhardt treats every phase of the Renaissance, but dwells particularly on what he believed to be the basic psychological trait of the period—the rise of individualism. Medieval society was characterized by group control, as every one was subordinate to a class, a

[24] G. Freytag, *Bilder aus der Deutschen Vergangenheit.*
[25] H. Lindau, *Gustav Freytag;* P. Ostwald, "Gustav Freytag als Politiker" in *Westermanns Monatshefte*, CXXXVIII (1925), pp. 253-259.
[26] J. C. Burckhardt, *Griechische Kulturgeschichte.*
[27] J. C. Burckhardt, *Die Zeit Constantine des Grossen.*
[28] J. C. Burckhardt, *The Civilization of the Renaissance in Italy.*

corporation, a guild, or a family, and prominent personalities were rare. But the Renaissance witnessed the advent of a spiritually-minded individual, the complete man who desired self-realization, desired to know everything and to do everything in the world. This new spirit was engendered by the intensity and fullness of urban life, the revival of Greek and Roman art and philosophy, the decline of traditionalism and authoritarianism, and the tendency toward secularization. Burckhardt's book has been criticized for such deficiencies as the lack of an adequate medieval background, a sufficient elucidation of the origin and development of the Renaissance, for the paucity of political material and its omission of material foundations. Yet the work is considered one of the most brilliant and penetrating pictures of the Renaissance ever painted by an historian. An ardent aesthete and individualistic spiritual aristocrat, Burckhardt naturally possessed a predilection for subjects and periods which were predominated by personality and culture.[29]

ANCIENT HISTORY

Mommsen. Among the great specialists in the field of Roman history, Theodor Mommsen (1817-1903) stands out as a marvel of scholarship and originality. A master of minute and accurate research, he also exhibited a capacity for bold generalization and could express himself with perfect artistry and verve. Mommsen's accomplishments both in quality and quantity were astounding. His publications number over fifteen hundred titles, including articles in various fields, a volume of Latin inscriptions, surveys of all sorts of source material, a history of the Roman monetary system, a detailed study of Roman constitutional and criminal law, and a general history of the Roman Republic. Mommsen not only made permanent contributions to epigraphy, numismatics, archaeology, Italian philology, law and history, but he was also a passionate liberal politician who fought for liberty as a writer in 1848 and as an active member of the Prussian Parliament in 1861 and of the German Reichstag in 1881.[30]

In his survey of the Roman Republic, Mommsen in a very vivid literary style reconstructs Italian antiquity, its racial background, early institutions and social life. He aimed to describe classical Rome as a realistic world, picturesque, and human, and he was eminently successful in producing a brilliant and vital account of ancient civilization. "History is neither written nor made without love or hate," declared Mommsen. Accordingly, the *History of the Roman Republic* is replete with candid bias and partiality and is devoid of difficult problems, debatable points and the discussion of the value of sources. Julius Caesar is idolized as a man of destiny who dominated the stage, an irresistible savior of society sent by Fate to reanimate the decadent, dying Republic. Caesar's ambition was not to be king and conquer the world but to generate a national renaissance—political, military, moral, and intellectual. His enemies were contemptible mediocrities who tried to prevent a great man from doing what was necessary to promote the welfare of the Roman people. Mommsen

[29] C. Neumann, *Jacob Burckhardt;* K. Joel, *Jacob Burckhardt als Geschichtsphilosoph.*
[30] L. M. Hartmann, *Theodor Mommsen;* W. Weber, *Theodor Mommsen.*

justified the overthrow of incompetent government and approved usurpation or revolution when history deems the latter effectual. The Romans, he believed, possessed no deliberate plan to dominate the world; sometimes they just drifted into war, and were forced by circumstances to conquer and annex territory. Roman methods of rule were praiseworthy, and even their brutality and oppression could be condoned occasionally because such policy was necessary, and because historical movements must never be judged by moral standards. Intended for popular consumption, this work was received with great admiration and delight by the public and was translated into every civilized language. However, scholars and specialists lamented its lack of references and footnotes, pointed critically at Mommsen's unorthodox treatment, his emotional and journalistic style, and his liberal political predilections, though everyone attested to his profound erudition.[31]

Another remarkable creation of Mommsen's scholarly genius was the constitutional history of Rome, a lengthy account of the evolution of the Roman system of government and administration. Thoroughly acquainted with Roman law and politics as well as historical sources, Mommsen produced one of the most exhaustive and most authoritative treatises on Roman government ever written. It contains over 3000 pages with minute details and an enormous number of notes, and hence was popular only among historians. Mommsen also wrote an important tome on Roman criminal law—a descriptive examination of ancient crimes and punishments, legal procedure and the character of court officials from earliest times till Justinian. While scrutinizing and elucidating the laws, the book also illuminates for the reader Roman customs and attitudes on morals, marriage and religion. Still another notable contribution of Mommsen was his history of the Roman monetary system, which strikingly reveals the value of the study of coinage in clarifying certain historical problems. In matters of government and politics, in which he was frequently and vehemently engaged, Mommsen was moderately liberal, opposing both the reactionary Junkers and the radical democrats and preferring rule by an aristocracy of intellect.[32]

Curtius. An important writer in the field of Greek history was Ernst Curtius (1814-1896), a professor at Goettingen and Berlin. After an extensive and intimate exploration of the Greek peninsula and a thorough study of the various collections of sources in art and literature, Curtius published his most significant book, *Peloponnesus.*[33] In this two-volume work he displayed his expert knowledge of the topography of that part of the world, and, as a disciple of Karl Ritter, he endeavored to demonstrate the relation between geography and the characteristics of Greek culture. Curtius believed that the Ionians originated in Asia Minor and emphasized the important part played by nature in the making of history. He showed how the Grecian peninsula served as a bridge between the East and the West and thus facilitated the growth of Hellenic civilization. Less scientific but more poetic and particularly appealing

---

[31] T. Mommsen, *Roemische Geschichte.*
[32] T. Mommsen, *Roemische Strafrecht; Abriss des Roemischen Staatsiechts; Roemischen Muenzwesens.*
[33] E. Curtius, *Peloponnesus.*

to the general, cultured public was his three-volume *Greek History*.[34] It is a vivid, romantic but accurate survey of the cultural aspects of the Greeks— their art, literature, philosophy, religion, their bonds of union and the character of their eminent men. Curtius wrote with poetic grace and apparent ease and with abounding and admiring enthusiasm for everything Hellenic. Intended for popular consumption, the book is without footnotes. It draws upon legends as sources of information about early history. Mundane matters, prosaic politics, economic problems, diplomatic events, and wars held no charm for Curtius and so those subjects are eschewed. His passion was for aesthetics and ideas and these are the topics which he treated with warmth and artistic fervor.

Other contributions of Curtius include an outline of the history of the city of Athens, the making of excellent maps of Attica and Athens, the establishment of an Athenian archaeological institute, his influence on research at Pergamum, and finally his work as director of a corps of specialists in their fruitful excavations of Olympia.

Friedlaender. Also very important and immensely popular was the picturesque and dramatic survey of Roman social and cultural history written by Ludwig Friedlaender (1894-1909), a disciple of Mommsen and Burckhardt.

Meyer. Another eminent authority on ancient history was Eduard Meyer (1855-1930). His most significant and scholarly work was the *History of Antiquity*, a classic in the field based principally on primary sources. Beginning with an anthropological treatment, Meyer deals with all phases of civilization— political, economic, social and cultural. He looked on history as the result of the interplay of chance and free will and as developing in cycles. Meyer did not believe that the historian can achieve objectivity.[35]

CHURCH HISTORY

Doellinger. An outstanding figure among the champions of Catholicism was the German ecclesiastical historian Johann von Doellinger (1799-1890), a professor and priest of Munich. In his first major work, four volumes of church history, he defended his faith zealously, not as theological dogma but as an institutional development. A well-documented and scholarly work, it was translated into English, French and Italian. Doellinger's next important productions were the books on the Reformation and Luther in which he minimized the value of the new theology, stigmatized the Protestant heroes and complained about the wicked and disastrous consequences of the Lutheran revolt. For the evil results, social and spiritual, he blamed Luther, bemoaning in particular the latter's belittling of good works. The Catholic Church, declared Doellinger, had experienced many reform movements and the sixteenth century reformation would have been just one more but for Luther's tenacious adherence to his doctrine of justification by faith. Christianity is the basis of civilization but its mission can be fulfilled only by a universal organization to include all devotees of the religion. All Christians are reminded of their common origin and common

[34] E. Curtius, *Griechische Geschichte.*
[35] E. Meyer, *Geschichte des Altertums;* W. Otto, "Eduard Meyer und sein Werk" in *Zeitschrift der Deutschen Morgenlaendischen Gesellschaft*, X, PP 1-24.

traditions, and non-Catholics are therefore invited to return to the Mother Church while Rome is asked to be more moderate toward nationalistic claims in order to reconcile the Protestants.[36]

Until the sixties, Doellinger was an enthusiastic defender of the Catholic point of view, but then he lost favor in the eyes of the ultramontane hierarchy because of his assertion that the unification of Italy and the consequent loss of the church states would not be fatal to the purely ecclesiastical power of the Papacy. His loyalty became more dubious when he suggested that the loss of the Pope's temporal power might be a wholesome purification and intimated that the Protestant Reformation perhaps had not been altogether baneful. This was followed by further critical remarks and, finally, when the Vatican Council was called with the object of announcing the principle of absolutism in the Catholic Church, Doellinger published his famous book, *The Pope and the Council,* in which he vigorously denounced the doctrine of papal infallibility.[37] The book was promptly placed on the Index, and, as Doellinger continued to castigate ultramontanism and the activities of the Council, he was excommunicated. As an opponent of papal infallibility, Doellinger contributed to the growth of Old Catholicism in Germany and inspired many disciples in that country and elsewhere.

Hefele. Another eminent ecclesiastical historian was the Catholic bishop and professor, Karl von Hefele, (1809-1893). In his *Biography of Cardinal Ximenes,* he apologized for the Inquisition, asserting that it was an instrument of secular totalitarianism forced upon the Church and that modern observers ought to consider the dissimilarity between current and medieval mores. Hefele's masterpiece was the *History of the Councils,*[38] in seven volumes, an objective and highly authoritative survey of Catholic dogma, canon law, liturgy, morals, political questions and ecclesiastical discipline. The work was universally recognized as a scholarly and valuable achievement and the author as an expert on church councils. In one of his pamphlets Hefele pointed out the possibility that the Pope could commit an error when interpreting doctrine but for the sake of peace he finally abandoned his stand against papal infallibility.

Hergenroether. An even stauncher champion of ultramontanism was Joseph Hergenroether (1824-1890), prefect of the Vatican Archives, who in 1883 helped make available to European scholars the enormous mass of historical material at the Vatican. In an exceptionally well-written monograph on Photius, the patriarch of Constantinople, Hergenroether places the primary blame for the Greek Schism on Photius rather than on Rome. He also replied to the attacks by Doellinger, defended the Vatican party, and was the author of a popular manual of Church history used by Catholic students.[39]

Janssen. A most momentous product of the Church historians of the late nineteenth century was the *History of the German People since the Ending of*

---

[36] I. Doellinger, *Die Reformation.*
[37] J. I. Doellinger, *Das Papstthum;* J. Friedrich, *Ignaz von Doellinger.*
[38] K. Hefele, *Conciliengeschichte.*
[39] J. Hergenroether, *Handbuch der Allgemeinen Kirchengeschichte;* J. B. Stamminger, *Zum Gedaechtnisse Cardinal Hergenroether's.*

the Middle Ages,[40] written by Johannes Janssen (1829-1891). According to Janssen the fifteenth century in Germany was not a period of intellectual and moral decay but an era of material prosperity and vigorous intellectual activity, abounding in creative art and progressive education, both secular and religious. Mercenary, greedy and licentious persons in the Catholic organization were not lacking; but on the whole the upper classes were prosperous and the peasants lived in comfort; for industry, trade and agriculture flourished during the fifteenth century. Then came the Protestant Revolution and Germany became materially and morally deranged; thus began its deterioration, reaching the nadir of decline during the destructive Thirty Years War. Janssen severely denounced some humanists as either heathens or skeptics and others as downright evil characters, but he was not chary about condemning wicked Catholics either, nor did he refrain from flaying and stigmatizing certain sanctimonious and unscrupulous German bishops. Luther was not the first German to translate the Bible, and his revolt was not an intellectual or ecclesciastical movement but was economic, social and legal. Though the peasants were unhappy even before the advent of Luther, their rebellion would not have been so fierce and savage were it not for the chaotic conditions engendered by the Protestant agitation. Interested in social and cultural life, Janssen devoted considerable space to the literature, crime, morals, and superstitions of the day. He deplored the decline of the universal empire and the corresponding increase of power of the princes, implying and asserting that the ruination of Germany in the seventeenth century was the result of the Reformation and not of the Thirty Years War. Janssen's writings were based on sound sources, but he used his material selectively and preferentially; the Catholics were pleased but the Protestants were reproachful.[41]

Denifle. Heinrich Denifle (1844-1905), the Austrian Dominican scholar, was also an eminent authority on phases of Church history. His first important work pointed out the relationship between scholastic thought and mysticisms and maintained that the mystics were not reformers and forerunners of the Reformation but stemmed from medieval scholasticism. Sixteenth century heresy, according to Denifle, was a calamitous consequence of the decline of religious life which had already begun to appear two hundred years before. The Austrian monk aimed to bring Luther down from the pedestal upon which the Protestants had placed him, asserting that historians had hitherto been biased and misinformed as to his character and career. Luther's constant fear of sin was either an indication of ignorance of true Catholic doctrine or symptomatic of a guilty conscience, and when he finally broke with the Church and renounced celibacy and papal authority he was probably impelled to do so by a desire to gratify his coarse and sensual passions. The reformers were all apostles of the flesh and Luther in particular was possessed of little learning, was prone to prevaricate and was the personification of contemporary decadence. Needless to say, these offensive allegations or revelations about the great German religious leader stunned the Protestants. The shock did arouse a re-examination of source material which led to a slightly altered attitude and appraisement of the heroic

---

[40] J. Janssen, *Goeschichte des Deutschen Volkes seit dem Ausgang des Mittelalters.*
[41] L. Pastor, *Johannes Janssen.*

heretic.[42] Denifle also wrote on the origin of the medieval universities and about the religious and social conditions of France and Germany following the Hundred Years' War.

Pastor. One of the most authoritative and scholarly of the Catholic historians was Ludwig von Pastor (1854-1928), a student of Janssen and an eminent professor at the University of Innsbruck. He was the author of numerous biographical sketches and magazine articles, and after an immense amount of research he produced his *magnum opus, The History of the Popes since the Middle Ages* in fifteen volumes.[43] The masterpiece was based on manuscripts and other materials thoroughly explored at the Vatican archives, although his scientific objectivity in the selection of documents has been questioned, as has been his belief that only a Catholic could understand and adequately interpret the lives of popes. Included in the work is a discussion of the new learning of art and literature in early modern times and of the extent to which humanism and heathenism influenced the Papacy of the Renaissance. Pastor does not absolve the notorious pagan popes, acknowledging that some of the pontifical princes did deviate from ecclesiastical constraint, while others were even entirely innocent of spiritual devotion.

Protestant Historians. Among prominent Protestant historians of the late nineteenth century who concentrated their attention on religious interests were Albrecht Ritschl (1822-1889), and Friedrich von Bezold (1848-1928). As the supernatural was gradually being delimited by the minatory advances of science, Ritschl sought to salvage the fundamentals of religion by divorcing Christianity from the dogmas of traditional theology, and by prescribing greater devotion to the ethical and empirical nature of religion. Bezold also investigated the significance of superstition in history and the conflicts between science and faith, and in his writings on the Reformation he stressed its social and economic aspects more than had been done hitherto.[44]

THE AUSTRIAN SCHOOL

Arneth. The Austrian school of history situated in the cities of Innsbruck and Vienna excelled in paleography and the study of diplomatics, and the latter city was proud of the Historical Institute, famous for its critical studies and sterling contributions to the field of medieval history. Alfred von Arneth (1819-1897), author of a monumental narrative of Austrian history, is regarded as an outstanding authority on the career of Prince Eugene and on the life and times of Maria Theresa.[45] His work on the memorable story of Eugene was one of the first productions of the Austrian school to be widely read, but Arneth's classic contribution and probably one of the most important issued in that country was the *History of Maria Theresa* in ten volumes. This brilliant book relates the Austrian record of the wars with Prussia and gives an admirable account of the illustrious empress—her personality and policies and vividly portrays the vicissitudes of the various sections of the Empire including all phases of eco-

---

[42] H. Denifle, *Luther und Lutherthum.*
[43] L. Pastor, *Geschichte der Paepste Seit dem Ausgang des Mittelalters.*
[44] F. Bezold, *Geschichte der Deutschen Reformation.*
[45] A. Arneth, *Prinz Eugen von Savoyen; Geschichte Maria Theresas.*

nomic, political and cultural history. Arneth was also the head of the Archives and compiler of the voluminous correspondence of Maria Theresa and members of her family. His students wrote ably on the development of the Austrian state, defending the unifying and constructive policies of the Habsburg and decrying the divisive and destructive practices of the Protestant princes, of Gustavus Adolphus and of Frederick the Great. Other worthy contributions of the school include writings on the era of the French Revolution and Napoleon, the post-Napoleonic period and the Revolution of 1848.

Habsburg Historians. The members of the Austrian school were not only competent scholars but were ardent apologists for the Habsburgs. Theodor Sickel promoted popular interest in the medieval history of Austria through his editorial work and his extensive studies of documents and manuscripts, and though a Saxon by birth, he championed the cause of the Habsburgs, against the encroachments of Prussia. Julius Ficker, a highly influential teacher, was a keen and erudite student of medieval law and government institutions of the Holy Roman Empire, of Germany, Italy and the Church, yet he found ample time to engage in vigorous controversy with Sybel, the eminent proponent of Prussian politics.

Recapitulation. The group of German historians treated in this chapter possessed a wealth of talent and considerable genius. All schools were represented, their products were exceedingly variable and the reader was offered a multifarious collection of outlooks, interpretations and syntheses. Among them were historians who were intensely patriotic and politically-minded and others who emphasized social and economic factors. There were those who stressed intellectual development, those who were factual and those who were philosophical. History was a science or an art, it was past politics or current propaganda. It was literature, it was philosophy, or it was the story of the life of a people in all its phases and ramifications. Sometimes these men wrote for the multitude with verve and literary brilliance and at other times for the professional pundit with grim drabness and scientific severity, but all of them made significant contributions to the study of history.

Chapter 16

BRITISH HISTORIOGRAPHY OF THE TWENTIETH CENTURY

By Matthew A. Fitzsimons

CHARACTERISTICS OF BRITISH HISTORICAL WRITING IN THE TWENTIETH
CENTURY

B RITISH historians have done their greatest work in the study of their
own history. In general the work has been done on more limited topics
and on a more complex and subtle scale than in the past. The non-academic
tradition has survived and has produced lively and valuable work ranging
from Winston Churchill's *The World Crisis* (1931) to Lytton Strachey's
Elizabeth and Essex (1928). But the most substantial work has been done
by academic writers. In carefully working over old sources and noting the
bias of their predecessors, in utilizing new sources or in studying interrelations
of movements and ideas, British historians have extensively reworked and
broadened the whole scope of their history. The burden of specialization has
rested strongly but gracefully upon them, for they have been rarely provincial
in time. The necessity of specialization has encouraged cooperation and
modern British scholarship presents an imposing line of collaborative works.
Not that a broader view has been lacking, for British scholars as a rule
have been more aware of their heritage from the distant past than American
scholars, who have often had to rediscover it. This difference is not only a
reflection of the aristocratic quality of British society but of other differences.
Historians as different as the profound medievalist, Sir Maurice Powicke
and the felicitous and urbane heir of the Whig tradition, George Macaulay
Trevelyan, have given memorable expression to their sense of the persistence
of the past into the contemporary world.[1] Places, place names and the constant necessity of adapting surviving laws and institutions, all have contributed
to this sense of the living past.

Before World War I. As writers of monographs and general works, British
historians have approached their subjects with all the preoccupations and
interests created by the development of their society. The New Liberalism
of the years before the First World War strengthened a tendency to be practical and to avoid the doctrinaire. Pressing social problems and the rise of
economic rivals inspired the re-study of British growth and hegemony. The
advent of political democracy and the appearance of a formidable Socialist
movement directed scholars to a more realistic historical study of the British
common people. The expanding role of the state suggested a study of the

[1] Trevelyan, George M., *An Autobiography and Other Essays*, p. 3; Powicke, *Medieval England*,
pp. 25-27.

bureaucracy of earlier ages, a subject which constitutional historians had ignored. Difficulties of Empire drove scholars to consider Britain's path to Empire and in the self-governing Dominions historians eventually turned from their tales of heroes and pioneers to the self-conscious study of their own unique societies. This latter change occurred after the First World War.

After World War I. The First World War served to make a large part of the Empire self-conscious and enormously emphasized the study of diplomatic history. In the post-war years there was a period of disillusionment, in which writers revenged themselves for the plight of the present by presenting sardonic pictures of the past, particularly the more recent Victorian past. This attitude, though it had unfortunate social and political effects, did not affect the mass of serious historical writing. By patient scholarly endeavors, often greatly assisted by American historians, a large part of the English past has been reworked. Indeed, it may be said that the Whig veils were removed from Stuart history and that seventeenth century England was rediscovered. The outlines of Anglo-Saxon England and the nature of its society and culture became known more intimately. Medieval institutions were studied with an imaginative thoroughness that remains one of the great triumphs of modern scholarship. Economic historians produced monuments of scholarly accumulation and of artistic history. Religious history received new impetus from an important Catholic revival and from the concern of Englishmen with their Established Church. The Second World War has already produced studies of international relations and the British Government has well under way a project for the publication of *Documents on British Foreign Policy, 1919-1939.* Finally, the feeling of crisis which has become an almost normal feature of our contemporary outlook has stimulated Arnold Toynbee to his imposing search for patterns and meaning in human history, while less ambitious efforts towards synthesis have been attempted by men as various as H. G. Wells and H. A. L. Fisher.

Learned Societies. Cooperative labors have characterized a large part of British historical activities. The Camden Society (founded 1837), which later (1897) amalgamated with the Royal Historical Society (founded 1868) had sponsored the publication of source material, and the printing of sources became a flood in the later nineteenth century with the publication of the Rolls Series, and the editions of such groups as the Selden Society, the Pipe Roll Society, the Naval Records Society and the Harleian Society. Apart from these, the works of the Scottish Historical Society, and a host of others, a company of national and county antiquarian societies issue publications which include very valuable sources, bibliographies and studies, and bumbling forays into the local picturesque.

Cooperative Histories: The Cambridge Series. These cooperative labors produced their most impressive monument in the various Cambridge histories, and first of all in the *Cambridge Modern History* (13 vols., 1902-1912). This work was inaugurated as an attempt to present a comprehensive and searching story of the modern western world, based on the individual contributions of specialists. Lord Acton's vision of cooperative specialist scholarship was in conscious reaction against the ambitious projects of individual historians like E. A. Freeman, who avoided the labor of searching far and wide for sources and, nonetheless, persuaded the readers by their high narrative talents. At the time (1896) when the project was first discussed, Acton, then Professor at Cambridge, wrote: "I have not hesitated as much as I ought to do on account of the difficulty because my office here makes it a duty not to be declined, and because such an opportunity of promoting his own ideas for the treatment of history has seldom been given to any man." As he saw it "universal history is not the sum of all particular histories, and ought to be contemplated, first in its distinctive essence, as the Renaissance, the Reformation, the Religious Wars." Instead of adhering to fairly strict chronological divisions for the volumes, he proposed to speak of countries "when they are important, and not, whether or no, according to date." Thus, when a country became important and contributory to a general movement, it would be introduced with an account of its past history, and a prospective survey would be provided for such states as Venice when it passed out of the main stream of history. The volumes of this set adhere closely to Acton's program: "I would . . . unite the moral and intellectual realm with that of political force, on the following plan. There would be a chapter, at intervals, on each branch of literature, when it attains supremacy and impresses its character on the age."[2]

The success of the *Cambridge Modern History* encouraged the continuation of the series, and, indeed, the *Cambridge Medieval History* (8 vols., 1911-1936) which numbered among its editors J. B. Bury, C. W. Previte-Orton, J. P. Whitney and Z. N. Brooke, and the *Cambridge Ancient History* (12 vols., 1923-1939) have had a greater success in their fields than the initial series in its own. Later, a series on the Empire, British Foreign Policy and Poland were projected and completed. Currently in preparation is the *Cambridge Economic History of Europe,* a work which could hardly have been attempted fifty years ago. This series, whose first volume (1941) was edited by J. H. Clapham and Eileen Power, will mark the first serious synthesis in English of the labors of several generations of economic historians, English and foreign.

Characteristic of the widening of historical inquiry is the contrast between the volumes in the *Politial History of England* series (12 volumes, edited by William Hunt and R. L. Poole), written in the first decade of the century, and the *Oxford History of England* (projected in 14 volumes under the editorship of G. N. Clark). The latter series consists of social histories, in which political events still loom large, but, as a rule, social structure and transformation are carefully noted.

Dictionary of National Biography. One of the most important influences in training and influencing a number of scholars was work done for the *Dictionary of National Biography* (66 vols., 1885-1901), edited by Sir Leslie

---

[2] Quoted by G. N. Clark, in "The Origin of the Cambridge Modern History," *Cambridge Historical Journal,* VIII (1945) pp. 61-62. The *Cambridge Modern History* revealed many of the weaknesses of earlier history—inadequate treatment of economic, intellectual and social history. The series is being rewritten.

Stephen and Sir Sidney Lee. The Dictionary Office itself with its specialized library inspired A. F. Pollard in his efforts to establish the Institute of Historical Research. The preparation of biographical notices enabled Pollard, T. F. Tout and James Tait, among others, to secure a wide knowledge of the sources of medieval and Tudor history. The necessity of terseness and restraint in writing the notices, also, permanently shaped their style of writing.

The Victoria History of the Counties of England is another example of cooperative scholarship. The county histories were begun to commemorate the Sixtieth Jubilee of Queen Victoria. They are invaluable because they present an approach to the history of England through local history. They include, as a rule, chapters on the geology and archaeology of the counties, as well as accounts of economic and social history. Some of the most prominent historians of England have contributed to these volumes. A contributor to many of the volumes on the subject of Roman Britain was Professor F. J. Haverfield (1860-1919), who published his general views in *The Romanization of Roman Britain*. As a worker in archaelogy, Haverfield strongly emphasized that the historian himself prepare his own materials.[3] For the study of early British agricultural history even the resources of aerial photography have been used with success. The Roman period has been most recently summarized by R. G. Collingwood in *Roman Britain and the English Settlements* (1936).

REVISIONISM IN ANGLO-SAXON HISTORY

In the Anglo-Saxon and medieval field, as elsewhere, new and more limited approaches were necessary, if historians were not to go on repeating themselves. The medieval period of English history had been sketched in bold and striking outlines by John Richard Green, an imposing but smaller section had been treated by Freeman, and Bishop Stubbs had surveyed the medieval constitution. Thus, the new demands of science and originality went hand in hand. Paul Vinogradoff (1864-1925), a Russian born scholar, had already analyzed early English institutions and the critical studies of J. H. Round (1854-1928) had contributed to the rediscovery of English feudalism. F. W. Maitland (1850-1906), who always professed the highest respect for the work of Bishop Stubbs, had also dealt with English law and institutions with a deep appreciation of social complexity and with imagination and sympathy.

Thus, the work of revision had already begun. In general, the result of their work and that of their successors was to wipe away the anachronisms which Stubbs and especially Freeman had introduced into the story of English political and social development. Stubbs had been too ready to see a fully developed parliament in the thirteenth century, and had repeated the seventeenth century view of the fifteenth century as the time of the free Lancastrian Constitution. Systematic study of the sources and new approaches

---

[3] "Some writers have urged, as the late Professor Freeman used to urge, that it is no business of the historian to prepare his own materials . . . It is not so. No historian can really understand materials at which he has not himself to some extent worked, just as no scholar can understand textual criticism unless he has himself collated at least a few manuscripts." Quoted by H. Craster in an obituary notice on Haverfield in *English Historical Review*, XXXV (1920), p. 65.

completely revised Stubbs' version of the Anglo-Saxon period, as a time of "rustic democracy" which was conquered by the Normans but "carried into the Norman age traditions of freedom which gave a distinctive character to the medieval English state."[4]

F. M. Stenton. The greatest of modern Anglo-Saxon historians, F. M. Stenton, characterized the revisionist work of Anglo-Saxon and medieval scholars in the following criticism. "What the modern critic feels when considering the work of Freeman, Stubbs and Green is not that these historians were misled by a false theory of social and institutional development, but rather that they idealized and over-simplified the history with which they were dealing. Many readers who do not wish to be critics have felt that there were subjects vital for the understanding of Old English history with which these historians never attempted to deal."[5]

Among the Anglo-Saxon subjects to which scholars devoted themselves were the study of Anglo-Saxon chronology, the significance of place names and social structure in determining the relative contribution of Germanic and Scandinavian settlers to the stream of English history. W. H. Stevenson lectured on the diplomatics of Anglo-Saxon history, and one of his auditors, R. L. Poole, was one of the English masters of diplomatics, having also published a study of the Papal Chancery. Archaeology, local studies and the religious history of the Anglo-Saxon period yielded fruitful results. These works were synthesized for a portion of the period by R. H. Hodgkin in his *History of the Anglo-Saxons* (2 vols., 1935). But the greatest work in the period is Professor Stenton's volume in the Oxford History series, *Anglo-Saxon England* (1943). Stenton not only knew the period before the Norman Conquest but had a considerable familiarity with the twelfth century, on which he had written a valuable book, *The First Century of English Feudalism.* Thus, he passed equable and moderate judgment on both Anglo-Saxons and Normans. The Whig interpretation had seen the Norman Conquest as the calamitous subjection of a free people. Other historians had been so impressed by the organizing talents of the Normans that the latter were viewed as a miraculously orderly people who had regenerated the declining, if not degenerate, Anglo-Saxons. Stenton's verdict is: "The Normans who entered into the English inheritance were a harsh and violent race. They were the closest of all western peoples to the barbarian strain in the continental order. They had produced little in art or learning and nothing in literature that could be set beside the work of Englishmen. But politically they were the masters of their world."[6]

MEDIEVAL ADMINISTRATIVE HISTORY

Medieval historians have similarly reworked their field, and have seriously revised the earlier interpretations of Stubbs and others. The most striking study on medieval constitutional history, devoted to a subject not touched upon

[4] F. M. Stenton, "Early English History, 1895-1920," in *Transactions of the Royal Historical Society,* Fourth Series, XXVIII (1946), p. 10.
[5] *Ibid.,* p. 12.
[6] Stenton, *Anglo-Saxon England,* p. 678.

by Stubbs, was the work of a student of Stubbs, T. F. Tout (1855-1929).
Tout had studied at Oxford under T. H. Green, one of the philosophers of
the New Liberalism. He taught at St. David's College before going to
Manchester (1890), where, with the cooperation of James Tait, he established a center of post-graduate study which almost rivalled London. In the
five years before coming to Manchester he contributed over 200 biographical
notices to the *Dictionary of National Biography*. Until past the age of fifty his
work showed no marked originality. He had, however, acquired considerable
experience, not only as a teacher and administrator, but also in the field
of local politics.

Tout. The first written evidence of the interest which prompted his
Chapters in the Administrative History of Medieval England (6 vols., 1920-
1933) appeared in Tout's review of *Etudes de Diplomatique Anglaise, 1272-
1485* by A. Deprez for the *English Historical Review* (1908). In his review,
Tout noted that this study revealed a whole new world for investigation.
To the same journal in the following year he contributed a list of the chief
officers of the King's Wardrobe down to 1399. Four years later, in the
Ford Lectures at Oxford, he made his first major study along the new lines,
The Place of the Reign of Edward II in English History (published in 1914).
With the historian's necessary optimism he underestimated the task, for he
did not complete it before his death in 1929. The experiences of his own
time shaped his interest, for, as he noted early in his study, the emphasis
on political history, parliament and narrative history, had precluded the study
of administration, although "even under modern conditions, administration
is more important than legislation."[7] His description of medieval administrative machinery gave new meaning to the parliamentary story of the
middle ages, and led to the extensive rewriting of the whole history of the
thirteenth and fourteenth centuries.[8] One of his concluding remarks may
serve to indicate the results which he achieved. He saw the king's experiments
with the privy seal and the signet as revealing the royal inability to distinguish between official and personal capacity. "In the collapse of the last
avowed attempt at autocracy in the revolution of 1399 we have a real reason
for drawing our study to a close. Henceforth, no manifestation of the royal
authority can be divested of its official character, can be freed from the constitutional control of the aristocratic and official class."[9]

Tout was rigid in his demands upon students, and also restricted himself in the area of the past which he sought to explain. In another book
review he wrote: "But, as always in medieval history, though we can carefully
record the acts of the period, we at once fall back into vain conjecture when
we begin to investigate the motives which inspired those acts."[10] He was

---

[7] Tout, *Chapters in the Administrative History of Medieval England*, I, pp. 4-5. The Fabian
Socialists, Sidney and Beatrice Webb, wrote a standard study of the machinery of local government,
English Local Government from the Revolution to the Municipal Corporations Act (8 vols., 2d ed.,
1924-1929).
[8] Prof. C. G. Crump in reviewing Vols. III and IV for the *English Historical Review*, XLIV
(1929), p. 134, cautiously said of the work: "No one will ever dare to touch any question or topic
connected with the period treated in it without looking at its pages."
[9] Tout, *op. cit.*, (1930), V, p. 229.
[10] *English Historical Review*, XXXIV (1919), p. 601.

not a speculative man, and developed no consistent theory of historical interpretation.[11]

It is appropriate that a work on diplomatics suggested his task to Tout, for the labors of several generations of English medievalists, J. H. Round, Helen Cam, A. L. Poole, James Tait, and many more, have involved a turning away from chronicles to charters, though, more recently, this new knowledge has itself led to more satisfactory interpretations of the chronicles themselves. Tout's colleague at Manchester, James Tait (1863-1944), was an able teacher, who shared Tout's rigorousness and restriction of the historian's field. Tait was particularly mistrustful of attempts to describe the "feeling and outlook" of an age.[12] Tait's major work was done in the field of local and institutional history, though in his teaching he was long concerned with Richard II. In 1936, he published his principal work, a collection of his essays on the *Medieval English Borough*. Tait's work directed considerable criticism at the thesis of the American scholar, Professor Carl Stephenson, who based his theory that the towns were revolutionary creations which developed with the revival of trade in the eleventh century, on the studies of Henri Pirenne in the Low Countries. Careful studies of Anglo-Saxon trade and coinage, and of the plans and archaeology of medieval towns, contributed to Tait's conclusion, which is much less simple than Stephenson's. There were towns, he believed, before the Norman Conquest, and they enjoyed self-government to a considerable degree. In other essays he marshalled the evidence on the origin and character of medieval town government. As a rule, Tait was opposed to any theory which rested upon analogies with continental developments.

English Medievalists

Powicke. The most distinguished of contemporary English medievalists is Sir Maurice Powicke, Professor Emeritus at the University of Oxford. Powicke in his Inaugural Lecture at Oxford (published, 1929) happily described himself as combining two vigorous schools of history, that of Manchester, with its rigorous professionalism and that of Oxford, with its rather more humane view of history. The amalgam is quite wonderful, for Powicke's work has all the painstaking detail of Tout and Tait, but is also filled with a disciplined and imaginative sympathy that makes his historical characters fully alive, revealed in the complexity which even a sensitive contemporary could hardly present. Powicke has written a number of small volumes, some of them, collections of essays, for example, *The Christian Life in the Middle Ages* (1935) ; and these essays present delightful portraits of such personalities as Giraldus Cambrensis. In dealing with *Stephen Langton* (1928), Powicke revealed a masterly knowledge of church-state relationships, and of the quarrel between the baronage and King John. Powicke is at his best in revealing the interplay of social institutions, inheritance and personality. In the Riddell Memorial Lectures, he defined his view of history, which he saw as the history of ideas.

---

[11] "He would stress one theory at one time, another at another, as he saw occasion or as recent experience had promoted. He did not worry much about consistency." Obituary notice on Tout by F. M. Powicke in *Proceedings of the British Academy*, XV (1929), p. 506.
[12] V. H. Galbraith's obituary notice, "James Tait," in *English Historical Review*, LX (1944), pp. 129-130.

We are interested in what men have done "as thinking beings . . . The origin or ground of our interest is this mental activity, not the external relations between this event and that."

In differing with Tout, whom he greatly respected, Powicke argued that a history of taxation should not primarily be a catalogue of kinds of taxes (though that would be a necessary part) but he would also like to know "what the men who levied taxes at various times had in mind when they levied them or when they discontinued them . . . Historical method, on the other hand, implies that it is the first duty of the historian to try to live through the events and to think the thoughts of those who acted them." . . . Above all, the historian must not "charge his description with emotion drawn from elsewhere." It is likely that historical relativists will deny the possibility of Powicke's objectives; nonetheless, his books carry an overwhelming conviction that his presentation is a true *apercu* of a vibrant past reality. Powicke's writing is permeated by a sense of tragedy. The "contrast between opportunity and achievement is at the root of the sense of frustration, of the tragedy, in history . . . History is full of the dead weight of things which have escaped the control of the mind, yet drive men on with a blind force."[13] Professor Powicke's objectives are magnificently achieved in his two volume study, *King Henry III and the Lord Edward* (1947). Rarely has a work of history ever combined such knowledge, profundity and interest.

Coulton. A very different approach to the Middle Ages was made by the late G. G. Coulton. Powicke's approach is paradoxically more sympathetic and detached. Coulton was passionately interested in the Middle Ages and had a remarkably wide knowledge of medieval sources. But in the course of his writings he was easily enraged especially by the romantic idealizers of the Middle Ages. Nonetheless, this polemical interest should not obscure the value of Coulton's work on subjects as various as village life, Froissart, and the scenes of daily life in the Middle Ages.

The fifteenth century has also been reworked in similar fashion by C. L. Kingsford, S. B. Chrimes and the economic historians M. M. Postan and Eileen Power (1889-1940). The last named in her charming Ford Lectures at Oxford, *The Wool Trade in English Medieval History* (1941) not only shed light on monastic and agricultural life, but provided a better understanding of diplomacy and the history of parliament. On the last point, she was partly following Stubbs, whose verdict was that an understanding of English constitutional development required a knowledge of the wool trade, the most important trading enterprise of medieval England.[14] As an illustration of this point, it may be mentioned that the meetings and deliberations of the wool merchants have an importance that compares with the early parliaments. Eileen Power's work is mentioned as an example, albeit a particularly distinguished one, of a multitude of specialized investigations of the medieval world. The labors of almost two generations of scholars in the field of the fourteenth

---

[13] F. M. Powicke, *History, Freedom and Religion*, pp. 6, 9, 12, 18-19.
[14] H. M. Cam, review of *The Wool Trade in English Medieval History* in *Economic History Review*, XI (1941), pp. 90-93.

and fifteenth centuries await a work of synthesis, which may be forthcoming in the Oxford History of England series.

Tudor Historians

Pollard. On the Tudor period, English scholars have made fewer striking changes. Albert F. Pollard, (1869-1948) had an impressive mastery of the sources of political and institutional history relating to the early Tudor Period. Pollard's most substantial works are his careful and vigorous biographies, *Henry VIII* (1905) and *Life of Wolsey* (1929). He has also written a useful study of Cranmer, and a stimulating book on *The Evolution of Parliament* (2nd ed., 1926). Pollard was an ardent supporter of graduate historical training. In a lecture (1904) he argued that the concentration of historical source material in London made it possible and desirable that the University there take a leading role in promoting and guiding historical research. His own strenuous labors, not always abetted by his aggressiveness and sharpness of manner, contributed to the realization of that end. Pollard, in characteristic fashion, attacked even the greatest representatives of the broader and more humane tradition of British learning. In 1922, he criticized that excellent student of the history of political theory, Sir Ernest Barker, for his "quaint conceit" in setting "up an antithesis between thinking and historical research . . . It might not require much thinking of the philosophical sort to produce a scientific edition of medieval English legislation, but it would save a number of people, including philosophers, if they studied it, from a whole morass of deductive confusion."[15] With all of his emphasis on political history and on the technical work of the historian, Pollard had a broad and undogmatic view of the historian's art.

> When we have all our documents collected, collated, sifted, and arranged, we still need the intuition and imagination to discover behind the parchment the play of human minds. For in all ages the most valid and intimate decisions are reached by unrecorded discussions and arranged by word of mouth, and even the spoken word often conceals the real intention. The sense of how things happen and what men mean is the supreme qualification of the historian.[16]

In this emphasis, Pollard approached Powicke, although Pollard's sympathies were more secular, Protestant and aggressively modern.

Apart from the political history of the Tudor Period, English literary historians have done valuable work in describing the social and intellectual background of the sixteenth and seventeenth centuries, but the advances have been largely the result of the joint efforts of English and American scholars. In the field of biography, two works are particularly preeminent. R. W. Chambers in *Thomas More* (1935) wrote an attractive picture of the Chancellor-Martyr and provided an especially interesting interpretation of *Utopia*.

---

15 A. F. Pollard, "An Apology for Historical Research," *History*, VII, (1922), p. 177.
16 Quoted by C. H. Williams, "A. F. Pollard," *Bulletin of the Institute of Historical Research*, XXII, no. 65 (1949), p. 8.

By using the concepts of the scholastic philosophy with which More was familiar, he argued that Utopia represents the perfection of society attainable by natural reason alone. Chambers' colleague at University College, London, J. E. Neale has written a vivid and sympathetic life of *Queen Elizabeth* (1934), which is based on an extensive knowledge of Elizabethan material. Neale's erudition is more obviously revealed in *The Elizabethan House of Commons* (1949), an important contribution to the detailed institutional history of parliament, which has been carried out by medievalists and seventeenth and eighteenth century historians.

New View of the Seventeenth Century

But the most sweeping changes in the picture of the English past have taken place in the work on the early seventeenth century. Historians, building on the careful political histories of S. R. Gardiner and C. H. Firth, and often drawing their inspiration from modern social problems and theories, have drastically revised the old conventional picture of a liberty-loving parliament and puritanism in conflict with a Divine Right monarchy. The revision is so much the product of the accumulation of a multitude of individual studies by American, English and even Danish economic, social and religious historians, that it is almost ungracious to single out a few names. In this work, however, the eminence of R. H. Tawney is indisputable. Tawney's best known book, *Religion and the Rise of Capitalism* (1926) is the work of a Christian and Socialist, who is interested in accounting for the failure of medieval social religious teaching to guide and restrain modern economic developments. The thesis of the book, that the traditional moral teaching was not restated to meet new economic conditions and that, with other individualist forces sapping it, the collectivist view of social life gave way before its own barren repetition, is often misrepresented and the misrepresentation is easily made because Tawney's thought is complex and subtle. In *The Agrarian Problem in the Sixteenth Century* (1912) Tawney gave a detailed account of the transformation of English rural economy, and particularly noted the role of the peasant himself in the enclosure movement. In more recent years, his article on "The Rise of the Gentry, 1588-1640" in the *Economic History Review,* XI (1941), recounted the story of the rise of that uniquely English class, the gentry, and provided a glimpse of social development, which has already inspired a number of studies. Tawney's lectures on the background of the Puritan Revolution have not been published but are awaited as the first synthesis of the revisionist work.

Possibly the most fruitful abettors of this revisionism were the economic historians who chose a particular industry or locality as Henry Hamilton,[17] A. P. Wadsworth and J. de L. Mann have done.[18] They cast new light on the social policies of the Stuart rulers and support the conclusion that English experience with large scale business and industry goes back beyond the second half of the eighteenth century to Tudor times. At a time of transition, Keith Feiling, himself the author of histories of the Tory Party, gave vivid ex-

[17] H. Hamilton, *The English Brass and Copper Industries to 1800* (1926).
[18] Wadsworth and Mann, *The Cotton Trade and Industrial Lancashire* (1931).

pression to his sense of the revisionist work in reviewing a somewhat conventional work by J. R. Tanner: "An extraordinarily high proportion of the 'unconstitutional' actions of Elizabeth and the first Stuarts passed in the shape of endless and multifarious demands upon the local authorities. Martial law, James' interference through Council with trade regulation, Wentworth's rule in the North, the history of wage assessments, from such tributaries the main stream on which Dr. Tanner sails could be swollen and enriched, and perhaps new conclusions drawn."[19]

On the seventeenth century in Europe, two writers have made important contributions and have paralleled those labors with studies of the Restoration period. G. N. Clark's *The Seventeenth Century* is an erudite comparative history of Europe. Clark divides his interests between commercial and economic history and social history, in which he has placed particular emphasis on the history of science and technology. *The Later Stuarts, 1660-1714* (1934), is a judicious synthesis of the period, although the reign of William III is still a relatively untilled field. David Ogg has written an excellent narrative history of the seventeenth century and a more conventional but very learned two volume work on *England in the Reign of Charles II* (1934).

New Directions in Eighteenth Century Studies

British history in the eighteenth and nineteenth centuries has not received the painstaking and systematic study which has been devoted to earlier centuries. The greatest advances in the political history of the early eighteenth century have been in the history of diplomacy, especially the work of Basil Williams and Sir Richard Lodge (1855-1936). The latter in his old age, yielded to the pleasure of "fitting together the jig-saw puzzle of diplomatic relations"[20] of a period which Carlyle had called "an unintelligible huge English and Foreign delirium . . . a universal rookery of diplomatists." L. B. Namier's studies, *The Structure of Politics at the Accession of George III* (2 vols., 1929) and the misnamed *England in the Age of the American Revolution* (1930), were based on herculean labors in the papers of the Duke of Newcastle, and are important for their revelation of the manipulations of influence in the period of the Whig Supremacy, about which Basil Williams wrote in the Oxford History of England. Namier's study was in the general line of detailed institutional history as practiced by Neale, for an earlier period, and A. S. Turberville, whose *House of Lords in the Eighteenth Century* (1927) is a fascinating account of the cliques within the Whig Aristocracy.

The Industrial Revolution and Economic History

The greatest of all changes have come in the conception of the Industrial Revolution, whose date is no longer arbitrarily set at the political date, 1760.

---

[19] In *English Historical Review*, XLIV (1929), p. 140. Feiling's most important study is his *History of the Tory Party, 1640-1714*. As a result of the studies, of Tawney, F. J. Fisher and others, the social policies of the Tudors and Stuarts are often placed in a background of depression and trade stagnation and the revelation of the economic interests of members of parliament elucidate the proceedings of the parliaments. Margaret James' *Social Problems and Policy during the Puritan Revolution, 1640-1660* is a good example of the work inspired by Tawney and Socialist thought.
[20] Lodge, "The Treaty of Seville, 1729," *Transactions of the Royal Historical Society*, 4th Series, XVI (1933), p. 43.

Studies have been made of business organizations, of individual industries, and of the social impact of industrialism.[21] The best known of the last class are the works of J. L. and B. Hammond, who in response to the social problems of their own day traced the origins of modern labor problems in a series, *The Village Labourer, 1760-1832, The Town Labourer, 1760-1832,* and *The Skilled Labourer,* 1760-1832, (1911-20). The Hammonds wrote excellent social history, although the dates of their economic and social studies are imposed by the accession of George III and the First Reform Bill. The most monumental of British economic histories is the *Economic History of Modern Britain* (3 vols., 1926, 1932, 1938) by Sir John G. Clapham (1873-1946). Clapham carried on in the field of Cunningham, Unwin and E. Lipson. He was urged on to his labors by the famous economist, Alfred Marshall, who in 1897 wrote to Lord Acton: "Clapham has more analytic faculty than any thorough historian whom I have ever taught."[22] Clapham noted that the earlier economic historians had largely concerned themselves with the political and legal framework within which economic activity had been carried on. As in the field of constitutional history, the earlier economic historians had drawn bold outlines which threatened to become the conventional divisions of the subject. Clapham and the later economic historians have stressed the quantitative approach as the distinctive method of economic history. In the hands of Clapham, this approach blurred a great many theoretical outlines but provided greater certainty about the highly qualified conclusions which he presented.

Diplomatic Studies

John Holland Rose centered his early studies on the French Revolutionary and Napoleonic periods. His *Life of Napoleon I* (1901) is backed by an impressive range of learning, and is deliberately devoted to the political, diplomatic and military aspects of his subject's career. It is strongly pro-British in judgments and is rather unsatisfactory in dealing with the personality of Napoleon, who has rarely been adequately treated by British historians. Rose followed this work with studies of the younger Pitt and later became the editor of the *Cambridge History of the British Empire,* a work which he regarded as a patriotic and scholarly duty.

The fields of nineteenth- and twentieth-century history are still dominated by the heavy, quasi-official biographies of political leaders. Important studies of diplomatic and political issues have been made, but doubtless in those fields a considerable work remains to be done. E. L. Woodward in *The Age of Reform 1815-1870* and R. C. K. Ensor, *England, 1870-1914* have attempted a first synthesis which is illuminated by the techniques of the social historian. Woodward with R. Butler is currently editing the *Documents on British Foreign Policy, 1918-1939.* This work continues the tradition established by Professors Gooch and Harold Temperley (1879-1939) in editing the *British Documents on the Origins of the War, 1898-1914* (11 vols., 1926-

---

[21] T. S. Ashton, *The Industrial Revolution,* draws upon this material.
[22] An unsigned notice in the *Cambridge Historical Journal,* VIII (1946), p. 115.

1938). Temperley had studied the career and foreign policy of George Canning and was particularly interested in the international problems created by the Turkish Empire. Diplomatic and military experience heightened his interest in the history of diplomacy. Along with G. P. Gooch, who became the Nestor of British diplomatic studies, he carried on research which enormously contributed to a re-evaluation of the origins of World War I and to a fair-minded and tragic conception of twentieth century world politics. Sir Charles Webster has done important studies of Castlereagh and Palmerston.

The Historian and the Reading Public

Trevelyan. Although British historical writing has been marked by a high literary standard, few British historians have had the prestige and wide audience of George Macaulay Trevelyan. Author of works ranging from *England in the Age of Wycliffe* and *British History in the Nineteenth Century* (1922) to three studies of revolutionary and nationalist Italy, he writes with charm and with great narrative power. His most ambitious work, *England Under Queen Anne* (3 vols., 1930-34), is a delight to read but historians have criticized many of his general judgments. The desire to make his characters live in all their fullness is often responsible for these occasional prostrations of science before art. Even in his earliest work the same is to be observed. The rigorous James Tait in reviewing *England in the Age of Wycliffe* (1899) observed that Trevelyan had chosen a wide field which he could not master completely.[23] But Trevelyan wonderfully represents the historian as artist, a conception which he has tirelessly defended. In his writings on English history he transforms the Whig tradition, of which he is heir, and perhaps exaggerates the ability of the British to profit from their historical experience, so that British history appears almost as the story of divine providence. Though his sympathies are wide and warm, the reader may be troubled by such passages as the following: "If the French noblesse had been capable of playing cricket with their peasants, their chateaux would never have been burnt."[24]

Strachey and Guedalla. In the nineteen twenties there was a vogue of debunking biographies. These, the product of a widespread cynicism, were modelled on the works of such suave practitioners of denigration as John Maynard Keynes (1883-1946) and Lytton Strachey (1880-1932). The most influential writing of the latter in this genre was *Eminent Victorians* (1918). In other works, in *Elizabeth and Essex* (1928) and in *Queen Victoria* (1921), Strachey revealed a broader sympathy and the same artistry. Philip Guedalla's (1889-1944) many works, *Palmerston* (1927), *The Second Empire* (1937), and his essays suffer from a disease which may be called "fallen archness." An individual scene or chapter is pleasant reading, but the author's tense effort to be amusing puts an unendurable strain on most readers today. In this condemnation, an exception may be made of Guedalla's *Wellington* (1931).

[23] *English Historical Review*, XV (1900), pp. 161-165.
[24] *English Social History*, p. 408.

HISTORIANS OF THE BRITISH COMMONWEALTH

The national self-consciousness of the dominions and the problems of Empire have produced very valuable results in historical writing. Some of these are evident in the *Cambridge History of the British Empire*. Such Canadian historians as Frank Underhill and J. B. Brebner have restudied the making of the Canadian nation and its special position in relation to Britain and the United States. Eric Walker and C. W. de Kiewiet have described the South African nation. De Kiewiet's interpretation has particularly stressed the race issue in South Africa. The history of South Africa, he wrote, "cannot be ignored because in a modern world beset by problems of race, and in an Empire that has made its subject peoples a special charge, South Africa, past and present, holds a uniquely instructive place. To the black man, not to the white man, does South African history owe its special significance." In a land, where the greatest social and economic fact is "the universal dependence on black labor," "frontiers were much less lines of separation than areas of absorption and fusion." [25] Typical of the self-conscious study of Australia by Australians are the works of Brian Fitzpatrick who in *The British Empire in Australia, 1834-1939* (1941), recounted the influence of British economic control on the development of the country. In *The Australian People* (1946) Fitzpatrick attempted an explanation of the general forces which made the Australian. W. P. Morrel, of New Zealand, has devoted himself to the development of British colonial and imperial policy.

Many of such imperial studies were synthesized in W. K. Hancock's excellent *Survey of British Commonwealth Affairs* (2 vols., in 3, 1937-42), which is itself an extraordinary example of the valuable contemporary studies published by the Royal Institute of International Affairs.

HISTORY AND MEANING

In the preceding pages an attempt was made to characterize some of the principal trends and advances in contemporary British historical writing. Comprehensiveness is impossible, and no mention was made of many important achievements such as P. S. and H. M. Allen's wonderful edition of the letters of Erasmus and N. H. Baynes studies on Constantine the Great. One further current, however, certainly deserves mention,—the serious search for a meaning in history

Fisher. The Liberal, H. A. L. Fisher (1865-1940), in the *History of Europe* (3 vols., 1935-1936), confessed that he could find no pattern and no recurring themes, but only "the play of the contingent and the unforeseen." To one who had to narrate the achievements of the Greek genius, the thirteenth century, the Renaissance and the eighteenth century, but whose story began "with neolithic man and concluded with Stalin, Mustapha Kemal, Mussolini and Hitler," progress, though "written plain and large on the page of history" is "not a law of nature." "The ground gained by one generation may be lost by the next. The thoughts of men may flow into the channels which lead to disaster and barbarism." [26]

---

[25] de Kiewiet, *The Imperial Factor in South Africa*, pp. 1-2.
[26] Fisher, *A History of Europe*, p. v.

Dawson and European Civilization. Other historians, especially Catholics, have told the history of the past in order to affirm again the unity of Europe against the divisive forces of nationalism. One of the most impressive expressions of this aim is Christopher Dawson's *The Making of Europe* (1932). Dawson applied the knowledge of the anthropologist and cultural historian to the Dark Ages in which, he believed, the unity of Europe was created. A number of Catholic and other scholars less successfully sought to deal with the history of European culture in Edward Eyre (editor), *European Civilization: Its Origin and Development* (7 vols., 1934-1939). This work was also intended as a corrective to the specialized, secular and nationally divided studies in the Cambridge Histories.

Toynbee. But the most famous essay in this field is A. J. Toynbee's still unfinished *Study of History* (6 vols., 1934-1939). Toynbee has a dazzling knowledge of phases of ancient history, the Near East and modern international affairs. In seeking a properly defined object of study for history he concentrated on the history of civilizations. He is in reaction against the rigidities of specialization and nationalism, and his religious tone has appealed to the changing temper of our century. Toynbee's own patterns, challenge and response, withdrawal and return, and his concept of civilization, have been widely criticized, although they are sometimes wonderfully suggestive. Nonetheless, he has encouraged men to be more spacious in their thinking about human experience, and the panorama of man's history which he has unfolded in the crisis of our age raises the question whether our society is now like the drowning man recalling his entire past or, following Toynbee himself, will draw resources from our past and respond creatively to the challenge.

Chapter 17

TWENTIETH CENTURY PROGRESS IN FRANCE
By Charles W. Hallberg

FRENCH historical writing of the first half of the present century has been influenced by a number of developments, some characteristic of the age, others peculiar to the country. Most of the leading historians, it should be noted, were born shortly before or after the Franco-Prussian War. Several of them had attained distinction by 1914. The span of their lifetime witnessed tremendous strides in science, social science and technology, the growth of democracy, the spread of nationalism, imperialism and socialism, the intensification of social and economic problems, great wars and depressions, revolutionary upheavals and idealogical conflicts. In addition to these, the thinking of French historians received the impress of certain trends and developments within France—the German invasions and the events and consequences of the wars, anticlericalism, Marxism, national sentiment, and the continuing influence of the Great Revolution and of republicanism.

The tradition of critical scholarship established by Aulard, Fustel de Coulanges, Monod and others has been carried forward by an increasing number of trained specialists. The French Revolution continues to be the center of attention although much work has been done in other periods. The coming of the first World War gave considerable prominence to diplomatic history, particularly for the period after 1870. But until very recently, French scholars have shown a tendency to neglect nineteenth and twentieth century history. A fairly large amount of French historical writing, especially the propaganda material written by historians in the First World War, is of a nationalistic character. During the Second World War scholars labored under severe handicaps. Many of the younger French historians entered military service, while others found it difficult to pursue their investigations or to publish their results. Yet, despite the interruptions of the war years, the volume of serious historical work in the form of monographs, articles in learned reviews, cooperative syntheses, bibliographies, sources, and official documents has been considerable in the past half century.

THE FRENCH REVOLUTION

Mathiez. Albert Mathiez, 1874-1932, is famous for his work on the economic and social aspects of the Revolution and as the defender of Robespierre. He studied at the Ecole Normale Superieure and later at the Sorbonne under Aulard. After a varied teaching career, he joined the faculty of the Sorbonne in 1926 and remained there until his death.

Mathiez' early interest was in religious history and his theses, prepared under

Aulard's direction, were on the revolutionary cults. To a certain extent, the break between teacher and pupil, which made such a stir among historians of the Revolution, was caused by a difference of interpretation concerning the significance of these cults.[1] Mathiez published a series of articles and several books on the religious history of the Revolution.[2]

His studies of the revolutionary cults led Mathiez to become interested in Robespierre. For nearly two decades he carried on a scholarly campaign to vindicate the famous Jacobin leader, if necessary, at the expense of his rival, Danton.[3] Drawing upon material uncovered by extensive research in the parliamentary struggle of the Convention period, Mathiez exposed Danton's graft and dealings with foreign governments. In this he appears less the impartial judge than the prosecutor.

Mathiez' third subject of interest was the origin and development of the policy of the maximum price control law. Here his most significant contribution was *La Vie Chere et le Mouvement Social sous la Terreur*[4] in which he showed that there was a link between the Terror of 1793-94 and the policy of price control.

In addition to these rather specialized writings, Mathiez published a history of the Revolution for the general reader, *La Révolution Française*.[5] He was the founder of the Société des Études Robespierristes and editor of its journal, the *Annales Révolunnaires* which, in 1924, became the *Annales Historiques de la Révolution Française*.

While Mathiez did not reach the eminence attained by Aulard, the two men rather neatly represent viewpoints characteristic of different generations. Aulard stood for the bourgeois, political Revolution, whereas the more socially conscious and radical, Mathiez was concerned with economic realities and in the name of social justice approved even violence and bloodshed. Mathiez' great contribution, then, was in describing the economic and social basis for the Revolution which Aulard and others had neglected.

Sagnac. Philippe Sagnac (1868) studied at Paris under Aulard. After teaching at the universities of Lille and Bordeaux, in 1923 he succeeded Aulard in the chair of the French Revolution. From 1926 to 1929 he was visiting professor at the University of Cairo during which time Mathiez gave the courses on the Revolution at the Sorbonne.

Sagnac's principal writings on the Revolution include *La Formation de la Société Française Moderne, La Fin de l'Ancien Régime et la Révolution Americaine* (1763-1791)[7] *La Révolution* (1789-1792),[8] and with Georges Lefebvre

---

[1] On this see the article by Georges Lefebvre, "Albert Mathiez" in *Annales Historiques de la Révolution Française*, IX (1932), pp. 98-102.

[2] His books in this field, some of which were based on articles previously published included: *Contributions a l'Historie Religieuse de la Révolution Française; La Révolution et l'Eglise;* and *Rome et le Clerge Français sous la Constituante.*

[3] The following books deal with the subject: *Etudes Robespierristes; La Corruption Parlementaire sous la Terreur;* and the second volume, *La Conspiration de l'Etrangere* (1918) ; *Danton et la Paix; L'Affaire de la Compagne des Indes,* (1921) ; *The Fall of Robespierre and Other Essays,* translated from the French; *Autour de Danton;* and *Girondins et Montagnards.*

[4] Albert Mathiez, *La Vie Chere et le Mouvement Social Sous laT erreur,* 1927.

[5] Albert Mathiez, *La Révolution Française,* 5 volumes, the last volume published posthumously.

[6] Philippe Sagnac, *La Formation de la Société Française Moderne,* 2 volumes.

[7] Philippe Sagnac, *La Fin de l'Ancien Régime et la Révolution Americane* (1789-1792).

[8] Philippe Sagnac, *La Révolution* (1789-1792). In Lavisse's *Histoire de France Contemporaine,* Vol. 1.

and Raymond Guyot, *La Révolution Française*.[9] In addition, he wrote on Louis XIV and Louis XVI for Lavisse's *Histoire de la France Depuis les Origines jusqu'à la Révolution* and on French history from 1661 to 1789 for *Peuples et Civilisations* of which he was co-editor with Louis Halphen. He also served as editor of *Cahiers de la Révolution Française*, *Révolution Française*, and *Revue d'Histoire Politique et Constitutionelle*.

Sagnac, a generally recognized authority on the history of the Revolution, emphasizes the influence of ideas, particularly American, and of economic factors in bringing on the Revolution, and gives less weight to political developments.[10]

Lefebvre. Successor of Aulard and Sagnac in the chair of French Revolutionary history at the Sorbonne and associated with Mathiez as editor of the *Annales Historiques de la Révolution Française*, Georges Lefebvre (1874—), like Mathiez, is primarily interested in economic problems connected with the Revolution.[11] In connection with the sesquicentennial of the French Revolution in 1939 he published a brilliant synthesis, *Quatrevingt-neuf*, which has been translated as *The Coming of the French Revolution 1789*.[12] In this, as in other writings, Lefebvre follows Mathiez, though without the latter's bias, in presenting a socio-economic interpretation.

Other Historians of the Revolution. While Mathiez, Sagnac and Lefebvre occupy first place among twentieth century French historians of the Revolution, significant contributions to a study of the economic conditions of the Old Regime have been made by Camille-Émile Labrousse (1895-).[13] Prosper Boissonade (1862-1935), published a volume on the economic history of the Revolution during the years 1789 to 1804.[14] The financial aspects of the Revolution have been dealt with by Fritz Braesch (1877-), Jean Bouchary and by Marcel Marion (1857-1940).[15] The agrarian history of the period has been studied by Lefebvre, Marion and others, while Robert Schnerb has contributed to the knowledge of taxation during the Old Regime. The *Commission Pour la Recherche et al Publication des Documents Relatifs à la Vie Economique de la Révolution*, founded in 1903, has published a large number of volumes dealing with economic aspects of the Revolution. It has also published many documents, including the *Cahiers de Doleances*. On the intellectual background of the Revolution the volume by Daniel Mornet (1878-), *Les Origines Intellectuelles de la Révolution Française* (1715-1787)[16] is especially im-

---

[9] Phillipe Sagnac, Georges Lefebvre and Raymond Guyot, *La Révolution Française*, XIII in the series, *Peuples et Civilisations*.

[10] Professor Louis Gottschalk believes that the prominence which Sagnac gives to the influence of the American Revolution may be his greatest contribution to historiography. Gottschalk, "Philippe Sagnac and the Causes of the French Revolution," *Journal of Modern History*, Vol. XX (June, 1948), p. 147.

[11] More recent ones include *Les Thermidoriens* (1937) ; *Le Directoire* (1946).

[12] *The Coming of the French Revolution, 1789*, translated by R. R. Palmer.

[13] Camille-Emile Labrousse, *Esquisse du Mouvement des Prix et des Revenus en France au XVIIIe Siècle and La Crise de l'Economie Française de la Fin de L'Ancien Regime et au Debut de la Revolution*.

[14] Prosper Boissonade, *Les Etudes Relatives a l'Histoire Economique de la Revolution Francaise* (1789-1804).

[15] Fritz Braesch, *Finances et Monnaies Revolutionnaires*; Jean Bouchary, *Le Marche des Changes de Paris à la Fin du XVIIIe Siècle*; and *Les Manieurs d'Argent à Paris à la Fin du XVIIIe Siècle*; Marcel Marion, *Histoire Financiere de la France Depuis 1715*, 6 volumes.

[16] Daniel Mornet, *Les Origines Intellecuelles de la Révolution Francaise* (1715-1787).

portant. The Marxist interpretation has been set forth by Daniel Guerin (1904-), in his study, *La Lutte des Classes sous la Premiere Republique*.[17] On the conservative side is the well known writer on the Revolution, Louis Madelin (1871-), whose study of Fouché[18] was crowned by the French Academy. Camille Bloch (1865-1949), noted historian and archivist, published both monographs and volumes of documents dealing with the Revolution before turning his attention to the causes of the First World War. The religious history of the Revolution was the subject of works by Pierre de la Gorce (1846-1934) and Rudolphe Reuss (1841-1924).

There are excellent studies of the Revolution in the provinces and of its influence in other lands. In the past few years, French scholars have re-examined the causes of the Revolution, particularly the relative influence of ideas and of conditions, and the value of the *cahiers de doleances*. Marxist writers, like Guerin, view the Revolution as a class struggle. Lefebvre and others emphasize the fact that there was actually a series of revolutions. Finally, there is a difference of opinion as to when the Revolution began.[19]

ECONOMIC AND SOCIAL HISTORY

See. During the nineteenth century, economic and social history did not attract much attention from French historians. Its increasing importance in the twentieth century is due in no small degree to the work of Henri See (1864-1936), who studied at the Sorbonne under Fustel de Coulanges, Monod, Lavisse and Luchaire, and for nearly thirty years taught at the University of Rennes.

See worked in several fields, including intellectual history and the philosophy of history. His early work was in agrarian history in which he contributed several studies, among them a monograph on the manorial regime in Brittany,[20] a larger work on the rural classes in France during the Middle Ages.[21] This, his most important monograph, deals with the rural classes in Brittany from the sixteenth century to the Revolution.[22] In preparing these studies, See used manuscript sources, including the medieval charters and cartularies. He concluded his work in agrarian history with the publication of the *cahiers de doleances* of Rennes.[23]

See's books in economic and social history appeared after his retirement in 1920. These dealt with the development of French commerce and industry from the seventeenth century to the Revolution, the social conditions of the Old Regime, economic and social conditions in France in the period from 1815 to 1848, the history of European capitalism, the economic interpretation of history, a survey of economic and social history of France from its beginnings

[17] Paris: Gallinnard, 1946.
[18] Louis Madelin, *Fouché, 1759-1820*, 2 volumes.
[19] Among other French scholars who have attained recognition in the field are: Octave Aubry, Paul Bastide, Henri Beer, Pierre Caron, Henri Carré, Antonin Debidour, G. Lacour-Gayet, Boris Mirkine Guetzevitch, Pierre Renouvin, Edouard Driault, Louis Madelin and Albert Pingaud.
[20] Henri See, *Études sur les Classes Rurales en Bretagne au Moyen Age, Annales de Bretagne*, XI (1896), pp. 367-412, 589-611 and XII, pp. 60-82 and 190-226.
[21] Henri See, *Les Classes Rurales et le Regime Domanial en France au Moyen Age*.
[22] Henri See, *Les Classes Rurales en Bretagne du XVIe Siècle á la Révolution*.
[23] Henri See and Andre Lesort (eds.), *Cahiers de Doleances de la Senechausees de Rennes pour les États-Generaux de 1789*, 4 volumes.

to the First World War, and a larger study on the economic history of France which is considered the best in the field.[24]

The excellence of See's scholarship, particularly in his writings on agrarian, economic, and social history, is generally recognized. In his research he consulted the best sources, generally manuscript materials, which he analyzed critically. The comparative method was employed in several of his books. He was a firm believer in the preponderance of the economic factor in history though he did not espouse Marxism. On the whole, his work attains a high degree of objectivity.

Other French Economic and Social Historians. Georges Jacques Weill (1865-   ), wrote on the social reform movement in France of the nineteenth century. Vicomte Georges d'Avenel (1855-1939) wrote extensively on the history of prices, transportation, and on the social classes in the time of Richelieu; Georges François Renard (1847-1930), was primarily interested in labor history. In addition to these scholars, Henri Haüser (1866-1946), professor of economic history at the Sorbonne, shortly before the outbreak of the Second World War, published outstanding works on the beginnings of capitalism, labor history in the period of the eleventh and twelfth centuries, the history of prices from 1500 to 1800, and on German industry and economic organization. Significant contributions have been made by François Simiand (1873-1935) on wages; Edouard Dolleans, Paul Louis (1872-   ) and Georges Dureau on the labor movement, by Paul Louis and Alexandre Zevaes (1873-   ) on the history of socialism; and by Charles Moraze (1913-   ), J. Aynard (1875-   ) and B. Groethuysen (1880-   ), on the middle classes, particularly for the eighteenth century. Important also is the scholarly work of Charles H. Pouthas (1886-   ).[25] A number of interesting volumes have appeared in the collection, "La Vie Quotidienne."[26] French scholars have also contributed many articles to learned journals as well as monographs covering many aspects of economic history.[27]

COOPERATIVE SYNTHESES

Hanotaux. Cooperative historical syntheses have come to occupy a prominent place in French historiography. A number of outstanding scholars of France have associated themselves with such works. Among them was Gabriel Hanotaux (1853-1944), who studied law before taking up history at the École des Hautes Études and the École des Chartes. After a brief period of teaching, he turned to politics and entered the Foreign Office, serving as Foreign Minister from 1894 to 1898 with the exception of a few months in 1896.

[24] Henri See, *Franzoesische Wirtschaftsgeschichte,* 2 volumes. A French edition was published with the collaboration of Robert Schnerb, *Histoire Economique de la France,* 2 volumes.
[25] Charles H. Pouthas, *Democratie et Capitalisme* (1848-1860), XVI of *Peuples et Civilisations.*
[26] Among these are the books by Robert Burnand, *La Vie Quotidienne en France de 1870 à 1900,* and Georges Mongredien, *La Vie Quotidienne sous Louis XIV.*
[27] Studies of agrarian developments of the Middle Ages have been made by Ferdinand Lot, Louis Halphen, Marc Bloch, Oliver Martin and Joseph Calmette, of the sixteenth century by Paul Robeau, and of the eighteenth century by Georges Lefebvre, Marcel Marion and others. The history of commerce has been treated by See, Boissonade, Paul Masson, Lefebvre and L. Vignols, industrial history by See, Georges Espinas, Haüser, Julian Hayen, Masson, Boissonade and Charles Ballot. Camille-Emile Labrousse has studied prices in the eighteenth century. The work of the Commission Pour la Recherche et la Publication des Documents Relatifs à l'Économique de la Révolution has already been mentioned.

As a young man, Hanotaux became interested in Richelieu, and the first volume of his *Histore du Cardinal de Richelieu,*[28] based upon fifteen years of research, appeared in 1893. The second volume was published three years later while the other volumes were delayed until the First World War. The first two volumes are the most scholarly of the series and, together with various articles relating to the period, constitute Hanotaux's main contribution to French historiography.

Hanotaux was well known as a writer on political and international relations. His numerous articles on current events were usually expressions of personal opinions and frequently based upon his own personal experience. A strong sense of nationalism characterizes much of his later writings. Along with his nationalistic sentiment and a warm admiration for Latin culture went a pronounced hostility for Germany.

In the field of cooperative syntheses, Hanotaux directed the preparation of a French national history and an extensive history of Egypt.[29] In addition to these cooperative works, his editing and his numerous writings, he published a massive history of the First World War[30] and, in collaboration with A. Martineau, a history of the French colonies.[31]

Lavisse. In connection with French cooperative works, no name is better known than that of Ernest Lavisse (1842-1922). Educated at the Lycée Charlemagne in Paris and the École Normale Supérieure, he served for a time as private tutor to the Prince Imperial and became an ardent Bonapartist. After the Franco-Prussian War, he spent two years in Germany, attending the lectures of Waitz and other scholars and studying the German educational system. His thesis was on the early history of Brandenburg. He became professor at the École Normale Supérieure in 1879 and five years later assistant to Fustel de Coulanges at the Sorbonne. Among his students were Charles V. Langlois and Charles Seignobos. In 1888, he was appointed professor of modern history at the Sorbonne.

For a number of years, Lavisse maintained his interest in German history and published studies on Germany of the medieval period and the nineteenth century. In 1891, appeared his famous biography of Frederick the Great,[32] a classic of French historical literature, which was continued in another volume of lesser merit.[33]

Lavisse's greatest contribution to historical scholarship, however, grew out of his editorship of cooperative syntheses of French history. In collaboration with Alfred Rambaud (1842-1904), he produced the *Historie Générale du 4e Siècle à nois Jours.*[34] This was followed by the *Histoire de France Depuis les Origines*

---

[28] Gabriel Hanotaux, *Histoire du Cardinal de Richelieu,* 6 volumes in 7.
[29] Gabriel Hanotaux (ed.), *Histoire de la Nation Française,* 15 volumes; *Histoire de la Nation Egyptienne des Origines pre-Historiques jusqu'à nos Jours,* 7 volumes.
[30] Gabriel Hanotaux, *Histoire Illustree de la Guerre de 1914,* 17 volumes.
[31] Gabriel Hanotaux and A. Martineau (eds.), *Histoire des Colonies Françaises et de l'Expansion de la France dans la Monde,* 6 volumes.
[32] Ernest Lavisse, *La Jeunesse du Grand Frederic;* an English translation was made by Mary Bushnell Coleman.
[33] Ernest Lavisse, *Le Grand Frederic avant l'Avenement.*
[34] Ernest Lavisse and Alfred Rambaud (eds.), *Histoire Generale du 4e Siecle a nos Jours,* 12 volumes.

jusqú à la Revolution[35] for which Lavisse wrote the section on the reign of Louis XIV to 1685. After the first World War, he edited a history of France from the Revolution to 1919,[36] considered one of the best cooperative syntheses of modern French historical scholarship.

Seignobos. One of the most distinguished of Lavisse's pupils was Charles Seignobos (1854-1942). Following his graduation from the École Normale Supérieure, he went to Germany where he studied the educational system. He began his long career as a teacher in 1879 at the University of Dijon, and four years later became a professor at the Sorbonne. To Lavisse's *Histoire Generale,* he contributed chapters on feudalism, the Crusades, the Revolution of 1848, and the Third Republic. In his own political history of the nineteenth century,[37] noteworthy for the excellence of organization and impartiality of treatment, he indicated his growing interest in this period, which is continued in his contributions to Lavisse's *Histoire de France Contemporaine.*[38]

Other Cooperative Syntheses. Several other distinguished French hsitorians participated in similar cooperative syntheses. Henri Berr (1863-   ) is editor of one of the most ambitious cooperative syntheses ever undertaken, *L'Évolution de L'Humanité.*[39] This work is a history of civilization, which will exceed the 100 volumes for which it was originally planned. The cooperative works of Georges Renard [40] (1847-1930), of Louis Halphen (1880-   ) and Philippe Sagnac [41] (1868-   ), and of Gustave Glotz (1862-1935), *Histoire Generale,*[42] covering antiquity and the Middle Ages, are fine examples of historical syntheses.[43]

FRENCH HISTORIANS OF THE MIDDLE AGES

French historians of the twentieth century have made notable contributions to the knowledge of medieval times. Ferdinand Lot (1866-   ) has won wide recognition for his studies of the late Roman Empire and the beginnings of the Middle Ages, the barbarian invasions, the Carolingian rulers, medieval warfare and early English history, and as an editor of Carolingian sources. Louis Halphen (1880-   ), known as a "scientific" historian, has written several volumes on the history of France in the later Middle Ages, and, like Lot, has edited sources for the Carolingian period. In the economic and social history of the Middle Ages, Marc Bloch (1886-1944), produced significant studies of feudal society and rural developments. Charles Edmond Petit-Dutaillis (1868-1947) wrote on medieval England and France, while Charles Bemont (1848-1939), who succeeded Monod as editor of the *Revue Historique,* was also a specialist

[35] Ernest Lavisse, *Histoire de France Depuis les Origines Jusqu' à la Révolution,* 9 volumes.
[36] Ernest Lavisse (ed.), *Histoire de France Contemporaine depuis la Revolution jusqu'à la Paix de 1919,* 10 volumes.
[37] Charles Seignobos, *Histoire Politique de l'Europe Contemporaine, Évolution des Partis et des Formes Politiques,* 1814-1896, 7th edition, 1924 in 2 volumes.
[38] *La Revolution de 1848, Le Second Empire (1848-1859),* vol. 6, *Le Declin de l'Empire et l'Establissement de la Troisieme Republique (1859-1875),* vol. 7 and *l'Évolution de la Troisieme Republique (1875-1914),* Vol. 8.
[39] Henri Berr (ed.), *L'Évolution de l'Humanité, Synthese Collective,* 1920.
[40] Georges Renard (ed.), *Histoire Universelle du Travail,* 8 volumes.
[41] Louis Halphen and Philippe Sagnac (eds.) *Peuples et Civilisations,* now complete in 20 volumes.
[42] Gustave Glotz (ed.), *Histoire Generale.*
[43] Another, among many important cooperative collections, is: "Clio's," *Introduction aux Études Historiques.*

on medieval England. Charles V. Langlois (1863-1930) contributed to the knowledge of the Capetian rulers, Alfred Coville (1860-1942) wrote on the Hundred Years' War, and René Grousset is an authority on the Crusades.

Among other French scholars who have achieved recognition in the medieval field are: Paul E. Guilhiermoz (1860-1922), an authority on the French parlements of the fourteenth century; Joseph L. A. Calmette (1878-   ), known for studies of Louis XI, Charlemagne, Charles VI and Charles VII, and of Carolingian diplomacy; Christian Pfister (1857-1933), who wrote on the early Franks and rather extensively on the history of Alsace; Edouard Jourdan (1866-1946), who succeeded Langlois in the chair of medieval history at the Sorbonne and was interested in late medieval Italy; Charles-Edmond Perrin (1887-), also of the Sorbonne, an authority on feudal society; and Georges Espinas (1869-1948), best known for his studies of Douai and of the textile industry of Flanders. Religious developments have been studied by Paul Fournier (1853-1935), Pierre Imbart de la Tour (1860-1925), Jean Leflon, E. Lesne, Dom O. Rousseau, Georges de Lagarde and others. On the Byzantine Empire, in addition to the significant work of Alfred Rambaud (1842-1905), there are studies by Gustave Schlumberger (1844-1929), Charles Diehl (1859-1944). Charles Bayet (1849-1918), and Louis Brehier (1868-   ). For the history of the Christian church there are such outstanding scholars as Louis Duchesne (1843-1922), Charles Guignebert (1867-   ) and Alfred Loisy (1857-1940).[44]

HISTORIANS OF THE MODERN ERA

History of Modern France. During the present century, and especially since the First World War, there has been an increasing volume of good historical work in the modern field as a whole and not simply in the revolutionary period. Leaving aside the work in economic and social history and on the Great Revolution, already discussed, French scholars have added much to the knowledge of their country's past in the modern period. For the sixteenth century significant contributions have been made by Jean Hippolyte Mariejol (1855- ?) in his writings on Margaret of Valois and Henry IV as well as on Spanish history in the time of Ferdinand and Isabella and Phillip II; by Felix Rocquain (1833-1925) and Lucien Romier (1885-   ) on the religious wars between France and the Habsburgs; by Pierre Imbart de la Tour (1860-1925) and Lucien Febvre on the Protestant Reformation; and especially by Pierre H. Champion (1880-1942) in his books dealing with Charles IX, Francis I, Henry III, Louis XI, Catherine dé Medici, and François Villon, the

---

[44] Though the history of antiquity occupies a less prominent place in twentieth century French historiography than the Middle Ages, it includes several outstanding scholars. Gustave Glotz (1862-1925), was an authority on Greece and editor of the famous *Histoire Générale*. His books on the Greek city and on the economic life of the Greeks, are familiar to many students. He also wrote on the political and cultural aspects of Greek history. Maurice Croiset (1846-1935) was another authority on Greece, particularly on Greek literature. Georges Radet (1859-1941), who taught Alexander the Great. Eugene Cavaignac, who is editing the *Histoire du Monde*, has also written extensively on antiquity. Other scholars in the history of antiquity include Auguste Bouche-Leclerq (1842-1923) and Alexander Moret (1869-1938) for studies of ancient Egypt, Camille Jullian (1859-1933), a pupil of Fustel de Coulanges, and Albert Grenier (1878-   ) on ancient Gaul, Louis Delaport (1874-   ) for his books on the Hittites, G. Contenau for the ancient Near East, Clement Huart (1854-1926) for ancient Persia, and Andre Bertholet (1826-1938) for the history of north Africa.

last of which was awarded the Grand Prix Gobert by the French Academy.[45] There are recent studies of sixteenth century institutions by Gaston Zeller, professor at the University of Strasbourg, and Robert Doucet (1885-   ), professor at the University of Lyon. Henri Hauser (1866-1946) has several volumes on the sixteenth century, while the massive volume of Fernand Braudel on the Mediterranean in the age of Phillip II is a scholarly contribution to the economic and social history of the period.[46]

The seventeenth century received the attention of Hanotaux, Lavisse, Georges Pages (1867-1939), Alexandre de Saint-Leger (1866-   ), Louis-Casimir André (1867-1948), Edouard Preclin, Pierre Gaxotte, and especially Henri Carré (1873-   ), whose books on Richelieu, Louis XIV and some of the famous women at the French court, are well known. For the eighteenth century there are studies by Sagnac, Henri Leclerq (1869-   ), Henri Vast (1847-1921), and Pierre Muret (1870-1944).

Nineteenth century France has been dealt with by Pierre de la Gorce (1846-1934) in his volumes on Louis XVIII, Louis Philippe, the Second Republic and the Second Empire; by Paul Gueriot and Octave Aubry (1881-1946) on Napoleon III; by Emile Bourgeois (1857-1934), known to American readers for his *History of Modern France, 1815-1913*,[47] in his various chapters in the *Cambridge Modern History;* by Georges Weill (1865-   ) in his excellent study of the republican party; by Albert Malet (1864-1915) on the period from 1789 to 1900; by Léon Cahen (1874-   ) on the years 1789 to 1848, and by Jacques Bainville (1879-1936) on the period 1815-1918.

There are a number of noteworthy studies on the Third Republic. In order to stimulate the interest of French scholars in this area there was established in 1936 the *Société d'histoire de la Troisieme Republique.* Still among the best works of this period are those of Hanotaux [48] and Seignobos.[49] Other works on the third French Republic include Alexandre Zevaes [50] (1873-   ) who presents a socialist viewpoint; Michel Lheritier (1889-   ), editor of a two-volume cooperative work and author of a study of France since 1870 [51] which deals with economic development, Robert David (1873-   ) for the conservative republican view, Maurice Reclus (1883-   ), for a general history of the period to 1918,[52] Georges Laronze on the Paris Commune, and the scholarly works of Daniel Halevy (1872-   ) and Robert Dreyfus (1873-1939).[53] There are also competent biographies of the principal leaders and a number of popular volumes dealing with special episodes in the history of the Third Republic.

[45] Pierre H. Champion, *Francois Villon, Sa Vie et son Temps,* 2 vols.
[46] Fernand Braudel, *La Méditerranée et le Monde Méditerranéen à l'Époque de Philippe II.*
[47] Emile Bourgeois, *History of Modern France, 1815-1913,* 2 vols.
[48] Gabriel Hanotaux, *Contemporary France,* trans. by John C. Tarver and E. Sparvel-Bayley, 4 vols. cover the years 1870-1878.
[49] In Lavisse's *Histoire de France Contemporaine,* volume 6: *Le Declin de l'Empire et l'Establissement de la Troisieme Republique (1859-1875),* and volume 7: *L'Evolution de la Troisieme Republique (1875-1914).*
[50] Alexandre Zevaes. *Histoire de la Troisieme Republique, (1870-1925).*
[51] Michel Lheritier, *La France Depuis 1870.*
[52] Maurice Reclus, *La Troisieme République, de 1870 à 1918* (Paris: A. Fayard, 1945). In 1948 appeared his *Grandeur de la Troisieme.*
[53] Daniel Halevy. *La Fin des Notables; La Republique des Ducs;* Robert Dreyfus, *Monsieur Thiers Contre l'Empire, La Guerre, la Commune;* and *La Republique de M. Thiers, 1871-1873.*

For the period between the two world wars attention has been given largely to economic and social problems, international relations, or colonial developments. Among those who have written on this period are Maurice Baumont, Léon Cahen, E. Mantaux, Charles Moraze, and Pierre Rain. The Second World War and the resistance movement have been dealt with by Baumont, Marc Bloch, Roger Ceree, Adrien Dansette and Charles Rousseau. However, most books on the recent period of French history are of a popular nature.

History of Other Countries. A number of French scholars became specialists in the history of countries other than France. Foremost among them was Élie Halévy (1870-1937), an authority on nineteenth century England. His first important work, *La Formation du Radicalisme Philosophique en Angleterre*,[54] won him recognition as a scholar. The study deals with the youth of Bentham, the development of Utilitarian thought and philosophical radicalism, and shows how Bentham's philosophy influenced the Classical School of economics. His chief contribution to historiography was *A History of the English People*.[55] The first volume on England of 1815 is considered the best of the series. Volume two covers the period from 1815 to 1832 and volume three covers from 1832-1841. The First World War had the effect of diverting Halévy's attention to the more recent period of English history. The next two volumes of the series are entitled *An Epilogue* and deal with the years 1895-1905 and 1905-1914 respectively. In a final volume, published after his death, Halévy returned to the earlier period (1841-1852).[56] Two more volumes were planned for the years 1853-1865 and 1866-1894. Halévy contended that it was the beliefs, emotions and opinions of the English people, particularly their nonconformity, which explained the development of their national life in the nineteenth century. His history remains the most important contribution to this subject.[57]

Diplomatic History. The study of diplomatic history made great advances as a result of the First World War. French scholars in this field include Edouard Driault (1864-   ) and Vicomte Eugene de Guichen (1869-   ) on Near Eastern affairs, Antonin Debidour (1857-1917) for the diplomatic history of Europe in the nineteenth century, Albert Malet (1864-1915) for the seventeenth and eighteenth centuries, Pierre Muret (1881-1944) on Louis XIV, and François Charles-Roux (1879-   ) and Georges Pages (1867-1939) on the period of the Second Empire. In regard to the origins of the First World War, French historians for the most part have upheld the innocence of their country. A good example of such writing is the volume by Bourgeois and Pages.[58] More scholarly is the well known study of Pierre Renouvin (1893-), *The Immediate*

[54] Élie Halévy, *La Formation du Radicalisme Philosophique en Angleterre*, 2 vols.
[55] Élie Halévy, *A History of the English People*, trans. by E. I. Watkin and D. A. Barker, 5 vols. Volume V was published by P. Smith, New York.
[56] Élie Halévy, *A History of the English People, 1841-1852*, trans. by E. I. Watkin. The volume was from Halevy's notes by Paul Vaucher.
[57] Besides Halévy, French authorities on other countries include Jacques Bardoux (1874-   ) who has written extensively on Anglo-French history, Edouard Dolleans and Paul Nicolle on England, Lavisse, Georges Blondel (1855-   ), J. Droz and Henri Brunschwig on Germany, Rambaud, A. Mousset, Bertrand Gille and G. Welter on Russia, Edouard Driault (1864-   ) and Michel Lheritier (1889-   ) on Greece, Ernest Denis (1849-1921) on Bohemia and Serbia, Louis Leger (1843-1923) and Louis Eisenmann (1869-1937) on Austria-Hungary and Slavonic countries, Georges Bourgin (1879-   ), Paul Matter (1865-   ) and Albert Pingaud (1869-   ) on Italy, Bernard Fay (1893-   ), Gilbert Chinard (1881-   ), Andre Siegfried (1875-   ), Edouard Preclin and Leon Lemonnier on America.
[58] Emile Bourgeois and Georges Pages, *Les Origines et les Responsibilites de la Grande Guerre.*

Origins of the War.[59] Renouvin is one of the most competent among contemporary historians of France and has written extensively on diplomatic history. Henri Hauser, Camille Bloch, Albert Pingaud, Henri Salomon (1861-   ), Maurice Baumont and Georges Michon have also contributed important studies on the War. The revisionist viewpoint is represented by Georges Demartial (1861-   ) and Alfred Fabre-Luce (1899-   ). The publication of the *Documents Diplomatiques Françaises, 1871-1914,* which began in 1929, has been of considerable value to scholars in this field. Nothing comparable has appeared in connection with the origins of the Second World War although such historians as Baumont and Roger Ceree have dealt with the subject. The *Revue d'Histoire Diplomatique* has published many scholarly articles on various aspects of diplomatic history.

Colonial History. Besides the earlier works of Hanotaux, Eugene Fallex (1862-   ) and Arthur Girault (1865-1931), there are recent studies of French colonial history by Henri Blet, G. Debien, Robert L. Delavignette (1897-   ), E. F. Gautier (1864-   ), Georges Hardy (1884-   ), Charles-André Julien (1891-   ), Pierre Lyautey and J. Saintoyant. The *Société d'Histoire des Colonies Françaises* through its publication. *Revue d'Histoire des Colonies Françaises,* which appeared from 1913 to 1939, contributed to the advance in this field.

French historical writing during the past fifty years reveals no sharp dividing line between the nineteenth and twentieth centuries. Up to the outbreak of the war in 1914, more or less the same influences can be traced since 1890 or since 1870. There was the tendency towards greater specialization, the gradual separation of history from *belles lettres,* the broadening of the historians' horizon, and the diffusion of critical standards of scholarship. The war interrupted the production of serious historical works as most historians were engaged in writing propaganda articles and books. In the period between the two great wars there were several major developments. An increasing number of scholars turned to diplomatic history, the study of economic and social problems, the growth of civilization, the history of ideas, and the history of the nineteenth and twentieth centuries. Not only were these fields greatly expanded. Historians of the Revolution and the Middle Ages displayed a greater interest in cultural, economic and social developments than heretofore. Political history no longer dominated the field as it did in the closing decades of the nineteenth century. Positivism, which had such an influence over Taine and others, was not an important factor, nor was the contemporary medievalist concerned with the question of whether feudalism was of German or Roman origin, a point much belabored by Fustel de Coulanges. For the twentieth century French historian other factors such as anti-clericalism, Marxism, and nationalism were more important.

The Second World War affected historical scholarship in France in various ways. It led to the suspension of a number of learned journals and of government publications and created a shortage of trained historians. It tended to

---

[59] Pierre Renouvin, *The Immediate Origins of the War,* trans. by Theodore Carswell.

reduce the volume of serious work because of paper shortages and the high cost of printing. The result has been that many historians have had to resort to articles in reviews and the publication of popular books. Among the latter are such collections as *Rayon d'Histoire, Les Figures, Joie de Connaitre, Reines de France, Colonies et Empires, Vie Quotidienne, Grandes Epoques,* and especially, *Que-Sais-Je?.* Interesting also are publications commemorating anniversaries such as the sesquicentennial of the Revolution in 1939 and the centennial of the 1848 Revolution. On the whole, the contributions of French historians during the past half century have been impressive. Nearly every field has been investigated. Great service has been rendered in collecting the sources for the history of France and in the publication of government documents, cooperative syntheses, serious monographs, and popular works. Such scholars as Berr, Hanotaux, Lavisse Halphen, Halévy, Lefebvre, Lot, Sagnac, See and Seignobos have won worldwide recognition.

Chapter 18

GERMAN HISTORIOGRAPHY IN THE TWENTIETH CENTURY

By Louis Kestenberg

Man muss das Leben erst praktisch
treiben
Will man über das Leben schreiben.

ALL IS WELL IN 1900

THE YEAR 1900 portended nothing startling in Germany; it seemed still to manifest the trend which had culminated in the years of 1870-71. German thinkers found the German scene good and safe. The German Army was lauded as a protective element of the State, which, in turn, was looked upon as "organized society," from which each individual could expect not only that it prevented evil, but that "it effected good. . . . It should not only protect the weak from iniquity; it should help them out. Perhaps we expect too much from it. . . . However, thanks to Kaiser Wilhelm I and his great Chancellor we take with us the duty of the Imperial command to bring about social reconciliation in the new era." [1]

Prosperity, happiness, and busy-ness typified Germany at the opening of the twentieth century. If political parties existed and if each had its own platform, these Conservative, Liberal and Centrist parties were proclaiming meaningless nothings. The Socialists' talk of a republic was dismissed as "so manifestly a mere catchword, or at best so shadowy a dream of immature brains, that it need not be seriously considered." The country was satisfied; only social justice—and no prattle about brotherhood of nations, enlightenment, freedom, and nationality—concerned its subjects.[2]

Is it any wonder that Goethe and Kant, Schiller and Fichte (who saw only the good in life), and Nietzsche (who preached *Lebensbejahung*) presumably served as cultural models for the German people of the time? [3]

Even in the literary sphere nothing momentous appeared in the year 1900. Except for Gerhart Hauptmann's *Michael Kramer* and Stefan George's *Der Teppich des Lebens* there is hardly another significant title to be listed. It was in this placid year that Friedrich Nietzsche died in Weimar.

NIETZSCHE: HISTORY AND PHILOSOPHY

The philosopher Nietzche (born in 1844) was a severe critic of prevalent German opinion. In accepting Schopenhauer's atheism and professing to be the

---

[1] Ulrich von Wilamowitz-Moellendorf, "Neujahr 1900" in Fritz Strich, *Deutsche Akademiereden*, pp. 342-351.
[2] Kuno Francke, *German Ideals of Today and Other Essays on German Culture*, pp. 12-19.
[3] Francke, *op. cit.*, pp. 34-37.

anti-Christ, he adopted a number of views of historical import—preaching of the *Übermensch,* his denunciation of shallow patriotism and his posing as the Good European. He felt himself to be the first modern psychologist fearlessly dissecting the mind of mankind. This led him to maintain that art, science, ethics—in other words, *Kultur*—are only barbarized by the masses, and that for a society to achieve the highest in the realm of Spirit—the model being Hellenism—slavery is indispensable.

Thus, Nietzsche's philosophy of history was basically aristocratic, anti-democratic and outspokenly anti-Socialist. For him history had "no meaning except as the servant of life and action . . . By an excess of history our life has become maimed and degenerate." [4]

He taunted the Germans; they would accept as great any statesman who constructs for them "a new tower of Babel, any monstrosity of a Reich and power." He scolded them for their nationalism and political ambitions, which he classified as "stupidities" because of their anti-French, anti-Jewish and anti-Polish twists. Nor did he appreciate Germany's Christian-Romantic, Wagnerian, Teutonic or Prussian manifestations. In connection with Prussianism, he jibed: "One ought to look at these poor historians, these Sybels and Treitschkes and their tightly bound heads." [5]

A Nazi in Spite of Himself

Nietzsche's political, social and historical views influenced, largely implicitly and in some ways explicitly, Oswald Spengler (1880-1936), author of the striking and famous *Untergang des Abendlandes,* which may be taken as sounding many of the *leitmotivs* of modern German history and thought. Spengler led the life of a *Privatgelehrter* in Munich after having been *Oberlehrer* in a Hamburg Gymnasium from 1907 to 1911. The genesis of the *Untergang des Abendlandes* is obscure. The work is verbose and is sprinkled with a jargon in part derived from Nietzsche,—Culture and Civilization, Caesarism, Faustian, Classical, morphology, money-thinking, and the born statesman. Spengler imbibed Nietzsche's aversion toward democracy, his preference for an elite group with "ability to command"—i.e., the ruling minority—his contempt for party life or the concept of equality. [6]

Spengler's Theory of History. Basic for Spengler's theory of history was his certainty that history will inform us "what *can* happen, and therefore—what *will* happen." He substituted for the historical concept of Europe ("the Ptolemaic system of history") a world-view ("the Copernican discovery in the historical sphere"). Although he recognized organic growth within each Culture, Spengler maintained there were limits in its development, which ultimately leads to the death of each Culture. He boldly makes an analogy between Cultures and the individuals within them. Individuals experience youth, growth, maturity, decay and so do Cultures. He distinguished between Culture and Civilization ("the inevitable destiny of the Culture"). He considered Civiliza-

---

[4] John Herman Randall, Jr., *The Making of the Modern Mind,* pp. 607-611; E. Troeltsch, *De Historismus und seine Probleme,* pp. 494-506; Ernst Cassirer, *An Essay on Man,* p. 179.
[5] Friedrich Nietzsche, *Jenseits von Gut und Böse,* pp. 169-183.
[6] *Ibid.,* pp. 37, 43, 45 *et passim.*

tion a last stage, with its actors having no choice; specifically, the present world is experiencing "the early winter of full Civilization." [7]

While eruditely discussing his own version of what Cultures in history constitute—at the same time cleverly juggling terminology to give them contemporaneity—Spengler interspersed his presentation with such gems as: ". . . The history of humanity has no meaning whatever. . . . Man is not only historyless before the birth of the Culture; he again becomes so, as soon as a Civilization has worked itself out fully to the definitive form. . . . The spans of time are gradually returning to the biological order . . ." [8]

History, he wrote, apparently thinking of the Nazis, has no comfort for "enthusiasts," because "history is not sentimental, and woe to him who takes himself sentimentally!" [9] Modern man fears to contemplate the loss of free-will in history. Writing, once again at a moment of crisis, the disintegration of the Weimar Republic, he described "the relentless course of things, senseless chance, real history with its pitiless stride through the centuries, into which the individual with his insignificant private life is irrevocably born." History favored "the will of the strong, healthy instincts, race, the will to possess and power." [10]

Spengler regarded his own times with hatred, and his hatreds make a great hodge-podge—Rationalism, Progress, Materialism, Idealism, democracy, the popular primacy of economics, the Versailles Treaty, the Weimar Republic and England. On the other hand, German, that is, Prussian instinct, "asserts that power belongs to the whole community: the community is sovereign, the individual serves the whole community. Some command and some obey. . . . Only German Socialism is *real Socialism*. . . . The old Prussian spirit and Socialism, although they seem to be opposed to each other, are really one and the same thing. . . ." [11]

Many of Spengler's ideas were congenial to the Nazis. However, his pessimism was opposed to their ostentatious display of confidence and strength, and he did not share their valuation of race or approve their Anti-Semitism. [12] His work built a foundation and a historical method for Nietzsche's philosophy. [13]

Influence of Nietzsche on Spengler. To summarize this very influential historical thinker of the first half of twentieth century Germany, we need to note that Spengler was basically influenced by Nietzsche. Spengler succeeded in using some terms in an original manner, although—for example, when he equated Socialism with Prussianism, both of which were to convey the notion of the individual's submission to the State—these ideas are often puzzling or even contrary to current usage. His ventures into contemporary political questions made him amenable to Nazi ideas in his analysis of statesmanship, in his anti-party, anti-democratic, and anti-constitutional biases. His Russophobia and Anglophobia gave Nazi chauvinism pseudo-philosophical fuel; his deprecatory views of America only furnished the Nazis more political ammunition. However, he

[7] *Ibid.*, pp. 115-129, 145.
[8] *Ibid.*, pp. 135, 137, 193.
[9] Spengler, *Jahre der Entscheidung*, p. ix.
[10] *Ibid.*, p. 4.
[11] S. D. Stirk, *The Prussian Spirit: A Survey of German Literature and Politics*, 1914-1940, pp. 60-62.
[12] Spengler, *Jahre der Entscheidung*, pp. 159, 160, 162; Emery Neff, *The Poetry of History*, p. 215.
[13] Troeltsch, *op. cit.*, p. 507.

was unpalatable to the Nazis because he dissociated race from physiological and genealogical considerations. Because he knew he had discovered the pattern of history, he nonchalantly indulged in prophecy. And, if one were to follow Spengler's pattern which involves the inevitable death of every Culture after it has declined into the stage of Civilization, a pessimistic attitude toward history is inexorable.

A CONSERVATIVE'S VIEW

Before the outbreak of World War I the Germans had acquired "an abundance of cultural values but were frightfully impoverished in cultural heights." Differences in political attitudes were widespread. Thus, there is no doubt where the economic and constitutional historian, Georg Anton Hugo von Below (1858-1927) stood. In 1913 he represented the Conservative view. He admitted that the Conservatives were losing political campaigns and their programs were labelled by the newspapers as antiquated. However, he took heart in that Bismarck had adopted elements of the Liberals' program and that the latter were left without a program. Their classical view of free trade and the individual's absolute freedom of movement had to be modified by consideration of the general welfare, of the expansion of State activity,—for example, protective tariffs, nationalization of railways, colonialism, all had to be accepted by the Liberals.[14]

Below's historiographical views seemed to be unaffected by the first World War. His Conservative view—fortified by Droysen's assertion that "all must become reactionary"—underwent no change during that conflict. Historians who depend on constitutional ideals, he asserted, are lost; only those able to attach themselves to "political life"—e.g. to monarchical Prussia—can become great. Democratic historians remain "unpolitical, cosmopolitan," searching for *Kulturgeschichte*.[15]

The year, 1878-79 Below considered to be a turning point in German historiography. With the appearance of Treitschke's work historians began to delve into economics and administration; Bismarck's policy took shape; and Manchesterian economics gave place to "the energetic concept of the national idea." Romanticism was the point of departure for nineteenth century historiography but it did not lack realism, whereas Positivism, he thought, had harmed such historians as Taine and Lamprecht.[16]

POSITIVISM REJECTED

Wilhelm Dilthey (1833-1911), a contemporary of Below primarily interested in the history of ideas, started out to study for the ministry but changed his chief field of interest to philosophy while at the University of Berlin. After having taught at several universities, he returned to Berlin in 1882 as a professor of philosophy. He is better known, however, in the fields of sociology and intellectual history. Schleiermacher basically influenced his views

---

[14] George von Below, "Vom konservativen Standpunkte," in Dr. Sarason (editor), *Das Jahr 1913. Ein Gesamtbild der Kulturentwicklung*, V, pp. 1-2.
[15] George Anton Hugo von Below, *Die deutsche Geschichtschreibung von den Befreiungskriegen bis zu unseren Tagen*, pp. 55-63.
[16] *Ibid.*, pp. 85, 95-98.

on religion and ethics. He wrote in many fields: philosophy, logic, metaphysics, the natural sciences, sociology, psychology, art, and history.

In the first place, Dilthey sought to establish the province of history. He rejected the Positivistic, naturalistic adaptations to history of Comte, J. S. Mill, Buckle, and Spencer as infringements upon the real task of history. Natural science has as its task the study of a unit—e.g. the atom; history's task is also a unit, but it is man.[17] Thus Dilthey arrived at an "autonomy of history," in which man looms importantly. When man begins to think of himself, his past and future, he is apt to write autobiography—with all its advantages and disadvantages. Biography is another type of historical endeavor. Historiography as a science reaches its apex in the eighteenth century, although writing history had its origin with primitive man. Any philosophy of history which attempts to explain more than human purpose was rejected by Dilthey. History only attempts to explain the whole man—in his actions, interactions, feeling, perceiving, imagining, and thinking—but no more. For this there are three essential steps: (1) facts, (2) theorems, (3) value-judgments and rules. By following these steps the complete study of man—his mind and body in their inner relation and relations to others—could be attained without applying Positivism or naturalism. The historian's task is not to produce absolute values, because "historical experience knows only the process . . .; on its own grounds it knows nothing of unconditional assertions."[18] Dilthey sought to find his historiography within ethical, idealistic bounds; he started with an optimistic view and probably became pessimistic toward the end of his life.[19]

A Historian and the Status Quo

Troeltsch. Before World War I Ernst Troeltsch (1865-1923), a professor at the University of Heidelberg, wrote on economics and religion as if he had been a Marxist—or at least an economic determinist. In 1913 he wrote that Jesus' ideals are meaningless without a consideration of "the climatic-naturalistic circumstances of Galilee"; they were unthinkable in modern urban life. Although he attributed Anglo-Saxon wealth to Calvinistic beliefs in immortality, piety and work, he pointed out that "modern economic man has no longer a religious home"—a decisive problem to be faced by the future.[20]

Troeltsch's seeming economic determinism evanesced with the outbreak of World War I. He considered the war as "an instinctive and loud national hatred," with the press as its medium; the war was "a crusade or cultural attack on Germany." After blaming England for the outbreak of hostilities, he cleared Treitschke, Nietzsche and Bernhardi of preaching war and cited English historians as instigators of war—of whom the only reputable one cited was Seton-Watson.[21]

[17] Alexander Goldenweiser, "The Relation of Sciences to Social Sciences," in Barnes, Becker and Becker, editors, *Contemporary Social Theory*, p. 94.
[18] Ernst Cassirer, *op. cit.*, p. 194; H. A. Hodges, *Wilhelm Dilthey: An Introduction*, pp. 29, 54, 113, 143. Among Dilthey's most important writings are his *Introduction to the Intellectual Sciences* (1883) and *Intuition and Analysis of Men in the Fifteenth and Sixteenth Centuries* (1891-1892).
[19] Friedrich Carl Sell, "Intellectual Liberalism in Germany about 1900," *Journal of Modern History*, XV (Sept. 1943), p. 228; E. Troeltsch, *op. cit.*, p. 516.
[20] E. Troeltsch, "Religion und Wissenschaft" in Strich, *op. cit.*, pp. 327, 334-338, 341.
[21] *idem*, "Der Geist der deutschen Kultur," in Carl H. Becker and Paul Darmstadter, editors, *Deutschland und der Weltkrieg*, pp. 52, 54.

France was dismissed by Troeltsch as being mere form (constitutions, parliaments) and pretense (phrases without spirit). Russia's pan-Slavism received harsher treatment: it lacked a cultural ideal; it embarrassed French and English Liberals because the Entente was "a victory of autocratic Russia's Peter and Paul fortress, Siberian exiles, pogroms and pretended Constitutionalism.[22]

German Historiography according to Troeltsch. These hostile countries were envious of Germany's recent unification and her rise to the position of a competitive Power. If the rest of the world would only realize that to the German "Kultur" signifies whatever "is characteristic of German thought and life" and that it is "something Romantic-Individualistic-Irrational," then it would be in a position to understand the chief characteristic of Germany: (1) Germans are a monarchial people with the Kaiser "the bearer and symbol of German unity," for whom parliamentarism is superfluous, and whose feeling of independence is satisfied in many respects. (2) German militarism is hereditarily and geographically determined with the army as the base of national unity. Since the German Army is a national one, there can be no thought of world domination. (3) Education—being directed toward Pestalozzi's principles of spiritual self-reliance, ethical self-control and intellectual self-development —promotes a "democratic and State socialistic" idea. (4) German administration—or bureaucracy—considers welfare measures, the only danger being a superfluity of officials, "bureaucratic compulsory happiness, immoderate respect for office and title, the habit [of depending] on the aid of the police, and a certain inclination toward subservience." (5) The German people are accustomed to working harder than others and produce quality goods. (6) A sense of order, connected with strict discipline and a feeling for duty *(Pflichtgefühl),* further distinguished the German people, "metaphysicians and dreamers by nature."[23]

Even if the French and English denounce German philosophy for propagandistic purposes, they neglect (Troeltsch reminded them) to admit that their own philosophers have been influenced directly by German thought.[24]

German historical science, Troeltsch assured all who could read, is inspired by philosophy and is comprehensive. It includes—in a cosmopolitan manner—the evolution of language, art, religion, and politics, and finally universal economics. Paradoxically, he maintained that German historians oppose "the democratic fictions that the State is an organization of individuals for the sake of their security and happiness."[25]

After World War I Troeltsch published *Der Historismus und seine Probleme.* Here he stated explicitly that the philosophy of history *(Geschichtsphilosophie)* is a part of formal philosophy. Though he paid Spengler a compliment for being "the last and most extreme branch or renewer of organology, purely contemplative, particularizing and individualizing," he differentiated between Spengler's basic idea and that of Schopenhauer-Nietzschean atheism and cultural criticism. Troeltsch proposed

[22] *Ibid.,* pp. 62, 64.
[23] *Ibid.,* pp. 59, note 7; pp. 70-79.
[24] *Ibid.,* pp. 82-83.
[25] *Ibid.,* p. 84.

to direct his efforts toward "the structure of a contemporary cultural synthesis [derived] from the historical heritage, for which task it is immaterial whether one belongs to a rising or declining branch of a cultural evolution."[26]

For those who are inclined to deprecate the prevailing crisis in historiography, Troeltsch warned that the crisis was not attributable to the plethora of new tools available to the historian nor to specialization nor to the multiplicity of problems. The crisis is inherent in the end of "senile cultures," in "historico-philosophical thought," but German "earnestness and objectivity, . . . thoroughness and honesty" will be the pillars of the spiritual position of the world.[27]

The war divided youth's historical attitudes into followers of Nietzsche (with his "conquest" of history, *Übermensch* and formal historic logic) and Marx (with his utopia based on Sociology and process of a structural nature). Troeltsch thought Nietzsche's historical philosophy was the more certain and clearer point of departure and approximated objective, generally more valid thinking. Yet, he accepted naturalism and historicism as tenable, though he rejected each of them individually.[28]

Finally, Troeltsch maintained that a universal *Kulturgeschichte* is impossible, since there exists no uniformity between cultures. He refrained from pontificating as to its possibility in the future. A "world history of Europeanism" is feasible but the thought of a universal history would convince one that "a journey around the world may be the shortest road to come to one's self."[29]

Unrevised Revisionists

Professor Barnes has itemized an impressive list of well-known German historians who, during World War I, permitted their patriotic fervor to push their historical equilibrium into the background.[30] His own fervor, however, led him to the questionable assertion that "It was purely accidental that history has since rather thoroughly vindicated their general position. It was not lack of emotion that made it possible for them to approximate the truth more closely than *Entente* scholars.[31]

That German scholars did not "approximate the truth more closely than *Entente* scholars" is clearly reflected in the critical articles of the *Preussische Jahrbücher* during World War I. What inherent "truth" is there in the contention that Germany would not sacrifice idealism and humanitarianism for the sake of a successful war, or that "the spirit of Schiller and Fichte still lives in us and our organizations"?[32]

Delbrück. Whenever th eeditors and contributors of the *Preussiche Jahrbücher* needed to bolster their patriotism with history, they had sufficient English

---

[26] *Der Historismus und seine Probleme*, Chap. IX.

[27] *Ibid.*, pp. 1-4, 6-7.

[28] *Ibid.*, pp. 26, 102-110.

[29] *Ibid.*, pp. 706, 709.

[30] Harry Elmer Barnes, *A History of Historical Writing*, pp. 277-278.

[31] *Loc. cit.*

[32] Walter Baetke, "Der Weltkrieg und der deutsche Geist," *Preussiche Jahrbücher*, CLIX (Jan.-Mar. 1915), pp. 1-9.

sources to quote copiously. (In other words, the opinions among Entente historians were so diverse that German publicists could use them "to approximate the truth more closely.") Hans Delbrück (1848-1929) who tutored Prince Waldemar of Prussia, 1874-79, was a professor at the University of Berlin, 1885-1921, and was editor of the *Preussische Jahrbücher*, 1883-1919, for which he wrote articles entitled "Politische Korrespondenz." Not only did he taunt the Entente that if they did win battles, was due to their numerical superiority, but he also denounced the English for striving to perpetuate a balance of power on the European continent and not on the high seas. With a German victory, on the other hand, there would ensue a balance on the high seas; only then will there come into being "world Kultur, freedom of peoples and lasting peace."[33]

What historical truth has Delbrück approximated when he maintains that the French military system is blameworthy because non-commissioned officers could rise to a captaincy, whereas the German system is better because the non-commissioned officers can win promotion only on the field of battle? Or, that militarism in France and Russia are "kulterfeindlich" but in Germany militarism has facilitated a situation in which "one can say in Germany there exists practically no proletariat"? Could a historian approximate the truth when he approvingly summarized a statement of four thousand educators who claimed that German militarism worked "for peace and security," that it led to training in a "sense of honor of the truly free man," individualism and self-reliance?[34]

Delbrück also indulged in much wishful thinking. When the German armies won at Przemysl and Lemberg in 1915, he was certain the Russian armies would never recover from these defeats and the war seemed won. The rationalization emerges when he quotes Clausewitz on the advisability of pursuing victory one step at a time because simultaneously the Germans had failed at the Marne and at Warsaw.[35] In connection with the age-old Polish issue, he was hoping that Germany would abandon Prussianization of German Poland, that Austria-Hungary might include her portion of Poland as an integral third of the Empire and that Germany would escape Polish irredentism.[36]

Schäfer. By 1914 even historians of repute had adopted the chauvinistic ideology of pan-Germanism. Thus, Dietrich Schäfer (1845-1929) suffered from the malady.[37] He bewailed Germany's plight in having so many of its nationals outside its own borders—25% of them, whereas vociferous Italy had only 3% of its population irredentist. He further noted that Germany is in the "middle of Europe," that the Germans "have received and given more than any other nation," that—despite their having been "the bearers and intermediaries of European spiritual Streams"—the Germans are readiest to surrender their

[33] Hans Delbrück, "Das Zahlen Uebergewicht unserer Gegner und die Politik Belgiens," *ibid.,* pp. 181-189, 337.

[34] Delbrück, "Das deutsche militariste System," in *Deutschland und der Weltkrieg,* pp. 176-178.

[35] "Der Krieg im Juni," *Preussiche Jahrbücher,* CLXI (Okt.-Dez, 1915), pp. 189-192.

[36] *Ibid.,* pp. 556-561.

[37] Professor Barnes lists him among the wayward German historians, *op. cit.,* p. 278.

Germanism, and that Germany's two thousand-year old obstacles had been hurdled only by "State union."[38]

Professor Schäfer explicitly demurred from attempting to reflect social and economic factors in history: History is no "struggle around the feed trough"; it is "neither applied psychology nor applied logic . . . [It is] the freest activity of human capability."[39]

The close of World War I and the establishment of the Weimar Republic brought many economic, social, political, and intellectual perplexities to the German people. None of these concerned them so much as the emotional question of *Kriegsschuld* (war guilt). Only the political Left gloated over Germany's sharing in the guilt in the outbreak of hostilities in 1914. Among historians no reputable one can be found who was even a "salvager."[40] Professor B. E. Schmitt points out in one of his articles on the origins of World War I that during the five-year period beginning in 1929 three hundred and sixty titles on the origins of the 1914 conflict were published by experts in the field, "yet the conclusions which they reach are easily the same as they would have drawn if they had written in August, 1914."

RESPECTABLE REVISIONISTS

For authoritative support of the thesis that Germany was not culpable in connection with the events of 1914 German historians had to wait till the publication of the *Groose Politik*. Here they found much to substantiate the Entente's culpability. One of the most respectable German historians on the question of war guilt was Erich Brandenburg (1868-1946), who was also one of the leading editors of the *Historische Reichskommission* which published five volumes on Prussian foreign policy, (1866-1871). In *Die Reichsgündung* he expressed doubt that the Zollverein was a direct or positive factor in Prussia's asumption of the initiative which led to German unification.[41]

Brandenburg. As a historiographer of the causes of World War I, Brandenburg is also catalogued as an uncompromising "revisionist,"[42] though in fairness to him it must be emphasized that he arrived at his condemnation of the *Entente* by a circuitous route. It must also be borne in mind that his chief accomplishment in this respect has been lauded as "one of the best studies of diplomacy in the era before the World War."[43]

It was Brandenburg's major thesis that Bismarck's policy was one of peace, that up to the period of his resignation Germany had nothing to gain even from a victorious war, that north and west all German nationals had been

---

[38] Dietrich Schäfer, *Deutsche Geschichte*, pp. 5-8. Apologists for Schäfer would probably prefer to consider it a slip-of-the-pen when he stated that the Germans entered history as "warrior nations" and that warlike strength "has not remained strange to our people," *loc. cit.*

[39] *Ibid.*, pp. 11-12. No one can quarrel with Schäfer for hoping that history, because of his belief in the future of his fatherland, will have a patriotic influence although his dedication to Waitz and Treitschke bespeaks chauvinism rather than patriotism.

[40] In Professor Barnes' scheme, which divided historians of World War I into "bitter-enders," "salvagers," and "revisionists." All the German historians are to be found among the uncompromising "revisionists," *op. cit.*, p. 289. A masterpiece of casting the whole blame on the Entente—Barnes calls it "the best indictment of the Versailles guilt clause"—is Alfred von Wegerer's *Kriegsschuldfrage, Ibid.*, p. 284.

[41] Eugene N. Anderson, "Recent Works on German Unification," *Journal of Modern History*, VII, no. 2 (June, 1935), p. 190.

[42] Harry Barnes, *op. cit.*, p. 284.

[43] *Ibid.*, p. 284; Bernadotte E. Schmitt, *op. cit.*, p. 160.

incorporated in the *Kaiserreich*, that no rational German coveted Switzerland or Holland, and that only the Catholic South—but not the Protestant North—desired Austria within the Reich. Only Poles in the east and some sections along the Baltic Sea were inimical elements within the Reich.[44]

Brandenburg observed two all-embracing disruptive factors in Europe before 1914: (1) Alsace-Lorraine, which touched French vanity at its most sensitive spot and (2) the Balkans, which required keeping Austria and Russia apart. To prevent difficulties over Alsace-Lorraine, Bismarck studiously isolated France. To prevent German involvement with her ally's Balkan adventures, he explicitly disclaimed any intention of supporting Austria's every territorial whim *(Expansionsgelüste)*.[45]

Having emphasized Bismarck's peaceful intent (which was "a well-thought-out system with quite simple aims . . . but often very complicated means for implementation"), Brandenburg unequivocally denied that the cause of the Chancellor's resignation was an ideological difference with the Kaiser; it was simply the Kaiser's personal desire to rule without having to work with an overpowering personality.[46]

With Nicholas II's succession to the Russian throne in 1894, the Kaiser felt closer to Russia and estranged from England. His fear of the Yellow Peril intensified his tacit support of Russia against Japan in 1904-05. However, he managed to retain neither Russia nor England as full-fledged allies. Between 1890 and 1905 the Kaiser launched a "world political" orientation and neglected the more important continental position of Germany. This was certain to find Germany on the opposite side of the greatest seapower, England. The pursuit of continental alliances was an "unrealizable utopia." The Triple Alliance weakened with Italy's defection, because of Italy's anxiety to retain good relations with England. This situation "pushed" Germany into accepting every Austrian move, thus hoping to impress Russia and prevent any rash acts.[47]

Brandenburg accepted the charge that in 1914 Germany indulged in short-sightedness, planlessness, lack of foresight, and impulsiveness; she cannot be accused of wanting war since a more propitious time for hostilities would have been 1904-05. He also cleared England of plotting war, although he attributed to her a fear of German continental hegemony. It was in Russia that an active war party operated—not the czar, but Izvolski was the *bête noire*. As ambassador to Paris, he pushed or was pushed by Poincaré to bring about a war situation. By rousing the press, by means of bribery and by flattery the Russian (and his French cohort, Poincaré) incurred personal responsibility for 1914. No German act, only Russian mobilization, had war as a direct consequence. The "deeper causes of the catastrophe" Brandenburg found in (1) the dearth of raw materials and (2) the incongruities between political borders and national-linguistic groupings.[48]

[44] Erich Brandenburg, *Von Bismarck zum Weltkriege. Die deutsche Politik in den Jahrzehnten vor dem Kriege*, pp. 2-3. In the course of the discussion of Bismarck's policies, the author indulged in no white-wash and even referred to his "Machiavellian statecraft."
[45] *Ibid.*, pp. 4-7, 13.
[46] *Ibid.*, pp. 15, 17.
[47] *Ibid.*, pp. 43-44, 52-53, 64, 456, 459.
[48] *Ibid.*, pp. 459-463.

Oncken. If Brandenburg managed to blame the *Entente* circuitously and decorously, Oncken is not so circumspect. Professor Hermann Oncken (1869-1946) started his career at the University of Berlin. In 1905 he was an Exchange Professor at the University of Chicago. Subsequently he taught at Giessen, Heidelberg, Munich, Berlin, and Göttingen. He edited or published *Allgemeine Staatengeschichte, Historische Reichskommission's* documents and *Forschungen zur neueren und neuesten Geschichte.* His earliest publications proved him to be more than a competent craftsman in historical biography. Sketches of Ferdinand Lassalle, Rudolf von Benningsen, Archduke Frederick I of Bavaria were among his successful contributions to historiography.

In his non-biographical works, Oncken eulogized Bismarck in unrestrained terms. He credited him not only with raising Prussia to unexpected heights but with having served the monarchy and simultaneously having dominated it; "indeed, as he dominated it he served it."[49] With Kaiser Wilhelm II Oncken had greater difficulties. He had to reject the prevailing delvings into "the dark passages of the unconscious" to explain the Kaiser's actions as psychological compensation for his physical defects. He is convincing when he reminds the reader that all individuals do not react similarly to given situations; harsh discipline may break the will of one individual and foster rebelliousness in that of another. Oncken also took issue with those who equate the debacle of 1918 with the Kaiser's inability to solve internal problems. As the foremost "representative of this newly German modernization of life," it is clear to Oncken that the hurdles were external and not internal. Nor was the crash due to the Kaiser's loss of self-confidence (as the Crown Prince wrote), since his marginalia on diplomatic documents and statements to his ministers reflected mental vigor.[50]

Oncken's reputation as an acute observer of all factors that constitute history—political, social, economic, and diplomatic—is borne out in his analysis of the temper of the world *circa* 1910: Diplomats—e.g. von Below—were optimistic regarding world events up to the last and expected no "Niagara." The social-economic conditions in Germany required peace. Conditions were so satisfactory that annual emigration was at a minimum. Although commercial rivalry with England was acute, each country remained the other's best customer. If superficial pleasures, sophistication and mechanization of life were to be deplored and if the Social Democrats were too harsh on imperialism, tariffs, and military budgets, there were some Socialists who "understood" the difference between aggressive imperialism and national needs.[51]

Oncken's *Des Deutsche Reich* has been praised as "the most pretentious effort of German historiography to explain the origins of war."[52] Now it must be pointed out that to acquit the Kaiser, Oncken emphasized Bethmann Hollweg's inexperience in statesmanship and ineffectual *Pflichtgefühl.* He admitted that documents do not support an official British policy of *Einkreisung,*

---

[49] Hermann Oncken, *Das Deutsche Reich und die Vorgeschichte des Weltkrieges* II, p. 355 et passim vol. I.
[50] *Ibid.,* II, pp. 356, 661-662.
[51] *Ibid.,* I, pp. 655-660.
[52] Schmitt, *op. cit.,* p. 160.

so he blamed publicists and scholars. He also dismissed the Versailles guilt clause as being directed only at 1914. Then Oncken concluded that the *Kriegsschuldfrage* was the Entente's ruse for attacking "the whole rise of the German Reich in the last generation."[53]

A German Maverick. Friedrich Meinecke (1862-   ) was an eminent contemporary of Oncken and was at various times professor at Strasbourg, Freiburg and Berlin. In 1903 he began editing the *Handbuch der mittelalterlichen und neueren Geschichte,* while in 1928 he helped found the *Historische Reichskommission* for the publication of documents on Prussian foreign policy. His earlier biographies have been overshadowed by subsequent political and historiographical contributions.

Criticism of German Foreign Policy. Like all other historians of the 1920's, Meinecke devoted considerable effort to the causes of World War I. Although he criticized the whole course of German foreign policy since Bismarck, there are two leaders he especially reproached in this connection: Holstein and the Kaiser. Holstein was particularly blamed for adhering to his *Kastanientheorie* regarding England's continental policy—that is, that England desired a war on the continent so that the contending powers would exhaust each other and leave England dominant. There are repeated references by Meinecke to Holstein's unreasonable distrust of England's policy, to his shortcomings as a diplomat (who pursued "cowardly boudoir politics"), and to his thinking that England was dependent on Germany's tolerance.[54]

Kaiser Wilhelm II fared no more gently in Meinecke's analysis. He was blamed for having lost "the torn thread of negotiation" with England. His testimony as to the course of events was dismissed as unreliable because of his personality. His drawing close to Turkey and Czarist Russia was attributed to ideological conservatism, Machiavellianism and expansionism. The Krueger dispatch was dubbed "the crude game of power," which was instrumental in alienating all of Europe. By 1900 the Kaiser's Machiavelianism vis-à-vis England and Russia appeared to Meinecke to be a case of vacillation. It lacked strength and experience but not "vanity and ruthless ambition."[55]

Meinecke's Historiographical Views. Although Meinecke's historiographical views are explicitly stated in some specialized works, his attitudes are also expressed in his general studies. Thus in his studies of Anglo-German relations, he "adapted" Planck's Quantum Theory to problems in history. He wanted it understood that he would refrain from telling the politician what he should have done—"after the event"—or demonstrate historical wisdom—"*post eventum.*" He thought that the historian's task resembled that of the politician: "Reason of state must be the measuring stick for all—political judgments [and] the controlling factor for all political desires."[56]

In *Weltbürgertum und Nationalstaat* (which went through seven editions

---

[53] *Ibid.,* II, pp. 662-670; 840-841; Schmitt, *op. cit.,* pp. 163-164. The bitterness with which Oncken resented all of Germany's enemies should have found a spot for him in Barnes' revisionist listing. He is not to be found there.
[54] Friedrich Meinecke, *Geschichte des deutsch-englischen Bündnis-problems* 1890-1901, ppp. 43, 58, 60-64, 92, 235-237. He even credited England with only desiring a "pax anglogermanica", *ibid.,* p. 252.
[55] *Ibid.,* pp. 50-54, 69, 100, 157, 234, 358.
[56] *Ibid.,* pp. 5, 7-9, 252.

from 1907 to 1928) and *Die Idee der Staatsräson in der neueren Geschichte* (1924 and 1929) Meinecke strove to express ethical and philosophical concepts of history. His view that realistic power politics is unavoidable was tempered with a deep respect for the moral and spiritual, a compromise between extremes. More vital and more daring is his work on historicism which appeared in 1936 in the face of Nazi authoritarianism. On this occasion he upheld the historian's task to be the search for individualization in history. This led him to a relativism which he found best expressed in Goethe.[57]

The origin of the idea of individualization in history Meinecke traced not too originally to the Middle Ages, Renaissance, Reformation and Enlightenment, which "brought this individualization process to consciousness itself, because (historicism) understood all historical life as the development of the individual even if it was always embedded in typical occurrences and regularity." Thus, in Möser he recognized French and English influences, and his enthusiasm for "his Germanic ancestors" he found to be typical of his age and Montesquieu's theories.[58]

Meinecke's own views seem to be clearest when he discusses Herder. In him he noticed the personification of the first and most creative synthesis of historicism—the search for antiquity in humanity, subjectivism from Pietism, Winckelmann's preparation for the new views, and the Platonic-Neoplatonic world of ideas in Leibniz and Shaftesbury—these are the elements that constitute historicism. These roused in Herder his interests in individuality as found in all nations, with not a thought given to racial theories. With approbation he quoted Herder to the effect that "humanity and the State are not synonymous" and "if you must, serve the State and if you can, serve humanity." The historian can best do that by making the past useful for the present.[59]

Götterdämerung. In the limited space of one chapter it is impossible to treat the flood of memoirs that appeared in Germany after World War I. Nor can space be adequately allotted to the cooperative historical publications that appeared. Such historians as Erich Marcks, Gerhard Ritter, Johannes Haller, Schwertfeger, and Ziekursch have to remain neglected. Emigrants like Kantorowicz and Valentin must be left undiscussed. Historiography from 1933 to 1945 needs to be dismissed with the observation that the motto of the *Monumenta Germaniae Historica* ("Sanctus Amor patriae dat animum") probably serves as a generalization.[60]

With the end of World War II German scholars occupied themselves not so much with war guilt as with guilt—i.e. the collective guilt of the German people. One of the first—and most worthy of attention—was the emigrant Wilhelm Röpke (1899—). He unqualifiedly accepted the thesis that Germany was morally guilty of the horrors ascribed to her under Nazism. But, he insisted

---

[57] Friedrich Meinecke, *Die Entstehung des Historismus*, p. 328; C. F. Sell, *op. cit.*, p. 233.

[58] *Ibid.*, pp. 327, 627-628.

[59] *Ibid.*, pp. 455, 474, 620, 629.

[60] By means of illustration Friedrich Alfred Beck's *Deutsche Vollendung*, VI, should suffice. Unequivocally he asserted that Chamberlain's *Grundlagen des 19. Jahrhunderts*, Krannhals' *Organisches Weltbild* and Rosenberg's *Mythus des 20. Jahrhunderts* are the three greatest achievements of German history. He sidestepped Hitler's *Mein Kampf* by saying that it was beyond any literary criticism "since it has become the living historical actuality."

the rest of the world was responsible too: it would not listen to the emigrants of 1933 and it admired the Autobahn and "social" experiments of the Nazis. Moreover, Hitler never attained a majority in elections and the German people were the first to suffer from concentration camps and tortures. Totalitarian ideas are not the exclusive property of Germany—that is to say, the German nation did not come to its contemporary status parthenogenetically.[61]

If one considers the exceptions which Röpke finds in Germany's guilt, the inescapable conclusion is that, since the rest of the world will not punish itself for "condoning" Hitlerism inside Germany, then Germany cannot be held morally responsible for anything that was perpetuated in the name of Nazism.

---

[61] Wilhelm Röpke, *Die deutsche Frage*, pp. 21, 26-28, 63, 205 *et passim*.

Chapter 19

THE LOW COUNTRIES

By Leslie F. Smith

BELGIUM, LUXEMBURG, NETHERLANDS

THE history of the Low Countries is complicated by nomenclature. The name Belgium, "Belgica," disappeared from history with the fall of the Roman Empire during which the Rhine had bounded the Empire. It did not reappear until the sixteenth century. The term Netherlands, now the official title of a kingdom we used to call Holland, was in the past applied to the territory included in the modern kingdoms of Belgium and the Netherlands. The Dutch themselves use "Holland" not only for the province of that name but loosely for the whole country. A part of what we call Belgium, the principality of Liège, was never a part of the Netherlands, but up to 1795 was ruled by a bishop-prince as a fief of the Empire. Luxemburg, curtailed in size in 1839 but an independent nation since 1876, was also a fief of the Holy Roman Empire.

When the Roman legions withdrew c. 400 A.D., barbarian Franks invaded the Low Countries but stopped short at the Silva Carbonaria so that Latin and Roman institutions were maintained South of a line running nearly East and West. This explains the "Linguistic Barrier," which has remained virtually unchanged since the fifth century. Belgium thus has two languages since the Walloons (Wala, cf. Welsh) developed dialects of Northern French, whereas Flemish, a low German tongue, is closely akin to Dutch. The Flemings and Dutch are regarded as descendants mainly of Franks but also of Saxons and Frisians. The characteristics of each group are said to be still discernible. The Walloons are, of course, descended from the Roman provincials of the Silva Carbonaria and South whose speech they preserve.

The partition of Charlemagne's Empire made Flanders a fief of the French crown, while the rest of our Belgium with the modern Netherlands and Luxemburg remained German or, at any rate, part of the Holy Roman Empire. Dutch Historians such as Blok and Belgian ones such as Pirenne have been much concerned with the break up of the countries into smaller fiefs and with the intricacies of feudal wars in general. The Dukes of Burgundy almost succeeded in reuniting the Lotharingia named after Lothaire II but their Spanish heirs lost the seven Northern provinces which became independent as a republic, the United Netherlands. Belgians deprecate the notion that their provinces made terms with Spain because of any "national" split between Walloons and speakers of Flemish and Dutch. They stress the fact that Belgian principalities included both Flemings and Walloons.

Belgium's union with Spain was, in the eighteenth century, transformed into

267

a similar union with Austria. Relations between Belgium and the United Netherlands were embittered by the Dutch closing of the Scheldt, which stifled Antwerp, and by the Dutch garrisons in Belgian fortresses in accordance with the Treaty of the Barriers. Both countries suffered a period of French influence under the Republic and then the Napoleonic Empire but the period was not altogether a loss to them. The Congress of Vienna brought the Netherlands, no longer a republic, and Belgium together under an Orange king. Belgian and Dutch historians agree that, though their countries shared the same vicissitudes up to 1588, the national cultures were quite different. It is not surprising, then, that in 1830-1831 Belgium rebelled against the union with Holland and acquired independence and a dynasty of her own.

BELGIUM

Archivists, Pirenne and his School. In its short national life, from 1830 on, Belgium has exploited not only its own archives but those of other nations, for example, Spain, which have had connections with Belgium. Even before the separation from Holland a Commission had been set up in Brussels to publish the *Scriptores Rerum Belgicarum.*[1] Among the best known Belgian historians of the nineteenth century were Alphonse Wauters (1817-1898), archivist of Brussels, and Louis Prosper Gachard (1800-1885), a French born archivist of Brussels.[2] They have been succeeded by a distinguished line of archivist-historians. It may be mentioned that both Belgium and the Netherlands established schools for training archivists soon after World War I.

Belgium is overwhelmingly a Catholic country though left-wing politics there are often associated with anticlericalism. It is not surprising that the popular historian, Kervyn de Lettenhove (1817-1891), was accused of strong Catholic bias. The Dutch historian, Robert Fruin, however, regarded him as quite sincere and his industry in finding documents was praised. Belgium has in the Bollandists Catholic historians whose supernational tradition is much older than Belgium as a nation.

In their number were Charles de Smedt (d. 1911), Albert Poncelet (d. 1912) and Hippolyte Delehaye (1859-1941). The last was not only historian of his order but himself the Bollandus of the twentieth century, a man who made great contributions to critical hagiography. The Belgian Historical Institute at Rome has been prolific in publications. Alfred Cauchie (1860-1922), professor of Ecclesiastical History at Louvain, was instrumental in founding the Institute and was in charge of it at the time of his death in a street accident. With L. van der Essen Cauchie inventoried the Farnese archives at Naples. He also investigated material concerned with the Principality of Liège, the Papal Nuncios in Flanders, and Joseph II's well-meant reforms for his Belgian subjects. In 1900 Cauchie helped found the *Revue d'Histoire Ecclésiastique.*

---

[1] H. T. Colenbrander, "The Work of the Dutch Historical Societies," *American Historical Association, Report for 1909,* pp. 245-256.

[2] The preparation of a volume of indices to Gachard's *Correspondance de Philippe II* was a project of H. Lonchay (d. 1918), but was produced by J. Lefevre. Joseph Cuvelier (1869-   ), Archivist-General of Belgium followed up Gachard's work with his *Correspondance de la Cour d'Espagne sur les Affaires des Pays-Bas au XVIIe Siècle,* 6 vols. His co-workers were Lonchay and Lefevre.

G. Kurth and Dom Ursmer Berlière (1861-1932) were also connected with the Institute at Rome.

Léon Vanderkindere (1842-1906) was an anthropologist as well as an historian. H. Pirenne described him as an "incomparable teacher," who introduced the scientific methods of the German school to Belgian historiography. He investigated the difficult problem of the origin of urban institutions. In this and in his liberal and anticlerical philosophy he seems to have influenced Pirenne. He sat on the left during two terms in the Belgian Chamber of Representatives.[3]

Léon van der Essen (1883-   ) is known for his work on Belgian hagiography but, above all, for his contributions to the history of the University of Louvain and to that of Alexander Farnese's governorship. He made a full analysis of the Farnese archives at Parma besides collaborating with A. Cauchie on those of Naples. Van der Essen's readable *Short History of Belgium* was the result of a course of lectures delivered at the University of Chicago early in World War I.[4]

Godefroid Kurth (1847-1916) was professor of Medieval History at Liège and in 1906 became director of the Belgian Historical Institute at Rome. His research tended towards the cultural, including the literary and linguistic, as, for example, the Walloon-Flemish language frontier. He was the first to introduce scientific German methods into Belgian historiography by means of a practical seminar. Kurth is credited with having turned H. Pirenne toward medieval studies.[5]

Paul Frédéricq (1850-1920) was born at Ghent but studied at Liège, teaching at Liège first and then at Ghent. This may help to explain why he wrote some works in French and others in Flemish. He became an ardent Flamingant but was arrested and deported 1916-1918 by the Germans when he resisted their attempt to divide and weaken Belgium by exploiting the Flemish movement. H. Pirenne, who also was deported, believed that Fredericq's life was shortened by this experience.[6] Fredericq's first work dealt with the Burgundian period but thereafter he specialized in a century eventful for the Low Countries, the sixteenth. As a teacher, he was the first professor in Belgium to introduce "practical" courses in history. He made a survey of history teaching in the universities of Belgium and the Netherlands, France and Germany, England and Scotland. The final examinations at Oxford and Cambridge won his admiration as regards the quantity and range of material to be memorized but he criticized the failure to bring the students into touch with actual sources.

Henri Pirenne (1862-1935) was a pupil of G. Kurth and P. Frédéricq but

---

[3] *Étude sur le Siécle des Artevelde,* "the first social history of Flanders and Brabant" (H. Pirenne). *La Formation Territoriale des Principautés Belges au Moyen Age* (2 vols.), also "of fundamental importance."

[4] Other works, *Étude Critique et Littéraire sur les Vitae des Séints Mérovingiens de l'Ancienne Belgique* and *Alexandre Farnèse, Prince de Parme, Gouverneur-Général des Pays-Bas 1545-1592* (5 vols.), the latter with preface by H. Pirenne.

[5] *Jean de Hocsem; Chronique des Évèques de Liège* (ed., completed by U. Berliere and J. Closon, Brussels, 1927). In connection with Liège, Eugene Hubert (1853-1931), for forty years a professor there, also deserves mention.

[6] See Pirenne, *History of Europe,* Preface by Jacques Pirenne, for incidental mention of Frédéricq's and details of H. Pirenne's own deportation. A. Cauchie of Louvain was also deported.

studied also at Paris and in Germany. He became easily the best known Belgian historian of this century. His forte was interpretation, though his capacity to do fundamental research was amply proved. His two best known ideas, namely the suburb origin of towns, and the closing of the Mediterranean by the Moslems, have swept the textbooks of medieval history, though both have been disputed. Pirenne argued against what was to him the "Germanist" heresy and stressed the persistence and importance of Roman factors. Yet he insisted that there was a complete break between the towns of the Roman Empire and those of the Middle Ages and a marked difference in spirit between the medieval city and the Greco-Roman city-state. A complete breakdown of trade was brought about by the Viking invasions and by the conversion of *Mare Nostrum* into a Moslem Lake. One English reviewer would put the breakdown of Mediterranean trade much earlier, namely in Vandal times.[7] Pirenne found his theories, which were originally derived from Belgian data, confirmed for other northern countries and indeed for Northern Italy and Provence.

His countrymen regard Pirenne's *History of Belgium,* which goes from the origins to 1914, as monumental and the same can be said of his *Bibliography of the History of Belgium.*[8] The author received much recognition in his own country as well as abroad. It is not every professor who can resign a chair at the age of sixty-eight and immediately obtain another. Foreign historical reviews conveyed the impression that Pirenne became emeritus at Ghent in 1930. The fact is that he had been refusing to lecture in Flemish, as was his duty every other year, and that when the university became completely Flemish-speaking, Pirenne resigned.[9] He was then appointed to Brussels.

In 1916, during their long occupation of Belgium, the Germans interned Pirenne. He was already so well known that various prominent people, including the Pope, interceded for him. Princeton University appointed him lecturer in the hope that the Germans would release him to the then neutral United States. They refused, however, and his visit to this country was delayed until 1922. During the worst part of his internment, Pirenne solaced his mind by composing a *History of Europe from the Invasions until the Sixteenth Century.* This was not published until after Pirenne's death. A German reviewer criticized the competence of Pirenne's son Jacques, who edited the work, and also his taste in putting so much about Pirenne's captivity into the preface.[10]

Pirenne's lectures at Princeton and elsewhere in the United States resulted in a notable book, entitled *Medieval Cities, Their Origins, and the Revival of Trade.*[11] The work is without the notes, which Pirenne usually provided in his articles, the basis of the book.

Henri Pirenne was a forthright, self-confident person. Reviewers described his thinking as rationalistic and positivist. He was accused of stopping just short of historical materialism. He was not a practicing Catholic but was

[7] Norman H. Baynes, *Journal of Roman Studies,* XIX (1929), pp. 230-235.
[8] *Histoire de la Belgique* (7 vols.); *Bibliographie de l'Histoire de Belgique* (3rd Ed.). H. Nowé and H. Obreen collaborated with him.
[9] My authority is a non-Belgian pupil of Pirenne's.
[10] Walther Kienast, *Historische Zeitschrift,* CLVII (1938), pp. 527-537.
[11] Princeton University Press, 1925.

reconciled with his Church on his deathbed. His death occasioned a crop of eulogies from Belgian historians and a volume of studies in his honor to which thirty pupils contributed, including five Americans.[12]

Jacques Pirenne (1891-   ) was trained in the law. He learned ancient Egyptian and applied his legal training to a problem of Egyptology. He has written an interpretative work on universal history.[13] A pupil of his famous father, Henri Pirenne, he has superintended posthumous publication of the latter's works. In the Spring of 1950, he was chief secretary to King Leopold III and prominent in the negotiations for the king's return to Belgium.

From considerations of space rather than of merit the following pupils of H. Pirenne are merely listed. G. Des Marez (1870-1931), archivist of Brussels, specialized in economic history of medieval Belgium, Herman vander Linden (1868-   ) dedicated to H. Pirenne and P. Frédéricq his best-known work which was translated into English as *Belgium, The Making of a Nation*. F. L. Ganshof (1895-) succeeded his teacher at Ghent. He contributed articles on Belgium to the *Encyclopedia Italiana*.

Belgium is very rich in learned periodicals. To mention a few, there are the *Revue Belge de Philologie et d'Histoire* (1922-   ), the *Revue Bénédictine* (1884-   ) and the *Revue d'Histoire Ecclésiastique* (1900-   ). The Bollandists not only continue their centuries' old labors on the *Acta Sanctorum* but also produce the *Analecta Bollandiana* (1882-   ). The Belgian Historical Institute at Rome produces the series *Analecta Vaticano-Belgica* (1906-   ) as well as the *Bulletin de l'institut historique belge de Rome* (1919-   ), the *Études de philologie, d'archéologie et d'histoire anciennes* (1934-   ), and the *Études de histoire économique et sociale,* all four published at Rome. Two cooperative histories can hardly be omitted, the *History of Flanders* and that of Antwerp.[14]

LUXEMBURG

There is room for a modern history of this little country by a native, though it is to be hoped that he will not write in the now official language, Letzeburgesch.[15]

NETHERLANDS

Conservatives, Liberals, Catholics. It seems fitting to begin modern Dutch historiography with Robert Fruin, termed the "Ranke of Holland." However, mention of Fruin inevitably recalls his older opponent in a controversy over government theory and politics, G. Groen van Prinsterer (1801-1871). Groen was archivist of the royal house of Orange-Nassau.[16] Both as historian and as politician he took the conservative, ultra-Calvinistic point of view.

[12] F. L. Ganshof, E. Sabbe and F. Vercauteren, editors, *Études d'Histoire dédiées à la memoire de Henri Pirenne.*

[13] *Histoire des Institutions et du Droit Privé de l'Égypte Ancienne* (3 vols.) ; *Les Grand Courants de l'Histoire Universelle* (3 vols.).

[14] R. van Roosbroeck, Ed., *History of Flanders* (in Flemish, 6 vols.). *History of Antwerp;* see *English Historical Review,* LVIII (January, 1943), p. 116.

[15] Paul Weber, *Histoire du Grand-Duché de Luxembourg,* is a short but recent work. Past historians include N. van Werveke, Paul Eyschen and Emmanuel Servais (the latter two both statesmen). Note the publications of the Institut Grandducal de Luxembourg.

[16] His greatest work was the *Archives ou correspondance inédite de la maison d'Orange-Nassau* (14 vols. Further series under the same name were edited by J. F. van Somren, T. Bussemaker and F. J. L. Kramer. When completed, in 1917, the work amounted to five series totaling twenty-eight volumes.

Fruin. Robert Fruin (1823-1899) was the grandson of Thomas Frewin, an Englishman who migrated to Rotterdam. His original idea had been to specialize in ancient history but when, in 1849, the teaching of Dutch history was for the first time separated from Dutch language instruction, at the Leyden Gymnasium, Fruin became its teacher. Similarly, when, in 1860, Dutch history and language were separated at the University of Leyden, Fruin became Leyden's first professor of Dutch history. For his inauguration he lectured on "Impartiality in History" and concluded that a historian must write history as he sees it and that a partisan must have leave to write in a partisan spirit. His voice and delivery were poor. It was said that he did not found a school, possibly because he never sought to force his ideas on others. Yet the names of the pupils who greeted his seventieth birthday with a volume of studies are those of scholars who in turn influenced many others. His greatest work and only book was the *Ten Years of the Eighty Years' War* which made his reputation while he was still teaching at the Leyden Gymnasium.[17] His essays, however, fill ten volumes.[18] Fruin edited the "dignified but heavy" monthly *De Gids* (1865-1874) and for some time also Nijhoff's series of *Historical Contributions.* After his retirement, he was offered the honor of tutoring Princess, later Queen, Wilhelmina but declined in favor of his pupil and successor at Leyden, Blok.

Nuyens. W. J. F. Nuyens (1824-1894) suffered from the prejudice which still hampered cultural activity among Dutch Catholics. He became a physician to support himself as a historian. Robert Fruin, who doubtless shared the opinion expressed by his pupil, N. Japikse, that "a Catholic sees our struggle against Spain differently from a Protestant and an anti-revolutionary sees the French Revolution differently from a Liberal or a Socialist,"[19] had been crying out for a Catholic Netherlander to write on the Eighty Years' War but when Nuyens' work[20] appeared, Fruin reviewed it scathingly as *A Specimen of Preposterous History Writing.* Nuyens' "errors," he thought, were the result of disingenuousness, not lack of ability.

Another Catholic historian, Father Gisbert Brom (1864-1915) may be mentioned. He taught history at Groningen and then at Utrecht and from 1904 on was director of the Netherlands Historical Institute in Rome. He was especially interested in the history of the old Episcopal see at Utrecht. While at Rome, he produced *Archive Material in Italy Concerning Netherland History* and *a Guide to the Archives of the Vatican.*[21]

The Dutch archivist tradition is as old as the Belgian. The cooperation of the personnel of the "noble archives of the Hague" was acknowledged by Macaulay in a footnote to his *History of England,* vol. 4. The standard work on the arrangement of archives, *Manual for the Arrangement and Description of Archives,* is by three Dutch archivists, S. Muller, Fz., J. A. Feith, and

---

[17] (In Dutch). It appeared in two successive issues of the Gymnasium's report, *c.* 1856, Fifth ed.
[18] One is available in English translation. R. C. Trevelyan tr. *The Siege and Relief of Leyden in 1574.*
[19] Japikse chapter, p. 33, in S. Steinberg ed., *Die Geschichtswissenschaft der Gegenwart in Selbstdarstellungen.*
[20] *History of the Netherlands Troubles in the Sixteenth Century* (in Dutch, 4 vols.).
[21] *Guide aux Archives du Vatican.*

R. Fruin.[22] Up to 1902 the plan put forward by Thorbecke in 1826 to publish the sources of Dutch history had been chiefly fulfilled by a private society, the Historical Society of Utrecht, which acted practically as a national society. In 1902 a royal commission to publish sources was appointed. H. T. Colenbrander was at first secretary and then director. N. Japikse succeeded Colenbrander as director when the latter became professor of colonial history at Leyden.

Colenbrander. Herman Theodor Colenbrander (1871-1945) had been one of Fruin's most gifted students. He specialized in the period 1795-1840. In 1918 he not only became editor of *De Gids* but gave up his publication of sources for the post in colonial history. In this connection he edited the *Reports and Correspondence of Jan Pieterszoon Coen,* founder of the Colonial Empire in the E. Indies, and also wrote a *Colonial History.*[23]

Nicolaas Japikse (1872-1944) felt that during his study-years philological training interfered with methodological training. When he entered Leyden, Fruin taught Dutch history, P. L. Muller all the rest that was taught. Japikse was impressed with Fruin's contribution to method but his successor, Blok, was livelier than the elderly Fruin and made the students more aware of method. In 1912, Japikse joined Blok in editing the oldest Dutch historical journal. Their teacher, Fruin, had long edited it.[24] In 1928, Japikse became Director of the Archives of the House of Orange. Major achievements were the editing of the correspondence of Johan de Witt and that of William III and Hans Willem Bentinck, First Earl of Portland. With these goes naturally, a *History of the House of Orange-Nassau.*[25]

Pieter Johannes Blok (1855-1929) was, as has been stated, a pupil of Fruin, who, after teaching Dutch history at Groningen, succeeded his old master at Leyden and taught there 1894-1925. He is credited with the foundation of the Netherlands Historical Institute at Rome. His *History of the Netherland People* in eight volumes[26] was recognized from its first volume as the answer to a great lack, namely, a full history of the Dutch people. His knowledge of the sources for all sides of controversial issues was the fruit of much research in archives. The first edition showed that he had mastered the work of previous Dutch historians, the second that he had kept up with subsequent work by his contemporaries. Blok's pupil, Japikse, who himself preferred political history, said that Blok was the first Dutch historian to insist on the importance of economic, social and cultural phenomena in the life of the people and to fit the whole into political history. Reviewers praised Blok for his lack of partisanship but might have preferred a little moral indignation in the manner of Fruin. One of them felt that, though Blok was full of facts, he did not quite show *how* the Dutch became a nation and that, though he had not evaded controversial political issues, he had

---

[22] Arthur H. Leavitt, tr. 2nd Dutch ed.
[23] The former, in Dutch (5 vols.) ; the latter, in Dutch, 3 vols. While serving the Royal Commission Colenbrander wrote a *Survey of the Gaps in Netherlands Historical Knowledge to Be Filled by Source-Publications.*
[24] The *Bijdragen voor Vaterlandsche Geschiedenis en Oudheidkunde.*
[25] In Dutch (2 vols.). He also wrote, with I. H. Gosses, *A Manual for the Constitutional History of the Netherlands 1887-1917* (in Dutch).
[26] In Dutch, Wolters, Groningen, 1892-1908.

played down the difficult religious issues of the Netherlands. Another praised his scholarship and lack of bias but found his style undistinguished.

The complete survey which Blok had made of his nation was repeated in a more concentrated form in the *History of a Holland City* (Leyden) in four volumes. He was an editor of the *New Netherland Biographical Dictionary* and cooperated with P. Frédéricq of Ghent and others on a *Historical Atlas of the Netherlands.*

Huizinga. Johan Huizinga (1872-1945) was professor of history, first at Groningen, and then, from 1915, at Leyden. He became president of the philological-historical division of the Netherlands Academy of Science. In 1942, the Germans took him as a hostage and thereafter banished him to Overyssel-Gelderland. His best known work is entitled in English, *The Waning of the Middle Ages, A Study of the Forms of Life, Thought, and Art in France and the Netherlands in the XIVth and XVth Centuries.*[27] Not all reviewers agreed with Huizinga that the period 1300-1500 A.D. was one of "fading and decay." At least the work will serve to correct the easy notion that civilization from the Renaissance of the twelfth century to the Renaissance proper was a continuous rise to better things. "So violent and motley was life," says Huizinga, "that it bore the mixed smell of blood and roses." In his *Violated World*[28] he argued against the belief in a continuous progress of our own civilization. His interest in cultural history was carried through the Renaissance, producing a work on Erasmus, to the seventeenth century. The author was interested in American problems.[29]

Romein. Jan Marius Romein (1893-   ) was a pupil of Huizinga. He and his wife Annie have been described as convinced Marxists. *The Uncompleted Past,* a volume of essays, was termed by A. J. Barnouw an attempt to write history from the standpoint of dialectical materialism. In *The Low Countries by the Sea,* political events are omitted though political forms find their place along with social organization, economic life, religion, art, letters and thought. *Legators of Our Civilization* illustrates the history of the Low Countries with biographies. Romein produced in cooperation with others a highly-praised *Eighty Years' War.*[30]

Geyl. Pieter Geyl (1887-   ), first professor of Dutch studies at London (1919-1935) and thereafter professor of modern history at Utrecht, was a pupil of Blok. Before his appointment in London, he had served there six years as a newspaper correspondent. He was taken by the Germans as a hostage on October 7, 1940, and held for over three years, the first thirteen months of which were in Buchenwald. As an historian, Geyl stresses the effectiveness of individuals and apportions praise and blame to them according to definite standards. He took sharp issue with Toynbee as an interpreter of history. Geyl's magnum opus, the *History of the Netherlands Race* (his own English), in the three volumes which have appeared, reaches 1751.[31]

[27] London, 1924. This is not an exact translation from the Dutch original of 1919 but has been adapted by the translator, F. Hopman, with the author's cooperation.
[28] Published posthumously (in Dutch).
[29] *America Living and Thinking* (in Dutch) ; *Man and Multitude in America* (in Dutch).
[30] All four in Dutch, Amsterdam, 1937, Utrecht, 1934, Amsterdam, 1938, Amsterdam, 1941, respectively.
[31] In Dutch, Amsterdam, Wereldbibliotheek, 1930, 1934, 1937.

Adriaan Jacob Barnouw (1877-   ), Queen Wilhelmina Professor at Columbia University, has written mainly in English. He even translated into English verse the medieval Flemish of the *Miracle of Beatrice,* a remarkable undertaking for one not a native speaker of English. It would be a pity to omit the names of G. W. Kernkamp, who, according to Japikse, first made Dutch historians aware of Marx's materialism, of Nicolaas W. Posthumus (1880-   ), professor of economic history at Amsterdam, and of the following who have written histories of the Netherlands. Hajo Brugmans (1868-   ) edited one in eight volumes. Also, like Barnouw, he wrote a *History of the Netherlands under Queen Wilhelmina.* Herman A. Enno van Gelder (1889-   ), who published a short treatment of the Netherlands from the crucial sixteenth century on, is praised by his countrymen. Bernard H. M. Vlekke (1899-   ) in the *Evolution of the Dutch Nation* [32] reverted to Nuyens' main thesis against Groen van Prinsterer, namely, the patriotism, of Dutch Catholics. Pierre Daniel Chantepie de la Saussaye (1848-1920) not only wrote *The Religion of the Teutons* but also a standard *Manual of the History of Religion.*[33]

Because the Netherlands once had a great colonial empire, the remains of which were put on a basis of equality with the mother country in 1922, Netherlanders have been interested in many parts of the world. F. W. Stapel, E. S. De Klerck, and B. H. M. Vlekke are the authorities on the East Indies, N. J. Krom on their medieval history. In the West, the archives of Surinam, Curacao and British Guiana have had attention. Since Afrikaans, the Boer language of South Africa, is a simplified form of Dutch, it is not surprising that Dutch or Flemish-speaking professors occasionally write of South Africa. G.-Molsbergen of Batavia, A. J. Barnouw of Columbia and Paul Frédéricq may be cited.

The Netherlands parallels Belgium in richness of scholarly periodicals as in other respects. The monthly *De Gids* has been published since 1837 and often has been edited by historians. The *Bijdragen voor Vaderlandsche Geschiedenis en Oudheidskunde* is the oldest Dutch historical journal (1836-1944). These *Contributions to National History and Archaeology* are continued by the *Bijdragen tot de geschiedenis der Nederlanden* (1946-   ), which is an amalgamation with the *Nederlandsche Historiebladen* of Antwerp. The Netherlands, Flemish-Belgium and South Africa are represented on the editorial board. The *Historisch Tijdschrift,* published since 1922, is specifically Roman Catholic. The *Nederlandsch archief voor Kerkgeschiedenis (Netherlands Archive for Church History)* is the best periodical for ecclesiastical history. It goes back to 1829.

As to series, the *Rijks Geschiedkundige Publication (National Historical Publication)* amounted to 118 volumes in 1937. The Linschoten Society, modelling itself on the Hakluyt, produced 57 volumes between 1909 and 1947. An important cooperative work entitled *Algemeene Geschiedenis der Nederlanden (General History of the Netherlands),* edited by J. Romein and others, has had the first volume of twelve published. The towns of Amsterdam and Rotterdam have been subjects of recent "definitive" works.[34]

---

[32] New York, Roy, 1945.
[33] *Lehrbuch der Religionsgeschichte* (2 vols.).
[34] H. Brugmans, *History of Amsterdam* (in Dutch, 8 vols.); H. C. Hazewinkel, *History of Rotterdam* (in Dutch, 3 out of 4 vols.).

Chapter 20

THE SCANDINAVIAN COUNTRIES

By Leslie F. Smith

DENMARK, SWEDEN, NORWAY, ICELAND, AND FINLAND

A COMMON characteristic of the Scandinavian countries, including Finland, is that they never formed a part of the Roman Empire. Viking times are the beginning of their written history. Norway as a kingdom begins with Harold Fairhair (860-930), Denmark with Gorm the Old (900-940), and Sweden with Olaf Skott-Konung (944-1022). Iceland, too, begins its history with Harold Fairhair, because chieftains who objected to the taxes Harold imposed settled Iceland in the period 870-930. With the formation of Norway, Denmark, Sweden, and Iceland came the process of conversion to Christianity. At this time it was decided whether Scandinavia was to be one nation or at least three. If King Canute's Empire based on England—comprising England, Denmark, and, after 1028, Norway—had continued, all Scandinavia would have been one and might also have continued its connection with the British Isles.

There was a union of the crowns between Norway and Sweden for a good part of the 14th century under Magnus, son of Eric, and under the Regent Margaret. Margaret became regent of Denmark in 1376, of Norway in 1380, and of Sweden in 1389. The Kalmar Union of all three countries began in 1397, Margaret continuing as regent until 1412. In 1450, Norwegians and Danes at Bergen signed a compact that their two countries should be "forever united under one king." Sweden, however, was liberated from the Kalmar Union by the Dalecarlian Engelbrekt Engelbrektsson. About the same time the foundations for Parliamentarism in Sweden were laid. Norway continued her union with Denmark until 1814, when, as a result of the Napoleonic Wars, she entered a union of the crowns with Sweden. Norwegians today resent the period of union with Denmark as one of *de facto* subjection. During the union with Sweden (1814-1905) Norway was also restive. In 1905 came a solution when, with Norwegians and Swedes mobilized against one another, the union was pacifically dissolved and a Danish prince was elected king of Norway as Haakon VII (1905-   ).

In the later Middle Ages and the Renaissance the Scandinavian countries had common problems in the Reformation of the Church, which all three eventually adopted, and the predominance of the Hansa merchants, which threatened the native middle class. In the nineteenth century, especially in connection with the Schleswig-Holstein question, there was a tendency to draw together in the "Scandinavist" Union movement but it did not come to fulfillment.

Greenland, the Faroe Isles, and Iceland had fallen to Denmark through the

1450 union with Norway. In 1918, Iceland severed all ties save allegiance to the Danish Crown. In 1944, it was proclaimed an independent republic. The Faroe Isles, population about 25,000, are free from Denmark except in foreign affairs.

Finland had a connection with Sweden from 1154 on but was finally lost to Russia in 1809, a consequence of the Napoleonic Wars. Since then, Finnish proponents of Swedish culture have tended to lose ground to the Fennomans.

The Norwegian, Didrik Arup Seip, declares that Norwegian, Swedish, and Danish are the same spoken language. Yet, Swedes and Danes have difficulty understanding one another's conversation. Worse, not all Norwegians can understand the New Norwegian (Landsmaal) in which the illustrious Halvdan Koht writes. Icelandic, close to Old Norse, is, without study, incomprehensible to Scandinavians. Finnish is not an Indo-European tongue. Consequently, Fennomans who will not write Swedish restrict the number of their readers sharply.

DENMARK

Quantity and Quality. Continuity is a characteristic of Danish historiography. Beginning with modern times the Danes trace an unbroken line from the Dano-Norwegian, Ludvig Holberg (1684-1754), comedian and historian, until the present day. However, within the nineteenth century breaks can be made at 1830 or 1840, and at 1870. The dominating figures in the "Middle Period" between these dates were N. F. S. Grundtrig (1783-1872), C. F. Allen (1811-1871) and C. P. Paludan-Muller (1805-1882). The last specialized in fundamental research whereas C. F. Allen was a synthesizer as his famous *History of the Three Northern Kingdoms 1497-1536*[1] proves.

Denmark's defeat in 1864 and loss of the Duchies of Schleswig, Holstein and Lauenburg, almost coincide with the introduction of modern methods of historical research, derived, of course, largely from conquering Germany. Edvard Holm (1833-1915), who wrote extensively on the history of Denmark-Norway with special emphasis on the period 1720-1814,[2] and J. A. Fridericia (1849-1912), who specialized on external issues and edited the Danish *Historical Periodical* from 1897 to his death, were, of course, young in those days.[3]

Kristian Sofus August Erslev (1852-1930) was trained in the German school, that of Waitz, Droysen and Nitzsch. He introduced the critical study of sources and made it the foundation of historical studies at Copenhagen. He specialized in the Valdemars and the Kalmar Union, in general, the fourteenth and fifteenth centuries.[4]

The Society for the Translation of Historical Sources was founded in 1875, that for the Publication of the Sources of Danish History in 1877. When the National Government Archives were established in 1889 A. D. Jørgensen, described as the foremost archivist of his generation, was put in charge. These archives became a school for historians. Jørgensen himself, like Erslev, examined

---

[1] In Danish, 5 vols. The work is incomplete.
[2] *Denmark-Norway's History from the Great Northern War's End till the Separation of the Kingdoms, 1720-1814* (in Danish), 7 vols.
[3] J. A. Fridericia, *Denmark's External Political History 1629-60* (in Danish, 2 vols.), and its continuation, *The Last Days of the Nobility's Rule 1648-60* (in Danish).
[4] *Repertorium Diplomaticum Regni Danici Mediaevalis.*

the basis of Danish claims to the lost duchies. Their sane estimate of these claims partly consoled their countrymen for the loss of the duchies.

Friis. Aage Friis (1870-1949) followed in their footsteps. He was a statesman as well as a professor, having been consultant to the Foreign Ministry (1906-1913) and working with the Germans for the reunion of North Schleswig with Denmark in 1918. He has specialized in the period of the Bernstorff family's influence and in the North Schleswig question (1863-1879). If Friis, described as Denmark's leading historian, has left anything to say about the latter question, that is history in itself. Friis also wrote a history of South Jutland, in spite of the fact that a cooperative history of the same area had been completed.[5]

Positivist Philosophy. In some ways the noted critic, Georg Brandes (1842-1927), was most responsible for introducing the Positivist philosophy into Denmark. Troels-Lund (1840-1921) wrote a work on *Daily Life in the North in the Sixteenth Century.* Sofus Otto Müller (1846-1934) was the creator of the Danish National Museum and the organizer of unrivalled research in pre-literary history. He disagreed with the absolute chronology of the Swede Montelius.

Johannes Steenstrup (1844-1935) was the son of Johann Japetus Smith Steenstrup, Danish zoologist and researcher in prehistory. His favorite study was the Oldest Period and the Early Middle Ages of Denmark. His industry may be judged from the *Festschrift* with which the Danish Historical Society honored his ninetieth birthday. A. Krarup contributed to it a Steenstrup bibliography of 665 items, 253 being books and articles or reviews in historical or scientific periodicals. In view of Steenstrup's production, it is no wonder that the sheer quantity of Danish historiographical production is admired.

Economic history has, of course, had its Danish devotees. In this connection the studies of the Tolls of the Øresund (between Denmark and Sweden) by Nina Ellinger Bang (1866-1928) have been analyzed and found on the whole reliable.[6] Mrs. Bang, in the Scandinavian, and indeed in the Western European tradition of the historian's profession, was a statesman as well as historian.

Ellen Jørgensen (1877-   ) has made the history of historiography in Denmark her field. She emphasizes the Danish tradition of solid achievement in the writing of history, which, despite Erslev's pessimism, she hopes will continue. She places the inspiration of the Danes below that of the greatest Swedish historians. Kay Schmidt-Phiseldeck (1894-   ) has studied the historical development of philosophies of history.[7]

SWEDEN

Hjärne and his School. According to Kay Schmidt-Phiseldeck,[8] the Swedes were early interested in the philosophy of history. Benjamin Höijer wrote on

---

[5] *History of South Jutland* (in Danish). The cooperative history was edited by la Cour, Fabricius, Hjelholt and Lund, 1930-1942, 5 vols. Frii's work on the Bernstorff family is paralleled by Louis Bobé's on the Reventlow family.
[6] *Statistics for Ship-passage and Transport of Goods* through the øresund 1497-1660 (in Danish, 2 vols.). Further statistics for the øresund 1661-1783 and the Great Belt 1701-1748, ed. N. E. Bang and K. Korst.
[7] E.g., *Swedish Historical Thinking* (in Danish).
[8] See unrer Deunmark, note 7.

the *Historian's Difficult Task* for his degree in 1788. Erik Gustav Geijer (1783-1847), poet, politician, economist, and "The Father of Historical Study" in Sweden relied on Höijer's views. C. J. Boström, however, dominated Swedish philosophy with his Rational Idealism for most of the century. When the influence of modern German historical schools became felt, Swedish historians debated Lamprecht's ideas of cultural history, but, while adopting German methods of historical research, decided to be empiricists in philosophy. Gunnar Aspelin (1898-   ), a Hegelian, is a noteworthy philosopher of history today.

Harald Hjärne (1848-1922) was described as the central figure in the empirical as against the philosophically-dogmatic schools of historiography in Sweden. Ludvig Stavenow says that "almost all later Swedish historians acknowledged Hjärne as their master." Hjärne believed that the health and strength of the State is the chief factor in the development of nations. He took an active part in politics and was in the Swedish Diet for many years. Schmidt-Phiseldeck would make Hjärne's *Charles XII, a Task for Swedish Source-Researches* compulsory reading for all students of Nordic history,[9] no matter what their specialty. It may be remarked that it was not necessary for Hjärne to stimulate Swedes to write on Charles XII. He and Gustavus Adolphus, both hero-kings, are the favorite subjects of the pacific Swedish nation.[10]

Emil Hildebrand (1848-1919) did not perhaps publish as many books as some of his contemporaries but he received recognition, e.g., in his editorship of and contributions to a great cooperative history. He was interested in the evolution of the Swedish constitution and in palaeography, among other things. He was editor from its inception (1881) of the *Historisk Tidskrift (Historical Periodical)*, organ of the Swedish Historical Association.

Johann Henrik Emil Schuck (1855-1947) has been termed a humanist and historian of literature. After a career as professor at Lund and then at Upsala he became president of the Nobel Foundation in 1918. He is credited with great influence on Swedish culture during his long life. In the field of general history, as against the history of literature, may be mentioned his *Swedish Memoirs and Letters,* his *History of the Swedish People* and his *Gustavus III*.[11] His grasp of world literature may be illustrated by his range in English from Beowulf to Shakespeare. No literature seems to have affected him as did the classics of Greece and Rome but he wrote a seven-volume *History of Swedish Literature*.[12] In special treatments he ranged over all of Swedish history, favoring the Middle Ages and the Reformation and, in modern times, the reign of Gustavus III (1771-92).

Stavenow. Ludvig Stavenow (1864-1950) in 1895 declared himself against a philosophy of history as such. History, he said, must form a conception of the existing culture and trace its evolution from as far back as possible.[13] He was associated with E. Hildebrand in the editorship of the great *Cooperative History*

---

[9] In Swedish, *Svenskt och Främmande,* 1908.
[10] The Caroline Association seems to be dedicated principally to studies connected with Charles XII.
[11] The first with O. Levertin (in Swedish, 10 vols.), the second (in Swedish) 1913-15, the third a critical study, 1904.
[12] Begun alone in 1890, continued with K. Warburg (in Swedish).
[13] Schmidt-Phiseldeck, *op. cit.,* p. 59.

of Sweden and was given a *Festschrift* for his sixtieth birthday. Stavenow, like the Norwegian, H. Koht, contributed to the *Cambridge Histories.*

For convenience De Geer, Montelius and Eli Heckscher will be considered together. Gerhard Jakob De Geer (1858-1943) bore a name famous in Swedish history. Primarily a geologist and geographer he was known for important contributions to prehistoric chronology. His chief study was the changes of level in Scandinavia since the Glacial Age and his chronology was based on the strata left by the Glacial torrents. He travelled extensively in Europe but also visited the United States of America. He declared that his European Time-Scale applies also to America.[14]

Oscar Montelius (1843-1921) began publishing in 1869 with his *Remains from the Iron Age of Scandinavia.* His researches led him all over Europe, especially to the Mediterranean area. A good linguist, he was especially at home in Italy. In 1880, he had become Professor at the Historical Museum. Montelius has been heralded as the founder of prehistorical research, especially of the typological method. He established a prehistoric chronology especially for his native Sweden and for Italy but also for much more of Europe and was busied with a work on pre-classical Greece at his death.[15]

Eli Filip Heckscher (1879-   ) was originally a follower of H. Hjärne.[16] He brought history and national economics together in economic history. He has written on *Economic History and Its Neighbor-Sciences* and contributed *An Economic History of Sweden from Gustavus Vasa (1521) On.*[17] Heckscher's most celebrated work is a study of *mercantilism* as a European-wide phenomenon.[18]

NORWAY

Statesmen-Historians. Scandinavian publishers may possibly be unduly modest about "pushing" their wares, witness the few reviews of Scandinavian works in the *English Historical Review* as compared with the many notices of authors from the Low Countries. In the *American Historical Review,* however, attention is more evenly divided. Danish publishers would seem to be the most conscious of the world market, the Norwegians far and away the least so, the Swedes in between.

Sars. Johan Ernst Welhaven Sars (1835-1917) belonged to the generation of Björnson and Ibsen and was a link with the Norwegian historians of the middle of the nineteenth century—Jakof Rudolf Keyser (1803-1864) and Peter Andreas Munch (1819-1863). His *Survey of Norwegian History*[19] correlated the development of classes in Norway with that country's loss of independence from the Kalmar Union on and again with Norway's vigorous self-assertion in the nineteenth century. Sars worked against the Scandinavist movement and was for nothing less than the complete independence of Norway. In 1905, the

[14] Bibliography of De Geer's works complete to 1918 (in Swedish), Transactions of the Geological Association XI.
[15] *On Determining Times within the Bronze Age* (in Swedish). *Chonology of the Nordic Iron Age* (in Swedish). *Civilization Primitive en Italie,* 5 vols.
[16] Schmidt-Phiseldeck, *op. cit.,* p. 58.
[17] The first an article in *Historik Tidskrift* (Sw.) 1947, 1, the second in Swedish.
[18] It was translated into English and published in London in two volumes.
[19] In Norwegian, 4 vols., Oslo, 1873-91, new ed., 2 vols., 1913.

year of independence, he was honored with a volume of studies. It was through a special appropriation of the Norwegian parliament that he had been named, in 1874, to the chair of history at Oslo.

Bull. Edvard Bull (1881-1932), Foreign Minister in Norway's first Labor government (1928), combined a severe, critical attitude toward the sources he used with a devotion to Karl Marx, about whom he had written, as well as to the socialist movement in Norway.[20] He specialized in the Middle Ages in Norway as is shown by his work, *People and Church in the Middle Ages,* Oslo, 1912.[21]

Koht. Halvdan Koht (1873-   ), also a socialist, has been a tremendously productive scholar. His range of interest is enormous. In time it begins at least as early as the first kings of Norway, over whose dates he had a controversy with the Icelander, Finnur Jónsson, and comes down to our own day, in the events of which, *"pars magna fuit."* In Scandinavian tradition he has been statesman as well as historian, and was Foreign Minister of Norway 1935-1941, sharing his government's exile after the German occupation, which began April 9, 1940. He was criticized for his behavior in connection with his advance knowledge of German intentions. While in exile, far from his study and his materials, Koht, like H. Pirenne, was still active as a historian. America was one of his interests long before 1940. He contributed a volume to the Danish cooperative work, *The Nineteenth Century.*[22] It was on American culture. He has dealt with the subjects of nationalism, including the formation of a Norwegian nation, democracy, socialism, and the class struggle, including the rise of the workers. Reviewers find his attitude "fully socialistic." As a biographer, Koht produced what was really the political history of Norway in the nineteenth century in his *Johan Sverdrup.*[23] Other biographies deal with the literary men of Norway; Wergeland, Vinje, and Ibsen. The *Letters* of Björnson and of Ibsen have been published by him. A bibliography of his works down to 1933 is to be found in a *Festschrift* for his sixtieth birthday in 1933. Besides his cooperation with Danish scholars Koht has contributed to the *Cambridge Medieval History.* His use of "New Norwegian" has been commented upon.

Johnsen. Oscar Albert Johnsen (1876-   ) has been interested in the sources of Norwegian history and the discovery of fresh ones in foreign, especially French, archives.[24] He has specialized in his country's economic history, particularly its commercial aspect as is evidenced by his *Norwegian Shipping from the Middle Ages to the Seventeenth Century.* He has also given particular attention to the Norwegian farmer (Bonde) and has written a local history, that of the town of Tönsberg.[25]

A. Bugge (1870-1929), a son of the philologist, Sophus Bugge, Johan

[20] In German, *Archiv für die Geschichte des Sozialismus und der Arbeiterbewegung*, III, 3.
[21] In Norwegian. Subtitle, *Studies in Norway's History.*
[22] In Danish, ed. Aage Friis.
[23] 3 volumes.
[24] *Introduction into the Sources for Norway's History until the Nineteenth Century* (in Norwegian). *Rapports de la légation de France à Copenhague, correspondance consulaire relatifs à la Norvège*, vol. 1 (1670-1748)).
[25] *Norwegische Wirtchaftsgeschichte. Survey of the Norwegian Farmer-Class* (in Norwegian). *History of Tönsberg* (in Norwegian). "Norway's Commerce and Shipping in the Middle Ages" (in Norwegian, *Nordisk Kultur*, XVI).

Schreiner (1903-   ) and A. W. Brögger (1884-   ) have dealt with Viking times. H. Shetelig (1877-   ) is the authority on Norwegian pre-history. Among Norwegian periodicals there is space to name only the *Historisk Tidsskrift* (same spelling as the Danish one) and among cooperative histories only the latest, to which W. Keilhau, after dealing with the period 1814-1920 in the last three volumes, added an eleventh to the series.[26]

ICELAND

Scanty Population, Great Traditions. Modern Icelandic historians seem to stress philology. Publication of sources and interpretation of the Old Northern tongue, for which Icelandic gives a natural aptitude, are their main business. General history develops from the necessity of providing historical introductions and explanatory footnotes. Much definitive work in Icelandic history has been done away from Iceland. Foreign universities lure away experts in Icelandic. Further, Iceland with its 130,000 inhabitants (1940) cannot afford to publish scholarly production as well as the United States of America, for example. The situation may change somewhat, for Iceland has had its own university since 1911.

Gudbrandur Vigfússon (1827-1889) was called to Oxford in 1864 to complete the Icelandic-English dictionary begun by Richard Cleasby.[27] Finnur Jónsson (1858-1934), namesake of a famous eighteenth century bishop and son of a self-taught local historian, was primarily an Old Norse philologist. His editions show the scientific methods of the German school and are tinged with anticlericalism.[28] Sigurdur Johannesson Nordal (1886-   ), professor of Icelandic at the University of Iceland since 1918, is a poet and essayist as well as historian. He is credited with a solid work on Snorri Sturluson and by far the best interpretation of the difficult *Völuspá Edda* (1922-27). He contributed introductions to Einar Munksgaard's reproductions of *Icelandic Manuscripts* and *Early Printed Books.* A new Icelandic society for publishing the ancient literature entrusted Nordal with the chief editorship. He began the series by editing *Egíls saga.*[29] Halldor Hermannsson (1878-   ), curator of the William Fiske Collection of Icelandic Books at Cornell University, and professor, himself published from 1908 to 1945 the annual volume, *Islandica,* demanded by Fiske's will. He published besides a *Catalogue* in three volumes and a special *Catalogue of the Runic Literature* in it. As volumes XXXII and XXXIII Stefan Einarsson wrote a *History of Icelandic Prose Writers 1800-1940.* He dedicated it to Hermannsson, whom he described as the greatest Icelandic bibliographer since Arni Magnusson (1663-1730).

FINLAND

Fennomans and Suecomans. Georg Zachris Yrjö-Koskinen (1830-1903) and

[26] H. Shetelig, E. Bull, S. Hasund, S. Steen, W. Keilhau, *The Norwegian People's Life and History through the Ages* (in Norwegian, 10 vols.), W. Keilhau, do. in *Our Own Time* (in Norwegian). Keilhau is specially good on the interplay of economic and political forces.
[27] Also *Chronology in the Icelandic Sagas* (in Icelandic), *Corpus Poeticum Boreale (1883) and Origines Islandicae* (1905) the latter both with F. York Powell, Eiríkur Magnússon (1833-1913) was at Cambridge while Vigfússon was at Oxford. He collaborated with William Morris in translating from the Icelandic.
[28] For him as for the other Icelanders see S. Einarsson, *History of Icelandic Prose Writers 1800-1940.*
[29] 1933. Under the auspices of the Faculty of Philosophy, Nordal started *Studia Islandica* in 1937.

Magnus Gottfried Schybergson (1851-1925) both produced histories of Finland.[30] Yrjö-Koskinen took part in public life and was known as anti-Swedish. Schybergson criticized his work entitled *Leading Ideas in the History of Mankind*. It appeared in the Finnish language in 1879 but in a Swedish translation not until 1906. The idea of nationality dominates it. Being above all an empirical historian, Schybergson rejected much of Lamprecht but recognized that history would even more than before scrutinize the economic conditions for the existence of nations. Bernard Rudolf Estlander (1863-1931) received considerable recognition for his *Eleven Decades of Finland's History, i.e.,* the period 1808-1918, the fifth volume being devoted to the critical years 1917-18. His work is paralleled by Per Olof von Törne's *Finland through One Hundred and Thirty Years 1809-1938*. Eirik Hornborg (1879-   ), a very productive historian and prominent in politics, is author of a *History of Sweden*—which covers the period of union between Sweden and Finland excellently and gives credit to his countrymen for the part they played in Sweden's wars. Gabriel Rein (1869-   ), grandson and namesake of an important historian (1800-1867) and Einar Wilhelm Juva (1892-   ) write in Finnish.

[30] Y. K., in German translation, *Finnische Geschichte von den frühesten Zeiten bis auf die Gegenwart;* S., *Geschichte Finnlands.*

Chapter 21

TWENTIETH CENTURY TENDENCIES—POLAND AND BALTIC COUNTRIES

By Anthony F. Czajkowski

HISTORIOGRAPHY in Poland and the Baltic States in the relatively brief span of half a century has already passed through three phases, determined by political conditions in central and eastern Europe. The successive periods of foreign domination, independence and occupation directed the minds and efforts of native historians to certain purposes which naturally color the products of their historical writing.

The first phase, beginning in the last decades of the nineteenth century and terminating with the winning of independence following the First World War, was marked by the domination of the Polish and Baltic nations by foreign powers. Partitioned Poland had been subject to Austria, Prussia and Russia, while the Baltic peoples in Lithuania, Esthonia, Livonia and Courland lived under Russian rule. The Polish and Lithuanian people could look back to days of independence and glory, but the Latvians and Esthonians had no such memories. Russia eventually conquered all the Baltic coast and during the second half of the nineteenth century, Russia proceeded systematically to russify her Baltic and Polish possessions. In reaction to foreign domination, native historians attempted to rouse national feeling by reliving the glories of the past. By fanning the rising flame of nationalism they contributed to the various movements for independence.

The defeat of Austria and Germany and the overthrow of the Tsarist regime resulted in the liberation of the Polish and Baltic peoples and in the establishment of independent republics. The second phase of historiography was thus ushered in. The organization of educational facilities, the training of cultural leaders, the establishment of museums, libraries and research centers were tasks assumed by the states which actively supported historical endeavor as an aid to the patriotic attachment of the people to the state, and to justify in foreign eyes their historical rights to existence.

The end of the war in 1945 found Poland, though reconstituted as a state, under Communist domination, with her eastern and western frontiers altered. The changed political, social and territorial conditions have canalized historical writing in certain directions. The Baltic nations of Lithuania, Latvia and Esthonia, however, were annexed to the Soviet Union and found themselves subject to another policy of russification, more ruthless than the Tsarist. The torch of national culture, including history-writing, must perforce be carried on by exiled scholars or by foreign sympathizers.

POLAND

To World War I. As the twentieth century opened, Poland was subject to three masters and her historiography reflected conditions under each of these. In the Russian portion, following the unsuccessful insurrection of 1863, a ruthless program of russification had begun, wherein Polish officials were removed from office. Russian was made the official language of the country, Polish law courts were abolished, Polish schools and the Warsaw University suppressed and the Greek Uniate rite abolished. From the west, Bismarck had similarly embarked upon a program of "Germanizing" the Poles under Prussia. The use of the Polish language in schools and church services was prohibited and forceful expropriation of land from Poles was fostered.

In contrast, Austria granted self-government to her portion of partitioned Poland in 1867 and paved the way for a period of rapid cultural revival. Here Polish learning and art were concentrated and scholars and artists found shelter from Prussian and Russian sectors. Throughout this period the Austrian sector became the focus for all Polish nationalism and contributed in great measure to frustrate the efforts to russify and Germanize the other two sectors.

University of Cracow. Poland's oldest university, Cracow, founded in 1364, assumed the leadership in the revival and became the chief seat of learning. The establishment of the Cracow Academy of Science (1872) made possible the coordination of effort which could cut across artificial political boundaries. A historical commission within the academy became the principal center for publishing historical documents which still remain invaluable for studying Poland's history. The Jagiellonian University concentrated on Polish medieval studies and in the pre-1914 period could boast of such men as Stanislaw Krzyzanowski (1865-1917), who treated the troublesome transition period of the thirteenth century and made notable contributions to the auxiliary sciences; Karol Potkanski (1861-1907), who examined problems of Poland's origins; Francis Piekosinski and Boleslaw Ulanowski (1860-1919), who published critical editions of medieval documents and specialized in the history of Polish and Canon Law; Stanislaw Zachorowski (d. 1918), specialist in medieval Church history; Anatol Lewicki (1840-1899) and Fredryk Papee (1856-1940), who probed into the fifteenth century; Vincent Zakrzewski, director of the Academy's publications, who treated religious and political history; Jan Ptasnik (1876-1930), who worked in the local archives to study Poland's past culture; and Waclaw Sobieski (1872-1935), whose studies spanned the Golden Age (15th and 16th centuries).

Lwow, as a Center of Historical Activities. Historical research also prospered in the other Austrian-dominated city of Lwow. Xavier Liske (d. 1891) founded the famous historical seminar in Poland to train future historians and provided the impetus for the founding of the Polish Historical Society in 1886 and of its organ *The Historical Quarterly (Kwartalnik Historyczny)* which shortly succeeded in concentrating about itself scientific historical research from all parts of the country. Prominent in Lwow were Ludwik Finkel, founder of a comprehensive *Bibliography of Polish History*;[1] Oswald Balzer, whose systematic investigations into legal and constitutional history illuminated Poland's origin;[2] Wladyslaw Abraham (d. 1912) who concentrated on Polish medieval Church History, using unedited Vatican materials; Tadeusz Wojciechowski (1838-1919), whose essays analyzed the most controversial problems of Poland's origins; and Stanislaw Zakrzewski (1873-1936) whose study of the Middle Ages was based on extensive use of the auxiliary sciences. Best known outside of Poland was Simon Askenazy (1866-1935) whose interests centered on the post-partition period, especially the times of Napoleon.[3]

Warsaw. The third historical center was Warsaw which under Russian occupation lagged behind the other universities. Some collections of sources were published, but it was only after the Russian political upheaval in 1905 that the Polish language was re-introduced and more freedom was permitted. The transition was marked by the founding of the *Historical Review (Przeglad Historyczny)* in Warsaw.

Historical Themes. The bulk of the pre-1918 historiography dealt with two principal topics, the origins of the state and the partitions. From the standpoint of the number of sources and studies published, medieval history occupied the predominant position. Historians collected and edited source material, developed auxiliary sciences and probed into the Piast period, the introduction of the Church into the country, the histories of medieval law, jurisprudence and business.

In the modern period, the effect of the Protestant movement, the Baltic question, the wars for outlet to the sea, Polish-Swedish relations, all received notice, but the historians, almost in self-defense, gravitated towards the partition period. German and Russian historians had justified the dismemberment by their interpretation of eighteenth century events and had presented the entire course of Polish history as a long series of shortcomings which had finally terminated in the inevitable dismemberment. Polish historians reacted sharply to this version of their history which ignored the periods of greatness in earlier centuries. Some found refuge in a messianic concept of Poland's history, but the majority sought an answer through critical research.

The Cracow School. Poland's past had been critically investigated by Joachim Lelewel (1786-1861) and Karol Szajnocha (1818-1868) but a new phase began after the unsuccessful insurrection of 1863. The sense of helplessness, futility and disillusionment which followed provoked a demand for a total re-evaluation of Polish history. In 1869 the young historian and rector of the Jagiellonian University, Joseph Szujski (1835-1883), started a wide-

---

[1] Ludwik Finkel, *Bibliography of Polish History,* 3 vols., and 3 supplements (in Polish). Presents bibliography of sources, of history of law, Church, civilization and political affairs up to 1815. After World War I it was continued to embrace the 1815-1865 period, and was one of the first projects resumed in 1945.

[2] Oswald Balzer is the author of the monumental and still indispensable *Genealogy of the Piasts* (in Polish), Cf. also Oswald Balzer, *Corpus juris polonici* and *Polish Kingdom 1295-1370* (in Polish).

[3] Among the works published outside of Poland were Simon Askenazy, *Die letzte polnische Konigwahl; Prince Joseph Poniatowski* (in Polish) was translated into several languages, as was his standard work *Napoleon and Poland,* 3 vols. (in Polish). He was the only Polish historian who contributed to the *Cambridge Modern History* (Vol. X, pp. 413-474, two chapters on Russia and Poland from 1815 to 1831).

spread and oftentimes bitter polemic by calling the insurrection a piece of political foolishness and challenging the entire Romantic version of the partitions.[4] The challenge found firm support in Michael Bobrzynski (1849-1939), destined to become the head of the socalled Cracow school of historians, who blamed the fall of Poland upon the Poles themselves. Their own weakness and faults, he contended, had brought on past disasters.[5]

In the ensuing controversy, national literature was investigated as a source of lessons for national thought and conduct. From this, came a comprehensive literary history by S. Tarnowski (1837-1917). Since Cracow possessed the greatest collection of old manuscripts and early printed books, the University librarian, Karol Estreicher (1827-1908) began compiling a voluminous bibliography.[6] Francis Piekosinski (1844-1906) and Stanislaw Smolka (1854-1924) made their contribution to the polemic by probing the social life of medieval Poland and the formation of the noble class.

The Warsaw School. In opposition to the pessimism of Bobrzynski's Cracow school, Warsaw became the center of historical optimism, led by Tadeusz Korzon (1839-1918),[7] who stressed the value of the federative and republican institutions of old Poland, and Wladyslaw Smolenski (1851-1926) who described the intellectual revolution in pre-partitioned Poland.[8] Poland was partitioned in a period of revival and the Warsaw school stressed the positive and constructive achievements, the essential virtues of the nation, rather than its past shortcomings.

Lwow also opposed Cracow's revisionism. Oswald Balzer presented a new evaluation of old Poland's constitutional structure upon which much "revisionist" criticism had been directed, while Ludwik Kubala (1838-1918) with his brilliant descriptions of Poland's heroic campaigns in the seventeenth century, inspired the historical novels of Henry Sienkiewicz. Most brilliant of all was Simon Askenazy, who demonstrated that the partitions had been the result of exterior factors.

The Warsaw-Lwow current of optimism developed until it reached its apogee in the First World War when it permeated even Cracow. In 1917 the Historical Society of Cracow organized a series of lectures which were published in 1918 as *Causes of the Fall of Poland, Lectures* (in Polish) wherein the pessimistic and optimistic viewpoints were synthesized.

The controversy stimulated scientific investigation, but in the process great syntheses were replaced by studies of specific problems. Recognition of this tendency occasioned lively debates in the Second (1890) and Third (1900) Historical Congresses between proponents of the particularistic and synthetic schools, but the particularistic viewpoint generally prevailed in the pre-1914 period. A Congress was to meet in Lwow in May, 1915, to re-examine the whole of Polish historiography, but the outbreak of war ended the first phase of Poland's historical science.

---

[4] In a pamphlet, *Stanczyk Portfolio* (in Polish), a symbolic name recalling a court fool of Sigismund I.
[5] Michael Bobrzynski, *Outlines of Polish History* (in Polish).
[6] Karol J. T. Estreicher, *Polish Bibliography* (in Polish, 24 vols.).
[7] Tadeusz Korzon, *Internal History of Poland in the Reign of Stanislas Augustus* (in Polish, 6 vols., 1887, 2nd edition).
[8] Wladyslaw Smolenski, *Intellectual Revolution in XVIIIth Century Poland* (in Polish).

Period of Independence, 1918-1939

Independence brought the problem of organizing educational facilities, with emphasis on training of teachers. Despite burdensome teaching duties, the learned societies and universities continued to encourage historical research. When new universities were founded, Cracow provided them with their first staffs. The Polish Academy of Cracow continued its monumental publications and Cracow scholars became the leaders of free Poland's historiography. But Warsaw, the new capital, also entered into the main stream of history-writing through its university and its National Library and Central Archives. The latter became one of the most important research centers in Europe. Lwow University continued as the eastern center of Research; Poznan University, founded in 1919, concentrated on Polish-German relations and on medieval history. When Lithuanian Wilno was annexed, its old university was restored; its historical studies emphasized Lithuania.

The studies and interests of pre-1918 historians were continued and expanded. The social and economic aspects of medieval Poland were studied by Karol Tymieniecki and Roman Grodecki, ecclesiastical relations with Rome and the ages of the early Piasts by Stanislaw Zakrzewski, medieval laws and institutions by Stanislaw Kutrezeba and Oswald Balzer, history of culture by Aleksander Bruckner, while the Later Middle Ages, including relations with Hungary, formed the theme of J. Dabrowski's researches. The Jagiellonian period and the Lithuanian federation were widely studied, especially by Antoni Prochaska, L. Kolankowski and Oskar Halecki. Waclaw Sobieski turned to the history of the Baltic, as did Leon Koczy, while Sladyslaw Konopczynski surveyed Poland's diplomatic relations with Sweden and Turkey and delved into internal constitutional problems. Marcel Handelsmann and Simon Askenazy continued to be known, even outside Poland, as outstanding scholars on the period of partitions and of Napoleon.

Polish Studies in Baltic History. A feature of postwar Polish historiography was the great interest in the newly-acquired outlet to the sea. Previously disorganized collections and records were catalogued and made available at Danzig, Torun, Elbing, and Frauenburg. Leading historians conducted studies of the area, *e.g.,* L. Kolankowski, W. Sobieski, K. Tymieniecki, S. Askenazy, S. Kutrezeba, K. Gorski and L. Koczy. Collective works were issued on special occasions and numerous periodicals were published by the leading cities in the region. To coordinate activity, the Baltic Institute in Bydgoszgz was founded in 1926 and it soon became an important center of research on the area. Its publication, *The Baltic and Scandinavian Countries,* in English, presented articles on the cultural and economic development of the Baltic and Scandinavian countries and peoples.

Military History. Another feature of postwar historiography was the attention to military history. In the previous period, Konstanty Gorski had conducted exhaustive studies into the organization of the infantry, artillery and cavalry, and Tadeusz Korzon had presented a comprehensive military history of the insurrections, but in the main lack of access to Warsaw and Moscow archives had proved a deterrent. After 1918, with the establishment of a national army, military historiography assumed a more organized status. The acknowledged authority was the editor of the monthly *Bellona*, Waclaw Tokarz whose *Armies of the Polish Kingdom* (in Polish, 1918) inaugurated a long series of military studies. Others followed, notably M. Kukiel, later director of the Historical Bureau of the General Staff and Otto Laskowski, who became editor of the *Historical-Military Review (Przeglad Historyczno-Wojskowy)*.

The National Struggle. To gather material on secret organizations which had fought for Polish independence prior to and during the war, the Institute into the Most Research in Poland was founded in 1923, and placed under the care of Polish Military Historical Bureau in 1926. Numerous records were amassed and a great number of works and memoirs were published.[9] In 1929 a quarterly *Independence (Niepodleglosc)* was founded to publish materials and studies on the 1863-1918 period. After Pilsudski's retirement from public life, the Institute was renamed in his honor and its work was divided into seven departments to cover the 1863-1935 period, with special emphasis on Pilsudski's activities.

Reference Works—Synthesis. Even while the specialized studies were being conducted, the Polish Academy recognized that the vast store of knowledge unearthed by over a half century of research should be synthesized. It took the lead by sponsoring first a two-volume composite *Polish Encyclopaedia* tracing the history up to 1775,[10] and then a greatly expanded Encyclopaedia in ten volumes to cover the entire Polish history. Meanwhile other handbooks were published, notably, *Poland, Her History and Her Culture,* wherein competent historians summarized the main results of recent research in three illustrated volumes.[11] The tendency toward synthesis also resulted in the preparation of a large historical atlas in connection with a new geographical dictionary and the initiation in 1935 of a dictionary of national biography, of which four volumes had appeared up to September, 1939.

Although Poland's historians generally probed their own nation's past, each university possessed scholars who delved into ancient and classical times or who studied the histories of other countries although this generation of Polish historians was immensely nationalistic. Great interest was always manifested in neighboring countries. J. Dabrowski devoted himself to the history of medieval Hungary, J. Grzegorzewski to the Balkans and F. Koneczny to Russia. Jan Kucharzewski, after a study of Russian rule in Poland, published an exhaustive study of Russia's evolution from Tsarism to Communism.[12]

Polish Historical Society. In the van of Polish historiography was the

---

[9] Most noteworthy being Joseph Pilsudski's *Writings, Speeches and Orders of the Day* (in Polish, 8 vols. and Supplements).
[10] *Polish Encyclopaedia* (in Polish). Vol. V, Polish History of Poland (in Polish, part 1), by S. Zakrzewski, S. Zachorowski, O. Halecki, J. Daborwski, S. Smolka and F. Papee; Part II, by O. Halecki, W. Sobieski, J. Krajewski and W. Konopczynski
[11] The trend toward synthesis is further noted in R. Grodecki, S. Zachorowski, and J. Dabrowski, *History of Medieval Poland* (in Polish, 2 vols.), and W. Konopczynski, *History of Modern Poland* (in Polish, 2 vols.).
[12] Jan Kucharzewski, *From White Tsardom to Red* (in Polish, 6 vols.). Three additional volumes were ready for publication in 1939 when the war broke out. A one-volume condensation was published as *Origins of Modern Russia.*

Polish Historical Society which had become a comprehensive federation of thirteen branches. It encouraged the tendency towards synthesis and interest in foreign history through cooperative work at home and abroad. National congresses were held every five years and proved useful for surveying past accomplishments and outlining future needs. The Congress of 1925 in Poznan concentrated on the history of western Poland, of 1930 in Warsaw on post-partition affairs, and of 1935 in Wilno on Polish-Lithuanian history. The Society also represented Poland in international congresses at Brussels (1923), Oslo (1928), Zurich (1928) and played host at Warsaw in 1933. Polish historians took the initiative in creating a federation of Historical Societies of Eastern Europe in 1927 and played an important role in the congresses of Baltic historians.

Polish Academy. The Polish Academy maintained research activities in Paris, where main interest centered on modern and contemporary events, and in Rome, where the Vatican archives were explored and the results published in the *Monumenta Poloniae Vaticana.* Meetings of Polish and British historians took place in Warsaw and Cambridge which resulted in the preparation of a two-volume history of Poland.[13] Closer relations were also established with Esthonian, Lithuanian, Hungarian, Czecho-Slovak and Ukrainian historians and by 1939 Polish historians were an influential group in European historical circles.

1939—PRESENT

The extensive work of Polish historiography came to an abrupt end with the German attack in 1939. Imprisonment, death, flight or underground activity was the fate of leaders of thought and culture. Such famous historians as Bruckner, Dembinski, Handelsmann, Kochanowski, Kutrzeba, Rutkowski, Siemienski, Zakrzewski and Zielinski died during the occupation. Material losses were also great. Archives, libraries, museums and art treasures were deliberately plundered, burned or carried away. Universities and high schools were closed and historical instruction was banned from public schools. Teaching continued but underground, clandestine research meetings were held and research activity was carried on secretly by scholars.

Halecki. To continue research and studies outside of Poland the Polish University in Exile was established in Paris. The fall of France caused further emigration of scholars to England, Scotland and the United States. In New York, the Polish Institute of Arts and Sciences was founded to continue the cultural activity of the Polish Academy. The career of its director, Oskar Halecki, well illustrates the three phases of Polish historiography in the twentieth century. Born in Vienna in 1891 he began his research and teaching at the University of Cracow in partitioned Poland. His original interests tended towards the later Middle Ages and his two-volume study on Jagiellonian Poland is very important.[14] In independent Poland, Halecki became professor of Eastern European history at the University of Warsaw and a

[13] Volume II, entitled, *Cambridge History of Poland, 1697-1935*, edited by W. F. Reddaway, J. H. Penson, O. Halecki and R. Dyboski, appeared first. This is by far the best history in English on the modern period in Poland.
[14] Oskar Halecki, *History of the Lithuanian Union* (in Polish, 2 vols.).

member of the Polish delegation to the League of Nations. His interest in the medieval period was again evidenced by his *Rome et Byzanc au temps due grand schisme d'Occident* (1937) and *Crusade of Varna* (New York, 1943). Forced to flee from Poland in 1939, Halecki became a member of the Sorbonne faculty and president of the University in Exile. In 1940 he joined the faculty of Vassar College and in 1944 accepted the chair of Eastern European History at Fordham University. His *History of Poland,* published in French, has been translated into English and several editions have appeared. In 1949 appeared his *The Limits and Divisions of European History.* Universally recognized as an outstanding scholar on Polish and Eastern European history, he has contributed to journals, periodicals and collective works.

Most publications by exiled Polish historians during the war years were of a semi-propaganda nature, to explain Poland's position on the "Polish Corridor" and to refute Russian claims in the East. Many works were also written on conditions under German occupation, one of the best being Jan Karski's *Story of a Secret State* (Boston, 1944).

The Cracow Thesis Revived. The catastrophe of 1939 revived the "revisionist" viewpoint, sponsored by Olgierd Gorka, who had first enunciated his opinions in a paper "Optimism and Pessimism in Polish Historiography—An Inversion of Ideas" at the 1935 National Congress. The events of 1939, more disastrous than those of 1863 which had prompted Szujski's and Bobrzynski's challenge, evoked a new demand by Gorka (in the London-published *New Poland)* for a total revision of the interpretation of Polish history and received support from the foremost English historian of Poland, William J. Rose.[15] Emulating Bobrzynski, Gorka blamed the catastrophe of 1939 upon the Poles themselves. Those responsible for national life and independence had lived in an atmosphere of complacent optimism, almost in a fool's paradise, but the writers and teachers of history had done virtually nothing to warn them because the realist Cracow historians had been superseded by the revived Romanticism of Askenazy, Balzer and others. In answer, Halecki defended the work and interpretations of Polish historians as being based on truly and honestly conducted research.[16]

Soviet Domination. The end of the war in 1945 saw Poland reconstituted as a national entity, but her eastern lands had been annexed by Soviet Russia, her western frontiers had been extended to include Silesia, half of eastern Prussia and most of Pomerania, her government was Communist-dominated and the country itself was a satellite in the Soviet orbit. These changed conditions were bound to affect postwar historiography and although it is as yet too early to posit definite opinions concerning their full impact, a few definite tendencies are apparent.

Activities After 1945. The first task undertaken by historians was the revival of pre-1939 periodicals and projects. Led by the Polish Historical Society's *Historical Quarterly,* various local historical associations revived their pre-war

---

[15] William J. Rose, "Realism in Polish History," *Journal of Central European Affairs,* II (October, 1942).
[16] Oskar Halecki, "What Is Realism in Polish History?", *Ibid.,* III (October, 1943).

journals. The initial articles for the most part surveyed the tasks that lay ahead, evaluated existing facilities, described the condition of archives, museums and libraries, contained obituaries of scholars and discussed various plans of reorganization. More space has been devoted to critical reviews of Polish and foreign literature and less to original contributions than in the prewar period.

Large prewar projects have also been assumed. The Polish Academy is continuing the *Biographical Dictionary of Poland (Polski Slownik Biograficzny)* which had reached the letter "D" by 1939. The *Bibliography of Polish History after 1815 (Bibliografia Historii Polski)*, Finkel's monumental work, has also been resumed. Aleksander Bruckner's *History of Polish Culture* received its fourth volume in 1946, seven years after the author's death.

Postwar Publications. A survey of postwar publications reveals the absence of great syntheses and the predominance of painstakingly written monographs, a throwback to pre-1914 times. The historians concentrate on their own national past, showing little interest in universal or foreign history. The Slav idea is strongly emphasized. A great number of studies have been devoted to the recovered lands in the west and special attention is drawn to Polish-German relations in the past. More work is being done on eastern Poland and Russia as scholars try to account for Poland's frontiers and her changed internal structure on historical grounds. The great economic and social changes since 1945 have produced new evaluations of social and economic history, although no predominance of Marxian historical conceptions is noted.

In number, most books deal with Polish-German relations. Typical are Zygmunt Wojciechowski's contributions wherein he defends through historical arguments the changed boundaries and geopolitical position of the "new Poland."[17] Joseph Feldman, who died shortly after the war, also studied Polish-German history and tried to determine the reasons which caused the hatred to flare up time and again between the two countries. A third noteworthy contributor is Marian Friedberg, who has studied the German influence on Polish culture and constitution.[18] The lands regained from the Germans have been studied by Kazimierz Piwarski and Wladyslaw Konopczynski. Medieval history, as an extension of Polish-German relations, bulks large in postwar historiography and every age of medieval times has come under scrutiny, with the exception of the Jagiellonian period, which was marked in its foreign policy by opposition to Moscow and in home affairs by the predominance of the magnates.

The modern period of Polish history has received less coverage than the medieval, but Henryk Wereszycki has written on political affairs and Witold Kula on economic events. The year 1948 inspired historical works devoted to the hundredth anniversary of the "Springtime of Nations," particularly on

[17] Much of Zygmunt Wojciechowski's work was completed during the war, while he was actively participating in underground activities. Since 1945 he has published four books, *Poland-Germany* (in Polish); a volume of essays, *Prussian Vassalage* (in Polish); *Zygmunt the Old* (in Polish); and with Maria Wojciechowska, *Poland of the Piasts, Poland of the Jagiellons* (in Polish). He is also the founder and director of the Western Institute and editor of its publications.

[18] Marian Friedberg, *Polish and German Culture* (in Polish, 2 vols.).

Polish affairs at that time.[19] In September 1948, the first postwar Congress of Polish historians met in Wroclaw (Breslau). In the same year, the Polish Academy celebrated its seventy-fifth anniversary by editing the *Chronicle of Gallus* from the most valuable codex. Currently pre-historians and archaeologists are engaged in a vast problem of research in preparation for the Polish "millenium" which will take place in the early 1960's.

Outside of Poland, historians pursue their researches and contribute to scholarly publications. Halecki's and Kucharzewski's contributions have already been mentioned. Waclaw Lednicki, authority on Polish literature, wrote *Life and Culture of Poland as Reflected in Polish Literature* (1943), while an attempt to synthesize Polish history resulted in a collective work, *Poland* (1945), edited by Bernadotte Schmitt for the United Nations Series. In the field of historiography can also be included the memoirs and accounts of former diplomats and statesmen. Jan Ciechanowski, wartime ambassador to the United States, has summarized the diplomatic relations of these years in *Defeat in Victory* (1947) and the United States Ambassador to Poland presented his postwar impressions in *I Saw Poland Betrayed* (1947). Wartime premier, Stanislaw Mikolajczyk, who returned as vice-premier in the Provisional Government only to flee after two years, issued *Rape of Poland, Pattern of Soviet Aggression* (1948). Wladyslaw Anders, commander of the Polish Army in the Italian campaign, wrote *An Army in Exile* (1949). The plight of the people under the Communist regime has evoked a number of books, the outstanding one being the anonymous *Dark Side of the Moon*.

THE BALTIC COUNTRIES

Although the same threefold chronological division might be followed for each of the three Baltic countries, actually historiographical tendencies in Lithuania, Latvia and Esthonia center in the period of independence. Prior to 1918 Baltic history was mainly the preoccupation of German historians, supplemented by Russian, Swedish, Danish and Polish scholars. German interest centered on the Hanseatic League and the cultural influence of German settlers on the eastern Baltic coast, while the Danish, Swedish, Russian and Polish historians occupied themselves with their nations' struggle for hegemony in the region.

Research into Baltic history was accelerated by the foundation of learned societies which published reviews on the subject.[20] Main emphasis was on large-scale publication of documents and sources.[21] Friedrich Georg von Bunge planned a great collection of historical documents on Livonia, Esthonia and Courland,[22] and also collaborated with Baron von Toll on a collection of

---

[19] A collective work, *The Year 1848 in Poland* (in Polish), edited by Natalia Gasiorowska, was issued in commemoration.

[20] Beginning with the *Kurlandische Gesellschaft fur Litteratur und Kunst* in 1817, other societies came into existence, emphasizing research and producing important material for future historians. Noteworthy periodicals were *Inland* (1836-1863) and *Baltische Monatsschrift*.

[21] *Monumenta Livoniae Antiquae* (5 vols.); *Scriptores rerum Livonicarum* (2 vols.).

[22] Friedrich Georg von Bunge, *Liv-Est-und Kurlandisches Urkundenbuch*. The first series, up to 1472, appeared in 12 volumes, but the second series (to 1570) was interrupted by the war in 1914 after three volumes had been published.

materials on the lands and the nobility of Esthonia and Livonia. Eduard Winkelmann also catalogued the sources and studies of the Livonian region.[23]

Interest in the Baltic region also produced interpretative studies, mainly in German. The outstanding worker in pre-1914 historiography was Karl Schirren (d. 1910), who, during a long career in St. Petersburg, Dorpat and Kiel, turned out numerous collections, articles and books, based on research in the most important archives of Europe. His student, Richard Hausmann, who followed him at Dorpat (Tartu) similarly based his studies on critical investigation of sources and gave a great impetus to the field of archaeology. The best presentation of Baltic history was Theodore Schiemann's *Russland, Polen und Livland bis ins XVII Jahrhundert* (2 volumes, Berlin, 1886-1887). Contemporary with Schiemann was Hermann von Bruiningk who concentrated on Livonian medieval history and edited numerous archival publications.

By 1914 the preliminary steps, in the form of monographs and large collections of documents and sources, had been taken. But political history far outweighed economic and social history and many *lacunae* still appeared in the historiography of particular regions. When three new states appeared on the eastern Baltic in 1918, the historians of each inaugurated the task of separating their own national background from that of the other Baltic people.

LITHUANIA

Historical literature in the Lithuanian language goes back to the early nineteenth century, but its progress was handicapped by Polish cultural influences, the absence of an educated Lithuanian class and an intensive policy of russification. Whereas scientific works were published either in Polish or in Russian, historical studies were written in Lithuanian by patriots and nationalists for political purposes. One of these amateur historians, but an eminent patriot, was Simanas Daukantas (1793-1864). Of little scientific value today, his works testify to the stupendous efforts then made to create a historical literature in the national language. Much superior as an historian was Maciej Kazimierz Wolonczeskis, better known as Valancius (1810-1875), a Polish bishop of Samogitia and an ardent opponent of russification. Besides numerous works on religion, ethics and other subjects, he wrote the *Bishopric of Samogitia* (in Lithuanian, 1848), which contained valuable material from episcopal, parochial and school records.

Progress after 1905. The political changes in 1905, which terminated the policy of russification, inaugurated a new scientific and literary movement in Lithuania. At Wilno, which became the center of the movement, was founded (1907) the Lithuanian Scientific Society to foster study of the language, folklore and history. The founder, Jonas Basanavicius (1851-1927), the father of the Lithuanian renaissance, also became editor of the Society's publication *The Lithuanian People* wherein were published studies in many fields, including products of historical research. Although many articles continued to be written by amateurs, the pages of the review saw the initial products of many men who were to become leaders of Lithuanian's historiography. In the war period,

---

[23] Eduard Winkelmann, *Bibliotheca Livoniae historica.*

1914-1918, the Scientific Society popularized the historical foundations of the nation through popular presentations and text books, including histories of Lithuania by M. Birziska and A. Alekna.

Independence and History's National Task. The birth of the modern Lithuanian state in 1918 was a natural turning-point in historical science. The amateur-historian gave way to the specialist. As Lithuania's political aspirations and the very basis of its existence rested on historical claims, the state fostered the establishment of research centers and publications and generally supported the work of historians. Further to coordinate and inspire academic and scientific effort, the government founded the Kaunas University in 1922 (rechristened Vytautas the Great University in 1930) which became the hub of historical research. Leading historians were appointed to chairs of history on the various faculties. In addition to their teaching duties, the professors pursued individual researches and published their results in university periodicals (each faculty published its own) or in other learned journals.

Societies and Journals. Another center was the Historical Society of Lithuania, founded in May, 1927. Its executive board included some of the leading historians in the country, A. Janulaitis, I. Jonynas, K. Jablonskis and P. Tarasenka. In 1928 the Society inaugurated a periodical *The Past (Pruetis)* edited by A. Janulaitis, which printed articles, source material, reports, reviews and bibliography. In 1933 a supplement, *Praeities Biblioteka,* was added to published historical works.

Archives. With the support of the state, archival materials were collected and unified. The Archdiocesan Archives, the oldest, contained episcopal, diocesan and ecclesiastical correspondence and records; the State Central Archives collected documents and records from the German and Russian periods, also archives of noble families and records of public offices; the Chief Notarial Archives gathered notarial deeds, court files and municipal records. Leading libraries also contained valuable materials for the historian.

The historians used these materials to probe into the national past— the main theme of free Lithuania's historiography. They distrusted the work of earlier non-Lithuanian scholars and projected a complete reexamination of the same materials so that all the problems of the nation's past could be elaborated independently of former studies. No startling new facts were brought to light, but different interpretations of source materials, regrouping of facts and new viewpoints did result.

Predominance of Medieval Studies. Most attention was concentrated on the period of complete independence, up to the union with Poland in 1385. Basanavicius and the great philologist, K. Buga, investigated the origins of the nation and its early relations with neighboring peoples. Here Lithuanian writers have attempted to refute Russian and German conclusions about the original settlers in the Baltic region. The first Lithuanian king, Mindaugas (1219-1263), was studied by J. Totoraitis, his victories over the Knights of the Sword of Livonia were examined by P. Zugiedelis and Z. Ivinskis, and his relations with western Europe by J. Stakauskas and K. A. Steponaitis. The hero of the struggle against the Teutonic Knights, Kiejstut, was the subject of numerous works, and the 550th anniversary of his death in 1932 inspired commemorative studies by J. Jonynas, A. Kucinskas, P. Slezas and A. Janulaitis.

But the greatest outpouring of historical essays, studies and books, to which every noted historian in the country contributed, marked the 500th anniversary of the great Lithuanian hero, Vytautas (Witold) the Great (1401-1430) .[24] Adulation for Vytautas led originally to a condemnation of his cousin Jagiello, king of Poland, but scientific investigation, led by Z. Ivinskis, reversed this viewpoint.[25]

Medieval Lithuania. Social and economic conditions in medieval Lithuania have been probed, especially by Z. Ivinskis, and M. Krasauskaite, who traced the genesis of the boyar class, and by J. Remeika, A. Pinka, and Z. Ivinskis who studied commercial relations with neighboring countries. Examination into the past made obligatory the study of auxiliary sciences, such as archaeology, heraldry, diplomatics and historical geography, which received attention in the university.

Modern History. The modern period has received less attention than the medieval and most works are short studies. Lithuania's final fusion with Poland was discussed by A. Sapoka, J. Zmujdzinas and J. Lappo, but the latter's work was colored by a bitter anti-Polish feeling. The insurrection of 1830 received treatment by A. Ruzancovas, P. Purenas, P. Slezas and A. Janulaitis, and the insurrection of 1863 by S. Matulaitis and P. Ruseckas. The period of russification was examined by P. Slezas in a monograph on the cruel administration of Russian Governor-General Muravieff, while others considered the various methods at russification. The National revival, the independence movement, the war and the early years of national existence formed the basis for many studies.

In addition to political history, studies on law, jurisprudence, and social and economic developments were also pursued. The chief contributor was A. Janulaitis, whose interests surveyed the Lithuanian tribunal of the sixteenth and seventeenth centuries, the history of the Jews from the sixteenth to the nineteenth centuries, the plans for the abolition of serfdom in the 1817-1819 period, and the rise of the nobility and the gentry in the 1795-1863 era. Histories of cities and towns were also compiled, with the capital city of Kaunas, because of its complete archives, receiving the most attention. A series on the larger cities was edited by J. Balkakevicius. The history of the Church, of the Protestant movement, of education and of schools is also well represented in historical writings.

Special studies marked the general trend of Lithuanian historiography. Until the middle of the 1930's there were only a few treatments of Lithuania as a whole, and of these, few were of high calibre. Recognizing the need, the Ministry of Education initiated a composite work, *History of Lithuania* (in

---

[24] A collective work *Life of Vytautas 1350-1430* (in Lithuanian), dealt with every aspect of Vytautas' reign. *Praetis* carried articles dedicated to the domestic and military achievements of the ruler, but probably the best monograph came from the pen of a German, Josef Pfitzner, *Grossfürst Witold von Litauen als Staatsmann.*
[25] The collective work *Jogailo* (in Lithuanian) represented the newer tendency.

Lithuanian, Kaunas, 1936) under the editorship of A. Sapoka, which covered the entire national history.

Soviet Control. As in Poland so in Soviet-annexed Lithuania a policy of cultural repression was followed. Underground activity, directed by the Supreme Lithuanian Committee of Liberation, appealed for world support, while in the United States the Lithuanian American Information Centre demonstrated the nation's historic claim to statehood by articles, pamphlets, brochures and books. But the end of the war, instead of bringing liberation, ushered in a renewed policy of russification. Since 1945 cultural activity has been carried on outside the country and several histories, mainly in English, have appeared.[26]

LATVIA

As in Lithuania, so in Latvia, history was considered to be an invaluable aid to the new state. The government, therefore, sponsored an intensive program of stirring up national pride by a rebirth of national culture. To foster an attachment to the national past, exhaustive studies were inaugurated and methodically conducted, relics were carefully collected and early cemeteries and ancient settlements excavated.

Preparatory work had been done by the few nineteenth century historians who attempted to apply the new western European research methods to their own studies. Thus, not only historical documents, but also folklore, inscriptions, archaeological excavations, old coins and similar materials were accepted as sources of history. The first Latvian historian of the nineteenth century was J. Krueger-Krodznieks (1854-1924), who not only wrote many essays on Latvian history, but also encouraged the collection of folksongs, legends, tales and riddles, local history and translation of all foreign works on Latvia, which were to prove of great value to later historians, philologists and ethnographers. Archaeological research was carried on, but since the findings had to be kept secret from Tsarist authorities, the work could not be systematized. Some coordination resulted from the founding of the Scientific Committee of the Latvian Social Society of Riga, but history still was studied by a relatively few workers who devoted themselves almost exclusively to ethnology and folklore. Prior to 1919, due to political and social conditions, scientific institutions and large scale research work were lacking.

Period of Independence. Independence brought systematization and organization of previously conducted labors. A Latvian State University was founded in 1919 and historical, archaeological, ethnographical departments were established, together with archives to collect and preserve materials from the past. Emphasis on archaeological research was prompted largely by the lack of published source material, for centuries of continuous warfare and devastation had destroyed much material on early history. Few original sources remained

---

[26] Thomas G. Chase, *The Story of Lithuania;* Constantine R. Jurgela, *History of the Lithuanian Nation;* Kazya Gecys, *Catholic Lithuania* (in Lithuanian) ; Owen J. C. Norem, *Timeless Lithuania;* A. Sapoka, *Lithuania Through the Ages;* T. J. Vizgurda, *Vilnius, The Capital of Lithuania;* E. J. Harrison, *Lithuania's Fight for Freedom;* F. W. Pick's *The Baltic Nations, La Tragedie des Nations Baltiques.*

and even these had not been systematically collected. To compensate for these losses archaeologists attempted to uncover other records of the past.

Balodis. Outstanding in this field was F. Balodis, director of the Latvian Historical Museum, founder and most competent interpreter of the modern Latvian school of archaeology. His systematic explorations enabled him to unearth convincing proof of an ancient, specifically Latvian culture. Using archaeological findings, plus chronicles, runes and treatises, Balodis reconstructed Lettish life from the ninth to the twelfth century.[27]

Balodis' work was continued by A. Svabe who wrote on the thirteenth century and traced the history of Riga from its origins. Like other students of Riga's history, P. Abers, A. Tentelis and I. Straubergs, Svabe described the role of the autochthonous Livonian population and furnished support to the rights of the Latvians to their own soil.

Historical Institute. It was recognized that there was need for an institute which could coordinate and aid in the scientific exploration of Latvian history, especially in unearthing, collecting and publishing the scarce documents and source materials. Sponsored by the Ministry of Education, the Latvian Historical Institute held its first public session on May 11, 1936, at which time the Minister of Education, A. Tentelis, outlined the tendencies of Latvian historiography. The Germans, who had been the principal research workers on the Latvian past, had aimed specifically at demonstrating German historical and cultural rights to Latvian soil. It was time, therefore, for the history of Latvia to be studied by the Latvians and for the relevant source materials to be re-examined and reported upon in the true spirit of historical investigation. The government-subsidized Institute was divided into three sections: one for the study of Latvian pre-history to the thirteenth century, second, up to the middle of the nineteenth century, and a third, for the study of recent history. A fourth section was envisaged, devoted to the study of world history.

Source Publications. The results of historical and archaeological researches by the Institute members were published in a quarterly, *Journal of the Latvian Historical Institute* (in Latvian), founded in 1937. A series of historical documents, *Les sources de l'histoire de Lettonie,* was also published by the Institute, consisting mainly of excerpts from archives in various European capitals. As enunciated by Tentelis, the purpose of this material was to throw light on Latvian history, which had formerly been represented as the history of a German colony and had ignored the Latvians as a nation. The same motives impelled historians to study the international position of their country and to visit foreign archives in order to trace the political and economic relations of the Baltic States with Sweden, England, Spain, France, Germany and the Netherlands. The conclusions drawn were that Livonia had always been in contact with western Europe and that its history was actually a part of western European history. The climax of Latvian historiographical progress came in August, 1937, when some three hundred historians from twelve countries met at Riga to launch the first congress of Baltic historians.

---

[27] F. Balodis, *La Lettonie du 9-me au 12-me siècle,* Det Aldsta Lettland, and in numerous essays and monographs.

The emphasis upon proving Latvia's rights to her land and the collecting of source materials did not allow much time or opportunity for great syntheses or for studying the histories of foreign countries. The outbreak of war in 1939 and subsequent annexation ended the fruitful progress of Latvian historiography. Some work has been accomplished by historians in exile, especially by Alfred Bilmanis, to keep alive the name of the nation, but Latvian output has lagged behind that of the other Baltic nations.

ESTHONIA

Nationalist Beginnings. The objectives of the Esthonian historians paralleled those in neighboring countries, namely, to controvert the historical judgments of the Baltic German school of historians. Prior to 1918, the German historians had probed deeply into Baltic affairs, methodically collecting source material on the eastern Baltic. As a result much source material was at hand when the historians of the reborn state undertook their research, giving them an advantage over their Latvian colleagues.

In addition to German workers, some native historians had begun to study their nation's past during the period of national revival toward the end of the nineteenth century. Outstanding was Villein Reiman (d. 1917) who examined various problems of the nation's existence through the use of western methods. His *History of Esthonia* (in Esthonian) was the first critical evaluation of Esthonian history. M. Kampmann in *The Principal Features of Esthonian Literature* (in Esthonian) traced the development of Esthonian literature from the appearance of the first book. Martin Lipp contributed a history of the Church and of native culture plus a genealogical study of a leading Esthonian princely family.

State Support of Historiography. With independence came state support for the development of historical knowledge. In 1919 the old University of Dorpat was reestablished as Tartu University and immediately became the main research center. Historical studies were organized by Arno Raphael Cederberg, who was invited from Helsinki to accept a chair at the restored university. A good organizer, Cederberg sponsored research into the state archives and his seminars afforded an opportunity for young historians to learn the techniques and methods of research, not only in Esthonian history, but also Baltic and Scandinavian history.

Periodicals and Reference Works. Archives, museums, educational and literary societies acquired and encouraged collection of materials in order to facilitate research activity. The University sponsored the establishment of the Academical Historical Society in 1920 with Cederberg as first president. The Society published a historical quarterly, two series of archive materials and in 1923 initiated a biographical dictionary to which prominent historians contributed. The last of four sections appeared in 1929, but supplements continued to be issued. The first edition of a "Who's Who" appeared in 1933, followed by a second edition in 1937. Another large work of synthesis was the *Esthonian Encyclopaedia,* published in eight volumes in Tartu.

Esthonian historians were in a better position than their Baltic colleagues to synthesize the vast store of knowledge almost from the beginning, for the preliminary work of collection had been done for them. All historical works and articles published from 1877 to 1917 were gathered together and listed in *Bibliotheca Estoniae Historica* (1933), edited by E. Blumfeldt and T. Loone. The work was supplemented by the *Esthonian Philological and Historical Annual Review* (in Esthonian) which listed all books, journals, writings and criticisms published from 1918 to 1923 and again from 1929 to 1930. The collection and publishing of documents and source materials, begun in the previous century by the German Baltic historians, were now continued on a much larger scale, especially by the National Central Archives.

The subject material of Esthonian historiography was, as in the other Baltic countries, concerned with the national past. This included archaeological studies to probe Esthonian national life and culture prior to the impact of German culture (M. Tallgren, H. Moor, R. Indren and M. Schmiedehalm) ; topographical and ethnographical researches (R. Kenkman and J. Ulvots) and an agrarian history of the country (J. Ulvots). Successive domination by Denmark, Sweden and Russia has been examined, but most interest centered on the Swedish phase. Paul Johansen concentrated on the late medieval period, J. Vasar on the seventeenth century and H. Seppe on Baltic military affairs during the Great Northern War. The economic and cultural aspects of Swedish domination found its historians in Otto Liiv. Interest in the Swedish period prompted the formation of the Swedish-Esthonian Academical Society in Tartu, with a journal *Svio-Estonica*. In 1929 a collective work in Swedish and Esthonian languages was issued to synthesize the contributions and influences of the Swedish period. The eighteenth century received less exploration, but the nineteenth occasioned great interest.[28]

By 1939 the horizon of Esthonian historiography was widening. Two years earlier a joint Polish-Esthonian Historical Congress gathered in Tartu to outline the practical measures needed to stimulate inter-change of information. Although the majority of studies was still concerned with the political, social, economic and legal problems of the nation's past, work of synthesis was progressing. The Esthonian Literary Society issued the *History of Lithuania* (in Esthonian, 1935) and a composite work, *History of the Esthonian Nation* (in Esthonian) was appearing in sections until 1939.

Russian-German occupation ended Esthonian research; teaching and learning for the professors and scholars suffered the same fate as their neighbors. Since 1939 very few books on Esthonian history have appeared. In 1941 J. Hampden Jackson's *Esthonia* was published, followed by Jack Survel's *Estonia Today* in 1947. F. W. Pick's *The Baltic Nations* (1945) and A. Oras' *Baltic Eclipse* (1948) included the story of Esthonia. The Baltic Humanitarian Association in Stockholm, Sweden, has published a number of pamphlets and periodicals, such as the *Baltic Review* and *Newsletter from behind the Iron Curtain,* which contain material on Esthonia and the other Baltic countries.

---

[28] The main points were covered by H. Kruus in *New and Most Recent History of Esthonia* (in Esthonian).

to synthesize the vast store of knowledge about from the beginning, for the preliminary work of collection had been done for them. All historical works and articles published from 1877 to 1917 were gathered together and listed in the then-known resource Horonze (1935) carried on E. Blumfield and I. Loose. The work was supplemented by the Estonian bibliography, and all serial Annual Research Bibliography which list all books, journals, writings and publications published from 1918 to 1922 and again from 1929 to 1930. The collection and publishing of documents and source-materials begun in the previous century by the German Baltic historians were now continued on a much larger scale, especially by the Lettland Central Archives.

The subject material of historical historiography covers, as in the others Baltic countries concerned with the general period, included archaeological studies to probe Estonian national life, and cultural periods the history of German culture (M. Vellgren, H. Moor, R. Indexina and H. Stenndelmann); topographical and ethnographical researches (A. Bielman and J. Olivers) and agrarian historography the country (J. Libots). Successive domination by Denmark, Sweden and Russia has been examined, but most interest centered on the Swedish phase. Paul Johansen concentrated on the late medieval period; J. Vasar on the seventeenth century; and J. Asped on Baltic military affairs during the Great Northern War. Various economic and cultural aspects of Swedish domination found its fullest result (h.). For historians in the Swedish period produced the formation of the Swedish historical Academical Society of Tartu who assisted Estonian work in historical studies work in Swedish and Estonian languages was taken to elucidate the topographics, and the numbers of the Swedish period which consequently require a great deal of exertion for the interpretation of sources and other assessment.

By 1940 the horizon of historical interpretation was widening. Two years earlier a joint Estonian-German Historical Congress gathered in Tartu to outline the practical bases needed in a sufficient exchange of information. Although the majority of writers dealt mainly with the political social, economic and legal problems of the nation, a great work of critical was progressing. The Estonian Literary Society carried the History of Estonia (in Estonian, 1932), and a companion work, History of Estonian Literature (in Estonian), was appearing in section until 1940.

Russian Estonian occupation ended both main research, teaching and learning for the past some time in their country although remnants of their condition. Since 1939 very few works on Estonian history have appeared. In 1941 J. Hampden Jackson's Estonia was published, followed by Jack Suvella's Estonia (1941), in 1944, K. W. Pääts, The Baltic States (1945), and A. Oras, Baltic Eclipse (1948). Included the story of Estonia. The Baltic Humanitarian Association in Stockholm, Sweden, has published a number of pamphlets and periodicals, such as the Baltic Review, and Acta Baltica. Noteworthy has been Caraat, which contain material on Estonia and the other Baltic countries.

Chapter 22

CZECHOSLOVAKIA

By Joseph S. Roucek

WESTERNMOST outpost of the Slavic world in Central-Eastern Europe, Czechoslovakia has always been a tiny island, almost entirely surrounded by a threatening German (and now-Russian) sea. Time and again, the mountain ranges of Czechoslovakia's borders acted as breakwaters against enemy pressure. Since the Czechs live in the very centre of the German *Lebensraum* of the late Hitler, and today are an important link in Soviet Russia's bloc of states behind the Iron Curtain, Czech history is a history of constant wars against the Germans and other invaders. Since the Czechoslovaks view their history in terms of centuries, there has not been a single century without their need to fight, either with sword or spirit, against foreign aggression. Frequently, and temporarily, the Czechs have lost. But, up to now, no invader, whether German or Austrian or Turkish or Russian, has succeeded in enslaving the country for good, thanks to the profound sense of Czech and Slovak nationalism.

In their efforts to survive, the Czechoslovak people have been able to present important cultural arguments (their main national ideology in modern times) to the world on their behalf. Long before Leipzig and Heidelberg became world famous university centers, and at a time when there were, in the whole of Europe, only four universities (Bologna, Avignon, Paris and Oxford), the "Alma Pater Pragensis" was founded by King Charles IV of Bohemia in 1348 with this significant dedication: ". . . that this Kingdom of Bohemia should abound in learned men as much as in worldly riches; that the faithful subjects of this Kingdom who ever hunger for the fruits of beautiful arts should not in foreign lands beg for alms, but that they themselves should always have a table set for all; that they should not be forced to seek enlightenment in foreign parts of the world, but themselves enjoy the honor of inviting others to participate in such happiness."[1]

That education and learning have always been good foundations of the Czech national life is demonstrated by the fact that the first printed novel in Czech, a popular version of the history of the Trojan war, came out a full quarter of a century ahead of the day Columbus made his first landing in the Bahamas. The famous Sorbonne Press was two years the junior of her Bohemian sisters, and in the British Isles they had still eight years to go without printed books.

The Czechs had had no history of their own (in the ideology of modern

---

[1] Translation in F. G. Weiskopf, *Hundred Towers, A Czechoslovak Anthology,* p. x.

Czech nationalism) ; their historical writing had been only a history of their princes and kings. But when Charles IV founded the Charles University, he made Prague a centre of European civilization, upon which the greatest glory was bestowed by Magister John Hus, both as Rector and as a popular preacher in the Czech language. He was the first Protestant religious reformer of Central Europe (preceding Luther by a century). But the fortunes of history eventually led to the destruction of the Czech state and of Czech Protestantism. In the Battle of the White Mountain (near Prague) in 1620, the freedom of the Czech people and the very life of its letters were to be buried for the next three centuries. "Extirpate that entire unholy and rebellious Czech nation," was the advice of the Spanish ambassador at the Court of Vienna after the news of the victorious battle reached the jubilant Habsburg capital. The advice was followed. A reign of terror was inaugurated; the leaders and nobility were killed. The Bohemian (Moravian) Brethren, the spiritual flower of the nation, were driven into exile. The schools were Latinized or Germanized. Father Konisch, S.J., a special envoy from the Imperial Court of Vienna, in anticipation of Dr. Goebbels' system, burned more than 60,000 books at the stake. At the time of Jonathan Swift and Voltaire, the children of the Czech nation did not even possess a primer to learn how to spell the words of their mother tongue. Only in the inarticulate talk of the half-slave peasants, only in their bitter songs did the native language and literature survive, at home. But abroad, the cultural reputation of the Czech people continued to live thanks to the world-famous reputation of John Amos Comenius (Komenský), exiled from his native Bohemia in 1621; this last bishop of the Moravian Brethren was invited to become president of Harvard University; his name in the history of education is recorded among the great ones in that field of human thinking and endeavor.

The bugles of the French Revolution and the clatter of the first industrial mills in Bohemia-Moravia aroused Czech national and cultural life from their deathlike sleep of centuries. The Czech and Slovak nationalist rebirth was under way in the nineteenth century. But the Czechs were more favored by the course of history, as they had more contacts with the Western world than the Slovaks, whose culture, for one thousand years, had been throttled by the Magyars and whose thousand years of history culminated in this modern era in cultural vacuity and political enslavement.

At any rate, under the spiritual leadership of a famed Czech teacher, philosopher and sociologist, Professor Thomas G. Masaryk, the Czech people eventually revolted against the domination over them by the Austro-Hungarian Monarchy, and formed a free, democratic and republican state in 1918.[2]

During the thirty-five years of Czechoslovakia's contemporary history, her ups and downs have reflected the hopes and disappointments of the world as a whole. Created in 1918, amid the optimism which most of mankind felt at the close of World War I, until then the country had been part of the Austro-Hungarian Empire. Established under the leadership of Dr. Masaryk

[2] For more detailed information on all the figures and topics discussed in this chapter, see Joseph S. Roucek, Ed., *Slavonic Encyclopaedia.*

and Dr. Eduard Beneš, another professor, and with the encouragement of the American President Woodrow Wilson, Czechoslovakia, imitating almost in their entirety the American concepts of democracy, set up a democratic government. It was a comparatively prosperous and progressive nation, and aimed to gear its nationalistic ideology with the Western concepts or liberalism and internationalism.

During the 1930's, when Hitler started the aggressive policies that eventually plunged Europe into war, Czechoslovakia was one of his early victims. Hitler demanded, in 1938, a fringe of Czechoslovakia's territory known as the "Sudeten region," which had never been part of Germany. At the famous Munich Conference of September, 1938, France and Britain agreed to stand aside and let Hitler seize that area.

This victory merely whetted Hitler's appetite. Within a short time Nazi Germany had absorbed nearly all of Czechoslovakia; Poland and Hungary took the rest. Soon Europe was engulfed in World War II. At the close of this conflict, Czechoslovakia was liberated by Russian and American troops. President Beneš came back from exile, and from 1945 to 1948 tried to revive a democratic government again. But communist influence, already strong in Czechoslovakia after World War I, served the Kremlin as the "fifth column" among the supporters of Beneš. The course of events in 1948 and the evidence that the Communists were losing their hold in Czechoslovakia led to the *coup d'état;* Beneš resigned (dying soon afterwards) ; Jan Masaryk, a son of the legendary Thomas G. Masaryk, anti-communist states-man and internationally famous as a diplomat, plunged to his death—apparently committing suicide in despair over his country's downfall. The late Klement Gottwald (who died in 1953) became president in June, 1948. For the second time in ten years, Czechoslovakia lost its liberty. Under the present communist regime, Czechoslovakia still calls itself a nation, although in reality it has no independence.

ORIGINS OF MODERN HISTORIOGRAPHY

Palacký, "The Father of the Nation." In the Czech and Slovak national revival, the historians played a leading role; among them, František Palacký; the leading Czech historian of the nineteenth century, was granted, in fact, the honorary title of "The Father of the Nation."

Palacký (1789-1876) was a contemporary of such great historians as Jules Michelet (1798-1874) and Leopold von Ranke (1795-1886). His contribution consisted of five volumes of a history of Bohemia from its dawn to the union of the Lands of the Bohemian Crown with the Habsburg domains in 1526; it became "a cornerstone of modern Czech historiography and a starting-point for the subsequent and more detailed studies of Czech national history."[3] In addition, Palacky produced a number of monographs and

---

[3] Otakar Odložilík, "Modern Czechoslovak Historiography," *The Slavonic and East European Review,* XXX, p. 75 (June, 1952), pp. 376-392, the best available short survey of Czechoslovakia's historiography available in English. See also: Hans Kohn, "Palacky, Frantisek," in *Slavonic Encyclopaedia,* pp. 915-916; Josef Fischer, *The Ideas and Work of Frantisek Palacky* (in Czech) ; Jaroslav Werstadt, "The Philosophy of Czech History," *Slavonic and East European Review,* III (March, 1925), pp. 543ff; Josef Pekar, "Historiography" (in Czech), in *Pamatnik na saslavu 50letého panovnického jubilea,* pp. 24ff, and *Frantisek Palacky* (in Czech) ; Jaroslav Werstadt, *Political Historiography of the 19th Century and Its Czech Representatives* (in Czech), pp. 7ff.

analytical studies, and sponsored editions of sources of the history of Bohemia in Czech, Latin and German.

His training and education included the reading of the works of the philosophers Kant and Hegel supplemented by the English historians Robertson and Gibbon, as well as the German, Luden. His European outlook as well as his good knowledge of Austrian history enabled him to place properly the history of Bohemia-Moravia in the main stream of mankind's development. History in the "highest sense" is the "teacher of life" and the ultimate court in which the judgment of mankind is expressed. The historian in the name of humanity is the servant of truth and justice. Thus it behooves him to plumb to the depths the historical forces and facts by means of which he reconstructs the past.

Palacký's concept of the interplay of historical forces was dramatic and idealistic. The content of history reflects the continuous struggle and byplay of opposing elements: the individual and society in mutual strife as well as with nature create makers of history as well as a number of cultural values, viz., science, nationality, law, the state, language, morality and religion. All of this in its ultimate aim is to achieve the good, the true, and the beautiful in reaching for liberty and the realm of God. This serves not only for the individual life but for all history.

The dual struggle in history is reflected in the history of the Czech nation not only by national struggle within the Slavonic world but a national struggle with Germandom. In the religious field a struggle arises between the Roman "universal" Church and the "Reformation," that is, between Catholicism and Protestantism. The religious struggle came to the fore in the days of Hus and remained a constant, leading factor until the disastrous Battle of the White Mountain. Palacký argued that while the Germans have stressed power, the Slavs had laid emphasis on voluntary and free agreement conditioned by the sentiment of social solidarity. For him, the Germans were primarily warriors and conquerors, who founded their society on inequality, whereas the Slavs did not know or recognize difference of estate or inequality before the law.[4]

Since all life is founded in struggle, for Palacký the struggle between the Hussites and the Catholics was really a war between Slav and German. Another facet of comparison was the struggle between liberty of conscience and ecclesiastical absolutism, but another aspect of the duel between "democracy" and "aristocracy." For Palacký, the Hussite wars were the first of the great struggles in the realm of ideas, which the Czech people were called upon to undertake.

The Importance of Palacký. Palacký's ideology of Czech nationalism became the backbone of the struggle for Czechoslovakia's independence and the foundation of the new state in 1918. His views were more or less faithfully, although not slavishly, reflected by numerous successors; there has been no end of studies on Palacký in Czechoslovakia and abroad;[5] numbered among these are

---

[4] Palacký later revised this thesis about the romantic national character of the Slavs, a view derived from Herder and the Czech and Polish Romanticists.

Tomek, Kalousek, and Rezek, and to some extent Antonín Gindély (1829-1892) ; the foremost critic has been Josef Pekař.[6] His romanticism helped to inspire his people to national awakening, and his successors built on his foundation.

Yet, at the end of his life, Palacký was bitterly attacked by the radicals of the National Party, known as the Young Czechs. After his death, his scholarly achievements came under criticism, especially his romantic concept of conceiving the early Czechs as peace-loving folk, gaining their livelihood by cultivation of the soil, in contrast to the autocracy and fundamentally different from the culture patterns of the neighboring Germans. The proponents of the "revisionism" were headed by Lubor Niederle (1865-1944), who received international recognition for his penetrating studies of Slavonic anthropology and archaeology.[7] Niederle placed archaeology on a scientific basis; under him, this discipline parted with history and was raised to the status of a special department with its own methods and aims. Another spokesman of the critical school was Jaroslav Goll (1846-1929), professor of general history at the Czech University of Prague (founded in 1882), who was actively supported by Jan Gebauer and T. G. Masaryk in the famed "Battle of the Manuscripts" (academic arguments over the right to use falsified documents for the promotion of the Czech national cause). Goll was inspired by Georg Waitz, the greatest of von Ranke's pupils; he also warned against sweeping historical generalizations and drew a sharp line between history and sociology which, in its beginnings at that time, fascinated T. G. Masaryk and the group around him; he also criticized the value of philosophy of history and stressed that the collection of facts was the primary task of the historian.

Rieger and Denis. Bohuslav Rieger (1856-1907), a grandson of the great Palacký, specialized in the legal and constitutional aspects of Austrian and Czech history. His studies in the history of public law in Central Europe still remain an important source of information in that field. At the end of the nineteenth century, there appeared the works of a Frenchman, interested in Bohemia's history. Ernest Denis' *Fin de l'Independance Bohème* (Paris, 1890) 2 vols., covered the period from 1434 to 1620; its continuation, *La Bohème Depuis la Montagne Blanche* (1903), 2 vols., covered the period from 1620-1900; its translation in Bohemia was evaluated as a continuation of Palacký's *History.* Denis paid special attention to religious and constitutional struggles of the Czech people with the Habsburgs and emphasized the progressive and democratic trends in modern Czech nationalism.

Jaroslav Goll. From the beginning of the nineties, Czech historiography experienced a fundamental change under the influence of Jaroslav Goll (1846-1929) ; among his pupils were some of the foremost Czech historians of the following period, such as Jaroslav Bidlo, Kamil Krofta, the successor of Beneš in the post of foreign minister, and many others. Indirectly, Goll transmitted

---

[6] For summaries of such studies, see: Count Francis Lützow, *Lectures on the Historians of Bohemia;* Jaroslov Werstadt, "The Philosophy of Czech History," *Slavonic and East European Review,* III. pp. 533-546; Otakar Vočadlo, "English Influences Upon Palacký," *Ibid.,* pp. 547-552.
[6] Pekar's obituary appeared in the *Slavonic and East European Review,* XVI (1938), pp. 203-205.
[7] Lubor Niederle, *Manuel d'antiquite slav,* in *Collection de Manuels Publiées par l'Institut d'Études Slaves.*

the fruits of the German school of Leopold von Ranke; and more directly the influence of the Vienna *Institut für Osterreichische Geschichtsforschung,* into Czech historiography.[8] He introduced into Czech historical writing an assiduous collection of the fundamental sources, helping the rise of the critical stream which flowed in modern Czech historiography, tuned to a realistic view of Czech national life, breaking away from the generation which had been influenced by romanticism. To this must be added a keen knowledge of the west as well as its historical methodology.

THE ERA OF MASARYK

T. G. Masaryk. Czech historiography in the latter nineteenth and early twentieth centuries was dominated to a remarkable degree by the ideas of Thomas G. Masaryk (1850-1937), for many years professor in Charles University. Indeed, he might be called the sole philosopher of history in Bohemia in our century. All his numerous and scattered writings are replete with profound reflections on the course of Czech history and current problems.

Masaryk started specializing in sociology, but soon transferred his interest to the formulation of historical and political theories, especially in their application to the historical events and problems facing his nation. In this he differed from the earlier Czech political thinkers who tended to take a historical approach and to whom historical experience alone dictated the course to be taken in the future; in turn, the critics of Masaryk pointed to Masaryk's philosophy of history being insufficiently grounded in the facts of Czech history, or questioned his methodology as applied to history.

In evaluating Masaryk's ideas and his influence, we must remember that his writings reflected Czech (and subsequently Czechoslovak) national and political conditions. He agreed with Palacký that "whosoever does not understand contemporary social life, cannot understand old or older societies." His approach to history was eminently pragmatic. Thus, before World War I, when Bohemia was under the domination of the Austro-Hungarian Monarchy, Masaryk directed his nation's energies toward strengthening and enhancing the nationalistic ideology. Everything in the field of national endeavor was to be measured by the standards of national utility. His interpretation of the religious influences in the history of the Czech people was the main pillar of his historical views—based in large part on the philosophy of Palacký. His influence on the post-Goll generation was to turn the Czech historians back to the principles of Palacký, who did not believe that it was possible to write a completely objective history and stressed the service which history could render to the nation by showing it "what it was, and what it might become." Masaryk, however, opposed the empty or false patriotism, as shown in his leadership in the "Battle of the Manuscripts."

Masaryk's conception of realism took the form of an effort to search for greater truth and deeper morality in life; in the belief that the world and mankind are ruled by certain principles and laws of absolute truth; that man

---

[8] Kael Stoukal, "Jaroslav Goll," *Cesky Casopis historicky (Czech Historical Review),* XLVII (1946), p. 1066; Josef Pekar, "Historiography," *op. cit.,* pp. 48ff; Jaroslav Goll, "History and Historiography" in his *Selected Writings* (in Czech), pp. 2ff.

is a living expression of these principles of God or Providence, and has to live in accord with these laws. All individuals, as well as nations, have an equal right to freedom. In its application history should teach the nation to seek a better educational, intellectual, moral, artistic, and especially a politically realistic outlook on life. Progress lies in evolution rather than in revolution. Masaryk's insistence on a basically moral and religious approach made him a bitter critic of Karl Marx, and the materialistic interpretation of history.[9]

Masaryk developed some of Palacký's ideas further in his insistence that the aims of the Czechoslovak people were also the aims of worldwide democracy. The ideas of the Czech Reformation and of Hussitism were basically involved in the rise of modern Europe and of the French Revolution—and hence the struggle against Austria-Hungary and later Germany was also a struggle for democracy—for these involved the hope of a better world, and for more human relationships among all peoples. Masaryk declared: "The problems of humanity are a specifically Czech problem."

From the standpoint of the present insistence of Russia that Czechoslovak historiography should reflect the Pan-Slav tendencies in Czechoslovakia's history, let us note that Masaryk was bitterly opposed to the Czarist system and later of the soviet experiment. He opposed Pan-Slavism and Slavophilism and rejected Lenin's revolution and the subsequent development of Sovietism in theory and practice, finding in Leninism more of Bakunin than of Karl Marx. For Masaryk, individual initiative and the right to think for oneself were the indispensable foundations of political and intellectual life.[10]

Eduard Beneš. The ideas of Masaryk found an able exponent in his brilliant follower and collaborator, Dr. Eduard Beneš (1893-1948), who held his chair as professor of sociology in Charles University even during the time of his term in office as foreign minister. He helped Masaryk to found Czechoslovakia as an adroit diplomat, then became foreign minister, and Czechoslovakia's second president (1935-1948). In general, he expounded Masaryk's practical philosophy which would be evaluated, in America, as "applied sociology." A former newspaper correspondent, he published his doctoral thesis, *The Austrian Problem and the Czech Question* (1908), in French at the University of Dijon; two years later appeared the first volume of an extensive study, *The Evolution of Modern Socialism.* During World War I his numerous articles propounded the cause of Czechoslovakia's independence; his memoirs, translated into English, appeared in America in 1928 as *My War Memoirs.* During World War II, his course of lectures at the University of Chicago, *Democracy, Today and Tomorrow* (1942) was a brilliant evaluation of the basic issues confronting the modern world. In the short period of his service after World War II, he produced two works of unique importance, namely, *Üvahy o Slovanství (Ou vont les Slaves?,* Paris, 1948) and his *Paměti: Od Mnichova k nové válice a ke novému viězství (Memoirs: From Munich to the New War, and the New Victory).* Here he reversed Masaryk's traditional

[9] Hans Kohn, "Roots of Czech Democracy," Chapter VI, pp. 91-105, in R. J. Kerner, ed., *Czechoslovakia: Twenty Years of Independence.*
[10] Hans Kohn, "The Heritage of Masaryk," *The Annals of the American Academy of Political and Social Science,* CCLVIII (July, 1948), pp. 70-73.

antagonism to Russia and tried to reach an ideological rapprochement with the Kremlin on the basis of a Slavonic policy. In *Paměti* Beneš recounted his efforts to restore Czechoslovakia during World War II.

Beneš interpretation of the basic currents of Czechoslovak history, and especially of their relation to the worldwide trends of contemporary history, led him to promote the pro-Western and pro-democratic policies of Czechoslovakia during the two decades just before Munich. But Munich, which led to the dismemberment of Czechoslovakia by Hitler and with the tacit approval of France and England, induced Beneš to modify his theories in favor of an activated and rejuvenated form of "Pan-Slavism."

CZECHOSLOVAK HISTORIOGRAPHY DURING THE FIRST REPUBLIC

Under the sponsorship and leadership of Masaryk and Beneš, special attention was given, soon after the formation of the Czechoslovak Republic in 1918, to the promotion of history (as well as all social sciences). Two universities— the Masaryk University at Brno and the Comenius University at Bratislava— were added to the Charles University at Prague. The government granted liberal subsidies to the history departments, and such learned periodicals as the *Český Casopis Historický (Czech Historical Review)* and the *Časopic Matice Moravske (Review of Moravian Mother-Society)*. The Comenius University started to develop Slovak historiography, favoring the thesis of a coordinated destiny of Czechs and Slovaks, while the Matice Slovenská, at Turciansky Sv. Martin, favored, after 1931, the clerical and nationalistic demands of the autonomists.[11] At any rate, the four principal chairs in history became the rallying points for Czechoslovakia's historiography during its independence.

Josef Pekař (1870-1937) broke with the Palacký-Goll-Masaryk school of historical interpretation and emphasized the role of Catholicism in the development of the Czech national awakening; he rejected Masaryk's thesis that the meaning of Czech history could be found in the religious principles, especially in the Czech Reformation. He also tried to deal realistically with the problem of the share that the Germans had, as a second largest ethnic element in Bohemia, in the historical development of the country.[12] He exerted his influence as editor of the *Czech Historical Review*. Pekař s critical attitude found support in Emanuel Rádl's *The Struggle of Czechs and Germans,* in Czech, whose appraisal of the contributions of the Germans to Czech history was bitterly criticized by many Czech patriotic historians.

On the whole, the Czechoslovak historians made remarkable contributions to historiography during this period. Václav Novotný continued Palacký's great work with specialized works on the importance and grandeur of the Hussite era. J. Susta headed the field of West European history and edited a monumental history of mankind in Czech, *Dějiny Lidstva.* F. Dvorník (1893-   ) contributed studies on Byzantine and early Slavic history; he is now living in the United States. Milada Paulova (1891-   ) worked in Byzantine and modern

---

[11] The autonomistic tendencies of the Slovaks seem to have found their refuge in Scranton, Pennsylvania. Some of the Slovak works belonging to this school are cited in Francis Hrušovský, *op. cit.,* pp. 107-110.

[12] R. W. Seton-Watson, "Josef Pekar," *The Slavonic Review,* XVI (July, 1937), pp. 203-205.

Slavic history; she edited the *Byzantinoslavica*. Josef Macourek (1901-1950) had a chair of Slavonic history created for him at the Masaryk University. Jaroslav Bídlo attempted to write a general history of the Slavs as a major work of historical synthesis.

Slovak Historiography. The Slovaks had no national historian such as Palacký was for the Czechs. Recently they became concerned with the problem as to whether the Czechs and Slovaks are one people, or separate entities. The most notable of the Slovak historians was Daniel Rapant.

CONTEMPORARY DEVELOPMENTS

After Munich (1939), the Czech and Slovak historians went on their separate ways. In Bohemia-Moravia, the higher institutions of learning were closed and publication was restricted.[13] In Slovakia, the pro-Nazi regime supported those historians who subscribed to the official ideology as derived from anti-Czech tendencies; at the same time, the Nazis allowed the publication of the historical periodical, *Historia Slovaca*.

With the restoration of Czechoslovakia, but already under the shadow of Soviet domination, *Český Časopis Historický* and *Časopis Matice Moravské*, were reorganized. But with the *coup d' état* by the Communists, two trends started to treat Czech historiography—one represented by Zdének Nejedlý (Goll's pupil), a Soviet spokesman, and the other by a few Czech historians who were lucky to escape abroad, and who are headed by O. Odoložilík, today T. G. Masaryk Professor of Czechoslovak Studies at Columbia University.

---

[13] For their list, see: Otaker Odložilík, "Clio in Chains: Czech Historiography, 1939-1940," *Slavonic and East European Review*, XX (1942), pp. 330-337.

Chapter 23

AUSTRIA

By Samson B. Knoll

A STRICTLY Austrian historiography did not really exist before the second half of the nineteenth century.[1] Prior to that period, Austrian history was conducted as part of German historical scholarship. Ficker and Sickel, who with Arneth were the most important Austrian historians of the earlier part of the century, were both of German origin and education, and the Ranke school dominated Austrian historiography as it did that of Germany.

HISTORICAL BACKGROUND

The divorce of Austrian from German historical writing coincided roughly with the final separation of the German and Austrian empires. This process had begun in 1806, when, under the impact of Napoleon's victories, the Habsburg Francis II abdicated as Holy Roman Emperor. It was decided in 1866 with the victory of Prussia, Austria's only serious rival in the long "struggle for supremacy in Germany." Five years later, the establishment of a new German Empire through Bismarck's "blood and iron" diplomacy wrote a climactic end to Austrian influence in the affairs of Germany.

Few countries, indeed, seem to illustrate as strikingly as Austria Ranke's dictum that successive generations will rewrite history in the light of their own experiences and ideologies. It is an essential factor in Austrian historiography, especially of the modern era, that in the short span of eighty years, Austria itself has undergone several fundamental changes which inevitably led to decisive reorientations of Austrian historical research. The far-reaching events marked by the dates 1866, 1918, 1938, and 1945, were turning points in Austrian history, and each involved a complete change in outlook upon the historical past.[2]

THE MEDIEVALISTS

Austrian historical scholarship of the nineteenth century had gained international reputation since the establishment of two important document centers: the Academy of Sciences at Vienna (Division of Philosophy and History), founded in 1847, and the Austrian Institute of Historical Research

---

[1] The term "Austrian" is limited here to those historians, mostly of German-Austrian descent, who became the exponents of a more typically Austrian historiography as distinct from that of Germany. Only the most representative historians are discussed in the text.

[2] R. John Rath, "History and Citizenship Training: An Austrian Example," *Journal of Modern History,* XXI (1949), pp. 227-238, finds that the *Heimwehr* regime of 1934 entailed similar changes in the teaching of history. This does not apply to historical writing on the academic level which was not subject to the textbook regulations of the Austrian Ministry of Education.

at Vienna, founded in 1854.[3] It is especially the latter, modelled after the famous *École des Chartes* in Paris, which grew into a unique school for the study of diplomatics and paleography. Around it rallied all medievalists of note, many of whom participated in such important German projects as the gigantic *Monumenta Germaniae Historica.* Here, too, prominent students of modern history were first initiated into the principles of historical documentation.

The majority of Austrian medievalists followed the traditions of the documentary school of research. Johannes Loserth (1846-1936), Oswald Redlich (1858-1944), Wilhelm Erben (1869-1933), and many others, made outstanding contributions to paleography and to a strictly documented historical narration. It was mainly with Ludo M. Hartmann (1865-1924) and Alfons Dopsch (1868-1953) that more original paths in historical interpretation were opened.

The work of Ludo M. Hartmann, one-time student of Theodor Mommsen, was characterized by an evolutionary and sociological approach to history which was influenced by the historical writings of Karl Marx and the psychological studies of Ernest Mach. Convinced of the continuity of historical development, Hartmann first turned his attention to the problem of the seemingly abrupt break in historical evolution caused by the fall of Rome. In several writings he asserted that the link between the ancient and the medieval world is found in the development of cities and in the survival of Roman, as well as Byzantine, legal and economic institutions.[4] Subsequent studies yielded his *Geschichte Italiens im Mittelalter (History of Italy in the Middle Ages,* 4 vols., Gotha, 1897-1923), and further confirmed Hartmann in his evolutionary approach. They "clearly impelled the historian toward what is commonly called the materialistic concept of history in which the individual must naturally appear as carried by the stream of mass phenomena."[5] Hartmann concluded that the entire content of history is given in the threefold unity of "progressive organization *(Vergesellschaftung),* progressive productivity, and progressive differentiation"; no judgment of historic events and personalities could be relevant without reference to these three fundamental principles.[6]

Alfons Dopsch, founder and director of the Seminar for Cultural and

---

[3] On the Academy of Sciences, see Alfons Huber, *Geschichte der Akademie der Wissenschaften,* and the centennial account by R. Meister, *Geschichte der Akademie der Wissenschaften in Wien 1847-1947.* On the Institute, see Hans Hirsch, *"Das österreichische Institut für Geschichtsforschung, 1854-1934," Mitteilungen des österreichischen Instituts für Geschichtsforschung,* XLIX (1935), pp. 1-14; also Leo Santifaller, *Das Institut für österreichische Geschichtsforschung.* Very important for medieval studies became the Austrian Historical Institute in Rome, opened in 1882 as a branch of the Vienna Institute. The Institute's editions of medieval documents are supplemented by the *Fontes Rerum Austriacarum,* valuable source material for Austrian history since the fifteenth century, published by the Historical Commission of the Academy of Sciences. These, in turn, are complemented by the document editions of the Commission for Modern Austrian History.

[4] Hartmann's *Untersuchungen zur byzantinischen Verwaltung in Italien (540-750)* placed him among the foremost Byzantine scholars. His stimulating *Untergang der antiken Welt* was incorporated in his *Römische Geschichte,* part of a *Weltgeschichte in gemeinverständlicher Darstellung* which he began to edit, in 1919. His brief study of medieval social institutions, *Ein Kapitel vom spätantiken und frühmittelalterlichen Staate,* was recently published by the British Historical Association as *The Early Medieval State.*

[5] Translated from a quotation in Stephan Bauer's biography of Hartmann, *Neue Oesterreichische Biographie,* III, p. 202.

[6] *Ueber historische Entwicklung,* p. 62. In 1903, Hartmann founded the *Vierteljahrschrift für Sozial—und Wirtschaftsgeschichte* which became the model for similar quarterlies in England and France.

Economic History at the University of Vienna, also began with searching studies of the early medieval period. His approach to history, like Hartmann's, was economic and sociological, though essentially non-Marxist. His basic and most original research covers the period from the fall of the Roman Empire through the Carolingian era. A critical examination of the sources, most comprehensively discussed in *The Economic and Social Foundations of European Civilization* (London & New York, 1937), led him to reject the prevailing view of the economic and social backwardness of the pre-Carolingian age.[7] Against this he asserted the continuity of the historical development from the fifth to the eighth century. In support of this thesis he maintained that the Germanic conquerors of Rome, after century-long association with Roman culture and gradual infiltration into all ranks of Roman society, had emerged from primitive barbarism. Thus they had become quite capable of inheriting, even carrying on, the declining Roman civilization. No violent break in historical continuity had occurred; West Roman civilization passed over, as it were unmourned and unnoticed, into the rising civilization of the early Middle Ages. Dopsch's theories, giving rise to much scholarly discussion, have stimulated valuable research in the early medieval field.

Among Austrian medievalists who more recently have made significant contributions are Hans Hirsch (1878-1940) with his studies in constitutional problems of the Middle Ages; Theodor Mayer (born 1883) in medieval economics and administration; Herman Wopfner (born 1876) in medieval agrarian history; and Otto Brunner (born 1898) with writings on medieval financial, constitutional, and legal history. Following the death of Alfons Dopsch, Leo Santifaller (born 1890) ranks as the most outstanding living Austrian medievalist. A scholar of international renown, Santifaller has since 1945 held the most honored offices open to a historian in Austria and abroad.[8] His work comprises a vast number of document publications for local, regional, and national medieval history. Among his theoretical discussions is a basic *Urkundenforschung (Document Research,* Weimar, 1937.)

THE PERIOD OF THE DUAL MONARCHY

By its very nature the field of modern history reveals most clearly the effects of political events and ideologies upon historical writing. In 1848, at Frankfurt, the *grossdeutsch* dream that had moved so many German and Austrian

---

[7] This English edition is a condensation of a two-volume work, *Die wirtschaftlichen und sozialen Grundlagen der europäischen Kulturentwicklung aus der Zeit von Caesar bis zu Karl dem Grossen* (2d ed.). It was preceded by *Die Wirtschaftsentwicklung der Karolingerzeit* (2 vols.). Dopsch is author of numerous works on economic and social history, mostly of the Middle Ages. Among his more recent publications are *Naturalwirtschaft und Geldwirtschaft in der Weltgeschichte* and *Herrschaft und Bauer in der deutschen Kaiserzeit.* An autobiographical sketch is contained in Sigfrid Steinberg, ed., *Die Geschichtswissenschaft der Gegenwart in Selbstdarstellungen,* I, pp. 52-90.

[8] Santifaller is Director of the Austrian Institute of Historical Research, Director General of the Austrian State Archives, and Chairman of the Historical Commission of the Austrian Academy of Sciences. His international prominence was confirmed by his recent election to the presidency of the *Comité Internationale des Sciences Historiques.* Important studies by Hans Hirsch are *Die Klosterimmunität seit dem Investiturstreit* and *Die hohe Gerichtsbarkeit im deutschen Mittelalter.* During the Nazi regime, Theodor Mayer became one of the editors of *Das Reich und Europa,* a series of "co-operative studies by German historians" published in Leipzig, beginning 1941. Herman Wopfner contributed the chapter on agrarian history to the well-known *Handwörterbuch der Staatswissenchaften,* and is author of an important *Urkundenbuch zur Agrargeschichte.* Otto Brunner's more recent publications include an investigation of feudal administration, *Land und Herrschaft. Gundfragen der territorialen Verfassungsgeschichte Südostdeutschlands im Mittelalter.*

historians, had collapsed in a manner none too flattering to the Austrian delegation and their government. A brief revival of Austrian prestige was followed by Austria's defeat in the "fractricidal war" of 1866 and the final triumph of Bismarck's unification policy in 1871. To the Habsburgs establishment of the Bismarckian Empire meant exclusion from further participation in the internal affairs of Germany; to the Germans of Austria it meant reduction to a minority position within the new Dual Monarchy. Multinationalism, hitherto characteristic only of the Habsburg family possessions— the *Hausmacht* as distinct from the old *Reich*—, now became the very essence of the Austrian state. In prospect as well as in retrospect, the historical outlook upon the Austrian problems thus was fundamentally changed.

Even before the political break had become complete, disappointment with the failure of 1848 had found expression in acrimonious controversy between Austrian and Prussian historians, in which patriotism frequently was more conspicuous than scholarship.[9] Yet, the historical reality of a new, predominantly non-German political entity demanded a thorough revision of the prevailing concepts of Austrian history. By the end of the eighties, hostile debate gave way to a more careful and dispassionate analysis of the personalities and events that had helped to shape the existing situation.

While August Fournier (1850-1920) critically studied the French Revolution and the Napoleonic era with their vital impact upon Austrian history, it was Heinrich Friedjung (1851-1920) who most thoroughly analyzed Austria's past in its relevance to the present.[10] His basic work, *The Struggle for Supremacy in Germany, 1859-1866* (London, 1935), offered a keen critique of the political developments along with a thorough analysis of the military campaigns of 1866.[11] Other publications examined the domestic policies of the Habsburgs and their vacillating and confused diplomacy.[12]

In all his writings Friedjung combined an intense nationalism with much genuine scholarship. Though a liberal by inclination, he was passionately convinced of the justice of the German cause in the Dual Monarchy. Like so many German Austrians in whom the memory of 1848 lingered on, he completely identified the cause of liberalism with that of the German contingent. This nationalistic liberalism made him highly critical of Metternich and influenced all his studies of recent Austrian developments.[13] Despite this bias, however, his writings have retained their value. They have been supplemented rather than superseded by the publication of documents which

---

[9] The classic scholarly controversy was that between Sybel and Ficker about the Holy Roman Empire. The pertinent writings of both have been re-edited by F. Schneider in *Universalstaat oder Nationalstaat*.

[10] Fournier's *Napoleon I* (3 vols., in English 2 vols.) was, until very recently, considered best in its field and is stil a classic. A new line of investigation was his *Die Geheimpolezi auf dem Wiener Kongress*.

[11] This is a condensed translation of the original two-volume work.

[12] *Oesterreich von 1848-1860* (2 vols.) and *Der Krimkrieg und die österreichische Politik*. Friedjung also wrote a chapter for the *Cambridge Modern History*, XI, pp. 393-411: "Austria, Prussia, and the Germanic Confederation."

[13] Friedjung's intense nationalism led to the one great blow to his prestige: the notorious "Friedjung Trial" of 1908. The Austrian government had used forged documents to prosecute a group of Serbo-Croat "conspirators." Called in as an expert, Friedjung had pronounced these documents genuine and had justified his government's actions in the press. In an ensuing libel suit against him, the forgeries were exposed, and Friedjung had to make a public retraction (see A. J. P. Taylor's introduction to the English edition of *The Struggle for Supremacy, op. cit.*).

the narrow-minded archival policy of the Habsburgs had withheld from scholarly scrutiny in his days.

The basic problem confronting the Dual Monarchy was that of holding together the many nationalities of which it was composed. All Austrian historians recognized this fact, and much of Friedjung's criticism of Metternich was directed at the latter's inability to have grasped it. The many aspects of the problem were searchingly studied in the period before 1914. Legal and constitutional implications of the Habsburg law of successsion were exhaustively analyzed by Gustav Turba (1864-1935) in his definitive editions of the Pragmatic Sanction of 1713.[14] The most comprehensive review of the historical bankground to the administrative problems of the Monarchy was undertaken with the still unfinished *Geschichte der österreichischen Zentralverwaltung (History of the Central Administration of Austria,* 6 vols., Vienna, 1907-1934). Of its successive editors, Heinrich Kretschmayr (1870-1941) had gained prominence with his near definitive *Geschichte von Venedig (History of Venice,* 3 vols., Gotha, 1905-1934).

Stimulated by the political questions of the day, an increasing number of historical studies were made outside the historical profession, as the twentieth century progressed. Among the few that can claim greater validity are the writings of an ardent admirer of Friedjung's, Richard Charmatz (born 1879). His *Deutsch-österreichische Politik (German-Austrian Politics,* Leipzig, 1907) was the ideological premise of his better known histories of Austrian domestic and foreign policy.[15] He preached a "new liberalism" which would solve the socio-economic problems of Austria by a consciously accelerated industrialization; the political problems of the Dual Monarchy could then be solved by uniting its many nationalities through ever progressing democratic equality.

More fundamentally challenging to the past and present social order in Austria were the historical analyses of the two Social Democratic leaders Otto Bauer (1881-1938) and Karl Renner (1870-1950), the latter president of Austria from 1946 until his death. Of the two, Renner undoubtedly was the more scholarly, while Bauer was more strictly Marxist in his approach. The writings of both, however, are of more than party-political significance. As early as 1889, a solution to the nationalities problem on the basis of national equality had been one of the major points in the Austrian Social Democratic platform.[16] In many respects similar to the liberal program presented at the ill-fated Kremsier Parliament of 1848, the Socialist position was discussed by Renner, under the pseudonym of Rudolf Springer, in *Der Kampf der österreichischen Nationen um den Staat (The Struggle of the Austrian Nations Over the State,* Leipzig & Vienna, 1902). Here, and in subse-

---

[14] *Die Grundlagen der Pragmatischen Sanktion* (2 vols.) and *Die Pragmatische Sanktion. Authentische Texte samt Erläuterungen und Uebersetzungen.*

[15] *Oesterreichs innere Geschichte von 1848-1907* (2 vols., the 3rd ed., revised, 1918, carries Austrian history ʹo 1895 only) ; *Geschichte der auswärtigen Politik Oesterreichs im 19. Jahrhundert* (2 vols.). Helpful to the student of Austrian history is his *Wegweiser durch die Literatur der österreichischen Geschichte.*

[16] A recent study of the Socialist position is Arʹhur G. Kogan's "The Social Democrats and the Conflict of Nationalities in the Habsburg Monarchy," *Journal of Modern History,* XXI (1949), pp. 204-217.

quent publications, he presented the Social Democratic solution to the
nationalities problem as one of the prerequisite steps toward the future
democratization of Austria.[17] At the same time, Renner, representative of
the Socialist right wing, proposed that this be accomplished well within the
framework of the Habsburg empire, whose position as a bulwark against
Russian absolutism and imperialism he wished to maintain. This view was
so well within the bounds of average German national sentiment in Austria,
that even intrinsically non-Socialist historians like Friedjung pointed to its
significance.[18] Against this, Otto Bauer wrote his *Die Nationalitätenfrage und
die Sozialdemokratie (The Nationalities Problem and Social Democracy,*
Vienna, 1910), where he presented the nationalities provisions of the Socialist platform as essentially provisional, until social change would become
a historical fact.

From Versailles and St. Germain to the Anschluss of 1938

History by-passed historiography, when the outcome of the World War
of 1914-1918 removed the problem of a multi-national empire from practical
reality and reduced the Austrian state to its German contingent. After 1871,
grossdeutsch sentiment, though never completely unpolitical, had survived
chiefly as the pride in the German "cultural mission" among the other
nationalities of the Dual Monarchy. Through the upheaval of 1918 it once
again received a vigorous political content in the form of the *Anchluss* movement. The resulting widespread identification of Austria's cause with that of
Germany and the general disappointment with the peace terms left their
imprint upon the writing of history. In the re-examination of the Austrian
past, an author's historical approach frequently was determined by his attitude
to the new political actuality.

The nationalistic appraisal of the pre-war era is well exemplified by Heinrich Friedjung's *Das Zeitalter des Imperialismus 1844-1914 (The Age of
Imperialism,* 3 vols., Berlin, 1920-1923), the last two volumes of which
were posthumously edited by Pribram. Commissioned as a continuation of
Schlosser's *World History,* this is Friedjung's only major study on problems
of general rather than Austro-German history. Although some attention is
paid to cultural and social trends, the work is devoted mainly to foreign affairs,
and Friedjung's nationalistic bias is fully apparent, especially in his hostility
to the United States and to President Wilson.[19]

Among the few historians who in this review of pre-war history retained
scholarly balance and objectivity, Alfred F. Pribram (1859-1942) stands out
with his detached analyses of Austrian and European diplomacy. Internationally
known even before the war, Pribram amplified his studies in diplomatic history with the new material available in the now freely accessible Vienna
archives.[20] His first post-war publication, *Secret Political Treaties of Austria-*

[17] Cf. Renner's *Grundlagen und Entwicklungsziele der österreichisch-ungarischen Monarchie.*
[18] In *Oesterreich von 1848-1860, op cit.,* I, p. 336.
[19] Like most Austrian and German historians, Friedjung doubted Wilson's sincerity and believed
that the Fourteen Points had only been bait to induce the Central Powers to lay down their arms.
[20] Among Pribram's earlier document publications are the important *Oesterreichische Staats-
verträge mit England* (2 vols.). A significant study of seventeenth century diplomacy is his *Lisola
und die Entwicklung der Tripelliga.*

Hungary, 1879-1914 (Vienna, 1920), was quickly translated into English (London, 1920) and French (Paris, 1923).[21] Pribram was also one of four historians chosen by the Commission for Modern Austrian History to select and publish the documents of the Austrian Foreign Office relating to the outbreak of the War of 1914-1918. Edited by Ludwig Bittner and Hans Uebersberger, the nine-volume work is the Austrian counterpart to the official document publications in England, France, Germany, and the Soviet Union.[22]

The war itself was discussed in a mushrooming of writings by qualified as well as unqualified observers. The more serious attempted to find the historical roots of the collapse of 1918, and even ardent supporters of the extinct monarchy now voiced strong criticism of Habsburg domestic policies.[23] Among professional historians, a significant exponent of the nationalist view was Viktor Bibl (1878-1948) whose approach to the Austrian past resembled Friedjung's in many respects.[24] In *Der Zerfall Oesterreichs (The Collapse of Austria,* 2 vols., Vienna, 1922-1924) he presented the disintegration of the Habsburg empire as a consequence of the legacy left by Emperor Francis and by Metternich's "system." The book clearly reveals his hostility to the Revolution of 1918, and Bibl's resentment of the non-German nationalities in Austria because of their conduct during and after the war. More dispossionate, though also partisan, was Otto Bauer's attempt to explain the growth of the revolution of 1918 out of the insoluble national and class conflicts of the Habsburg empire.[25]

The most profound and essentially non-partisan approach to the Austrian past is that of Josef Redlich (1864-1936). Historian and jurist of international repute, Redlich had become known before the war through his books on English government and parliamentary procedure. With his legal and historical background he undertook to investigate the causes of the dissolution of the Dual Monarchy in the light of the newly available documents. Two volumes of his imposingly planned, but unfinished, `Das österreichische Staats—und Reichsproblem (The Austrian State and Imperial Problem,* Leipzig, 1920-1926) carry his investigation to the *Ausgleich* of 1867, and are indispensable to the student of Austrian history in the nineteenth century. They are complemented by his *Austrian War Government* (Vienna, 1925; English edition, New Haven, 1929), a careful analysis of the transformation and final disintegration of the Habsburg government under the impact of war.

During the war years 1914-1918, the concept of *Mitteleuropa* had been revived in Germany and had found an echo in Austria. After the war, this con-

---

[21] Highly regarded in England, Pribram contributed several English publications. Among them are *Austrian Foreign Policy, 1908-1918* and *England and the International Policy of the European Great Powers, 1871-1914;* the latter were his Ford lectures given at Oxford, in 1929). Posthumously published was his *Austria-Hungary and Great Britain, 1908-1914.*

[22] *Oesterreich-Ungarns Aussenpolitik von der Bosnischen Krise 1908 bis zum Kriegsausbruch 1914.* The fourth of the historians was Heinrich von Srbik.

[23] Examples are F. G. Kleinwächter's *Der Untergang der österreichisch-ungarischen Monarchie* and Edmund Glaise von Horstenau's *Collapse of the Austro-Hungarian Empire.* The latter, who in the crisis of 1938 played a rather unsavory part as Hitler's go-between, was also co-author and editor of the official war history published by the Austrian General Staff under the title *Oesterreich-Ungarns letzter Krieg, 1914-1918* (15 vols.).

[24] Bibl had become known for his research in the revolutionary period of 1848. A notable product of these earlier studies is *Die niederösterreichischen Stände in Vormärz.*

[25] *The Austrian Revolution,* condensed version of the original German edition.

cept spread and merged with the *Anschluss* sentiment. Much of Austrian history was re-written under the impact of the longing for Greater German unity, which resulted.[26] The most notable exponent of this trend became Heinrich von Srbik (1870-1951), whose exhaustive learning and scholarship placed him among the outstanding contemporary Austrian historians. An intense German nationalist, his outlook yet was European, while at the same time he was deeply convinced of a particularly Austrian tradition within the Greater German "cultural mission" in Europe.

The collapse of the Habsburg monarchy with its ancient traditions led Srbik to devote his studies with increasing exclusiveness to the history of the ancestral German *Reich*. To Srbik, the union between the Habsburg monarchy and the Holy Roman Empire had made possible the accomplishment of the transcendental purpose of Germany's existence in the heart of Europe. The inclusion of so many different nationalities within the Habsburg possessions only heightened and increased the importance of Austria as the eastern bulwark of *Mitteleuropa*. Reestablishment of the traditional union between Germany and Austria, abandoned in the "fatal hour" of 1806, thus became to Srbik an indispensable prerequisite for the preservation of Europe.[27]

Much of his research attempted to demonstrate the existence of such a European mission in the traditions of the "Holy Empire" and in the consciousness of the great men of the Austrian past. After idealizing Wallenstein in this manner, Srbik produced, in two exhaustive volumes, what may be termed the classic conservative interpretation of Metternich.[28] He upheld him as the great conservator: Guided by an idealistic vision of the concert of Europe, Metternich attempted to stem the threatening tide of revolutionary chaos by preserving that dynasty which, as bearer of the most glorious tradition in Europe, was the natural leader in a common struggle for peace and order.

The controversy aroused by Srbik is indicative of the conflicting trends within the Greater German school of historiography. The radical nationalist Bibl challenged the conservative nationalist Srbik in writings which passionately denounced the ill-fated abandonment by the Habsburgs of their German responsibility.[29] Bibl charged Metternich with direct responsibility for the Revolution of 1848, because the latter's reactionary and selfish policies made him unable to understand, let alone cope with, the growing German and European nationalism. Since out of that failure grew the ruinous "struggle of the nationalities," Bibl held Metternich at least indirectly responsible for the collapse of 1918. Thus the study of the Austrian past became increasingly expressive of the conflicting ideologies of the present.

HISTORIOGRAPHY UNDER NAZI RULE

In 1938, *Anschluss* was finally accomplished, though under conditions far

---

[26] An opposing trend emerged in the late twenties and early thirties, which upheld Austrian individualism against German Prussianism. Its influence, however, was not comparable.
[27] Cp. Srbik's *Die Schicksalsstunde des alten Reiches*, condensation of an earlier article. An important key to Srbik's interpretation of European history is given in his *Mitteleuropa, das Problem und die Versuche seiner Lösung in der deutschen Geschichte*.
[28] *Wallensteins Ende* and *Metternich, der Staatsmann und der Mensch*.
[29] *Metternich in neuer Beleuchtung* and *Metternich der Dämon Oesterreichs*.

different from those that had prevailed in 1918. For Austrian historiography the Nazi triumph was as deplorable as it had earlier been for that of Germany.[30]

Medieval studies, which received new impetus from the Nazi glorification of the German past, were on the whole less affected. Straight documentary research maintained its traditional high standing, but teaching and interpretative writing suffered severely. In some writers the influence of Nazi doctrines led to little more than an exalted view of Germanic leadership in medieval civilization, but others succumbed far too uncritically to Nazi racial theories.[31]

The colorful past of the Austrian lands, the great wealth of documents preserved in Habsburg and provincial archives, had given to the study of *Volkskunde* in Austria a widespread impetus, long before Nazi ideology made it the fashion of the day. An important pioneer in this branch of history was Viktor von Geramb (born 1884), whose steadfastly unbiased and scholarly approach to folk history resulted in his dismissal from office in 1938.[32] Not so immune to the lure of Nazi lore was Adolf Helbok (born 1883), whose work was one of the most comprehensive efforts to view early history in the new racist orientation. Long before Anschluss, Helbok had begun research in regional settlement; his *Grundlagen der Volksgeschichte Deutschlands und Frankreichs (Foundations of the Folk History of Germany and France, 2 vols., Leipzig & Berlin, 1937)* is an attempt to lay the basis for a folkish, geopolitical and regional approach to history. But the author's very real achievement is greatly minimized by his obvious racial bias. His conclusion that France is culturally a "guest land," whereas Germany is culturally a "mother land," can hardly be taken seriously. And the impression of scholarship and scientific thoroughness is spoiled by the author's quoting of the familiar Pan-German battle cry: "Through Germany the world shall live."[33]

In the modern field, radical nationalists early adapted themselves to the new trend. Nazi nationalism had long held its appeal to the *grossdeutsch* and *Mitteleuropa* sentiments of many Austrian historians. After *Anschluss,* the Nazi demand for a *gesamtdeutsch* (All-German) historiography was echoed in Austria. A host of publications now tried to prove that the separation of Austria from Germany had not only been against the desire of the Austrian people, but counter to the very laws of history. Apart from those who went into either actual or spiritual exile, only a few among the better known Austrian historians were able to maintain scholarly balance and the freedom of research and of interpretation.

The change to historico-political activism is well expressed in the preface to Viktor Bibl's new edition of his *Collapse of Austria,* where he saw "the task of

---

[30] For a preliminary estimate see Felix Gilbert, "German Historiography during the Second World War," *American Historical Review,* LXIII (1947), pp. 50-58. A factual compilation is now being prepared in Germany under the editorship of Gerhard Ritter and Walther Holtzmann, and part of it has been published: *Die deutsche Geschichtswissenschaft im zweiten Weltkrieg,* I:1 and I:2.

[31] This influence is evident in the post-*Anschluss* publications of Otto Brunner and Theodor Mayer, among others. A telling example is *Der Vertrag von Verdun, 843,* ed. Th. Mayer (series *Das Reich und Europa).*

[32] Since 1945, von Geramb (now emeritus) has been reinstated at the University of Graz. His most complete study is *Die Kulturgeschichte der Rauchstuben.*

[33] The book actually ends with this phrase *("Am deutschen Wesen soll die Welt genesen!")*

the historian in furnishing factual material from which the politician must draw
his conclusions." [34] Even earlier, in 1935, Heinrich von Srbik had responded to
the overtures of Nazi *gesamtdeutsch* historiography by ostentatiously joining the
official Berlin *Reich* Institute for History of the New Germany. Yet, *Anschluss*
could not solve the conflict between his Austrian patriotism and Greater German
nationalism. He continued to eulogize the Austrian tradition within the Greater
German *Reich;* above all, he never surrendered that thoroughness of research
which gives importance to all his writings.

The *Anschluss* period saw the completion of his most cherished work,
Deutsche Einheit (German Unity, 4 vols., Munich, 1935-1942), where he
attempted to trace the evolution of the "Holy Empire" as a concept and as reality
through Greater German history. In his vision, German Unity became an ideal
of almost metaphysical dimensions, unaffected by the time-bound character of
historical actualities. Through such an abstraction he was able, though in cautious and lofty terms, to allude to Hitler's Greater Germany and its "New
Order" for Europe as the spiritual and political manifestation of the eternal and
universal *Reich.* Controversial as such an approach and its inferences naturally
are, the work contains a wealth of material and is provocative of new study.[35]
But this political idealism, in its complete divorce from political reality, led
Srbik to conclusions of an abstruse transcendence which seriously detracts from
his unquestionably profound and extensive scholarship.

HISTORICAL WRITINGS SINCE 1945

In 1945, the Greater German dream was shattered; Austria once again was
separated from Germany. For their political misjudgment a number of prominent Austrian historians lost the privilege of teaching, although they could
continue research and publish their findings. Among them were Viktor Bibl,
Otto Brunner, Theodor Mayer, Heinrich von Srbik, and many others.

It is still too early to define the historiographic trends now in the making in
Austria. Emerging from the unprecedented material and spiritual destruction of
Anschluss, world war, and defeat, Austrian historiography is now vigorously
continuing the scholarly projects of earlier years. Two new volumes, edited by
Friedrich Walter, have been added to the *History of the Central Administration
of Austria* (Vienna, 1950) ; and the latest two volumes of the *Fontes Rerum
Austriacarum* (Ferdinand Maass, *Der Josephinismus,* Vienna, 1951) have made
available important material for the history of the Enlightenment in Austria.
But no really new direction of historical writing seems to have emerged so far;
the majority of the publications since 1945 are reminiscent of the conflicting
trends of the past.

The humiliation of a common defeat has not allowed German nationalism to
wane completely. Yet, seven years of Nazi *Anschluss* were bound to have a
sobering effect upon *grossdeutsch* sentiment, and a new, more narrowly Austrian,
nationalism inevitably resulted.[36] Srbik's first post-war publications again tried

---

[34] The book, bringing Austrian history to the *Heimwehr* regime of 1934, is a one-volume condensation of the earlier edition, now renamed *Die Tragödie Oesterreichs.*
[35] The last two volumes are based upon one of Srbik's most important document publications, his
edition, with Oskar Schmid, of the *Quellen zur deutschen Politik Oesterreichs* (6 vols.).
[36] The individuality of the Austrian character is again stressed in Renner's *1950 Jahre Oesterreich.*

to conjure up the great figures of Austrian history, from Prince Eugene to Emperor Francis Joseph.[37] A broader, more European, view is discernible, but its relationship to the old *Mitteleuropa* complex is not yet clear. As formulated in the posthumous writings of Karl Renner, this view, which identifies Austria with Western Europe in the new struggle between East and West, seems to be little more than a revival of the familiar persuasion of Austria's mission as the "guardian of Europe's eastern frontier." [38]

Yet, it is with respect to eastern Europe that the Austrian position has been most fundamentally challenged. In view of Austria's geography and earlier history, Slavic studies necessarily made up an important part of Austrian historical research.[39] The new power relationships logically force Austrian historians to review their concepts of Eastern European history. Thus a basic reorientation of Austrian historiography in the Slavic field may well be taking shape. An effort in this direction, though shortlived, was made by Heinrich Felix Schmid and Josef Matl when, from 1948-1949, they published the *Eastern Review* in parallel German, French, and English editions.

Among the several attempts to fit the most recent events into the pattern of Austrian history, perhaps the most dispassionate is Richard Charmatz's *Vom Kaiserreich zur Republik (From Empire to Republic,* Vienna, 1947). As indicated by its subtitle, "Austria's Struggle for Democracy, 1747-1947," the book tries to point out the continuity in the tortuous road travelled by Austrian democratic liberalism, from the days of Maria Theresa to the present. Not so broad in scope, but more penetrating in its approach, is Karl Renner's posthumously published *Oesterreich von der ersten zur zweiten Republik (Austria from the First to the Second Republic,* Vienna, 1953). Tracing Austrian history from 1918 to 1945, the book points to the political irresponsibility of a nationalistic and reactionary bourgeoisie which, by sanctioning the crushing of the Socialists in 1934, prepared Hitler's conquest of Austria. That at least some of the blame must be shared by the Social Democrats themselves, has now been made clear in Joseph Buttinger's compelling history of the Revolutionary Socialists of Austria *(In the Twilight of Socialism,* New York, 1953).[40] Despite its highly personal approach, this soul-searching account of the inner party struggles among Austrian Socialists in their defensive efforts against the Dollfuss and Hitler regimes is indispensable for an understanding of the ultimate failure of Austrian Social Democracy.

---

[37] *Aus Oesterreichs Vergangenheit;* a collection of essays which, with one exception, had been previously published.

[38] Renner's acceptance of the *Mitteleuropa* idea, unusual in a Socialist, had as early as the first World War involved him in bitter controversy with Otto Bauer (Cp. Renner, *Oesterreichs Erneuerung,* 3 vols., and Bauer, *The Austrian Revolution, op. cit.).*

[39] The best known Slavic scholars are Heinrich Felix Schmid (born 1896), authority on Slavic church and constitutional history, and Hans Uebersberger (born 1877) in modern Russian history. Together with Joseph Matl (born 1897), predominantly a student of Yugoslav culture and history, they were the editors of the *Jahrbücher für Kultur und Geschichte der Slawen* and their continuation, the *Jahrbücher für die Geschichte Osteuropas.*
Uebersberger's publications include *Oesterreich und Russland seit dem Ende des 15. Jahrhunderts* (2 vols.) and *Russlands Orientpolitik in den letzten zwei Jahrhunderten.* Removed from office because of his Nazi sympathies, he is now with the Free Ukrainian University, an anti-Soviet institution in Munich.

[40] Buttinger is the pseudonym of an Austrian Revolutionary Socialist now living in the United States. The English edition, and possibly the German trade edition unavailable to this writer, is a condensation of the original *Am Beispiele Oesterreichs,* printed as manuscript only, in 1951. (See the review by Franz L. Neumann, *Political Science Quarterly,* LXVII (1952), pp. 138-141).

While these writings are intrinsically of documentary value, a truly historical analysis of the Austrian past is the recently continued work by Hugo Hantsch (born 1895), *Die Geschichte Oesterreichs (History of Austria,* 2 vols., Graz, 1950-1951). This broadly conceived, and still unfinished, study confirms Hantsch as one of the ablest and most scholarly representatives of the conservative Catholic tradition in Austrian historiography.

Whatever the reasons, the conservative tradition has indeed emerged as the strongest trend in Austrian historical writing of the new post-war era. It has, in fact, produced one of the outstanding contributions to historical thought with the, partly posthumous, publication of Heinrich von Srbik's *Geist und Geschichte vom deutschen Humanismus bis zur Gegenwart (Mind and History from German Humanism to the Present,* 2 vols., Munich & Salzburg, 1950-1951). One of the most mature achievements of Austrian historical scholarship, the work is a discussion of the history and the meaning of German historiography which in scope and profundity surpasses anything hitherto presented in this field. Srbik has justly been criticized for having dealt too seriously with the Nazi pretense at a new concept of history, and no doubt Srbik here spoke in defense of his own political indiscretion.[41] Nevertheless, in this legacy from Srbik's pen he dissociated himself with cogent arguments from the fallacies of racist and nationalistic historiography. Too wise to believe that absolute objectivity in historical writing could ever be more than an unattainable ideal, Srbik saw the redemption of history in its innate spirituality; in the end he quoted Ranke's demand that history must become "a matter of conscience," if the historian would approach its essentially humane goal.

A similar call for a conscience in the writing of history had earlier been made by a Viennese writer, who pointed out the dangers which a political historiography has presented to society.[42] These dangers must increase in the age of atomic warfare, when political disagreements may result in the destruction of all mankind. The failure of the political approach to history demands a revision of the contemporary view of history through the creation of a new historical consciousness and conscience. It must result in a "turn toward ethics," a new concept of the ethical responsibility of men everywhere "to their time, to God, and to mankind." The historian's task must be to lead in this profound searching of the souls *(Gewissensforschung).*

The article confirms what was stressed at the beginning of this chapter: the profound influence of political history upon Austrian historical scholarship. There can be little doubt, however, that the implied flight from politics was motivated by the deeply disturbing experiences of the last decade, and thus is itself not without political connotations. It seems indeed doubtful that an ethical historiography totally divorced from political actualities is really possible. The further question arises whether such an approach, even if feasible, would not ultimately create its own, though different, dangers both to political history and to the validity of historical writing.

---

[41] *Cf.* Walther Hofer, "*Heinrich von Srbiks letztes Werk*," *Historische Zeitschrift,* vol. 175 (February, 1953), pp. 55-66.

[42] Adam Wandruszka, "*Die Problematik der Geschichtsschreibung in der Gegenwart*," *Europa-Archiv,* IV (1949), pp. 2453-2456.

Chapter 24

HUNGARY

By Stephen Borsody

Broader Background of the Problems

FOLLOWING the *Ausgleich* of 1867, Hungary entered the twentieth century as a kingdom of the Austro-Hungarian Empire. With the collapse of the empire in World War I, Hungary became first a democratic republic (1918), next a Bolshevik state for four months (1919), and then, following a counter-revolution (1919), a restored monarchy under a regency. The Treaty of the Trianon (1920) reduced the country to a third of its prewar size and put a fourth of the Hungarian people under the succession states, Czechoslovakia, Rumania, and Yugoslavia.

Trianon Hungary was ruled by a reactionary oligarchy which resisted any democratization of the country, and made the foreign issue, namely, revision of the Trianon Treaty, the central problem of national life. Hungary's neighbors, needless to say, defended the *status quo* obstinately. After Italy and Germany favorably revised the Trianon Treaty with the two Vienna awards (1938, 1940), Hungary joined the Axis power in the Second World War (1941). In the last phase of the war, Germany occupied the country, and Hungary's attempt to make a separate peace failed (1944)

Following the Second World War, Hungary became a republic (1946), and the Peace Treaty of Paris (1947) restored the Trianon frontiers. After a Communist *coup d'état* (1947), which frustrated hopes of the long awaited democracy, Russian-occupied Hungary was rapidly integrated into the Soviet totalitarian system.

It is against this political background that we can best understand the work of Hungarian historians; for Hungarian historiography developed under the double influence of Western ideas and local political conditions.

National Liberals and Scientific Positivists

Hungarian historiography during the period of the *Ausgleich* (1867-1918) presents a very heterogeneous picture. The two great historians of the nineteenth century, Ladislas Szalay (1813-1864) and Bishop Michael Horváth (1809-1878), both of whom were politically active in the 1848-1849 revolution against Austria, are typical of the European national-liberal school. To them the dominant theme of Hungarian history was the struggle for national freedom and independence. They were influenced to a considerable extent by the French liberal historians; Guizot, for example, had a marked effect on Horváth. They were also pioneers in the use of primary sources, and Szalay, who somewhat followed Ranke, was especially successful in reaching objective conclusions from the study of sources. Consequently, his *History of Hungary* (1851-1862; 2d ed., 1866) never became popular. Horváth's *History of Hungary,* on the other hand, was regarded as the standard historical work in liberal Hungary, achieving eight editions from 1842 to 1882.

The national-liberal school was soon outnumbered by the adherents of scientific positivism, but the establishment of the modern historical sciences was the joint achievement of both groups. At the Academy (founded in 1825) and the National Museum (1802) new historical sections were created after the *Ausgleich* of 1867 when the cultural and economic life of the country developed in rapid strides. In 1874 the Historical Society was founded, and in the next year the *Századok (Centuries),* the review of the Society, the first in a long line of scientific periodicals, was established. Of especial importance was the *Monumenta Hungariae Historica,* a series of source editions started by the Academy in 1880. The study of sources was accompanied by a rapid development of the auxiliary historical sciences and related fields.

The positivistic-scientific school with its materialistic trend flourished until the end of the century, at which time the new methods of Below, Meinecke, Lavisse, Aulard and others, aiming at wider and deeper synthesis, were gaining ground in European historiography. The long era of positivism was useful, however, inasmuch as the study of sources, involving the methodical discovery and collection of facts and documents, made considerable headway during those years.[1]

The historians of the scientific school were excellent in detailed research and analysis; they made lasting contributions to the study of various segments of the past, but in synthesis they did not achieve anything similar to the works of the earlier national-liberal authors. The great collective work of this generation, the ten-volume *History of the Hungarian Nation* (in Hungarian, Budapest, 1895-98), edited under the direction of Alexander Szilágyi, the dean of the historians, was more or less a chronological record of events.[2]

THE "LAY" CONCEPT OF HISTORY

The general concept of history during the period of Austro-Hungarian dualism was saturated with the spirit of independence and hostility toward Austria. It emphasized the "liberal" and "national" aspects of the past; in a sense it identified the nation with liberty—a habit freely practiced nearly everywhere in Central Europe.

This concept was called the "lay" interpretation of history, the word "lay" expressing not only a contrast to earlier theological concepts but even to a greater extent the contempt later critics felt for its unscientific nature. By the turn of the century this "lay" concept overshadowed all the other contemporary trends in historiography. Institutions and university chairs passed into the hands of politician-historians, devotees of the "lay" concept, who did not continue the scientific work of the positivists. They busied themselves in adjusting history to

[1] On the role and character of positivism see Theodor Thienemann, "Positivism and the Hungarian Historical Sciences" (in Hungarian), *Minerva,* I, (1922).
[2] The "Millenium History," so called because it was published while the country celebrated the thousand-year anniversary of the conquest of Hungary by the Magyars, set at 896 A.D.

current political needs and failed to maintain contact with the development of Western scholarship.

During this period of so-called decadence *(ca.* 1890-1920), only Henry Marczali (1856-1940) among the historians of position and influence fought against national isolation. Calling himself the pupil of Waitz, Wattenbach and Monod, he stood for continued cooperation with the foreign schools. His seminar at the Budapest University was the center of the study of sources. Marczali himself was the most prolific Hungarian historian, the finest exponent of scientific historical writing.[3]

HISTORICAL CRITICISM AND MATERIALISM

The period of "decadence," however, was not altogether decadent. Under the noisy surface dominated by the "lay" concept, the silent work of the scholars continued.

Historical criticism was one of the cherished tendencies among the serious scholars. German positivism was rejected as being bogged down in sheer recording of facts. The more "spiritual" positivism of Spencer and Comte was followed instead. Among the exponents of historical criticism, Charles Tagányi (1858-1924) had a decisive influence. Although Tagányi never held a professorial chair, the younger generation regarded him as their teacher and master. He specialized in the social and economic problems of medieval Hungary, depicting also the analogous developments and relationships among the Hungarian, Germanic and Slavìc peoples. Among other things, Tagányi established the fact that Hungary did not experience feudalism proper but adapted only many feudal social forms, like other nations living outside the truly feudal area of Europe.[4]

Tagányi, together with Ignatius Acsády (1854-1906), founded Hungarian economic history. Acsády specialized in the period of the sixteenth to the eighteenth centuries, and his *History of the Hungarian System of Serfdom* (in Hungarian, Budapest, 1908) was the first of its kind. Though written with some of the democratic bias of the twentieth century, it is a remarkable synthesis, and so is his *History of the Hungarian Empire* (in Hungarian, Budapest, 1903-4). Alexander Takáts (1860-1932) also made a valuable contribution with his studies concerning the economic and social conditions during the Turkish occupation (1526-1686).

A rather isolated group consisted of the radicals who followed to a varying extent the theories of historical materialism; their interest was focused on the social and minority problems, the two neglected aspects of both the past and present. Grouped around the review *Huszadik Század (Twentieth Century,* 1901-1919), they were the extreme antithesis of everything for which contemporary Hungary stood. Well trained in western sociology, they applied Western standards of measurement to Hungary. Their conclusions, pointing out

---

[3] Marczali's *History of Hungary* (in Hungarian) was a basic work on the political history of the country. Outstanding among his many monographs were *Hungary in the Eighteenth Century* and *Ungarische Verfassungsgeschichte.*

[4] Tagány's chief works are available also in German. See: K. Taganyi, *Lebende Rechtsgewohnhetten und ibre Sammlungen in Ungarn.*

as they did the backwardness of the country, made their authors unpopular. The contributions of this group to the historical sciences were rather limited. They interpreted rather than searched the past; seldom did they understand the problems of the past in their original setting because of the emphasis they put on current politics. Their bitterness—and the bitterness against them—was aggravated after the failure of the democratic experiment in 1918-19; sooner or later they were all forced to emigrate.

Oscar Jászi (1875-   ), who became professor at Oberlin College in 1925, was the leading spirit of this group. The wide range of his scholarly works covered the nationality problem, the miscarried revolution and the fall of the Habsburg Empire. Bitter political experience did not undermine Jászi's striving for objectivity. His recent analyses offer not only a clear historical presentation of the Danubian problems (concerning which much has been written from a propaganda viewpoint) but also a lucid sociological evaluation of the present confused situation.[5]

An outstanding member of this group was Rustem Vámbéry (1872-1948), a sociologist of international fame, whose last historical work, however, was a rather unfortunate exhibition of personal grudge.[6]

HUNGARIAN VERSION OF "GEISTESGESCHICHTE"

Among the historians working in silence since the turn of the century, some followed the German currents known under the name of *Geistesgeschichte*. Dilthey, Schmoller, Georg V. Below, Lamprecht, Max Weber, Troeltsch and Sombart were their models. The excesses, however, of what is known as German *Geistesgeschichte* were checked in its Hungarian version. The new school of *Szellemtörténet*, as *Geistesgeschichte* is called in Hungarian, was a rather happy mixture of French and English inspired historical criticism and German *Geistesgeschichte*. In other words, the new school, although German in name, was essentially a Hungarian phenomenon. It became all-powerful in the period between the two world wars.

According to the new school, the task of the historian is not merely to establish the facts but to penetrate into the spiritual background of the facts. Human history, said Julius Szekfü, who first essayed Hungarian *Geistesgeschichte,* is the history of the human soul. The spiritual approach encouraged the historians to reconstruct the ideas of the past and evaluate the facts in the spirit of the times when they occurred. As Elemer Mályusz, the best social historian of the postwar period, expressed it: It is the *"Weltanschauung"* which is to be properly understood. He even proposed that the new school be called "History of the Weltanschauung." [7]

The favorite slogan of the new historians was "synthesis." They wanted to

---

[5] Jászi's chief works are: *The Formation of the National States and the Nationality Problem* (in Hungarian) ; *Revolution and Counter Revolution in Hungary; The Dissolution of the Habsburg Monarchy.*

[6] *Hungary; To Be or Not to Be.*

[7] For the "credo" of the new school see: Valentin Hóman, "The Road of History" ; and Julius Szekfü, "Political Historiography" ; both in Hóman, Ed., *New Ways of Hungarian Historiography* (in Hungarian), pp. 7-53, and pp. 397-445 respectively. Cf. also J. Bartha, "Spirit, Spiritual Science, Spiritual History," (in Hungarian). *Athenaeum,* XVII (1931) ; considered one of the most important studies on *"Geitesgeschichte"* in Hungary.

recreate the past in its fullness. They rejected the romanticism of the national-liberals, held insufficient the rigid fact-finding methods of the scientific-positivists, detested the narrow-mindedness of the "lay" conception, and condemned the radicals, both for their ahistorism and their disregard of Hungarian peculiarities. Their work began in times of stress. The lost war and its consequences left Hungary in a desolate situation. Nevertheless, thanks to the sympathetic understanding of an able Minister of Education, Count Cuno Klebelsberg (1873-1932), and the enthusiasm of the scholars, the disrupted organizations of the historians were rapidly rebuilt. Klebelsberg's aims were primarily political (he launched the haughty and unfounded slogan of "Magyar cultural superiority"), but the historical sciences benefited from his interest in culture.

Work of the Historical Society. The Historical Society assumed the responsibility for the editing of sources with the first publications in 1923 of the *Fontes Historiae Hungaricae Aevi Recentioris 1686-1918.* The huge volumes of the *Fontes* with exact reproduction of the sources and scientific commentaries were justly regarded as the pride of Hungarian historiography. Another important venture of the Society, the *Manual of the Hungarian Historical Sciences* (in Hungarian, Budapest, 1923), standardized the methods of research. A new society and review, called *Minerva,* was founded by the new school in 1922. Foreign contact was established in the research institutions at Vienna, Rome, Berlin, Paris and Warsaw, and also by means of several foreign language publications, such as the *Ungarische Jahrbücher* (1920) and the *Revue des Études Hongroises* (1923).

With an organization relatively better developed than those of many greater nations, Hungarian historiography after World War I pursued a double objective: specialization and synthesis. Not only in the cultural-intellectual field but in the neglected areas of economic and social relations as well, the work of the specialists was significant.

THE HISTORIANS OF THE NEW SCHOOL [8]

The representative work of the new school was the *Hungarian History* (in Hungarian, Budapest, 1st ed. in 8 vols., 1928-34; 2d and 3d eds. in 5 vols., 1935-36). The ancient and medieval parts were written by Valentin Hóman and the modern part by Julius Szekfü. Written in a brilliant style, it was tremendously successful; nearly 10,000 copies were sold in a country with less than 10,000,000 people. A synthesis of the labor of more than one generation, it was the first work which integrated the political, economic, social and cultural aspects of the past into one great picture.[9] Hóman and Szekfü portrayed—by scientific and not ideological argument—the history of the multi-national Hungarian state as showing distinctive marks of the Magyar nation and possessing organic ties

[8] "New school" is used here as a substitute for *szellemtörténet*, the Hungarian word for *Geistesgeschichte.*
[9] Shorter syntheses of Hungarian history were given by Francis Eckhart, *A Short History of the Hungarian People;* Alexander Domanovszky, *Die Geschichte Ungarns;* Alexander Pethö (1885-1939), *History of the Hungarian Nation* (in Hungarian); George Balanyi (1886-....), *The History of Hungary;* Count Paul Teleki (1879-1941), *The Evolution of Hungary and Its Place in European History;* Dominic G. Kosáry, *A History of Hungary.*

with the Christian-Germanic, *i.e.* Central European brand of Western civilization. Szekfü's narrative ends with 1914; the ensuing chapters were written but remained in manuscript.[10]

Szekfü. Julius Szekfü (1883-   ) was the dominant figure of Hungarian historiography in the period between the two World Wars. His first synthesis of Hungarian history, written during the First World War,[11] already clearly set forth his national-christian concept, which, often linked together with the so-called "christian-national" trend of the postwar reactionary regime, was branded as Catholic, pro-Habsburg, and anti-liberal.

It is true, that Szekfü rehabilitated the royalists and Catholics whose real historical value had been neglected by the "lay" concept. Moreover, Szekfü, and the entire historiography of the postwar independent Hungary, was more "dualistic" in spirit than the historiography of the prewar period when Hungary was a partner of the Dual Monarchy. But this reflected more often the historical realism of the new school than its political conformism with the counter-revolutionary regime. The historians, of course, could not escape the effects of the oppressive political climate in which they lived and worked. The discussion of the postwar period in Hungary was possible only under the condition of sacrificing scholarly integrity. In Hungary, the discussion of the prewar past, however, was free, and the scientific results of the new Hungarian historiography in this field were undeniable.

Influence of Bethlen on Szekfü. Szekfü's much criticized "anti-liberalism" consisted mainly in the exposure of liberalism's failure to live up to its own ideas. Liberalism drifting away from its spiritual springs and devoted to egotistic materialism was, in Szekfü's view, a worldwide phenomenon and one of the principal causes of the crisis of democracy. His severe but constructive criticism of the Hungarian social conditions made him popular both with the enlightened conservatives and the progressive democrats. He supported the conservative policies of Count Stephen Bethlen (1874-1948), was editor of *Magyar Szemle (Hungarian Review),* a prominent politico-sociological monthly sponsored by Bethlen. During the second World War, Szekfü became a rallying point of spiritual resistance. He edited *What Is Magyar?* (in Hungarian, Budapest, 1939), a collective work of Hungarian scholarship presenting a challenge to totalitarianism on the eve of Hungary's entrance into the war on the side of Germany, 1941. Until the German occupation of Hungary (1941) he was editorial writer for the anti-Nazi daily, *Magyar Nemzet (Hungarian Nation).* After spending the year of German occupation in hiding, Szekfü in 1946 became democratic Hungary's first envoy to Moscow. In his latest book, *After the Revolution,* written partly in Moscow, he was at his best in describing the inglorious end of the old regime. However, his analysis of Russian Communism, corroboratng the views of the "red dean," Hewlett Johnson, whom he cites

---

[10] Szekfü dealt with the recent period, with a quasi-sociological approach, both in his *Three Generations* (in Hungarian; enlarged under the title *Three Generations and After),* and *After the Revolution* (in Hungarian). His other chief works are: *Rákóczi in Exile 1715-1735* (in Hungarian); *Gabriel Bethlen* (in Hungarian). Szekfü greatly encouraged the study of minority (nationality) problems; his own studies in this field were collected in *State and Nation* (in Hungarian; in French: *État et Nation).*

[11] Julius Szekfu, *Der Staat Ungarn;* in Hungarian: *The Biography of the Hungarian State.*

with approval, was a grave disappointment to his old friends and adherents. In 1948, Szekfü resigned his post in Moscow and returned to his professional chair at Budapest University.

Hóman. The career of the co-author of the *Hungarian History* was very different. Valentin Hóman (1885-1952) was convicted as a war criminal and sentenced to a life term for his wartime collaboration as Minister of Education and leader of pro-Nazi political movements. Hóman's political views were by no means characteristic of the Hungarian historians; his case was a rather isolated one. The fact that Hóman is a convicted war criminal cannot alter the fact that he was the great medieval historian of the new school. He started— like most members of the new school—as an advocate of historical criticism. Besides the great syntheis he presented in the *Hungarian History,* he wrote many important monographs and was an efficient organizer and editor.[12]

Specialization brought substantial results in the study of the different periods. Ancient history was explored by exemplary teamwork of historians, archaeologists, anthropologists, ethnographers and linguists. A valuable contribution to the exploration of the Middle Ages was made by Alexander Domanovszky (1877-   ), the many results of whose profound studies were incorporated into the Hungarian History by Hóman.[13] Elemer Mályusz (1898-   ) did outstanding work with his studies both of medieval and modern times. He clarified many problems of the medieval minorities in Hungary; his main interest, however was in the bourgeoisie.[14] He maintained that the middle class was the prisoner of the nobility until the end of the nineteenth century. Himself a Protestant, he was often out of step with the new school, and his criticism of Catholics, Habsburgs and nobles was decried by Szekfü as "a historic antipathy."

STUDENTS OF MODERN TIMES

Among the students of modern times, Francis Eckhart (1885-   ) has explored economic problems, and Imre Lukinich (1880-   ) has widened the horizon of Hungarian historiography with studies concerning relations with Hungary's neighbors, especially the Rumanians.[15] Gustav Gratz (1875-1946) in his excellent monograph, *The Age of Dualism, 1867-1918* (in Hungarian, Budapest, 1934) produced the long-awaited pragmatic work on the period of *Ausgleich.* Gratz, a liberal statesman-historian, had ready in manuscript the history of Hungary between the two world wars, but after his return from a German concentration camp in 1945 he looked in vain for a publisher. Stephen Szabó (1898-   ) specialized in the study of the peasantry;

---

[12] Hóman's chief works were: *Towns in Hungary under the Arpads* (in Hungarian) ; *History of Hungarian Money* (in Hungarian, 1916) ; *Financial and Economic Policy of Hungary Under Charles Robert, 1308-1342* (in Hungarian) ; *Settlement of the Hungarians* (in Hungarian) ; *King Stephen the Saint* (in Hungarians) ; Hungary, 1301-1490," in the *Cambridge Medieval History*, vol. VIII, ch. xix (1932).

[13] Domanovszky edited two volumes on the *History of Hungarian Culture* (1st vol. *The Middle Ages,* 2d vol. *Hungarian Renaissance*), in Hungarian.

[14] Cf. "Geschichte des Burgerstums in Ungarn," *Vierteljahrschrift fur Sozial—und Wirtschaftgeschichte,* XX, 1928. Mályusz has also written a biography of *Mattias Corvinus* and an outstanding work entitled *Development of the Community Turocz* (in Hungarian).

[15] *Territorial Changes of Transylvania* (in Hungarian).

with firm historical sense he maintained a scientific point of view in treating the sorry plight of the peasant.[16]

Among the younger historians, outstanding works were produced by Domonic Kosáry (1913-   ), whose latest studies dealt with Kossuth,[17] and by Julius Mérei (1911-   ), who made valuable contributions to the understanding of the social and political background of the nineteenth century.[18] Many other historians, trained in the "new school," undertook with great skill the detailed examination of the past—sometimes so detailed that, as Szekfü once put it, the more general follower of the past had to "pull himself together" to follow them.

The art and literary historians contributed much to the synthesis of the new school. Tibor Gerevich (1882-1954) was one of the real builders of Hungarian *Geistesgeschichte;* his major contribution was the reappraisal of medieval Hungarian art.[19] Anthony Hekler (1882-1942), the other leading art historian, was an authority on the Hungarian baroque. Among the literary historians, an outstanding name is that of Eugene Pintér (1881-1940), author of a precise, scholarly, ten-volume *Hungarian Literary History.*

THE COMMUNIST TREND

The aftermath of World War II threw Hungary into the Russian sphere of influence. In 1947, Hungarian historiography was described by an American expert on Eastern European affairs as "iconoclastic, partisan, and dialectical," rebelling against the trend prevalent between the two wars and emphasizing the importance of Russia.[20] This same expert cites as a "prime example" the work of the Hungarian Communist writer Erik Molnár, (1894-   ), whose study of early Magyar society was largely an attempt to apply all the familiar Marxist dogmas to that simple, early period.

Since the *coup d'état* of May, 1947, the Iron Curtain has sealed off Hungary completely from the West, and Hungarian historiography has been forced to break its traditional Western ties. The local political scene, often a factor in history writing during the past, has now changed in a way which makes the influence of politics greater than ever. The historical organizations gradually passed under the control of the Communists. Elizabeth Andics (1902-   ), the new president of the Historical Society, and thus far an unknown historian, assuming her post in 1949, denounced the old historiography as being the servant of the ruling classes.[21] As a matter of fact, the approach of the "new school," which might well be called the "old school" today, was indeed conservative and national. But there is no

---

[16] *History of the Hungarian Peasantry* (in Hungarian). Less scientific was the approach of the so-called "village explorers," a group of progressive writers, poets and folklorists, who in the thirties exposed with great courage the social ills of Hungary and made frequent excursions into the past. Although none of these was a trained historian, the group displayed more courage than did the historians.

[17] *Kossuth in the Age of Reform* (in Hungarian).

[18] *Political Party Programs, 1867-1914* (in Hungarian) ; and *The Agricultural and Agrarian Society, 1790-1848* (in Hungarian).

[19] Tibor Gerevich, *L'arte antica ungherese.*

[20] Leslie C. Tihany, "Post-Armistice Hungarian Historiography" (in manuscript) ; the bibliographical part of the study was published in *The American Slavic and East European Review,* VI (May, 1947), pp. 158-178.

[21] Elizabeth Andics, "Some Problems of Hungarian Historiography" (in Hungarian), *Forum* (May, 1949).

denying that it reached a high scientific level and showed a growing sense of realism and objectivity.

It is too early to sum up the results of the Communist trend. The "five year plan" of the Hungarian historians is now directed to the exploration of neglected fields and the revision of distortions. No doubt there are such neglected fields, and there are certainly distortions favoring the former ruling classes. But it is highly improbable that Communist historiography, with its known prejudices, will be able to either fill the gaps or correct the distortions.

Chapter 25

RUMANIA AND THE BALKANS

By George Waskovich

A T THE beginning of the nineteenth century, only Greece and Serbia among the Balkan countries had made progress toward becoming national states. Rumania was next when, in 1861, the European powers gave recognition to the joint-hospodarship of John Cuza. It was not until 1878, however, with the Russian victory over Turkey and the Congress of Berlin, that the foundations of Bulgaria were laid. Even then, the national aims of the Kingdoms of Serbia and Bulgaria were far from satisfied. Moreover, no settlement occurred in the area of the Balkans that could not be challenged by nations bordering them. The process of national integration was accompanied by the decline of Turkish power and the elevation of the ailments of the "sick man of Europe" into a major concern of the Great Powers. As a result of the Balkan Wars of 1912, Albania appeared as a state, whose geographic position was of concern to Italy and whose ethnic and historic backgrounds were of concern to Greece.

HISTORIOGRAPHY AND NATIONAL REVIVAL

The rise of historical writing in the Balkans is associated with the return of national life and state sovereignty, which for so many centuries had been stifled by Turkish domination. If the stimulation of the latent energy in a nation and the evocation of national pride in past achievements is the proper function of the historian, then the historiography of the Balkan peoples had many worthy representatives. The historians of this area worked in close harmony with the general and specific needs of their own fatherlands, grounding their activities in a deep knowledge of the psychology of their countrymen. Many of them took part in political life, linking their knowledge of the past with present political yearnings and aspirations.

POLITICAL AND CULTURAL FORCES

The re-discovery of the "Roman" tradition in Rumania had its counterpart in Greece, where those striving for the future turned a nostalgic eye to the "glory that was Greece." The Slavs of the Balkans, lacking the traditions of classical antiquity, found the *Slavonic idea* attractive. Russian interest in the lesser Slavic brethren ebbed and flowed, being conditioned largely by the greater considerations of European policy. All the Balkan nations had the common problems of defending themselves against the imperial ambitions of the greater European powers while striving to establish a *modus vivendi* among themselves. The one common element, except for Croatian Catholicism, the Moslem remnants, and other religious particles, was the Eastern Orthodox

Church. Thus the Balkan historian did not write in a vacuum; he was fully conscious of the many contemporary factors affecting the destinies of his nation. And on top of this regional, historical consciousness, he often showed a broad knowledge of the development of the art of history in the Western countries.

GREEK HISTORICAL WRITING

The country with the longest historical continuity and tradition was Greece, both extremely old and yet quite new in the European family of nations. The awareness of this past and its recovery were not alone the work of the Greek historians, but in their hands became the basis of the Hellenistic principle, or the *Great Idea*. The modern worship of Clio, clothed in the garb of nineteenth century romantic nationalism, became indeed something of a cult.[1] The study of antiquity became a burning passion, almost a religious duty; while the Middle Ages were largely ignored, for they provided little that was intrinsically complimentary to national pride or prestige. But national independence here, as elsewhere in the Balkans, tremendously stimulated the investigation and writing of history. Among the outstanding accounts of this time we find the work of Spiridion Trikoupis (1788-1873), which must indeed be regarded as a document of the times.[2] But Greece was to suffer a cruel blow to its "religion of history" from the almost contemporaneous attacks of the German historian, Fallmerayer, on the concept of the continuity of the Greek people as a race.[3] Fallmerayer contended that the modern Greeks are preponderantly of Slav, perhaps even somewhat of Albanian blood, *i.e.*, Greek-speaking Slavs. While some historians have professed to see in these theories a valuable contribution to the understanding of medieval Greek history, modern Greek historians have been prone to reject indignantly such shabby constructions. Thus Constantine Paparrhigopoulos (1815-1891) made the refutation of this "slander" his life work and wrote one of the first great works on modern Hellenism.[4]

THE HISTORIANS OF HELLENISM

The dominant note struck by Paparrhigopoulos served not only to establish the basic theme of modern Greek historiography, but assisted as well in encouraging a large number of minor historians to delve into all the nooks and crannies of local history in search of material, the better to substantiate the theses of the master. These stokers of the historical fires supplied fast increasing data to the outstanding followers of the Hellenism theme, such as Diomede Kyriakos,[5] M. Dendia, and A. Ephtaliotis, who perhaps came closest to the spirit of Paparrhigopoulos, while G. Frangoudis tried to establish the

---

[1] Cf. William Miller, "Modern Greek Historians of Modern Greece," *History* X (July, 1925), pp. 110-124. Cf. also J. W. Thompson, *History of Historical Writing*, Vol. II, pp. 641-643. Cf. also Eduard Driault & Michel L'Heriter, "Greece," in *Histoire et Historiens depuis cinquante ans*, pp. 193-208.

[2] Spyridion Trikoupis, *The War of Independence* (in Greek).

[3] See the attempt to refute Fallmerayer by George E. Mylonas, *The Balkan States: An Introduction to Their History*, appendix. Cf. also the criticism of Fallmerayer by George Finlay, *History of Greece in the Middle Ages*, pp. 2-4, 14-31.

[4] Constantine Paparrhigopoulos, *The History of the Greek People* (in Greek). Later enlarged by a supplement (1876), it has been carried down to the recent past by Paulos Karolides.

[5] Diomede Kyriakos, *Histoire ecclesiastique*. This is a three-volume work of which a portion has been translated into German as *Geschichte der orientalischen Kirchen*.

place of Hellenism historically by an examination of the relations of East and West.[6] But soon all the periods of Greek history had their specialists as the stimulus of historiography was more broadly felt. One of the more representative was A. Gennaudius who busied himself with the national awakening, while D. J. Drossos dealt with the European diplomatic repercussions of the same movement.[7] Greek historians soon developed a specific sympathy for the Byzantine period, and the names of Karolides, Bikela, Dragoumis, and K. Amantos are the most prominent in the field. Bikela, in addition, was attracted to and shed light on the Turkish period of Greek history.

LATER NINETEENTH CENTURY HISTORIOGRAPHY

For the period of the nineteenth century probably the outstanding historian was Constantine Sathos, (1841-1914), trained in Venice and Paris where he became familiar with the archival material of those cities. The duty of searching the library collections of Europe with a view to gathering such basic materials as appertained to Greece he carried out with the greatest assiduity. An example of the research type of historian, his life became one long historical safari through the sometimes parched mountains and deserts of "source materials." Trained originally in medicine, he lacked both the philological and the auxiliary historical sciences. Despite this, his monumental labors bore fruit not only in the field of Byzantinology, but in Russian history as well. For he helped to establish the interrelationship between the two fields, and to encourage the further pursuance of the subject by the publication of the Byzantine chronicles of Michael Constantine Psellus (1018-1079), a forerunner of the later Renaissance Platonists.[8]

Among the followers of this trail-blazer may be mentioned such writers as D. Bikelas whose work on Byzantium showed a sure competence. The neighbors of the Greeks were studied by D. J. Drossos, especially the Bulgars, while Greece's position in the diplomatic struggle incident to the rise of Bulgaria became the concern of S. T. Lascaris.[9] The diplomacy of the critical period before the First World War came in for examination by A. F. Frangulis and S. Phocas-Cosmetatos, who showed the same acumen in their discussion of the subsequent postwar situation.[10]

The specialists in various aspects of Greek history were led by A. M. Andreades (1876-1935) whose mastery of both English and French enabled him to publicize his nation's problems in various European periodicals. He was equally at home in the field of economic history and finance whether in ancient, Byzantine, or modern Greece, writing very prolifically in all three. On the other hand, specialists such as Nicolaides could deal with the intricacies of the Macedonian question or explain the significance of the relation of

[6] G. Frangoudis, *L'Hellenisme en lutte contre L'Orient et l'Occident.*
[7] A. Gennadius, *Modern Greece and the Greek Insurrection* (in Greek, French translation). D. J. Drossos, *European Diplomacy and the Greek Insurrection* (in Greek, French translation).
[8] Sathos' edition of Psellus' *Chronographia* was issued in 1899 by Methuen of London.
[9] D. Bikelas, *La Grece byzantine et moderne;* D. J. Drossos, *La fondation de l'alliance balkanique: etude d'Histoire diplomatique;* S. T. Lascaris, *La politique exterieure de la Grece avant et apres le Congres de Berlin, 1875-1881.*
[10] A. F. Frangulis, *La Grece et la crise mondiale* (2 vol.); S. Phocas-Cosmetatos, *L'Entente et la Grece pendant la grande guerre.*

Greece and Turkey for general European peace, not only with charm and grace but with accuracy as well.[11] The Greeks, a nation close to the sea, deserved the excellent maritime history written by Constantine Rados. Nor on the other hand was historical writing confined to the professional teachers of history, but any one with an easy pen, such as journalists, amateur archaeologists, retired businessmen, might try his hand. Local patriotism inspired many lesser works, some of them containing no inconsiderable material for the historical hamper. What occurred in local history was repeated in historical biography and not even classical mythology was excluded. All became grist to feed the historical mill. The concentration on purely Greek interests preponderantly has resulted logically in a paucity of works by Greeks on other subjects of a historical nature. But this is explained largely by the necessity for a small nation, recently become free after a long alien rule, to establish its historical identity and individuality.

The preparation for systematic work in history as in other social sciences was often difficult in Greece due to the essential poverty of the country. However, Lambakis founded the *Society for Christian Archaeology* in 1884; while Kalogeropoulos became the first president of the *Association for Byzantine Study*, founded in 1919. A *Society for Cretan Studies* was founded in 1924.[12]

HISTORIOGRAPHY IN RUMANIA

With the rise of Rumania to independence, the historians there soon discovered the hidden or latent culture of ancient Rome as a factor preeminent above others in the history of their own country. While the Roman cultural descent of the western Romance peoples is easy to establish, that of Rumania presented many problems. Systematic effort, strengthened by the developing national outlook, soon concentrated on proving the thesis that the culture and language were of Latin origin.

ROMANISM AND HISTORIOGRAPHY

For if the Greeks had been affronted by the theories of Fallmerayer, the Rumanians had a vexing problem also in the question of the priority of their arrival in Transylvania. Their contention, fought out mainly with the Magyar historians, was first stated by a Swiss, Franz Josef Sulzer, in a work published in 1781, dealing with the historical background of transalpine Dacia. Later this thesis was augmented by J. Ch. Engel, who based his conclusions on Rumanian as well as non-Rumanian materials.[13] It fell eventually to G. Sincai (1753-1816) to take up the cudgels in defense of the idea of Rumanian priority and earlier appearance in his *Chronica Românilor,* published in 1853 on the eve of Rumanian independence. Sincai, an intellectual of the Enlightenment of Joseph II, stoutly defended the theory of the Roman origin of his people under the Emperor Trajan, and stressed the later coming of

---

[11] C. Nicholaides, *Die geschichtliche Entwicklung der Macedonischen Frage im Alterthum, im Mittelalter und in der Zeit.* See, also, his *Die neuste Phase der Macedonischen Frage.*

[12] For a good survey of what was planned by the various Balkan countries in the field of social science, including history, up to 1930, see Robert J. Kerner, *Social Sciences in the Balkans and in Turkey.*

[13] Franz Josef Sulzer, *Geschichte des transalpinischen Daciens;* cf. Johann Christian Engel, *Geschichte der Moldau und Walachei.*

the Germans and the Magyars. According to him, these elements were entitled only to lesser rights on the "national" soil. P. Maior (1760-1831) insisted on the direct cultural and racial continuity of the modern Rumanians with ancient Rome. According to Maior, even the introduction of Christianity was a Roman and not a Slav or Byzantine contribution.

In view of the fierce nationalism developed in the Balkans during the nineteenth century, it would be unrealistic to underestimate the political and social force of the idea of Roman origin. It had a sustained and progressive influence on the national consciousness as well as the character of historical scholarship. This notion paid dividends in that it helped to generate a revolutionary spirit useful in the struggle for independence from the Turks.

THE EARLY NINETEENTH CENTURY

In the later progress of historical writing in Rumania we encounter the name of Bogdan P. Hasdeu, who was among the first to make an attempt at historical synthesis. Educated in Russia, conversant with a number of Slavonic languages, and, in the words of Jorga, "a fanatic of Latinism," he was a proponent of Romanism while still recognizing the influence which others besides the Romans had exercised on the development of his country. In addition to his synthesis, he gathered materials for a comprehensive study of the ancient laws and customs of Rumania, expanding them later with "acta" on political and military matters.[14] Thus, in his collection of the *Archives of the History of Rumania,* he furnished a prime source for the study of the national history from the fourteenth through the sixteenth centuries.

The first Rumanian historian of European reputation was A. D. Xenopol, who possessed not only an unusual breadth of view, coupled with power of organization, but also philosophical balance, and the intellectual equipment for historical synthesis. He was thoroughly grounded in the seminar method of German scholarship in Berlin, but at the same time managed to retain, in his general approach, the clarity inherent in the French intellectual method and philosophical outlook. He was an admirer, but not a slavish follower, of the geographical approach of the English scholar, Henry Thomas Buckle. We thus find that one of his main works deals with the problem of historical causation.[15] Xenopol was a writer of no mean literary ability, and his works are prized by his fellow-countrymen because he combined this with unusual narrative skill in unfolding the main stream of cultural development not only in his own country, but in that of adjacent neighbors as well. In some of his earlier works, he was concerned with the traditional Russian "urge to Constantinople," as well as such matters as the foundation of the Bulgarian Empire. Trained in jurisprudence, he nevertheless avoided a dry, legalistic approach, but was sensibly aware of the economic forces at work in the whole of the Balkans. His great work, rather elaborate in character, is at once an attempt to present the story of the Rumanian element regardless of province, and at the same time to refute the German historian, Rossler's, stand on that

---

[14] Bogdan P. Hasdeu, *The Critical History of Rumania* (in Rumanian).
[15] A. D. Xenopol, *Les principes fondamentaux de l'histoire.*

hardy perennial: Rumanian or non-Rumanian priority in the settlement of the provinces of Wallachia, Moldavia, and especially Transylvania. His national zeal was fully equalled by the devotion of his readers, who were hardly aware that this work, to which he added a supplement bringing the story down to 1866, did not always reflect the greatest possible historical objectivity. Xenopol owed much to Hasdeu, especially in bibliography, but found it difficult to overcome the handicaps imposed by his inability or lack of opportunity to do research in other countries. Thus, while Rumanian historical writing owes much to Xenopol, its main task henceforth was to improve not only the presentation but also the basic methodology of his followers and his critics.

THE WORK OF NICHOLAS JORGA

The most widely celebrated of Rumanian historians is the extremely versatile and prolific Nicholas Jorga (1871-1940) whose venerable age and European reputation proved no deterrent to his brutal murder at the hands of Iron Guard underlings of the Nazi German overlords.[16] Jorga was trained in Paris and at the University of Leipzig, but he was more inclined to impart to Rumanian history and cultural development the Romantic tradition of the mid-nineteenth century. His concept of the historical process and the function of the historian took into account the unending national struggle to achieve independence, establish the language, preserve the national values, and to toughen the national consciousness. History had "purpose" and he himself, as a public character, took part in public polemics, in the tradition of the European intellectual, on many occasions. He imparted an ineluctable, semi-mystical concept to his treatment of the history of the Rumanian people, thus making himself not only the intellectual, but in a sense the moral, leader of his nation. To be sure, serious objections and penetrating criticisms have been made of some of his generalizations, but the debt owed to Jorga by western European and American historians of the Balkan area is and will still continue to be enormous. Like others before him, Jorga laid great stress on the Roman or Latin element in Rumanian civilization, even going to the extent of denying that Rumania was a Balkan nation at all. In this and other contentions he sought to prove that modern Rumania is the custodian of the ancient Roman tradition, shared in the West by Italy, France, and Spain.

The historians of small nations like Xenopol and Jorga are hard put to justify, or to place in its proper framework in the universal history of mankind, the particular history of their own nation. Thus Jorga, like his older contemporary Xenopol, tried to evaluate the position of Rumania in an elaborate work aiming at universal synthesis.[17]

A still earlier work was a part of a series edited by the distinguished German historian, Karl Lamprecht, and only belatedly translated into Rumanian.[18] Later attempts at synthesis or interpretation resulted in his interesting work establishing the place of Rumania in general history.[19] However, English readers may

[16] J. C. Campbell, "Nicholas Jorga," *The Slavonic Review*, XXVI (November, 1947), pp. 44-59.
[17] N. Jorga, *Essai de synthese de l'histoire de l'humanite.*
[18] Nicholas Jorga, *Geschichte des rumanischen Volkes.*
[19] Nicholas Jorga, *La place des Roumains dans l'histoire universelle* (3 vols.).

glean a picture, however inadequate, of the power of Jorga by consulting either his numerous articles or his only general history in the language.[20] Jorga's crowning achievement, the *Istoria Romanilor,* which reached ten volumes, has been published in French with the translation of the first four volumes, carrying the story of Rumania down to the sixteenth century.

Jorga as a Byzantinologist. Although Jorga ranked very high as a Byzantinologist, his output in this field was not of uniform quality. Nevertheless, it was a field in which he was prolific and which widened his reputation by bringing him a European following. One of his most interesting works in this field was actually an elaboration of a small work published as early as 1907 in English, but rewritten for a French edition in 1934 in three volumes.[21] The historical and cultural tradition of Byzantium came in for elucidation in a series of *Etudes,*[22] while his interest in the subsequent development of Turkish power in general and in the Balkan peninsula at large resulted in a work which still remains indispensable for students of the region.[23] This logically led, in turn, to his study of the rise of the Balkan states as separate entities.[24] Jorga understood the necessity of studying the larger framework of Rumanian history with the histories of Bulgaria, Hungary, and Yugoslavia, while at the same time devoting himself to many problems common to all. Perhaps his greatest handicap was his relative non-acquaintance with the history of Slavic civilization, especially in those nations bordering on his homeland. While Jorga had undoubted literary ability, some of his work suffers from a plethora of rhetoric.

THE SUCCESSORS OF JORGA

It is perhaps not entirely accurate to say that Jorga founded a school of historiography in Rumania; but it is entirely just to say that without his efforts historical writing would be immeasurably poorer in inspiration, scope, power, and method. Many of his students became lesser known but none the less potent members of the so-called "critical school." Among them we find Constantin C. Giurescu (1875-1918), whose *Istoria Romanilor* reveals a deep understanding of the medieval period, and his fellow medievalist D. Oncuil (1856-1923); while Byzantine studies are connected with the name of D. Russo (1869-1926). V. Parvan's archaeological study of the Gotho-Dacian field did much to clear up some of the vexing problems of Rumanian foundations. Working as a team, their combined efforts were also devoted to the gathering of sources, added to those already issued by E. Hurmuzaki; Jorga himself contributed some twenty-three more volumes of documents and six volumes of *Notes et extraits.*

AFTER THE FIRST WORLD WAR

In the period following the first World War, Rumania was faced with the political problem of coordinating the newly acquired territories; hence, from

[20] Nicholas Jorga, *A History of Roumania: Land, People, Civilization; Histoire des Roumains et de la Romanite orientale.*
[21] Nicholas Jorga, *Histoire de la vie Byzantine: empire et civilisation.*
[22] Nicholas Jorga, *Études Byzantines.*
[23] Nicholas Jorga, *Geschichte des osmanischen Reiches* (5 vols.).
[24] Nicholas Jorga, *Histoire des l'états balcaniques jusqu'à* 1874.

the national point of view, their inclusion in any new historical synthesis would necessitate the documentation of such acquisitions. It was not unnatural for this to lead to an expansion and an intensification of activity on the part of the historians. The twenty years between 1919 and 1939 represent indeed not only a quickening of the aims of the historians, but a sharpening of national life in all of its aspects. Not all of the materials for the achievement of this purpose were in Rumania; hence, a search in foreign archives had the double result of providing an answer to the immediate problems, and of acquainting Rumanian scholars with the western world at first hand. Jorga founded the South-Eastern European Institute in 1913, and became the body and soul of it. Subsequently the various universities of Rumania laid the foundations of a number of "historical institutes" all of them quickened with a new purpose. The roster of scholars connected with them would indeed be not inconsiderable, and their number increased with the spread of the enthusiasm for historical studies.

This newer historiography blazed trails and departed in some instances radically from the traditional outlook. The New History in Rumania acquired a humanistic tone and a breadth of treatment which attested the new interdependence of the social sciences as far as they had developed in the Balkans. Such special fields as the Rumanian relations with the Slavs produced workers such as C. C. Giurescu, G. Bratianu, and A. Lapedatu. Other specialties such as the history of warfare, the history of art, archaeology, Byzantinology, and historiography found exponents who stressed the stream of cultural development, social and economic institutions, principles, ideas, and the role of the social classes. The patriotic urge which had enveloped the whole of historical writing with an aura of pseudo-grandeur did not give way entirely to rigid objectivity, but it was somewhat modified by the necessity of conforming to more exacting criteria. Among the most noteworthy of the exponents of the "new history" were such scholars as G. Ghibanescu, L. T. Boga, Gr. Toscilou, S. Dragomir, and P. P. Panaitescu. The Second World War in these circumstances dealt not unnaturally a mortal blow to many activities. We can only conjecture the turn of Rumanian intellectual activity under the present impact of a Communist social order.[25]

THE BULGARIAN BACKGROUND

Unlike the Greeks and the Rumanians, the Bulgarians had no classical antiquity to which they could appeal in the revival of historical studies. Indeed, their national cultural revival began rather slowly, and until about 1835 their basic problem was largely linguistic. Once established as a European state, following the Berlin Congress, despite some later involved diplomatic tangles, Bulgaria was open to new cultural influences, tending to enrich her national life. Thus besides the stream from Russia, we find elements of Slavism from Central Europe, from Serbia, even from Poland; while the reception of political ideas from France via Serbia and Greece created a constant ferment.[26]

Thus, although the Bulgarians at the beginning of the nineteenth century

[25] See the account of Josef Macorek, *Historiography of Eastern* (in Czech), pp. 236-241, 272-279. Cf. also N. Iorga, "Roumanie," in *Histoire et Historiens depuis cinquante ans*, pp. 320-340.
[26] Cf. C. E. Black, *The Establishment of Constitutional Government in Bulgaria*, pp. 7-51. Cf. also D. Mishew, *The Bulgarians in the Past: Pages from Bulgarian Cultural History*, pp. 292-328.

possessed the minimum of historical awareness, once developed it proceeded forward with an unusual velocity. The interest in Bulgaria's historical past was shared in large part by a number of able scholars of other nations.

BULGARIAN HISTORIOGRAPHY

Among the early champions of Bulgarian studies was George Venelin, some-time member of the University of Lvov, a Ukrainian by birth, who in Galicia had become acquainted with a number of Bulgarian political emigrés. The author of a work in philology, *Vlacho-Bulgarian Grammar,* as well as a historical account which first appeared in 1829, his *The Old and New Bulgaria* clearly reflects the prevalent romanticism of the day. In the work on grammar he tried to establish the roots of the science of Bulgarian linguistics in the language spoken in the days of Saints Cyril and Methodius, that is, in the middle of the ninth century, and furthermore tried to prove that the Bulgarians were of pure Slav descent. While these works would not be considered scholarly by the standards of today, they attracted some notice in Russia, where the St. Petersburg Academy was so impressed that Venelin was provided with the means to travel and study in Bulgaria.

The intensification of intellectual activity in Bohemia was likewise reflected in Bulgarian studies, where the celebrated work, *Slavonic Antiquities* of the Slovak scholar P. J. Safarik, was published in 1840, after a great deal of intensive research. It was some time later before the scholarly efforts of Constantine Jirecek produced the *History of the Bulgarian People* (in German, 1876). The most recent Czech scholar in this field was Francis Hybl of the Charles University of Prague. However, the chief credit for establishing scientific standards and the necessary critical approach undoubtedly belongs to Jirecek.

Probably the earliest of the purely modern, semi-scientific Bulgarian historians was George Stojkov Rakovski (1818-1868) who, like a number of his contemporaries, acquired a Russian background by virtue of his long residence in the Moscow Bulgarian quarter. A man of many accomplishments, he was driven by patriotism, his journalistic activities, and his work as agitator to the study of his country's past. It was not, however, until the coming of Marin Drinov (1838-1906) that Bulgarian historical writing was established on a basis comparable to that of western Europe. Following the establishment of Bulgarian independence, Drinov and the Czech, Jirecek, collaborated not only in the field of history, but in the establishment of cultural, scientific, and educational institutions so necessary to raise the level of national life.[27]

M. S. DRINOV

Some of Drinov's works were written in Russian, for from 1873 to his death he was professor at the University of Kharkov. During this period he wrote of the settlement of the Slavs in the Balkans, and closely related subjects, such as the influence of Byzantium on the Southern Slavs in the tenth century, and the religious and cultural origins of the Bulgarian people. In addition to

---

[27] Gaston Cahen, "Bulgarie" in *Histoire et historiens,* pp. 72-85.

his writings on history and the evolution of church doctrine, Drinov wrote on the evolution of the Bulgarian alphabet and was one of the founders of the embryo organization which became the Bulgarian Academy of Sciences.[28] In all that he did, Drinov upheld the best traditions of the Slavic savant.

V. N. ZLATARSKI AND ASSOCIATES

The foundations laid by Drinov were carried on by Zlatarski (1866-1935) and his associates such as N. S. Bobchev, I. Shishmanov, and L. Miletic on a uniformly high level of accomplishment. Zlatarski specialized mainly in the medieval period of Bulgarian history, but also became one of the foremost Balkan scholars on the relations of Byzantium to Bulgarian development. Since in some respects the medieval period was the most "honorable" in Bulgarian history, a great deal of attention was devoted to it. But the national renaissance claimed its historians as well. In this latter field the studies by Shishmanov of the patriot Rakovski, and those of S. Georgiev, on the elements of the diplomatic history in the formation of Bulgarian unity, constitute typical examples. Simeon Radev, a follower of Zlatarski, has done well in maintaining the high level of accomplishment in his work on the establishment of the principality of Bulgaria. On the other hand, N. Stanev's study of recent Bulgarian history during its subjection and liberation, 1793-1878, despite its evident carefulness, is not quite so useful from the point of view of the scholar.[29] Other scholars like S. Bobhev, in the field of Bulgarian law, and Popov and Kacarov, dealing with obscure aspects of pre-history or ancient history, have shed considerable light on recondite problems of Balkan history, such as the place of the Celts, or the religion of Thrace in ancient times.[30] P. Nikov's work in the field of Bulgarian historiography is basic spade work, but must be augmented by his studies in Bulgarian sources; while his studies in ecclesiastical history have been honored by the Bulgarian Academy of Sciences.[31]

As in other Balkan countries, general historiography soon broke into a number of constituent branches such as institutional, ecclesiastical, economic, social and constitutional. Thus N. V. Mikhov's work on the population of Turkey, the legal studies of N. P. Blagoev, and the study of I. Snegarov concerning the last Bulgarian See at Ochrida, shed considerable light on moot questions. Economic and social theorists have been responsible for a number of works; the earliest and most representative is the application of Marxian historical dialectics, by D. Blagoev to Bulgaria and to Bulgarian social development.[32] More orthodox in its approach in the same field is the scholarly work of Ivan Yankov Sakuzov (1895-1935) ; while Zhak Natan in his own studies endeavored to integrate economic and political factors in their reciprocal

[28] Drinov's main works in the field of Slavic history: *The Historical View of the Bulgarian Church from Its Foundation to Today* (in Bulgarian) ; *The Settlement of the Balkan Peninsula by the Slavs* (in Russian) ; *Southern Slavs and Byzantium in the Xth Century* (in Russian).
[29] Cf. also his evaluation of the influence of other nations on Bulgarian culture in *Rodina* 1 (1938-1939) ; and N. Stanew, *The Newest History of Bulgaria* (2 vols. Sofia, 1924-1925, 29; in Bulgarian).
[30] Cf. S. S. Bobchev, *Byzantium and Bulgaria: the Struggle of Popular Law Against the Influence of Byzantium* (Sofia, 1934) ; and his *The Struggle of the Bulgarian People for a National Church* (in Bulgarian).
[31] P. Nikov, *The Problem of Bulgarian Historiography;* and *Report on Some of the Works of N. P. Blagoev* (in Bulgarian).
[32] See D. Blagoev, *A Contribution to the History of Socialism in Bulgaria* (in Bulgarian).

relations. The labor movement in this preponderantly agricultural country was studied by Ivan G. Klincharov.[33]

HISTORIOGRAPHY AND NATIONAL INDEPENDENCE

Bulgarian historians have endeavored to treat in all of its aspects the most important fact in their modern history: the achievement of national independence. Hence the course of the revolutionary movement leading up to this as well as other related facts of national life has been done by various hands, notably by B. Yotsov on its general aspects; while such writers as M. Arnaudov, Ilarion Makariopolski, and S. Romanski have done individual sketches or historical portraits of the most influential leaders of the "renaissance."

The contributions of other nations have interested Bulgarian writers in their effort to reconstruct the history of the national independence movement.[34] Thus Nikola Stanev, L. I. Dorosiev, and N. Dontchev have emphasized the French cultural and political stream into Bulgaria, while numerous works have dealt with the Russian background. Suffice to say that the eastern influence is regarded as paramount by the post-Second World War historiographers, dominated as they are by Russian Communist influence.[35] Perhaps the most elaborate work is that of Peter Nikov (1884-1938) who endeavored to trace the spread of European Romanticism not only in Bulgaria but in Slavonic literature and culture in general.[36] N. Penev labored, however, to give not only a sociological but a philosophical answer to the question concerning the nature of the Bulgarian national tradition. In another work of keen intellectual insight he sought to evaluate the historical place of the educated element or the *intelligentsia* in Bulgarian cultural development, laying no inconsiderable emphasis on the contributions of Germany. Digging rather deeply, Iv. Minkov endeavored to treat the foundations of Bulgarian social life by tracing the elements of the domestic democratic tradition.[37]

Additional works in this same field have bordered on the closely related domains of physical anthropology, political ideas and theories, and the conception of the philosophy of history. Thus the history of political ideas, especially those of Rakovski, was described by M. Arnaudov. While not coming up to the standard of Jovan Cvijic, the work of St. Romanski, a study of the Bulgarian population in Wallachia and Moldavia, is a good example of the methods employed in contemporary physical anthropology, which in the Balkans has always political connotations and overtones. One of the ablest

---

[33] Ivan Y. Sakuzov, *Bulgarische Wirtschaftsgeschichte;* Zhak Natan, *Economic History of Bulgaria* (in Bulgarian, 2 vols.) ; Ivan G. Klincharov, *History of the Labor Movement in Bulgaria* (in Bulgarian).

[34] For a discussion of these factors in English see, C. E. Black, *The Establishment of Constitutional Government in Bulgaria*, pp. 23-50.

[35] For an account of Czarist influence see B. H. Sumner, *Russia and the Balkans, 1870-1880;* cf. also N. Stanev, *The Influence of French Culture on Bulgarian Public Life and Literature* (in Bulgarian).

[36] Petur Nikov, *The Bulgarian Renaissance at Varna and Its Environs* (in Bulgarian) ; similar ground was covered by N. Penev in his *On the Beginning of the Bulgarian National Awakening* (in Bulgarian, 3rd ed.) and *European Romanticism and Its Reflection in Slavonic Literature* (in Bulgarian).

[37] Iv. Minkov, *The Historic Roots of Our Democratic Tradition* (in Bulgarian).

students of ethnogeography was Anastas Ishkirov (1866-1937) who attempted also an analysis of the social institutions of the typical village in Bulgaria.[38]

Proceeding along this path another writer, already mentioned, N. S. Bobchev, made a study of the Bulgarian gentry or *Tschorbajis* appraising their role in the social structure and seeking to evaluate the influence of the Ottoman occupation on the character, spirit, and structure of Bulgarian society.[39]

THE BACKGROUND OF HISTORIOGRAPHY IN YUGOSLAVIA

Two basic intellectual centers existed in that part of the Balkans destined to become Yugoslavia after the First World War: Old Serbia with its capital at Belgrade, and Croatia with the more westerly capital of Zagreb. Slovenia and its capital city of Ljubljana, or Laibach, was always more within the cultural orbit of Austria and the universities of Graz and Vienna. Early in the nineteenth century there developed a strong cultural movement denominated *Illyrianism,* not only in Serbia, but in practically all of the provinces, stirred to a new life by the impact of the French Revolution, and the burgeoning of a powerful nationalism. Thus it is that individuals like Bartolomej Kopitar and Vuk Karadzic are not only the symbols but the actual heroes of a resurgent national life, for they encouraged the development of literature, scientific works, political and sociological studies, and the institution of a national drama. Philology became the forerunner, and then the handmaiden of historical studies, in a splendid effort to restore and burnish something of the cultural and intellectual tradition of the South Slavs. Nevertheless, Illyrianism lacked the classical appeal of Hellenism, and had shallower roots than Rumanian Latinism.

The intellectual influence of Vienna is reflected in some of the eighteenth century predecessors of Croatian national historical writing. Such forerunners as B. A. Kroelic (1715-1778) and the Franciscan, Kacic Miosic (1702-1760), wrote panegyrics rather than history. The first attempt at a "scientific" work was made by another priest, a Jesuit, J. Mikoczi (1730-1800), in a work which appeared in the early years of the nineteenth century. It had little appeal to the mass of the people, and this transition to the colloquial was achieved in the writings of I. Svear (1775-1839), who in his survey of "Illyria" tried to establish the direct descent of all South Slavs from the ancient Illyrians.

Croat historiography had still another facet which strongly influenced its direction; the struggle with the Magyars involving the nature of the constitutional relationship of the province to the Kingdom of St. Stephen. Croat historians emphasized the concept of autonomy, while on the other hand the Magyars, particularly after 1848, stressed the centralistic aspect of this relationship. However, here as in Bulgarian historiography, a certain impetus was imparted by the Slovak scholar, Paval Josef Safarik, through his great work on Slavonic antiquities. These studies, once the proper atmosphere was created by the fall of the Bach regime, were at once utilizd by L. Kukuljevic-Sakcinski

---

[38] A. Ishkirov, *Bulgarian, Land and Leute.* An English edition is also available: *Land and People of Bulgaria.* Cf. also A. Ishkirov, *Characteristic Traits of the Town in the Kingdom of Bulgaria* (in Bulgarian).

(1816-1889) who published a series of source collections of noteworthy character.[40]

But the foremost historian was undoubtedly Francis Racki (1828-1894) whose prolific pen touched every aspect of Croatian history, and had an immense influence on the efflorescence of Croat national consciousness. Whether it was Croatian historiography, Cyril and Methodius, the origin of Bogomilism, or simply Croatian origins, his busy pen had a message to convey. In 1876, with the cooperation of the famous Bishop Strossmayer, and that of T. Smicklas as well as that of V. Jagic, the Yugoslav Academy of Science was founded, and Racki long remained its guiding spirit. Through its auspices were issued the source materials, such as the *Documenta historiae Croaticae* (1887) and the necessary and indispensable secondary works for popular education.

Francis Racki believed ardently in the historic and political necessity of Serb and Croat unity. Only national woe could come from a pro-Magyar outlook; "Slav and Yugoslav" solidarity would alone be capable of achieving a harmonious national life.

The momentum given by Racki was carried on by T. Smiciklas, in a series of notable works which gave him a well-deserved fame. The earliest, a popular account, was published as early as 1877.[41] But he also assisted the expansion of historical studies by his compilation of the "Codex." When the work of Vjekoslav Klaic (1849-1928) appeared, another milestone was laid in Croat writing. This account of the history of Croatia became immediately one of the most authoritative and detailed on the subject, and eventually was made accessible to western Europeans by translation into German; exhibiting the same faults and merits as all of Klaic's work: the ultimate in comprehensiveness and a veritable Teutonic passion for detail. With the advent of the writings of F. Sisic the genetic approach came into vogue. Sisic (1869-1940) had as early as 1916 appeared with a preliminary work later incorporated in a much more elaborate work,[42] reflecting a more catholic view. From 1912 to 1918 he edited the acts of the legislature, and in the meantime issued his larger work in the German language, just before the end of the war.[43]

The primary need of systematising the sources engaged the energies of a number of workers such as M. Sufflay (1879-1931) who was a fellow researcher with Smiciklas and the Czech historian Jirecek. A. V. Bogisic wrote and worked in the field of public law, while Croat-Hungarians like S. Barabas and A. Horvath collected material for a diplomatic "codex."

The attempt at synthesizing the development of the Croat national renaissance engaged the constant attention of historians. Among the most able was

[39] For a discussion in English see, Philip E. Mosely, "The Post-War Historiography of Modern Bulgaria," *Journal of Modern History*, IX (Sept., 1937), pp. 348-356. Cf. also C. E. Black, *The Establishment of Constitutional Government in Bulgaria*, pp. 275-299. Cf. also Gaston Cahen, "Bulgarie" in *Histoire et historiens*, pp. 72-85, and Josef Macurek, *op. cit.*, pp. 246-248, 288.

[40] *Jura regni Crotiae, Dalmatiae et Slavoniae* (3 vols.).

[41] T. Smiciklas, *The History of Croatia* (Zagreb, 1877) ; *ibid., Codex diplomaticus regni Croatiae, Slavoniae et Dalmatiae.*

[42] F. Sisic, *History of Croatia* (in Croatian).

[43] F. Sisic, ed. *Acta comitalia regni Croatiae, Dalmatiae et Slavoniae.*

D. Surmin.[44] This subject has attracted many non-Croatians like the Russian Kulakovski, the Czech Jiricek, and the American Robert J. Kerner.

SERBIAN HISTORICAL WRITING

As in Croatia, so in Serbia, the rise and expansion of historical writing is associated intimately with the extension of national feeling, and the development of a national outlook. It remains a moot question just how much this outlook was due to the early work of Brankovic, whose *Sloveno-Serbian Chronicle* appeared in manuscript form in the early part of the eighteenth century. However, this is hardly true of Jovan Rajic (1726-1801) in whom the Serbs found their first thorough, systematic, yet devoted, servant of the national cause. His work is not blindly nationalistic, nor merely devoted to specific laudatory aspects of Serbian history, but on the contrary takes account of the broad factors of Balkan history. Jovan Rajic met the celebrated Bulgarian historian-monk, Paissi, during a visit to Mt. Athos in 1758, and the result of this in large part was the inspiration to write his principal work.[45] Although in the perspective of subsequent historical accomplishment this work lost stature, it exercised some scholarly influence, down to the sixties of the nineteenth century. Moreover, it clearly established the necessity of collecting the sources if further progress were to be made. Thus the first half of the nineteenth century was largely characterized by the systematic collections of materials. And it is not until the turn of the century that two outstanding names appear in Serbian historical writing.

The first of these, Il. Ruvarac (1832-1905) belonged to the rigidly scientific, relentlessly analytic school of historiography which held that the sources must be exposed to the most exacting kind of external and internal criticism. Obviously popular tradition, so much a part of the national awakening, was exposed to some rude shocks. In Panta Sreckovic (1834-1903), however, we perceive a different approach. As a student of theology and philology, he ardently defended the validity of the national songs (an enormous collection) and the historical traditions which were contained in them. Ruvarac achieved a measure of notoriety as an anti-patriot because of his demolition of such legends as the treason of Vuk Brankovic at the Battle of Kossovo in 1389, where Serbia was conquered by the Turks. Despite his apparent disrespect for the treasures of the national culture, the school of Ruvarac triumphed in the end, and by the early 1880's Serbian historiography was definitely founded in a more critical approach and the relentless examination of the elements of national history.

THE CRITICAL SCHOOL

The seed thus sown bore fruit in the work of Stoyan Novakovic (1842-1915) whose remarkable versatility and catholicity of interest is attested by the large number of works which issued from his pen. In common with other Balkan historians, he published many documents; made studies of the diplomatic relations of the Kingdom of Serbia with Hungary, and with Venice;

---

[44] D. Surmin, *The Croatian Rebirth* (in Croatian).
[45] Jovan Rajic, *The History of Various Slav Peoples especially Bulgars, Croats and Serbs* (in Croatian).

studied the influence of Byzantium on national life and published the famous *Zakonik* of Tsar Dushan *(The Legal Code of Tsar Stephen Dushan)*. His study of village life from the thirteenth to the nineteenth century, in his *Selo (The Village)*, while not up to Western standards still is an important work. He further found time to interest himself in Serbian literature, and to serve his country in a political capacity, as Prime Minister, as Minister of Education and as President of the Serbian Academy.

In view of the rapid multiplication of works, only a few of the succeeding historians will be mentioned. Jovan Radonic and Stanoje Stanojevic became the pillars of scholarship in the newly founded University of Belgrade (1905) and Stanojevic's *History of the Serbian People* (1910) soon achieved the status of a standard work, despite its neglect of the cultural elements of history. The author attempted to utilize the pioneer efforts of such writers as Sreckovic, Kovacevic, Jovanovic, and others. His training was mostly in the school of Jirecek and V. Jagic, one of the great monuments of Slavonic learning in Europe. With the development of Serbian Russophilism in the 80's the way was prepared for such studies as that of Stayan Dimitrijevic on Russo-Serbian relationships. The neighbors of the Serbs also came in for attention. Thus R. Grujic (b. 1878) became interested in the Hungarian Serbs, and Rumanian-Serb relationships. The ever fascinating subject of the influence of the western European states upon Serbia attracted J. Tomic, mostly a self-trained historian.

The influence of the First World War, the turmoil attendant upon the effort to establish the Yugoslav regime, and the disastrous Second World War have hardly contributed positively to the furtherance of historical studies. However, the foundation of the Yugoslav Historical Society in 1927, and the establishment of the Yugoslav Historical Review in 1935 as a general repository of the efforts of historians were steps in the right direction.

SLOVENIA

The rise of historical writing in Slovenia, as such, is comparatively recent. The people were not numerous, and their territory was divided by or integrated within the influential or dominant Germanic element. The cultural capital is Ljubljana, where the University concentrates much of the national intellectual effort.[46]

---

[46] The following are typical examples of Slovenian historiography: Franc Kos, *Materials for the History of Slovenia in the Middle Ages;* continued by Milka Kos. F. Erjavec, *Slovenia;* Josip Gruden, *History of the Slovenian People.* All in Slovenian.

Chapter 26

RUSSIA AND SOVIET RUSSIA

By Alfred A. Skerpan

Pre-Revolutionary Russia

T HE major historians of pre-revolutionary Russia, those wielding influence at the beginning of the twentieth century, represented a pursuit that had not been marked by any high order of achievement prior to the reign of Nicholas I (1825-1855). There had been, to be sure, an early period of chronicle writing in Russia, extending from the eleventh through the seventeenth centuries. This had been followed by a hundrd years of invaluable and necessary critical labor, both in the gathering of the raw documentary materials of history and in tentative efforts at presentation of the historical process. It was the nature of this process, however, that was responsible for the delay in the flowering of a historiography that could bear comparison with the best in Europe.

The problems of foreign policy, and the relation of these problems to those of the national economy, had signified for Russia a pattern of development that was more complex, more slowly paced and of longer duration than that of the Atlantic states. In the pattern, also, the state power was destined to play a greater and more enduring role than it had played in western Europe. The very outline of the development had begun to form clearly only toward the end of the reign of Catherine II (1762-96). By that time Russia had achieved the major goals of her diplomacy, while her more advanced citizens had begun to awaken to a new consciousness of history under the influence of the Enlightenment.

As the role of the state in the historical process was to become the chief concern of the major Russian historians, it is noteworthy that two of the more significant accomplishments in the formative phase of modern Russian historiography centered on this theme. The first of these, the work of V. N. Tatishchev (1686-1750), published posthumously as *Russian History from Earliest Times* (in Russian; 5 vols., Moscow, 1768-1848), was begun originally under the personal encouragement of Peter the Great (1682-1725). It achieved no distinction in content or style and had no influence on later writers, but in its seriousness of purpose and its broad vision it represented the first real effort at a synthesis of Russian history. At the close of the formative period appeared the work of N. M. Karamzin (1766-1826), entitled *History of the Russian State* (in Russian; 12 vols., St. Petersburg, 1816-1829). Written in the spirit of romantic nationalism, it was the most readable and the most popular of all writings by amateur historians to that time. However, in its panegyrical style it gave free reins to poetic imagination and rhetoric and praised uncritically the work of Russian autocrats, particularly Ivan IV, the Terrible (1547-1584).

THE LEADING HISTORIANS AT THE BEGINNING OF THE TWENTETH CENTURY

Ultimately the real significance of Karamzin's *History* lay in its service as a target for the criticism of enlightened and educated opinion and as a starting point for succeeding historians. The work appeared at the very dawn of the new critical consciousness that appeared in the reign of Nicholas I. This new critical consciousness was a product of French social thought and German idealism, which influenced Russian universities and Russian society and stimulated searching debates on the essential nature of Russian historical development. These debates, which took place mainly in the eighteen-forties, have taken their own place in history as the intellectual struggle of the Western-izers and the Slavophiles. As far as historiography was concerned, it was the liberal Westernizers, with their organic approach to history, that triumphed. Typical products of this period of intellectual ferment were two scholars who, at the turn of the century, were still of prime significance for students of Russian history: Sergei Mikhailovich Solovyev (1820-1879) and Boris Niko-layevich Chicherin (1828-1904).

Solovyev. S. M. Solovyev, who has been called the greatest Russian historian of the nineteenth century, even by Soviet scholars, was the son of a priest and was educated at Moscow University, where he was strongly influenced by the Hegelian view of history. This preliminary training in Western organic thought was strengthened by work at Berlin, where he studied under the great Leopold von Ranke, and in Paris, where his teachers were Jules Michelet and F. P. G. Guizot, who was his favorite. In 1847 he was made professor of history at Moscow, and in 1851 he published the first of the twenty-nine vol-umes of his *History of Russia.*[1]

This enormous work made great use of the archival material that the Russian Academy of Science had been collecting for a century. The scope was so broad, however, and the pace of writing so rapid that much of the material remained undigested. Despite this weakness and the faults of an unattractive style, the *History,* governed by an Hegelian approach, presented Russian history for the first time as something more than a series of episodes. As he himself stated, "anatomic" study was replaced by a "physiological" approach that sought to fuse into one "organic whole" parts that had formerly appeared dis-united. On the basis of his method he showed interrelations between the peculiarities of Russian geography, chiefly flatness and great space, the loose and imperfect development of early social organization, and the creative role of state power in making up the latter's deficiencies.

Chicherin. Solovyev's views of the state's function in Russia owed much to the work of his younger contemporary, B. N. Chicherin, "the basic theoretician of the state school."[2] Chicherin was not a historian in the precise sense, but

---

[1] S. M. Solovyev, *History of Russia from Earliest Times* (in Russian; 29 vols.). The work ended with 1774; an additional six volumes, never completed, were to cover down to the nineteenth century.
[2] N. L. Rubinshtein, *Russian Historiography* (in Russian), pp. 301, 314.

a student of philosophy and political science and of the history of law and political institutions. Nevertheless, his extensive monographic work, and particularly his *Provincial Institutions of Russia in the Seventeenth Century* (in Russian; Moscow, 1856) and his *Essays in the History of Russian Law* (in Russian; Moscow, 1858), both written while he was still a young man, wielded a great influence on Russian students of history. His appeal was due largely to his rigorous philosophical and legal discipline. From his university days on he was a thorough Hegelian and as such he was a staunch supporter of the state principle, which he saw as the culmination of Russia's historical process. At the same time, he believed that the state had experienced over-development, repressing instead of working with the creativity of the people, and that modification was necessary in the direction of political freedom and the broader rule of law.

Klyuchevsky. Solovyev and Chicherin both helped mold the work, thought and ideology of the best known and most readable of the greater Russian historians, Vasily Osipovich Klyuchevsky (1842-1911). There were other influences on his work, including an economic (non-Marxian) interpretation of history; Klyuchevsky lacked true originality, and in fact has been frequently charged with eclecticism. Nevertheless, he was not by any means a slavish follower of his masters; rather, he showed considerable independence of thought and in his integration, grasp and presentation—written and oral—of the Russian historical process, as shown in his master work, *Course of Russian History*,[3] he stood alone.

The son of a poor provincial priest, Klyuchevsky grew into intellectual maturity after the Crimean War and in the age of reforms and revolutionary movements. Thus, the era of great social change was responsible for his original research into social-economic problems within the general framework of Solovyev's *History*. Those studies were pursued under Solovyev himself, and the monographic by-products, considered by some authorities to be his best scientific work, included *The Russian Ruble of the XVI-XVII Centuries in Relation to Today's* (in Russian; Moscow, 1884), and *The Boyars' Duma of Early Rus* (in Russian; Moscow, 1883). His own investigations ended in the eighties, and from then on he devoted his attention to his survey history of Russia, which appeared originally as a series of lectures lithographed for the benefit of students and then subjected to constant revision. In his general view the basic historical forces were human personality, human society, and the nature of the country in which these operated. Under the special Russian conditions, he felt, these produced a distinctive society moving at a different tempo from that of the West. His concern with the popular forces, particularly colonization, led him to give somewhat less importance to the state than did Solovyev.

Milyukov. The last of the major historians to appear before the 1917 revolutions was Pavel Nikolayevich Milyukov (1859-1943), the son of an architect. Although he was influenced by the work of Solovyev and more by Chicherin

---

[3] The latest and most useful edition appeared in Moscow in 1937 (in Russian; 5 vols.). An imperfect translation into English from earlier editions, by C. J. Hogarth, appeared as *A History of Russia* (5 vols.).

and Klyuchevsky, under whom he studied, Milyukov's approach to history came to be his own. Under the influence of economic determinism and of the positivist thought of Auguste Comte and Herbert Spencer, he decided that the processes of history were too complex to be presented as an organic unit, even though he came to recognize—even to illustrate—that human evolution was motivated by the necessity of adjusting to the total environment. His views were responsible for the monographic nature of even his major work.

Milyukov died an octogenarian, but his significant historical research and writing were crowded into a space of about ten years. These began with his pioneering study, *State Economy of Russia in the First Quarter of the Eighteenth Century and the Reforms of Peter the Great* (in Russian; St. Petersburg, 1892); they ended with the appearance in 1903 of the last part of his brilliant *Outlines in the History of Russian Culture* (in Russian; uniform edition in 3 vols., St. Petersburg, 1904-1909).[4] Revealing some indebtedness to Chicherin, Milyukov gave greater significance to the creative role of the state in Russia's past than did most of his predecessors. He observed that whereas in studying western European states one had to begin with the economic order and then proceed to state organization, in Russia the procedure was reversed.[5] Nevertheless, he was convinced that ultimately Russia would follow the same path of development as the West, and this belief accounted for his liberal-democratic political activity after 1904.

THE OCTOBER REVOLUTION AND HISTORIOGRAPHY

The seizure of power by the Bolsheviks in November, 1917, did not bring an immediate revolutionary change in the writing of Russian history. New prominence was given to M. N. Pokrovsky,[6] an uncompromising Marxist historian who had also been an early supporter of V. I. Lenin, but down to 1924 many able, although obscure, representatives of older schools continued their research and even teaching. This toleration existed partly because government interest was centered on current economic and political problems. It was also true, however, that, with the exception of Solovyev and Chicherin, most of the historians active or in repute on the eve of the revolution were not idealist in their approach, but were positivist or materialist or economic-determinist (whether Marxian or non-Marxian), and in general were social-minded.

Nevertheless, the establishment of Communist power in 1917-1918 was the work of men who were convinced they were being guided by telefinalistic laws of history. The full impact of the Communist Party on historical study was felt eventually in the thirties. This union of politics and historical study was the work mainly of three men: G. V. Plekhanov, Leon Trotsky, and V. I. Lenin. These were not so much historians in the traditional sense as they were students of Marxian-interpreted world and Russian history, with aims that were utilitarian.

---

[4] There were several editions of individual volumes. A revised "Jubilee" edition was projected in 1930, and at the time of Milyukov's death all but a major portion of volume I had been republished. The chief conclusions of the study appeared in his *Russia and Its Crisis*. A partial translation of the "jubilee" edition, edited by Michael Karpovich, has appeared as *Outlines of Russian Culture* (3 vols.).
[5] Milyukov, *Outlines, I* (in Russian; 5th edition), pp. 133-34.
[6] See special section below, on Pokrovsky.

Plekhanov. Georgii Valentinovich Plekhanov (1856-1918) was, in his earlier days, a devotee of the belief that a reconstruction of Russian society on the basis of the existing communal land organization would spare the country many of the evils of industrial capitalism. In 1880, however, he went abroad and, after making a study of the work of Marx and Engels, came to the conclusion that Russia also would, like the West, experience capitalist development. As a consequence, he helped organize in 1883 at Geneva the first Russian social-democratic group, "The Liberation of Labor." More significant than this party work were his voluminous writings.[7] These on the one hand denounced opinions that were similar to his own earlier beliefs, and on the other hand expounded the new Marxian ideology for Russians. On these works, as Lenin wrote later, "were founded a whole generation of Marxists."

In respect to history Plekhanov produced three notable studies: *On the Question of the Monistic View of History* (an exposition of the Marxian approach) ; *On the Question of the Role of Personality in History;* and *History of Russian Social Thought* (three volumes).[8] In the last work, which dealt specifically with the Russian scene, he appeared to depart somewhat from his earlier, more rigid Marxism. Now, instead of centering attention on the growth of productive forces, as the "logic" underlying social development, he preferred to begin with determining geographical conditions peculiar to Russia. On this and on matters of Russian social development, he followed such historians as Klyuchevsky and Milyukov, but principally Solovyev. On these and other points, which brought him closer to the Menshevik camp, Plekhanov and the later official Soviet Marxists parted company.

Trotsky. Leo Davidovich Trotsky, born Bronstein (1877-1940), Lenin's chief lieutenant in the Bolshevik seizure of power in 1917, had early decided on history as the most fruitful field of study. He was much less a scholar than Lenin, but he was as passionately interested in the historical forces that could swing revolutionary social democracy into power in Russia. For this reason he drew his lessons not only from Marxism but also from standard historians who had helped mold Plekhanov's later thought, chiefly, it appears, Klyuchevsky and Milyukov. Summaries of these lessons and the political conclusions derived from them appeared in several of his works.[9]

Trotsky accepted, first, the thesis that the natural environment had impeded Russian economic and social growth and that the correction of this deficiency, in the face of external danger, had led to an overdevelopment of state power. The state had become strong and centralized, he wrote, had made itself relatively free of dominating social classes, and had become the leading entrepreneur within the country. Proceeding from this he evolved his version of the idea of permanent revolution. Thus, although Russia was a backward country in terms of industrial and political class development, and was not, strictly speaking, ripe for social revolution, the notion of the conquest of

---

[7] G. V. Plekhanov, *Works* (in Russian; 24 vols.).

[8] Plekhanov, *Works,* vols. VII, VIII, XX-XXII.

[9] L. D. Trotsky: *1905* (1st edition, in Russian; 4th edition, in Russian) ; *The Permanent Revolution,* translated by Max Schachtman; *History of the Russian Revolution,* translated by Max Eastman (3 vols.).

power by the proletariat was as immediately applicable in that country as in the West. The further fate of socialism in Russia, under the proletarian dictatorship, depended ultimately on the fate of capitalism in the remaining sectors of the world economy. Paul Milyukov suggested in the thirties that without this theory it was impossible to understand such an event as the October (N.S., November) Revolution, which by-passed the economic evolution of capitalism in Russia.[10]

Lenin. Vladimir Ilyich Lenin, born Ulyanov (1870-1924), was originally more of a student of history in the academic sense than was Trotsky, but from the start his approach was more inflexibly Marxian. His most significant original work of investigation was *The Development of Capitalism in Russia* (in Russian; published under the pseudonym Vladimir Ilin, St. Petersburg, 1899), a technical work on economic growth after the emancipation of the serfs in 1861. Scholarly as this study was, it had a direct political purpose, to discredit those in Russia—the Populists—who not only believed that Russia could avoid the Western pattern of capitalist economic development but also were the leading competitors for the leadership of Russia's mightiest revolutionary force, the peasantry.

Less scholarly and less original, but of far greater political significance was Lenin's *Imperialism: The Highest Stage of Capitalism. A Popular Outline* (in Russian, Petrograd, 1917; in English, revised translation, International Publishers, New York, 1925). It is generally accepted by Soviet and Western scholars as a continuation of Marx's and Engels' examination of capitalism and its application to the period of imperialism after 1870. The conclusion that Lenin reached, and one highly significant for his strategy in respect to the seizure of power, was that imperialism was dying capitalism and represented therefore the eve of proletarian social revolution.

More pertinent to the Russian scene and its part in proletarian world revolution was Lenin's acceptance of a statement by the Austrian Marxist Rudolf Hilferding. This was that areas under exploitation by imported capital (*i.e.,* areas least developed economically, like Russia) were just the areas where the popular resistance that was excited by this exploitation could be transformed into "dangerous measures" against foreign capital. However, this view of Russia's possible role in revolution appears to have been in Lenin's own mind much earlier. Although his interpretation of the Russian state as a class state was and remained a rigid Marxian view, thus differing from Trotsky's, as early as 1902 he saw the Russian autocracy as a "bulwark of European and Asiatic reaction." From this he concluded that the immediate task of destroying this bulwark placed the Russian workers "in the vanguard of the international revolutionary proletariat." [11]

Under the influence of these men, and of the stimulus of a successful revolution, revolutionary Marxian history dominated the field by the time of Lenin's death. For a while, however, there was considerable confusion in

---

[10] P. Milyukov, "The Greatness and Fall of M. N. Pokrovsky," *Contemporary Notes*, vol. LXV (in Russian), p. 375.

[11] V. I. Lenin, *What Is to Be Done?* (in English), p. 30.

the teaching and writing of history. This rose on the one hand from the difficulties created by the lack of personnel and materials, and on the other, from the confounding, by many inexperienced Marxists, of scholarly history with politics and propaganda. From the Revolution to the early thirties only one scholar of stature could be said to have predominated in Russian historiography.

POKROVSKY (1868-1932)

Pokrovsky, who can be said to have represented the Leninist view of Russian history, came from a middle class family. He was given an excellent education in a Moscow classical gymnasium and at the University of Moscow. His most important teachers were V. O. Klyuchevsky and P. G. Vinogradov, a specialist in medieval English social history, later at Oxford. Quite early he fell under the influence of economic materialism but he definitely entered the Marxist camp only at the turn of the century. After spending some years teaching in secondary schools and at a pedagogical institute, he was forbidden in 1903 to give public lectures. From this time his political interests became more active, to the extent even of helping to organize the Bolshevik uprising in Moscow at the end of 1905.[12]

This direct experience with revolutionary politics gave his interest in history a decisive fillip. In 1907 began to appear his Marxian master work, *Russian History from Earliest Times to the Rise of Commercial Capitalism* (in Russian; first edition, 4 vols., Moscow, 1907-1910).[13] A brief and in some respects newer version appeared after the revolution as *Russian History in Its Most Concise Outline* (in Russian; 3 parts, Moscow, 1920-1923).[14] The latter publication was immediately pressed into service as a textbook in Soviet schools.

Pokrovsky had parted with the Bolsheviks in 1907 but reentered their ranks in 1917, after which he performed yeoman service for the new state. He was a member of the Soviet peace delegation at Brest-Litovsk in 1918 and the director of the reorganization of the Central Archives. He organized new associations of historians and became the editor of such historical journals as *The Red Archive, Marxist Historian,* and *Class Struggle* (all in Russian) ; in 1929 he became a member of the Academy of Science.

Pokrovsky's Theories. The view of Russian historical development that characterized Pokrovsky's original work and thought, down to about 1925, had been determined by his interpretation of Marxism well before World War I. Essentially his view—shared by other historians before and after the 1917 revolutions—was one of, not dialectical but, economic materialism, that is, the explanation of all human development on the basis of economic organization and change.[15] Among the consequences of this interpretation

---

[12] Thomas R. Hall, "Mikhail Nikolayevich Pokrovsky (1868-1932)" in Bernadotte E. Schmitt, ed., *Some Historians of Modern Europe* (pp. 349-366), pp. 350-51.
[13] An abridged and uncompleted English translation of the 7th edition, by J. D. Clarkson and M. R. M. Griffiths, appeared in 1931 (1 vol.).
[14] This was translated into English from the 10th edition by D. S. Mirsky as *Brief History of Russia* (2 vols., 1933).
[15] Dialectical materialism places stress on change—quantitative and qualitative—and allows for the reaction of the social and cultural results of economic development on that development. This did not become official Soviet doctrine until 1929.

were the rejection of nationalism and what may be called the de-personaliza-
tion of history. These ideas, particularly the last, which was of great significance for Pokrovsky's ultimate professional fate, were expressed succinctly
by him in May, 1923, when he stated in a lecture: "Commercial capital was
the actual tsar that stood behind the—in essence—crowned phantom . . . or
mannequin; it was the true guiding force which created both the Russian
Empire and serfdom."[16] In Pokrovsky's historical surveys none of the tsars,
not even Peter I, was allotted any creative role.

Pokrovsky did not leave the class struggle conception out of his scheme.
In fact the use of this notion proved to be one of the most fruitful devices
in his re-interpretation of the past, while later Soviet critics even charged
that he made such excessive use of it that he rendered Soviet historical study
"subjective." Nor did Pokrovsky look upon historical study as an academic
pursuit. For him it had direct utility, since such a study, he believed, would
reveal the laws of social change and these could be used in helping determine
the future of society.[17]

The belief of Pokrovsky that historical study should be politically pur-
poseful involved a denial of the validity of all earlier Russian historical
theories. Indeed he can be said to have waged a revolutionary war of his
own against these ideologies, which he considered as representative of class
interests and as products of class struggle.[18] His basic view of the responsibility of commercial capital for the establishment of autocracy and of
serfdom, in Russia, ran partly or wholly counter to the theses not only of
most of the leading pre-revolutionary historians, but also of such theoreticians
as Plekhanov and Trotsky, whom he was already attacking vigorously at the
beginning of the twenties.[19] The bitterness, contempt and unscrupulousness
which entered into his verbal assaults may very well have been due, as
Milyukov suggested in another context, to desire for personal glory and
prestige.[20] His hostility to Klyuchevsky was partly personal and stemmed
from conflicts that had led to Pokrovsky's leaving Moscow University.[21]

Pokrovsky and Lenin. Much of Pokrovsky's assurance was based on the encouragement and trust he had from Lenin in the first years of Soviet power.
When his short history was completed, Lenin urged that it be made a text
book. And Pokrovsky himself was to state later that the "original plan and
original conception were approved by V. I. Lenin,"[22] and that the historical
views with which he was associated, and which were called Marxism, were
really Lenin's and not his own.[23]

Early Criticism of Pokrovsky. Despite the support and enthusiasm for his
work, Pokrovsky had difficulties with Soviet critics very early, and not only
from Trotskyists. The main position that was assailed was his stand on the

[16] M. N. Pokrovsky, *Historical Study* and *The Class Struggle* (in Russian: 2 vols.) I, 28.
[17] Pokrovsky, *Brief History*, I, 24; *Historical Study*, II, pp. 284f. Also compare Hall, "Pokrovsky," pp. 352-53.
[18] Pokrovsky, *History of Russia*, Clark and Griffiths translation, pp. ix-xiii; *Historical Study*. I, pp. 12-13.
[19] Pokrovsky, *Historical Study*, I, pp. 29f.
[20] Milyukov, "Pokrovsky," p. 373.
[21] Hall, "Pokrovsky," p. 350.
[22] Pokrovsky, *Brief History*, I, pp. 5, 11-13.
[23] Pokrovsky, *Historical Study*, II, pp. 274, 283.

importance of commercial capital in Russian history. More significant, this was related to a mechanistic materialism whose leading exponent was N. I. Bukharin (1888-1938), one of Stalin's chief foes in the later twenties.[24] In the face of the political work of Lenin and Trotsky, the Bolshevik seizure of power in 1917, the consolidation of Stalin's authority, and the introduction of the economic program of the first Five-Year Plan by the state in 1927, Pokrovsky's theoretical judgments were almost palpably false. They became politically so after the philosophy of dialectical materialism, which allowed for these changes, had been made official in 1929.[25] In 1922 Pokrovsky had been ready to admit that his major four-volume work was not in accord with contemporary Marxism; from 1924 on he made increasing efforts to adjust his conceptions, and in 1931 he granted that his own views were occasionally non-Leninist.[26]

In two special lectures given in 1930-31[27] he attempted to correct several points in his theories, although the situation now called for complete revision. He defended his view of the role of merchant capital in Russia and cited Lenin in support. However, he accepted the argument that the Russian monarchical state had been pliable and could change, and made a special point of declaring that the autocracy had given the country Peter I and Alexander II. As for the creativity of political action, he now granted that "true Marxism" allowed for it at all stages of development, and that without contingencies— such as the character of the people at the head of movements—history would be mystical in aspect. He admitted, too, that he had forgotten Engel's rhetorical question: Why is the dictatorship of the proletariat needed if it cannot hasten economic development? And lest there be any doubt concerning his view of economic materialism, he declared that it and Leninism—"the recognition of the revolutionary dialectics of history"—were incompatible.[28]

MONOGRAPHIC HISTORIOGRAPHY IN THE NINETEEN-TWENTIES

Despite the revolutionary changes that 1917 and the years to 1930 brought, many specialists through the whole field of history were able to continue their researches, or else to deal with new topics, without much difficulty. One of the most brilliant of the older scholars was N. Ya. Marr (1864-1934), the son of a Scotch father and a Georgian mother, who made a study of Caucasian and South Asian languages. With these tools, and also with the conception that language is both an instrument and a creation of social consciousness, he re-explored whole areas of linguistics, archaeology, philosophy and history.[29] He established in this way the autonomy of early Caucasian culture, and its significance in joining the ancient East with the world of the Aegean Sea and Asia Minor.

Another scholar of exceptionally broad learning was V. V. Barthold (1869-1930) who made the Moslem-Turkic world and its culture his specialty. His

[24] Bukharin was to attack Pokrovsky in the thirties.
[25] John Somerville, *Soviet Philosophy: A Study of Theory and Practice* (New York), pp. 213-31.
[26] Milyukov, "Pokrovsky," pp. 373, 380; Rubinshtein, *Russian Historiography*, p. 579.
[27] One of these appears in English as an appendix to Pokrovsky, *Brief History*, I, pp. 281-95.
[28] Pokrovsky. *Historical Study*, II, pp. 274, 283.
[29] N. Ya. Marr, *Selected Works* (in Russian; 5 vols.)

most famous work available in English is *Turkestan Down to the Mongol Invasion* (2nd edition, translated from the Russian and revised by the author with the aid of H. A. R. Gibb; London, 1928). A third specialist of great ability is B. Ya. Vladimirtsov (b. 1884), an expert in Mongolian history best known for his *Chingis-Khan* (in Russian; Moscow-Leningrad, 1922).[30]

In the field of Russian history proper A. A. Shakhmatov (1864-1920) continued to direct his philological training to the examination of chronicles. There appeared posthumously his *Survey of Russian Chronicle Collections* (in Russian; Moscow-Leningrad, 1938). M. M. Bogoslovsky (1867-1929) did further work on sources pertaining to Peter the Great, but only in 1940 did his compilations begin to appear in print.[31]

The revolutionary movement itself came under investigation, with immediate emphasis being given to the publication of source materials. In 1923 M. K. Lemke completed his edition of the *Complete Collection of the Works and Letters of A. I. Herzen* (in Russian; 22 vols., Petrograd, 1915-1923). Bakunin proved to be of exceptional interest. There appeared a definitive biography by Yuri Steklov, *Mikhail Aleksandrovich Bakunin* (in Russian; 4 vols., Moscow, 1926-1927), and later, the work of a group of scholars, *The Collected Works and Letters of M. A. Bakunin* (in Russian; 4 vols., Moscow, 1934-1935). Documents on socialists of the 1840's were published by P. E. Schegolev in *The Petrashevtsy* (in Russian; 3 vols., Leningrad, 1928).

THE CONSOLIDATION OF PARTY INFLUENCE ON HISTORIOGRAPHY IN THE NINETEEN-THIRTIES

Although attacks on Pokrovsky were increasing toward the close of his life, and although he himself took steps to meet them and to correct his earlier tenets, the main assault came after his death. As late as 1934 a fifth edition of his brief survey of Russian history could still be published, but in that year the voices that had hailed and defended Pokrovsky abruptly fell silent. In the preceding months a new and menacing world political situation had arisen with the entrenchment in power of the German National Socialists, who were frankly expansionist and frankly anti-Soviet. And in the course of 1934, as in subsequent years, the Communist Party intervened directly in the field of historical writing.[32] The aim appears to have been basically, in the face of the new German danger, to intensify the new Soviet nationalism, which had been growing from the late twenties, and to join it to Stalinist conceptions of world revolution.[33] For this, Pokrovsky's anti-nationalist approach to history was definitely unsuitable.

Party Intervention. A step in the new direction had in fact been taken in 1931 when, in a letter to a Soviet journal, Joseph Stalin dealt with the history of the Communist Party. There he stressed the early view of Lenin that the

---

[30] Vladimirtsov, *The Life of Chingis-Khan*, translated from the Russian by Prince D. S. Mirsky.
[31] M. M. Bogoslovsky, *Peter I: Materials for a Biography* (in Russian; 2 vols.)
[32] Between 1931 and 1937 there were seven basic pronouncements by leading Communists on historical matters. These, cited below, were brought together in *Toward the Study of History: A Collection* (in Russian).
[33] This is, in brief, the gradual extension of the Sovietized sector of the globe through the decay of the sector under capitalism and through conflicts between the sectors. See for a fuller statement: A. A. Skerpan, "The Idea of World Revolution," *South Atlantic Quarterly*, Vol. XLVIII, pp. 169-191.

problems of the Russian workers, in respect to the Tsarist state, made them the vanguard of the world proletariat. He suggested also that, as a consequence, the basic question of the Russian revolution was even "now" the basic question "of the world revolution." On May 16, 1934, the Council of Peoples' Commissars and the Central Committee of the Soviet Communist Party published a joint declaration on the teaching of history in Soviet schools. In this were summed up the criticisms that had been made of the writing of Pokrovsky and his followers: textbooks and teaching were not dealing with "living forms," important events, facts or with historical figures, but only with "abstract sociological schemes." A series of new textbooks was called for, including one on "dependent and colonial peoples."

New Textbooks. As a result of these and other actions by the government and the Communist Party, there began to appear, from 1937 on, a series of new textbooks on history for the elementary and intermediate schools and for the higher educational institutions. Also a new edition of V. O. Klyuchevsky's *Course of Russian History,* which was a master work and had nationalist overtones besides, was published in 1937. On the outbreak of war between the Soviet Union and Germany, only the text on Russia in the twentieth century for university students had not yet appeared. The competition for a textbook at the elementary level brought forth forty-six manuscripts, but none of these was judged worthy of a first prize. A second prize was awarded to a group of writers headed by A. V. Shestakov, and their work was approved for adoption for school use.

Shestakov's book (like the others) went a good way toward filling the needs of the ruling authorities. On the one hand Russia was shown to have followed in the past the same pattern of historical development as had the countries of the West. Abstract theories of social change were left out and close attention was paid to events, dates, and the achievements of historical figures; the Russian past no longer appeared as backward. On the other hand, great attention was paid to the Soviet period, which in the elementary text occupied one-half of the volume. All the Bolshevik leaders who had fallen from power and influence, in the years since the Revolution, were denounced and reviled while frequent mention and praise were accorded those in control after the party purges.[34]

Despite the changes the judges were not completely satisfied with the results, since the works that had been submitted still revealed "deficiencies." The faults and omissions cited were obviously a disservice to the political aims of the Communist Party. These, as revealed further by the criticism, looked to fuller development of nationalism among the Russians and the larger nationalities, greater appreciation of historical figures and of the roles of Lenin and Stalin—with their followers—since the beginning of the century, and a greater emphasis on the interdependence, or interaction, between Russia and other capitalist countries before and after the Revolution.

Important for the control of historical, as well as the social and political,

---

[34] See Skerpan, "The Idea of World Revolution," *South Atlantic Quarterly,* Vol. XLVIII, pp. 169-191.

thinking in the Soviet Union was the publication in 1938 of *The History of the All-Union Communist Party (Bolsheviks): Short Course.* Following the original edition in Russian there had appeared by September 1946 editions in sixty-one Soviet languages and dialects and sixteen foreign languages, with a total printing of 31,317,000 copies.[35] According to one of the leading Soviet historians, the appearance of "this genuine pearl of Marxist-Leninist science" was a festive occasion for all historians of the U. S. S. R. and had a "tremendous significance for the entire historical front." Histories of the Communist Party had appeared earlier, but in 1937 it was decided to subject them also to revision. Stalin came to guide this work and to produce for it a chapter on dialectical and historical materialism.[36]

New Assaults on Pokrovsky. After the successive proddings of the professional historians through the declarations and instructions of the Communist Party leadership, the historians had turned resolutely to the problem of mending their fences. Criticism of Pokrovsky now mounted to new peaks. The academic historians proceeded to examine all of Pokrovsky's work in the light of the official position. At the beginning of World War II the results were published by the Soviet Academy of Sciences in a collection of articles entitled *Against the Historical Conceptions of M. N. Pokrovsky* (in Russian; 2 vols., Moscow-Leningrad, 1939-1940). Denunciations, using terms and phrases from official decrees and statements, were made also in all new work covering Russian historiography. One critic, writing in time of war, commented on the "pernicious" and "retarding" effect Pokrovsky had had on the development of historical study, and on the injury his school had done to the younger generation in matters of patriotism: "It ignored the study of the heroic traditions of the great Russian people and did not arm the youth with feelings of love for their motherland and hatred for its enemies."

The Historian's Function at the End of the Thirties

The historian in the Soviet Union could, by 1941, discern the basic patterns that the Communist Party was determined he should follow in his work. He was instructed, first, that Lenin had shown that historical study was bound up with the revolutionary struggle of the working class. Then he was taught by Stalin that by penetrating to the "essence of Marxism," *i.e.,* class struggle, he could transmute Marxism into a vital and creative principle growing and developing "together with life" and achieving realization "in conformity with circumstances." Thus, the historian was required to see as the basic scheme of history the development and then the decay of world capitalism, the role of Marxism in showing the way to a new society, the leadership of Russia in the creation of this society, and the Soviet Communist Party—now headed by Stalin—as directing this leadership. Stalin and the Communist Party, therefore, were helping to develop Marxism "in conformity with circumstances,"

---

[35] *New York Times*, September 24, 1946.
[36] In 1946 (*New York Times*, as cited) he was called the author of the entire book.

and the interests of the Party and the state were to serve as a gauge in determining both the past and future development of Russia and the world.[37]

MONOGRAPHIC HISTORIOGRAPHY IN THE NINETEEN-THIRTIES AND -FORTIES

The instructions of Party leaders, the new emphasis on nationalism and the discrediting of Pokrovsky, all served to restore the authority of many pre-Soviet Russian historians and to establish a new trend in the preparation of special studies. The hero was restored to his former place in historiography. The materials that M. Bogoslovsky had prepared for a life of Peter I began to appear in print eleven years after the scholar's death. Another old scholar, R. Yu. Vipper (b. 1859), saw his biographical essay *Ivan Grozny* (*i.e.,* the Terrible) pass into a third edition.[38] Ivan, who had been subjected to a series of contradictory interpretations by early historians, was now hailed as "a remarkable statesman" who had consolidated the state in the face of "internal treachery and attempts at foreign intervention"—a suggested analogy with Stalin which could escape only the most obtuse.

New Views of Early Russian History. The end of Pokrovsky's influence, and the new national feeling, further made possible a re-examination of Russian feudal history and the process of her growth into a national state, both of which had been given little stress by the former master. And the Party's insistence that the periodization (Marxian) of Russian history parallel that of the West—stressing that the feudal epoch was an epoch of serfdom—met head on the contention of earlier historians and of Pokrovsky that there were no serfs prior to the sixteenth century.[39] The historian B. D. Grekov (b. 1882) now achieved the greatest prominence in these fields. He provided a new interpretation of the meaning of the Kievan state, arguing that it was based not on commerce, as had been the prevailing earlier view, but on agriculture.[40] Although this and other data signified that the origins of serfdom and the beginnings of feudalism were to be found five hundred years earlier than had been maintained formerly, it also meant that the recognized enserfment process of the fifteenth and sixteenth centuries represented new problems for study.

New study of the Russian past involved also a study of two basic questions, the factors responsible for the appearance of the Kievan state and the origins of the Slavs. Using new materials and the Marxian ideas of social-economic relations, specialists like Grekov and P. N. Tretyakov promoted the thesis that it was the growth of an agricultural social order among the early Eastern Slavs that produced an internal development of society and of state forms. This, of course, served the new nationalism by denying directly the long-debated theory that these were the product of the impact on the Slavs of the Huns, or of Germanic peoples like the Goths or Normans. Grekov himself declared that, well before the traditional coming of Rurik (862 A.D.), the Eastern Slavs had experienced state organization and had fused into the

---

[37] Compare Max N. Laserson, *Russia and the Western World*, pp. 152-53.
[38] R. Yu. Vipper *Ivan Grozny;* translated by J. Fineberg from the 3rd edition (in English).
[39] Pokrovsky, *Historical Study,* I, p. 108.
[40] The principal work by Grekov is *Kievan Rus* (in Russian; 4th edition).

state of Kiev. He argued, as well, that culturally and socially Kievan Rus was at equal level with the state of western Europe of that time.

With official encouragement there continued to appear, in these years, monographs on every aspect of the world's economic, social, and diplomatic history. Particular interest centered on French history. There were published such works as E. V. Tarle's *The Fatherland War of 1812 and the Defeat of the Napoleonic Empire* (in Russian; Moscow, 1941), and *The French Bourgeois Revolution, 1789-1794,* edited by V. P. Volgin and E. V. Tarle (in Russian; Moscow, 1941). In reference to Asia, historians were urged to study Marx, Engels, Lenin and Stalin on imperialism and revolution in China and India. One noteworthy monograph that was published in this general field was Sh. Lif's *War and the Economy of Japan* (in Russian; Moscow, 1940).

WORLD WAR II AND THE AFTERMATH

The very nature of the emphasis in historical writing after the middle thirties was, as had been calculated, a service to the moral rearming of the Soviet peoples against the likelihood of war. The new textbooks were aimed at promoting a sense of unity within the country and support of the regime and its aims. However, much broader and more "scholarly" works had been planned. Apart from a new "Universal History," a twelve-volume work was projected to survey the history of the country and all its national groups from the earliest times,[41] and the writing of a complete history of the Bolshevik Revolution and the Civil War had been begun under the editorship of such Party leaders as Stalin, Vyacheslav, Molotov, and Andrei Zhdanov.[42]

By 1942 there had been completed a *History of Diplomacy* under the editorship of V. P. Potemkin (in Russian; 3 vols., Moscow, 1941-45). This work won a Stalin prize. The third and largest volume, dealing with the years between the two world wars, contained no information not already available in non-Russian sources or in Soviet newspapers. At the outbreak of the war (and down to the present) on the other hand, nothing had been produced on the general history of the whole Soviet period, apart from the third volume of the textbook for intermediate schools and the history of the Communist Party. The latter remained, therefore, as one historian called it, the "sole model of Marxist investigation" of the period.

With the coming of the war itself, Soviet historians had a two-fold task. They had to keep their eye on the general perspective of history and at the same time to apply themselves to studying and writing "as warm patriots." Lenin was cited on the necessity of "not losing oneself in the individual zigzags of history" and maintaining a clear view of "the crimson thread in the development of events." He was also cited to the effect that there were historically progressive wars that brought gains to humanity.

In contributing to the general propaganda in support of the war, historians prepared great numbers of articles, pamphlets and works on heroic

---

[41] Four volumes had been prepared by 1942, but as late as 1949 none had been published.

[42] M. Gorky, G. Aleksandrov, *et al.* eds., *History of the Civil War in the U.S.S.R.* (in Russian; to date, 2 vols.; English translation, 2 vols.).

events and figures, particularly military, of the Russian past. However, they also went beyond the confines of the Soviet Union in contributing to a great acceleration of work on other Slav peoples. This in turn was joined with propaganda work among these peoples that was aimed at creating a sense of a common cause against the Germans with the Russians and under their leadership. A periodical entitled *Slavdom,* a monthly magazine published in Russian but under the auspices of an "All-Slav Committee," began to appear in Moscow in June, 1942. Edited by leading Russian Slavists its contents were heavily weighted with articles on Russia and on the achievements of the Soviet regime. The periodical continued to appear after the war.

The Postwar Position. The end of active conflict with Germany, and the establishment of a new Soviet position in world affairs, immediately brought new political intervention in Soviet investigation and writing of history. Amid the pronouncements and declarations that have been made from 1945, there appears, however, a policy which represents merely an intensification of what had existed on the eve of the Second World War. This is the subordination of historical study to the political ends of the Communist Party, which involves acceptance of the views that the Soviet period in world history is something distinctly new and apart from the past, while springing from it, and that each act of the Party re-illumines the past while serving the future. Objectivity in the Western sense was denounced in 1946 by Andrei Zhdanov, who was a member of the Politburo before his death. For him politics was the true function of scholars. This was not, for him, a denial of "true" objectivity since the interests of the workers, *i.e.,* as led by the Communist Party, coincided with the "objective course of historical development."

The year 1949 brought a four-month interruption in the publication of *Problems of History* and the dismissal of nine of its thirteen editors, including such long-established figures as V. P. Volgin and N. L. Rubinshtein. Some of these scholars were associated with the failure to produce any substantial work on Soviet history since 1917 and may have represented resistance to the political interpretation of "objectivity." However, these historians, several of whom appear to be of Jewish background, were assailed in *Problems of History* on its reappearance as "rootless cosmopolites." In this attack, which might be associated with the Soviet Union's attack on world Zionism, the historians were accused of having attempted to demean "the leading role of the Russian proletariat in the history of the revolutionary struggle both of our motherland and of the entire world."[43]

RUSSIAN HISTORIOGRAPHY OUTSIDE THE SOVIET UNION

The writing of Russian history was continued by many Russian scholars who emigrated after the Revolution, although their most valuable contributions lay perhaps in teaching in Western universities. However, free of governmental pressure and detached from events within the Soviet Union, one group among them was able to create a new tendency in Russian historiography that is still rich in its suggestiveness. The group was associated with the socalled

---

[43] *Problems of History,* 1949, No. 2, p. 6; also see *New York Times,* September 25, 1949.

Eurasian school, or movement, begun at Sofia, Bulgaria, in 1921, and represented a mode of thought that was the direct product of the Russian revolutionary experience.

Eurasianism generally concerned itself with the uniqueness of the broad land mass embraced, roughly, by the Soviet Union of 1921. Various members of the movement sought this uniqueness in all realms of human existence including geography and politics, hemology, linguistics, law, and economics, as well as theology and history.[44] The spirit that marked much of their labors possessed considerable affinity with early Slavophilism and with the statist tradition in Russian historiography. The historians, chiefly N. S. Trubetskoi, P. N. Savitsky, and George Vernadsky, have approached the past of Eurasia as the past not only of Russians but of all peoples who have promoted the economic and political organization of the area and who have contributed to its cultural and social pattern and development. They thus see the Soviet period as being in the same geo-political tradition as the Mongol Empire of the thirteenth through the fifteenth centuries and the successor Russian Empire.

The most productive of these historians has been Professor George Vernadsky (b. 1887) who is also, probably, the leading Russian historian in America. Apart from a long series of monographs, articles and biographies, he has produced two one-volume histories of Russia and is now engaged, with Professor Michael Karpovich, on a broad ten-volume *History of Russia*. The first two volumes, the only ones that have appeared thus far,[45] have made full but judicious use of the positive achievements of Soviet historical research.[46]

[44] Stepan Lubensky, "L'Eurasisme," *Le Monde Slave*, January-March, 1931, pp. 69-91; D. S. Mirsky, "The Eurasian Movement," *The Slavonic Review*, VI, pp. 311-20.
[45] George Vernadsky, *Ancient Russia, Kievan Russia*.
[46] The Soviet Journal *Problems of History*, 1949, No. 2, denounced both Eurasianism and the work of Vernadsky and Karpovich.

Chapter 27

TWENTIETH CENTURY TRENDS IN ITALIAN, SPANISH, AND PORTUGUESE HISTORIOGRAPHY

By Charles E. Nowell

ITALY

Introduction. Italy opened the twentieth century having recently attained an imperfect and incomplete national unity. The Italians thought largely in terms of their cities, localities or sections, and the famous words of Cavour still held true: "We have now created Italy; it is necessary next to create Italians." The major events of the twentieth century—the attempt to build a colonial empire, the effort to rule the Mediterranean, the intervention in both world wars, and the upsurge of Fascism—all represented attempts to carry out the dream of Cavour, though not perhaps in the way he would have wished.

Italy through this period was generally considered a great power, although the rest of the world doubted that the country had wealth and resources enough to sustain such a role under pressure. The Italian collapse in World War II showed that these doubts were well founded.

In the twentieth century, Italy has suffered from internal stresses and strains. Radical forces, culminating in the present strong Communist movement, have been aided by the national poverty, unequal distribution of wealth, and the repeated failure of Italian governments to find solutions for the basic national problems. Conservative tendencies have been represented by the church, the Italian industrialists, the landholders, and the conservatism innate in the limited middle class.

ITALIAN HISTORIOGRAPHY BEFORE THE RISE OF FASCISM

No one doubts the importance of Italian history, yet it cannot be said that the modern historiography of Italy has lived up to its splendid opportunities. Foreign scholars have been attracted by many phases of the peninsula's great past, and for some periods the best known works are by Germans, Englishmen, and Frenchmen. G. P. Gooch, in his *History and Historians of the Nineteenth Century,* could find little to say about Italian historians and confined his remarks to a few paragraphs in the chapter on "Minor Countries." Any examination of twentieth century developments will at least show that substantial advances have been made.

An interesting feature of Italian historiography during the present century has been the conflict between the "narrative-philological" school on the one hand and the "philosophical" school on the other. The narrative-philological school is the one primarily concerned with the orthodox search for and appraisal of documents. The philosophical school has been built largely around the views of two well-known thinkers: Benedetto Croce (1866-1952) and Giovanni Gentile (1875-1944). Though these philosophers have not thought alike, having both a philosophical and political basis of difference, their influence has been similar in one respect: each has helped demolish the Italian historiography that flourished at the turn of the century.

In 1900, and for some years later, the philological historians were in possession of the Italian field. Gone were such nineteenth-century writers as Cesare Balbo and Cesare Cantu, who combined a taste for long-range history with a flair for literary style. In their place had come a host of narrow historical specialists, who closely investigated minute subjects and wrote up their findings in the matter-of-fact way typical of specialists. These experts wrote primarily for each other and had lost touch with even the intelligentsia of Italy. They had no appreciable influence on either current thought or national policy. Of historical philosophy or breadth of view there was little symptom, save for a vaguely positivist idea that the historian, by providing all this information, was somehow contributing to human welfare.

The two principal journals devoted to history were the *Italian Historical Archive*[1] and the *Italian Historical Review*,[2] which still exist and which were founded respectively in 1842 and 1884. By 1900, these had grown scarcely distinguishable from each other, and were devoted to the same essential purpose —reviewing learned books and publishing erudite articles on narrow subjects. There were also many local historical reviews; these corresponded in general to the areas that had made up the Italian states before the unification of the kingdom in 1861. They followed, substantially, the policies of the main reviews, except that they confined their attention and interest to limited geographical areas.

Changing Trends. An important step toward changing the trend in historiography was made almost at the start of the century by Guglielmo Ferrero (1871-1942), who had previously been a journalist and a sociologist. Ferrero wrote the well-remembered *Greatness and Decline of Rome*, a five-volume work dealing with the last decades of the Roman republic and the founding of the empire by Augustus. Specialists in Roman history did not like the book and found it full of flaws. Orthodox reviewers had little good to say of it, declaring that Ferrero was inadequately prepared in philology and sound historical method. But Ferrero was at least read, and was translated into several foreign languages, including English. In the words of his friend and one-time collaborator, Corrado Barbagallo, Ferrero's was "the greatest and most abused of . . . heretical books";[3] the term "heretical" referring here, of course, to his departure from accepted historical opinions. Ferrero's work flourished because it was interesting; because it dealt with history in broader sweeps than Italian historians were accustomed to employ; and be-

---

[1] *Archivio Storico Italiano.*
[2] *Rivista Storica Italiana.*
[3] Corrado Barbagallo, "The Conditions and Tendencies of Historical Writing in Italy Today." *Journal of Modern History*, I (June, 1929), p. 237.

cause it provided an antidote to the famous views of the German, Theodor Mommsen, of Julius Caesar as the perfect man, or man of destiny. Ferrero's dislike for dictatorships, as brought out in his writing, caused him to fall into the bad graces of the Mussolini regime years later.

In the meantime, Benedetto Croce, the Neapolitan philosopher, was becoming an important figure in Italy through his writings. He applied his philosophy first to literary criticism, then to the study of historiography, and finally to the writing of narrative history itself. This is hardly the occasion for reviewing Croce's philosophy, but a rew remarks can hardly be dispensed with. The famous thinker believes that history is not a science and can never be one, since at its highest level it is an art. Art being a matter of intuitions stemming from the imagination, "it is futile to attempt to translate imaginative intuition into scientific concepts."[4] History and philosophy are really one and the same, and the only history there can be is contemporaneous history. Croce explains this by saying that the only reality is the "eternal present." There is no real past; only the past acting in the present. What the historian does, therefore, is widen the reader's apprehension of the present and enrich it.

Croce illustrated his ideas of how history should be written with several works of his own, two of which are the *History of Italy from 1871 to 1915*[5] and the *History of the Kingdom of Naples*.[6] Both these works have gone through several editions. Though the Crocean philosophy is rather stiff for the average Italian reader, or for any average reader, the philosophical author knocked the main props from under the old narrative-philological school of historians. They were visibly on the decline before the outbreak of World War I.

Italy entered that war early in 1915, and it soon became evident that the Italian people, even the learned, were in no way prepared to understand the crisis that had suddenly descended on their country and Europe. A group of thoughtful Italian scholars believed that the public's lack of historical knowledge accounted for this confusion. To remedy the lack, they founded the *New Historical Review*, early in 1917.[7] The purpose of this journal was to strike out on a new path; not merely to collect learned articles for specialists but to devote itself "mainly to interpretation and understanding of social events."[8] Though the *New Historical Review* directors did not despise erudition, they refused to regard it as an end in itself, and announced a policy of accepting only contributions that had relevance to large movements and great events. The extent to which the Italian public was influenced in its thinking is a question that can hardly be answered here. Examination of the files of the *New Historical Review* over a long period of years shows that though it stuck for awhile to its originally announced program, by World War II, it displayed ominous signs of becoming merely another historical journal.

[4] E. E. Aubrey, "Social Psychology, History, and Sociology," *American Historical Review*, XXX (January, 1928), p. 263.
[5] Benedetto Croce, *Storia de l'Italia dal 1871 al 1915*.
[6] *Idem, Storia del Regno di Napoli*.
[7] *Nuova Rivista Storica*.
[8] Barbagallo, *op. cit.*, p. 240.

ITALIAN HISTORIOGRAPHY UNDER FASCISM

The Fascist revolution in 1922 made it necessary for conscientious Italian historians in many cases either to revise their standards of values or to break with the regime. Some went to foreign countries, as did Gaetano Salvemini (b. 1873), who is the author of a distinguished work on Mazzini and who became a professor at Harvard University. Croce, on the other hand, continued to live and work independently in Naples, and though he was out of favor with the government, no apparent check was placed on his activities. Meanwhile, Giovanni Gentile, a one-time disciple of Croce, who had parted company, intellectually speaking, with his old master, became Italy's Minister of Education and proceeded to reform the Italian school system by a series of decrees. Gentile's philosophy of idealism could be reconciled, and was reconciled, with Fascism, and it called for laying a great deal of emphasis on history. As a result, Italian historiography received, with a vengeance, a dose of those qualities which it had so lacked at the turn of the century. It threatened to become all philosophy, and many books by so-called philosophical historians began to appear, based on no honest historical investigation but merely on preconceived notions, into which the facts of history had to be forced even at the cost of severely warping them. This is merely another way of saying that Fascist ideology was trying to swallow the Italian historians and was succeeding in the case of the lesser ones.

In justice, however, it must be said that the Mussolini regime did not altogether stifle independent historical work. Between 1922 and the Second World War, Italian scholars were usually able to write unmolested if they did not write in open opposition to the government. All through this period the principal Italian historians were men trained before the coming of the Fascists.

MAJOR HISTORICAL WORKS OF THE TWENTIETH CENTURY

The history of Italy is so long and complicated that no historian today would try to cover it all on any except an abbreviated plan. As a result, we have merely summaries of general Italian history. Of these, the most recent and probably the best is that of Luigi Salvatorelli (b. 1886), entitled *A Concise History of Italy from Prehistoric Times to Our Own Day.*[9] It was written shortly before the late war and closed with Italy's withdrawal from the League of Nations in 1937. Salvatorelli's work has been translated into English and may be recommended to the American student who wishes to gain a quick working knowledge of Italian history.

Roman studies have flourished in twentieth-century Italy, and the flourishing has been in some part due to the rather benevolent attitude of the Fascist government, anxious to revive the glories of imperial Rome.

Although the late Ettore Pais (1856-1939) was once regarded as the man on whose shoulders Mommsen's mantle had fallen, his numerous works on the Roman republic are today considered rather unreliable and full of erratic interpretations. Gaetano de Sanctis (b. 1870) is the best historian of republican

---

[9] Luigi Salvatorelli, *Sommario della Storia d'Italia dai Tempi Preistorici ai Nostri Giorni.*

Rome, with a four-volume *History of the Romans* which covers the field from the beginning to the battle of Pydna in 168 B.C.[10] Carolina Lanzani has made important contributions to late republican history, especially with her fine biography of the dictator Sulla. Roman imperial history still suffers from the lack of available source material that once caused Mommsen to shun the task of writing it. But Arnaldo Momigliano's book on the Emperor Claudius is an outstanding work, and the same is true of the study by Roberto Paribeni (b. 1876) of the Emperor Trajan. Interesting, too, is Momigliano's valuable monograph on *The Formation of Modern Historiography regarding the Roman Empire.*[11] This is a survey of all the main writings about the empire from Tillemont and Montesquieu to contemporary times. Momigliano's personal conclusion is that the history of the empire and the rise of the church should be regarded as essentially one and the same historical problem, a far cry from the purely secular interpretations of Gibbon.

Publication of History of Rome. In 1938, the *Institute of Roman Studies* began publication of a thirty-volume history of the city of Rome in all ages— ancient, medieval, and modern—the first sixteen volumes to survey the political history and the remaining ones to deal with religion, Roman law, military science, language development and art. The Duce took a personal interest in the publication, and the director of the series, Carlo Galassi Paluzzi (b. 1861), otherwise little known in the scholarly world, seems to have been chosen mainly for his Fascist orthodoxy. But some of the volumes were assigned to scholars of good reputation, such as Roberto Paribeni,[12] Giuseppe Corradi (b. 1880),[13] and Ottorino Bertolino (b. 1892).[14] A few of the volumes had appeared before Italy entered the war in 1940, and several have appeared since. There is no reason to call this anything but a good series, although it is safe to say that some of the volumes will not now be published; at least not in the form originally announced.

Another series planned and begun before the war was directed by the Fascist statesman, Arrigo Solmi (1873-1941), already known as the leading modern historian of Italian law.[15] The Solmi series is entitled *Political History of Italy from the Origin to Our Day.*[16] As originally planned, it was to consist of twelve volumes, of which six seem actually to have been published, dealing respectively with Italian prehistory, the Roman republic, the Roman empire, the period of foreign domination from 1500 to 1700, the Napoleonic era, and the origins of the *Risorgimento.*

The Italian Middle Ages have recently been surveyed in a pair of attractive, well-documented works by the late Romolo Caggese (1882-   ?).[17] These

[10] Gaetano de Sanctis, *Storia dei Romani,* 4 vols. in 7.
[11] Arnaldo Momigliano, *La Formazione della Moderna Storiografia Sull' Impero Romano.*
[12] Roberto Paribeni, *Da Diocleziano alla Caduta Del'Impero d'Occidente (From Diocletian to the Fall of the Empire in the West.)*
[13] Giuseppe Corradi, *Le Grande Conquiste Mediteranee, (The Great Mediterranean Conquests).*
[14] Ottorino Bertolini, *Roma di Fronte a Bizancio e ai Longobardi, (Rome Facing Byzantium and the Lombards).*
[15] Arrigo Solmi, *Storia del Diretto Italiano (History of Italian Law).*
[16] *Storia Politica d'Italia dale Origine ai Giorni Nostri.*
[17] Romolo Gaggese, *L'Alto Medioevo (The High Middle Ages); idem, Dal Concordato di Worms alla Fine della Prigionia di Avignone (From the Concordat of Worms to the End of the Avignon Captivity).*

covers almost a thousand years of Italian history, from the fall of the Roman empire in the west to the end of the Babylonian captivity of the popes in 1377.

There is no good history of the Italian Renaissance written by an Italian; nothing comparable to the old nineteenth century work by the Swiss Jacob Burckhardt. Yet minor Renaissance studies have flourished in Italy to such an extent that in 1938 a new review was started, edited by the famous writer, Giovañni Papini (b. 1881) and devoted entirely to the publication of such studies.[18]

Italian contributions to the great geographical discoveries of the fifteenth and sixteenth centuries were numerous, and these have naturally appealed to modern Italian historians. Alberto Magnaghi (1875-1945) [19] has produced the best study of Amerigo Vespucci ever made, and Roberto Almagia (b. 1884)[20] has clarified many details concerning Italian participation in the discovery of America. For an older period, Luigi Benedetto (b. 1886) has prepared a new and critical edition of Marco Polo, which appears to have superseded all earlier ones.[21]

The period of foreign domination in Italy, covering the sixteenth and seventeenth centuries, has been adequately surveyed by Romolo Quazza;[22] the eighteenth century by Ettore Rota (b. 1883)[23] and the Napoleonic era by Francesco Lemmi.[24] These works are all parts of the series on Italian political history edited by Arrigo Solmi, to which reference was previously made.

Historical Review of Modern Italy. The *Risorgimento* (resurgence), which was the principal modern Italian political movement before the advent of Fascism, has its own historical review, founded in 1914 and recently revived following a temporary eclipse during the war.[25] *Risorgimento* studies have thriven in the twentieth century. Of the numerous works to appear on Cavour, special attention is due the study by Alberto Cappa.[26] Though Cappa highly esteems the work of Cavour, he abstains from hero worship. He is careful to point out that the great statesman had many collaborators in the making of Italy, and that at the time of his early death the task was far from completed. A *Dictionary of the Risorgimento,* dealing in great detail with both the main events and the main persons involved, was published in four volumes from 1930 to 1937, directed by the late Professor Michele Rosi (1864—?) of the University of Rome.[27] This is a handy work of ready reference, from which a reader can easily extract information. Cesare Spellanzon (b. 1884) has tried with a great deal of success to give Italy a definitive *History of the Risorgimento and of Italian Unity.*[28] In four tremendous volumes (1933-

[18] *La Rinascita (The Renaissance).*
[19] Alberto Magnaghi, *Amerigo Vespucci.*
[20] Roberto Almagia, *Gli Italiani, Prima Esploratori dell'American (The Italians, First Explorers of America).*
[21] Luigi Benedetto, *Il Milione, Prima Edizione Integrade (Marco Polo's Work).*
[22] Romolo Quazza, *Preponderenze Straniere (Foreign Predominance).*
[23] Ettore Rota, *Le Origine del Risorgimento (The Origins of the Risorgimento).*
[24] Francesco Lemmi, *L'Eta Napoleonica (The Napoleonic Era).*
[25] *Rassegna Storica del Risorgimento (Historical Review of the Risorgimento).*
[26] Alberto Cappa, *Cavour.*
[27] *Dizionario del Risorgimento Nazionale,* 4 vols., Director Michele Rosi.
[28] Cesare Spellanzon, *Storia del Risorgimento e Dell'Unita d'Italia,* v. 1-4.

1938) he has produced an interesting and magnificently documented work, still to be completed, which runs at present to the year 1848.

For the years between Italian unification and the first world war, there is Benedetto Croce's Italian history already mentioned. Writings about Fascism and its history are so violently partisan that they are surely ephemeral. Italy since 1922 awaits its historian, and it will probably be years before a sound and balanced account of these critical recent years can become possible.

In the meantime, reports from Italy indicate that historical research and writing still go on abundantly. All the major reviews appear to have survived the war, and there is no sign that the great Italian past will cease to be vigorously investigated.

SPAIN

Introduction. Spain has run an interesting gamut during the first half of the twentieth century. It began as a declining monarchy, with prestige further weakened by the ignominious defeat suffered at the hands of the United States in 1898. For the first thirty years, liberal tendencies prevailed in the country, which were in general reflected by the historians' output. But the overthrow of King Alfonso XIII in 1931, instead of placing Spain firmly on the road to progress and prosperity, merely precipitated further crises. The short-lived republic, with undeniably liberal aspirations, was ground to pieces between the forces of extreme radicalism on the one side and those of extreme reaction on the other. The three-year revolution and the installation of the Franco regime in 1939 put an end, for the time being at least, to Spanish liberal development. The weakened condition of the country prevented intervention in World War II, but no doubt existed concerning the extreme partiality of the Spanish government toward its Fascist friends, Germany and Italy. Since the war, Spain has remained a country of forthright Fascist policies. This has been inevitably reflected in Spanish historiography.

General History

Historical work in great abundance has poured from Spain during the twentieth century. He who attempts to survey its main results in a few pages is under the necessity of making a careful selection, and even then finds many omissions necessary.

There exists no complete account of Spanish historiography, though an interesting beginning in that direction was made a few years ago by Benito Sanchez Alonso. According to that scholar's announced plan, the three volume *History of Spanish Historiography,*[29] when completed, would proceed in detail to the end of the eighteenth century and then provide a brief epilogue showing the main characteristics of nineteenth and twentieth century historiography. In 1944, Sanchez Alonso finished his second volume, carrying the account to the year 1684. But then, instead of proceeding with the final volume, the author elected to revise the first, which surveys Spanish historiography only to 1543. He produced a small third volume in 1950; apparently a lesser one than originally planned.

[29] Benito Sanchez Alonso, *Historia de la Historiografía Española,* v. 1-3.

Spain began the twentieth century possessing a Royal Academy of History that was already old, for it had been founded by the Bourbon King, Philip V, in 1738. Since 1877 the Academy has published a *Bulletin,* devoted to the usual learned articles and reviews, with occasional supplements for the publication of valuable documents.[30] This *Bulletin* has continued to appear regularly, despite the vicissitudes of modern Spanish politics.

Historical Center. In 1900, Señor Garcia Alix, then Minister of Public Instruction for Spain, created in the universities of the country a section called "Historical Sciences," which were thereby definitely separated from the linguistic, literary, and philosophical disciplines of which they had previously been a part.[31] Ten years later, the same Ministry founded at Madrid a Center of Historical Studies, to serve as a finishing or graduate school for budding Spanish historians. The Center has been described as a "laboratory of historical studies, where the masters of established reputation work together . . . with the young men . . . who wish to complete their historical training . . . by being initiated into the methods of research."[32]

From its establishment in 1910 until the Spanish revolution in 1936, the Center was the strongest driving force in Spanish historiography, devoted to stimulating publication and to raising the standard of research. Nevertheless, the most renowned names in recent Spanish historiography are those of men who received their training before the establishment of the Center. Unquestionably the three leading historians of Spain in the present century are Rafael Altamira y Crevea (1866-1951), Ramón Menéndez Pidal (b. 1869), and Antonio Ballesteros y Beretta (1880-1949). Of these, the first two had become active scholars before the turn of the century.

Leading Historians. Altamira, the oldest of the three, is chiefly known for his *History of Spain and Spanish Civilization,* which appeared in four volumes from 1909 to 1914.[33] As the title implies, this is a cultural synthesis rather than a work of straight political history. Though Altamira provides a political framework, he is mainly interested in the non-political achievements of Spain. Literature, art, institutions, customs, dress, and manner of living are the matters principally stressed. The work has become a classic and has been translated, all or in part, into various languages, including English.

Menéndez Pidal, though once known primarily as a philologist and student of literature, has transferred his main interest to history. Students of both literature and history are well acquainted with his *Spain of the Cid,*[34] a masterful reconstruction of the life and institutions of the peninsula in the eleventh century. In more recent years, Menéndez Pidal has undertaken to edit an ambitious *History of Spain,* with contributions from many scholars. Volumes one to four, dealing respectively with Pre-Roman, Roman, Visigothic, and Arabic Spain, have thus far been published, but these bring the country only to the beginning of the eleventh century.[35]

---

[30] *Boletín de la Real Academia de la Historia.*
[31] José Deleito y Piñuela, "Quelques données sur l'historiographie en Espagne de 1900 a 1930," *Revue de Synthèse Historique,* new series, XXIV (December, 1930), pp. 29-30.
[32] *Ibid.,* p. 31.
[33] Rafael Altamira y Crevea, *Historia de España y de la Civilización Española,* 4 vols.
[34] Ramón Menédez Pidal, *La España del Cid,* 2 vols.
[35] *Historio de España,* v. 1-4, Director Ramón Menéndez Pidal.

Ballesteros y Beretta is the author of an eight-volume *History of Spain and Its Influence in Universal History,* which appeared from 1919 to 1936.[36] The Ballesteros history is a more orthodox work than that of Altamira, and, though not wholly lacking in economic and cultural analysis, deals mainly with the political events of Spain. The terminal point is the year 1931 and the end of the monarchy. The earlier parts of the work are the stronger parts, and the value diminishes as the author reaches more recent times. For twentieth century events, Ballesteros confines himself to a slender thread of narrative and makes small attempt to weigh or analyze. In his last years this historian was busy supervising and editing a set of twenty-three volumes dealing with the Spanish discovery and conquest of the New World and with the individual histories of the American republics, including the United States. It is worth noting here that instead of preparing a new history of the United States for their purpose, Ballesteros and his associates have elected to translate into Spanish, the long-obsolete history by Henry W. Elson. At the present date, nine volumes of the series have been published.

Twentieth Century History. Spain has felt the twentieth century trend toward collaborative ventures in history writing. In addition to the unfinished Menéndez Pidal effort, there is the completed five-volume *History of Spain,* which is subtitled *Great General History of the Spanish Peoples,* edited and published by Luis Pericot García (b. 1899) between the years 1936 and 1943.[37] Each of the five volumes deals with a distinct epoch in Spanish history and each is the work of a group of authors, except for the first, covering the prehistoric and Roman period, which Pericot García writes alone. Once more the work concludes with the fall of Alfonso in 1931. The scholarship is adequate and the volumes are most attractive, due in part to their beautiful format and the abundance of illustrations.

The most ambitious economic history of Spain to appear recently is the encyclopedic *History of Spanish Economy* by Jaime Carrera Pujal of which five volumes were published from 1943 to 1947.[38] Carrera Pujal begins his economic survey with the reign of Charles V and carries it to the beginning of the nineteenth century. Presumably more volumes are in the offing.

Since the latest revolution in Spain and the elevation of the Franco government to power in 1939, the Spanish historical output, far from showing any sign of slackening, continues greater than ever. Several generalizations occur to anyone who examines any considerable part of this mass of historical literature. It appears that Spanish scholarship has concentrated more than ever on the Middle Ages and the age of discovery, to the comparative exclusion of the nineteenth and twentieth centuries. Moreover, there is a general tone of national self-laudation, which is best displayed by the tendency to explain Spain's "historic mission" in glowing terms and by the trend toward glorification of the famous characters of the past. This is accompanied by the apparent determination to exalt and revindicate those very national qualities

---

[36] Antonio Ballesteros y Beretta, *Historia de España y su Influencia en la Historia Universal,* 8 vols.
[37] *Historia de España, Gran Historia General de los Pueblos Hispanos,* 5 vols. Director Luis Pericot García.
[38] Jaime Carrera Pujal, *Historia de la Economía Española,* v. 1-5.

which outsiders have generally considered the most objectionable of the Spanish characteristics. There is no doubt, however, that much of the writing is addressed to Spanish American audiences quite as much as to those in Spain.

LOCAL HISTORY

Castilian history is not the only Spanish history, and valuable research has gone on in the non-Castilian parts of Spain. Catalan history has usually had a local nationalistic slant, never to the liking of whatever authorities, past or contemporary, have held power in Madrid. An Institute of Catalan Studies, which began its existence in 1907, was suppressed by the Primo de Rivera dictatorship in the twenties, but reappeared after the dictator's fall. The most noted Catalan historian of the twentieth century has no doubt been Pedro Bosch y Gimpera (b. 1891), whose work has been mainly devoted to clarifying the pre-history of Spain, with heavy emphasis on Catalonia.[39] Antoni Rubio y Lluch (1856-1937) has performed a great service to the scientific history of Catalonia by collecting two volumes of valuable documents illustrating the development of Catalan science.[40] To date, the principal beneficiary of his work has been a contemporary Catalan scholar, Gonzalo de Reparaz-Ruiz, who has used the documents extensively in studies concerned with the development of Catalan concepts of geography. Besides in Catalonia, historical studies have made progress during the twentieth century in Galicia, the Basque provinces, Valencia, and the island of Majorca. Scholarly reviews, devoted to local history and culture, have existed until recently in all these places, but at the moment it is extremely difficult to learn which, if any, have survived the late Spanish political difficulties.

Arabic studies have been cultivated in twentieth-century Spain to such an extent that in 1933 a journal called *El-Andalus* was founded in Madrid to assist in their propagation. *El-Andalus* is the organ of schools of Arabic studies in Madrid and Granada, and has served both as a medium for the publication and translation of Arabic sources and for the publication of original articles dealing with the history and culture of Moslem Spain.

PORTUGAL

Introduction. Portugal, like Spain, opened the twentieth century with a monarchy approaching its last gasp and with a lowly position in the world. The substitution of a republic in 1910 failed to help matters, as the small country, poor, staggering under a load of debt, and burdened with a largely illiterate population, proved entirely unequal to the task of maintaining democratic government. Revolutions and political upheavals followed in monotonous succession until, in 1926, a clique of military leaders seized control. Two years later, feeling themselves unable to cope with Portugal's economic problems, they invited an economics professor from the University of Coimbra, António de Oliveira Salazar, to take charge of the state, with virtually unlimited powers. Since then Salazar has ruled Portugal, maintaining

---

[39] Pedro Bosch y Gimpera, *Etnologia de la Peninsula Iberia (Ethnology of the Iberian Peninsula).*
[40] Antoni Rubió y Lluch, *Documents for the History of Medieval Catalan Culture* (in Catalan), 2 vols.

a government of a mildly Fascist type. He has given the nation at least an outward look of prosperity, has improved the colonial administration and evidently made substantial progress in paying off the debt. However, Salazar's detractors accuse him of juggling figures and falsifying the record.

GENERAL HISTORY

Two brilliant scholars, Alexandre de Herculano e Carvalho and Luiz Augusto Rebello da Silva, dominated Portuguese historical writing through most of the nineteenth century. Herculano specialized in the Middle Ages and Rebello, in the seventeenth century. Each of the two, before the end of his life, virtually gave up straight history to deal in a more popular literary commodity—romantic historical fiction. Though both Herculano and Rebello wrote good novels, they unfortunately had imitators. The historical romance steadily deteriorated in the hands of these inferior writers until the whole movement grew absurd. The realistic novelist, Eça de Queiroz, finally laughed this species of romance out of existence in his *Illustrious House of Ramires,* much as Cervantes had once put an end to the Spanish romance of chivalry.

In the last quarter of the century, predominance among Portuguese historians was held by Joaquim Pedro Oliveira Martins (1845-1894), who, in his numerous writings, ranged the whole field of national history and at times even ventured outside it. Oliverira Martins, who was by no means a romanticist, felt that his country had made its great mistake by electing to build a colonial empire in the fifteenth and sixteenth centuries, since by doing so it had destroyed the original spirit of Portugal. His way of telling Portuguese history was to paint brilliant word pictures of various crucial episodes in the past. The two-volume *History of Portugal,* which is his best known work, followed that plan.[41] Though the contemporary scholar does not find the Oliverira Martins treatment wholly satisfactory, the fact remains that he was widely read, and that he influenced public opinion.

Twentieth-Century Historians. In the present century, Portugal has produced several good historians, though none as influential or outstanding as the older literary masters. The best full-length national history to appear is that of Fortunato de Almeida (1869-1933), a six-volume work published from 1922 to 1929. Almeida's *History of Portugal* carries the story from Pre-Roman times to the republican revolution of 1910.[42] Though lacking in brilliance and by no means distinguished for originality, the work is sound, being chiefly based on the monographic work of other scholars. While Almeida writes orthodox political history in the main, he devotes a good deal of space to national institutions and their development. The same author has also published a *History of the Church in Portugal,* in four volumes.[43]

As in many other countries, Portuguese efforts in historiography have recently turned toward collaborative works. The seven-volume *History of Portugal,* edited by Professor Damião Peres (b. 1889) of the University of

---

[41] Joaquim Pedro Oliverira Martins, *Historia de Portugal,* 2 vols.
[42] Fortunato de Almeida, *História de Portugal,* 6 vols.
[43] *Idem, História da Igre-ja em Portugal,* 4 vols.

Coimbra and contributed to by many scholars, appeared during the years 1928-35.[44] Though it promised to be the best history of Portugal thus far produced, the work on appearance turned out to be rather disappointing. It is decidedly thin in spots and gives the impression of hasty scholarship. Peres himself is the author of several valuable studies, one of his best being a hundred-page monograph entitled *How Portugal Was Born,* which is a close and careful survey of those years in the late eleventh and early twelfth centuries, immediately before the first national ruler, Alfonso Henriques, rose to power.[45] That period is involved and confused, but Peres, fully master of the sources, steers a true course through the jumble of evidence and provides a clear picture of the national origins.

Portugal like Spain has an Arabic background, and though Arab studies have not flourished to the same extent there, much progress has been made since Herculano, whose ignorance of the language forced him to neglect important Arabic sources. The best known Portuguese Arabic scholar of the twentieth century has been David Lopes (1867-1942), principally noted for his translations of documents and for his extensive and valuable studies of Portuguese conquests and administration in Morocco.

The history of nineteenth- and twentieth-century Portugal has been, on the whole, neglected, and no historian has dealt fully with the building of the present important Portuguese empire in Africa. Julio de Vilhena (1845-1928) has written a three-volume work on *King Pedro V and His Reign,* referring to the brilliant and promising monarch who governed from 1853 to 1861.[46] But such topics as the constitutional struggles of the nineteenth century, the rise of republicanism, and the development of the "New State" under Salazar await their historians.

PORTUGUESE IMPERIAL HISTORY

In view of their splendid past and rather humble present, it is perhaps natural that the Portuguese should concentrate heavily upon their great oceanic discoveries. Of the numerous writers on this theme, a few seem worthy of special mention. The Cortesão brothers, Jaime (b. 1894) and Armando (b. 1891), have worked for years to clarify the results of early Portuguese voyaging in the Atlantic and the rise of the Portuguese school of cartography. Joaquim Bensaude has devoted his life to proving the priority of the Portuguese in scientific discoveries bearing on the development of navigation. Abel Fontoura da Costa (1869-1941), himself a seafaring man, has studied and described the sailing methods and techniques used by the Portuguese in their fifteenth- and sixteenth-century voyages. Luciano Pereira da Silva (1864-1926), a mathematician turned historian, produced in 1915 an admirable study of the astronomical concepts of the great national poet, Luiz Vaz de Camães, as they appeared in his immortal *Lusiads.*

Two important collaborative works have appeared in the twentieth century devoted to Portuguese overseas achievements. The first, edited by Carlos

[44] *História de Portugal,* 7 vols. Director Damião Peres.
[45] Damião Peres, Como *Nasceu Portugal.*
[46] Julio de Vilhena, *D. Pedro V. e o Seu Reinado,* 3 vols.

Malheiro Dias (1875-1941), surveys in three volumes the Portuguese discovery and early colonization of Brazil.[47] The second, also in three volumes, is supervised by António Baião (b. 1876) and deals with Portuguese expansion in the world from the national beginnings to the present.[48] These cooperative works are spotty, in that they intersperse brilliant chapters with others of inferior quality. Both are permeated with too nationalistic a spirit, with too much effort devoted to an attempt to prove Portuguese priority in all things related to discovery.

Historical reviews have not flourished in Portugal, and the few that have been started have withered and died after a brief existence. The deficiency has been partly made good by such publications as the *Bulletin* of the Lisbon Geographical Society and the *Memoirs* of the Lisbon Academy of Sciences, both of which devote a considerable part of their offering to history.

---

[47] *História de Colonizãçao Portuguesa do Brasil,* 3 vols., Director Carlos Malheiro Dias.
[48] *História da Expanão Portuguesa no Mundo,* 3 vols., Director A. Baiao.

Chapter 28

HISTORICAL WRITING IN MODERN JAPAN
By James William Morley

DURING the past century Japan has been undergoing a revolution, her traditional ideas and institutions being subjected to powerful influences from the West. How to control and use these influences so that they will not destroy, but rather enrich, the older patterns of thought and action, has been the essential problem facing all modern Japanese leaders. At times they have sought solutions by rejecting western ways. At others they have gone to the opposite extreme of accepting only Western ways. Many modern Japanese historians, for example, when imperial rule was first restored in 1868, sought guides in the purely native tradition of writing "official histories." Others swung to the other extreme and emulated the exotic Western school of *Kulturgeschichte*. In the end, most Japanese historians, like most leaders in other fields, have tended to find a satisfying solution in those patterns of behavior in which the native tradition and the Western impact complement each other. For historians, those patterns have been found primarily in the fields of compiling records, editing texts, and writing specialized monographs.

THE "OFFICIAL" TRADITION

When the Restoration leaders, after nearly a thousand years of aristocratic and feudal rule, restored power to the emperor in 1868, they naturally attempted also to restore many of the practices of the days of imperial greatness in the sixth, seventh, eighth and early ninth centuries. One of these was the practice of compiling official court chronicles. The oldest, the "Six National Histories" (in Japanese)[1] were compiled at imperial command by official bureaus in the seventh, eighth and ninth centuries. They were written in Chinese and partly modelled on the Chinese dynastic histories. For the period from the legendary Age of the Gods and the founding of the empire (traditionally 660 B. C., but probably *ca.* 40 B. C.) to the year 887 A. D., they recorded chronologically the events at court in the forms of annals and biographies.

The gradual assumption of power by the court nobles in the tenth and eleventh centuries and then by the provincial warriors in the twelfth to the nineteenth centuries, reduced the Kyoto Court for long periods to impotence and sometimes to poverty. Moreover, with the termination of official embassies

---

[1] The earliest official dynastic history, that compiled by Crown Prince Shotoku and Soga no Umako was in part destroyed by fire and otherwise lost. The oldest extant history, *Records of Ancient Matters*, recorded from the memory of *Hieda no Are*, is more informal in style and more limited in aim and scope, and so traditionally has not been ranked with the "Six National Histories."

Japanese works are indicated in this chapter by descriptive English titles. Most of them have not been translated into Western languages, but for the few that have consult *A Selected List of Books and Articles on Japan in English, French, and German*, compiled by Hugh Borton, Serge Elisseeff and Edwin O. Reischauer.

to the Chinese Court in the ninth century, the fever to mimic Chinese practice subsided In consequence, the practice of writing official court histories was discontinued; the tradition, however, was not allowed to die. In every century, partisans of the court have compiled voluminous records for "national histories." Two later histories in this great tradition were compiled outside the court in the Tokugawa Period (1600-1868). One was sponsored by the *Shogun* himself, *A General Mirror of Japan* (in Japanese, 1670), a monumental work in 237 sections, written in Chinese style and form, chronicling Japan's history from where the "Six National Histories" ended in 887 down to 1610. The compilation of this work was entrusted to the Hayashi family, who were assisted by many students at their school, *Shohei Gakko*. The second "official history" whose compilation was begun during the same period was *A History of Japan* (in Japanese, writing begun 1657, publication first completed 1906). This work, whose 2466 sections were finally published in 17 volumes (Dai-Nihon Yuben-kai edition, 1928-29), was originally sponsored by the Lord of Mito, Mitsukuni Tokugawa (1628-1700).[2] Chinese in language and form; it follows the official tradition more closely than the former, for it makes the imperial descent the heart of its account. It is especially valuable, for the "Mito School" was very careful in establishing authentic texts and meticulous in citing sources.

This is the official tradition to which the Meiji reformers turned first of all. Historical bureaus were set up within various administrative departments and were charged to search Tokugawa records for precedents and suggestions to help formulate current policy. As a result, several important studies were published in the 1880's, among them the *History of Japanese Taxation* (in Japanese, 1882), by the Department of Finance, and the *Draft History of Diplomacy* (in Japanese, 1884), by the Department of Foreign Affairs. More important than these departmental bureaus was the Historical Compilation Bureau *(Shushikyoku)*, established by Imperial rescript under Prince Sanetomi Sanjo in January 1868. It was attached to the highest governing body, the Great Council of State *(Dajokan)*, and assigned the job of compiling the official national history in continuation of the "Six National Histories."

INTERPRETATIVE HISTORY

A second departure in the early Meiji period was the attempt to write broad, interpretative history. Objective synthesis was not a highly developed native art. Indeed, rarely had Japanese historiography distinguished itself from the arts of recording, compilation, biography, autobiography and romance. Outside of the writing of chronicles and the compiling of records, historical writing in the feudal period had taken the form of "mirrors" *(kagami)*, "narratives" *(monogatari)*, and "war records" *(gunki)*,[3] being usually intimate romantic

---

[2] Standard Japanese practice is to list family names first, given names last; however, in this chapter, to avoid confusion, Western practice is followed in the order of given name first, family name last.

[3] Among the best known "mirrors" reflecting court life from the ninth to the fourteenth centuries are the so-called "Four Mirrors": *Great Mirror, Water Mirror, Clear Mirror,* and *Present Mirror* (all in Japanese). The most useful today is perhaps the *Mirror of Eastern Japan* (in Japanese), which describes the organization, administration and policies of the Shogunate in the late twelfth and early thirteenth centuries. Among the best known "narratives" are such feudal romances as *Tales of the House of Taira* (in Japanese), *Records of the Rise and Fall of the Minamoto and Taira Families* (in Japanese) and *Records of Great Peace* (in Japanese).

glimpses of court life, Buddhist tales, yarns about warring clans and knightly battles, in which historical accuracy was frequently sacrificed for literary appeal. Interpretative history as distinct from chronicles and stories had had only four significant exponents.

The first was Jien Fujiwara (Abbott Jichin, 1155-1225). An Abbott of the Enryakuji monastery, four times head of the Tendai sect, son and brother of Civil Dictators at Court and uncle by another brother's marriage to the shogun, Jien knew intimately the affairs of his day. It was with this information that he wrote *Miscellany of Personal Views of an Ignorant Fool* (in Japanese, 1220). In it he surveyed Japanese history, analyzing the changing relationship between emperor and subjects, and between civil and military authorities. He found these relationships to change in cycles expressive of a single principle, "dori" (reason, idea, truth, principle, right).[4] The second was Chikafusa Kitabatake (1293-1354). As chief counsellor to Emperor Daigo II, he guided policies and led armies in that ruler's vigorous, but unsuccessful effort to wrest control of the country from the shogunate. During his campaign in the *Kanto* region, he also wrote a *History of the True Succession of the Divine Monarchs* (in Japanese, 1339). While uncritical in its use of sources, Chikafusa's work has been extremely influential for its attacks on the shogunate and its glorification of the Japanese islands, people and emperors. The third was Hakuseki Arai (1659-1725), who was high in the councils of the Tokugawa shogun in the early years of the eighteenth century. Upon his retirement from active service, he made extensive researches in geography, linguistics, ethnography, archaeology, genealogy, and history. Perhaps his most outstanding work was his *Treatises on Japanese History* (in Japanese, 1912),[5] originally conceived as a series of lectures to the young shogun, Ienobu. In this book he relates the decline during the Middle Ages of the power of the court aristocracy and the rise of the military families. His critical handling of sources, objectivity, use of auxiliary sciences and skill in interpretative synthesis, make Hakuseki Arai a truly modern historian. The fourth pre-Meiji scholar to write interpretative history was Sanyo Rai (1780-1832). While Sanyo was sloppy in his research methods (he copied much of his data from earlier works by other authors), his works, like the *Informal History of Japan* (in Japanese) and the *Political Account of Japan* (in Japanese) were extremely influential. Throughout the nineteenth century they were prized by politicians as much as by historians, for they denounced the shogunate, glorified the court and argued for the restoration of complete authority to the emperor.

Except for these four, Jien, Chikafusa, Hakuseki and Sanyo, modern Japanese historians could look back on few native scholars who had organized large bodies of knowledge interpretatively. Perhaps, because they felt their

---

[4] Jan Rahdar, "Miscellany of Personal Views of an Ignorant Fool (Guk(w)ansho)," by Fujiwara Jien, *Acta Orientalia*, 15, p. 182.
[5] Besides his autobiography and the above-mentioned *Treatises*, Hakuseki compiled a 20-volume set of *Clan Records* (in Japanese, 1701), and an additional 6 volumes of *Clan Records, Genealogies* (in Japanese), tracing especially the seventeenth century families related to the Tokugawa. In his *Notes on Ancient History* (in Japanese, 1716), he offered a rational interpretation of the Age of the Gods, applying higher criticism to the ancient classics. The more debatable points he took up in *Some Questions and Notes on Ancient History* (in Japanese).

own tradition so weak in this respect, several early Meiji historians turned eagerly to Western *Kulturgeschichte*. One of the first Western histories to be translated was François Guizot's *Histoire Générale de la Civilization en Europe* (1828, first translated into Japanese in 1875). Guizot's reputation as promoter and editor of *Documents Inédits,* his critical handling of sources, his emphasis on the middle class and his nationalism all appealed to the Japanese, but most attractive was his skill in synthesizing. It was this which also drew the Japanese to Henry Thomas Buckle's *History of Civilization in England* (1857, translated into Japanese, 1875). Several works were written in imitation of those of Guizot and Buckle. One of the earliest was the *Outline of Civilization* (in Japanese, 6 vols., 1875) by the ardent Westernizer and publicist, Yukichi Fukuzawa (1835-1901). Another was the *Short History of Japanese Civilization* (in Japanese, 1877) by Dr. Ukichi Taguchi (1855-1905), noted economist, historian, lecturer and publisher. In his *Short History,* he attempted to combine Guizot's emphasis on the middle class with Buckle's broad cultural view.

By the end of the century foreign *Kulturgeschichte* had practically died out. Likewise, the initial project of the official historiographic bureau, that of writing "national history," was abandoned. The task of collecting and evaluating the records of the Imperial Government, shogunates, noble families and military lords since the ninth century proved so gigantic—and, perhaps more important, so congenial—that the bureau decided to devote itself to that task alone. In giving their major attention to source compilation, Japanese historians were returning to an already deep-rooted national habit.

SOURCE COMPILATION

Throughout the feudal period and before, it was the practice of all in authority to keep extensive records (*kiroku*) and documents (*monjo*). These became the subject of intense study by historians in the Tokugawa period, who with the aid of contemporary literary and linquistic scholars, developed a highly perfected, critical methodology. The contribution of Tokugawa Sinologists and Japanologists, like Mabuchi Kamo (1697-1769), Norinaga Moto'ori (1730-1801) and Nobutomo Ban (1775-1848), to contemporary and later historians was to provide philological methods of source analysis. Among the many scientific compilers of records in the Tokugawa Era were the above-mentioned "Hayashi School" and "Mito School." Most impressive of all was the work of a third group of scholars, the Source Study School *(Shiryo Gakuha),* which was led by the greatest of all Japanese compilers, the blind Hoki'ichi Hanawa (1746-1821). In his Seminary for Japanese Studies *(Wagaku Kodansho),* organized in 1793, Hoki'ichi and his associates compiled voluminous genealogical records and historical materials of all kinds.[6] This long-established and critically developed habit of source compila-

---

[6] Outstanding among the compilations of Hoki'ichi's Seminary are: *Family Records* (in Japanese, started in 1799) in 178 sections, *Catalogue of Military Families* (in Japanese, started in 1804) in 700 sections, the unfinished *Sources* (in Japanese, started in 1801) in 430 sections, and, most important of all, *Japanese Sources Classified by Subjects* (in Japanese, 1893-94), a collection of 1270 historically valuable works or manuscript fragments in 665 sections, the last of which was completed in 1819.

tion has been perhaps the strongest single influence shaping modern Japanese historiography.

This traditional influence was powerfully supplemented by knowledge of Western practice. Whether by going abroad to study, reading translations of Western works, or working with and studying under Western historians in Japan, Japanese historians of the late nineteenth and early twentieth centuries have been strongly influenced by the critical methodology and penchant for writing monographs of the West, particularly of the German School. Leopold von Ranke, the University of Berlin, the Bavarian Historical Commission, the *Monumenta Germaniae Historica*—these became models for modern Japan. Two handbooks of Western methodology have been particularly influential. One of the first Japanese ministers to England, Kencho Suematsu, was very anxious to make Japanese scholars "acquainted with the style, plan and methods pursued by the most eminent historians of Western nations, in order for them to write the history of their own country in accordance with these models."[7] He made the acquaintance of George Gustavus Zerffi (1821-1892), an Hungarian lecturer on art history in South Kensington, England; and prevailed upon him to write a handbook for this purpose. Finally translated into Japanese by 1887 under the title, "History," it was not published, but presented in manuscript to the official historiographic bureau. Much more influential was the manual written by the noted Japanese historian, Dr. Kumazo Tsuboi (1858-1936), entitled *The Method of Historical Research* (in Japanese, Tokyo, 1903). Strongly influenced by Bernheim and Seignobos, Tsuboi returned from his study abroad in 1891 to become a professor of Western history at Tokyo Imperial University. "Pure history," he maintained, "begins with Leopold von Ranke."[8] Through his *Historical Research* and his lectures and other writings, Tsuboi spread the new gospel. The purpose of "pure history," he went on to explain is not to instill moral lessons but "to reflect the appearance of the world and . . . to explain the cause of things."[9] For Tsuboi, his students and most of his colleagues, Niehbur and von Ranke had eclipsed Guizot, Buckle, Macaulay and Carlyle.

The most influential exponent of the German school in Japan at the turn of the century was Tsuboi's colleague, Dr. Ludwig Riess (1861-1928). Born in Prussia, Riess studied at Berlin under von Ranke, and upon completion of his doctoral dissertation in the field of English history, was invited in 1886 to Japan to teach in the history department of Tokyo Imperial University. He taught off and on until 1902, when he returned to Berlin to accept a position as professor extraordinarius at the university. His influence on Japanese historiography would be difficult to exaggerate. Under him, Tsuboi and their colleagues, notably Doctors Kunitake Kume (1839-1931), Yasutsugu Shigeno (1827-1910) and Tsune Hoshino (1839-1917), Tokyo Imperial University was made a veritable Japanese University of Berlin. When the university was established in 1877, history was taught in the division of literature. The dis-

---

[7] Toshiki Imai, "The Influence of Western Historiography on Japanese Historiography," *Essays On Japanese Historiography*, compiled by the Society for Historical Science (in Japanese), II, p. 1442.
[8] *Ibid.*, p. 1450.
[9] *Ibid.*, p. 1457.

tinction between history and literature was not sharply drawn and history was generally taught from literary sources. In 1882, Japanese history was included in the classics department of the Education Ministry. Following Dr. Riess' arrival, a separate history department was organized in the university in 1888. In the same year, the official historiographic bureau was likewise transferred to the university, thus bringing together physically the native and foreign practices already so close intellectually.

Abandoning the writing of "national history," the official historiographic bureau thereafter devoted its entire efforts to collecting and publishing historical source material. A catalogue of extant materials was drawn up, then various historians were assigned the tasks of collecting and collating them for particular periods. In 1901, publication began of a projected 300-volume set, *Great Collection of Historical Source Materials* (in Japanese, Tokyo), including extracts from this major work and a framework into which the data of future volumes is to be fitted. The year before, it had begun publication of another 200-volume series of records, *Ancient Documents of Japan* (in Japanese, Tokyo).

The publication of large bodies of source material became a kind of mania. Many sources were published in the form of collectanea *(sosho),* that is, single collections of books on various subjects, like our own "Five Foot Shelf" or Modern Library series. Hoki'ichi's *Japanese Sources Classified by Subjects* (in Japanese, 1893-94), for example, and its *Supplement* (in Japanese, 1923-28), were republished and extended with a supplement to the supplement.[10] A quite different type of source publication is the Japanese encyclopedia. Modeled on the Chinese *lei-shu,* it consists of selected quotations from classical works, arranged by subject. An outstanding example is the *Classified References from the Past* (in Japanese, 1866-1914). Compiled by Junjiro Hosokawa (1834-1923) and others, it was first issued in 51 volumes, and has twice been republished. Moreover, to help the searcher in using these sources, modern Japanese scholars have developed many outstanding research tools.[11]

---

[10] Among the most important of these *collectanea* is the official historiographic bureau's series of useful works on the feudal period under the title, *Historical Works of the Faculty of Letters* (in Japanese, 1897). Biographies of 22 feudal leaders were included in the *Collection of Biographies of Great Men* (in Japanese, 1896-98). Memoirs of the feudal epoch were also gathered and published by the Philosophical Book Store in its *Great Mirror of Historical Source Materials* (in Japanese, 1898-1900). The Kondo's, father and son, compiled an *Historical Collection* (in Japanese, 1881-85). The Journal of Economics Publishing House issued a 32-volume set of standard Japanese histories, under the title, *Omnibus of Japanese History* (in Japanese, 1897-1904). More specialized is the *Collection of Works relating to Ancient Customs* (in Japanese, 3 series, 1900-03), which contains twenty-nine works on costumes, weapons, customs and notes of ancient scholars. From 1905 to 1922, the Society for the Publication of Japanese Books published eight series of historical sources, classified as to subject. Examples of collectanea in auxiliary fields are the *Complete Works on Buddhism in Japan* (in Japanese, 1912-22), a series of 953 titles published in 160 volumes; the *Collection of Works on Meiji Period Culture* (in Japanese, 1927-30), a series of sources, commentaries and biographies in 24 volumes; and the 54-volume set of the *Omnibus of Japanese Economic Works* (in Japanese, 1929-30).

The above list is merely suggestive. For a fairly complete list and analysis of Japanese collectanea, see the *Catalogue of Japanese Collectanea* (in Japanese, 1927) and the *Index to Japanese Collectanea* (in Japanese, 1939), issued by the Society for the Publication of Japanese Books.

[11] Among the more important modern reference works are indices, including those to the abovementioned collectanea; dictionaries, like the *Dictionary of National History* (in Japanese), compiled by Kuniji Yashio (1873-1914), the *Dictionary of Geographic Names of Japan* (in Japanese), a 7-volume set by Professor Togo Yoshida (1864-1918), and the Journal of Economics Publishing House, *Biographical Dictionary of Japan* (in Japanese); bibliographies, like the *Annotated Bibli-History* (in Japanese), on modern works, and Yasujiro Koizumi's *Chronological Table of Works on the History of Japan* (in Japanese); and the catalogues of the great governmental and university libraries. The most complete list and description of Japanese reference books and other standard works, in English, is a manuscript by Osamu Shimizu, at Columbia University, entitled, "An Annotated Bibliography of Selected Japanese Reference Works."

HISTORICAL MONOGRAPHS

The collecting and publishing of historical sources and the writing of reference works was only the first half of the program proposed by Dr. Tsuboi. The new history, he felt, must also "explain the cause of things." How this might be done and to what end was explained by his colleague, the first president of the Historical Society, Dr. Yasutsugu Shigeno. "We desire," he told the society, "to benefit the nation by examining and compiling our national records . . . using the Western historical method."[12] The "Western historical method" for explaining the "cause of things" has lead modern historians in Japan, as in the West, to devote themselves to highly specialized research. Nearly every phase and period of Japanese history has attracted its own students.[13] Other scholars have devoted themselves to a study of the broader fields of Oriental and Western history.

No assessment or even list of the more important modern Japanese historical monographs is here possible. Some have appeared as separate books. Others have appeared as integral parts of larger works, such as the encyclopedia compilations, *History of Japan by Eras* (in Japanese, 1926-27), a 14-volume history, primarily of Japan's political development, to which twelve different specialists each contributed; and the *History of Japanese Civilization* (in Japanese, 1922), a 12-volume collection of monographs by various authorities on non-political phases of Japanese history. In the 1930's another many-volumed type of publication of specialized articles became popular, the "lecture series" *(kosa),* in which articles by special students were published according to a scholarly plan. One, the *Iwanami Lecture Series on Japanese History* (in Japanese, Tokyo, Iwanami shoten, 1933-   ), was edited by Dr. Katsumi Kuroita (1874-1946), influential professor of history at Tokyo Imperial University, whose own *Studies in National History* (in Japanese, Tokyo, Iwanami shoten, rev. ed., 1931) has guided a generation of scholars in Japanese sources. Another outstanding "lecture series" is the *Lecture Series of History Teaching* (in Japanese, 1935-   ), issued by the Society for History Teaching.

The outlet for the great bulk of the research has been the learned journals. In 1889, Dr. Riess and his Japanese colleagues established the first historical society *(Shigakkai)* in Japan. Dr. Yasutsugu Shigeno became its first president. To encourage the new scholarship, the society undertook to publish some of the specialized writings of its members in its own *Journal of Historical Science* (in Japanese, 1889-   ). Developments at Tokyo were quickly copied else-

---

[12] Imai, *op. cit.,* p. 1447.

[13] For example, Takematsu Otsuka, Shigeo Inobe and others at the Bureau for Compiling the History of the Restoration, set up in the Education Department in 1911, have concentrated on the mid-nineteenth century. Takeshige Kudo, Jun'ichiro Otsu, Tsunego Baba and others have been working especially on modern political history. Social and economic history has attracted such men as Eijiro Honjo, Yasuhiko Kinomiya, Yosaburo Takekoshi, Masajiro Takikawa. Various phases of diplomatic history have been subjected to intense study by other scholars, including Nagao Ariga, Kenzo Akiyama, Yasuhiko Kinomiya, Chozo Muto, Michiyo Naka, Masamichi Royama, Jumpei Shinobu, Kiyoshi Tabohashi, Kijiro Tatsumi, Zennosuki Tsuji, long-time head of the official historiographic bureau, and Jin'ichi Yano. In cultural fields, Tsuji and others, including Masaharu Anesaki and Sadao Kiyohara, have made pioneer studies.

where. History departments, source publications, societies and journals sprang up in all major universities.[14]

RECENT TRENDS IN HISTORICAL WRITING

While the studies made in the late nineteenth and early twentieth centuries were generally careful and objective, they rarely took up problems which might have a bearing on contemporary social issues and rarely criticized prevailing Shinto, Buddhist and Confucianist concepts of religion, philosophy and politics. In the 1930's, when expansion on the Continent brought new psychological strains, historians were subjected to strong official and unofficial pressure to concentrate on "spiritual history"; the history of ancient and feudal cultural subjects, particularly of those relating to sentiment and institutions which might be conceived as peculiarly Japanese. The Department of Education established an Institute for the Study of National Culture. The wealthy Mr. Kunihiko Okura sponsored the Okura Institute for the Study of Spiritual Civilization. The Society for History Teaching used its organ, *History Teaching* (in Japanese, 1925-   ) to give nationalistic guidance to secondary school teachers.

Japanese historians have not yet entirely freed themselves from this decade and half of "spiritual history"; but, one significant effect of the defeat of Japan in World War II and the greater academic freedom inaugurated under the Allied Occupation since 1945 has been to encourage a scientific reexamination of Japan's history. In particular, the acceptance of early Japanese mythology as an objective description of historic events has been undergoing sharp attack.[15] A second major tendency in post-war Japanese historical writing has been the great increase in attempted interpretations of Japanese history according to Marxist teachings.[16]

How productive these new departures will be remains to be seen. World War II left many of the large libraries and universities disorganized, and some destroyed. Many of the old scholars have been dismissed or have died. Those remaining are overworked, underpaid, and uncertain. Nevertheless, depending on recovery of political and economic stability, psychological health and the attainment of academic freedom, the promise for historians in Japan is extremely encouraging. Through a combination of native tradition and

---

[14] The Faculty of Letters at Kyoto Imperial University, for example, began to publish its *Ancient Documents* (in Japanese, Kyoto, 1933-   ), and *Rapports sur les recherches archeologiques* (Kyoto, 1917-   ), and two reviews: *Historical Forest* (in Japanese, Kyoto, 1916-   ), and *Art and Literature* (in Japanese, Kyoto, 1910-   ) ; and from Keio University came *Historical Science* (in Japanese, Tokyo, 1922-   ). Outside the universities, the Greater Japan Historical and Geographical Society began publishing *History and Geography* (in Japanese, Tokyo, 1900-   ). Many other journals, like Dr. Taguchi's *Historical World* (in Japanese, Tokyo, 1891-96), *Historical Opinion* (in Japanese, Tokyo, 1892-   ) and *Historical Views* (in Japanese, Tokyo, 1892-   ) were begun. In specialized historical fields, there were to appear such publications as *Studies in Economic History* (in Japanese, Kyoto, 1929-   ), begun by Dr. Eijiro Honjo and his Society for the Study of Economic History at Kyoto Imperial University; and *Social and Economic History* (in Japanese, Tokyo, 1931-   ), the organ of the Society for Social and Economic History in Tokyo. These are only a few of the major kinds of learned journals relating to history published in modern Japan. For journals being published in Japan since 1945, see the latest study in English: Andrew Y. Kuroda, "Periodicals in Occupied Japan," *Pacific Affairs*, XXII (March, 1949), 43-52.

[15] For example, by Iwasaburo Okino in his *Japanese History that Should be Revised* (in Japanese, Tokyo, Kin-no-hoshi-sha, 1947), Tosaku Miura in his *A View of Early Japanese History* (in Japanese, Tokyo, Nihon Keikoku-sha, 1947) and Shuichi Goto in his *An Examination of Early Japanese History in the Light of Archaeology* (in Japanese, Tokyo, Yamosa shoten, 1947).

[16] A useful guide to recent "left-wing" historical writing in Japan is the *Handbook for Research in Japanese History*, edited by Toyama Shigeki (in Japanese, Tokyo, Tokyo University Press, 1949).

Western inspiration, generations of scholars have made vast quantities of materials readily available. Many basic monographs have already been written. Many more should follow. They can be expected to contribute richly, both to an interpretative synthesis of Japan's own history and to an increased understanding of man and society in general.

Chapter 29

MODERN CHINESE HISTORIOGRAPHY
By Philip Yampolsky

INTRODUCTION

THE historic period in China begins with the Shang dynasty (*ca.* 1523-1027 B.C.). However, no accurate chronology is available until the ninth and eighth centuries B.C., when the Chou dynasty (1027-256 B.C.) held nominal control over China. Although the Chou endured for a longer period than any other dynasty, its power after the first two or three centuries was purely nominal, inasmuch as actual control was in the hands of various feudal lords. Until recently, the sole source of information on Chinese antiquity has been a literature describing fabulous rulers who bestowed basic knowledges and inventions upon their peoples and listing the names of the rulers of the as yet unverified Hsia dynasty as well as those of Shang and Chou. Recent archaeological discoveries have verified the existence of a Shang dynasty and have added to what little was known of the Chou. The first unification of China was effected in 221 B.C. by the short-lived Ch'in dynasty (221-207 B.C.). The feudal system was destroyed and a strict dictatorship enforced. The Han period (divided into Anterior Han, 207 B.C.-9 A.D. and Posterior Han, 25-220 A.D.) has been called the "imperial" age of China. Feudalism was revived, and the period witnessed the establishment of many of the institutions which have endured until modern times. At this time, the writing of history became an official government function and a pattern of writing was set which has lasted until most recent times.

History has been regarded by the Chinese as one of the four major divisions of literature.[1] A tradition of history writing has long been established and, with calendar making, was one of the important functions of Chinese governments. However, as a governmental function, it was regimented along certain lines; it was required not merely to record events, but also to pass judgment upon them. When Confucianism became the state cult, it served to throttle all ideas detrimental to the government. The historian was not only required to itemize fact and event, but also to pass judgment upon these facts and events from an ethical viewpoint in order that the rulers might learn thereby what conduct to follow and what to avoid. History was emasculated of all concepts of change and growth and was presented as a series of events within a framework of static ideas. It is against this tradition of history that present day Chinese historians have revolted. To understand the trends of contemporary

---

[1] The traditional division is: 1. Classics, *ching*; 2. history, *shih*; 3. philosophers, *tzu*; 4. literature, *chi*. This system was first established by Hsun Shu (died 289 A. D.) and was adopted with some modifications by later writers.

Chinese historiography, it is first necessary to trace briefly the development of historical method in China.

EARLY HISTORICAL WRITING

At the time of Confucius (551-479 B.C.), the various feudal kingdoms into which China was divided maintained hereditary positions for archivists and historians whose duty it was to chronicle significant events. The only work remaining from this period is the celebrated *Spring and Autumn Annals* [2] of the State of Lu, which until most recent times has been attributed to Confucius. It records chronologically in terse language, important military events, natural disasters, and astronomical and meteorological phenomena. Historians of the Han period (B.C. 202-220 A.D.) attributed ethical significance to the annals, implying that Confucius's intention was to pass judgment upon the events described in order to bring about governmental and social reforms. Thus, a pattern was set, which endured until the present century, in which the historian judged the events he described.

The *Narrative of the States,* of unknown authorship and dating from the fourth century B.C., follows a chronological arrangement but departs from the *Spring and Autumn Annals* in that it treats of more than one state. The first general history of China is the celebrated *Historical Records* (first printed 994-1004) [3] by Ssu-ma Ch'ien (B.C. 145-86). Treating the period from remote antiquity until 99 B.C., it served as a model for all later dynastic histories. The work is divided into five parts: (1) Imperial annals, (2) Chronological tables, (3) Discussions of rituals, laws, music, etc., (4) Records of distinguished families, and (5) Biographies and discussions of foreign lands. This arrangement had disadvantages, because it destroyed chronological continuity and placed various aspects of related events under separate headings.

A chronological arrangemnt of history was adopted by the Sung scholar, Ssu-ma Kuang (1019-1086), who treated the period from 403 B.C. to 959 A.D. in his famous *Mirror for Aid in Government* (1084). The first treatment of history on a topical basis was by Yuan Shu (1131-1205). Classifying the contents of Ssu-ma Kuang's work under 239 different categories, he provided a more logical and useful grouping of subjects and events. His book, *Complete History* (1173), was used as a model by many later writers.

Seventeenth and Eighteenth Century Writings. The seventeenth and eighteenth centuries witnessed the growth of sound scholarship. Devoting themselves primarily to textual criticism, phonetic studies, and historical geography, scholars of the Ch'ing (Manchu) dynasty established a scientific method of approach that set the direction for later historians. Historical study at this time was carried on individually and sporadically by scholars who were largely ignored by their contemporaries, and who, moreover, were required to work under the handicap of a rigid governmental proscription against any work which might reflect unfavorably upon the government or upon Confucian

---

[2] Translated by James Legge, *The Chinese Classics,* Vol. 5, pt. i-ii.

[3] Translated in part by E. Chavannes, *Les memoires historiques de Se-ma Ts'ien,* 5 Vols. Hereafter, unless otherwise noted, all titles mentioned in the text will be translations of titles of Chinese works.

teachings. Yao Chi-heng (1657-1715), of whom little is known and most of whose works are lost, wrote a significant book, *Forgeries of Ancient and Modern Times,* in which he discusses the authenticity of almost a hundred works. Perhaps the outstanding historian of the eighteenth century was Ts'ui Shu (1740-1816), who was the first to call attention to the artificiality of the legendary history of the model emperors by demonstrating that the more ancient a ruler, the more modern was the literary reference to him.

The trend towards a scientific approach to the study of history was brought to a temporary halt around the year 1800 by the growing degeneracy of the ruling dynasty and the increasing pressure of the Occidental nations upon China. Following the Anglo-Chinese war of 1842, a nationalistic sentiment arose, aimed at the preservation of the national heritage in the face of external aggression. There was a growing tendency to reexamine and to preserve the past; literature was written on the basis of classical forms. Even translations of Western works were written in the archaic Chinese of pre-Han times, which was unintelligible to the greater part of the population. Despite the influx of Western ideas and the return of Chinese students from studies abroad, it was not until the removal of the Manchu rulers and the subsequent establishment of the Republic that the study of history made significant strides in terms of Western historiographical method.

Ku Chieh-kang, in his *Present-day Chinese Historiography* (Shanghai, 1947), has treated modern Chinese historiography during the past one hundred years.

Development of Chinese historiography in the past hundred years.[4]

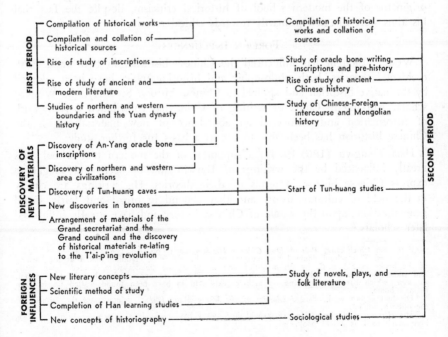

This period he divides into two, the first extending from 1850 until the establishment of the Republic; the second extending from 1911 until the present.
Development of Chinese historiography in the past hundred years.[4]

FIRST PERIOD

The first period set the direction for later study. It was marked by sporadic and individual scholarship rather than by a general trend in historical writing. To some small extent, contemporary events were dealt with; the main emphasis, however, was placed on the supplementation, revision, and annotation of old works. The study of stone and bronze inscriptions occupied the time of antiquarians. Stimulated in part by Occidental scholars, interest in the areas of Central Asia and the lands contiguous to China was awakened. Mongol history for the first time drew the attention of scholars.

Around the turn of the century, the critical study of Chinese classics was given a new impetus by the work of Kang Yu-Wei (1858-1927). The scholars of the seventeenth and eighteenth centuries had not dared to criticize the Confucian classics, and it was in this field that Kang conducted his research. As the leader of the modern text school[5] which held that Confucius was not merely the transmitter of a series of ancient documents designed to maintain ancient values, he held that Confucius himself was a great ethical teacher. With this viewpoint, Kang Yu-wei reopened the question of the authenticity of ancient texts.[6] His aim was not primarily scholarly, for he wrote within the framework of Confucianism with the intention of placing Confucius in what he believed to be his true perspective. K'ang was the originator of the modern school of historical criticism, despite the fact that his aims were directed primarily towards ethical reform.

FOREIGN INFLUENCES

Western thought has influenced the Chinese historian in two ways. First, occidental theories, both philosophic and historiographic, have been adopted by the native historian and applied to Chinese history. Secondly, the Western scholar working in China or writing of China has contributed a framework of information and uncovered an abundance of new material which the Chinese historian has been able to use as a basis for further study.

Hsia Tseng-yu (1865-1924), a supporter of the modern text school, was greatly influenced by the writings of Darwin and Spencer, and sought to express Chinese history in terms of their theories. His writings are chiefly in the field of cultural history and they abound in broad and fairly sound generalizations upon the whole of Chinese history and have greatly influenced later scholars.[7]

---

[4] After Ku Chieh-kang, *Present Day Chinese Historiography*, pp. 4-5.

[5] *Chin wen.* This school doubted the authenticity of the old texts, claiming that after the burning of the books in 213 B. C. by Ch'in Shih-huang, many of the classics were handed down orally and transcribed by later scholars in modern script. They were opposed by the old text school, *ku wen*, which based its teaching on archaic texts said to have been found walled up in Confucius's home.

[6] His best known work, *Forged Classics of the Wang Mang Period*, demonstrates the fallacies of the old text school.

[7] His *History of Ancient China* (first published 1904) has appeared in numerous editions and has been much used as a text book.

Liang Chi'i-ch'ao (1873-1928), a student of K'ang Yu-wei's who, together with his teacher is considered largely responsible for promoting sound scholarship and research technique, was greatly influenced by Western historical method. He travelled widely, visiting and studying in Europe, America, and Japan, and wrote several articles calling for the abandonment of old Chinese historical methods. He advocated the adoption of Western techniques and stressed the need for monographic studies on specific subjects.[8]

Hu Shih, recognized as the leader of the new culture movement, is perhaps most conversant with Western techniques and his writings, particularly in the field of literature and philosophy, have had great influence on contemporary scholars. One of his greatest contributions is as the leader of the new culture movement which swept away the antiquated classical language, substituting a vernacular, *pai hua,* which gave impetus to great new literary expression. Not only was the way opened for the study of plays, drama, and folk literature, which long had been neglected, but a more flexible and intelligible language was substituted for the classical.

The progress of scientific and historical studies in China has been severely handicapped during the past twenty years by the constant turmoil in which the country has found itself. The tendency has been to sacrifice historical accuracy for nationalistic and ideological prejudice. Conservative and radical schools of historical interpretation exist, each of which adopts concepts in accord with its own expediencies. Both, however, "tend to believe again in China's past and have blessed the legendary history with historical finds and scientific terms." [9]

DISCOVERY OF NEW MATERIALS

During the present century a vast new body of material, both archaeological and documentary, has been made available to the historian. The scope of Chinese history has been greatly enlarged and these new finds, coupled with the adoption of Western historical techniques, have contributed greatly to the reinterpretation of Chinese history.

Westerners have added much to the knowledge of prehistoric China. Their work, in conjunction with Chinese scholars, has brought abundant evidence of paleolithic and pleistocene age cultures to light within the past few decades. Excavations in 1929 showed that at one time, North China was inhabited by the species of sub-man known as *sinanthropus pekinensis.* Andersson, in his surveys in Honan in 1930 and 1931, uncovered sites dating to the new stone age. The Chinese scholar was thus presented with an antiquity of which he had hitherto had no conception.

Besides China proper, contiguous areas to the north and west received the scrutiny of students. Central Asia was studied and the relationship of China to the ancient empires of this area was investigated. Here again, the initial workers were non-Chinese. Sir Aurel Stein in 1907 discovered at Tun-huang,

---

[8] See *Research Method in Chinese History.* This work has been translated into Japanese by Ohase, Tatsukichi.

[9] S. Y. Teng, "Chinese Historiography in the last Fifty Years," *Far Eastern Quarterly,* VIII, 2, p. 139.

a remote outpost in Kansu, a walled-up library containing a vast amount of material none of which was later than the mid-eleventh century (A.D.). New light was thus thrown on Chinese relations with Central Asia. So important are these documents that the study of Tun-huang material is in itself referred to as a separate science by Sinologists.

In China itself, new historical materials relating to the Grand Secretariat, *Nei ko,* and the Grand Council of State, *Chun chi ch'u,* of the Ch'ing or Manchu dynasty (1644-1912) have been uncovered in the form of literary documents. A vast number of publications, primarily collections of source materials, have been drawn from the Ch'ing archives within the past quarter century.[10]

The acquisition of this vast new body of knowledge, together with the knowledge of how to make use of it, has been one of the basic influences on Chinese historiography in the past one hundred years.

SECOND PERIOD

Since the establishment of the republic in 1912, the scope of historical writing has broadened considerably. Importation of Western historical methods opened new fields of research. No longer was emphasis centered on the ruling dynasty, but cultural, economic, and social histories began to be written.

Various efforts have been made to write a general history of China; as yet, however, there seems a need for additional work on specific aspects and periods of Chinese history. General works, when attempted, usually suffer from the political bias of the author. Perhaps the best is *A General History of China Written in Pai-hua Style,* by Lu Ssu-mien, which is largely a factual presentation of the subject.

Although no important work on the history of the Republic has appeared, the modern history of China has received the attention of several authors, among whom the best known are probably Cheng Hao-sheng and Chiang Ting-fu.[11] These two disagree in their ideas of where modern China begins; Cheng thinks in terms of the last three or four hundred years; Chiang begins his history with the Opium War of 1839-1842.

Much has been written in the field of cultural history. Ch'en Tun-yuan and Liu I-ching have each compiled two-volume surveys of the subject under the title *Cultural History of China.* The field of Chinese philosophy is represented by two outstanding scholars, Hu Shih and Fung Yu-lan. Fung is well known for his *History of Chinese Philosophy* which was translated into English and published in 1937. Hu Shih's *Outline of Chinese Philosophy* is a work of real significance. The history of Chinese Buddhism has only recently begun to attract the attention of native scholars; previously Europeans and Japanese did most of the work on this subject.[12] As for Chinese literature, the prolific Hu Shih's *History of Chinese Literature in Pai-hua Style,* and

---

[10] For a discussion of available documents, see J. K. Fairbank and S. Y. Teng, "On the Types and Uses of Ch'ing Documents," *Harvard Journal of Asiatic Studies,* V, 1 (1940), pp. 1-71.
[11] Each has written a work entitled *Modern Chinese History,* a title which has been used by at least three other writers.
[12] The most noteworthy recent work is T'ang Yung-t'ung's *History of Buddhism during the Han, Wei, Tsin, and Northern and Southern Dynasties Period.*

Cheng Chen-t'o's *History of Chinese Literature* are outstanding.

The study of social and economic history is another new phenomenon in China, and gained its momentum from the revolutionary movement of the early 1920's. Quo Mo-jo and T'uao Hsi-sheng are the most important writers in this field. Kuo has followed the Marxian interpretation and his *Study of Ancient Chinese Society* is an important, though occasionally inaccurate, discussion of the subject. T'ao Hsi-sheng has written prolifically[13] with perhaps a more scholarly attitude than Kuo, who has been accused of occasionally sacrificing accuracy for the sake of destroying traditional concepts. Other important contributions have been made by Meng Ssu-ming, whose *Class Systems in Yuan Society* is a detailed exposition of the subject.

HISTORICAL CRITICISM

The first three decades of the present century witnessed continued advance in historical criticism. The classics, once regarded as above criticism, were virtually discredited. Works formerly attributed to Confucius have been presented in their true historical light. The distortions which the state cult of Confucianism had imposed on Chinese history have been exposed. The entire literary past is now looked upon with skepticism and no effort is spared in bringing to light literary forgeries and works of dubious value. The recovery of lost works, the annotation and punctuation of old texts together with a comparative study in related fields, has characterized the advances in historical criticism.

REFERENCE WORKS

There has been great progress in the compilation of reference tools and indexes to various classical texts. The *Harvard-Yenching Sinological Index Series* has greatly facilitated reference work. Bibliographies, biographical and geographical dictionaries, chronological tables, and tables for conversion from lunar to solar calendar have appeared in considerable number in recent years.[14] However, despite a considerable quantity of reference works, there is ample room for improvement. The student of Chinese is still handicapped by the lack of adequate tools and the difficulty of using those that exist.[15]

During the twentieth century, history as well as the study of history in China has undergone an almost complete revision. Not only has its scope been enormously broadened, but by the adoption of Western historiographical method, adequate exploitation of this enlarged range was made possible. The basic factors which implemented this change were the adoption of Occidental historiographical methods and concepts, the discovery of a vast body of new source materials, the adoption of a national language, and the impetus furnished by Western and Japanese scholars in the field.

---

[13] T'ao's works include *Analysis of Chinese Society, History of Chinese Feudal Society,* and *Economic History of the Southern and Northern Dynasties.* He is also the author of numerous articles in periodicals.

[14] See Teng, S. Y. and Biggerstaff, K., *An Annotated Bibliography of Selected Chinese Reference Works.*

[15] Such works as the *Dictionary of Far Eastern History* compiled by Heibon-sha (in Japanese, 9 vols.), Mochizuki's *Dictionary of Buddhism* (in Japanese, 5 vols.) among numerous others are invaluable for the study of Chinese history.

Chapter 30

AMERICAN HISTORIOGRAPHY BEFORE THE TWENTIETH CENTURY

By Phillip R. Shriver

INTRODUCTION

A MERICAN historical writing has passed through four general phases. The first extended over the colonial period and was characterized by a product that was usually both meagre and primitive. The colonial historian could command no large audience, and his work, especially in the New England colonies, was utilitarian, often autobiographical, and profoundly influenced by religious preoccupations. Even the American Revolution and the foundation of an independent government did not put an abrupt end to this historical barrenness.

The second phase of American historical writing emerged in the period of national self-consciousness, democratic and humanitarian enthusiasm, and party conflict which began in the last years of the eighteenth century and accelerated with the War of 1812. This writing was animated by patriotism, filiopietism, and party loyalty. It was marked by bias, inaccuracy, and frequent plagiarism. Though no monumental works were produced, the quantity of output increased and a wider audience was acquired.

With the advent of the fourth decade of the nineteenth century, American historical writing entered its third and classic phase. History was now regarded as a branch of literature, as it had long been recognized in Europe, particularly in England. Narrative writing on a panoramic scale was executed by masters such as Francis Parkman, William H. Prescott, and John L. Motley. Style was paramount; ideas attracted little interest. The American historian acquired both a high degree of respect and the widest voluntary audience in proportion to the population that he has ever known. The United States continued to produce antiquaries and collectors, such as Jared Sparks, but most of its historians of the mid-nineteenth century regarded themselves primarily as artists.[1]

The Civil War produced the impetus for a torrent of memoirs and sectional writings of a highly partisan nature which would continue until the last years of the century. Yet paradoxically in the wake of the war, critical and scientific historical investigation and writing began to win dominance over the literary and patriotic school that had dominated for several decades. In 1876 the German-trained scholar, Herbert Baxter Adams, inaugurated the first graduate program in this nation for the training of professional historians at Johns Hopkins University. In 1880 John W. Burgess commenced a seminar at Colum-

---

[1] John Spencer Bassett, *The Middle Group of American Historians*, pp. vii-viii.

bia to provide similar training, while others at Harvard, Pennsylvania, Cornell, Michigan, and Wisconsin soon followed suit.[2]

With the founding of the American Historical Association in 1884 the fourth phase of American historiography was well launched. Historical writing, long a literary avocation, was being transformed into a highly professionalized discipline with its aims and standards now dictated by academic scholars.[3] Soon the scope of the historian would be broadened far beyond the former "past politics" and "drum and trumpet" emphases to include explanations and interpretations of the social, economic, religious, and intellectual developments of mankind. Due to the vastness of collected materials, the necessity for careful scholarship, and the complexity of the "new" history, few American historians could hope to cover great periods of history in their writings. Instead, they turned to specialization in areas or institutions, or supplemented individual effort with cooperative writing. A glance at the titles of recent doctoral dissertations in history will illustrate the lengths to which this specialization has been carried in America's twentieth century historiography.

THE COLONIAL HISTORIANS

The first writers of history in the region now included in the United States were European emigrants or the sons of emigrants who were "so near to the days of colonial foundation that they could not easily take the backward glance of the historian without also taking the forward view of the prophet. To them God had let His countenance shine upon the New World, and for decades to come historians continued to wonder at the marvel of divine intercession in the affairs of America."[4] To them was given the task of recording the events they had witnessed to insure that future generations would know of the hardships incident to the settlement of a new world. Their work was almost exclusively provincial in scope and autobiographical in method. Not until the Revolution did colonial writers begin to take a comprehensive view of all the colonies.

John Smith. Of the colonies none were more assiduous in the preservation of their records than Virginia and Massachusetts. For the history of the founding of the former colony we are indebted to the writings of Captain John Smith. A representative of the heroic Elizabethan period, an adventurer of the cut of Francis Drake, Smith belongs less to America than to England. His stories comprise a record of a mismanaged province and a personal narrative of his many hair-raising adventures. The first of his histories, *A True Relation . . . ,* was written in Virginia and published in England in 1608. It describes briefly the founding of Jamestown, the misery and suffering of the settlers, and the beginning of trade relations with the Indians. The best known of Smith's writings and the first widely-read history of English colonization was his *Generall Historie of Virginia, New-england and the Summer Isles* (1624). A work of some two hundred fifty pages, it was a compilation of anecdotes

---

[2] John Herman Randall, Jr., and George Haines, IV, "Controlling Assumptions in the Practice of American Historians," *Theory and Practice in Historical Study: A Report of the Committee on Historiography* (Social Science Research Bulletin 54, 1946), p. 23.
[3] *Ibid.,* p. 24.
[4] Michael Kraus, *A History of American History,* p. 3.

and reminiscences of the Jamestown settlers, including those of Smith himself. Here is found a description of the "starving time," the beginning of tobacco culture, the introduction of Negro slavery to British America, and the story of Smith's rescue by Pocahontas, which most modern historians reject as a fabrication. Indeed, the captain's boastfulness and addiction to embellishment has prompted J. Franklin Jameson to remark that "what is historical is not his, and what is his is not historical." [5]

Robert Beverley. Fully eight decades elapsed before any significant historical writing about Virginia was produced. In the meantime the colony had prospered through tobacco growing, a leisured class had appeared, but a callous indifference had developed so far as its history was concerned. Only through chance was this indifference ended. A prominent planter and a native Virginian, Robert Beverley, was visiting in London when the publisher of John Oldmixon's *The British Empire in America* asked him to read that part of the work relating to Virginia. Long acquainted with the colony's documentary sources through his service as secretary of Virginia, Beverley was aghast at the numerous errors he found in the Oldmixon volume, remarking: "It would take a Book larger than his own to expose his errors." [6] This prompted him to write his own *History of Virginia* (1705), a well-written work which contains an excellent comprehensive view of contemporary colonial society and a scholarly summary of the documentary records available to this government official.

William Byrd. A scion of one of Virginia's fine old aristocratic families, William Byrd II was another colonial planter who put his hand to the writing of history. Possessing the largest library in the colonies, a collection of some four thousand volumes at "Westover," Byrd turned to literary pursuits while in his advanced years. Commissioned in 1728 to settle the boundary dispute between Virginia and North Carolina, he kept a journal of his adventures which subsequently served as the basis for two books, *History of the Dividing Line betwixt Virginia and North Carolina* and *The Secret History of the Line.* In them he immortalized border life during the reign of George II, describing the Norfolk rum-traders, the careless agricultural practices, and the general shiftlessness of the Carolinians (for whom he had little use).

William Stith. The last of the important historians of colonial Virginia was the Oxford-educated, Anglican minister, William Stith. A man of sound scholarship, he published in 1747 *The History of the First Discovery and Settlement of Virginia.* Based upon the records of the London Company and the works of John Smith, his work carried in considerable detail the story of Virginia to the year 1624. Though he had intended to complete the history of the colony, his first book was so poorly received that he carried his researches no further. In point of his scholarship, however, Stith's work remains a standard in Virginia's colonial history. [7]

---

[5] J. Franklin Jameson, *The History of Historical Writings in America,* p. 11. See also Allan Nevins, *The Gateway to History,* pp. 139-140, and William C. Spielman, *Introduction to Sources of American History,* pp. 79-80, for a fuller recounting of the discrepancies in the narratives of John Smith.

[6] Kraus, *op. cit.,* p. 70.

[7] *Ibid.,* p. 95.

HISTORIANS OF SEVENTEENTH CENTURY MASSACHUSETTS

Turning to the settlements at Plymouth and Massachusetts Bay, which in 1691 united as the Province of Massachusetts, we find a much steadier development of historical writing than was the case in Virginia. Both the Separatists and the Puritans were intellectual and idealistic. Both groups saw the need for the preservation for their posterity of the records of the trials and triumphs incident to the settling of a new world. Both saw need to thank God on the written page for the guidance which He had rendered them in their work.

William Bradford. The leader of the Plymouth Colony from 1621 to 1657 and its principal historian was Governor William Bradford, sometimes styled the "Father of American History." [8] The possessor of a fine intellect, Bradford had gathered documents for his *History of Plimoth Plantation* over many years and his work is highly reliable. He describes the aid given the *Mayflower* colonists by the friendly Indians, Squanto and Samoset, who showed the settlers how to take furs and plant native crops. He denounces the behavior of Thomas Morton and laments the "errors" of Roger Williams of the Bay Colony. Bradford faithfully recounts some of the hardships of his settlement—a midsummer hurricane, a plague of locusts, a smallpox epidemic—but his faith in divine intercession in behalf of the colony remains unshaken. By its very piety and modesty his account helps to give us insight into the Pilgrim mind. Covering the story of the settlement to 1646, Bradford's work has served for three hundred years as the principal source for Plymouth's early history even though a complete edition was not published until 1856.

Edward Winslow. In 1622 there was printed in London a little book co-authored by William Bradford and Edward Winslow and entitled *Mourt's Relation,* or *Journal of the Plantation at Plymouth.* It faithfully chronicled the daily adventures of the little group of Separatists in their first year in the new world, and was aimed at arousing English interest in the settlement across the sea. Edward Winslow, its principal author, had joined the group in Holland and would one day become the colony's governor. Signing his journal "G. Mourt" to avoid the appearance of boastfulness, he recounts the story of the Mayflower Compact and the circumstances surrounding its origin, a matter in which both he and Bradford had had prominent roles. He also tells of the difficulties of the first winter, the exploration in the bay area, and the meeting and peace treaty with Massasoit. Writing easily and vividly, Winslow has left us an authoritative account of the establishment of the Pilgrim settlement.

John Winthrop. The most valuable chronicle of the Massachusetts Bay Colony is the *Journal* of John Winthrop, the founder and for nineteen years the governor or deputy governor of the colony. Subsequently published as *The History of New England from 1630 to 1649,*[9] the book lacks objective interest. There is a continuous reference to the author in the third person, the narrative is frequently broken, and there is little of the literary verve found in Bradford's

---

[8] *Ibid.,* p. 33.
[9] Winthrop's original manuscript was in three volumes. For some time the third was lost, though historians had used the first two for a number of years before Noah Webster published them in 1790. The third volume was discovered in 1816, and in 1825-1826 it was included in the complete edition published in two volumes with notes by James Savage. *Cf.,* John Spencer Bassett, *The Middle Group of American Historians,* f. n. 1, p. 10.

writings. Nonetheless, much that relates to the establishment of the Puritan theocracy and its social and political organization can be found in its pages. The birth of trade with the West Indies to meet economic exigencies, the heresies of Roger Williams and Anne Hutchinson, the Pequot War, relations with the Indians, French, and Dutch—all are described in the Winthrop *Journal*.

Edward Johnson. Unlike most of the other New England historians of the colonial period, Edward Johnson was not a foremost political or social leader. Indeed, his *Wonder-Working Providence of Sion's Savior in New England,* treating the development of the Bay Colony from 1628 to 1651, evidences his little education and the limitations of the middle-class Puritan mind. Despite its heavy phrasing, its numerous errors, and poor arrangement, this history has value in its exposition of the life of the average citizen in the Puritan commonwealth and for its portrayal of the founding of churches and towns in Massachusetts, Rhode Island, and Connecticut. The militant Puritanism of the author is evident throughout this book, which was first printed anonymously and under another title in London in 1654 as the first published history of Massachusetts.

Cotton Mather. Perhaps the most important single volume written in the colonial period by any American historian was Cotton Mather's *Magnalia Christi Americana: or the Ecclesiastical History of New England . . .*, which was written from 1693 to 1697 and published in London in 1702. Its author, the third in succession of one of the Bay Colony's most prominent Puritan families, was one of America's most prolific writers with more than four hundred books and pamphlets to his credit. A comprehensive affair, his *Ecclesiastical History* runs from the planting of the New England colonies to the Salem witchcraft trials. It includes biographical sketches of educators, ministers, and governors, the history of Harvard College (his alma mater), the Indian wars, and an elaborate defense of Puritan theology. For dissenters such as Quakers and Anabaptists, Mather evidences the greatest detestation. For the lowly red man he shows no compassion. Despite his bloodthirsty piety and the absence of proof-reading, Mather's volume remains the most authentic voice of seventeenth century New England theocracy.

HISTORICAL WRITING IN MASSACHUSETTS IN THE EIGHTEENTH CENTURY

With the advent of the new century the increasing preoccupation of men's minds with matters material rather than spiritual prompted a change in the nature of historical writing in the Bay Colony. While there was still much writing by ministers and much emphasis upon the evidences of God's Providence in the founding and development of the colony, to an increasing degree nontheologians were turning to the writing of secular history of a political and economic nature.

Thomas Prince and Thomas Hutchinson. Of the eighteenth century historians of Massachusetts, two deserve especial consideration, Thomas Prince and Thomas Hutchinson. The first held a pastorate in the old South Church in Boston until his death in 1758. As a minister he did not excell. As an antiquarian zealous in the collection of the records and documents of the past he made an enduring contribution to subsequent generations. Despite the loss of much of his collection (which he had stored in the tower of his church) during the British occupation of Boston in the Revolution, a number of his priceless manuscripts are now to be found in the Boston Public Library. So far as Prince's historical writing is concerned, he is best remembered for his meticulous but dull anthology of New England antiquities to 1633 entitled *Chronological History of New England in the Form of Annals,* volumes of which were published in 1736 and 1755. Far superior in literary skill and historical perception was Thomas Hutchinson, perhaps the greatest American historian of the eighteenth century. A Tory aristocrat who held high office in the colony for a third of a century (he was its last royal governor), he was paradoxically a direct descendant of Anne Hutchinson. Despite his stand in favor of loyalty to the crown which brought the destruction of his house by stamp act rioters, Hutchinson's three volume *The History of the Colony of Massachusetts Bay* evidences an amazing lack of political bias or prejudice. The work encompasses the history of the colony from 1620 to 1774, the year that Hutchinson went into exile in England. Happily absent are the genealogical minutiae that haunted the pages of most of the writings of earlier American historians. Instead his chapters give insight into the economic, political, religious, and geographic aspects of the development of Massachusetts. Particularly outstanding is his treatment in Volume III of the forces bringing on the Revolution which he regarded as essentially a popular uprising.

Historians of Other Colonies in the Eighteenth Century: Carolina and Rhode Island. Not all of the foremost colonial historians lived in Massachusetts or Virginia. John Lawson, surveyor general of North Carolina, published in 1709 *A New Voyage to Carolina* that was at once a history of the colony, a propaganda device to attract settlers, and an anthropological examination of Indian customs (always of great interest to Europeans). Self-governing Rhode Island boasted a Baptist clergyman, John Callender, as its historian. Reflecting the religious tolerance of this colony, Callender's *An Historical Discourse on the Civil and Religious Affairs of the Colony of Rhode Island . . .* (1739) was more "a sermon in praise of liberty of conscience" than it was a history of the colony.[10] Yet it excels in its consideration of the religious disputes incident to Roger Williams' banishment from Massachusetts and consequent founding of Rhode Island.

New Jersey and New York. The history of early New Jersey was first presented in scholarly fashion in *The History of the Colony . . . of New Jersey . . . to the Year 1721, . . .* by Samuel Smith, a Quaker. The lengthy book is filled with extensive quotations and has a chronological narrative that makes for dull reading. A good deal of space is devoted to genealogical documentation, to immigration, and to relations between the settlers and the Indians. Far abler was the work of another Smith—William, of New York—entitled *The History of the Late Province of New York* which carried the story in two volumes down to 1762. A Tory official who fled New York during the Revolution, William Smith was primarily concerned with the political history of that colony. His

---

[10] Kraus, *op. cit.,* p. 92.

work, while generally good, is marred by frequent editorializing reflecting his royalist sympathies. The ablest of the historians of the middle colonies was Cadwallader Colden, one-time lieutenant governor of New York. In his best-known work, *The History of the Five Indian Nations depending on the Province of New York*, Colden was both historian and propagandist. His efforts were bent in persuading the British and the colonists to establish the Iroquois nations as buffers against the French and to gain control of the fur trade from the French. While so doing he has left us with an excellent account of the history and customs of the Iroquois.

Historians of the Revolution. During the Revolution and shortly thereafter, little history was written in the new United States. Instead, it was a period of confusion and unsettlement, of exodus for thousands of Tories (from whose members most of the earlier histories had come). Little attempt was made in the former colonies to preserve records of the struggle. As a consequence, after peace had been made and historians had commenced the work of portraying the struggle and its causes, it was to the British archives and particularly Edmund Burke's account of the controversy in the *Annual Register* that they repaired for their sources of information. Most notable of these historians were the Reverend William Gordon and Dr. David Ramsay. The former, a Boston clergyman, published in 1788 his four volume *History of the Rise, Progress, and Establishment of the Independence of the United States of America.* A Charleston, South Carolina, physician, author, and politician, Dr. Ramsay was the most assiduous historian of his day. His work which reached the greatest vogue was the two-volume *History of the American Revolution.* Both Gordon and Ramsay drew heavily upon Burke's writing. In fact, since plagiarism was not regarded as a vice at this time, both lifted huge quantities of their materials directly out of the *Annual Register* without care as to the use of quotations or citation as to source. Not until the turn of the present century was the fact discovered. Since then both have been largely ignored.

THE PATRIOTIC, FILIOPIETISTIC PERIOD OF AMERICAN HISTORIOGRAPHY

As the eighteenth century drew to a close a new phase of American historical writing emerged with the advent of a growing spirit of nationalism and democracy. Marked by a zealous patriotism and filiopietism, much of the writing of this period was inaccurate and woefully biased. Increasing attention was placed by historians on the popularization of their product with marketability in mind. Emphasis was also placed on biographical writing and state history.

John Marshall and Parson Weems. Among the best known works of this period was the five-volume *Life of George Washington* by Chief Justice John Marshall. Lifting large quantities of his product from Jeremy Belknap, Thomas Hutchinson, and the *Annual Register,* Marshall produced a heavy though well constructed work of pronounced Federalist and filiopietistic tone. Writing for the middle and lower classes of American society was Mason Locke Weems, a Maryland parson who found popular biography more to his calling. His objectives were two-fold: to inculcate in his readers the virtues of patriotism, temperance, thrift, obedience, morality, industry, and frugality; and to make money. He succeeded in doing both. Frequently embellishing his writing with imaginative anecdotes, he caught the popular fancy such as few have been able to do. His well-known *Life of Washington,* which first appeared in 1800 and included the famed but fictitious stories concerning hatchets, cherry trees, and cabbage-beds, certainly reached forty and may have reached as many as seventy editions. Succeeding biographies of Benjamin Franklin, William Penn, and Francis Marion were just as fanciful though not as well received. Although his works are now all rejected as historically worthless, the popular pictures Weems created of colonial and revolutionary heroes have survived to the present.

Washington Irving. Far surpassing Weems in literary and historical ability was Washington Irving, though even his works are sadly inaccurate. Lacking the ability for the interpretation of the men and the events about which he wrote, he nontheless excelled in style and became one of the ranking men of letters of the nation. Commencing with his burlesque of the early Dutch settlers in *A History of New York . . .* (1809), he advanced through *The History of the Life and Voyages of Columbus* (three volumes, 1828), the *Conquest of Granada* (1829), *Astoria* (two volumes, 1836), the *Adventures of Captain Bonneville* (1837), *Mahomet and His Successors* (1849), and the *Life of Washington* (five volumes, 1855-1859). The last was to have been his magnum opus but disappointingly added little to earlier biographies of the first president.

State Histories of the Late Eighteenth and Early Nineteenth Centuries. With the acquisition of independence, local pride became assertive with much writing of state history. Outstanding among the works in this field was Jeremy Belknap's *History of New Hampshire* (three volumes, 1784, 1791, 1792). Easily and agreeably written by a first-rate scholar who had been a student of Thomas Prince and had access to his library in the Old South Church, the study was based on original documents and remains today one of the finest of our state histories. Others of note were George Minot's *Continuation of the History of the Province of Massachusetts Bay from the Year 1748* (two volumes, 1798, 1803) which picked up the narrative where Thomas Hutchinson had left off, and his *History of the Insurrections in Massachusetts in the year 1786 . . .* (1788), giving the story of the Shays' rebellion as viewed through partisan Federalist eyes; Benjamin Trumbull's *A Complete History of Connecticut . . .* (1797; two volumes, 1818) ; John Daly Burk's *History of Virginia from Its First Settlement to the Present Day* (three volumes, 1804, 1805) ; Hugh Mc-Call's *History of Georgia* (two volumes, 1811, 1816) ; Hugh Williamson's *History of North Carolina* (two volumes, 1812) ; David Ramsay's *The History of South Carolina . . . to the Year 1808* (two volumes, 1809) ; and Robert Proud's *History of Pennsylvania . . .* (two volumes, 1797, 1798).

Historical Societies. With the development of the patriotic impulse as reflected in the afore-mentioned increasing number of historical writings, there developed a consciousness of the necessity for the preservation of original source materials. Collectors of documents, such as Peter Force, a Washington editor and compiler, and Jared Sparks, editor of the *North American Review* and later President of Harvard, noted with alarm the rapid disappearance of many of the nation's priceless records and called for the creation of depositories where remaining manuscripts might be forever preserved. Doubtless the greatest service to scholarship in history prior to the Civil War was the establishment of historical societies to serve this purpose. Commencing with the founding of the Massachusetts Historical Society by Jeremy Belknap and John Pintard in 1791, the movement grew slowly with only two others founded before 1820: the New York Historical Society (1804), and the American Antiquarian Society at Worcester, Massachusetts (1812). By 1860, however, the movement had spread so rapidly that sixty-five societies, in every state east of Texas with the exception of Delaware, had come into existence. Unfortunately, a number soon became preoccupied in the collection of genealogical materials to the detriment of state and national records.

The First Histories of the United States. As early as 1707 an Englishman, John Oldmixon, had made a feeble attempt to write a history of all the British North American colonies, while another from the same nation, George Chalmers, followed it with his *Political Annals of the Present United Colonies, from Their Settlement to the Peace of 1763 . . .* (1780). The first American historian to treat the new United States with broad, sweeping strokes in a significant work was Abiel Holmes, father of Oliver Wendell Holmes, who in 1805 published his two volume *American Annals.* Dull, lifeless, but accurate, the work was little more than a chronology, leaving citizens still searching for a good national history. An attempt was made by Benjamin Trumbull to fill this need with his *General History of the United States of America from the Discovery in 1492, to 1792 . . .*, originally intended for three volumes of which but one was published in 1810, bringing the story as far as 1765. Timothy Pitkin, a Connecticut lawyer and statistician, published in 1828 his two-volume *Political and Civil History of the United States . . . from . . . 1763 to . . . 1797,* a work as drab and unimaginative as that of Holmes. A truly acceptable national history had yet to appear. Two men, George Bancroft and Richard Hildreth, soon filled the gap.

George Bancroft. The chief figure in the patriotic, filiopietistic school of American historical writing and the first to produce a national history on the scale of the heroic epic was George Bancroft. The son of a cleric-historian, Aaron Bancroft (*Life of Washington,* 1807), George Bancroft was one of the first Americans to receive his training in a German seminar, this at Göttingen. Schoolmaster and politician (he was Secretary of Navy under Polk and later Minister to Germany), Bancroft was a passionate nationalist, a believer in manifest destiny, and an egalitarian democrat. In philosophy he believed that "God rules in the affairs of men," that each historical event could be considered as a "separate manifestation of the will of Providence." [11] Throughout his monumental twelve-volume *History of the United States from the Discovery of the American Continent* (1834-1883) there run the threads of these political and religious convictions.[12] In his lifetime his work was exceedingly well-

[11] Watt Stewart, "George Bancroft," in *The Marcus W. Jernegan Essays in American Historiography* (Chicago, 1937), pp. 8-9.
[12] Bancroft condensed and revised his work into a six-volume *The Author's Last Revision,* of 1883-1885.

received. Judged by present-day standards his volumes are full of flaws. His emphasis is largely on political, military, and religious matters with very little attention to social or economic forces. His foot-noting is haphazard, his use of quotations meaningless, his intense patriotism oppressive, his generalizations often unsubstantiated, his suppression of unpleasant facts misleading. A critic has observed:

> To Bancroft, . . . the history of the formation of the American re-public was no modest secular achievement of ordinary mortals, but a veritable *Aeneid*. In it Augustus was replaced by Washington. . . . In florid rhetorical style, Bancroft represented the process of coloniza-tion as the flight of brave spirits from oppression, characterized the American Revolution as a crusade of wholly virtuous and disinter-ested patriots in behalf of the liberties of civilized humanity, described the American Constitution as the creation of a group of unique mental giants, never before equaled and not to be matched at any later epoch, and regarded their work as even more notable than its makers. The pathetic inaccuracy of all of his major dogmas can only be appreciated after a careful perusal of the scholarly treatment of the same topics by George Louis Beer, C. H. Van Tyne, Carl Becker, S. M. Eliot, M. C. Tyler, H. L. Osgood, C. W. Alvord, C. M. Andrews, S. G. Fisher, Max Farrand, C. A. Beard and A. M. Schleisinger among others. The damage done to sane perspective in American history by his works was almost incalculable, if not irreparable.[13]

So far as his method of writing is concerned, John Spencer Bassett has observed:

> He had blank books, quarto in size, and gave a day of the year to each page. Then he read vastly, setting down on each page all the events that happened in the year to which it was devoted. He let no event slip, even putting in the phases of the moon; for they some-times had bearing on the actions of men. When he wrote, these books served as skeleton outlines. His mass of transcripts do not seem to have been indexed, and he probably relied on memory to reproduce the ideas in them, using his chronological arrangement of events to correct errors. He had an unusual memory, and it is to his credit that it rarely failed him. Although he was many times criticized, it was generally for bad judgment rather than for mistakes in fact.[14]

Despite all his faults and the ease with which he can be criticized in the light of our modern standards, George Bancroft blazed a broad trail for other writers of national history to follow. "His work greatly strengthened the popular devotion to the institutions of the republic. His ideas were the ideas of his time. His *History,* therefore, becomes a valuable document for our under-standing of the national psychology in the first half of the nineteenth century." [15]

Richard Hildreth. A contemporary of Bancroft and another who wrote in epic fashion was Richard Hildreth, the first eminent historian who started his

[13] Harry Elmer Barnes. *A History of Historical Writing* (Norman, Oklahoma, 1938), pp. 231-232.
[14] Bassett, *Middle Group of American Historians,* p. 208.
[15] Watt Stewart, *op. cit.,* p. 24.

career in journalism. After helping found the Boston *Atlas* in 1832 and writing editorials for it until 1840, his health gave way and he turned to the less exacting but more personally rewarding field of history. After pamphleteering against slavery for several years he commenced his major work, *The History of the United States of America*. In 1849 the first three volumes appeared, followed three years later by three more, the last of which brought the story down to the Missouri Compromise of 1820. The reader is at once struck by the wide gulf separating Hildreth's work from that of the more illustrious George Bancroft. In style Hildredth was dryly severe and rigidly factual. In politics he was an arch Hamiltonian who denounced Jeffersonian Democracy as demagoguery. In religion he expressed extreme contempt for orthodox trinitarian views of Christianity. Hildredth deplored Bancroft's liberties with facts, his wordy rhetoric, and his frequent mis-quotations. He sought to strip American history of its emphasis upon extreme patriotism. In an era in which most Americans were highly nationalistic the works of Bancroft were received with far greater acclaim. Today, however, they are seldom read while those of Hildreth, built upon the solid substance of fact, are still being used.

The Literary and Romantic Period of American Historiography

By mid-nineteenth century, history in America as in Europe had come to be regarded as a branch of literature by most of its students and its readers. Dry, factual chronicles were little noted nor widely read. Style in writing had become paramount. Narratives in the romantic vein found the largest audience. To the forefront stepped such literary masters as William H. Prescott, John L. Motley, and Francis Parkman. The former, though nearly blind, possessed great will power and with the aid of a reader was able to turn out such masterpieces as *Ferdinand and Isabella* (three volumes, 1836), the *History of the Conquest of Mexico* (three volumes, 1843), and the *History of the Conquest of Peru* (1847).

John L. Motley. Like Prescott not properly a subject of this brief review of the history of American history, John L. Motley deserves attention as another whose artistry in words made him a giant among writers. As a boy he studied under Bancroft who urged him to go to Germany for professional training. After study at Göttingen and Berlin he returned to Boston, there to be drawn into his life's principal work, the investigation of the rise of liberty and revolution in the Netherlands. Highly imaginative, a skillful portrayer of the scenes and characters of his narratives, and ever sympathetic to his subject of the Dutch struggle for independence from Spain, Motley turned out in succession the *Rise of the Dutch Republic* (three volumes, 1856), the *History of the United Netherlands* (four volumes, 1860, 1868), and the *Life and Death of John of Barnevald, Advocate of Holland* (1874).

Francis Parkman. One of the greatest, if not the greatest, of America's historians was Francis Parkman. Nine years younger than Motley, twenty-seven years younger than Prescott, and like both a Boston "Brahman," he owed his prime allegiance to their school of literary writing. Yet, seeking after primary sources and employing critical methods in his selection of materials, he was to be claimed by the historians of the new scientific school in late nineteenth century as one of their own. Thus Parkman, with Henry Adams and perhaps John Fiske, may be regarded as a bridge connecting the third and fourth periods in American historical writing.

It was while he was a student at Harvard that Francis Parkman first conceived his life's principal work, the task of narrating the titanic Anglo-French struggle for the control of North America with the American Indian a hapless participant. Never of robust health, an invalid with impaired eyesight for most of his life, Parkman nonetheless devoted his restricted energies to the collection of manuscripts; to the compilation of notes on former French and British forts, most of which he personally visited; to interviews with Indians and old settlers; and to exhaustive study of French archives and British colonial records to prepare himself for his monumental task. Ever a devotee of field, forest, and stream, he roamed the region of the St. Lawrence, the Great Lakes, and the Ohio Valley where so much of the struggle had taken place. With geographers he could agree that physiography had had much to do with the shaping of the events he was portraying.

Commencing with *The Oregon Trail* in 1846, a steady stream of narratives poured forth from the Parkman pen including *The Conspiracy of Pontiac* (two volumes, 1851); *Pioneers of France in the New World* (1865); *The Jesuits in North America in the Seventeenth Century* (1867); *La Salle and the Discovery of the Great West* (1869); *The Old Regime in Canada* (1874); *Count Frontenac and New France under Louis XIV* (1877); *Montcalm and Wolfe* (two volumes, 1884); and *A Half Century of Conflict* (two volumes, 1892).

In explaining the veneration which has come to Parkman, with some enthusiasts styling him the "Herodotus of American history," and "a Tacitus," one recent historiographer has noted:

> The genius for literary expression, the accurate portrayal of geographic scenes, the lively delineation of characters, the correlation of events into a coherent unity, and the vast use of primary documents may go far to describe Parkman's accomplishment but do not explain the spirit of critical analysis and impartiality—the warp and woof of historical writing—which pervades his works. Commentators are agreed that Parkman's detachment from the movements of the world accounted, in the main, for his great analytical powers. Indubitably, his training in law, with its rules of evidence closely akin to the principles of historical criticism, aided him in untangling conflicting statements, while his zeal to tell the truth lay at the base of his impartiality.[16]

Emphasizing the grandeur and distinctiveness of his style another has noted:

> Acquaintance with Parkman's writings as well as with many of his favorite writers leads me to conclude that he studiously avoided the style and the mannerisms of historians while absorbing their facts and their ideas. On the other hand his style was markedly influenced

---

[16] Joe Patterson Smith, "Franic Parkman" in *The Marcus W. Jernegan Essays in American Historiography*, pp. 43, 55.

by the idiom and the verbal techniques of Scott and Cooper and the romantic poets. He developed style consciously and deliberately to serve his own ends, and one need only glance at the writings of the historians who could have been his models to see how much his differed from theirs.[17]

So that the student may form his own opinions respecting Parkman's literary capacities, the following excerpts from two works written a third of a century apart are offered. The first, from *The Conspiracy of Pontiac*, is Parkman's description of the scene in the area around Detroit after Pontiac had ordered the siege of the English-held post temporarily ended in the late fall of 1763:

> The summer had long since drawn to a close, and the verdant landscape around Detroit had undergone an ominous transformation. Touched by the first October frosts, the forest glowed like a bed of tulips; and, all along the river-bank, the painted foliage, brightened by the autumnal sun, reflected its mingled colors upon the dark water below. The western wind was fraught with life and exhilaration; and in the clear, sharp air, the form of the fish-hawk, sailing over the distant headland, seemed almost within range of the sportsman's gun.
>
> A week or two elapsed, and then succeeded that gentler season which bears among us the name of the Indian summer; when a light haze rests upon the morning landscape, and the many-colored woods seem wrapped in the thin drapery of a veil; when the air is mild and calm as that of early June, and at evening the sun goes down amid a warm, voluptuous beauty, that may well outrival the softest tints of Italy. But through all the still and breathless afternoon the leaves have fallen fast in the woods, like flakes of snow; and everything betokens that the last melancholy change is at hand. And, in truth, on the morrow the sky is overspread with cold and stormy clouds; and a raw, piercing wind blows angrily from the northeast. The shivering sentinel quickens his step along the rampart, and the half-naked Indian folds his tattered blanket close around him. The shrivelled leaves are blown from the trees, and soon the gusts are whistling and howling amid gray, naked twigs and mossy branches. Here and there, indeed, the beech-tree, as the wind sweeps among its rigid boughs, shakes its pale assemblage of crisp and rustling leaves. The pines and firs, with their rough tops of dark evergreen, bend and moan in the wind; and the crow caws sullenly as, struggling against the gusts, he flaps his black wings above the denuded woods.[18]

The second is his stirring description of the climactic struggle for the Plains of Abraham at Quebec in 1759 which witnessed the deaths of both commanders, Montcalm and Wolfe.

> It was towards ten o'clock when, from the high ground on the right of the line, Wolfe saw that the crisis was near. The French on the ridge had formed themselves into three bodies, regulars in the centre, regulars and Canadians on right and left. Two field-pieces.

---

[17] Otis A. Pease, *Parkman's History* (New Haven, 1953), p. 80.
[18] Volume II, 1909 edition, pp. 119-120.

which had been dragged up the heights at Anse du Foulon, fired on
them with grape-shot, and the troops, rising from the ground, prepared to receive them. In a few moments more they were in motion.
They came on rapidly, uttering loud shouts, and firing as soon as
they were within range. Their ranks, ill ordered at the best, were
further confused by a number of Canadians who had been mixed
among the regulars, and who, after hastily firing, threw themselves
on the ground to reload. The British advanced a few rods; then
halted and stood still. When the French were within forty paces the
word of command rang out, and a crash of musketry answered all
along the line. The volley was delivered with remarkable precision.
In the battalions of the centre, which had suffered least from the
enemy's bullets, the simultaneous explosion was afterwards said by
French officers to have sounded like a cannon-shot. Another volley
followed, and then a furious clattering fire that lasted but a minute
or two. When the smoke rose, a miserable sight was revealed: the
ground cumbered with dead and wounded, the advancing masses
stopped short and turned into a frantic mob, shouting, cursing,
gesticulating. The order was given to charge. Then over the field
rose the British cheer, mixed with the fierce yell of the Highland
slogan. Some of the corps pushed forward with the bayonet; some
advanced firing. The clansmen drew their broadswords and dashed
on, keen and swift as bloodhounds. At the English right, though the
attacking column was broken to pieces, a fire was still kept up, chiefly,
it seems, by sharpshooters from the bushes and cornfields, where they
had lain for an hour or more. Here Wolfe himself led the charge, at
the head of the Louisbourg grenadiers. A shot shattered his wrist.
He wrapped his handkerchief about it and kept on. Another shot
struck him, and he still advanced, when a third lodged in his breast.
He staggered, and sat on the ground. Lieutenant Brown, of the
grenadiers, one Henderson, a volunteer in the same company, and
a private soldier, aided by an officer of artillery who ran to join them,
carried him in their arms to the rear. He begged them to lay him
down. They did so, and asked if he would have a surgeon. "There's
no need," he answered; "it's all over with me." A moment after, one
of them cried out: "They run; see how they run!" "Who run?" Wolfe
demanded, like a man roused from sleep. "The enemy, sir. Egad,
they give way everywhere!" "Go, one of you, to Colonel Burton,"
returned the dying man; "tell him to march Webb's regiment down
to Charles River, to cut off their retreat from the bridge." Then,
turning on his side, he murmured, "Now, God be praised, I will die
in peace!" and in a few moments his gallant soul had fled.

Montcalm, still on horseback, was borne with the tide of fugitives
towards the town. As he approached the walls a shot passed through
his body. He kept his seat; two soldiers supported him, one on each
side, and led his horse through the St. Louis Gate. On the open space
within, among the excited crowd, were several women, drawn, no
doubt, by eagerness to know the result of the fight. One of them
recognized him, saw the streaming blood, and shrieked, *"O mon
Dieu, mon Dieu! le Marquis est tué!"* "It's nothing, it's nothing,"

replied the death-stricken man; "don't be troubled for me, my good friends." (*"Ce n'est rien, ce n'est rien; ne vous affligez pas pour moi, mes bonnes amies."*) [19]

From these excerpts it can be observed that the abiding power with Parkman was his vividness. He saw history as a series of pictures to be painted with words by the literary artist. Few American historians have ever approached him in descriptive ability.

THE ADVENT OF THE SCIENTIFIC SCHOOL OF AMERICAN HISTORICAL WRITING

Before Francis Parkman had completed the last of his volumes a new school of American historical writing had emerged to claim him as its own. Characterized by critical investigation of sources, the application of German seminar methods to American graduate school training of professional historians, and the dominance of academicians in the realm of historical writing, the "scientific school" was to be led by men such as Herbert Baxter Adams of Johns Hopkins, John W. Burgess of Columbia, John Bach McMaster of the University of Pennsylvania, James Ford Rhodes, Hermann Eduard von Holst of the University of Chicago, James Schouler of Johns Hopkins, Woodrow Wilson of Princeton, John Fiske of Washington University at St. Louis, and Henry Adams of Harvard. The latter, though he taught at the Cambridge school for only a very few years, inaugurated doctoral studies in history there. These men, whose lives bridged the nineteenth and twentieth centuries, had much to do in shaping the tendencies of American historiography in the new century.

---

[19] *Montcalm and Wolfe,* II, 1911 edition, pp. 295-297.

Chapter 31

TWENTIETH CENTURY TENDENCIES IN AMERICAN HISTORIOGRAPHY

By Glenn S. Dumke and James C. Findley

INTRODUCTION

A MERICAN historical writing went through three fairly distinguishable stages before the twentieth century, which saw American historical activity largely in the hands of trained scholars, who were also, as a rule, college teachers.

In the first stage, which extended over the colonial period and through the first decades of the federal union, the historian could look to no large audience; and his work, especially in the New England colonies, was profoundly influenced by religious preoccupations.

Indeed, the historian might consider his story significant as the story of deeds done beyond the sea (the writings of John Smith) or as a great manifestation of God's providence (Bradford's *History of Plymouth Plantation*). But he could not look to a wide audience which would recognize the general importance of his subject. As this colonial period developed, there was a considerable degree of historical literacy, especially in classical and English history, but no monuments of historical literature.

Even the Revolutionary War and the foundation of an independent government did not put an abrupt end to this historiographical barrenness. The second phase of American historical writing emerges in the period of national self-consciousness, democratic and humanitarian enthusiasm and party conflict which began in the decades after the conclusion of the War of 1812.

This historical writing, which was animated by American impulses and interests, was history as literature, as it was generally recognized in Europe, particularly England. The United States produced its antiquaries and collectors, such as Jared Sparks, but the historians of the middle period of American history thought of themselves as artists and stressed narrative history, with a strong nationalistic bent.

The Civil War produced the impetus for memoirs and sectional justifications until the closing years of the century. Almost all of this writing was, if not uncritical, then so selective as to be classified as partisan history. Perhaps, the most provocative American historian in the early decades after the Civil War was Henry Adams (1838-1918) who, while teaching at Harvard, inaugurated doctoral studies in history there. Later, Adams wrote a historical study of the Middle Ages and *The Education of Henry Adams*. His greatest historiographical work was *History of the United States during the Administration of Jefferson and Madison.*[1] The dissatisfied spirit, which led him to give up his position at Harvard, drove him to ironical attempts to secure the certainty of science in history and culminated in restless self-questioning and the gravest doubts about the course of modern civilization.

Henry Adams may stand as the bridge between the older tradition of historical writing and the third stage of American historiography, the development of critical history.[2]

With the dawning of the twentieth century, American historiography faced a new era. With the development of the scientific attitude, historians began to broaden their outlook and to envelop many of the social and natural sciences in their considerations. This tendency was a late development in the field of American historiography and did not actually find its inception until the decade of the 1870's with the application of German seminar methods to graduate studies at John Hopkins University. With the founding of the American Historical Association in 1884, the principles and methods of American history received great impetus, and the turn of the century found many students busily engaged in historical research. To a large extent, however, the nationalistic and politically dominant schools of the previous era still held sway. Thus nineteenth century backgrounds of American history gave little indication of the great changes which were to occur in the first four decades of the present century.

American Historiography before the First World War

The beginning of the twentieth century saw a rising emphasis on realism in history. This realism consisted largely in a scientific approach to historic problems which had previously been considered from a purely nationalistic or romantic point of view. For example, the patriotic bias of George Bancroft's nineteenth-century history of the United States was now being replaced by the more objective studies by James Ford Rhodes and John Bach McMaster. In addition, there was an increased emphasis on problems which up to that time had been considered outside the province of history—notably social questions, racial issues, and other factors influencing the course of society. There was still a major emphasis on politics in most of the major works, but it was becoming slightly diluted; although the dilution was not always productive of a smooth or evenly-balanced result, the attempts were significant.

Rhodes. One of the outstanding products of American historiography in the prewar period was the *History of the United States from the Compromise of 1850* (1893-1906), by a retired Cleveland businessman, James Ford Rhodes. Although not a professional historian, Rhodes produced a major work which surveyed in a fairly objective manner the political history of the nation during the final half of the nineteenth century. Like all historians, Rhodes had certain preferences and biases, notably a failure to pay attention to the history of the frontier and a tendency to overemphasize the importance of New England

---

[1] Ernest Samuels, *The Young Henry Adams;* William H. Jordy, *Henry Adams: Scientific Historian.*
[2] Many phases of historical activity in the last quarter of the century may be found in W. Stull Holt (ed.), *Historical Scholarship in the United States, 1876-1901: As Revealed in the Correspondence of Herbert B. Adams, Johns Hopkins Studies in History and Political Science,* LVI, No. 4.

in the development of America. Since the latter technique is still a vital issue among certain schools of American historians, it is perhaps not fair to criticize him too severely on this point. One of the chief contributions of the work was its inclusion, to a certain extent, of social history—tremendously significant in illustrating the new trend toward synthesis.

McMaster. Another contribution of major importance, this time by an academician, was the *History of the People of the United States from the Revolution to the Civil War,* in eight volumes (1883-1913), by John Bach McMaster of the University of Pennsylvania. McMaster recognized the needs of professional historians by having voluminous and helpful footnotes to analyze his sources of information, and he too produced a fairly objective and interestingly written treatment of his subject. He also realized the importance of the American West, and included social history. But one critic said that "his realism . . . was marred by a nationalist tone and a predominantly descriptive treatment based heavily on newspapers." [3] Since many historians do not consider reliance on newspapers a fault, McMaster must be given credit for helping to inaugurate the use of this highly valuable and interpretative source of historical information. The same period saw, too, the beginning of the *History of the United States,* in eight volumes, by Edward Channing of Harvard, another excellent master reference on national growth.

Myers and Semple. An important addition to social history was contributed by Gustav Myers, whose *History of the Great American Fortunes,* published in 1911, tried to advance the thesis that many of America's troubles were due to the possession of power by an hereditary plutocracy. Another point of view was illustrated by Ellen C. Semple, who in the years preceding World War I turned out two works defending the geographical approach to history: *American History and Its Geographical Conditions* (1903) and *The Influences of Geographic Environment* (1911), based on the approach of the German, Friedrich Ratzel.

Turner. Probably the chief contribution to American historiography during the period was made by Frederick Jackson Turner, a professor at the University of Wisconsin, who stressed the importance of American frontier history. He has been characterized as one "who rebelled against the overemphasis given at John Hopkins to the Teutonic origins of American institutions," [4] and his influence was first felt in 1893, when he read a paper to the annual meeting of the American Historical Association at Chicago, entitled "The Significance of the Frontier in American History." Turner attempted to veer the emphasis of American historians from colonial New England and seaboard culture to a consideration of the "westward movement." He felt that the American character, based as it was on individualism, democracy, inventiveness, and aptitude at material and technological skills, had been shaped largely by the influence of the great west. "The existence," said Turner, "of an area of free land, its continuous recession and the advance of American settlement westward, explain American development."[5] He chose the proper time to present

[3] Harvey Wish, *Contemporary America*, p. 51.
[4] Harvey Wish, *op. cit.*, p. 51.
[5] Frederick Jackson Turner, *The Frontier in American History*, p. 1. First published in 1920.

his thesis, for the Census of 1890 for the first time showed no definite frontier line, and indicated that most of the good free land which had attracted immigrants throughout the nineteenth century was gone. By recognizing its end, Turner climaxed the American "westward movement."

Research in History of American West. The influence of Turner on American historiography is difficult to overemphasize, for he was followed by a group of historians who devoted their researches to the history of the American west. Leaders in this field were concentrated in several institutions, notably the University of Wisconsin and the University of California at Berkeley. Men like Frederick L. Paxson, with his *History of the American Frontier* (1924), Clarence W. Alvord, and others followed Turner to the extent of making American frontier history a legitimate and respected field of historical research. Although there was a tendency to overemphasize the influence of the frontier as a result of this new attention paid to it, the fresh viewpoint had important significance. A corollary result of the Turner influence was the increased production of much local and regional history.

Another trend evident in American historiography before the First World War was the publication of sets and series of collective works. The first and, according to some authorities, the best of the sets was *The American Nation: A History from Original Sources by Associated Scholars,* 28 vols. (New York: 1904-18), edited by Albert Bushnell Hart. This publication presented volumes by such recognized experts as Edward Gaylord Bourne on the Spanish colonies, Charles M. Andrews on colonial history, Reuben Gold Thwaites on the French influence in America, C. H. Van Tyne on the American Revolution, Albert Bushnell Hart on slavery, and Edward Channing on Jefferson. The series was described by Herman Ames, of the University of Pennsylvania, as a "comprehensive, fairly consecutive, reasonably well-proportioned survey of the history of the country from the discovery down to 1917 . . . the average of excellence is high."[6] *The American Nation* series set a noteworthy standard for subsequent collective works to follow, and it ranks as the most notable achievement of its type in the prewar years.

The characteristics of American historiography preceding World War I were therefore a tendency toward realism and a broader approach in the larger works, with a continuation of the emphasis on politics, the inception of a new theory of American history which stressed the effect of the frontier on American culture, and the beginning of production of collective works and series. These tendencies were intensified as the century progressed.

AMERICAN HISTORIOGRAPHY DURING WORLD WAR I

The beginning of the First World War saw American history with recognized professional status but also saw historians confronted with the problem of how to approach their subject. Although some historians managed to maintain a coldly objective outlook during the period of hostilities, most of them became partisan and therefore contributed to a new emphasis upon national history. As propagandists, they were able to reach an entirely new

[6] *A Guide to Historical Literature* (George M. Dutcher, et al., eds.), p. 1012.

audience, since much of their work was published by the National Board for Historical Service or by the Creel Committee on Public Information.

The historical societies and journals were also affected by the war. The presidents of the American Historical Association, fearing the effect of jingoism on history, criticized non-objectivity in their addresses between 1915 and 1917, and taxed the non-scientific, nationalist historians with responsibility for bringing about the current unfortunate situation. By 1918, however, the point-of-view had changed, and Secretary Waldo G. Leland was able to state:

> A national historical society with no thoughts above the level of antiquarianism might better not convene in such days as these, but a national historical society with the right spirit could not hold an annual meeting without sending its members home heartened to the performance of every patriotic duty, nor without extending in some measure throughout the nation the inspiring and clarifying influence of sound historical thinking and right patriotic feeling.[7]

With the adoption of the new point of view, papers read at the annual meeting of the Association covered such subjects as ancient and modern imperialism, military history, the Far East, and Latin America. In 1917 the *American Historical Review* decided "That the quarterly would neither ignore the war nor open its pages to partisan argument against Germany, but would welcome scholarly contributions on the background of the struggle, or on the experience of the United States in its earlier conflicts." Previous to the war, only two percent of the articles in the journal had been devoted to European history after 1815; during and after the war that percentage rose to eighteen.[8]

In April, 1917, in order to make their contributions more effective, historians organized the National Board for Historical Service which immediately made itself felt by sponsoring lectures, printing pamphlets, aiding the Creel Committee, offering prizes for essay contests, outlining academic courses on peace aims, and organizing war history commissions in practically every state.

Although official sponsorship of historical activities never reached the proportions attained in World War II, the War and Navy Departments somewhat tardily set up historical branches, and comprehensive plans were laid for producing a full official history of the war. These plans never got beyond the outline stage, however, and although through the influence of the National Board many records were preserved that otherwise would have been destroyed, most of the materials were put into "dead storage."

REINTERPRETATION OF AMERICAN HISTORICAL THEMES

Reinterpretation of favorite American historical themes was an important characteristic of the war years. England, which had been previously considered a tyrannical nation against which a freedom-loving group of American

---

[7] William T. Hutchinson, "The American Historian in Wartime," *Mississippi Valley Historical Review*, XXIX (1942), p. 167.
[8] *Ibid.*

colonies revolted, was looked upon with new respect and even "the hitherto
maligned Tories were at last dusted off and made respectable."[9] Conyers
Read and others pointed out that England had, during the nineteenth century,
gone further along the path of social reform and democratization even than
had America. "Taking at their face value the many articles written in this
vein," said one authority, "the conclusion is inescapable that the American
people are almost exclusively English in ancestry, other immigrant groups
have contributed little if anything to America's heritage of liberalism, and
Frederick Jackson Turner's emphasis upon the frontier origins of American
democracy is scarcely worthy of consideration."[10] In addition, there was a
corresponding effort on the part of British historians to establish new contacts
with their colleagues in America. The Royal Historical Society welcomed
American lecturers, and in 1917 Henry E. Malden edited *Magna Carta
Commemoration Essays,* published in London as a joint British-American
project. Other tendencies were illustrated in the practice of giving France
better treatment in historical essays, of considering the British navy as
America's first line of defense, in treating isolation as a myth, in recalling
the Holy Alliance as a basis for the League, and in rehashing past wars as
examples and models for the current conflict. Military history also came into
prominence, and it is significant that the 1918 Pulitzer Prize in history was
won by James Ford Rhodes for his one-volume treatment of the Civil War.

Publication of sets continued during the war years. One of the most important was the *Chronicles of America,* 50 vols. (New Haven: 1919-21),
edited by Allen Johnson. This set consisted of brief volumes in small format,
written by a group of thirty-five experts, some seasoned historians and
others of a more popular bent. As in all collective works, the texture varied;
but volumes such as Max Farrand, *Fathers of the Constitution* (Vol. XIII),
F. A. Ogg, *The Reign of Andrew Jackson* (Vol. XX), and W. Wood,
Elizabethan Sea-Dogs (Vol. III), stand out with especial brilliance. With
the impact of the "New History" in mind, certain volumes were devoted to
non-political fields, such as Burton J. Hendrick, *The Age of Big Business*
(Vol. XXXIX), and S. P. Orth, *The Armies of Labor* (Vol. XL).

The tendency of the war period to approach history broadly was also
indicated by the publication of items like Seymour Dunbar, *History of Travel
in America* . . . 4 vols. (Indianapolis: 1915) and Charles A. Beard, *Economic
Interpretation of the Constitution of the United States* (New York: 1913),
which last, although appearing the year before the war began, can be said
to characterize the wartime approach.

In summary, the historical activity in America during World War I was
characterized by less official sponsorship, a higher degree of jingoism and
patriotic slanting of effort, cooperation with the war effort not only by
individual historians but also by historical societies and journals, and a
readjustment of traditional American historical views. It is safe to say that

[9] *Ibid.,* p. 174.
[10] *Ibid.,* p. 172.

the historiography of World War II was in general much more mature than its counterpart in World War I.

THE PERIOD OF THE 1920'S

The outstanding characteristic of the postwar decade was a reaction to many of the attitudes fostered by the war years. The cynicism and "lost generation" feeling, typical of the literature of the period, found its counterpart in historiography with the popularization of traditional historic themes, the production of many "debunking" works, the revisionist interpretation of war guilt, and a tendency toward synthesis of other social sciences with history.

Although the so-called popularization of history has increased as the century has progressed, it has usually suffered from two great faults. First, it is often attempted by amateurs who sacrifice accuracy for popularity; second, even when accuracy is maintained, it is often mocked by the warped effort to emphasize only those episodes of history which lend themselves to dramatic treatment. The output of large numbers of popular works for the general reader characterized the decade. Two of the better examples were Carl Burgess Glasscoack's *Bandits and the Southern Pacific* (New York: 1929), and Stanley Vestal's *Kit Carson: The Happy Warrior of the Old West* (Boston, 1928).

A second tendency of the "postwar debauch of the 1920's,"[11] was the enthusiasm for debunking. George Washington, previously revered as the father of the nation, it was now pointed out, had poorly-fitting false teeth, a lurid vocabulary, and a terrible temper, besides being the representative of an aristocratic class that produced, in the Constitution, a document for the preservation of its own economic interests. This tendency, said Dixon Ryan Fox, "seemed to change the literary emphasis from drum and trumpet history to bum and strumpet history."[12] In addition, debunking was carried to a new extreme in the so-called "vogue for fictionized biography." [13] Based on the new interest in psychology and psychoanalysis, many praiseworthy items were produced. However, many examples of the regulation, conservative biography, based on scientific evaluation of sources, were also written during the period. Albert J. Beveridge won the Pulitzer Prize in 1920 with his *Life of John Marshall.* Perhaps the greatest biographical achievement of the decade was the commencement of publication of the massive and authoritative *Dictionary of American Biography,* 20 vols. (New York: 1928-44), edited by Allen Johnson. This master work was turned out under the auspices of the American Council of Learned Societies, and was modeled after the British *Dictionary of National Biography.* It achieved great success in maintaining a high quality of scholarship throughout, and has become one of the standard reference works on American history.

The third tendency of history during the 1920's was to alter measurably the attitude which it had maintained toward the problems of nationalism imposed

---

[11] William C. Binkley, "Two World Wars and American Historical Scholarship," *Mississippi Valley Historical Review,* XXXI (1946), p. 10.
[12] *Ibid.*
[13] Wish, *op. cit.,* pp. 340-41.

by World War I. It must be admitted that the war brought about an attitude of narrow patriotism which held over into the early 1920's. With the Hearst Press taking the lead, great criticism was heaped upon teachers of American history, and many state legislatures passed laws regulating in one way or another the type of history which appeared in school textbooks. Such a process brought an official rejoinder from the Council of the American Historical Association which in part stated: "In the opinion of this Association, the clearly implied charges that many of our leading scholars are engaged in treasonable propaganda and that tens of thousand of American school teachers and officials are so stupid or disloyal as to place treasonable textbooks in the hands of children is inherently and obviously, absurd." [14] Although the attacks soon diminished, similar episodes following the Second World War seem to indicate that they are indicative of the reaction which follows any modern conflict.

As the cynicism of the decade began to make itself felt, however, this jingoistic approach met less and less response, and finally a group of historians emerged who had altered radically the prevalent views of the war years. Many decided that the Allies were equally responsible for the war, and fulminations against the war guilt clause of the Treaty of Versailles became rife. Harry Elmer Barnes, for instance, concluded that Russia was largely to blame for the diplomatic muddle which preceded the outbreak of war, and Sidney B. Fay, who wrote *Origins and Causes of the World War,* 2 vols. (New York: 1926), adopted an attitude midway between casting responsibility on the Central Powers and the Allies. The modification of attitude grew in intensity as the decade progressed, and with the coming of the depression blossomed out in frank apologia for the Central Powers.

"New History" of the 1920's. The "New History" also made itself felt in the decade of the 1920's. "Contemporary advances in the other social sciences," said one writer, "compelled the professional historian to bring his specialty abreast of the times or be threatened with the eclipse that overtook philosophy during the decade." [15] Charles A. Beard and his wife, Mary, applied a somewhat narrow approach, based chiefly on an economic viewpoint, to *The Rise of American Civilization,* 2 vols. (New York: 1927), but this, too, illustrated the synthetic trend. Outstanding among the collaborative works was the *History of American Life,* 12 vols. (New York: 1927-   ), edited by Arthur M. Schlesinger and Dixon Ryan Fox. This series frankly attempted to treat American history from the new viewpoint, and volumes by Allan Nevins, Ida M. Tarbell, and others so successfully applied the principle of synthesis that the set immediately gained a tremendous reputation. Although "scientific history" still remained the basis for professional training, there was an increasing awareness of the necessity of broadening the approach to historical study. The presidential addresses of the American Historical Association demonstrated this attitude clearly enough; between 1920 and 1934 only three stressed the application of the scientific method to past incidents; the others either cast doubts on the traditional concepts of the scientific method or emphasized the synthetic approach.

---

[14] Preston William Slosson, *The Great Crusade and After,* p. 316.
[15] Wish, *op. cit.,* pp. 350-51.

In summary, the decade of the 1920's saw an intensification of the fundamental trends already expressed in the prewar years. Perhaps the best example of this was the widening acceptance of the "New History" and its application by skilled professionals to various fields. Collective works increased in number and specialization was accentuated. The most significant departures were in the field of popularized and "debunking" history, and in the reinterpretation of many historical attitudes crystallized during the war years.

HISTORY DURING THE DEPRESSION

The new keynote of American historiography was struck by the publication in 1932 of a volume by the American Historical Association fully analyzing the field. This important document, entitled *Historical Scholarship in America: Needs and Opportunities,* merits rather full and specific consideration.

In surveying the current developments in the various fields, the report concluded that American research in ancient history needed the least change. Already the various branches of that subject were interrelated, and the "New History" ideas of Robinson were already being applied by scholars who had realized for years that the paucity of materials in their specialty made whole civilizations their province. Most of the areas of ancient and medieval history, it was said, were being given adequate consideration and attention. In the European and American fields, however, a broader approach and better contact with scholars in related fields were needed. The report recommended that sessions in American Historical Association meetings be devoted to related fields and their contributions to history. It was clear, as well, that modern European history was being given over to a political emphasis, but this was the natural result of the First World War, and the committee concluded that "it need cause no uneasiness, and that students would in due course revert to other fields of investigation."[16]

Differences of Opinion regarding American History. With regard to American history as such, however, there was some difference of opinion. Two committees had been appointed to investigate current trends, one meeting in the East, and another in the Middle West. The middlewestern conference was most optimistic, concluding that current studies represented "surprisingly well" the broader interests of American history. The eastern group disagreed, maintaining that the lists of doctoral theses showed a deplorable working-over of old themes, to the point of diminishing returns. It was generally agreed that new fields of history needed attention, especially Eastern and Southeastern Europe, local history in both Europe and America, social and intellectual history, racial movements, the development of morals, commerce, industry, transportation, law, and administration, the evolution of national economic policies, histories of propaganda, journalism, and educational and religious institutions. "Vast areas," the report said, "of historical investigation have, up till now, been allowed to lie fallow." [17]

In the section devoted to the historical profession, the report stated that not

---

[16] *Historical Scholarship in America, op. cit.,* p. 14.
[17] *Ibid.*

enough superior students were attracted and that every effort should be made to induce men of outstanding merit to become professional historians. From the standpoint of research methods, the report emphasized the "New History" concept, and decided that more attention should be paid to language requirements to prevent a narrow approach to the field. In addition, good writing and literary style should be stressed more than they had been in the past.

This 1932 report was of especial significance because it indicated a fair degree of self-satisfaction among members of the profession, and yet a recognition of certain outstanding weaknesses. It indicated that all fields of history were being given attention in the United States, and that attention was taking a scholarly form.

Trends during the Mid-1930's. The mid-1930's saw several historical trends develop and emerge. Perhaps the most important was the appearance of a social consciousness in historical treatment of familiar themes, brought to the attention of historians by the influence of the depression and the New Deal upon American life and society. One of the forms which this social consciousness took was intensified examination, often in a critical vein, of existing institutions of American and world society. Typical was Matthew Josephson's *The Robber Barons* (New York: 1934). Perhaps the best example of an historian who involved himself with social and economic as well as political problems was Charles Beard. His first epoch-maker was the *Economic Interpretation of the Constitution of the United States,* published in 1913 and previously mentioned. In 1927, with the aid of his wife, he published *The Rise of American Civilization,* which made a conscious attempt to apply the principles of the "New History," and in 1939 the Beards wrote *America in Mid-Passage,* a searching investigation of American development during the 1930's. Beard began as a frank economic determinist, but his later writings indicated that he was departing from that limitation. He deliberately adhered to the principles of the "New History," and integrated his material with as much social, economic, cultural, and literary history as possible.

In addition to social consciousness in history, the integration of various related fields with history continued. This movement to break down the lines of specialization was manifested in many ways. The *Encyclopedia of the Social Sciences* was begun, edited by Edwin R. A. Seligman and Alvin Johnson. This was a comprehensive work in fifteen volumes, aimed at discussing the major items in the fields of the social sciences in an authoritative manner. The "New History" idea was also seen in more conservative volumes by Charles M. Andrews, *The Colonial Period of American History,* 4 vols. (New York: 1934-38), in which the economic influences of Europe on the New World were carefully assessed. The movement toward integration was seen as well in course work, and the most evident trend toward the end of the decade was away from history courses as such, especially in elementary fields, and toward social science courses, which emphasized a broader treatment and the pulling together of many related subjects.

Renewed Interest in Local History. A third movement in American historiography during the 1930's was a renewed interest in local and regional history. Tremendous impetus was given to this by the depression and the consequent government activity in subsidizing writers and researchers under the Works Progress Administration. In addition to an excellent set of guide-books to the various states and chief cities of the nation, the government sponsored bibliographies and checklists of local and regional archives, thus placing much new information at the disposal of local historians. This government attention influenced historians to devote more attention to local and regional history, and for the first time this subject became the focus of trained historians, rather than enthusiastic amateurs. As a result, top-notch local history was written in the late 1930's, such as John Walton Caughey's *California* (New York: 1940).

A fourth trend in the 1930's was the collection and preservation of historical records. The WPA impetus toward production of checklists and bibliograph-ical information informed the trained historians of the nation that much material was not being cared for properly and would eventually disappear unless more attention were paid to it. For instance, almost four times as much material went into the War Department archives during World War I as had been collected in the entire history of the nation under the Constitution. The tremendous increase of material since that time led to much experimenta-tion in microfilming, which gave promise that former bulky files, such as newspapers, and large documents, could be reduced eventually to manageable size.

Contemporary Problems. A final characteristic of history in America during the depression was a concentration on contemporary problems. The instability of the international situation, the economic issues that filled the days of the average citizen, and the new communications which made the layman aware as never before of what was going on in the world, combined to emphasize current topics and contemporary affairs in much the same way that they had been emphasized during World War I. In general, in the final years of the decades, there appeared some of the danger-signals that had characterized American historiography during the first great international cataclysm.

Along with these outstanding trends, there continued to be produced in America during the 1930's much standard, scientifically-based, orthodox his-tory. Much of it was influenced by the new trends, but an equal amount of it was not. Biographies, for example, lost their psychoanalytical approach and returned to a more conservative technique; and the appetite of the public for historical romance was removed from the field of history as such and shifted to the area of historical fiction, which underwent a great vogue in the latter part of the decade.

The depression years resembled the 1920's, therefore, in having the older twentieth-century trends reemphasized. There was, however, a new note in governmental attention to historical problems, and a new appraisal by his-torians themselves of their own field and its contributions to American life. Social consciousness seemed to be the keynote of history during this period; problems existed, and historians did their best to apply their craft to the solutions.

AMERICAN HISTORIOGRAPHY DURING WORLD WAR II

The onslaught of hostilities again disrupted American historical scholarship and revived many problems that had vexed the professional historian during the first world conflict. However, government was much more active in directing the work of American historians than it had been twenty years earlier. War agencies, in attempting to use the records of the preceding wars for precedents and guideposts, came to the conclusion that better methods of filing would have to be adopted if they were to be of any practical value. In 1941 historian Arthur Schlesinger suggested to Archibald MacLeish, the Librarian of Congress, that an historian or archivist be attached to every important official agency to preclude some of the difficulties that had hindered effort up to that time. The first government bureau to appoint an official historian was the Priorities Division of the Office of Production Management, and in 1942 the Bureau of the Budget chose similar assistance. Forty others soon followed suit. Outside of monthly meetings of the experts involved, no attempt at similarity of techniques was attempted, and therefore the Budget Bureau fostered the formation of the Committee on Records of War Administration in order to centralize policy. In 1943 the Social Science Research Council started the Committee on War Studies to foster historical work along private lines, in much the same way that the National Board had directed effort during World War I, and finally the Committee on Records was merged with the Committee on War Studies to form the Advisory Council on War History. Although there was some conflict with Selective Service procedure which resulted in highly trained personnel sometimes ending up peeling potatoes in army camps, it was true that "most of the trained historians who went into the Army were eventually involved in historical work of some capacity.[18]

The work of the Navy and War Departments in historiography began about the same time as the creation of the other government advisory boards. In 1942, the former service set up a new office, that of Historian of Naval Operations, and the army in the same year ordered its commanding generals to establish historical sections in their outfits. The War Department also utilized the services of professional historians in connection with the Army War College and the Service, Ground, and Air Forces. Eventually a superior coordinating body was established, the Historical Branch of the Military Intelligence Division of the War Department General Staff; this served to pull together all army historical activities.

WORLD WAR II HISTORIANS

In general, the activities of historians in World War II were much more successful than in the previous conflict, and it might be said that historical efforts in connection with World War II formed the most "adequately subsidized historical project of all time." [19] The result was an accumulation of records and data which, when analyzed, sifted, and studied, will provide later historians with a mass of material to enable them to assess World War II more accurately

[18] Binkley, *op. cit.*, p. 23.
[19] *Ibid.*, pp. 25-26.

from an historical standpoint than any similar event has ever been appraised in world annals.

World War II also served to shake up the traditional attitudes toward the teaching of American history. A survey conducted by the *New York Times* during the early part of the war seemed to indicate that the average American college student had little command of the factual information of American history. Although various professional organizations, including the American Historical Association, followed the *Times* investigations with a less pessimistic report of their own (1944), new emphasis was placed upon the study of American history in the schools of America. Various states passed legislation which added to history requirements, and constitutional study was increased in most of the institutions of higher learning.

World War II also saw the influence of James Harvey Robinson's "New History" in the curricula of American colleges and universities. It became possible to take "fields" of study such as Hispanic America or the Far East, in which a number of different departments participated. Many institutions abandoned departmental lower-division requirements, and combined the work of many fields into social science and humanities courses, which involved not only history, but also economics, political science, philosophy, religion, and in some cases psychology and literature.

A new interest in economic history was very marked. In May, 1941, there appeared the first issue of the *Journal of Economic History,* and Louis M. Hacker wrote *The Triumph of American Capitalism* (1940). Intellectual and cultural history also attracted some attention, an outstanding example of which was Oscar Cargill's *Intellectual America: Ideas on the March.* Items which obtained a wide circulation were Carl Sandburg, *Abraham Lincoln: The War Years* (1939), and Arthur M. Schlesinger, Jr., *The Age of Jackson* (1946).

On the borderline of history appeared dozens of "war books," usually produced by journalists or correspondents, but sometimes written by military personnel themselves. Most of the major phases of the war were thus covered, and many of the items attained best-seller status. One such example was William L. White's *Queens Die Proudly* (1943). Many were of great value from both literary and historical standpoints, but an equally large number had a justifiably ephemeral popularity. The war was better covered journalistically than any previous conflict, but obviously both time and future re-evaluation will be necessary before the historicity of many of these popular items can be known.

HISTORY IN AMERICA SINCE WORLD WAR II

It is still too early to assess clearly the trends that will characterize postwar historical production in America. At this writing, there has been no revolutionary change in approach, save that the ending of war priorities and shortages and the rapid refilling of graduate schools have increased historical production markedly. New editions of older texts have appeared in considerable numbers, bringing them up-to-date and continuing the emphasis upon "New History," with long discussions of cultural, intellectual, religious, and economic influences. Another characteristic of postwar history has been an increasing tendency toward popularization, through such series as "The Rivers of America" and "The Sections in History." This newer type of popular history has made a greater contribution than did many of the earlier popular items. Much of it is dramatized, to be sure, but often it constitutes a really novel approach or synthesis of data, besides furnishing new and interesting emphasis on the history of sections or regions. A thoughtful consideration of the deeper problems of the peace is also evident in careful analyses of economic problems of various wartorn areas, in patient consideration of philosophical works like Arnold Toynbee's *Study of History,* and in the serious attention now given to history as a whole, its presentation to the student, and its traditional treatment.

Chapter 32

TWENTIETH CENTURY TENDENCIES—LATIN AMERICA
By Harold E. Davis

GENERAL MOVEMENTS

ALTHOUGH the volume of historical studies and the intensity of historical interest in Latin America are greater today than ever before, other social sciences, notably anthropology, have also greatly increased their claims on contemporary scholarship. Thus, although Latin America shares the great preoccupation with history and its meaning which characterizes modern civilization in general, history is not the predominant social science it was half a century ago.

Fifty years ago, historical writing was done largely by men of wealth, leisure and literary inclination, frequently retired from political life. It found little place in the universities. Today, the number of historians is larger. They are much more likely to have received professional training, and their work centers to a larger extent in the universities, in historical archives or libraries, or in other historical organizations. The number of historical reviews has increased and their scholarship has improved. National archives have increased in number and improved in organization and housing. Historical libraries have grown. Provincial and local historical societies have increased in numbers. Two aspects of historical organization are especially notable: the appearance of national conferences of historians on the professional level in some countries, e.g. Mexico, and the growth of inter-American historical activities.

The study of history in Latin America is characterized by a deep preoccupation with the meaning of history and particularly the meaning of the history of America. The institutional approach to historical study is so widespread that we might speak of it as a "school" of historians. Its roots go back to the pre-civil war Center of Historical Studies in the University of Madrid, to Rafael Altamira and Ramón Iglesia. It has outstanding representatives in Silvio Zavala of Mexico and Ricardo Levene of Argentina. But other cross currents of political, social and historical philosophies are reflected among church historians, apologists of the Mexican Revolution, literary Apristas (the reforming party of Peru) and students of Indian and Negro sociological development.

A deep preoccupation with the history of America and its meaning characterizes Spanish America especially. The "new history" has made its appearance in the form of an emphasis upon the history of ideas, social and economic history, and the history of art. Colonial history and preconquest history (reflecting progress in archaeological and anthropological studies) are predominant interests. In both, the elements of revaluation and revision of the Black Legend of Spanish colonial administration are important elements. Questions of historical method and the philosophy of history are matters of intense discussion.

HISTORY AT THE TURN OF THE CENTURY

By the end of the nineteenth century, historical scholarship in Latin America had witnessed a remarkable half century of development. Growth of historical research and writing was due in considerable measure to the increased historical consciousness which came with greater political maturity and the consequent increase in the sense of nationalism, a development experienced in some degree by every country in the area. As might be expected, historical scholarship achieved its highest expression in Mexico, Chile, Peru, Colombia, Argentina and Brazil. Research interests centered in the independence movements and other aspects of national origins. For these earlier phases of national history, such writers as Bartolomé Mitre (1821-1906) in Argentina, Lucas Alaman (1792-1853) in Mexico, and Francisco Adolpho Varnhagen (1816-1878) in Brazil, were able to draw upon their own recollections, since they either remembered or had been active participants in the events. Others drew upon their acquaintance with the older leaders, or upon collections of contemporary documents which came to them through family ties or ties of friendship.

Unconsciously, therefore, this history often reflected the political and social views of the authors and of the groups, usually creole, that had led the independence movements and had generally thereafter controlled the destinies of their nations. Until the early part of the twentieth century, literary history dominated the scene although such scholars as Vicente Riva Palacios (1832-1896) of Mexico, Diego Barros Arana (1830-1907) of Chile, and Manoel de Oliveira Lima (1865-1928) of Brazil reflected the influences of the scientific history of the Ranke school, or complete developments in England, France, or Spain. Much of their writing was cast in the idealistic, frequently heroic and romantic mold of the nineteenth century.

Under the influence of these nineteenth century scholars, national archives were developed and a beginning was made with historical libraries. But the archives were poorly housed and supported, while the richest collections of books and manuscripts were in the hands of private collectors, from whose hands they often found their way into foreign libraries. They enriched the opportunities for the study of Latin America in the United States, England, France, Germany and elsewhere, but impoverished historical scholarship in Latin America.

Positivist social thought increasingly dominated intellectual life and found some expression in historical literature. Most historians, however, resisted positivism, holding to the earlier patterns of thought which came out of the independence movements and mid-nineteenth century liberalism. Both from the literary standpoint and from the standpoint of history, Justo Sierra's

Political Evolution of the Mexican People is an outstanding representative of this positivist influence, which also found expression in university courses in national or American sociology, and in numerous quasi-historical works on these subjects.

TWENTIETH CENTURY TRENDS

Archives. Today, eighteen countries maintain national archives, many of them long-standing collections, rich in documents relating to the colonial and early independence periods. In some places, a tendency to make more recent records available may be observed, but in general the national archives house materials relating to the period prior to the middle of the nineteenth century. They are usually small institutions, inadequately housed. In this respect, the archives of Argentina, Brazil, the Dominican Republic, Ecuador and Cuba (with a new building) are exceptions. However housed, they are generally headed by scholars of national or even international reputation, and frequently issue good publications, either serials or separate volumes of documents, indexes, articles of general historical information, or a combination of these. Good documentary material is currently being published by the National Archives of Venezuela, Chile, Colombia, Mexico, Uruguay and Argentina.[1]

General Historical Libraries. Historical libraries developed more slowly. The best ones open to the general public were developed in Argentina. National and some state and provincial libraries in Mexico, Brazil, Colombia, Chile and elsewhere have come to house valuable historical materials. Some of the valuable collection in the National Library of Peru was lost in the fire which destroyed the library in 1943. Much of the material was salvaged, however, and international assistance, under the direction of Jorge Basadre, helped to rebuild this collection and to make it again a valuable center for historical studies. In many cases, still, the most valuable historical collections are the private property of scholars or men of wealth rather than public collections. The recent purchase by the National Library of Peru of the rich private library of former President Justo of Argentina may be indicative of a new trend to bring such collections into libraries open to historical scholars.

Inter-American Historical Activity. The growth of the Pan-American movement stimulated an increase of inter-American historical activity. The Pan-American Scientific Congresses and other international conferences provided opportunities for historians of the hemisphere to meet and share the results of their studies. As a result of the Sixth Inter-American Conference at Havana in 1928, for example, The Pan-American Institute of Geography and History was established (1930) with headquarters in Mexico City, supported by official contributions of the participating governments.

The Hispanic Tie. The tendency to renew cultural ties with the European mother countries became strong, especially in Spanish America, after the War of 1898. In historical studies, this influence was reflected in several ways,

---

[1] See Roscoe Hill, "Archives," in *Handbook of Latin American Studies,* 1943, and his *National Archives of Latin America,* recently translated into Spanish and published by the National Archives of Cuba.

but particularly in a movement to re-examine Spanish colonial history and the history of the colonial church. Carlos Pereyra of Central America published in Madrid, an eight-volume history of Spanish America, and the Spanish historian, Antonio Ballesteros y Beretta (1880-1949), enlisted the cooperation of a group of Latin American scholars in a similar enterprise which is still not complete.

Chief Interest in Early Nineteenth Century. The great increase of historical activity was concerned chiefly with independence and early aspects of national consolidation. There was little study of the history of the late nineteenth and early twentieth centuries. Reluctance of governments to permit use of recent archives and the lack of vigorous historical institutions engaged in the collection of materials relating to the more recent historical period tended to discourage careful studies of developments after 1900. In some countries historians did little significant work beyond 1850. Dictatorial political regimes sometimes frowned upon studies of recent developments as likely to have political implications. Slowness in developing the archival science which would make the documentary collections accessible to scholars was also a retarding factor. Some important work had been done in colonial history, as in the monumental *Mexico Across the Centuries* edited by Vicente Riva Paalcios in Mexico, but interests centered chiefly in early national history.

Biography. Some good biographies were written on personages from this recent period, but the best ones were of non-political figures. Most of the important political figures have, of course, received biographical treatment, but usually of a popular and superficial character. Prominent figures like Porfirio Díaz, Ruy Barbosa, Hipolito Irigoyen, José Balmaceda, Francisco Madero, and Venustiano Carranza, to mention only a few, still await fully documented study, even today.

NEW DIRECTIONS

Latin American historians today evidence great interest in the underlying social forces and processes which have conditioned national development, as well as in the history of ideas, of literature, and more recently of art and music. Interest in revaluation of the colonial period and in social and economic history is currently strong. This latter interest has roots in the long-standing preoccupation with national or American sociology. Some, but not much, reflects the penetration of the Marxist philosophy. Along this latter line may be noted a number of studies of revolutionary theory which have appeared in Argentina and elsewhere.

Marxist Interpretations. Although not a professional historian, Carlos Mariátegui, the intellectual father of Peruvian *Aprismo,* in his *Seven Essays of Interpretation of Peruvian Reality*[2] gave a quasi-Marxist interpretation to Peruvian history which continues to influence the thinking and writing of the *Aprista* political party. The work of Alfonso Teja Zabre in Mexico has given a similar interpretation to Mexican history, in line with concepts which found considerable currency in the Mexican Revolution. Both of these inter-

---

[2] *Siete ensayos de interpretación de la realidad peruana.*

pretations have highly indigenous characteristics, however, and few, if any, Latin American historians follow the straight Communist line in their writings.

Historical Synthesis. While the preoccupation of Latin American historians with the sociological aspects and bases of Latin American history is very marked, and frequently of a profound character, it has not yet resulted in the formation of an acceptable historical synthesis, either for the history of individual nations or for the history of the national period of Latin America as a whole. The Comtean-positivist interpretations, so prevalent in the sociology of the turn of the century, were never accepted by a majority of the historians, who retained more of the idealistic natural law concepts of the American and French revolutions. The philosophical assumptions of positivism moreover, are currently undergoing severe criticism, almost amounting to a general rejection, by Latin American intellectuals. Phenomenological, existential, personalistic and neo-Thomistic concepts tend to replace them. Especially interesting is the way in which voluntaristic Catholic social thought has tended to capture the optimism characteristic of earlier American thought. But historical studies, on the whole, seem less affected by these trends than the other social sciences, except in relation to the history of ideas, or as it is reflected in the discussion of the question: Is there a history of America?

Hemispheric History. The hemispheric approach to the writing of American history had found an able nineteenth century exponent in Diego Barros Arana of Chile. Professor Herbert Eugene Bolton of the University of California gave vigorous expression to the concept in his presidential address before the American Historical Association at Toronto in 1932. Bolton's influence was, of course, greatest in the United States, but it had some effect in Latin America. Ricardo Levene of Argentina enlisted scholars of the continent in a collaborative history of the Americas, and Argentine historians were active in urging the Commission on History of the Pan-American Institute of Geography and History to undertake its projected history of the Americas. During the early years of the twentieth century, courses on the history of the Americas had found their way into many Latin American universities.

In spite of the continued prevalence of intellectual and literary Pan-Hispanism, current interest in Argentine historical circles and in the Pan-American Institute of Geography and History would seem on the whole to show a livelier interest in the formulation of a synthesis for hemisperic history than for that of the Latin American family of nations. However, during the decade of the forties, the Center of Hispanic Studies in Buenos Aires and Estudios Centro-America in El Salvador stimulated historical re-examination of American ties with Spain, and these two opposing interests have given rise to a conflict of historical interpretations which will be noted later.

Ricardo Levene's fourteen-volume *History of America*[8] has been noted. The only comparable work is the monumental twenty-four-volume *History of America* projected by the Spanish historian, Antonio Ballesteros y Beretta and associates, mentioned above. José Luis Romero, known among other things for his excellent recent *History of Political Ideas in Argentina* (1946), has

---

[8] (Buenos Aires: Jackson, 1940).

prepared a brief collaborative *History of America*. In fact, the emphasis upon the study of the history of the Americas, which appeared in striking fashion in the meeting of the Commission on History of the Pan-American Institute of Geography and History in 1947, and continues in the program of its activities, may well be noted as an important trend among Latin American historians. In the University of Panama, the chair of history of the Americas was occupied from 1940 to 1948 by the Spanish refugee historian and well-known student of the life of Miranda, Juan María Aguilar y Calvo (died 1948). Another increasingly well-known exponent of the hemispheric synthesis is Professor Eugenio Pereira Salas of the National University of Chile. National history is still the main concern, however. Rarely do Latin American historians go outside the hemisphere for their areas of study.

Independence Movements. A number of questions relating to the period of independence are the subject of great historical interest and controversy. In 1940 what purported to be sensational development in the history of the independence movement occurred when Colombres Marmol published what he claimed was new documentary evidence of the interview of San Martín and Bolívar at Guayaquil. The National Academy of History of Caracas repudiated the claim, and most historians now accept the view that these documents were forged. Other questions concerning the history of independence which currently engage the attention of historians are the career of Santander, the assassination of Sucre, various aspects of the lives of Bolívar and San Martín, the May (1810) Revolution in Argentina, the history of the Bolivarian Congress at Panama in 1826, and the economic and social bases and results of independence.

The view of the independence movements as the work of an aristocratic ruling class in Spanish and Portuguese America and as essentially a civil conflict in its American aspects has gradually crystallized. But the role of the "inert" populations of Negro slaves and Indians challenges increased attention, especially in Mexico, Peru and Brazil.

Jaime Eyzaguirre of Chile rejects traditional views of colonial discontent and interprets the Chilean independence movement as the work of a small minority with few real grievances. He is the author of a biography of Bernardo O'Higgins, the principal Chilean liberator, and collaborates with Ricardo Donoso, Eugenio Pereira Salas and others in the publication of the *Archive of Don Bernardo O'Higgins*. His view of Chilean independence is substantiated in the main by Francisco Antonio Encina.[4]

Vicente Lacuna began publishing the *Letters of Bolivar* in 1929, and has continued publication of additional letters in the *Boletin* of the National Academy of History of Venezuela. Lecuna's motive appears to be one of interest in and admiration of the career of the great Liberator, and the various accompanying studies which this Venezuelan scholar has made are largely military in nature.

Pre-conquest and Indian History. The Mexican Revolution of 1910-20

---

[4]."Breve bosquejo de la literatura histórica chilena," *Historiografía chilena*, ed. Luis Durand and others, pp. 27-68.

TWENTIETH CENTURY TENDENCIES: LATIN AMERICA

brought a great increase of interest in the history of the Indian of Pre-Conquest America, which has been further stimulated by archaeological and anthropological studies in Mexico, Central America, and the Andean republics. The study of Indian history has assumed a prominent place in the Mexican schools, and there are indications that it will assume similar importance in Peru and Guatemala.

Interest in the social and economic history of the Indian during the national period and in the history of Indian uprisings, both colonial and national, in those countries where *Indianismo* becomes important[5] is another trend of importance.

Two Peruvians, Julio Tello (1880-1948) and Luis Valcarcel (1891-   ), have made outstanding studies of pre-Conquest Peru.[6] Luis Chavez Orozco of Mexico republished the out-of-print *Codice Osuna* with new documentation from the Mexican National Archives and studied democratic institutions in pre-Conquest Mexico.[7]

Colonial History. It is in studies of colonial history that the spirit of revisionism is most apparent and strikes deepest. Here, also, the institutional "school" is most evident. The extent of interest in colonial history is shown by the many new editions of chronicles of the Conquest which are appearing. Charmion Shelby listed one hundred nine, published mostly since 1937 (*Hispanic American Historical Review,* May, 1949). José María Ots Capdequí, outstanding Spanish historian of colonial political institutions, and former director of the Center of Historical Studies in Madrid, came to Colombia in 1939. Ramón Iglesia, who came to Mexico as a refugee, has stimulated students to study colonial historiography, while the example of Rafael Altamira has aroused increased interest in critical studies of the Laws of the Indies. Peruvian historians have made colonial studies of outstanding importance. Jorge Basadre's (b. 1903) scholarly study of seventeenth century Peru in his *El Conde de Lemos y su tiempo*[8] is perhaps the most important. But Manuel Belaúnde Guinassi has published an important study of the *enconomienda,* and Raúl Porras Barrenechea has made significant studies of the historiography of the conquest. In Chile, the excellent biography of Valdivia by Jaime Eyzaguirre is worthy of special note.[9]

Negro History. Studies of American Negro history increasingly occupy the attention of historians in Cuba, Haiti, Mexico, Peru, and most of all in Brazil.[10] In Mexico, G. Aguirre Beltrán has studied the Negro population, especially of the colonial period, showing that it was much larger than has

---

[5] For a good brief statement on *Indianismo* in English, see Bette Salz, "Indianismo," *Social Research* XI (November, 1944), pp. 44-69. Alejandro Lipschutz, in his *Indoamericanismo y raza india* and his *El indoamericanismo y el problema racial en las Américas* has given the most comprehensive and philosophical discussion of the subject. There is also a good discussion in the Introduction to Aída Cometta Manzoni, *El indio en la poesía de América española.* The important *Handbook of South American Indians,* published by the Smithsonian Institution, is fundamental to the subject. See also under various nations, *infra.*
[6] See especially, Valcarcel, *Historia de la cultura antigua del Perú.*
[7] *Codice Osuna;* "Las instituciones democràticas de los indigenas mexicanos en la epoca colonial," *América Indígena,* III (January, 1943), pp. 73-82, (April, 1943), pp. 161-171, (July, 1943), pp. 265-276, Ocłober, 1943), pp. 365-382.
[8] (Lima: Ed. Huascarán, 1945).
[9] *Ventura de Pedro de Valdivia.*
[10] See "The Negro in Continental America," *Hispanic American Historical Review,* XXIV (1944), pp. 547-559, for an excellent bibliography. Many of the works listed are by Latin Americans.

been hitherto believed. Francisco Romero, emphasizing the nineteenth century, has made similar studies for Peru. What is virtually a school of historians of the Negro in Brazil has grown up among the disciples of Arthur Ramos (died 1950). A foremost living Brazilian authority on the history of the Negro and the institution of slavery is Gilberto Freyre (b. 1900). Fernando Ortiz has made important studies of Negro influence in the social and cultural history of Cuba.

Other Aspects of Social and Economic History. Francisco Vetancourt Aristigueta has studied public finance in Venezuela from 1810 to 1821. Several Venezuelan scholars have made significant studies of colonial trade, and the National Archive has published a documentary guide to the important colonial Guipuzcoa Company. One of the most important collections of historical source materials to be published recently in Latin America is the *Sources for the History of Labor in New Spain,* edited by Silvio Zavala and María Castelo. Moisés Poblete Troncoso of Chile, known for his studies of social legislation, has written a brief pioneering summary of the labor movement in Latin America. Pedro Calmon (b. 1902) has published a three-volume social history of Brazil.[11] A renaissance of interest in church history is represented, among others, by Rubén Vargas Ugarte of Peru.

Art and Literature. It was natural that the development of the Mexican school of painting should produce an interest in the history of art in Mexico, because of the extent to which it drew on colonial and indigenous elements. Augustín Velásquez Chávez's *Tres siglos de pintura colonial mexicana* is a work of beauty and distinction. In Colombia, another land of Indian background, Gabriel Giraldo Jaramillo has written a good history of the national painting, while in Peru Emilio Harth Terre has made a carefully documented study of indigenous contributions to Peruvian sculpture and painting.

National histories of literature are abundant, and examples could be cited freely from practically every nation. A new note has been struck, however, by Angel F. Rojas, himself an Ecuadorian novelist, in his work on the novel in Ecuador,[12] in which literature is used to interpret national social history. Pedro Henríquez Ureña, distinguished man of letters of the Dominican Republic, has written a history of Latin American literature which is in reality a critical analysis of the development of Latin American culture.[13]

History of Ideas. Closely connected with the great interest in historical interpretation, which will be discussed in the next section, is a growing interest in the history of ideas. Some of the scholars doing significant work in this field will, therefore, be mentioned later. There is a notable group in Mexico, including Edmundo O'Gorman, José Gaos, and particularly Leopoldo Zea, whose *History of Positivism in Mexico*[14] was an important and provocative contribution. *A History of Political Ideas in Chile* by Ricardo Denoso and a *History of Political Ideas in Argentina* by José Luis Romero, both recent

---

[11] *Historia social do Brasil,* 3 vols.
[12] *La novela ecuatoriana.*
[13] Lectures given at Harvard University, 1940-41, and published originally in English as *History of Culture in Hispanic America.* Subsequently (1949) published in Spanish by the Fondo de Cultura Económica in Mexico.
[14] (México: El Colegio de México, 1943).

publications of the Fondo de Cultura Económica, are important even though semi-popular works. Interest in this field is also especially keen in Argentina, where it embraces an interest in the history of science. There it is also closely connected with a keen debate over philosophy in general.

HISTORICAL INTERPRETATION AND HISTORIOGRAPHY

Argument over the Meaning and Nature of History. Many nineteenth century Latin American historians, such as Diego Barros Arana of Chile, as we have seen, came to accept the principal tenets of the von Ranke school. But for the most part, Latin American scholarship retained an addiction to historical interpretation, "philosophical" history, and to the pursuit of the "meaning" of history. Yet, in spite of this predilection for the philosophical, Latin American historians have accepted far less completely than the sociologists the contemporary prevailing neo-Hegelian and neo-Thomistic idealistic patterns of thought, although these latter influences are currently growing in historical studies.

It would be premature to attempt to assess at this time the extent to which these tendencies will go, but a few tentative observations may be ventured. The new trend is away from the determinism and evolutionism ("positivism" to Latin American critics) which increasingly characterized historical thought around the beginning of this century. There is a notable tendency to search for the meaning of national history in colonial and pre-Conquest history, historical science joining hands with cultural anthropology for the latter. In Mexico, for example, a School of Anthropology and History is maintained by the national government. Interest is growing in religious history, especially as related to Spanish missionary activity, while revolt against materialistic history and history inspired by what some Latin Americans refer to critically as English psychological philosophy seems to be connected with the growing emphasis upon a history of the "spirit" and upon intellectual history.

The study of American or national sociology which became so striking an aspect of Latin American intellectual life and higher education, although not accepted as history by many historians, was, nevertheless, an important work of historical interpretation. Unfortunately, its positivist patterns of thought tended frequently to identify it with the defense of such enlightened dictatorial regimes as that of Porfirio Díaz of Mexico, where it was represented by the party of the *científicos*. Sometimes it was gradually assimilated into one or another of the Marxist revisionisms. As a result, "positivist" sociology and any historical writing connected with it, is in quite general disrepute in Latin America today.[15]

Yet one of the strongest lines of contemporary historical interest is in the broadest sense sociological. This is the interest in institutional history, an interest derived from Spanish historical scholarship and stimulated in no small degree by the influx of Spanish refugee historians. Rafael Altamira, José

---

[15] For a thorough critical discussion of this subject by a "non-positivist" see Alfredo Poviña, *História de la sociología en Latinoamérica.*

María Ots Capdequí and Ramón Iglesia have been outstanding influences in this direction. These institutional studies have usually had a juridical basis and have been directed especially toward the study of colonial institutions. Quite significantly, they have laid great stress on the ideas represented in institutions.

A lively argument goes on as to the nature and directions of history in general and of the history of Spanish America in particular, as well as concerning the nature of historical thinking, historical method, and the uses and purposes of historical study. The importance attached to the subject is indicated by the prominence given it in two quite dissimilar international conferences in 1949: The National Conference on Philosophy held in Mendoza, Argentina, in April, where the philosophy of history and the teaching of history were major subjects of discussion, and the Conference of United States and Mexican Historians in Monterrey, Mexico, in September.

Nelson Werneck Sodré, in his *Orientations of Brazilian Thought*,[16] traces the intellectual history of Brazil along lines of continued development and evolution which would probably be termed "positivist" in Spanish America. Alfredo Poviña's anti-positivist *History of Sociology in Latin America*, one of the most important works of this genre, has already been mentioned. In Argentina, Enrique de Gandia has written of history as art, and has attracted attention with an enthusiastic book on the "new history," by which he means essentially more attention to the history of ideas.[17]

Jorge Basadre (b. 1903) has speculated on the meaning of Peruvian history in his *Meditations on the Historic Destiny of Peru*,[18] and in his *The Multitude, the City, and the Country* in the *History of Peru*.[19] Luis Alberto Sánchez (b. 1903), also Peruvian, in his numerous writings presents an interpretation difficult to classify. Characteristically optimitsic, it combines the sense of an American spirit derived from experiences on American soil with elements of Marxian socialism, with overtones of rationalism, free-thinking and liberalism reminiscent of the great Peruvian writer, Manuel Gonzalez Prada (1848-1918).

Mario Briceno-Irragorry speaks of "the duty of bringing the world of history to life with immediate objectives of social understanding, not in its [history's] mere sense of a cultural discipline, but in its profound and permanent value of facts which speak in the continuing existence of society. To interpret the present, that is to say, the visible life of the people, we must know the reactions which occurred in the epoch which time veils from us."[20]

The Argument in Mexico. But it is in Mexico that the greatest argument over the nature and meaning of history, especially of American history, centers. Antonio Caso, in his *Concept of Universal History and the Philosophy of Values* (1933) and in his *Philosophy of Culture and Historical Materialism*

---

[16] *Orientações do pensamento brasileiro.*
[17] *La historia como arte* and *Introducción al estudio del conocimiento histórico.*
[18] *Meditaciones sobre el destino histórico del Peru.*
[19] *La multitud, la ciudad y el campo en la historia del Peru,* (2d. ed.)
[20] "Apuntes sobre los estudios históricos en Venezuela." *Revista de Historia de América,* Num. 24 (December, 1947), pp. 303-312.

(1936) appeared as the leading Mexican opponent of Marxian historical interpretation. Alfonso Teja Zabre's recent *Dynamic of History and the Inter-american Frontier* (1947), on the other hand, searches for the theory of dynamics in history. Although less rigid than some of his previous works, it is still fundamentally Marxist. José Vasconcelos's (b. 1882) *Short History of Mexico* attracted more attention for its application of some of his historical concepts than for its comments on the events of national history.[21] Vasconcelos's search for absolutes and universals and his effort to recapture the sense of the spiritual value of the individual, while fundamentally esthetic in approach, are founded to a large degree upon concepts of new values arising from the conflicts and adjustments of cultures in the New World. His writing, full of contradictions and paradoxes though it is, has been one of the most stimulating influences upon the contemporary mind of Latin America.

Edmundo O'Gorman gives a philosophical interpretation of the problem, in his *Crisis and Future of Historical Science,* from a point-of-view which seems to be generally non-Hegelian.[22] O'Gorman shares the historical views of Heiddiger and Ortega y Gasset, searching for a history of the being, or spirit. The whole structure of ideas upon which historical study has rested, as well as the concept of an American history, to which O'Gorman addressed himself in an earlier work, *Fundamentals of the History of America,*[23] is involved in this argument.

Mexican interest along these lines, as noted, has been inspired by the Spanish refugee scholars, including the late Ramón Iglesia and Leopoldo Zea, as well as O'Gorman and José Gaos. All of them reflect something of the recent lively interest in the philosophy of history and often something of Ortega y Gasset's concept of intellectual history. Rafael Altamira contributed to this Mexican interest in the philosophy of history by a series of lectures at the Colegio de México, later published as *The Historic Process of Human Historiography.* Altamira insisted on the dominance of the political factor in history which embraces the integrated story of all man's past endeavor.

---

[21] *Breve historia de Mexico.*
[22] *Crisis y porvenir de la ciencia historica.*
[23] *Fundamentos de la historia de America.*

Bibliography

A

Akiyama, Kenzo, "Orientation in the Study of Japanese History," *A Guide to Japanese Studies,* compiled by Kokusai Bunka Shinki Kai (Tokyo Kokusai Bunka Shinko Kai, 1937, pp. 1-54. An introduction to modern Japanese historiography and standard works, for Western students.

———————, *Studies in the History of Sino-Japanese Relations Nisshi Kosho-shi Kenkyu,* (Tokyo, Iwanami Shoten, 1939). Useful for Japanese historiography in the feudal period.

Alexander, Fred, *Moving Frontiers* (Victoria: Melbourne University Press, 1947). In this work, Professor Alexander of the University of West Australia attempted to determine how far Turner's frontier theory was relevant to Australian development.

Anderson, E. N., "Meinecke's Ideengeschichte and the Crisis in Historical Thinking," in Cate, J. L. and Anderson, E. N., Eds., *Medieval and Historiographical Essays in Honor of James Westfall Thompson* (Chicago: University of Chicago Press, 1938). An important chapter on Meinecke by an American scholar quite conversant with German historiography.

Armstrong, E., "Pasquale Villari," *English Historical Review,* Vol. XXXIII (1918), pp. 197-209. A good summary.

Ausubel, Herman, Brebner, J. B., and Hunt, E. M., (editors), *Some Modern Historians of Britain* (New York: Dryden Press 1951). Useful essays on Tawney, Namier, Power and Holdsworth.

Abbott, W. C., "Macaulay and the New History," *Yale Review,* XVIII (March, 1929), pp. 539-557. A brilliant summary of the greatness of Macaulay even in the glare of the New History.

Anonymous, "Michelet as an Historian," *Quarterly Review,* Vol. 193 (London, 1901), pp. 130-150. A description and analysis of all aspects of Michelet as an historian, based on his writings. A mine of valuable information critically assessed.

A travers les Ameriques Latines. With an introduction by Lucien Fevre. Cahiers des Annales, No. 4 (Paris: Armand Colin, 1949). The most important recent French survey of the field by a group of French and Latin American historians.

The Americas. A quarterly review, published by Academy of American Franciscan History, Bethesda, Maryland, is useful for critical reviews of recent publications.

B

Balzani, Ugo, *Early Chroniclers of Europe: Italy* (London: E. & J. B. Young, 1883). Rather cursory.

Barbagallo, Corrado, "The Conditions and Tendencies of Historical Writings in Italy Today," *Journal of Modern History,* I (June, 1929), pp. 236-244. An extremely helpful brief study.

Barnes, Harry Elmer, *A History of Historical Writing* (Norman, Oklahoma: University of Oklahoma Press, 1937). "At times the book degenerates into a catalogue of names" said Carl Becker in "What is Historiography?", *American Historical Review* (A.H.R.) SSIV (October, 1938), pp. 20-28. This is true of pp. 255-256, 258 which treat the Low and Scandinavian countries.

———————, "History, Its Rise and Development," *Encyclopedia Americana* (New York: Encyclopedia Americana, 1942) XIV, pp. 205-264. A full and concise history of historiography, especially good on trends in the philosophy of history. Good bibliography appended.

—————————, *The New History and the Social Studies* (New York: The Century Company, 1925). An execellent attempt to relate history to the other social sciences along the lines of Robinson's New History theory.

Beard, Charles Austin, *The Rise of American Civilization* (New York: Macmillan Company, 1930). A brief, but searching, section is included on recent trends in American historiography.

Behar, D. y R., *Bibliografia hispanoamericana: historia y bellas artes* (New York: Macmillan Company, 1937) I, pp. 301-320. Still a fundamental guide.

Beers, Henry A., *A History of English Romanticism in the Eighteenth Century* (New York: Henry Holt, 1916). A useful survey of the literary origins and chief aspects of early English romanticism, with special stress on the revival of medieval songs and poetry.

Bellorini, Egido, *Discussioni e Polemiche sul Romanticismo* (Bari: Gius-Laterza & Figli, 1943). A symposium of articles by a variety of Italian critics on the literary aspects of the movements.

Benz, Richard E., *Die deutsche Romantik* (Leipzig: Philipp Reclam, 1937). A circumstantial account of the German movement as a whole, with large sections devoted to its religious implications and its eventual decay.

Beck, Thor J., *Northern Antiquities in French Learning and Literature (1755-1855)* (New York: Institute of French Studies, 1934-1935). Shows French tendencies, especially in Montesquieu, towards belief in Nordic origins of freedom.

Becker, Carl L., *The Heavenly City of the Eighteenth Century Philosophers* (New Haven: Yale University Press, 1932). Chapter 4, "The New History" is indispensable. His chief thesis in this chapter does not sufficiently allow, however, for the indifference of Hume, Gibbon, and Montesquieu to social reform.

Belloni, Georges, *Aulard, Historian de la Revolution Francaise* (Paris: Presses Universitaires de France, 1949). By a former student of Aulard's. Part I on Aulard's training, work and influence as a historian is especially recommended.)

Below, G. A. H., *German Historiography from the Wars of Liberation to the Present* (Berlin: Oldenbourg, 1924). A keen but biased estimation of German contributions to history in the nineteenth century.

Below, Georg Anton Hugo von, *Die deutsche Geschichtschreibung von dem Befreiungskriegen bis zu unseren Tagen* (Munches und Berlin: Oldenbourg, 1924), Maintains conservatism with Romanticism as a base is the only guide for the historian.

Bernard, L. L., "Latin America," *Encyclopedia of the Social Sciences* (New York: Macmillan Company, 1937), I, pp. 301-320. Still a fundamental guide.

Beza, Marcu, "The Rounanian Chroniclers," *The Slavonic Review*, IX (June, 1930), pp. 124-132.

Black, J. B., *The Art of History: A Study of Four Great Historians of the Eighteenth Century* (New York: Crofts, 1926). The best volume on the subject in English. Includes essays on Voltaire, Hume, Gibbon, and Robertson.

Blankennagel, J. C., Havens, G. R., Fairchild, H. N., McKenzie, K., and Farr, F. C., and Mitchie, E., "Romanticism: A Symposium," *Proceedings of the Modern Language Association* (March, 1940), pp. 1-60. An excellent series of articles on literary romanticism in the major countries of Europe during the period of the Romantic Movement. As a synthesis of such knowledge at that date they are indispensable to the student of the period.

Black, C. E., *The Establishment of Constitutional Government in Bulgaria* (Princeton: University Press, 1943). Contains, besides a bibliographical essay, excellent background material of political and social forces in Bulgaria.

Binkley, William C., "Two World Wars and American Historical Scholarship," *Mississippi Valley Historical Review*, XXXIII (June, 1946), pp. 3-26. An excellent survey of the effect of war on American historiography, with additional information about the inter-war period.

Bourgin, Georges, "Histoire Contemporaine d'Italie," (Contemporary History of Italy), *Review Historique,* CLXXV (January-June, 1935), pp. 316-317. A detailed summary of Italian historical writing of recent years, all dealing with the nineteenth century.

Bourne, Henry E., "A Decade of Studies in the French Revolution," *Journal of Modern History,* Vol. 1 (1929), pp. 256-279. A good bibliographical article containing works of French historians.

Brailsford, H. N., *Voltaire* (London: Home University Library, 1935). Excellent chapter on the "Liberal History" of Voltaire. His view that Voltaire had a doctrine of historical continuity is questionable.

Brandes, Georg, *Main Currents in Nineteenth Century Literature* (London: Macmillan Company, 1904). Volumes V and VI, on the romanticist movement in France and Germany provide a good orientation on the continental aspects of the movement.

Brebner, J. B., "Elie Halevy," in Herman Ausubel, Brebner and Hunt (eds.), *Some Modern Historians of Britain* (New York: Dryden Press, 1951), pp. 235-254. A first rate essay.

Brehier, Louis, "Constantine Sathos," *Revue historique,* CXVI (May-Aug., 1914).

Briceno, Iragorry, Mario, "Apuntes sobre los estudios historicos en Venezuela," *Revista de historia de America,* No. 24 (Diciembre, 1947), pp. 303-312. A keen analysis and survey of Venezuelan trends.

Brinton, Clarence Crane, *The Political Ideas of the English Romanticists* (London: Oxford University Press, 1926). An excellent appraisal of the political concepts of Coleridge, Southey, Scott, Byron, Keats and Wordsworth by an outstanding American authority on the era of the French Revolution.

Butterfield, H., *The Englishman and His History* (Cambridge: Cambridge University Press, 1944). pp. 31-82. Interesting reflections on the Whig Interpretation of History.

Bush, Douglas, "History and Biography," Chapter VII, pp. 209-231, in *English Literature in the Earlier Seventeenth Century, 1600-1660* (New York: Clarendon Press, 1945). Chapter V which deals with character writing is valuable for understanding Clarendon's approach to history.

Bryson, Gladys, *Man and Society: The Scottish Inquiry of the Eighteenth Century* (Princeton: Princeton University Press, 1945). Useful for comments on the "conjectural history" used by Dugald Stewart, Adam Ferguson, and Hume. This is the doctrine that when facts are lacking, the history can be imaginatively reconstructed according to the author's view of what is normal and reasonable to expect.

Bryce, James B., *Studies in Contemporary Biography* (London: Macmillan Company, 1903). Sections on Green, Freeman and Acton are recommended.

C

Cambridge Medieval History: IV. *The Eastern Roman Empire* (New York: Macmillan Company, 1927); V. *Contest of Empire and Papacy:* VI. *Victory of the Papacy* (New York: Macmillan Company, 1929). Bibliographies for each chapter include lists of sources without comment.

Campbell, Lily B., *Shakespeare's Histories: Mirrors of Elizabethan Policy* (San Marino: Huntington Library, 1947). This interpretation of Shakespeare's progmatic purpose links his work with the historical writing of the sixteenth century.

Campbell, John C., "Makkai, Ladislas, Histoire de Transylvanie," *Journal of Central European Affairs,* VIII (April, 1948), pp. 99-101. A book review pointing out the difficult task of the Central European historian in observing objectivity when writing about topics which involve rival nations.

——————, "Nicholas Jorga," *The Slavonic Review,* XXVI, No. 66 (November, 1947), pp. 44-59.

Cahen, Gaston, "Bulgarie," in *Histoire et historiens depuis cinquante ans* (Paris: Felix Alcan, 1927), pp. 72-85.

Carson, George Barr, "Changing Perspective in Soviet Historiography," *South Atlantic Quarterly,* Vol. XLVII, pp. 186-195. Concerned largely with events of the nine-teen-thirties.

Caughey, John W., "The Mosaic of Western History," *Mississippi Valley Historical Review,* XXXIII (March, 1947), pp. 595-606. An evaluation, tabular and other-wise, of the attention being paid by scholars to certain phases of frontier history. Interesting and significant.

Carbia, Romulo D., *Historia critica de la historiografia argentina* (La Plata, Buenos Aires: Imprenta Lopez, 1939), and *Historia de la historografia argentina* (La Plata, Buenos Aires: Casa Edit. Coni, 1925). Works of importance for Argentine trends.

Chambers, R. W., *Thomas More* (London: Jonathan Cape, 1935). A modern biograph-ical classic, which gives an excellent account of the ferment of English humanism.

Cecil, Algernon, *Six Oxford Thinkers* (London: John Murray, 1909). Has a good essay on Froude—his work as a historian and his critics.

Chase, Eugene Parker, "Recent English Political Biographies," in *Journal of Modern History,* III (1931), pp. 614-626. Valuable as a survey of a genre which has been less prominent in the last fifteen years.

Chiu, A. K., "Chinese Historical documents of the Ch'ing dynasty, 1644-1911," *Pacific Historical Review,* II (September, 1932), pp. 324-336. A brief discussion of the important available documents for study of this period.

Clark, G. N., "Classical and Historical Studies," Chapter XVI, pp. 270-287, in *The Seventeenth Century* (New York: Claredon Press, 1929). A comparative survey of seventeenth century historical and classical studies. Rather lacking in illustrative detail on historical writing.

Collingswood, R. G., *The Idea of History* (Oxford, England: Claredon Press, 1946). The medieval section is weak, but the general views are suggestive.

Cohen, Morris R., *The Meaning of Human History* (LaSalle, Ill.: Open Court Pub-lishing Co., 1947). Contains a useful discussion of weaknesses in "The Liberal Interpretation of History "

Coulton, G. G., *Four Score Years* (New York: Macmillan Co., 1944). A surprisingly restrained and interesting autobiography of a controversial English medievalist. Contains some reflections on the functions of the historian.

Coleman, Marion M., "Problems of Polish Historiography," *Bulletin of the Polish Institute of Arts and Sciences in America,* II (January, 1944). Paper presented at conference on historiographic problems of eastern and central Europe in Polish Institute.

Corovic, Vi., "Histoire Yougoslave," *Review Historique,* CLV (May, 1927), pp. 112-162.

Correa, Filho, Virgilio, "Desenvolvimento dos estudos historicos no Brasil," *Revista de historia de America,* no. 27 (junio, 1949), pp. 45-58. A brief, useful, survey of trends in Brazil.

Croce, B., *History: Its Theory and Practice* (New York: Harcourt, Brace, & Company, 1921). Presents an interesting viewpoint.

—————, "The Historiography of the Renaissance," Chapter IV, Part II, pp. 224-242, in *History: Its Theory and Practice* (New York: Harcourt, Brace & Company, 1921). More valuable for generalizations than for discussion of in-dividual historians.

Curtis, Morris R., *The Meaning of Human History* (La Salle, Ill.: Open Court Pub-lishing Co., 1947). Contains a useful discussion of weaknesses in "The Liberal Interpretation of History."

—————, "Gibbon's Paradise Lost" in *The Age of Johnson: Essays Presented to Chauncey Brewster Tinker* (New Haven: Yale University Press, 1949). Search-ing analysis of what Gibbon was trying to say.

Creighton, Louise, *Life and Letters of Mandell Creighton* (London and New York: Longmans, Green, 1904). 2 vols. Volume I for Creighton's work as a historian; volume II, pp. 517-522 for his writings.

D

Dawson, D., *The Making of Europe* (London: Sheed & War, 1939). Brilliant interpretation of the period.

David, Jean, "Voltaire et les Indians d'Amerique," *Modern Language Quarterly,* IX (March, 1948), pp. 90-103. Analysis of the *Essai sur les Moeurs* showing Voltaire looking for the favorable in the aborigines.

Davis, H. W. C., *The Political Thought of Heinrich von Treitschke* (New York: Scribner's & Sons, 1915). A very comprehensive and minute account of Treitschke's political philosophy. See also the valuable essay "Treitschke" in Hans Kohn, *Prophets and Peoples* (New York: Macmillan Co., 1946), pp. 105-130.

Davis, John H., "Sir Richard Lodge, 1855-1936," Chapter XII, pp. 256-278, in *Some Historians of Modern Europe,* ed. Bernadotte Schmitt (Chicago: University of Chicago Press, 1942). Temperley's many-sided activities and interest are adequately described in this essay.

Douglas, David C., *English Scholars* (London: Jonathan Cape, 1939). A delightful book on English medievalists of the late seventeenth and early eighteenth century, written by a distinguished medievalist.

Droysen, J. G., *Outline of the Principles of History* (Boston: Ginn & Co., 1893). A scientific analysis of historical studies deprecating the value of determinism and objectivity and emphasizing the value of interpretative history.

Dutcher, George M., *et al.* (eds.), *A Guide to Historical Literature* (New York: Macmillan Company, 1936). One of the best of the newer bibliographies of American and other history. Comments by experts on series and individual volumes. Highly selective, but authoritative.

Dunham, Arthur L., "The Economic History of France, 1815-1870," *Journal of Modern History,* vol. XXI, no. 2 (June, 1949), pp. 121-139. A critical bibliographical article listing not only works published in the field but also bibliographies and leading journals.

E

Encyclopedia Britannica, Ninth and Eleventh Editions. Lists of Historians will be found under such headings as Norway, Norwegian Literature.

Engel-Janosi, Friedrich, "Politics and History in the Age of the Enlightenment," *The Journal of Politics,* V (Nov., 1943), pp. 363-380. Thorough coverage both of continental and English phases. One of the few discussions which has used Meinecke carefully.

————————, *Soziale Probleme Der Renaissance* (Stuttgart, 1924); a noteworthy study by the historian before his exile to the United States.

————————, *The Growth of German Historicism* (Baltimore: John Hopkins Press, 1944). Has good chapters on Herder, Hegel, Ranke and Marx. Chapter V discusses German romanticist historiography.

Ergang, Robert R., "Möser and the Rise of National Thought in German," *Journal of Modern History,* V (March, 1933), pp. 172-97. Discusses Möser as an outstanding German opponent of classicism. The author especially stresses Moser's interest in the lower classes, in folkways and folklore, attitudes which are believed to distinguish him as a German nationalist.

F

Farrar, C. P., and Evans, A. P., *Bibliography of English Translations from Medieval Sources* (New York: Columbia University Press, 1946). Records of Civilization, XXXIX. Unique and Valuable.

Farmer, Paul, *France Reviews Its Revolutionary Origins. Some Politics and Historical Opinions in the Third Republic* (New York: Columbia University Press, 1944). Particularly good on significance of the French Revolution and for accounts of Taine and Tocqueville.

Ferguson, W. K., *The Renaissance in Historical Thought* (New York: Houghton Mifflin, 1948), pp. 46-58. Brief but useful notices of Melanchthon, Flacius Illyricus, Burnet, Foxe, Beza and of the contribution of the Reformation to the conception of the Renaissance.

Firth, C. H., "Burnet as an Historian," Chapter VI, pp. 174-209 in *Essays Historical and Literary* (Oxford: Clarendon Press, 1938). An estimate which deals with Burnet as historian both of the Reformation and of his own time.

————————, "Edward Hyde, Earl of Clarendon," Chapter IV, pp. 103-128, in *Essays, Historical and Literary* (New York: Clarendon Press, 1938). An extremely competent job. The author dealt with the same subject more technically in three articles in the *English Historical Review* (1904).

Fleischhacker, Hedwig, *Die Staats- und Voelkerrechtelichen Grundlagen Der Moskauischen Aussenpolitik (14.-17. Jahrundert)*, (Breslau, 1938); *Beiheft 1* of *Jahrbuecher Fuer Geschichte Osteuropas*. An interesting analysis by this Slavic scholar who with her husband, Hans Uebersberger, taught at the University of Berlin.

Flint, Robert, *Historical Philosophy in France and French Belgium and Switzerland* (New York: Scribner's Sons, 1894). Among Turgot, Montesquieu, and Voltaire his preference is for Turgot. Still worth using.

Fairbank, J. K. and Teng, S. Y., "On the types and uses of Ch'ing documents," *Harvard Journal of Asiatic Studies,* V. 1 (January, 1940), pp. 1-71. A discussion of the various official documents required and compiled by the government and its officials, with an annotated bibliography of the more important published compilations.

————————, "On the Transmission of Ch'ing Documents," *Harvard Journal of Asiatic Studies,* IV, 1 (January, 1939), pp. 12-46. Discussion of the means and facilities for transmission of documents during the Ch'ing period.

Friedell, Egon, "Truth in History," The Living Age, CCCXXXVIII (August, 1930), pp. 674-82. A severe criticism of the methodology of Ranke and the attitude of the Positivists. The author admits the difficulty of accurately reproducing the past. He argues that history cannot divest itself of a certain poetic quality and that it is the function of the historian to give history a meaning. He sees in every intelligible account of the past a continuity of causes and claims that without this concept of continuity there can be no history.

Fowler, W. W., *Roman Essays and Interpretations* (Oxford: Clarendon Press, 1920). Contains an enlightening essay on Mommsen's life and work.

Forst de Battaglia, Otto, "Polish Post-War Historiography," *Eastern Review,* I (October-December, 1948), pp. 22-43. A survey of the nature, schools and merits of Polish historiography from May, 1945 to the Autumn of 1948. Mainly concerned with writers within Poland, little mention of the historians in exile.

Fueter, E., *History of Modern Historiography* in German (Munich, 1936); in French (Paris, 1914). The page references are to the 1911 (German) edition; pp. 186-189; 201-204; 246-291; and 312-316. Fueter judges past historical works by modern critical standards, and is often harshly unable to understand religious figures.

————————, *Geschichte der Neueren Historiographia* (Munchen und Berlin: Oldenbourg, 1911). Best survey in any language. Not superseded by Meinecke for the eighteenth century.

Fulnes, Oscar J., *National Romanticism in Norway* (New York: Columbia University Press, 1933). Has several especially valuable chapters on old Norwegian folklore and a good account of leading national historians.

G

Gambrill, J. Montgomery, "Cultural History," *The Study and Teaching of American History, op. cit.,* pp. 156-172. An examination of the growing emphasis on cultural history, with especial relation to American historiography.

Gautier, G., "Histoire de Russe: Publications des annees 1917-1927," *Revue Historique,* CLVII (Paris, 1928). Essentially bibliographical.

Giraud, Jean, L'ecole Romantique in Norway (New York: Columbia University Press, 1933). A short sketch of the origin of French romanticism, essays on the outstanding French representatives of that school and a chapter on the influence of French romanticism on religion, history, etc.

Godfrey, Eleanor Smith, "Sir Charles Firth, 1857-1939," Chapter XXII, pp. 495-518, in *Some Historians of Modern Europe,* ed. Bernardotte Schmitt (University of Chicago Press, 1942). Useful survey of a highly competent scholar of the seventeenth century.

Gooch, G. P., "Burnet and the Stuart Kings," and "Burnet and William III," Chapters V-VI, pp. 70-101, in *Courts and Cabinets* (New York: A. A. Knopf, 1946). A good appreciation of Burnet as the historian of his time.

——————, "Saint-Simon and Louis XIV," and "Saint-Simon and the Regency," Chapters VII-VIII, pp. 102-126, in *Courts and Cabinets* (New York: A. A. Knopf, 1946). An excellent estimate of the famous memorialist.

——————, *History and Historians in the Nineteenth Century,* 4th impression (New York: Longmans Green, 1928). A standard comprehensive textbook on the nineteenth century which is dated in interpretation and style and largely superseded by Thompson.

——————, *Studies in German History* (New York: Longmans Green, 1948). This work contains an important new essay, pp. 210-266, on Ranke's writing and interpretation of German history including an analysis of his works and his place in German history as distinguished from his international accomplishments. It is a fine addition to Ranke bibliography.

Grant, A. J., (ed.), *English Historians* (London: Blackie, 1906). Has selections from historians illustrating methods.

Guilday, P., editor, *Church Historians* (New York: Kennedy & Sons, 1926). Highly illuminating and critical account of the lives and contributions of Hergenroether, Janssen, Denifle, and Pastor.

Guilland, Antoine, "German Historical Problems, 1914-1920," *American Historical Review,* XXV (July, 1920), pp. 640-659. Vital problems in German historical thinking by a Swiss observer of Germany.

Guilland, A., *Modern Germany and Her Historians* (London: Jarrold and Sons, 1915). Very critical but clear and stimulating discussion of the eminent nationalistic historians.

H

Halecki, Oskar, "What is Realism in Polish History?," *Journal of Central European Affairs,* III (October, 1943), pp. 322-328. Author defends the work and interpretations of Polish historians in refutation of article by William J. Rose.

——————, "Problems of Polish Historiography," *The Slavonic and East European Review,* American Series, XXI (March, 1943), pp. 223-239. Brief but excellent survey of the accomplishments of Polish historians in the past century. Written mainly to offset Russian-German historiographical disparagement of things Polish.

Handbook of Latin American Studies (Cambridge: Harvard University Press, 1935). Annual volumes, the best general guide to recent literature in the field, with several sections on history in each volume.

Handelsman, Marcel, "Les etudes d'histoire polonaise et les tendances actuelles de la pensee historique en Pologne," *Revue de synthese historique,* XXXIX (1925).

Handelsman, Marcel, "La methodologie de l'histoire dans la science polonaise," *Revue de synthese historique,* XXXIV (1922). Both articles present an analysis of Polish studies and tendencies in the late nineteenth and early twentieth century. Good for the period up to the beginnings of historiography in independent Poland.

——————, "Pologne," Chapter in *Histoire et historiens depuis cinquante ans. Methodes, organisation et resultats du travail historique de 1876 a 1926* (Paris, 1927). A brief survey of Polish historiography in partitioned and independent periods. Considers work done by universities and learned societies and the methods employed in treating domestic and universal history.

Harrold, C. F., *Carlyle and German Thought* (New Haven: Yale University Press, 1934). This volume is an exhaustive analysis of the influence of German thought on Carlyle. It is especially valuable to students of Carlyle.

Haskins, Charles H., *The Renaissance of the Twelfth Century* (Cambridge: Harvard University Press, 1927), especially chapter on "Historical Writing." Brilliant description of historiography of the period with good bibliographical notes at end of each chapter.

Hazard, Paul, *La Pensee Europeene au XVIII eme Siecle* (Paris: Boivin & Cie, 1946). Important for general orientation in the century but has nothing original on the historiography.

Heaton, Herbert, "The Progress of Historical Studies in Australia," *Journal of Modern History,* XV (1943), pp. 303-310. A first rate account of the history of advanced studies and research in Australia.

——————, "Recent Developments in Economic History," *American Historical Review,* XLVII (1942), pp. 727-746. Although not restricted to English historians, this article is valuable, especially on Clapham.

Historical Scholarship in America: Needs and Opportunities, (New York: American Historical Association, 1932). This is the classical survey of the status of American historiography in the early 1930's. Committees labored many weeks to produce the thorough study incorporated here, headed by the Committee on the Planning of Research, chaired by Arthur M. Schlesinger.

"History and Historiography," *Encyclopedia of the Social Sciences,* 15 vols., (New York: Encyclopaedia of the Social Sciences, 1930-35), VII. Various authorities have contributed to this series of articles; the one on American historiography is capably done by Allan Nevins, pp. 385-389.

Hook, Sidney, "The Contemporary Significance of Hegel's Philosophy," *Philosophical Review,* XLI (May, 1932), pp. 237-260. An excellent re-evaluation of Hegel's thought and influence on the centenary of his death.

Huch, Ricarda Octavia, *Blutezeit der Romantik* (Leipzig: H. Haessel, 1913). A standard history of the rise, flowering and decay of German romanticism, with special reference to its impact on religion, politics, folklore and philosophy.

Hummel, A. W., *The autobiography of a Chinese historian,* translation of the preface to Ku Chieh-kang's *Symposium on ancient Chinese history* (1927-46, 7 vols.). An annotated translation, including an excellent preface on the development of modern Chinese historiography.

Hovde, Bryn J., *The Scandinavian Countries,* 1720-1865 (Ithaca: Cornell University Press, 1948), vol. II, pp. 444, 457, 462-466, is enlightening on historiography in Denmark, Sweden, and Norway up to 1865.

Hyslop, Beatrice, "Historical Publications since 1939 on the French Revolution," *Journal of Modern History,* vol. XX (1948), pp. 232-250. The best bibliographical article on the subject.

——————, "Recent Works on the French Revolution," *American Historical Review,* vol. XLVII (1942), pp. 488-515. First-rate survey.

J

Jaszi, Oscar, "Horvath, Mihaly," *Encyclopedia of Social Sciences,* VII, p. 461. That Horvath is regarded as "the founder of Hungarian history" seems to exaggerate his role. Perhaps he is rather, as Prof. Jaszi himself states, the "representative in historiography of Hungarian liberalism and democracy."

Joachimsen, P., *Historical Interpretation and Historical Writing in Germany Under the Influence of Humanism in German* (Leipzig, 1910). Indispensable in the study of German humanism.

Joesten, Joachim, ed., *German Book News* (New York: May, 1947, no. 1). A semblance of prevailing trends and news in the cultural activities of post-World War II, Germany is provided by this service.

Jonas, Hans, "Die Entwicklung der Geschichtsforschung in der Soviet-Union seit dem Ausgang des Weltkrieges," *Zéitschrift fur osteuropaische Geschichte,* V (N. F., Band I) (Berlin, 1931). An excellent guide to Soviet historical journals, museums, institutes, libraries, chief historians, etc., for the period covered.

Jones, C. W., (ed.), *Bedae Opera de Temporibus* (Cambridge, Mass.: The Medieval Academy, 1943). Valuable introduction.

Jones, L. W., "The Influence of Cassiodorus on Medieval Culture," *Speculum,* XX (1945), pp. 433-442.

Jorga, N., "Roumania," *Histoire et historiens depuis cinquante ans* (Paris: Felix Alcan, 1927), pp. 320-340.

K

Kantorowicz, Ernst, *Kaiser Friedrich II* (Berlin: Bondi, 1928).

Karpovich, Michael, "The Russian Revolution of 1917," *Journal of Modern History,* II (Chicago: 1930). A useful bibliographical article.

Kerner, Robert J., (ed.), *Yugoslavia* (Berkeley: University of California Press, 1949). Contains articles by various authors on aspects of Yugoslav politics, history, ethnography, etc.

——————, *Slavic Europe, A Selected Bibliography in the Western European Languages* (Cambridge: Harvard University Press, 1918). Chapter III, "The Poles," pp. 149-188, gives titles of studies on history, life and culture of Poland by western European scholars, and lists works of Polish authors which have been translated. Old but still useful for reference for the pre-1918 historiography.

Kiesewetter, A., "Histoire de Russie: travaux des savants russes emigrés (1918-1928)," *Revue Historique,* CXXIII (Parish, 1930). Essentially bibliographical.

Kingsford, C. L., *English Historical Literature in the Fifteenth Century* (Oxford: Oxford University Press, 1913). pp. 253-274. Good material on Polydore, Vergil, Hall, and John Stowe.

Kirsch, Karl, "The World Historians," *Partisan Review,* IX (Sept.-Oct., 1942), pp. 354-371. Shows origins of secular world histories among the eighteenth century historians and traces through to Spengler and Toynbee.

Klingbert, Frank J., "A Survey of Recent Books on British Africa, with Special Reference to the Native Problem," *Journal of Modern History,* X (1938), pp. 77-93. Good material on South African historians.

Knight, M. M., "French Colonial Policy. The Decline of Association," *Journal of Modern History,* vol. V (1933), pp. 203-224. A bibliographical article containing useful information about French works in the colonial field.

Kohn, Hans, *Prophets and Peoples, Studies in Nineteenth Century Nationalism* (New York: Macmillan Company, 1946). Chapter 2 is a splendid appreciation of Michelet as a romantic nationalist.

Kosary, Dominic, "Gabriel Bethlen, Transylvania in the XVII Century," *The Slavonic Review,* XVII (1938), pp. 162-163. In this study of 17th century Transylvania, the author summarizes the treatment of the problem by the new Hungarian historiography.

L

Lach, Donald F., "China and the Era of the Enlightenment," *Journal of Modern History,* XIV (June, 1942), pp. 209-222. Reviews the literature, shows Voltaire mirrored prevalent opinion on China.

Lamprecht, K., *German History* (Berlin: Gaertners, 1891-1909). Lamprecht's imposing effort to illustrate his laws of periodization with emphasis on economic and cultural forces in German History.

——————, *What Is History?* (New York: Macmillan Company, 1905). An abstruse exposition of Lamprecht's views and doctrines on history.

Langlois, Charles and Seignobos, Charles, *Introduction to the Study of History,* trans. by G. G. Berry (New York: Henry Holt & Company, 1898). A standard handbook on historical methods.

Lanson, G., "Historic Method of Jules Michelet," *International Quarterly* XI (1905), pp. 71-101. This is a detailed study of the formative period of Michelet, based on his works and showing the early development of his method. It is excellent as far as it goes, but it is too brief for an evaluation of either the historian or his method.

Laprade, W. T., "The Present State of the History of England in the Eighteenth Century," *Journal of Modern History,* IV (1932), pp. 581-603. Excellent bibliography which incidentally provides historiographical information.

Lapsley, Gaillard, "Some Recent Advance in English Constitutional History (before 1485)," *Cambridge Historical Journal,* V (1936), pp. 119-121. This article is richly informative about the important research in constitutional and allied fields.

Lednicki, Waclaw, *Life and Culture of Poland, As Reflected in Polish Literature* (New York: Roy Publishers, 1944). Excellent treatment on the manner in which Polish literature reflects the times and conditions in which the writers lived. Especially interesting is Chapter I on interpretations of Polish history.

Lavisse, Ernest, *Souveniers* (Paris: Calmann-Levy, 1912). Autobiographical with no discussion of his writings.

Lefebvre, Georges, "Histoire de la Revolution et de l'Empire," *Revue Historique,* vol. CLXXVI (1935), pp. 63-90, vol. CLXXXVII (1939), pp. 63-112; 184-224; 225-256. Surveys important writings on the Revolution.

——————, "L'Oeuvre Historique de'Albert Mathiez," *Annales Historiques de la Revolution Francaise,* vol. IX (1932), pp. 193-210; and in the same volume, pp. 98-102, "Albert Mathiez." Both articles are excellent.

Lepsius, Johannes, Mendelssohn Bartholdy, Albrecht and Thimme, Friedrich, (eds.), *Die grosse Politik der europaischen Kabinette* 1871-1914 (Berlin: Deutsche Verlagsgesellschaft fur Politik und Geschichte, 40 vols., 1922-1926). The editors assure the scholars that only those secret documents remain unpublished which were not germane to establishing causes of the conflict in 1914.

Lesage, Georges L., "La Production Historique en Italie de 1940 a 1945," (Historical Production in Italy from 1940 to 1945), *Revue Historique,* CXCVII (January-March, 1947), pp. 79-117. A mere listing of Italian historical works appearing during the war.

Lisio, Guiseppe, La Storiografia (Milan, no date), especially Chapter VII, "La Storia Durante la Lotta Tra l'Impero e il Papato," and Chapter VIII, "La Storia Durante la Lotta tra i communi e l'Impero." Quite full of accounts of Italian writers with many interesting quotations.

Loeb, Classical Library of about 300 volumes, projected and subsidized by James Loeb beginning in 1912. Most of the classical writers are available in this collection with Greek or Latin texts accompanied by English translations.

Longaker, Mark, *English Biography in the Eighteenth Century* (Philadelphia: University of Pennsylvania Press, 1931). The first five chapters contain much material on the seventeenth century.

Lorenz, Reinhold (born 1898), *Tuerkenjahr 1683. Das Reich im Kampf um den Ostraum* (Vienna, 1933). The most original study of the one time professor of the University of Vienna. His later publications suffered greatly from his frank espousal of Nazism, as evidenced in his *Drei Jahrhunderte Volk, Staat und Reich* (Vienna, 1943).

Loserth, Johannes, (1846-1936), ed., *The Works of Wyclif* (10 vols., London: 1886-1922) ; sponsored by the Wyclif society, this is one of the most important editions of sources for the history of the Reformation period in which Loserth specialized.

Lowith, Karl, *Meaning in History* (Chicago: University of Chicago Press, 1939). Chapter VII, pp. 137-144, of this valuable and profound book gives a brief account of Bossuet's historical conceptions.

Lubensky, Stepan, "Bibliographie de l'Eurasisme," *Le Monde Slave*, 1931, (January-March), pp. 388-422. A very useful supplement to Lubensky's article on Eurasianism in the same volume.

Lucas, H. S., *The Renaissance and Reformation* (New York: Harper & Brothers, 1934), pp. 345-419. Valuable for its background material on the Northern Humanists. Not very much interpretation.

Lukinich, Impre, *Les Editions des Sources de l'Historie Hongroise 1854-1930* (Budapest: Academie, 1930). List of source editions with short commentaries.

M

MacDonald, Janet L., "Sir William Ashley, 1860-1927," chapter II, pp. 20-44, in *Some Historians of Modern Europe*, ed. by Bernardotte Schmitt (Chicago: University of Chicago Press, 1942), Elementary survey of a British economic historian.

Magyary, Zoltan, ed., *Die Entstehung Einer Internationalen Wissenschaftspolitik. Die Lage der Ungarischen Wissenschaftspolitik* (Leipzig: F. Meiner Vlg., 1932). Collective work on the state of Hungarian sciences, including historiography.

Maitland, Frederic W., "William Stubbs, Bishop of Oxford," *English Historical Review*, 1901, Vol. XVI (1901), pp. 417-426. An excellent account.

Malowist, Marian, "Baltic Affairs in the Sixteenth and Seventeenth Centuries in the Light of Historical Literature," *Baltic and Scandinavian Countries, III* (September, 1937), pp. 417-427. Survey of what German, Russian, Swedish, Polish, Dutch and English historians have written on early modern Baltic affairs.

Mangan, J. J., *The Life, Character, and Influence of Desiderius Erasmus of Rotterdam* (New York: Macmillan Company, 1927), 2 vols. A sympathetic, careful but rather wordy study of Erasmus by a Catholic, who argues that Erasmus was an orthodox Catholic.

Manitius, M., *Geschichte der Lateinischen Literatur des Mittelalters*, Teil II (Munich: 1923). "Von der mitte des zehnen Jahrhunderts biz zum Ausbruch des Kampfes Zwischen Kirche und Staat": III Teil (1931), "Von Ausbruch des Kirchenstreites bis zum Ende des Zwolten Jahrhunderts." Very good and full accounts of the writers of the period with excellent bibliographies.

Marcks, E., *Maenner und Zeiten* (Leipzig: Quelle und Meyer, 1912). Enlightening essays on Dahlmann, Sybel, Treitschke and Mommsen.

Mannhardt, Francis, S. J., "Bollandus (1596-1665)," pp. 190-211 in *Church Historians*, ed. Peter Guilday (Kennedy, 1926). Very apologetic in tone.

Marburg, Clara, *Sir William Temple* (New York: Yale University Press, 1932). Temple wrote historical works and speculated about the causes of different national temperaments. Miss Marburg's study provides useful material on seventeenth century historical thinking.

Margoliouth, D. S., *Lectures on Arabic Historians* (Calcutta: The University of Calcutta, 1930). Eight lectures delivered at the University of Calcutta, in a popular style. Only Moslem chronology is used. No references and no bibliography. Printing errors in names and titles of books.

Matl, Josef, *Die Agrarreform in Jugoslawien* (Berlin: 1927); an investigation of the most pressing problem in Yugoslav history.

Mitis, Oskar von, *Studien Zum Aelteren Oesterreichischen Urkundenwesen* (Vienna, 1906-1912). Very useful paleographic studies by the onetime director of the Vienna archives.

Meinecke, Friedrich, *Entstehung des Historismus,* 2 vols. (Munchen und Berlin: Oldenbourg, 1936). A scholarly treatise of the origin and prevailing trends in German historiography through Dilthey.

——————, "The Year 1848 in German History: Reflections on a Centenary," *Review of Politics,* X (1948), pp. 475-492. The reflections of a German master on a decisive moment of his country's history.

Mossner, Ernest C., "Was Hume a Tory Historian?," *Journal of the History of Ideas,* 2 (April, 1941), pp. 225-236. The conclusion is that Hume was not, on the basis of a special study of Hume's revisions of his *History of England.*

Mosley, Philipe E., "The Post-War Historiography of Modern Bulgaria," *Journal of Modern History,* IX (September, 1937).

Muller, William, "Modern Green Historians of Modern Greece," *History,* Vol. X, No. 38 (July, 1925), pp. 110-124.

N

Neff, E., *The Poetry of History* (New York: Columbia University Press, 1947). A unique study in modern historiography of the literary masters of history as an art and a critique of history as a science, at Ranke's expense. Chapters IV, V and VI are valuable for this period, especially the informative account of Offried Müller and the sparkling study of Michelet.

Nicholson, R. A., *A Literary History of the Arabs* 2nd ed., (Cambridge: Cambridge University Press, 1930). Perhaps the best work of the kind in English. Its aim was to serve as a history of the development of ideas in Arabic literature.

Nietzsche, Friedrich, *Jenseits von Gut und Bose* (Leipzig: Korner, 1930). Aphoristic essays that yield a surprisingly large amount of materials on the author's attitude toward Germany.

O

Oman, Sir Charles, *On the Writing of History* (London: Methuen, 1939). Chapter 12, "History at Oxford," is interesting.

Ottenthal, Emil von, "Autriche," in *Histoire et Historiens Depuis Cinquante Ans* (Paris, 1927), I, pp. 39-50. A detailed account of Austrian historical scholarship in the fifty years up to 1926.

Orosius, *Seven Books of History against the Pagans,* translated with an introduction by I. W. Raymond (New York: Columbia University Press, 1936).

P

Parker, Donald Dean, *Local History, How to Gather It, Write It, and Publish It.* (Bertha E. Josephson, ed. New York: Social Science Research Council, n.d.). This item is an illustration in itself of the growing interest in local history which has characterized American historical scholarship since 1930.

Parsons, Talcott, "Capitalism in Present German Literature: Sombart and Weber," *Journal of Political Economy,* XXXVI (1928), pp. 641-661; XXXVIII (1929), pp. 31-51. A self-explanatory title dealing with two economic oracles in German economic thought.

Pastor, L., *The History of the Popes since the Middle Ages* (London: Hodges, 1891). Monumental and scholarly research on the papacy from 1378 to 1800.

Pattison, M., *Isaac Casaubon,* 2d ed. (Oxford: Clarendon Press, 1892). A classic study of the career of a scholar, whose very eminence in classical studies drew him into the controversies involved in church historical writing.

Paul, Herbert, *Life of Froude* (London: Sir Isaac Pitman & Sons, Ltd., 1905). Excellent. Chapters 4, 5, 6, 8, and 10 are the most pertinent.

Peardon, Thomas Preston, *The Transition in English Historical Writing 1760-1930* (New York: Columbia University Press, 1933). Chapter VIII on the English romanticist historians gives a critical account of Turner, Scott, Southey, Godwin and Chalmers.

Peers, Edgar A., *A History of the Romantic Movement in Spain* (Cambridge: Cambridge University Press, 1940). A good two-volume account of the clash between classicism and romanticism in Spain. Chapter VII, on the main features of Spanish romanticism, is especially useful.

Perrin, Charles-Edmond, "L'Oeuvre Historique de March Bloch," *Revue Historique,* vol. CXCIX-CC (1948), pp. 161-188. An excellent analysis. See also, Bloch, Marc, *Apologie pour l'Histoire ou Metier d'Historien* (Paris: Colin, 1949).

Pick, F. W., "Tartu, the History of an Estonian University," *The American Slavic and East European Review,* V (November, 1946), pp. 150-161. Survey of the long history, including Swedish and Russian domination, of the university which became the center of Esthonian education and research.

Plassman, Thomas, "Baronius, 1538-1607," pp. 153-189 in *Church Historians,* ed. Peter Guilday (Kennedy, 1926). A pleasant uncritical account of the career and writings of Baronius.

Powicke, F. M., "Henri Pirenne," *E.H.R.* LI (January, 1936), pp. 78-89. Few historians, British or foreign, are accorded such notices by the E.H.R.

Putnam, Ruth, "Robert Fruin 1823-1899, A Memorial Sketch," *American Historical Association, Report for 1899.* (Washington, 1900), Vol. 1, pp. 515-526. Detailed account by a historian who knew Fruin personally.

Q

Qualey, Carlton C., "Newer Interpretations of American History to 1860," *The Study and Teaching of American History, op. cit.,* pp. 102-120. An excellent survey of recent trends in American historiography on topics in American history from the colonial period to the Civil War.

R

Rand, E. K., *Founders of the Middle Ages,* (Cambridge, Mass.: Harvard University Press, 1928). Has a valuable essay on the humanism of St. Jerome.

Rand, E. K., "The New Cassiodorus," *Speculum,* XII (1938), pp. 433-447.

Rebellon, A., "Necrologie et bibliographie des travaux de Henri See," *Annales de Bretagne,* vol. XLIII (1936), pp. 3-11 on See's Life, pp. 12-33 for a list of See's works.

Ritter, Gerhard, "The German Professor in the Third Reich," *Review of Politics,* VIII (1946), pp. 242-254. Ritter describes the experiences of a history professor in the Third Reich.

——————, *Die Entwicklung der Geschichtswissenschaft* (Munich: Oldenbourg, 1919). Interesting and informative comment on Lamprecht.

Riegel, Robert E., "The Frontier and the West," *The Study and Teaching of American History,* pp. 133-142. This article, by one of the outstanding authorities on the American West, discusses newer interpretations of the Turner theory as applied by historians in the United States.

Robertson, J. G., "Muratori," Chapter III, pp. 60-95, in *The Genesis of Romantic Theory* (Cambridge: Cambridge University Press, 1923). Helpfully relates Muratori's historical and literary works.

——————, *Buckle and His Critics. A Study in Sociology* (London: S. Sonnenschein, 1895). Corrects some misconceptions concerning Buckle.

Robinson, Edgar Eugene, *Scholarship and Cataclysm: Teaching and Research in American History, 1939-1945.* (Stanford: Stanford University Press, 1947). This is the report of the findings of the Institute of American History at Stanford, a group organized to discover the status of American History in both teaching and research during the war years.

————, "A New American History," *School and Society,* LXIII: pp. 73-76 (February 2, 1946). Robinson is director of the Institute of American History at Stanford and has used his experience in that position as a basis for this article.

Robinson, James Harvey, *The New History* (New York: Macmillan Company, 1916). This is the provocative series of essays which made the New History important. Robinson's broad viewpoint is still worthy of careful consideration.

Rose, William J., "Polish Historical Writing," *The Journal of Modern History,* II, no. 4 (December, 1930), pp. 569-585. A brief, general survey of Polish historical writing during the various medieval and modern periods of history. Good for background information.

————, "Realism in Polish History," *Journal of Central European Affairs,* II (October, 1942), pp. 233-249. The author subscribes to the demand for a realistic revision of Polish historiography.

Roucek, Joseph S., *Balkan Politics* (Stanford: Stanford University Press, 1948). Practical politics with the national and sociological background.

————, (ed.), *Slavonic Encyclopaedia* (New York: Philosophical Library, 1949). Includes article on "Historiography, Czechoslovakia," and the related topics: "Czechoslovak Sociology," Chapter XXV, pp. 717-731, in G. Gurvitch and W. E. Moore, (eds.), *Twentieth Century Sociology,* (New York: Philosophical Library, 1946). A systematic study of the Czechoslovak sociologists.

S

Sabine, G. H., "Hegel's Political Philosophy," *Philosophical Review,* XLI (May, 1932), pp. 261-282. An excellent re-evaluation of Hegel's political thought and influence, comparable to that of Hook, on the centenary of his death.

Sakuragi, Akira, "Survey of the Japanese Historical World for the Past Forty Years," *(Kako Shijunenkan ni okeru kokushi Gakkai no Gaikan). Magazine of the Kokugakuin University (Kokugakuin Zasshi,* XIII (1907), pp. 67-79; 185-195; 378-397. Surveys historical studies in Japan during the period from about 1868 to 1907; includes list of works in Western languages, better consulted in revised version in Kuroita, *op. cit.*

Salomon, Henri, and Bloch, Marc, "Christian Pfister (1857-1933). Sa vie, ses oeuvres," *Revue Historique,* vol. CLXXII (1933), pp. 548-563 (life of Salomon), pp. 503-570 (works by Bloch).

Sandys, Sir John E., *A History of Classical Scholarship* (Cambridge: Cambridge University Press, 1908), vol. II. A monumental volume in an extremely difficult field.

Schapiro, J. S., *Liberalism and the Challenge of Fascism, Social Forces in England and France 1815-1870* (New York: McGraw Hill Book Company, 1949). A splendid new evaluation of the social forces of the period 1815-1870. Chapter IX on Carlyle, an unsympathetic critique, is of value to students of Carlyle.

Schargo, N. N., *History in the Encyclopedie* (New York: Columbia University Press, 1947). Suggests similarity in outlook of Voltaire and of the *Encyclopedie.* Slightly weakens the case for Voltaire's originality. Of 66,660 articles in the *Encyclopedie,* 6,199 were historical.

Schevill, Ferdinand, "Voltaire, Historian of Civilization and Exponent of Rationalism," in Stuart A. Rice, *Methods in Social Science* (Chicago: University of Chicago Press, 1931), pp. 424-436. Well-balanced presentation, especially valuable for comments on causation.

Schmid, Henrich Felix (born 1896), *Wesen und Aufbau der Detuschen Slawistik* (Breslau, 1927). An important summary of Slavic scholarship by the Director of the *Osteuropa-Institut* at the University of Vienna.

Schmitt, Bernadotte E., (ed.), *Some Historians of Modern Europe* (Chicago: University of Chicago Press, 1942). Essays on Halevy, Hanotaux, Mathiez, See and Seignobos are recommended.

Schnerb, Robert, "Napoleon III and the Second French Empire," *Journal of Modern History*, vol. VIII (1936), pp. 335-355. A good review of the historical literature on the Second Empire.

See, Henri, "Recent Work in French Economic History (1905-1925)," *The Economic History Review*, vol. I (1927-1928), pp. 137-153. A first-rate descriptive account of works in economic history by French scholars.

Seton-Watson, R. W., "The Abbot Trithemius," Chapter III, pp. 75-89, in Seton-Watson, ed., *Tudor Studies* (New York: Longmans Green Company, 1924). Pleasant description of one of the scholarly associates of Maximilian, and of his patriotic and religious works.

Sell, Friedrich Carl, "Intellectual Liberalism in Germany about 1900," *Journal of Modern History*, XV (Sept. 1943), pp. 227-236. Ideas of the more important thinkers—including sociologists—are discussed. A few birth dates are inaccurate.

Simkhovitch, Vladimir G., "Approaches to History," *Political Science Quarterly*, XLIV (December, 1929), pp. 481-498. A plea for something more than what the author calls a historicogenetic attitude. In a sequel to this article, appearing under the same title in the *Political Science Quarterly*, XLV (December, 1920), pp. 481-527, the author reviews various philosophies of history, emphasizing the contributions of modern European writers.

Slosson, Preston W., *The Great Crusade and After* (New York: Macmillan Company, 1930). One of the best social histories of the decade of the 1920's. Includes a brief survey of what happened to American history at that time.

Smith, P., *Erasmus: A Study of His Life, Ideals, and Place in History* (New York: Harper and Brothers, 1923). An important appraisal of Erasmus by a liberal Protestant

————, *A History of Modern Culture: The Enlightenment, 1687-1776* (New York: Henry Holt & Company, 1934). Includes excellent chapter on historiography which is, on the whole, notable for comments both on research methods and the philosophy of the historians.

Sorel, A., *Montesquieu* (Chicago: McClurg, 1888). Still the best short biography and analysis of his works.

Souriau, Maurice Anatole, *Histoire du Romantisme en France* (Paris: Spex, 1927). A three-volume survey of the literary movement and its impact on French art and drama.

Spengler, Oswald, *Jahre der Entscheidung* (Munchen: Beck, 1933). Brings up-to-date the views of the most provocative German thinker of the twentieth century in not quite such ponderous (or "original") language as his first important work.

Stavrianos, L. S., *Balkan Federation: A History of the Movement Toward Balkan Unity in Modern Times* (Northampton: Smith College Press, 1941-1942). A good survey of diplomacy of the Balkan peoples, and the effect to find the way out.

Steinacker, Harold, *Zur Frage Nach Der Rechtlichen Natur der Oesterreichisch-Ungarischen Gesamtmonarchie* (Vienna and Leipzig, 1910).

————, "Die geschichtlichen Voraussetzungen des osterreichischen Nationali-taten-problems und seine Entwicklung bis 1867," in Karl G. Kugelmann, ed., *Das Nationalitaechrecht des Alten Aesterreich* (Vienna and Leipzig, 1934). Two important publications on Austria's most pressing domestic problem by an author who, after *Anschluss*, became one of the most uncritical eulogists of Adolph Hitler.

Stenton, F. M., "Early English History, 1895-1920," in *Transactions of the Royal Historical Society,* series 4, vol. 28 (1946), pp. 7-20. A fine historiographical sketch by a master.

Stephen, Sir Leslie, *Letters of John Richard Green* (London: Macmillan Company, 1901). Green's letters give details of his life and historical writings. His works are listed on pages 494-503.

Stephens, W. R. W., *Life and Letters of Edward A. Freeman* (w volumes., London: Macmillan Co., 1895). A first-rate biography with a complete list of Freeman's writings.

Stirk, S. D., *The Prussian Spirit: A Survey of German Literature and Politics, 1914-1940* (London: Faber and Faber, 1941). Exposes crypto-Prussianism of emigres and other "Prussians."

Strakhovsky, Leonid I. (ed.), *Handbook of Slavic Studies* (Cambridge: Harvard University Press, 1949). Contains useful bibliography and a brief account of English contributions to history of Poland by Oskar Halecki.

Summers, Montague, *The Gothic Quest: A History of the Gothic Novel* (London: Fortune, 1938). The genesis of English literary interest in Gothic art is especially stressed.

Symonolewicz, Konstanty, "The Studies in Nationality and Nationalism in Poland between the Two Wars (1918-1939). A bibliographical survey," *Bulletin of the Polish Institute of Arts and Sciences* in America, II (October, 1943). Useful for a survey of accomplishments in field of nationalism in independent Poland.

T

Tapper, B., "Dilthey's Methodology of the Geisteswissenschaften," *Philosophical Review.* XXXIV (1925), pp. 333-349. Serious and useful account of the method of an important but difficult German historian.

Taylor, E. G. R., "Camden's England." Chapter X, pp. 354-386, in H. C. Darby, ed., *Historical Geography of England* (2d ed., Cambridge: Cambridge University Press, 1948). Gives a good picture of Camden's account of England in *Britannica.*

Taylor, H. O., *Thought and Expression in the Sixteenth Century,* 2 vols. (New York: Macmillan Company, 1920). Recounts the work of both humanists and reformers. Highly conventional intellectual history

Teggart, Frederick J., *Theory and Processes of History* (Berkeley and Los Angeles: University of California Press, 1941). Contains a brief examination of "The Method of Hume and Turgot," Suggests influence of Hume on Turgot.

Teng, S. Y., "Chinese historiography in the last fifty years," *Far Eastern Quarterly,* VIII, 2 (February, 1949). Survey of the most recent trends in Chinese historiography with critical comments on various historians and their works.

Thomson, S. Harrison, *Czechoslovakia in European History* (Princeton: Princeton University Press, 1953). Stresses the period since the Battle of the White Mountain.

Thompson, A. H. (ed)., *Bede, His Life, Times and Writings* (Oxford, England: Clarendon Press, 1935). See particularly the essay on "Bede as historian" by Levison, W., pp. 111-151.

Thompson, J. M., "Albert Mathiez," *English Historical Review* (1932), pp. 617-621. An excellent article which includes an account of the break between Aulard and Mathiez and the latter's socialist views.

Thompson, J. W., with Holm, B. J., *A History of Historical Writing* (New York: Macmillan Company, (1942): ch. xii, 'German Historians of the Saxon, Salian, the Hohenstauffen, Period; ch. xiv, "Historians of Feudal France; ch. xv, "Norman and Angevin England;" ch. xiii, "Italian Historiography (900-1200); ch. xvii, "The Historiography of the Eastern Roman Empire;" ch. xviii, "The Latin Historians of the Crusades;" ch. xix, "Medieval Syrian and Armenian Historians;" ch. xx, "Arabic Persian and Mongol Historians of the Middle Ages." Running accounts of very many historians with descriptions of their work, lives and bibliography.

Tihany, Leslie C., "Istvan Borsody, Magyar-szlovak kiegyezes (Hungarian-Slovak Compromise,") *The American Slavic and East European Review,* V (1946), pp. 198-201. Comments on a ". . . product of modern Hungarian historiography which was not conceived in the original sin of anti-democratic revionist propaganda."

Tompkins, S. R., "Trends in Communist Historical Thought," *Slavonic Review,* XIII (London, 1935). An objective and sober account; for the earlier period.

Tout, T. F., "The Study of Mediaeval Chronicles," *The Collected Papers of Thomas Frederick Tout,* III (Manchester, 1934), pp. 1-26. A good discussion of the characteristics of medieval historiography.

Trevelyan, G. M., *An Autobiography and Other Essays* (London: 1949). A brief but interesting sketch. The volume also contains a notice on Sir John Clapham and a number of essays which either defend or represent the author's views on the historian's function.

Trimble, William R., "Early Tudor Historiography, 1485-1548," in *Journal of the History of Ideas,* XI (1950), pp. 30-41. A carefully argued, scholarly and original piece of work.

Turner, Frederick Jackson, *The Frontier in American History* (New York: Henry Holt, 1945). This series of essays ranks with James Harvey Robinson's in setting one of the strongest tones of twentieth-century historiography in America. The first essay is especially significant.

Tymieniecki, Casimir and Handelsman, Marcel, "Cinquante ans de travail historique en Bologne," *Revue Historique* (Paris, 1939), pp. 325-344, 364-406. In the main, a French translation of historiographical survey in *Kwartalnik Historyczny.* Because of the outbreak of war only three articles appeared.

U

Uhlirz, Mathilde (born 1881), *Handbuch der Geschichte Oesterreichs und Seiner Nach-barlaender Boehmen und Ungarn* (4 vols., Graz, 1927-1941. An important handbook based upon the initial studies by the author's father, the well-known Graz historian, Karl Uhlirz (1854-1914).

Usher, R. G., *A Critical Study of the Historical Method of Samuel Rawson Gardiner* (St. Louis: Washington University Studies, 1915), Volume III, pt. II, no. 1. Good analysis of method, accuracy, handling of details and value of Gardiner's works.

V

Van Tiethem, Paul, *O'ere romantique: le romantisme dans la litterature europeen* (Paris: Albin Michel, 1948). An excellent history of the romanticist ideology, with special reference to its literary aspects.

Viatte, Auguste, *Les Sources occultes du Romantisme, illuminisme—théosophie, 1770-1820* (Paris: H. Champion, 1928). An interesting two-volume study of the pietistic and mystic elements in romanticism.

Volker, Karl, *Die Kirchengeschichtsschreibung der Aufklarung* (Tubingen: J. C. B Mohr, 1921). Valuable for showing the extent to which even in the writing of church history, the human secular approach of the Englightenment was influential also show that Mosheim and Semler were using history for Christian apologetic against Deism.

W

Ware, Caroline F. (ed.), The Cultural Approach to History (New York: Columbi. University Press, 1940). This symposium was undertaken at the suggestion of the American Historical Association. Part VI is especially important—"Sources and Materials for the Study of Cutural History."

Weisinger, Herbert, "Ideas of History During the Renaissance," *Journal of the History of Ldeas* VI (1945), pp. 415-435. Surveys some of the basic interpretative ideas of the sixteenth century historians.

Warnier, R., "Les Publications Yugoslav," *Le Monde Slave*, IV (July, 1933; September, 1933; October, 1933), pp. 142-160, 116-141, and 392-421.

Waskovich, George, "Historiography Bulgaria," *Slavonic Encyclopedia* (New York: Philosophical Library, 1949), pp. 419-432; and "Historiography Yugoslavia," *ibid.*, pp. 444-447.

Weisinger, Herbert, "The Middle Ages and the Late Eighteenth Century Historians," *Philological Quarterly*, XXVII (January, 1938), pp. 63-79. Limited to minor English historians: Joseph Berington, James Harris, Thomas Warton, Adam Anderson.

Welleck, Rene, "Carlyle and the Philosophy of History," *Philological Quarterly*, XXIII (Oct., 1944), pp. 55-76. A penetrating critique of Carlyle's present value as historian by a leading Carlyle authority.

Wereszycki, Henryk, "The Pilsudski Institute of Warsaw," *Baltic and Scandinavian Countries*, III (May, 1937), pp. 332-333. Brief account of the work and the purposes of the Institute.

Wormald, B. H. G., *Clarendon: Politics, History and Religion, 1640-1660* (Cambridge, England: Cambridge University Press, 1951). Difficult to read and over-subtly argued but based on deep knowledge.

Wright, L. B., *Middle Class Culture in Elizabethan England* (Chapel Hill: University of North Carolina Press, 1935). An extensive study of bourgeois culture. One of the chapters gives a good account of popular historical literature.

Y

Yakobson, Sergius, "Postwar Historical Research in the Soviet Union," in *The Soviet Union Since World War II*, edited by Philip E. Mosely (*The Annals of the American Academy of Political and Social Science*, vol. 263) (Philadelphia, May, 1949). An exceptionally thorough statement on the position of the Russian historian since 1945; useful and illuminating.

Young, L. M., *Thomas Carlyle and the Art of History* (Philadelphia: University of Pennsylvania Press, 1939). An exhaustive presentation and sympathetic evaluation of Carlyle's thought based on a comprehensive study of his writings. Indispensable to the study of Carlyle as an historian.

Z

Zajaczkowski, Stanislaw, "The Historical Sciences in Lithuania," *Baltic and Scandinavian Countries*, IV (May, 1938), pp. 239-246. Good English account of free Lithuania's historiography.

Zeeveld, W. G., *The Foundations of Tudor Policy*, (Cambridge: Harvard University Press, 1949). An original and stimulating account of the secular interest of a group of humanists who worked for Henry VIII's government.

Zerffi, G. G., "Voltaire in His Relation to the Study of General History, from a Philosophical Point of View," *Transactions of the Royal Historical Society*, X (pp. 344-370. Brings out Voltaire's pessimism and his lack of a sense of historical continuity.

SUBJECT INDEX

NAME INDEX

Abbott, W. C., 194
Acominatus, 79
Acropolites, 79
Action, Lord, xxix, 144, 205, 226
Adams, Eleanor N., 124
Adams, Henry, 413, 415
Adams, Henry M., 183
Aemilius, Paulus (of Verona), 114
Africanus, Sextus Julius, 11
Agathias, 72
Alaman, Lucas, 430
Alfred the Great, 30
Allen, C. F., 278
Almeida, Fortunato de, 377
Alonso, Benito Sánchez, 53, 57, 373
Altamira, Rafael, 437
Ammianus, 10
Anderson, Eugene N., 261
Andics, Elizabeth, 332
Andreades, A. M., 337
Andreas, Willy, 113
Andrews, Charles M., 424
Appion, 7
Arai, Hakuseki, 383
Arana, Diego Barros, 433, 437
Aristigueta, Francisco Vetancourt, 436
Arnakis, G. Georgiades, 67, 81, 87
Arneth, Alfred von, 223
Arnold, T., 46
Arrian, 7
Ashikpashazade, 89
Ashton, T. S., 236
Attaliates, 77
Aubrey, E. E., 369
Augustine, St., 13, 15, 16
Aulard, Alphonse, 199
Aventinus (Johannes Thurmaier), 112

Babcock, E. A., 39
Babinger, Franz, 89
Bacon, Francis, 135, 136
Baelke, Walter, 259
Balbo, C., 193
Bale, John, 124
Balodis, F., 299
Balzani, Ugo, 40, 44, 46, 47, 60, 61, 91
Balzer, Oswald, 287
Bancroft, George, 407
Bang, Nina Ellinger, 279
Barante, Baron de, 179
Barbagallo, Corrado, 368
Barber, G. L., 5
Barnes, 42

Barnes, Harry Elmer, 259, 261, 408, 422
Barnes, Sherman B., 147
Barnouw, Adrian Jacob, 275
Baronius, Caesar, 126
Barthold, V. V., 359
Bartholomeus, 54
Basadre, Jorge, 435, 438
Bassett, John Spencer, 399, 402
Bataillon, M., 116
Bauer, Otto, 317, 319
Baynes, Norman H., 270
Beard, Charles, 424
Beazley, C. R., 52
Becker, Carl L., 159
Beddie, J. S., 38, 42
Bede, 22, 23, 41
Beers, Henry A., 176
Bekker, 76
Belknap, Jeremy, 406
Below, Georg Anton von, 256
Beltrán, G. Aguirre, 435
Beneš, Eduard, 305, 309, 310
Beretta, Antonio Ballesteros y, 375, 432
Berossus, 2
Berr, Henri, 247
Berry, Thomas, 151
Bethman, D. L. C., 42
Beveridge, Albert J., 421
Beverley, Robert, 401
Bewer, Julius A., 2
Bezold, Friedrich von, 223
Bibl, Viktor, 319, 321
Biggerstaff, K., 397
Bilmanis, Alfred, 300
Binkley, William C., 421, 426
Biondo, Flavio (of Forli), 98, 108
Black, C. E., 342
Black, J. B., 155, 158
Bloch, Herbert, 6
Blok, Pieter Johannes, 273
Bobchev, N. S., 346
Boccaccio, Giovanni, 95
Bodin, Jean, 135
Boehner, Philotheus, 62
Bogoslovsky, M. M., 360
Boissier, Gaston, 10
Bollandus, John, 129
Bolton, Herbert Eugene, 433
Borsody, Stephen, 325
Bossuet, Jacques Benigne, 132
Bourgin, G., 44
Bouthal, G., 88
Bradford, William, 402